HUMAN–COMPUTER INTERACTION AND MANAGEMENT INFORMATION SYSTEMS: APPLICATIONS

Advances in Management Information Systems

Advisory Board

HUMAN–COMPUTER INTERACTION AND MANAGEMENT INFORMATION SYSTEMS: APPLICATIONS

DENNIS GALLETTA
PING ZHANG
EDITORS

FOREWORD BY IZAK BENBASAT

ADVANCES IN MANAGEMENT
INFORMATION SYSTEMS
VLADIMIR ZWASS SERIES EDITOR

Routledge
Taylor & Francis Group

LONDON AND NEW YORK

First published 2006 by M.E. Sharpe

Published 2015 by Routledge

2 Park Square, Milton Park, Abingdon, Oxon OX14 4RN

711 Third Avenue, New York, NY 10017, USA

Routledge is an imprint of the Taylor Francis Group, an informa business

Copyrights © 2006 Taylor & Francis. All rights reserved

References to the AMIS papers should be as follows:
Carroll, J.M., and Rosson, M.B. Dimensions of participation in information systems design. D. Galletta and P. Zhang, eds., *Human-Computer Interaction and Management Information Systems: Applications. Advances in Management Information Systems*, Volume 6 (Armonk, NY: M.E. Sharpe, 2006), 337–354.

ISBN-13 978-0-7656-1487-2

ISBN-10 0-7656-1487-1

ISSN 1554-6152

ISBN 13: 9780765614872 (hbk)

ADVANCES IN MANAGEMENT INFORMATION SYSTEMS

AMIS Vol. 1: Richard Y. Wang, Elizabeth M. Pierce, Stuart E. Madnick, and Craig W. Fisher
Information Quality
ISBN-13 978-0-7656-1133-8
ISBN-10 0-7656-1133-3

AMIS Vol. 2: Sergio deCesare, Mark Lycett, and Robert D. Macredie
Development of Component-Based Information System
ISBN-13 978-0-7656-1248-9
ISBN-10 0-7656-1248-8

AMIS Vol. 3: Jerry Fjermestad and Nicholas C. Romano, Jr.
Electronic Customer Relationship Management
ISBN-13 978-0-7656-1327-1
ISBN-10 0-7656-1248-1

AMIS Vol. 4: Michael J. Shaw
E-Commerce and the Digital Economy
ISBN-13 978-0-7656-1150-5
ISBN-10 0-7656-1150-3

AMIS Vol. 5: Ping Zhang and Dennis Galletta
Human-Computer Interaction and Management Information Systems: Foundations
ISBN-13 978-0-7656-1486-5
ISBN-10 0-7656-1486-3

AMIS Vol. 6: Dennis Galletta and Ping Zhang
Human-Computer Interaction and Management Information Systems: Applications
ISBN-13 978-0-7656-1487-2
ISBN-10 0-7656-1487-1

AMIS Vol. 7: Murugan Anandarajan, Thompson S.H. Teo, and Claire A. Simmers
The Internet and Workplace Transformation
ISBN-13 978-0-7656-1445-2
ISBN-10 0-7656-1445-6

Editor in Chief, Vladimir Zwass (zwass@fdu.edu)

CONTENTS

Part VII. Methodological Issues and Reflections

SERIES EDITOR'S INTRODUCTION

VLADIMIR ZWASS, EDITOR-IN-CHIEF

As the second volume devoted to human-computer interaction (HCI) research in the *AMIS* monographs, the present work makes a major contribution to the objectives of the series. Its companion volume presented analytically the theoretical foundations of HCI in MIS; this volume establishes this research stream on a firm ground.

HCI research in MIS is an organic part of the IS discipline. Indeed, MIS centers on the study of information systems, rather than on information technologies, which are these systems' constituent. Human actors play an essential role in information systems. In the MIS field, HCI studies humans in their interactions with information technologies in the organizational context or for organizational benefit. We need to study humans both as individual actors—say, companies' design engineers or e-tail customers, and as members of groups—say, technology-coordinated members of international virtual teams, members of organizations at large, and members of supraorganizational entities such as the collaborators in global supply chains.

The users of a system have a vital role to play in that system's success or failure, and thus in the organizational outcome. This is particularly so as these outcomes begin to depend on the discretionary use of many systems. Cooperation, collaboration, community building, and innovation can hardly be elicited through compliance. Here is a regrettably typical scenario: An organizational memory information system has been implemented with an intranet and would help in addressing the marketplace with the accumulated experience contributed by the engineers, marketers, and salespeople. The incentives for contribution have been put in place by a new motivation program aiming to enhance the level of innovation. We want to share cases across the functional units, and we need to learn from the customers. However, the system is cumbersome to use, the way the accumulated knowledge is classified is unnatural, and the use mode disrupts the way people work. Although seeded with several contributions and evangelized by its champions, the system is simply adjudged not worth bothering with. As such discretionary systems depend on network effects, the system will fall into disuse.

Explicitly or implicitly, information systems are built around a user model. For example, the ARPANET protocols and the Internet-Web compound they gave rise to were intended for information sharers; it is hard to protect them from subversives and it is difficult (generally for certain types of governments) to discourage access and sharing. In an organizational setting, the absence of task analysis can lead to the development of systems that—even if implemented—will produce suboptimal outcomes, because they do not rely on an appropriate user model. In the extreme cases, as illustrated before, the systems fall by the wayside. It is therefore important that the user model underpinning an information system be constructed, prototyped, and validated across the user community.

In the advanced and advancing economies, issues such as ease of use, fun, support for flow experiences, and design aesthetics come to the fore. Indeed, you will find Amazon.com advertising the position of "user-experience specialist," and SAP America searching for a "senior user-experience designer," whose responsibilities include the "design of user interfaces based on research, human-factor principles, platform-style guides, and industry experience."

The aim of HCI research in MIS is to learn how to design organizational information systems that support humans to the greatest extent possible. The editors of the present work, Dennis Galletta and Ping Zhang, have made a signal contribution to our field with their two-volume project. The first volume laid the theoretical foundations for the present work that contextualizes and applies HCI theories to e-commerce, teamwork support, health care, e-learning, and other areas of human pursuit. We would want the field to be able to train people suitable for the positions cited above. It would then function as translational medicine does by converting the findings of scientists into actionable knowledge. Of course, considering the aim, this work can never be completed. Izak Benbasat, a leading authority in our field, and not only in the HCI domain, offers a notable foreword. The volume editors offer an extensive research introduction. The series editor needs to say no more.

FOREWORD

IZAK BENBASAT

I enjoyed very much reading this book and its companion (*Foundations*) that together make significant, timely, and valuable contributions to HCI research in management information systems (MIS). These two excellent volumes are being published at a time when HCI scholars in MIS are experiencing a renaissance. After years of dormancy, the field is experiencing a burst of new activity. Major MIS conferences are including HCI in their core coverage. Leading HCI and MIS academic journals have published, or will be publishing, special issues based on the best papers presented at these conferences, as well as at the workshop devoted to HCI research in MIS—the pre-ICIS Annual Workshop on HCI Research in MIS. MIS academics have a new home base from which to launch new activities: The Association of Information Systems (AIS) Special Interest Group on HCI (SIGHCI), established in 2001, aims to promote and support HCI research, teaching, and practice in MIS. These two volumes are the crowning touches to this exciting era of renewal. The chapters, written by the leading scholars in MIS and HCI, not only capture and synthesize the new knowledge generated from recent academic work, but also put forth the visionary and novel ideas of senior academics that will shape MIS HCI work during the next decade.

The rich tapestry of topics that comprise MIS HCI is captured very well in this volume with its comprehensive introduction and seventeen informative chapters representing the state of the art in the field. These chapters cover key HCI application issues that are beyond the "one person–one computer model" of early MIS HCI studies, such as the literature on graphical interfaces, to encompass broader issues dealing with organizational, cultural, and global issues influencing technology design, use, and adoption. While the person-computer model is still being investigated, for example, in the chapters on Internet download delays and pop-up ads, the person-computer-person model is also prominent in the chapters on virtual teams, collaboration technologies, and distributed teams, dealing with individuals or groups connected with or communicating through information technologies. The research and design challenges of the latter are more difficult because they focus not only on people interacting with technologies but also with each other via technologies. The three chapters on the topic of technology-based learning are interesting because they examine HCI issues in contexts where the objective is different from the performance of an activity, such as shopping on the Internet or making a decision, typically examined in MIS HCI studies. There are chapters on design methodologies that can be applied to systems analysis and design in general; but here specifically examined from an HCI or interface design perspective, they represent topics of increasing interest to MIS HCI researchers.

These topics also reveal another issue that we do not normally consider to be part of traditional HCI, namely the interface between users and technologists who are responsible for building systems and interfaces. Although the issues of Business-IT communication or linkage (i.e., the problem of the two solitudes) have been extensively researched in MIS, to my knowledge user-technologist communication has attracted less scholarly attention. The chapters covering public policy issues, health-care systems, and people with disabilities attest to the wide coverage of the book, the former topic addressing a problem that is consuming a significant amount of public resources and the latter dealing with the difficulties some of our fellow citizens face in accessing the information and services available via the Internet. Lastly, the book covers topics on adoption, where the emphasis is on identifying the factors that influence the utilization of new technologies.

Other significant contributions of this volume are found in the chapters dealing with philosophical issues, experimental methodology prescriptions, and measurement or metrics, since these provide the foundations of high-quality research endeavors. Developing new measures is a crucial activity that is a *sine qua non* for good research; unfortunately some leading journals in MIS have dampened the enthusiasm of those interested in pursuing such activities by somewhat discouraging such submissions. The inclusion of measurement-related topics in this volume will create a much-needed impetus to encourage the MIS HCI community to emphasize the development of new measures in its workshops and journal special issues.

I would like to mention three important aspects captured in this volume and its companion that are worth noting. The first is that it represents the work of individual researchers and research teams who focus on a program of research rather than one-shot individual studies. It is encouraging to observe that the volumes describe many such programmatic research efforts. The second is the importance of developing a critical mass of studies within the MIS HCI community by combining the efforts and coordinating the activities of groups of individual researchers. There are many chapters in the two volumes that comprehensively integrate the work of a community of HCI researchers. The AIS SIGHCI community and its workshops and meetings would be the appropriate venues to continue adding to the fine examples we find in these volumes by discussing and debating important issues facing practice, and planning a series of coordinated research activities to tackle them as a community of scholars. The third is to focus, where appropriate, on practice-related issues in HCI; that is, we need to learn how to design the interaction or the interface between individuals or groups and the technological artifact in order to assist practitioners. Robert Zmud and I have been emphasizing this need recently. Fortunately, there are many fine examples in the volumes of research efforts that lead to actionable information for practice.

I hope that these volumes will initiate a series of books that, by conveying current and future accumulated knowledge in MIS HCI, will guide and encourage scholars in the field to advance their research work. It is an excellent choice as the main textbook, or as a supplementary one, for advanced undergraduate or graduate courses in MIS HCI, and one that would be most suitable for an advanced doctoral topics seminar. I would like to thank the scholars who have contributed their excellent work to make these volumes a success. I congratulate Dennis Galletta and Ping Zhang for their vision and hard work in bringing them to fruition, and commend Vladimir Zwass for providing the platform for this work to be published.

HUMAN–COMPUTER INTERACTION AND MANAGEMENT INFORMATION SYSTEMS: APPLICATIONS

CHAPTER 1

APPLICATIONS OF HUMAN-COMPUTER INTERACTION IN MANAGEMENT INFORMATION SYSTEMS

An Introduction

DENNIS GALLETTA AND PING ZHANG

Abstract: *In this introduction to the second of the two complementary volumes, we provide a general context of applications of HCI research in MIS and then preview all papers in the second volume. This volume represents applications of HCI from the point of view of MIS research. Applications take particular courses that are carved out by researchers; we find that MIS researchers have taken HCI work in the directions of electronic commerce, team collaboration, culture and globalization, user learning and training, user-centered system development, and information technology in health care. Two reflective pieces at the end of this volume provide ample food for thought for researchers in this area.*

Keywords: *WWW, Electronic Commerce, Collaboration, Culture and Globalization, Training and Learning, User-Centered System Development, Health Informatics, Research Methodology*

INTRODUCTION

This book is one of two complementary volumes that present scholarly works from a variety of thought leaders in HCI, especially those who have ties to the field of management information systems (MIS). The first volume (*AMIS* Vol. 5) covers concepts, theories and models, and general issues of human-computer interaction studies relevant to MIS. Addressing perspectives on HCI from different disciplines, the first volume's topics include the nature and evolution of our understanding of who users are; theoretical understanding of how to design systems to support humans; theories and models of cognitive and behavioral aspects of using information technology (IT); and fundamental understanding of the affective, aesthetic, value-sensitive, and social aspects of HCI. This volume (*AMIS* Vol. 6) covers applications, special case studies, and HCI studies in specific contexts. Topics in this volume include HCI studies in electronic commerce and the Web context; HCI studies for collaboration support; culture and globalization issues; specific HCI issues in IT learning and training; theoretical understandings of system development processes; HCI issues in health care and health informatics; and, finally, methodological concerns in HCI research.

Each volume concludes with thoughtful reflections by well-known authors. In the first volume, Fred Davis discusses the connection between the technology acceptance model (TAM) and HCI, and Jonathan Grudin provides a historical reflection of the development of three closely related disciplines. In the second volume, an early, influential, and visible debate on soft versus hard science in HCI studies is revisited and updated from the perspective of one of the original debaters, John Carroll.

Application of theories, frameworks, and principles is crucial to the HCI-MIS field. Without theory, research would be haphazard, inconsistent, and inconclusive. Because of that undesirable potential, the MIS field has explicit requirements from editors of all of the major journals to provide adequate theory in performing studies.

Applications of human-computer interaction (HCI) theories, frameworks, and principles to MIS problems can be considered to be an organizationally based "proving ground" of sorts for those tools. Theories, frameworks, and principles provide an understanding of an issue or problem, while applications supply not only some partial evidence of whether or not the principles hold, but also some solutions, additional extensions, and new questions.

Therefore, in some ways, this second volume completes the story that was started in the first volume by complementing the perspectives and theories with those selected application areas that several of our most respected colleagues have chosen to examine. In other ways, this volume should stimulate the emergence of new applications and problem areas as it raises new questions—most papers suggest the need for additional research and even new areas of theory. Thus, this volume provides for tomorrow's conceptual work and applications. Such is the hallmark of a vibrant and progressing field.

RESEARCH CONTEXT

It is important to establish an appropriate disciplinary base for studying HCI issues. In the introduction to the first volume, we assert that HCI is an interdisciplinary research arena. Several papers in this volume underscore the multifaceted and interdisciplinary nature of the field. These papers import theoretical perspectives and tools from a variety of reference disciplines. The astute reader will recognize theories from several areas, including such fields as psychology, sociology, computer science, economics, health science, cultural sciences, and organizational sciences.

There is one interesting benefit to the interdisciplinary nature of HCI. There is a highly publicized and dramatic trend towards outsourcing system development (and many other) tasks to offshore vendors, and hiring is down. At the same time, enrollments in systems-related academic programs have declined sharply. Fortunately, Schwartz (2005) provides a preview of an upcoming government report that indicates that "work that crosses multiple disciplines" and requires creativity, ingenuity, and, most interestingly, "integration of business processes with IT," is less likely to be cast offshore in the foreseeable future. The HCI designer's task fits with all of these notions.

In addition to being multidisciplinary, HCI is also a strong practical and application-oriented area. Applications requiring interactions with human users can be found everywhere in our surroundings, and are therefore of significant concern to both researchers and practitioners in a wide variety of disciplines. Long-term efforts are under way to pull these researchers and practitioners under a single metaphorical umbrella where duplication of effort can be avoided and synergies can be exploited (DevCon, 2005; Galletta et al., 2005; Instone, 2005). The MIS field's main academic association, the Association for Information Systems (AIS), is participating in the dialog and movement. Other professionals include ergonomists, graphic designers, business analysts, product designers, engineers, and health professionals. There are few fields that escape the task of designing for a user's experience, and the time has come to share important findings among these fields.

While efforts are under way to pool resources, the disciplines will remain distinct. Ergonomists will continue to examine physical impacts in human factors work, graphic designers will retain their skill base on layout and presentation, and mechanical engineers will not yield their ability to

Table 1.1

Framework for Applying Theory

	The Academic Researcher	The Practitioner
Goals	Generalization	Problem solving
Activities	Theory development and testing	System design and evaluation

analyze materials that will go into a physical product. At the same time, it is striking that all of them need to be concerned with usability and users' experience of their products. All need to ask if people will understand the product with little training, if the product will behave as users expect, and if the product will be appealing. These concerns are indeed also shared by systems designers in the MIS field. What distinguishes MIS researchers is the organizational context.

Both MIS researchers and practitioners are interested in the organizational context. That context provides a notion of an organization's strategic goals and users' tasks. For researchers, the organizational context drives the choice of research problems and suggests methods for learning more. In a similar fashion, for practitioners, the organizational context bounds the problems that are examined and leads to approaches for solving them. The differentiating factor is that researchers are most often interested in acquiring generalizable knowledge, while designers are focused on providing a solution to the organization, with systems that have improved usability or enjoyment.

The rest of this paper is organized as follows: First, the notion of applying theory is described. Then each of the papers in this volume will be described, in order by section.

APPLYING THEORY

Theory is applied in a multitude of ways by researchers and practitioners, and there are important differences in the purpose and the application itself. Each part of the framework in Table 1.1 will now be discussed.

Generalization versus Problem Solving

Both academic researchers and practitioners are concerned with issues that arise at the organizational, system, user, and task level. What differentiates them is the level of generalization and problem solving that each desires.

Academic researchers who study a particular organizational system, user, or task are interested in what it will teach them about future systems, users, and tasks. Generalizability is of primary concern for building models and publishing papers. If the knowledge is not generalizable in some way, it is unlikely that other researchers will take an interest in that knowledge. Lessons learned can be shared with others and progress can be made for the entire field.

On the other hand, practitioners want to solve organizational problems. They need to build a system or make a particular decision. Sometimes theories published in journals are not immediately useful or visible to practitioners. However, some research undoubtedly filters through to practitioners, as many attend conferences, hear presentations by researchers, or read materials generated by researchers. In that case, pieces that they find useful could drive their problem solving.

The difference between the researcher's and practitioner's purpose is actually unexpectedly unifying. Applying theory to an organization's problems should allow practitioners to develop systems that are responsive to the needs of the organization and its members. This puts MIS in a unique position to provide the necessary organizational focus. Stated another way, MIS needs HCI and HCI needs MIS, as mentioned in the introduction to the first volume. It is worthwhile to examine each part of this assertion in some detail.

HCI Needs MIS

Historically, HCI research has included some explicit consideration of organizational issues, especially with respect to managing a project for greatest usability. For example, the classic piece by Gould and Lewis (1985) specifies that the first step in designing usable systems is identifying users and their tasks. Failing to gain such an understanding could lead to vexing design problems, such as presenting dialog boxes or prompts that use terminology unfamiliar to users, or requesting users to follow steps that they cannot find in any documentation or training materials. Equally as vexing, designers sometimes err by providing detailed instructions for performing well-known tasks such as selecting File-Save to save a file or File-Print to print a document. Amidst the obvious instructions, it might be difficult to find the key aspect of help needed, or that key aspect might have not been provided.

Such a focus has existed in the MIS field for a long time in work on systems analysis and design. The organizational context for practical problems is often provided by a business analyst (i.e., an MIS person). A business analyst is a compelling candidate for designing a user's experience. He can speak the user's business language to gain a quicker and more accurate representation of the task. He can develop more effective design specifications with richer organizational knowledge. He can produce test goals and benchmarks that are meaningful to the organization. He can determine if usability is of adequate quality for release to users.

From the perspective of applying theory, the MIS field has models that would benefit the HCI field by providing such context more systematically. For instance, the unified theory of acceptance and use of technology (UTAUT) (Venkatesh et al., 2003) contains both effort expectancy and performance expectancy. As described by Davis (2006), the former had been called "ease of use" and the latter "usefulness" in the past. In this model, performance expectancy, along with outcomes of these expectancies, provide useful context for effort expectancy. Effort expectancy by itself seems to provide a focus that is incomplete.

As an example, the famous "Ernestine" project (Gray et al., 1992) provided evidence that support calls could be handled more quickly by avoiding purchase of a new system. The new system had touted an "HCI friendly" design (with an easier-to-use interface and faster connection speed), but in reality, several steps that were previously done in parallel (computer and human) would now have to be done sequentially. Broadening the analysis to organizational needs for overall efficiency helped provide the proper decision, and helped save several million dollars. Further, additional analysis of customer satisfaction, company image, and IT strategy might have provided crucial input to the decision as well. The context provided by MIS is valuable and necessary, hence, HCI needs MIS.

MIS Needs HCI

The converse is also true, that MIS needs HCI. We have models that would, and do, benefit from more detailed notions in HCI. Again, using the UTAUT (Venkatesh et al., 2003) example, neither MIS researchers nor practitioners should stop after making an overall assessment of effort expectancy. They should make use of HCI principles and theoretical perspectives for their application work. MIS researchers should drill deeper and specify more elements of usability. For example, some systems are easy to learn but hard to use (putting everything into deeply nested but understandable menus) while others are hard to learn but easy to use (forcing memorization of shortcuts). While that crucial notion has received broad coverage in the HCI literature, it has not in the MIS literature. Therefore, for similar deepening of issues that might not be explored in the MIS literature, MIS needs HCI.

DEVELOPMENT AND TESTING OF THEORY

Theory is addressed in different ways by researchers and practitioners. While researchers attempt to develop and test theory, practitioners will use theory to design systems or evaluate products.

Researchers have provided theory in many areas, but that work is not complete. Likewise, theory that has been developed has not been applied in every potential area. The latter shortfall is caused by sheer numbers; there is perhaps an infinite set of application areas for the HCI theories, frameworks, and principles defined in the first volume. Not only can broad types or categories of systems be investigated, but a bewildering array of highly detailed aspects of those systems can be studied too. Researchers should be concerned with two basic questions: Where (i.e., to what kinds of problems) is theory applied? How is it applied?

Where Is Theory Developed?

Categories of systems, at several different levels, have been examined. The categories have tended to include shortlists that are mutually exclusive and exhaustive. For example, the HCI field studied graphical, menu, and command-based interfaces as three general ways to manage a dialog with the user. Within menu-based systems, researchers have subdivided the types into static and dynamic menus. Within static menus, researchers have investigated different arrangements of menu items, such as alphabetical order, functional or categorical order, frequency order, temporal order, and even random order.

Detailed aspects of systems have also served to define our understanding of systems, and although many very interesting studies have been conducted, only some areas have been covered. These considerations are not as well defined or exhaustive as the categories. Perhaps inspired by the categories, they represent phenomena that are observed by researchers. When studying menu-based systems, for instance, several researchers noticed that response time differed substantially among different systems and among different times of day when using one particular system. When studying graphical interfaces, some researchers noted that reading speed and comprehension differed when comparing paper against CRT screens of the 1980s.

Browsing the titles of these two volumes will provide ample testimony of the diversity in the application of theory by researchers and practitioners. The next concern is *how* it is applied.

How Is Theory Developed?

Combining a large set of options and outcomes enabled early researchers to explore without many expectations. In the early days (e.g., see Dickson et al., 1977), researchers listed options for presentation of information such as summarized versus detailed, or paper versus screen. They also examined outcomes such as "confidence" and "accuracy." As time passed, the MIS discipline began to mature. Researchers began to apply theory by "borrowing" and adapting theoretical developments from other fields, or even by developing new ones from previous studies.

UTAUT (Venkatesh et al., 2003) is an example of a perspective adapted from outside the field. Its predecessor model TAM (the technology acceptance model) (Davis, 1989) was derived from the theory of reasoned action (Fishbein and Ajzen, 1975) from social psychology. Many other models have been imported and adapted in this manner.

By contrast, an example of a theoretical development that originated in the field is the theory of cognitive fit (Vessey, 1991; Vessey and Galletta, 1991). Seeds for that study were sown in 1981, when Professor Gary Dickson at the University of Minnesota required PhD students at that time to reconcile the disparate findings of previous "graphs versus tables" studies. Coursework on organizational psychology with Professor John P. Campbell, also at the University of Minnesota, provided another seed. Professor Campbell taught that disparate findings usually demanded a contingency approach. The following cycle seemed to hold in many disciplines: (1) new management tools are introduced and heralded as the "next big thing"; (2) the tools sometimes work and sometimes do not work; and (3) someone finally discovers why, by identifying situations (contingencies) in which they will and will not work. A third seed was planted in the mid-1980s when Vessey and Galletta were auditing a well-known cognitive science course taught at Carnegie Mellon by the late Nobel Prize winner Herbert Simon. They discussed the possibility of capitalizing on the previous two seeds and launched the experiments. Vessey demonstrates her formidable research and writing instincts in the first volume, and her expertise and leadership provided a sensible framework and name for the theory. As the experiments were under way, she then went on to analyze the previous studies in that light (Vessey, 1991), making a seminal and frequently cited contribution to the field of MIS and HCI.

System Design and Evaluation

Practitioners have developed, over the years, new creative interaction techniques or tools, such as ergonomic keyboards, special dials on handheld devices, and new pointing devices (e.g., Briggs et al., 1993). The creativity of designers has propelled these developments, and few, if any, of our current theories could have formulated the new tools. As Shneiderman pointed out in the first volume, theories describe objects and actions, explain processes, predict performance, prescribe guidelines, or generate agendas. They do not allow the practitioner to plug in parameters and view the resultant 3D design for a new product on a screen.

It would be difficult to expect theories to create new products or systems. For example, existing theory could not have *specified* the IBM ThinkPad "pointing stick" and its location between the G and H keys on the keyboard. Indeed, Rutledge and Selker (1990) point out the trial-and-error process that led to its design and final placement. Alternative solutions—such as integrating the pointing stick with the "J" key, or placing it below the space bar or above the function keys— were explored.

Application of theory was quite useful to the ThinkPad team. The GOMS model (Card et al., 1983) and Fitts' Law (Fitts, 1954), both derived from psychological theory, allowed the designers to *evaluate* the device systematically and in a standard way. They measured the extent to which "mental time," having to pause and think about how to initiate the "J" key pointer, disturbed the efficiency of that option. Their designs were evaluated in Fitts' time-versus-difficulty plots.

Such events are not relegated to hardware design. Practitioners have also benefited from analysis of design alternatives by applying Fitts' Law. Callahan et al. (Callahan et al., 1988) designed a "Pie Menu," which does not require users to move to the top of the screen as in a pull-down menu. By clicking the mouse button, a menu surrounds the pointer at its current location. The menu requires only slight movement in any direction to choose the desired option. Several software packages make use of such menus, and theory was helpful to practitioners in evaluating the general type.

OVERVIEW OF THE VOLUME

Researchers and practitioners alike can benefit from the application of theory. Researchers can develop and apply theory to generalize to other situations. They develop and test models that are either derived from applications of theory, or that lead to new theory. Practitioners can use it to solve problems, often for evaluation of new software or hardware.

Several applications of theory are described in this volume. The areas are diverse, interesting, and important, and have either direct or indirect relevance to researchers and practitioners alike.

This volume contains monographs that cover several specific areas of HCI and MIS. The topics included have evolved over an extended time or over an extended set of studies. The application areas include electronic commerce, team collaboration, culture and globalization, user learning and training, system development, and health care. Following these papers are two highly appropriate pieces to conclude the two volumes. One provides strong methodological advice for HCI/MIS researchers, and the other revisits, and perhaps settles, a famous debate in the HCI field over "hard" science and "soft" science.

Each section of the book is introduced below, and each paper within each section is described.

Electronic Commerce and the Web

The Web and electronic commerce have become important areas in HCI MIS. The MIS researchers' interest in studying hypertext or the Web has expanded from the early days of building decision support systems (Minch, 1990) to a much broader range of research interests. According to Galletta (2006), electronic commerce has taken computer usage to many more users than ever before. Adding to the importance of usability is the problem that these new users are not able to benefit from corporate training for their systems. Previously, users were business professionals or clerical individuals, a rather specialized segment of the population. Today, an unprecedented number of regular citizens are Internet users: Statistics from February 2005 show that about two-thirds of Americans have Internet access (Internet World Stats, 2005).

Because computer users exist in greater numbers than ever before, but have less training than ever before, electronic commerce provides an unprecedented and rich research laboratory for HCI in MIS. The three papers in this session examine complementary and important aspects of electronic commerce and HCI.

The first, by Izak Benbasat, outlines several studies on various difficulties imposed by the physical decoupling of retail stores from their customers. Benbasat first explores types of communication, and then describes various tools that can enrich the experience. These tools include ways in which service can be provided virtually, how customers can browse with another person, and how customers can experience products more thoroughly.

The second, by Dennis F. Galletta, Raymond M. Henry, Scott McCoy, and Peter Polak, focuses on the phenomenon of Web delay. Delay is examined in a progression of four experiments: a study to determine how long users will wait until they lose patience, a study that examines user reactions to delay in two different cultures, and two studies that include factors that interact with delay. Interacting factors included user familiarity with Web site terminology and depth of the site in the first experiment, and feedback on page loading progress and variability of the delay in the second experiment.

The third electronic commerce study, by Ping Zhang, addresses animation in pop-up advertising, and describes eight years of research in that area. Three studies during that period found consistent evidence that animation impairs performance because it diverts a user's limited attention capacity for her primary task. The first study examined other related factors such as task diffi-culty, relevance of the animation to the task, and bright versus dull colors. The second study examined the timing, location, and repetition of the animation. The third study focused on user experience with animation.

Collaboration Support

Collaboration through electronic means is easier and cheaper than ever before. People who can-not be near each other have been brought together electronically, but even people who are physi-cally together can accomplish a variety of tasks more effectively using certain technologies. This topic has received widespread attention and has a semiannual conference devoted to it.[1] Due to the large number of tasks that are too large or complex for a single individual to perform, this area is quite important.

The first collaboration paper, by Judy and Gary Olson, examines several challenges faced by distributed teams, based on several studies in both the field and in the laboratory. In their early work, the challenges included the nature of work, the common ground of team members, the com-petitive/cooperative culture, the level of technological competence of team members, and the level of technical infrastructure. The paper focuses on new challenges, including alignment of incentives and goals, difficulty of establishing trust, awareness of colleagues and their context, the motivational sense of the presence of others, and the need for explicit management. Data from two hundred "collaboratories" are used to construct conceptual technical and social "bridges" to solve the difficulties.

The second paper on collaboration, by Starr Roxanne Hiltz, Jerry Fjermestad, Rosalie Ocker, and Murray Turoff, focuses on groups that are separated by time and distance (also known as asynchronous teams). Results from several field and laboratory experiments are described, and the results push in a variety of directions. Future research needs are outlined to help uncover a model for understanding this area better.

Ilze Zigurs and Bjørn Erik Munkvold contributed the third collaboration paper, which exam-ines collaboration technologies, tasks, and contexts, and provides an analysis of how these three elements have been addressed in MIS research. They review several typologies, as well as the evolving nature of these concepts. They also thoroughly review the literature, which should help researchers who are interested in this area.

Culture and Globalization

As information is passed among more and more people, it sometimes crosses cultural boundaries. Multinational firms find that people need to understand people of other cultures to ensure that they are communicating accurately. Software and hardware design should be culturally sensitive, or designers might create the technological equivalent to trying to sell the Chevrolet "Nova" in Mexico several years ago. The literal translation of "Nova" from Spanish to English is "will not go," as General Motors later found.

Two studies focus on culture and globalization. The first, by Jinwoo Kim, Inseong Lee, Boreum Choi, Se-Joon Hong, Kar Yan Tam, and Kazuaki Naruse, represents a collaboration of researchers in three Asian countries on the subject of the mobile Internet. Specifically, metrics for examining cultural aspects of technology are proposed and tested. Rather than force-fit the estab-lished dimensions of culture, the authors develop a layered approach that assumes that most ele-ments of culture exist in deeper layers that cannot easily be observed. The metrics are adapted from two sets of cultural dimensions in the previous literature. The researchers tested the instrument by examining logs of 1,075 actual mobile Internet users in Korea, Hong Kong, and Japan. Thorough examination of the instrument is provided.

The second cultural study was contributed by Geoffrey S. Hubona, Duane Truex III, Jijie Wang, and Detmar Straub. The group collected data that are complementary to the Asian mobile Internet study. The paper focuses on organizational use, and includes several countries throughout the world. Hubona et al. demonstrate that North American models of technology acceptance are not necessarily applicable in other countries. They examine sociocultural factors (for example, motivation and norms) and globalization factors (for example, government policy and national economics) in a framework to understand adoption and use of IT in other countries.

Learning and Training

Over the years, a small but dedicated community has examined user learning and training (e.g., Cronan and Douglas, 1990; Davis and Davis, 1990; Kang and Santhanam, 2004; Sein and Bostrom, 1989). Their work is becoming more important as the years pass, as more and more technology reaches the physical but perhaps not the cognitive grasp of users. Evidence that supports investing in training research can be found in legends about users who make errors, such as the famous tale of the user who believed a CD drive was a cup-holder. A humorous Web site entitled Computer Stupidities (http://www.rinkworks.com/stupid) provides several more potentially true tales about users: One photocopied a floppy disk, another held up a printer to his monitor so that the computer could "see" (and thus find) it, and still another misinterpreted a request to right-click on an icon and used a permanent marker to write the word "click" on her video display. If even a small proportion of the dozens of stories are actually true, the serious need for training is obvious.

It is important to provide a firm understanding of technological capabilities to prevent some of these errors. It is also important to provide a better glossary of the terminology used when referring to technologies to avoid misunderstandings. Some of the training might be needed to make up for failures in design, and the need could pass after these difficulties are eliminated. However, interactions with hardware and software are quite complex, and making each system self-tutoring could result in systems that are quite cumbersome after extended use.

A paper by Sharath Sasidharan and Radhika Santhanam reviews the literature on technology-based training. Early studies seem to have focused on the technologies themselves, to determine how the outcomes of training might be improved. Later studies, however, have devoted their attention more to learners than to technologies. Taken together, the existing studies provide background in understanding characteristics of the learner, the instructor, the technology, and the course. Much more research is needed to make significant progress in this area.

The second learning paper is offered by Lorne Olfman, Bob Bostrom, and Maung Sein, who examine how to develop a training strategy from an HCI perspective. The approach outlines how to design, implement, and deliver software training that is consistent with a framework that extends from corporate strategy to learning strategy to training strategy. The authors present their original model from several years ago, and describe several studies related to that model. They take the unusual step of providing a detailed critique of their own work. Finally, after discussing the framework and industry best practices, they provide an agenda for future researchers.

Conrad Shayo and Lorne Olfman provide the final paper on learning and training, offering a perspective on "learning objects," small chunks of digitized instructional content that can be delivered online. The authors review the literature in this area, focus on the benefits and difficulties of such a technology, and suggest what needs to be done in this area from a "Value Chain" perspective.

User-Centered Information Systems Development

Most systems are developed in response to a need that is determined to exist. That need could originate from the organizational level, as in an enterprise-wide system, or at the individual level, for making decisions more accurately, strategically, or quickly. In either case, individuals will use the system, facing its screens and needing to understand and respond to its prompts. Developing systems from the perspective of users is therefore a logical, yet sometimes neglected, strategy.

Glenn Browne supplies us with a review of research in information requirements determination, a framework of the requirements determination environment, and an inventory of research questions that have or have not been addressed satisfactorily. The four stages of IRD are used to understand the environment: pre-elicitation conditioning, elicitation, representation, and verification. The second and third stages have received most of the attention. Browne points out additional research needed to better understand cognitive, emotional, communication, experience, environmental, organizational, task, and individual issues in requirements determination.

John Carroll and Mary Beth Rosson survey participative design (PD) under a framework of six dimensions of participation: participatory impetus, ownership, scope of design, nature of the participatory process, scope of cooperation, and expectations about learning and human development. The framework provides for an analysis of traditional and emerging PD models, some of which date back two decades. Contemporary studies throw all of the models into a new light, and provide for an up-to-date view of PD.

Health Care and Health Informatics

The health-care arena is one in which technology decisions can have powerful impacts on the well-being of people. There are many interesting IT issues to study in a health-care context; yet only a limited number of studies exist (e.g., Hu et al., 1999). Information technologies for health care can either address health records or the process of treatment. Inaccurate records can result in complications for a patient, especially when urgent steps must be taken and little information is available about drug allergies or current medications being used. From the treatment side, new advances provide exciting prospects for people who might have given up hope without the new opportunities in receiving leading-edge care. This section provides a paper about each of those areas.

The first paper in this section, by Ritu Agarwal and Corey M. Angst, defines and discusses health information technology and illustrates opportunities for MIS research in this area. Focusing on adoption decisions on an electronic personal health record (PHR), Agarwal and Angst report on an empirical study that supports the notion that different demographic and health conditions lead to different perceptions of value of a PHR, and ultimately to adoption of the technology.

The second health-care paper, by Adriane B. Randolph and Geoffrey S. Hubona, reports on significant cutting-edge efforts for developing assistive technologies for people with disabilities. Randolph and Hubona examine organizational adoption and diffusion of such technologies, to perhaps minimize the disproportionate levels of unemployment and poverty of the millions of working-age people with disabilities. Eight predictive models and two case studies are presented. The first case study addresses BrainBrowser, a promising but developing technology that will eventually allow people with motor disabilities to control certain functions with brain impulses. The second relies on galvanic skin response to accomplish the same goal in users who are not good candidates for BrainBrowser due to complicating diseases.

Methodological Issues and Reflections

The last two papers in the book provide useful advice for researchers interested in HCI/MIS applications. Researchers are often interested in making sure they are examining appropriate problems, and are examining those problems in the correct manner.

MIS scholars have utilized a large number of different research methods. A recent survey of published HCI studies in seven top MIS journals from 1990–2002 (Zhang and Li, 2005) revealed that almost all of the methods in Alavi and Carlson's research type framework (Alavi and Carlson, 1992) have been used. The most commonly utilized method, however, is the controlled lab experiment (used by 35.6 percent of the HCI papers in the period), followed by surveys (by 25.5 percent of the HCI papers) and field studies (by 12.5 percent of the HCI papers) (Zhang and Li, 2005). In this volume, Alan Dennis, Monica Garfield, Heikki Topi, and Joseph Valacich provide a paper on conducting lab experiments, from initial conception of a study to publication, that should be on every experimenter's desk. Four main issues are addressed: how to find and select ideas for studies, how to use theory, how to design an experiment, and how to write (and revise) the experimental paper.

John M. Carroll provides the paper that wraps up the two-volume set. He provides a unique retrospective of his and Robert Campbell's famous "soft versus hard science" debate with Allen Newell and Stuart Card from twenty years ago. Although Allen Newell has since passed on and Stuart Card was not available for a similar retrospective, Carroll's account and analysis helps us to think more thoroughly about the prospect that predictive mathematical or technical studies could drive out social and behavioral approaches. This paper serves as the missing final rebuttal by Carroll, with whom Campbell decided many years ago not to debate the matter further.

Carroll refers to the debate as an "essential tension," and two key questions are examined. The first question is whether there is a problem introduced by soft sciences in a multidisciplinary field, and the second is whether "hardening" all of the contributing sciences is desirable. Carroll demonstrates that additional "soft" sciences have entered the HCI milieu, and HCI's base in science is actually more eclectic and softer than it was during the initial debate. Cognitive modeling is no longer the default paradigm for HCI studies. Even with this happily multifaceted emergent discipline, Carroll notes that some less confident researchers will, even today, shy away from "soft" studies and pass up interesting opportunities because of this debate, and closes the thoughtful piece by asserting that long-running crises sometimes lead to what Kuhn calls extraordinary science, where researchers question assumptions, abandon conventions, and routinize innovative practices.

CONCLUSION

It is our hope that with these two volumes, researchers in MIS HCI will be better prepared for a possible period of extraordinary science. There seems to be no end to the development of exciting new technologies, and developers should be able to make them usable and useful to people in all walks of life. It is our responsibility to develop and impart to our students and/or colleagues the principles that enable and enrich these applications. We are proud to have edited these volumes and hope that they inform and energize you as much as they have informed and energized us.

NOTE

1. See Grudin (1994) for a detailed history of the CSCW (computer-supported cooperative work) conference.

REFERENCES

Alavi, M., and Carlson, P. A review of MIS research and disciplinary development. *Journal of Management Information Systems*, 8, 4 (1992), 45–62.

Briggs, R.O.; Dennis, A.R.; Beck, B.S.; and Nunamaker, J.F. Whither the pen-based interface? *Journal of Management Information Systems*, 9, 3 (1993), 71–90.

Callahan, J.; Hopkins, D.; Weiser, M.; and Shneiderman, B. An empirical comparison of pie vs linear menus. In *Proceedings of the Conference on Human Factors in Computing Systems (CH)*, Washington, DC: Association for Computing Machinery, 1988, pp. 95–100.

Card, S.; Moran, T.P.; and Newell, A. *The Psychology of Human-Computer Interaction*. Hillsdale, NJ: Lawrence Erlbaum Associates, 1983.

Cronan, T.P., and Douglas, D.E. End-user training and computing effectiveness in public agencies: an empirical study. *Journal of Management Information Systems*, 6, 4 (1990), 21–39.

Davis, D.L., and Davis, D.F. The effect of training techniques and personal characteristics on training end users of information systems. *Journal of Management Information Systems*, 7, 2 (1990), 93–110.

Davis, F. Perceived usefulness, perceived ease of use, and user acceptance of information technology. *MIS Quarterly*, 13, 3 (1989), 319–340.

DevCon, CHI Development Consortium. 2005 (available at http://uxnet.org/devcon/, accessed on December 15, 2005).

Dickson, G.W.; Senn, J.A.; and Chervany, N.L. Research in management information systems: the Minnesota experiments. *Management Science*, 23, 9 (1977), 913–923.

Fishbein, M., and Ajzen, I. *Belief, Attitude, Intention and Behavior: An Introduction to Theory and Research*. Reading, MA: Addison-Wesley, 1975.

Fitts, P.M. The information capacity of the human motor system in controlling the amplitude of movement. *Journal of Experimental Psychology*, 47 (1954), 381–391.

Galletta, D.; Zhang, P.; and Nah, F.F.-H. AIS HCI position paper. In *Proceedings of the ACM Conference on Human Factors in Computing Systems*. Portland, OR: Association for Computing Machinery, 2005, pp. 1080–1082.

Galletta, D.F. Human factors and e-commerce. In M. Shaw (ed.), *Electronic Commerce and the Digital Economy*. Armonk, NY: M.E. Sharpe, 2006.

Gould, J.D., and Lewis, C. Designing for usability: key principles and what designers think. *Communications of the ACM*, 28, 3 (1985), 300–311.

Gray, W.D.; John, B.E.; and Atwood, M.C. The precis of Project Ernestine or an overview of a validation of GOMS. In *Proceedings of the ACM CHI*. Monterey, CA: Association for Computing Machinery, 1992, pp. 307–312.

Grudin, J., CSCW: History and Focus. 1994 (available at http://www.ics.uci.edu/~grudin/Papers/IEEE94/IEEEComplastsub.html, accessed on June 6, 2005).

Hu, P.J.; Chau, P.Y.K.; Sheng, O.R.L.; and Tam, K.Y. Examining the technology acceptance model using physician acceptance of telemedicine technology. *Journal of Management Information Systems*, 16, 2 (1999), 91–112.

Instone, K. User experience: an umbrella topic. In *Proceedings of the ACM Conference on Human Factors in Computing Systems*, Portland, OR: Association for Computing Machinery, 2005, pp. 1087–1088.

Internet World Stats. 2005 (available at http://www.internetworldstats.com/am/us.htm, accessed on June 6, 2005).

Kang, D., and Santhanam, R. A longitudinal field study of training practices in a collaborative application environment. *Journal of Management Information Systems*, 20, 3 (2004), 257–281.

Minch, R.P. Application and research areas for hypertext in decision support systems. *Journal of Management Information Systems*, 6, 3 (1990), 119–138.

Rutledge, J., and Selker, T. In-keyboard analog pointing device: a case for the pointing stick. *Technical Video Program of the CHI '90 Conference*, *SIGGRAPH Video Review*, 55, 1 (1990).

Schwartz, E. Dire Forecast for IT jobs. *Infoworld*. 2005 (available at http://www.infoworld.com/article/05/05/17/21OPreality_1.html, accessed on December 15, 2005).

Sein, M.K., and Bostrom, R. The influence of individual differences in determining the effectiveness of conceptual models in training novice users. *Human-Computer Interaction*, 4 (1989), 197–229.

Venkatesh, V.; Morris, M.G.; Davis, G.B.; and Davis, F.D. User acceptance of information technology: toward a unified view. *MIS Quarterly*, 27, 3 (2003), 425–478.

Vessey, I. Cognitive fit: a theory-based analysis of the graphs versus tables literature. *Decision Sciences*, 22 (1991), 219–240.

Vessey, I., and Galletta, D.F. Cognitive fit: an empirical study of information acquisition. *Information Systems Research*, 2, 1 (1991), 63–84.

Zhang, P., and Li, N. The intellectual development of human-computer interaction research in MIS: a survey of the MIS literature (1990–2002). *Journal of Association for Information Systems* 6, 11 (2005), 227–292.

PART I

ELECTRONIC COMMERCE
AND THE WEB

CHAPTER 2

HUMAN-COMPUTER INTERACTION FOR ELECTRONIC COMMERCE

A Program of Studies to Improve the Communication Between Customers and Online Stores

IZAK BENBASAT

Abstract: *In electronic commerce the user-company interface is the Web site that represents the online storefront of an e-tailer. This Web interface is the company's "window to the world," through which communication with customers takes place and relationships are built. Therefore, electronic commerce gives rise to new HCI challenges mainly associated with how to design the Web interfaces for effective communication between customers and online retailers. This paper describes a series of studies conducted to investigate topics associated with HCI design for electronic commerce, mainly concerned with improving customer-company communications on the Web, including customer-product, customer-customer, customer-salespeople, and customer-recommendation agent communications. The main objectives and findings of these studies are discussed, and how they can be incorporated into an overall research framework for conducting HCI studies in the age of electronic commerce is described.*

Keywords: *Human-Computer Interaction, Electronic Commerce, IT-Mediated Communication*

INTRODUCTION

Human Computer Interaction (HCI) is a sub-discipline of computer and information sciences that has been an important area of study since the early 1960s. According to the ACM special interest group on computer-human interaction (ACM SIGCHI) "human-computer interaction is a discipline concerned with the design, evaluation and implementation of interactive computing systems for human use and with the study of major phenomena surrounding them" (Hewett et al., 1996). This definition focuses on the interaction between people and computing systems. It also characterizes to a large extent the kind of HCI research management information systems researchers have conducted for the last three decades. Historically, MIS researchers have investigated designs for both person-computer interaction (e.g., direct manipulation interfaces, command abbreviation methods) and computer-person interaction (e.g., graphical information presentation, use of colors, multimedia interfaces, response time). Design quality was measured in terms of effectiveness, efficiency, and satisfaction.

Electronic commerce (e-commerce) has changed the research emphasis associated with HCI studies in MIS. In the e-commerce context, the design of efficient and effective interactions between a technological artifact (e.g., a Web page) and a person continue to be important; download delays, navigational problems, and the look and feel of a Web site are still relevant issues to study. However, it is as important that we now direct our attention to the *communication* between the user and the online store and the components of that communication.

In the e-commerce context our key design focus should not be on the interaction between a person and a computer, but rather the communication between a person and an online company, that is, a non-IT artifact. Consequently, the new HCI design objectives for e-commerce are concerned more with the relationship-based aspects of communication, such as creating a positive company image and a favorable shopping experience. Even though technology is still the main conduit between a customer and an online company, the shift in focus from the interaction with a computer to communication with an online store is not unlike the case of group support systems or computer-supported collaborative work, where the main goal is to facilitate communication for collaborating individuals.

To understand why there is a shift of emphasis, we need to understand the nature of communications in an e-commerce context. E-commerce imposes several proximity constraints on the communication between the customer and an online company. They include the proximity to the online store, to the service personnel, to other customers, and to the product. When shopping online, one is segregated from the online store, its salespeople, and the other customers. Furthermore, the online settings provide little support for the physical examination of products. To a large extent, in e-commerce the user-company interface is the Web site that represents the online storefront of an e-tailer. This Web interface is the company's "window to the world," through which communication with customers takes place and relationships are built. Therefore, e-commerce gives rise to new HCI challenges mainly associated with how to design the Web interfaces for effective communication between customers and online retailers. MIS researchers are particularly suited to investigate these issues given their expertise both in HCI and individual, group, and organizational behavior.

In summary, HCI design in the context of e-commerce can be examined from two perspectives: (1) the transactional view that emphasizes the speed, accuracy, and efficiency of the exchange, and (2) the relationship-enhancing view that emphasizes the richness and rhetorical aspects of the exchange between the company and its customers. The former focuses on the customer's interaction with a Web page (as a technological artifact), and is more concerned with the traditional HCI goals of efficient and effective exchanges. The latter focuses on better communications between a customer and the online company, including communications with the personnel and other customers of this company. It is more concerned with design objectives such as enhancing trust, company image, product description, and service. These two perspectives are not so much contradictory as complementary. Ideally, HCI practitioners should understand how to design e-commerce interfaces that facilitate both the execution of transactions and the development of relationships among customers and organizational entities by creating tools for utilizing and communicating information.

In a series of studies conducted at the Sauder School of Business, University of British Columbia, my students and I have together investigated topics associated with HCI design for e-commerce, mainly about customer-company communications on the Web, including customer-product, customer-customer, and customer–recommendation agent communications. This paper will confine itself to discussing only these studies and describing their individual objectives, their overarching goal of improving company-customer communications, and their findings, with the

Figure 2.1   **Types of Interactions in an E-Commerce Context**

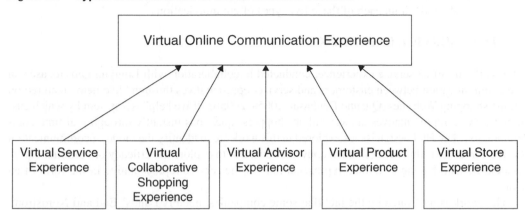

objective of providing a research framework for conducting HCI studies in the age of electronic commerce. Due to space limitations, it will not provide a complete coverage of the literature, or a broad picture of all research conducted in each study and its general topic area. However, readers desiring more information can access it via the papers referenced in the following sections that describe each study fully.

TYPES OF COMMUNICATIONS

Qiu (2002) identified several types of communications that take place in an e-commerce context, as illustrated in Figure 2.1. They are:

1. *Virtual Service Experience* (VSE): communication between a customer and a service-person to obtain assistance
2. *Virtual Collaborative Shopping Experience* (VCSE): communication between one or more customers, for example, between two friends in different cities shopping together, either for social interaction and/or for obtaining shopping advice
3. *Virtual Advisor Experience* (VAE): the interaction between a customer and an online rec-ommendation agent (software) that provides product recommendations to the customer
4. *Virtual Product Experience* (VPE): communication between a customer and a product to gain better product experience and understanding
5. *Virtual Company Experience* (VCE): communication between a customer and the Web site representing an online company.

   The Web site can be a difficult concept to define exclusively of its parts, such as virtual prod-uct experience, in the context of relational interactions (Al-Natour and Benbasat, 2004). The first four and the fifth category of e-commerce communications listed above are not mutually exclu-sive, since the former four (user-serviceperson, user-user, user-product, and user-agent) are a sub-set of one's communication with the Web site, that is, a customer first visits a Web site before reaching these other entities. Hence, one's communication with a given entity (e.g., a salesperson) will affect the overall perception of the Web site in addition to a specific type of communication.

With this caveat in mind, in the next sections of the paper I will discuss the research studies that we have conducted within each of these five types of communications.

VIRTUAL SERVICE EXPERIENCE

The work on virtual service experience, conducted in collaboration with Lingyun Qiu, focuses on the communication between customers and service representatives through "live help" featured on online shopping Web sites (Qiu and Benbasat, 2005a, 2005b). "Live help" is a system by which customer service representatives answer online shoppers' questions instantly through real-time communication. The HCI design issues explored in this work are to identify the mode of communication (voice versus text) that better fit such conversations, and to explore the efficacy of communication associated with having a "human representation" of the service representative in the form of an avatar.

This work is motivated by the fact that some companies, notably Lands' End and Nordstrom, have gained significant benefits from using the "live help" feature. The average dollar value of an order increases by 6 percent when a potential customer uses the "live help" function. An online visitor who uses Lands' End's instant messaging feature is 20 percent more likely to complete a purchase than one who does not (Dukcevich, 2002). "Live help" distinguishes itself from other online customer support functions by involving human assistants. Aberg and Shahmehri (2000, 2001, and 2003) demonstrated that integrating human assistance into Web pages makes a Web site more fun to use, increases the user's trust in the site, and improves enjoyment.

The Gartner Group predicts that "by 2002, only 20 percent of call centers will have integrated live Web contacts or e-mail response management systems with their telephone-based agents; by 2005, 70 percent of call centers . . . will support integrated live Web contacts and e-mail response management systems for their telephone-based agents" (Elliot, 2001). Therefore, the expected proliferation of such support indicates the need to investigate the best means to design them. Currently, most "live help" services are implemented through instant text chatting between shoppers and customer service representatives. A laboratory experiment was designed (Qiu and Benbasat, 2005b) to empirically test the hypotheses that voice communication and 3D avatars will have significant effects on three dependent variables: (1) perception of social presence, or the extent to which users sense the existence of other people in distant locations; (2) telepresence, or a user's experience of being in another environment by means of a communication medium; and (3) flow, "the holistic sensation that people feel when they act with total involvement" (Csikszentmihalyi, 1975, p. 36). The experiment was conducted in the context of online stores for digital cameras and accessories, using a 3×2 full factorial design to test the hypotheses. While shopping for digital cameras, customers interacted with a sales representative using text communication. The response from the sales representative in text format was communicated to the customer in three ways: "text only," "text-to-speech (TTS) voice conversion only," and "text + TTS voice." A TTS synthesizer refers to a device that reads text aloud. TTS, rather than a pure voice communication, was explored because TTS can significantly improve the customer service representative's productivity and reduce the call center's operating costs by enabling the serviceperson to service several customers simultaneously with the help of predetermined scripts containing answers to frequently asked questions, just as is done in text-based "live help."

The second interface feature investigated is the use of naturalistic[1] 3D avatars to "animate" a customer service representative in the process of communication. This type of avatar can emulate minimal natural protocols to achieve recognition of regular gestures, such as a smile, a waving hand, and a nodding head.

The findings indicate that the presence of TTS voice only significantly increases users' perceptions of flow, while 3D avatars enhance users' feelings of telepresence (of the sales representative). The lack of a significant impact of TTS voice communication and avatars on users' perceptions of social presence might be a result of the relative immaturity of the technology itself.

VIRTUAL COLLABORATIVE SHOPPING EXPERIENCE

The work on virtual collaborative shopping, conducted with Lei Zhu, focuses on the communications of two or more individuals, in distant locations, shopping together online, where one person is the shopper and the other is assisting him or her (Zhu and Benbasat, 2004). The motivation of the study is based on the fact that collaborative or social shopping, such as one sharing ideas about particular products with friends to obtain their feedback, is an important social experience in consumers' shopping activities. The constraints imposed by distance on traditional collaborative shopping have created an impetus for Web collaboration technologies that can enable people to shop with friends and family who are far away.

The HCI research questions explored in this study aim to identify the mode of instant communication support (voice versus text) that is best suited for such conversations and to explore the benefits of having collaborative browsing support (also known as co-browsing), a software-enabled technique that facilitates communication among shopping partners by allowing individuals using different workstations to view the same Web pages synchronously.

To investigate the effects of collaborative browsing support and instant communication support, a mixed 2×2 design was used in a laboratory experiment. In this design, collaborative browsing support is a between-group factor (without collaborative browsing support vs. with collaborative browsing support), and instant communication support (instant text chatting support vs. instant voice chatting support) is a within-group factor. The task studied by the experiment was to buy two products: schoolbags and watches. Participants who volunteered were asked to bring a friend to the study; one person was randomly assigned to play the role of the shopper and the other his assistant. The dependent variables were perceived ease of use and perceived usefulness (cognitive factors), telepresence (social factor), and shopping enjoyment (emotion factor).

The results indicate that there are significant benefits associated with collaborative browsing support. Its use enhances both shopping enjoyment and telepresence in online shopping. Voice chatting is superior to text chatting in terms of both perceived ease of use and perceived usefulness of collaborative online shopping support tools. It also leads to higher enjoyment and feelings of telepresence in online shopping activities. The relationships between the dependent variables were also investigated as part of the technology acceptance model (TAM) to apply and extend it to collaborative online shopping contexts. Telepresence improves perceived usefulness and shopping enjoyment, while shopping enjoyment increases the perceived ease of use of collaborative online shopping support tools. Furthermore, perceived usefulness, perceived ease of use, and enjoyment all positively influence consumer intentions to shop online collaboratively.

VIRTUAL ADVISOR EXPERIENCE

Two studies on communications with virtual advice-giving systems, conducted in collaboration with Sherrie Xiao Komiak and Weiquan Wang, focus on the communications between customers and product recommendation agents (Komiak and Benbasat, 2004; Wang and Benbasat, 2004). Recommendation agents are personalized computer agents that advise a customer about what to buy (product-brokering), or from which company to buy (merchant-brokering), based on the customer's individual needs (Ansari et al., 2000; Maes et al., 1999). They are sometimes characterized as customer decision support systems (CDSS) (Grenci and Todd, 2002).

The HCI design issues associated with communicating with a software agent are different from those that arise when communicating with a person, as is the case with the virtual service and the virtual collaborative shopping experiences discussed earlier. In those two instances, communication among individuals is mediated by a technology, for example, people collaborating via a group support system. Although designing the interaction between a software agent and a user appears to be within the domain of traditional HCI, the major focus of our studies of the virtual advisor experience has been *relationship-based* issues, namely, the *trustworthiness* of the agent, rather than on designing efficient and effective exchanges, such as information display or menu interfaces, between people and technology.

Trust is an important topic in the recommendation agent (RA) context for two reasons. First, the RA has more information than the user about the logic it uses to generate advice. Accordingly, the user may not have sufficient knowledge to evaluate the RA's performance. Second, there could be goal incongruence between the RA and its users: Because the RA is provided and owned by the Web site and e-vendor, it may have been designed to generate higher profits for the e-vendors, rather than to benefit its users. Furthermore, in order to trust the RA, a customer wants assurance that it has effectively internalized her needs. Perceived internalization is defined as (1) an RA fully understands individual customers' true needs, and (2) the RA fully adopts customers' needs as its own preferences (Komiak and Benbasat, 2004).

Therefore, the goal of the RA designer is to enhance trust by creating a sense of mutual understanding between the user and the RA. The design objectives corresponding to the two concerns described above are: (1) the user wants to understand the RA's decision-making behavior and criteria, and (2) the user wants to perceive that the RA understands her needs. In terms of HCI design, the first is accomplished by having the RA communicate its behavior to the user by providing explanations about its competence, goals, and intentions. For example, the RA might state that it is working on behalf of the user rather than the online store. The second is accomplished by designing RA-customer communication so that users can describe what they need rather than having to specify the level of attributes they want. These are discussed more fully below.

Wang and Benbasat (2004) identified a mechanism for a technological artifact (i.e., an RA) to communicate information about its goals and behaviors to its users so as to enhance mutual understanding between the user and the RA. To accomplish this objective, Wang and Benbasat empirically tested how three types of explanations affected consumers' initial trust in online RAs: (1) *how* explanations, which provide information about how recommendations are derived; (2) *why* explanations, which provide information about why the RA elicits certain user inputs; and (3) *guidance,* which helps the user with the trade-offs associated with expressing product-related attribute needs. By extending interpersonal trust to trust in technological artifacts,[2] consumer trust in recommendation agents is defined to include three belief components: *competence, benevolence*, and *integrity.* The results of a laboratory experiment, conducted using a $2 \times 2 \times 2$ factorial design, support the hypothesis that the explanation provision facilitates consumers' initial trust-building in RAs and indicate that different types of explanations increase different trusting beliefs: The availability of *how* explanations increases consumer beliefs in RA competence, the availability of *why* explanations increases consumer beliefs in RA benevolence, and the availability of *guidance* increases consumer beliefs in RA integrity.

Komiak and Benbasat (2004) studied how users can communicate their needs to the RA so that users perceive that the RA understands them. To accomplish this objective they empirically compared two types of RAs. To both RAs, the customers first specified all the product features they desired.

Using the same strategy to choose from the products available over the Internet, both then gave each customer a list of products, ordered by how well the products satisfied the customer's constraints.

The study used two types of RAs. The first, needs-based, RA utilized a "get advice" feature that asked customers questions about their needs. For example, the customer could state that he needed a digital camera that could take pictures of objects far away, rather than having to specify the level of zoom he required. In addition, the need-based RA allowed customers to specify the relative importance (weight) of each attribute, if they wished. The RA would then suggest products that met the desired specifications. The other, attribute-level specification, RA asked customers to specify a preferred level for each product attribute. For example, a customer could state that she wanted a $3\times$ zoom. It was expected that the needs-based RA would be perceived to have higher internalization than the attribute-level specification RA, because the availability of needs-based questions and specifying weights would elicit the customers' perception that it could more accurately and fully represent their needs.

When Komiak and Benbasat (2004) compared these two types of RAs in a laboratory study, they found that the needs-based RA led to higher perceived internalization of customers' needs by the RA. Perceived internalization was a significant predictor of customers' trust, which in turn significantly affected the intention to use RAs.

VIRTUAL PRODUCT EXPERIENCE

The study of virtual product experience, conducted in collaboration with Jack Zhenhui Jiang, focuses on the communications between customers and product recommendation agents (Jiang and Benbasat, 2005). The development of electronic commerce has been partly hampered by online consumers' inability to feel, touch, and sample products through Web interfaces, as they can do in stores. We argue that this limitation could be partly alleviated by providing consumers with virtual product experience, which would enable them to experience products virtually by using software and hardware technologies.

Virtual service, virtual collaborative shopping experiences, and virtual software-based advisors engage in two-way communication with the consumer, but the communication between the consumer and a product is more akin to a direct manipulation interface: The product reacts to a user's inputs by changing its form or behavior. Here, HCI explores the kinds of user inputs and product responses that can improve how a customer understands a product displayed on a Web page.

This study investigated the efficacy of providing virtual control that is composed of two dimensions, visual control and functional control, enabled by multimedia and direct manipulation technologies, respectively. Visual control enables consumers to manipulate Web product images, to view products from various angles and distances; functional control enables consumers to explore and experience different features and functions of products.

The individual and joint effects of visual and functional control were investigated in a laboratory experiment using a 2×2 factorial design. The results indicated that both visual and functional control increased perceived diagnosticity (i.e., the extent to which a consumer believes the shopping experience is helpful to evaluate a product) and that both increased flow. More specifically, visual control increased the perceived diagnosticity of appearance-related attributes of the product, and functional control increased the perceived diagnosticity of functionality-related attributes. In addition, functional control increased the perceived diagnosticity of appearance-related factors slightly, but only in the absence of visual control. In general, however, functional control dominated visual control in terms of diagnosticity, and the impact of visual control was evident only in the absence of functional control.

VIRTUAL COMPANY EXPERIENCE

The study on virtual company experience, conducted in collaboration with Nanda Kumar, focuses on the communications between customers and Web sites (Kumar and Benbasat, 2004). The goal is to explore the type of information exchanges between customers and online companies that emphasize the relationship-based aspects of communication, such as creating a positive company image, trust, and a favorable shopping experience. We are interested in whether or not a customer views a Web site as a social entity—that is, is it appropriate to draw a parallel between relationships among humans and the relationship between a Web site and its users?

In this study we attempt to identify the perceived communication characteristics that will result in the Web site being perceived as a richer communication partner, leading to higher levels of social presence and perceived usefulness. By synthesizing research from media choice and technology adoption literatures, we propose perceived usefulness as the utilitarian construct and social presence as the experiential construct that will mediate the relationship between the medium's communication characteristics and the customer loyalty they produce, that is, customers' tendency to revisit the store.

Usefulness is considered to be utilitarian because it represents the benefit or utility one expects to get from shopping via the Web. Social presence is considered experiential because it refers to how well a medium allows an individual to experience personal connections with others (Short and Christie, 1976). Recent research that elicited participants' beliefs about the goals that can be achieved through the Internet found that they attached considerable importance to better social relationships and new friendships (Capozza et al., 2003). Furthermore, Gefen et al. (2003) have adopted social presence in their study on Web site shopping. They label the construct as social presence–information richness (SPIR) and use it in the manner consistent with the original definition proposed by Short and Christie (1976). Because social presence has similar connotations to affect in expressing the experiential aspect of a relationship while capturing "a sense of connection" among multiple parties, such as other consumers, it is an important construct to study in the Web shopping context.

The HCI design objective of this research is to investigate the effects of personalization and of consumer reviews (one form of virtual community) on the strength of the relationship between e-tailers and customers. We argue that if a social actor (including a Web site) helps another social actor (a visitor to a Web site) connect with others who share similar interests (a virtual community), this would then foster a positive relationship between those actors (the Web site and the visitor to that site). We posit that IT-enabled support for personalization systems and virtual communities has a significant impact on two perceived communication characteristics of a Web site: perceived adaptiveness (the potential of the Web site to adjust itself to a particular receiver) and perceived connectivity (the ability of a medium to bring together people who share common interests or goals).

Two studies were conducted to test this hypothesis (Kumar and Benbasat, 2004). The first study showed that while adaptiveness influences both the experiential (i.e., social presence) and utilitarian (i.e., perceived usefulness) constructs, connectivity has an impact only on social presence. Social presence and perceived usefulness both significantly affect customer loyalty. The second study found that support for personalization has a strong impact on perceived adaptiveness, whereas support for consumer reviews has a strong effect on perceived connectivity. It also showed that IT-enabled personalization and virtual communities do have a significant impact, not only on perceived communication characteristics, but also on customer loyalty through social presence and perceived usefulness.

Figure 2.2   **A Model for Conducting HCI Research in E-Commerce**

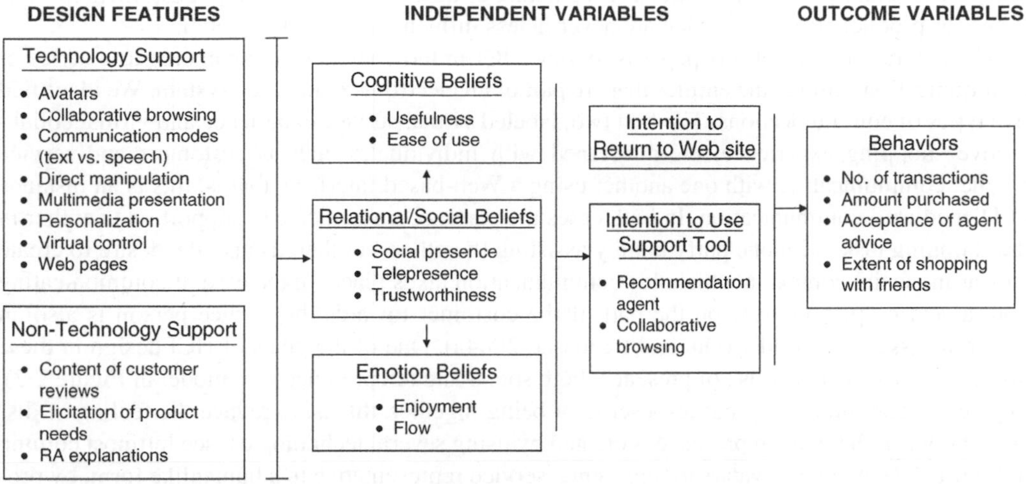

DESIGN FEATURES

INDEPENDENT VARIABLES

OUTCOME VARIABLES

Technology Support
- Avatars
- Collaborative browsing
- Communication modes (text vs. speech)
- Direct manipulation
- Multimedia presentation
- Personalization
- Virtual control
- Web pages

Non-Technology Support
- Content of customer reviews
- Elicitation of product needs
- RA explanations

Cognitive Beliefs
- Usefulness
- Ease of use

Relational/Social Beliefs
- Social presence
- Telepresence
- Trustworthiness

Emotion Beliefs
- Enjoyment
- Flow

Intention to Return to Web site

Intention to Use Support Tool
- Recommendation agent
- Collaborative browsing

Behaviors
- No. of transactions
- Amount purchased
- Acceptance of agent advice
- Extent of shopping with friends

DISCUSSION AND CONCLUDING COMMENTS

One way to organize the constructs investigated by the studies described in this paper into a cohesive whole is to incorporate them into a technology adoption model, such as the technology acceptance model (TAM), theory of reasoned action (TRA), or the theory of planned behavior (TPB) (Venkatesh et al., 2003). In Zhu and Benbasat (2004) we extended the TAM model by adding emotion and social beliefs to the cognitive ones (e.g., ease of use and usefulness) that are part of TAM. In Figure 2.2, we present such a model that serves as a framework to guide HCI studies in e-commerce, and later illustrate its use in the context of the studies described in this paper.

The central focus of this paper is on designing communications between customers and online companies to effect relationship-building in e-commerce. In Figure 2.2, the social or relational beliefs—namely, social presence, telepresence, and trust—measure the extent of relationship-building. These constructs influence two adoption variables, intention to return to the Web site and intention to use a support tool, such as a collaborative shopping tool. Intentions, in turn, lead to behaviors, such as an increased number of transactions with and purchases from the online store, accepting the advice provided by the recommendation agents, and an increase in collaborative shopping. Adoption is also influenced by cognitive—for example, usefulness—and emotional—for example, enjoyment—beliefs. Since the relational beliefs are central to relationship-building when customers and companies are separated by distance, we posit that their key role will also influence cognitive and emotional beliefs; for example, one will find it useful being with a friend (social presence) when shopping, and will also enjoy the feeling of interacting or shopping with a friend in close proximity.

The cognitive, relational, and emotional beliefs are influenced by the various hardware and software technologies utilized in e-commerce settings: Web pages, voice over IP, text-to-speech conversion, avatars, collaboration software ("what you see is what I see"), multimedia presentations, direct manipulation interfaces, and virtual reality tools. The investigation of these features' influence in e-commerce HCI research provides a technological anchor (Benbasat and Zmud, 2003) that is missing in the generic forms of TAM. However, the model also includes design parameters that are *not* normally considered to be technology-based manipulations, such as developing the content of RA explanations or the nature of questions posed to elicit customers' preferences for product attributes, which are nevertheless influential in forming beliefs.

The central premise of this paper is to view HCI in the context of e-commerce as a series of communications among the entities that are part of an electronic commerce system. We identified five types of communications. The first two, labeled virtual service experience and virtual collaborative shopping experience, are concerned with individuals, such as customers and service people, communicating with one another using a Web-based interface, that is, this is an instance of IT-mediated communication. In both cases the parties communicate to support one another in the shopping task, with one party mainly assisting the other, but there is also the desire to create a pleasant social context in which this communication takes place. In the case of communicating with a service person, trust on the part of the customer towards the service person is also an important issue to consider (Qui and Benbasat, 2004a). One of the goals of HCI design in these instances is to create a sense of presence, both social and telepresence (see model in Figure 2.2), to give the communicating parties a sense of being together, that is, to reduce the feeling of distance between them. Such presence is created by using several technologies (see leftmost column in Figure 2.2), by using avatars to represent a service representative in a humanlike form, by providing a tool for two shopping buddies to see and navigate through the same Web pages simultaneously, and by allowing for voice-based communications over the Internet in both instances.

The third type of interaction, virtual advisor experience, is a direct interaction between a software agent, that is, a product recommendation agent, and a consumer. In this type of interaction we assume that humans will treat an information technology artifact as a social entity and ascribe human properties to it, such as honesty. We also view the agent as an entity that will engage the customer in a two-way dialogue to identify the customer's product needs. Because there is an agency problem, as described earlier, trust (see Figure 2.2) is the central construct of interest here, more so than the social aspects and the presence issues discussed for the two types of communication experience between individuals. The HCI design problems are less about hardware or software design concerns than about designing the content of the communication as contained in the explanations provided, and about the nature of describing one's needs to an agent (see leftmost column in Figure 2.2). The overall objective is to have customers adopt the recommendation agent in order to reduce their effort and increase their effectiveness when making product choices (see rightmost column in Figure 2.2).

The fourth type of interaction, virtual product experience, is a two-way interaction between a customer and a product represented on the Web. The HCI design issues are concerned with how to enable the user to manipulate the form of the product and probe its functionality, and for the product reveal its new form and behavior in response to users' actions. The technologies used are direct manipulation and multimedia interfaces, and virtual reality (see the leftmost column in Figure 2.2). The main design goal here is to increase the extent to which the customer understands the product, a form of usefulness in this setting, and adopts online stores that provide support for improved product understanding (see the rightmost column in Figure 2.2).

The fifth type of interaction, virtual company experience, concerns the communication between a customer and an online company's Web site. Here we view the Web page as a social entity, as we did in the case of recommendation agents. The design objectives are similar to those for the first two types discussed above, namely, enhancing perceptions of social presence (see Figure 2.2) in order to increase user's intentions to return to the Web site (rightmost column in Figure 2.2). This is enabled by manipulating the Web page's perceived communication characteristics—that is, connectivity to others and adaptiveness to one's personal needs—to convey the feeling that the Web site is a richer communication partner—that is, a relational belief. The HCI design objectives are to provide for connectivity and adaptiveness through the use of technologies such as personalization and provision of consumer reviews (see the leftmost column in Figure 2.2).

In conclusion, this paper attempts to offer an alternative view of what HCI research might become in the age of e-commerce. This perspective exists alongside the traditional one of efficiency and effectiveness focused on issues such as download times and navigational ease, though it is the perspective that we view as more important for the success of e-commerce and more in line with MIS scholars' outlook on the world and their comparative strengths in HCI research.

ACKNOWLEDGMENTS

The studies reported in this paper were funded by grants from the Natural Sciences and Engineering Research Council of Canada (NSERC) and the Humanities and Social Sciences Research Council of Canada (SSHRC). I would like to acknowledge the support of the Canada Research Chairs Program. I thank my research collaborators, Zhenhui Jack Jiang, Nanda Kumar, Sherry Xiao Komiak, Lingyun Qiu, Weiquan Wang, and Lei Zhu for their efforts, and Dennis Galletta, Vanessa Liu, and Ping Zhang for their valuable suggestions for improving this paper.

NOTES

1. Naturalistic avatars are usually humanoid in form, but have a degraded level of detail.
2. A challenge in this study was to argue that technological artifacts, such as RAs, can have humanlike attributes, such as benevolence. Wang and Benbasat (2004) provide a detailed literature review and analysis to support this argument.

REFERENCES

Aberg, J., and Shahmehri, N. The role of human web assistants in e-commerce: an analysis and a usability study. *Internet Research: Electronic Networking Applications and Policy*, 10, 2 (2000), 114–125.

Aberg, J., and Shahmehri, N. An empirical study of human web assistants: implications for user support in web information systems. In *Proceedings of the SIGCHI conference on Human factors in computing systems (SIGCHI '01)*. Seattle: ACM Press, 2001, pp. 404–411.

Aberg, J., and Shahmehri, N. Live help systems. In J. Ratner (ed.), *Human Factors and Web Development*. Mahwah, NJ: Laurence Erlbaum Associates, 2003, pp. 287–309.

Al-Natour, S., and Benbasat, I. Relationship building in e-commerce: a dynamic systems perspective. Working paper 04-MIS-014, Sauder School of Business, University of British Columbia, 2004.

Ansari, A.; Essegaier, S.; and Kohli, R. Internet recommendation systems. *Journal of Marketing Research*, 37, 3 (2000), 363–375.

Benbasat, I., and Zmud, R.W. The identity crisis within the IS discipline: defining and communicating the discipline's core properties. *Management Information Systems Quarterly*, 27, 2 (2003), pp. 183–194.

Capozza, D.; Falvo, R.; Robusto, E.; and Orlando, A. Beliefs about Internet: methods of elicitation and measurement. *Papers on Social Representation*, 12, 1 (2003), pp. 1.1–1.14.

Csikszentmihalyi, M. *Beyond Boredom and Anxiety*. San Francisco: Jossey-Bass, 1975.

Dukcevich, D. Lands' End's instant business. 2002 (available at http://www.forbes.com/2002/07/22/07221 andsend.html, accessed on Nov 19, 2003).

Elliot, B. Call center internet contact integration: business issues. Gartner Group Intraweb, 2000 (accessed on Nov 19, 2003).

Grenci, R.T., and Todd, P.A. Solutions-driven marketing. *Communications of the ACM*, 45, 3 (2002), 65–71.

Hewett, T.; Baecker, R.; Card, S.; Carey, T.; Gasen, J.; Mantei, M.; Perlman, G.; Strong, G.; and Verplank, W. *ACM SIGCHI Curricula for Human-Computer Interaction*, 1996 (available at http://sigchi.org/cdg/cdg2.html#2_1, accessed on November 17, 2005).

Jiang, Z., and Benbasat, I. Virtual product experience: effects of visual and functional control on perceived diagnosticity in electronic shopping. *Journal of Management Information Systems*, 21, 3 (2005), 111–147.

Kumar, N., and Benbasat, I. The impact of adaptiveness and connectivity on customers evaluations of a web site. Working Paper 04-MIS-012, Sauder School of Business, University of British Columbia, 2004.

Komiak Xiao, S., and Benbasat, I. The effects of internalization and familiarity on trust in and adoption of recommendation agents. Working Paper 04-MIS-002, Sauder School of Business, University of British Columbia, revised 2004.

Maes, P.; Guttman, R.H.; and Moukas, A.G. Agents that buy and sell. *Communications of the ACM*, 42, 3 (1999), 81–91.

Qiu, L. How to provide "live help": the effects of text-to-speech voice and 3D avatars on perception of presence in electronic shopping. Master's thesis, University of British Columbia, Vancouver, Canada, 2002.

Qiu, L., and Benbasat, I. The effects of text-to-speech voice and 3D avatars on consumer trust in the design of "live help" interface of electronic commerce. *International Journal of Human-Computer Interaction*, 19, 1 (2005a), 75–94.

Qiu, L., and Benbasat, I. An investigation in the effects of text-to-speech voice and 3D avatars on the quality of live help in electronic commerce. *ACM Transactions on Computer Human Interaction*, 12, 4 (2005b), 399–455.

Short, J.; Williams, E.; and Christie, B. *The Social Psychology of Telecommunication*. New York: John Wiley and Sons, 1976.

Venkatesh, V.; Morris, M.; Davis, G.; and Davis, F. Use acceptance of information technology: toward a unified view. *MIS Quarterly*, 27, 3 (2003), 425–478.

Wang, W., and Benbasat, I. Impact of explanations on trust in and adoption of online recommendation agents. Working Paper 04-MIS-002, Sauder School of Business, University of British Columbia, 2004.

Zhu, L., and Benbasat, I. Let's shop online together: an empirical investigation of collaborative online shopping support. Working Paper 04-MIS-013, Sauder School of Business, University of British Columbia, 2004.

CHAPTER 3

UNDERSTANDING THE DIRECT AND INTERACTION EFFECTS OF WEB DELAY AND RELATED FACTORS

A Research Program

DENNIS GALLETTA, RAYMOND M. HENRY, SCOTT MCCOY, AND PETER POLAK

Abstract: *The benefits of using the Internet are partially offset by one aspect of its usability: highly variable, intermittent, but frequent inter-page delay. For several years, the HCI literature has studied user reactions to long computer response time in clerical applications, but few studies have examined this problem in the domain of the Web. Examining the delay problem in a Web context is important, because the Web touches many more users, most of whom have little formal computer or task training. Hence, we have examined in our labs consequences of delay, along with factors that interact with delay. Some of our experiments have been published and some are still under review. Consequences of delay that we examined include user attitudes, behavior, and performance. Factors that we examined for possible interactions included site depth, familiarity with terminology used in organizing the site, variability of the delay, and feedback (continuous and gradual filling of the screen to make it obvious that the page is indeed loading). Experiment 1 (n = 196) provided seven levels of delay, ranging from zero to twelve seconds (in two-second increments), and discovered that ill effects began as delay exceeded two seconds. Experiment 2 (n = 206) again compared reactions to the same levels of delay, but this time with Mexican subjects. It was found that Mexicans were more patient than subjects in the United States. In both studies, the outcomes differed when comparing a familiar site with an unfamiliar site, suggesting that interactions should be examined more formally. Experiment 3 (n = 160) introduced two other factors from the HCI literature, and with a 2 × 2 × 2 ANOVA, we assessed the interactions between delay, site depth, and familiarity with the terminology in the site. As predicted, we found a significant three-way interaction. Consistent with more traditional literature, we also found strong direct effects. Experiment 4 (n = 152) employed another 2 × 2 × 2 design, but along with delay we analyzed the effects of variability and feedback as interacting variables. Analysis revealed that page-loading feedback is only important when there are long delays, and variability does not seem to be important in influencing attitudes, behavior, and performance of users. Conclusions from the four studies are that user impatience is high; that the results of delay can differ with culture; and that the variables that interact with delay are familiarity with site terminology, depth of the site, and feedback (in a slow site). Variability does not seem to interact with delay.*

Keywords: *Electronic Commerce, Response Time, Web Site Design, Web Delay, Attitudes, Performance, Intentions, Cross-Cultural Research*

It is perhaps *de rigeur* to acknowledge the business opportunities afforded by the World Wide Web. The number of investment alternatives in the late 1990s was exceeded only by the number of newspaper articles about those opportunities. Today, the activity is no less frenetic, as firms not only provide information about their products and services online, but also make sales, transact internal business, and order from trading partners. Although the "dot-com bust" has vaporized many anticipated dot-com opportunities, virtually all firms have some kind of online presence. Online shopping reached $22.3 billion in the United States in the third quarter of 2005 (Commerce Department, 2005), and new records seem to be broken every year.

Many resources are devoted to attracting the browsing public to Web sites that sell products or services. However, this constitutes only the first step in turning visits into revenue-producing events. The second step, transforming visitors into online buyers, is proving to be even more difficult (Forrester, 2001; U.S. Bureau of Economic Analysis, 2001). The current record-breaking level of online sales amounts to only 2.3 percent of total retail sales (Commerce Department, 2005).

Obstacles to completing a successful purchase on the Internet are both technical and human. While many of the technical barriers—such as client identification, secure transactions, and integration with back-end systems—are largely solvable, human factors have been slow to change. Some of the human issues include habit, trust, and impatience.

The last issue, impatience, is the subject of four studies that we have performed in our laboratories. One of the most important limitations to online shopping is the delay when navigating from page to page (GVU, 1999; Wonnacott, 2000; Nielsen, 1999). The physical world rarely imposes delay when looking from one item to another next to it, but Web pages offer no such adjacency advantage. Regardless of whether a link points to a site across an ocean or to the very next file on the server, there is often a similar delay—taking several seconds. Even after waiting for the next page to load, a user will often discover the need to proceed to yet another page on the way to his or her target. The seconds add up quickly, and turn into many minutes per session.

The business world has recognized the difficulties caused by delay. One highly publicized and quoted estimate from 1999 might have caused many designers to focus more carefully on latency of their pages: Macroeconomically speaking, losses from download times of eight seconds and higher were estimated at $4.35 billion each year (Zona, 1999). Although such a claim might seem outlandish, one study revealed that traffic is indeed highly dependent on page load speed. Improving page load speed from eight seconds and higher to between two and five seconds doubled the traffic of some sites (Wonnacott, 2000). An analysis of the most popular sites led Nielsen (1999a) to conclude that the most popular sites are not coincidentally the fastest sites, that is, the enhanced usability of a fast site leads to increased usage.

Speed difficulties have a variety of causes. Because the ultimate speed of loading a page is only as fast as the slowest link in the chain, slowdowns are quite common. If we consider only the server that contains the content of interest, the host and local network that provides the user with Internet connectivity, and the user's PC, some of the causes for slow page loads include:

- Congestion at the user's host
- Congestion in the user's local network
- Narrow bandwidth between the user's host and the browsing PC
- Congestion between the host and the server (Internet backbone)
- Congestion at the server, due to high popularity
- Problems with the desktop, including slow processing capabilities, viruses, or spyware

- Pages with excessive data (often occurring due to extensive, unnecessarily large graphics)
- Misconfiguration of the server, which can in some cases triple the page loading time (Koblentz, 2000)

For all or some of these reasons, slowly loading Web pages will probably continue to vex users for some time to come. If they are not victims of telecommunications congestion, users could find themselves in a global waiting line at the server or fall victim to design or configuration errors. Even users who acquire much faster Internet connections might see fewer overall speed increases than expected because of other factors outside their control.

Finally, search capabilities have improved a great deal, but it is not likely that searching will solve the problems of delay. Thanks to innovative and successful entrepreneurs from Google and other firms, many average citizens have rapid access to sophisticated search tools that can take them to single pages, avoiding the difficulties of browsing a site. Unfortunately, searching is not a silver bullet; some important difficulties somewhat tarnish the silver.

One difficulty is operational, where users have trouble with searching (Olston and Chi, 2003). Keywords cause some of the problem, as does users' proficiency. Each search tool seems to introduce its own syntax and behavior (Lohse and Spiller, 1998), and search engines have low usability (Lee, 1999). Even if standardized, searching is still a difficult task for most users (Muramatsu and Pratt, 2001; Gauch and Smith, 1991). One difficulty is caused by the large yield that each search provides, causing users to have to browse through long lists of "hits" (Kaindl et al., 1998). User preference and performance are also issues; a recent study found that users prefer browsing, and their search time was not improved by using a search engine (Katz and Byrne, 2003).

Without a ready solution to the problem of delay, either by its reduction, or avoiding browsing for pages, it becomes especially important to investigate the effects of delay on user attitudes, performance, and intentions to return to a site. The authors have conducted four studies to investigate these outcomes as well as other related factors that could moderate the relationships between delay and those outcomes.

INTRODUCTION

Delay imposes upon its users an unwelcome and negative aspect of human life—waiting time. Waiting is nearly universally disliked because time is a precious and unrecoverable resource. Waiting has been studied in retail outlets such as banks, restaurants, and fast-food shops. The phenomenon has stretched to airline lounges, which is a timely focus given the recent difficulties of the 2004 holiday traveling season. (See Katz et al., 1991; Davis and Vollman, 1990; Dubé et al., 1991; Gail and Lucey, 1995; and Taylor, 1994.)

This distaste for waiting applies to the online environment as well as the physical world. In fact, people turn to the Web believing they can save time with an online transaction. Web delays diminish shoppers' ability to save time, leading to user dissatisfaction (Hoxmeier and DiCesare, 2000; Rose et al., 2001; Ramsay et al., 1998).

Although complete elimination of delays is infeasible, some previous research seems to indicate that it is also unnecessary (Kuhmann, 1989; Kohlisch and Kuhmann, 1997; Dellaert and Kahn, 1999). Customer dissatisfaction with waiting was found to be closely related to perceptions of the wait and to negative affective reactions experienced during the waiting situation. In other words, other factors besides the actual length of the wait influence the experience. Fortunately, this means that a designer has at his or her disposal some tools to provide proper trade-offs among conflicting needs. This series of studies attempts to identify the difficulties, quantify them, and make useful trade-offs to minimize the problems.

Theoretical Perspectives on Waiting, from Marketing

Following a stream of analytical work on waiting lines, a psychological and behavioral stream of work began with a conceptual article "The psychology of waiting lines" (Maister, 1985). Maister identified factors that were likely to influence service satisfaction in a waiting line situation. Many subsequent studies were based on Maister's initial explorations and anecdotes.

One such study was Larson's (1987) description of factors that affect the experience of waiting. Together the two authors identified the following among their lists of perceptual issues involved in waiting:

- Customer expectations towards the wait
- Filled time during the wait
- Experienced anxiety
- Uncertainty about the wait length
- Value of service waited for
- Position in the service process
- Fairness and social justice
- Presence or absence of others during the wait

Each of the factors will now be reviewed, along with subsequent studies that were conducted along the way.

Expectations

Expectations are well understood in studies of satisfaction, based on the theory of disconfirmation (Anderson, 1973; Parasuraman et al., 1994; Swan et al., 1981). These studies view satisfaction as the difference between expectations and perceptions, so modifications in either can increase or decrease satisfaction. In the restaurant and amusement industries, it is common to encounter over-estimates of expected waiting times, then a pleasant surprise when the actual waiting time is less.

Filled Time

In many cases, external stimuli can capture a person's attention. James (1891) described unfilled time as that which causes a person to focus on the passage of time itself, which makes a person more aware of the amount of time that passes. Not surprisingly, several studies have found that occupied time feels much shorter, but it is difficult to determine how to choose an appropriate activity to occupy the time. Larson (1987) suggested making that time useful, accounting for the popularity of mobile phones. Zakay (1989) proposed that a person has a "cognitive timer" that activates when a person is aware of the passage of time, and estimates its length. If the person is distracted, it interrupts the timer and the estimate decreases.

Anxiety and Uncertainty

Many waiting situations involve anxiety, which has many antecedents, including loss of control (Boucsein et al., 1984; Osuna, 1985), the fear of being forgotten (or otherwise the lack of satisfying a need; see Sawrey and Telford, 1971), and uncertainty over the duration. If the wait is precisely known, then a person can make plans for that time. Otherwise, the person does not know whether he or she must wait one more hour, minute, or second. Outcomes of anxiety and uncertainty can include annoyance, irritation, and frustration (Sawrey and Telford, 1971).

In some cases, information can be provided about the duration of the wait, which would raise a customer's control over the situation. Stressful situations can be alleviated by control (Hui and Bateson, 1991; Langer, 1983). Averill (1973) reviewed several ways in which control can be exercised: behaviorally (influencing the waiting event), decisionally (choosing to wait or stay), or cognitively (reappraising how to cope with the situation). Information about the duration of the wait increases controllability and affect, and decreases stress. Information also stimulates the cognitive reappraisal process, which is effective for coping when there is no way to escape from the situation (Folkman, 1984).

Value of the Service

Maister (1985) speculated that people have more tolerance for services that are highly valued. A well-known example is that of an airline, where people will wait in their seats for hours upon hours while in flight. However, as soon as the door opens, people scramble to their feet to get out. Once the flight is over, the perceived value of the service has been depleted, and tolerance is reduced dramatically.

Position in the Service Process

After the service is rendered, impatience is at its peak, perhaps due to the sudden loss of value in waiting. Pre-process waits are nearly as negative, perhaps due to anxiety about being forgotten and anticipation of getting started. In-process waits find greatest tolerance, perhaps because people's attention is on the service that they are receiving.

Fairness and Social Justice

Larson (1987) provided a strong focus on fairness and social justice as factors that can affect dissatisfaction with waiting. A person who skips ahead causes others to slip back, causing one of the most frustrating situations in waiting lines.

Presence or Absence of Others

Maister proposed that solo waits seem much longer than group waits. It is possible that this is a result of the greater ability to fill time during a group wait. Also, the others provide a benchmark for the individual to assess the level of social justice in the situation.

Empirical Studies on Waiting

Empirical studies of the waiting process explain many facets of waiting in a variety of situations. Those that are most useful in a Web context are described below.

Attribution

When customers can reconcile a wait with the number of customers in a store, they were more tolerant of delay (Davis and Vollman, 1990). If the customer load was low and the wait was long, lower levels of tolerance and lower service satisfaction resulted from the wait. Findings also showed that perceived waiting time predicted overall satisfaction more strongly than actual waiting time. Davis and Heineke (1998) provided additional support for this phenomenon, but also provided evidence that actual waiting time still explained more variance than did perception or disconfirmation, and management should still focus on reducing the actual waiting time.

Uncertainty

Maister (1985) proposed that unexplained waits feel longer than explained waits because an explanation gives individuals the capacity to estimate wait duration based on their experiences and knowledge of the situation. Similarly, Larson (1987) argued that "customers usually 'feel better' about queuing when they are provided information that allows them to estimate in advance their waiting time in queue" (p. 900). Indeed, Taylor (1994, 1995) found that filled time plays a role in reducing uncertainty in the wait. Also, people in a waiting situation assess the stability of the cause and the controllability of the situation by the service provider. The poorest evaluations of service resulted when the cause is perceived to be within the control of the service provider, and waiting time is unfilled.

Feedback

Feedback provides a way to reduce anxiety. Interestingly, feedback does not have to be explicit or quantitative (Larson, 1987). A checkout line example supports this point, where a customer could either enter a line behind ten individuals who are being served at an interval of one minute each, or could enter a line behind one person who takes ten minutes to be served. Even though the waiting time still totals ten minutes in either case, the steady progress of the first situation would be preferred to the second situation. The waiting parties can estimate their total waiting time by the movement of customers and visible action at the counter. Through feedback, uncertainty associated with the wait duration is reduced, anxiety level is decreased, and the wait is more tolerable.

Type of Feedback

Hui and Tse (1996) provided or withheld feedback in three different delay situations (five, ten, and fifteen minutes) in the use of a computer system, and assessed affective reactions toward the delay. Two kinds of feedback were provided: positional and estimated time remaining. In the short delay condition, neither kind of information improved affective reactions toward the wait. In the medium delay condition, both types of information improved affective reactions. Only in the long delay condition was queueing information (position in line) more effective in providing an estimate of the amount of time remaining. It is likely that the time estimate was still "bad news," and queueing information was more neutral.

Causal Attributions

Causal attributions emerged as an important factor contributing to the wait experience, important because people need to predict and control their environment (Harvey and Weary, 1984; Ross and

Fletcher, 1985; Weiner, 1980, 1985, 1986; Wrightsman and Deaux, 1981). Based on research by Weiner (1985), causal attributions can focus on the locus (who is responsible), the control (how much they can make a difference), and stability (how often this recurs). Several studies (Bitner, 1990; Folkes, 1984, 1988; Folkes et al., 1987) showed support for a relationship between attributions and affective and behavioral responses.

Summary

In summary, the marketing literature has studied the concept of waiting time throughout the last two decades. It has identified several factors that affect consumers' reactions to delay, such as feedback, causal attributions, and fairness. Subjective issues of waiting situations had stronger effects on satisfaction with services than the objective issues involved. It is important to note that "people's perceptions of time, and subsequent evaluations of the service, can be strongly affected by attributes that are not time-specific" (Polak, 2002, p. 25). Although the factors covered by expectations, attributions, and occupied time have strong effects, they are actually not inherently time-specific.

Delay Studies in Human-Computer Interaction

There is a long tradition of research on computer delays in the human-computer interaction literature. In striking similarity to the marketing literature, time-sharing computers stimulated a concern for maximizing the utilization of the service provider (a machine in this case) itself, but later researchers grew interested in the social and psychological dimensions of how delays impacted users. Of primary interest were the length of system delay and the variability of the delay.

Length of Delay

Also in striking similarity to the marketing literature, a conceptual piece had lasting impact on the area. Miller (1968) proposed a set of guidelines for the maximum allowable delay for a set of various user tasks that were meaningful and common at the time. Theoretically, humans have the need for psychological closure. They organize their mental activities into "clumps" and keep the scope of their short-term memory within the boundary of the currently active clump.

One of Miller's most important guidelines was to keep delay under two seconds when engaged in a conversational transaction with a computer. That level has been cited well into the 1990s (Nielsen, 1999), and is based on the limits of tolerable delays in human conversations.

After Miller's original article, many researchers studied problems inherent in computer delay. Their conclusions vary to a surprising degree, and seem to be dependent on the outcome being studied. Early studies focused on performance, which provided an interesting contrast to the focus on attitudes in the marketing literature.

The initial focus in the HCI arena was in user strategies in problem-solving situations under different levels of delay. Grossberg et al. (1976) showed that longer delays changed user work strategies to accommodate the response characteristics of the system. Users took longer but reached their solution in fewer steps. As delay increased, users used computer resources more sparingly; they were forced to learn more efficient strategies.

Goodman and Spence (1978) found that time to solution increased by 50 percent when response time doubled from 0.7 seconds to 1.5 seconds. A further doubling had the same effect, and reduced performance was accompanied by complaints of the system's intrusiveness.

Thadhani (1981) found significant impacts of system delay on productivity and user response time. User productivity and user response time were significantly higher in the 0.25-second to one-second response range than they were in the response range greater than one second. Thadhani found that lower user performance was caused by an imbalance in the human and computer components. That is, the user and the computer require the capability of the system to generate responses to match the user's capability to generate tasks.

Contradictory findings were provided by Bergman et al. (1981), who experimented with system response times of zero and ten seconds, and found no positive effects of short delay on human performance measures such as total time and total number of trials to reach a solution, total and per trial user response time, and number of trials per minute. Contrary to expectations, more trials were needed to solve a problem in the immediate response condition than in the ten-second-delay condition. One possible reason for this contradiction with previous results was the complicated nature of the task, compared to the simple tasks of previous work.

Even more equivocality resulted from Butler's (1983) experiments with differing task difficulty and computer delay (two, four, eight, sixteen, and thirty-two seconds). A simple data entry task was compared against a demanding set of steps involving information retrieval and record modification. Performance variables were similar to those in previous studies, and included typing time, the percentage of incorrect entries, and user response time. Amount of delay did not seem to affect mean typing time and the percentage of incorrect entries for either task. Butler concluded that performance degradation was similar even for tasks that were very different in cognitive demands.

An interesting finding by Dannenbring (1984) was that users performed more corrections when delay was reduced. With slower response time comes more deliberate and measured user actions, probably due to the punishing delays of each action. This finding was consistent with those of Bergman et al. (1981). Performance obviously appears to have strong ties to the affective domain.

Kuhmann (1989) investigated delay for a pattern-finding task. He compared delays of two, four, six, and eight seconds, and found that a moderately demanding task had an optimum delay point; a six-second delay was optimum for performance (error rates, completion time, user response time).

Barber and Lucas (1983) supported these findings, and reported their own U-shaped relationship between system response time and errors. However, the optimum was around twelve seconds. The key in both studies seems to be task complexity; although both were complex, Barber and Lucas's task was even more complex, implying the need for more thinking time on the part of users.

Polak (2002) describes the system's control over users:

> At the very short end of the delay continuum, users tend to adopt the working speed of the system (Shneiderman, 1984) . . . the system is rushing them along . . . sacrificing performance and generating a higher number of errors. Negative performance effects under fast response times occur mainly when the task at hand is cognitively quite demanding. In the case of low task complexity, instantaneous response could be the optimum level of system delay. (p. 34)

Polak explains further that:

> "At the other end of the delay spectrum is a situation when users are ready for the next task but the system is still delayed. This extra time spent waiting is not used for relaxation or as preparation time for the next step, but it produces psychological and physiological stress reactions." (p. 34) "Another factor playing a role in the users' negative self-assessment might be their realization of loss of control over the temporal work flow (Boucsein et al., 1984; Osuna, 1985)." (p. 35)

Kohlisch and Kuhmann (1997) conclude that a philosophy of making the system as fast as possible does not seem to be a good idea. Users need to be ready to execute the next task, and they should not be rushed by short system response time. Their recommendation is to impose a short delay to match task demands.

The opposite desire is expressed by computer users, who seem to demand the fastest possible system response time. Rushinek and Rushinek (1985) found in their survey that fast system response time was first of seventeen other variables that induce greatest user satisfaction.

Variability of Delay

Also of interest in the literature has been the variability of system delay. Several of the authors cited above also examined variability.

Miller (1968) cited Woodrow (1958) and other careful interval perception experiments in postulating how much variability would be noticeable. Delays that were less than 5 to 30 percent over or under a comparison rate would not be noticed.

It is possible that the uncertainty and predictability discussed earlier in the marketing literature bring some bearing to this issue. Carbonell et al. (1968) observed that users prefer having a constant delay to one that is usually shorter but unpredictable. Using Simon's (1966) idea of memory swapping, they supposed that predictable delay would allow users to plan for temporary cognitive activity while waiting for the system to respond.

Nickerson (1981) reported on a designer who found it advantageous to slow a system artificially to make sure the user would never experience a range of response time. Even if only one user was on the time-sharing system, the system behaved normally. Experiencing large delay variation would have been confusing and would have led to elevated expectations, and then disappointment, with future use.

Empirical results under carefully controlled conditions vary in their results. Grossberg et al. (1976) found that response variability did not impose performance problems, although Miller (1977) found such problems. Goodman and Spence (1981) reconciled the findings by stating that delay length and variability were simultaneously varied in both studies, making separate main effects impossible to isolate. Also, task demands were not controlled carefully enough.

Goodman and Spence (1981) performed their own study, and found no effects on any dependent measures. Dannenbring (1984) also found no effects on a complex debugging task.

A study by Bergman et al. (1981) fixed the mean delay time at ten seconds and deviated by 25 percent and 75 percent above and below that mean. One dependent measure showed a significant difference: user response time. However, a second experiment with a more difficult task resulted in no findings.

Butler (1983) found that task complexity was also important in the realm of variability of delay, not just in the study of its magnitude. When the task was simpler, user response time increased with variability of system delay. However, in a second experiment with a more complicated task, the differences disappeared. It appears that more complex tasks have more of a focus on human processing, and system variability is not noticed as much. If tasks reach a level of simplicity, then system response variability starts disrupting a user's focus.

Making use of physiological and self-reported measures of mood, Johansson and Aronson (1984) found evidence of stress caused by variability. The staff members were unable to tell if the system had "gone down" or whether it was merely under high load. The task in this study was simple, and subjects could not adapt to changing conditions and compensate for long delays. Work rhythm was also noted to have been impaired.

Subsequent studies by Treurniet et al. (1985) and Planas and Treurniet (1988) were rather equivocal in their findings. The earlier study found only effects on the manipulation check questions. The later study examined the role of "time feedback" to better inform users about the delay they would encounter, and "system feedback" to verify that the system acknowledged their inputs. Delay length and system feedback were found to interact; users became most annoyed with little feedback.

In conclusion, variability research suggests that similar factors are important in studying both delay length and delay variability. The most important variables are task complexity and cognitive requirements imposed on the user's short-term memory. Users' experience and expertise are also important for assessing delay length and variability. It is interesting that modern computer users have multiplied in numbers to a staggering degree, and many use the Internet in both corporate and personal applications. Delay has lengthened, and average user experience has declined. Therefore, four studies in Web-related delay have been conducted to study these issues in the context of the Web.

Web Delay Studies

Web delay studies have been performed in conjunction with three important outcome variables, including attitudes, behavior, and performance (Galletta et al., 2004). Previous literature will be reviewed for each of those outcomes.

Attitudes

Attitudes are pervasive in MIS research. Attitudes are related to satisfaction, however, as described by Galletta et al. (2004):

> Attitudes should not automatically be equated to satisfaction, although a sharp distinction cannot always be found. We might draw a useful base from dictionary definitions: "satisfaction" is usually defined as a consumer's gratification or fulfillment of a need (consistent with Oliver and Swan, 1989), and most definitions of "attitude" refer to a general disposition with many dimensions (consistent with Hilgard, 1980). That is, satisfaction usually fits a discussion about an experienced product, while an attitude can either precede or follow that experience. (pp. 5–6)

Web sites are an interesting application area for satisfaction and attitude studies. Use of a Web site often has an end goal: A user wants to find information or to purchase a product. However, the site itself is consumed on the path towards that ultimate goal. Therefore, the site itself will affect attitudes as part of the consumption process.

The perspective that seems to fit is that of Au et al. (2002), where a user will formulate his or her attitude about shopping at the site, and form an intention to return (or not return) to the site. Our focus is therefore on both attitudes and intentions to return to the site.

Studies of Attitudes and Web Delay

Theories for examining attitudes as an outcome of delay were taken from the interpersonal communication literature by Rose (2000) and Rose and Straub (2001), where nonverbal cues account for a large proportion of variance in attitudes. Rose and colleagues demonstrated strong effects of delay, employing levels of zero, five, and thirty seconds, but did not find that delay affected a person's attitude toward a retailer.

Ramsay et al. (1998) found that users considered pages that loaded faster to be more interesting and easier to scan. Their study used delays that ranged from two seconds to two minutes.

Hoxmeier and DiCesare (2000) asked users to perform an information retrieval task on the Web while varying delay from zero to twelve seconds. Satisfaction was highest at zero seconds, remained fairly constant from three to nine seconds, then dropped off dramatically at twelve seconds.

Palmer (2002) broke from the tradition of creating fictitious sites. He measured delay of real sites using a panel of judges, a rating by an external firm, and a software agent. Delay affected the success of the sites.

Weinberg (2000) formed expectations in two groups of users by warning them of either a five- or ten-second wait. The actual wait was 7.5 seconds for both groups. Those in the five-second expectation group reported lower estimates of the waiting time (5.6 seconds) than users in the ten-second expectation group (8.7 seconds). No significant differences in perceived site quality were found between conditions.

Jacko et al. (2000) found that when pages have lots of graphic elements, users blame Web designers when they experience long delays. When pages do not make heavy use of graphics, users perceived that the designer could not do much to help, and blame delays on technical problems outside of the designer's control.

Behavioral Intentions

Fewer studies have been conducted on intentions to revisit a site under varying levels of delay, as compared to attitudes. It is worthwhile to study intentions, as it is an excellent summary variable that indicates the success of the content or design of a site (Devaraj et al., 2002).

Rose et al. (2001) and Nah (2003) found that users tended to abort page loads when delays increased. According to Ranganathan and Ganaphy (2002), slower pages led users to go elsewhere. Hoxmeier and DiCesare (2002) that subjects' intentions to revisit diminished as delays increased from nine to twelve seconds.

The levels of delay varied quite a bit in the studies of behavioral intentions. On the conservative side, Hoxmeier and DiCesare (2000) varied delay among conditions built with zero, three, six, nine, and twelve seconds. On the other hand, Rose et al. (2001) used zero, fifteen, thirty, forty-five, sixty, and seventy-five seconds.

Performance

In concert with the Card et al. (1983) view that performance is the "ultimate concern" (p. 404) for the field, the study of performance predates the Web. The general findings are that delays cause people to be more cautious, that people slow down a great deal when there is delay, and that complex tasks forgive many delay sins.

Two Web-related studies have also been conducted with performance as a dependent variable. Davis and Hantula (2001) found that delay actually assisted learning performance, as less experienced subjects had more time to read and perhaps reread text while waiting for graphics to load. Nah (2003) found that subjects would tolerate long delays before giving up, thus their performance was not impaired until delays became extremely long at the first encounter. Subsequent non-loading links resulted in much shorter intervals before users aborted their tasks.

Other Factors

In our laboratory, we have examined other factors besides attributes that only involve delay (such as length, variability, and feedback). We have also examined the scent, or familiarity, of the terminology.

In navigating a Web site, the structure is an important constraint for users (Bernard 2002; Chi et al., 2001). Three types of structure are important to users: inherent structure (physical), internal structure (based on domain knowledge), and navigational structure (based on navigational aids). There are strong design implications of each type of structure.

As a user reaches each decision point, where links point downward toward the goal end node, they often evaluate how much effort it will take to reach the target via each link, or candidate path. Johnson and Payne (1985) and Todd and Benbasat (1999) found that people develop strategies to limit their cognitive effort and find the path (or even the site) with the lowest "cost" (in terms of effort or time). The theoretical basis for this factor comes from information foraging theory (Pirolli and Card, 1995). The theory asserts that individuals develop strategies to minimize the costs and maximize the rate of finding information (Katz and Byrne, 2003; Larson and Czerwinski, 1998).

Information scent is "the 'imperfect' perception of the value, cost, or access path of information sources obtained from proximal cues" (Pirolli and Card, 1995, p. 646) such as links. Words or images used in links or in a page layout provide the scent (Card et al., 2001). When the scent is strong, users can determine the proper path more easily, that is, with low effort and cost. If the scent is too low, users can become lost in the site. The two most-cited reasons for becoming lost given by Otter and Johnson's (2000) subjects include site depth and unfamiliar terminology. Open-ended responses provided additional evidence of the importance of those two measures.

Disorientation requires backtracking and choosing alternative paths to find a stronger scent. Delay weakens the scent and raises the cost of navigating. Unfamiliar terminology in links and content weakens the scent as well, as does a higher number of levels in the site. Each will be discussed in more detail.

Familiarity

Widespread heterogeneity of users makes it difficult to control familiarity (Chau et al., 2000). Galletta et al. (2006) defined familiarity as "the ability of users to discern, from the terminology presented on the site, their next move to reach their goal."

High-level pages provide general identifiers that users examine when making judgments about scent and about the search cost of seeking the bottom-level page (Paap and Roske-Hofstrand, 1988; Katz and Byrne, 2003; Pardue and Landry, 2001). Understanding the page's categories will decrease the search cost (Somberg and Picardi, 1983) and make it much easier to reach the goal (Dumais and Landauer, 1983).

Disorientation is extremely common and widespread, and is explained by users having to spend some of their limited processing capabilities on navigation rather than on comprehending the content itself (Thuring et al., 1995).

Trial and error comes with unfamiliarity (Schwartz and Norman, 1986), and the search cost rises wildly when users choose many incorrect paths and become lost in the hierarchy of the system (Norman and Chin, 1988; Robertson et al., 1981).

Unfortunately, some firms are so preoccupied with their internal terminology that they fail to predict their customers' lack of familiarity with those terms. When searching for a Dell Latitude laptop on www.dell.com, users may not know whether to look under "Home and Home Office," "Small Business," or "Medium and Large Business." Under the first option, the user will see only

Inspiron models. The user will then have to try the second option. Corporate-defined groupings escape many users, and such brute force searching is sometimes required.

A brute force search will be extremely costly if a site is very deep, with few links per page, but will be made less prohibitive if a site contains many links per page and fewer levels. In either case, there could be an identical number of bottom-level nodes, but more levels would need to be traversed to find the links to those pages. Therefore, the final issue, depth, is discussed next.

Depth

Galletta et al. (2006) provide two formulas to assess the impact on C (the number of clicks) when having to revert to a brute force search in a site, given L levels to traverse and n links per page. In a perfectly familiar site, $C = L$ because there will be no errors moving down the hierarchy. In a completely unfamiliar site, requiring brute force, C is more complicated:

$$C_{unfam} = \left(\sum_{i=1}^{L-1} n^i \right) + 1$$

At each level i, there are n^i intermediate pages. A brute force search requires the user to traverse each of these pages to find a direct link to the target bottom-level node. If the user is unsuccessful, he or she would stop at level $L-1$, one level above the bottom, because there would not be a link to the desired node. That is, links will point to all of the incorrect bottom nodes, and the user can immediately go back up to explore the next intermediate page. When the page is encountered that provides a link to the actual target, one final click is required (hence the $+1$ at the end of the formula).

Backtracking is required at each dead end, so two clicks per intermediate page are needed (one down and one back up). However, on average, a randomly placed goal would be found halfway through the search. Therefore, both multiplying and dividing by two will cancel each other, so the rather simple formula provides the average number of clicks to arrive at the goal.

A site with eighty-one bottom nodes can be arranged as four levels with three links each, or two levels with nine links each. Calling the first a "deep" site and the second a "broad" site, consistent with menu design research, the formulas reveal that the broad site would require two clicks if the links and content are familiar and ten clicks if they are unfamiliar. The deep site would require four clicks if familiar and forty clicks if unfamiliar.

Adding delay to the picture causes an expectation for a strong three-way interaction (Galletta et al., 2006), where an eight-second delay on each page will accumulate to such an extent that 320 seconds (nearly six minutes) of delay will be imposed for each search in the deep, unfamiliar site, and only eighty seconds of delay in the broad, unfamiliar site. For the familiar site, a deep structure will lead to thirty-two seconds of delay while a broad structure will lead to sixteen seconds of delay. If the delay is zero, then the aggregate delay for each cell is therefore also zero.

Four experiments were performed to investigate Web delay in a comprehensive research program. The first two examined the magnitude of delay that should be considered in our studies. The last two examined several factors that exacerbate delay.

EXPERIMENT 1: HOW IMPATIENT ARE USERS?

A fictitious Web site was created on compact discs to precisely control the delay that would be encountered by participants. The site included eighty-one target nodes that were arranged into four levels with three links, as a relatively "deep" site. We did not employ a "broad" site in this study because there would not be enough navigation to fully examine the effect of delay. We employed a familiar site to focus on the levels of delay, but because it was possible that there would not be enough navigation in that site, participants were also asked to navigate an unfamiliar site. Half of the subjects encountered the familiar site first, and half encountered the unfamiliar site first (and no learning effect was found).

Operationalization of Outcome Variables

Performance was operationalized using an average score for nine search tasks that were developed for this study. The nine tasks were specifically designed to require subjects to visit each third of the site's hierarchy the same number of times. This was done to ensure that subjects were exposed to a reasonably balanced overall view of the site. The questions for each site differed in the search object names (general store products versus software products), although their answers were located at the same point within each site. One point was assigned for each correct answer. The KR-20 test score (analogous to alpha, but for dichotomous items) was quite high in this study (.90).

Attitudes about the sites were measured by averaging the responses to a set of seven nine-point Likert-type questions adapted from Part 3 of the long form of the QUIS (Questionnaire for User Interaction Satisfaction) (Shneiderman, 1998, p. 136). This instrument has demonstrated reliability and validity in prior studies (Chin et al., 1988). Reliability for our subjects was also quite high (Cronbach's alpha = .95).

Behavioral intentions were measured using the average of two original questions. These items focused on two related future behaviors: how readily the subject would visit the site again and the likelihood he or she would recommend the site to others (seven-point scales). The alpha score for this very short instrument was also extremely high, at .94.

Method

Delay was manipulated by assigning subjects to treatments randomly via code numbers on their questionnaire packets. The code number was entered into a welcome screen, which triggered the proper delay via Javascript code. Experimenters ensured that the proper code was set up by visiting each workstation when subjects reached that portion of the protocol.

The Web sites utilized a linear design where lower child pages were accessible only through their parent page. We did not provide the ability to search or skip levels with shortcuts or other nonlinear methods of navigation. The only exception was a link to the site's home page located on every page to provide a lifeline to a well-known starting point.

Possible delays ranged from zero to twelve, using even numbers. Given the large number of researchers who considered eight seconds to be an upper limit, we wanted to provide two additional values above that limit. Our simple site did not contain enough graphics to justify longer delays, and we wished to avoid provoking too much anger at design attributes (Sears and Jacko, 2000).

The familiar site ("Pete's General Store") included products that would be found in a grocery store, arranged into easily understood categories such as "food products," and within that category, "snacks." The unfamiliar site ("A.C.T. Systems") made use of corporate division labels, and one major category was "Novo Products" with a subdivision of "Normalizers." The terms had as much meaning as a set of corporate labels such as Dell's "Latitude" and "Inspiron" laptop series.

Figure 3.1   **Error Bars for Behavioral Intentions**

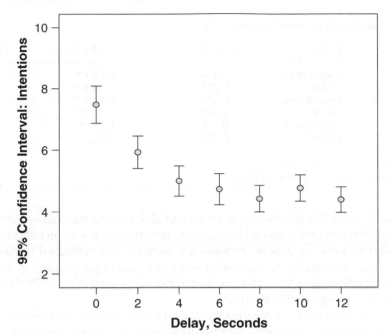

Subjects

A total of 196 upper-level undergraduate business students at a large university in the northeast United States volunteered to participate in the study.

Manipulation Checks

We included manipulation check items for both familiarity and speed. The mean of the familiarity manipulation check was 5.67 for subjects in the familiar condition and 1.98 for subjects in the unfamiliar condition, on a scale from one to seven. The difference was significant ($F(1,387) = 871.3$, $p = .000$). We ran a regression with delay (in seconds) as the independent variable and the manipulation check as the dependent variable. Delay was found to be a significant predictor of the manipulation check responses ($F(1,387) = 398.4$, $p = .000$; adjusted $R^2 = .506$).

Independence of Variables

We performed factor analyses on all dependent variable measures. All of the performance measures loaded clearly on one factor, and all attitudes and intentions measures loaded on a second factor, indicating poor discriminant validity between attitudes and intentions. The two variables have an extremely high correlation, above .8.

Results

We show the basic results in Figure 3.1 as error bars defining means and 95 percent confidence intervals at each time setting for behavioral intentions. There is a small increase at the

Table 3.1

Regression Results—Explained Variance (R^2)

Dependent	Method	All Subjects	Unfamiliar Only	Familiar Only
Performance	Logarithmic	0.019**	0.061***	0.012
Performance	Linear	0.017**	0.053***	0.018
Attitudes	Logarithmic	0.052***	0.058***	0.155***
Attitudes	Linear	0.050***	0.037**	0.176***
Intentions	Logarithmic	0.079***	0.050**	0.177***
Intentions	Linear	0.064***	0.029*	0.154***

***$p < .001$; **$p < .01$; *$p < .05$
Source: Adapted from Galletta et al. (2004).

ten-second-delay level. The results are similar for attitudes. Performance has unexpected perturbations at the eight- and twelve-second levels, where performance moves up rather than continuing to decline. Otherwise, in general, performance, attitudes, and behavioral intentions decline smoothly as delays increased. The unexpected small increases in performance at the eight- and twelve-second levels could indicate changes in strategies (Grossberg et al., 1976), but there is not sufficient evidence to support this assertion.

Analysis of the unfamiliar site revealed that the explained variance in performance improves dramatically. Regressions for attitudes and behavioral intentions remain significant, but less variance is explained than in the pooled analysis.

Our expectation was that the effects of delay would decrease with longer delay. We performed curvilinear regression and compared the results to the results of linear regression. A logarithmic function always provided nearly the best fit.

We show the results of our regression testing in Table 3.1, adapted from Galletta et al. (2004). The curvilinear regressions explain somewhat more variance than the linear approach. The logarithmic and linear regression equations are significant for all dependent variables, but explained variance is relatively modest.

Separate analysis of only the unfamiliar site resulted in much higher explained variance in performance. Regressions for attitudes and behavioral intentions remain significant, but less variance is explained than in the pooled analysis. For completeness, the familiar site was also analyzed in this manner. Regressions for attitudes and behavioral intentions remain significant, but performance loses significance. Curvilinear equations for attitudes and behavioral intentions explain substantially more variance (15.5 percent and 17.7 percent, respectively) in the familiar sub-sample than in either the overall sample or the unfamiliar sample, as shown in Table 3.3. The increased strength of the relationship indicates that familiarity has strong influence over the relationships. Familiarity will be studied more formally in Experiment 3.

Sensitivity Analysis

We analyzed both familiar and unfamiliar cases to learn at which point delays cease to have an effect on the dependent variables. To do this, we repeatedly ran linear regressions after removing data from the lowest remaining time delay. After removing the zero-delay subjects, regressions were significant for attitudes and behavioral intentions ($p < .005$), but not for performance. Explained variance was 2.4 percent for both attitudes and behavioral intentions. After removing the two-second

Table 3.2

Sensitivity Analysis

	0 & Up	2 & Up	4 & Up	6 & Up	8 & Up	10 & 12
Performance	Both (except familiar)					
Attitudes	Both	Both	Familiar Only	Familiar Only		
Behavioral Intentions	Both	Both				

Source: Adapted from Galletta et al. (2004).
Note: For each subset of time delays, this table shows for which tasks a significant linear regression equation could be found.

subjects, no regressions were significant. Across both sites, one could argue that any delay above two seconds ceases to be detrimental, and the outcomes have "bottomed out."

This iterative analysis was repeated for the separate sites. In the unfamiliar site, only performance survives the loss of the zero-delay subjects. The linear regression ceases to be significant. This illustrates that users in an unfamiliar site have significant reductions in attitudes and behavioral intentions with any delay, and suffer performance degradation when delay exceeds two seconds.

For the familiar site, only attitudes and behavioral intentions are significant to start. Dropping the zero-delay subjects results in regressions that continue to be significant and explain variance. Delay from two seconds and above explains 10.6 percent of the variance in attitudes ($p < .001$) and 6.8 percent of the variance in intentions ($p < .001$).

Dropping the two-second-delay subjects revealed that the only significant regression equation was provided by the attitude data. Results were nearly identical from both linear and nonlinear regression. From four to twelve seconds, 6.4 percent of the variance in attitudes ($p = .003$) is explained by delay. From six to twelve seconds, 3.7 percent of the variance in attitudes ($p = .041$) is explained by delay. After dropping the six-second subjects, regression ceased to be significant.

Discussion

Subjects are much more impatient than might have been expected. Table 3.2, adapted from Galletta et al. (2004), indicates that all slopes are significantly negative when considering the full range of data, from zero to twelve seconds. If the no-delay subjects are removed, then attitudes and intentions regressions have a significant negative slope, as does performance, but only for the unfamiliar treatment. Attitudes seem to bottom out at the six- to eight-second range, and only hold out beyond two to four seconds in the familiar group. Therefore, this should provide caution to designers about delays designed to be above two seconds.

EXPERIMENT 2: IS IMPATIENCE CULTURALLY DEPENDENT?

The popular press has painted an image of American culture as hurried and impatient. Whether this image is correct or not, it is indeed easy to make a scholarly argument that too many studies are based in a single culture. Significant previous research has highlighted important differences between cultures.

Table 3.3

Generally Accepted Cultural Dimensions

Hofstede's Dimension	Short Definition
Uncertainty Avoidance	Preference for structured over unstructured situations.
Power Distance	Degree of equality or inequality permitted or nurtured within a society.
Masculinity	Not gender, but prevalence of "masculine" values (e.g., achievement, control, power) and gender differentiation.
Individualism	Society's reinforcement of individual achievement and importance of individual (vs. collective) rights.
Long-Term Orientation	Degree to which people in a country have long-term versus short-term values.

Source: Hofstede, 2005.

The best-known differentiation among cultures was provided by Hofstede (1980), and was the result of a survey of over 116,000 IBM employees located in sixty-six countries. Hofstede's findings from this and a second study (Hofstede and Bond, 1988) concluded that people of the world differed along five dimensions: uncertainty avoidance, power distance, masculinity/femininity, individualism/collectivism, and long-term orientation. Table 3.3 summarizes the essence of each.

The significance of this differentiation is that we cannot count on people in a single country to represent the world. In this study, Mexico was chosen as a useful contrast to the United States, where Experiment 1 took place.

Mexico served as a useful and convenient initial basis for considering culture and Web delay because of its proximity and because its citizens differ substantially on three of the five scales. When compared to the United States, Mexican culture is obviously[1] much higher on uncertainty avoidance, power distance, and collectivism. Unfortunately, there is not a long-term orientation score available for Mexico.

None of the dimensions exactly address urgency or impatience. An argument could be made that Web delay is at least partly related each of the other dimensions, but this has not been studied. We speculate the following: Long delays can create more uncertainty and anxiety if a culture is high on uncertainty avoidance (Mexico). Delays can be tolerated more in a culture with higher power distance (Mexico), as people might be more accepting of the provider of Web information's authority and assume they must endure delay without questioning it. Delays could be more disturbing for those in individualistic cultures (United States[2]) because of the personal inconvenience they cause. Finally, long-term thinkers (*not* the United States[3]) could rank the longer-term benefits of perusing the information above the immediate waiting costs of browsing.

Lacking a particular measure for patience, popular culture and researchers (e.g., Stephens and Greer, 1995) have reported that Mexico's "mañana image is real" and that there is "little sense of urgency" (p. 48). That would indicate a higher amount of patience.

Such speculations and views of Mexico could readily lead one to believe that Mexican subjects might be more tolerant of delay (with cautions about uncertainty avoidance, which would predict the opposite effect). Therefore, we conducted Experiment 2 by repeating Experiment 1 in Mexico.

Figure 3.2   **Error Bars for Behavioral Intentions, Mexican Subjects**

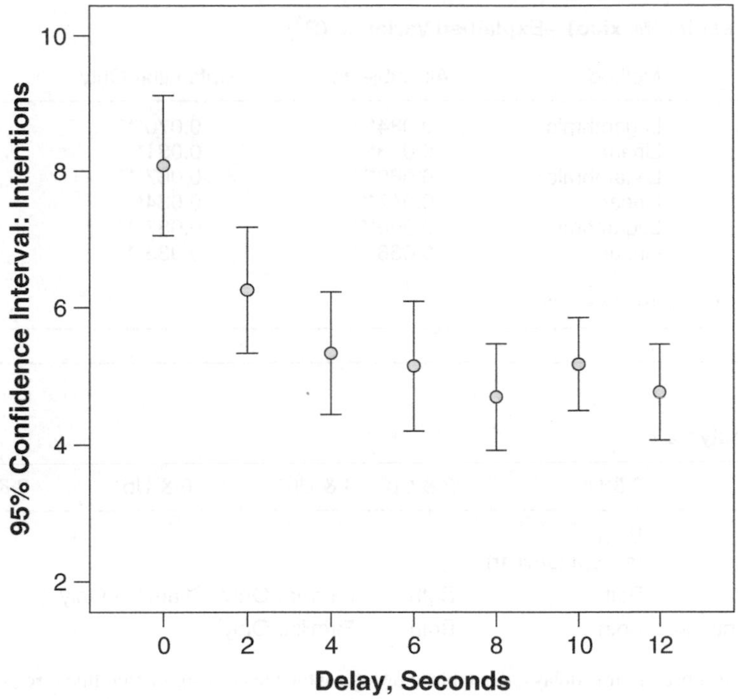

Subjects and Method

The site used for our U.S. subjects was translated into Spanish and then translated back into English by native Spanish speakers. After making modifications to increase its accuracy, the Spanish version was provided to the Mexican subjects. Nearly 100 percent of the subjects agreed to participate in the study, which was conducted during class. A small number of the 206 participants were disqualified because they were not native Mexicans.

The method was identical to that of Experiment 1. We used a lab at a highly regarded Mexican university, to which faculty brought students at the beginning of their class session. All students signed an attendance sheet and were candidates to win a prize of US$100. Data collection took place over two days, and one winner was drawn at random each day.

Results

Figure 3.2 provides the results for behavioral intentions, which look strikingly similar to the U.S. sample in Experiment 1. The inexplicable upward movement at ten seconds seems to have recurred in the Mexican sample, but to a greater extent.

Table 3.4 provides the same regression results as Experiment 1, which also appear very similar. It is interesting that all regressions are significant at the .05 level or better except for both performance results in the familiar-only subgroup.

The sensitivity analysis in Table 3.5 shows, once again, strikingly similar results as Experiment 1. Regressions are significant for performance, attitudes, and intentions when all levels of delay are

Table 3.4

Regression Results (Mexico)—Explained Variance (R^2)

Dependent	Method	All Subjects	Unfamiliar Only	Familiar Only
Performance	Logarithmic	0.034***	0.070***	0.009
Performance	Linear	0.013*	0.031*	0.002
Attitudes	Logarithmic	0.060***	0.067***	0.093***
Attitudes	Linear	0.047***	0.034**	0.103***
Intentions	Logarithmic	0.096***	0.087***	0.137***
Intentions	Linear	0.066***	0.035**	0.127***

***$p < .001$; **$p < .01$; *$p < .05$.

Table 3.5

Sensitivity Analysis

	0 & Up	2 & Up	4 & Up	6 & Up	8 & Up	10 & 12
Performance	Both (except familiar)					
Attitudes	Both	Both	Familiar Only	Familiar Only		
Behavioral Intentions	Both	Both	Familiar Only			

Note: For each subset of time delays, this table shows for which tasks a significant linear regression equation could be found.

Figure 3.3   **Overall Comparison in Intentions—United States vs. Mexico**

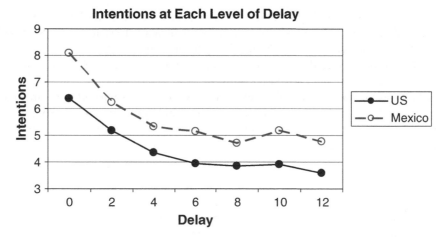

in the analysis. When the no-delay subjects are eliminated from the analysis, only attitudes and intentions have significant regressions. The regression for attitudes is significant until the delay meets or exceeds eight seconds. The regression for behavioral intentions is significant until the delay meets or exceeds six seconds.

Figure 3.3 provides a visual comparison between the subjects from Mexico and those from the United States. Overall, the data set from Mexico shows higher levels of performance, attitudes,

Table 3.6

Mean Performance, Attitudes, and Intentions for United States vs. Mexico

Dependent Variable	U.S. Subjects	Mexican Subjects	F (df)	Significance
Performance	7.09	7.52	7.2 (1, 1205)	.007
Attitudes	28.16	32.24	19.55 (1, 1189)	.000
Behavioral Intentions	5.03	5.60	7.74 (1, 1179)	.005

Figure 3.4   **Error Bars (Performance)—United States vs. Mexico**

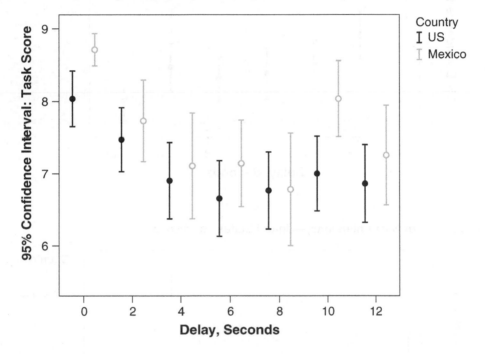

and intentions. Table 3.6 compares the overall mean for each sample for each dependent variable. There is a significant difference in all outcome variables; Mexican participants, very comparable in academic level and major, were more positive overall about delay.

Figure 3.3 illustrates the means for intentions for each level of delay, comparing subjects from the United States with those from Mexico. The bias appears to apply to each level of delay. Performance and attitude graphics are similar.

Figures 3.4 through 3.6 provide 95 percent confidence interval error bar graphs for each of the outcome variables to provide a more complete picture. Each chart shows a similar pattern, where the subjects with zero delay in the United States seemed strikingly lower than the subjects with zero delay in Mexico. Once delay is imposed, there is much overlap between the samples. Analysis indicated that at zero delay, performance and attitudes are significantly more positive for Mexican subjects than for U.S. subjects (Performance: F = 5.43; 1,159 df; p = .021; Attitudes: F = 5.91; 1,159 df; p = .016). Intentions were not significantly different at zero delay (F = 1.84; 1,155 df; ns). No other comparisons were significant except for performance and attitudes at ten seconds of

Figure 3.5   **Error Bars (Attitudes)—United States vs. Mexico**

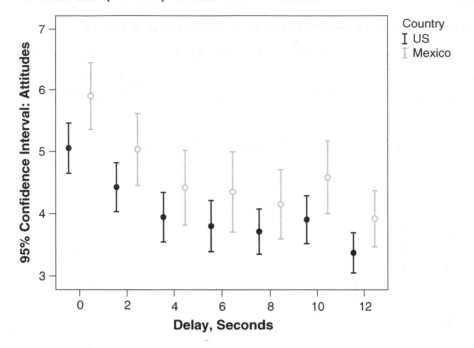

Figure 3.6   **Error Bars (Intentions)—United States vs. Mexico**

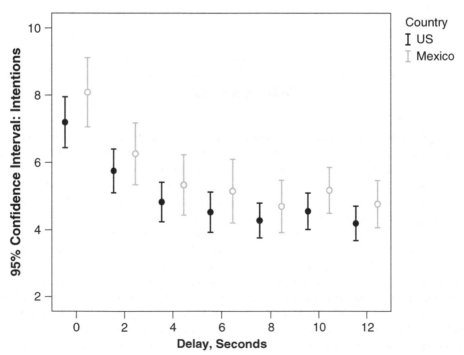

delay. Until the marked unexpected upward perturbation at ten seconds is understood, neither conclusions nor speculations are proposed for this pattern.

Discussion

Mexicans appeared on the surface to fulfill the stereotype of greater patience. However, although they performed generally better than U.S. subjects, and had more positive attitudes and intentions to return to the site, those outcomes sunk in similar patterns for each country. Interestingly, Mexican subjects seem to have reacted more severely to delay, because above zero delay the overlap between Mexican and U.S. subjects seems to increase dramatically.

One of the most intriguing outcomes was the second appearance of an upward perturbation at a ten-second delay, more serious in the Mexican sample than the U.S. sample. There seems to be something about the ten-second level that led the outcomes to improve at least slightly in two different countries with a large number of subjects who used the same materials (except for language).

Two further experiments will incorporate additional factors into the experiment, and will move behavioral intentions to an ultimate outcome variable that is affected by attitudes, as discussed in Galletta et al. (2006). Performance is also posited to affect intentions.

EXPERIMENT 3

Although delay can be caused by many factors, site designers can make choices that can alleviate or exacerbate the frustration that users experience. This experiment examines how two Web site design variables, familiarity of terminology and site depth, interact with delay to impact users' performance, attitudes, and ultimately behavioral intentions. All three independent variables were discussed earlier in this paper, and have been shown to impact users' reactions to a Web site. This experiment focuses on the interaction among these variables.

In searching for target information, users are faced with a series of decisions where they must evaluate the likely effort and probability of reaching their target via each link (candidate path). The assessment of costs is therefore an important part of users' experiences with Web sites, and Web sites providing lower cost—in terms of time and effort—will be preferred over those with higher cost. Familiarity, depth, and delay each individually increase the chance of a penalty for incorrect choices, but together these variables can have an even greater effect.

Although a single delay may not be noticeable, repeated delays are extremely frustrating. When users are unfamiliar with the terminology on a site, they cannot determine the appropriate path and are forced to find their way through trial and error. If delays are present, the penalty for each incorrect path goes up significantly. Similarly, "deep" sites require users to pass through many more levels to reach the target node. Delays increase the costs incurred by users of passing through additional levels of depth. In both of these situations repeated clicks on each site to arrive at the target will add up to a sizable time investment in viewing what might be a blank screen for several seconds. Deep sites, requiring more clicks to reach a target node, will impose greater penalties when users are unfamiliar. When there is a delay in loading each page, these costs become even greater. This suggests that in addition to direct effects, there will be interaction effects from the combination of these factors as the overall costs to users increase. Because users prefer low to high costs, the following hypotheses are tested.

H1: *There will be an interaction between delay, familiarity, and depth on user attitudes.*
H2: *There will be an interaction between delay, familiarity, and depth on user performance.*

One of the key Web design goals is to influence potential users to visit and to return later. Recent research suggests that the use of behavioral intentions is appropriate in a Web context (Song and Zahedi, 2001), where a user's behavioral intention (to return) serves as a useful summary variable indicating design success. Based on work concerning technology acceptance (Davis, 1989; Venkatesh et al., 2003; Taylor and Todd, 1995) and social cognitive theory (Compeau et al., 1999) we also expect attitudes and performance to impact behavioral intentions.

H3: *More favorable user attitudes will lead to more favorable behavioral intentions about the site.*

H4: *Higher user performance will lead to more favorable behavioral intentions about the site.*

Methodology

An experimental design was chosen to control delay, site depth, and familiarity. This design also allowed for measurement of outcome variables. The site used in Experiment 1 was also used in this experiment, but an additional "broad site" treatment was created. In all, the three factors are summarized as follows:

- Site Depth: The deep site made use of three levels, each with nine links, to provide eighty-one target nodes; the broad site made use of five levels each with three links to provide the same eighty-one target nodes.
- Familiarity: The "familiar" and "unfamiliar" sites were the same as those described in Experiment 1.
- Delay: A "fast" site had no delay and a "slow" site had an eight-second delay. We thus avoided the troublesome "ten-second boost" that occurred in Experiments 1 and 2, and also avoided uncomfortable delays for our participants.

Thus the sites covered two levels of each of three factors, providing a $2 \times 2 \times 2$ design with two between-subjects factors (delay and depth) and one within-subjects factor (familiarity). A completely counterbalanced, fully factorial design, providing all thirty-two combinations of order, delay, depth, and familiarity, was used. One hundred and sixty students in an upper division MIS class in the northeastern United States participated in the experiment and were randomly assigned to one of the thirty-two conditions. Manipulation checks revealed that differences between our conditions were discernible for all three experimental variables.

Results

Hypotheses H1 and H2 predict three-way interactions between familiarity, depth, and delay, suggesting that the combination of these three factors increases the negative effects on users beyond the effects of the factors individually. The results support both hypotheses, demonstrating a three-way interaction for both attitudes ($F = 5.9$; $p < .016$) and performance ($F = 7.98$; $p < .005$). The cell means reveal that unfamiliarity and deep sites interact to exacerbate the performance and attitudinal disadvantages of a slow site.

H3 and H4 assert that behavioral intentions can be predicted by attitudes and performance, respectively. Both attitudes and performance were included as predictor variables in a regression on intentions. The regression model was significant and explained significant variance in intentions

Table 3.7

Summary of Findings

	Expectation	Effect of Factors	Result
H1	Attitudes: Interaction between Delay, Depth, and Familiarity	3-way	**Supported**
H2	Performance: Interaction between Delay, Depth, and Familiarity	3-way	**Supported**
H3	Attitudes as an Antecedent of Behavioral Intentions	Direct	**Supported**
H4	Performance as an Antecedent of Behavioral Intentions	Direct	Not supported

(adjusted $R^2 = .597$). However, only the attitude measure contributed significantly to the model ($t = 18.8$; $p < .001$). In a stepwise regression, only attitudes entered the model (adjusted $R^2 = .598$). Supplemental analysis using partial least squares (PLS) regression found a significant relationship between attitudes and behavioral intentions, but not between performance and behavioral intentions. Performance, however, did have a significant effect on attitudes. In a mediation test, Galletta et al. (2006) determined that attitudes are an important mediator between the experimental treatments and behavioral intentions, which in this case cannot be left out of a model predicting behavioral intentions.

A summary of the results is shown in Table 3.7.

EXPERIMENT 4

In a design similar to that of Experiment 3, delay and two other factors were considered in predicting user attitudes, behavior, and performance. The other two factors included inter-page delay variability within the Web site (as manipulated by the experimenters) and process feedback that was provided to or withheld from the end users during the delay. When feedback was provided, users could see the page partially loading; when it was withheld, the page seemed to be blank for the delay duration. Only after the delay time was it displayed in its entirety all at once.

Hypotheses for delay are not provided, given that the first three studies found strong support for delay as a factor. Although it was hypothesized that each of the other factors would have an effect in its own right on users' attitudes and performance, more interesting research questions emerged when considering the interactions of the factors. In other words, besides the main effects, interaction effects (two-way and three-way) were expected to shed more light into the understanding of how the factors contribute to users' perception and performance measures.

Delay Variability

Research on user reactions to delay variability, covered in detail earlier in the review of the literature, is far more equivocal than research on delay's mean duration. However, several convincing studies suggest that low variability in delay length should be accompanied by positive effects on users. Low variability is in line with tuning theory, which states that users react positively when they can tune in with the timing of events in their environment (Roast, 1998). Shneiderman (1998) suggests positive outcomes when regularity is present in the task at hand; low variability in timing reduces uncertainty, which in turn reduces anxiety about the current situation (Carbonell et al.,

1968; Nickerson, 1969, 1981). Thus, low variability in timing (delay length) is expected to have positive effects on the dependent measures:

> H1a: *A Web site with low variability in delay will result in more favorable user attitudes than a Web site with high variability in delay.*
> H1b: *A Web site with low variability in delay will result in higher user performance than a Web site with high variability in delay.*

Feedback

The role of feedback given to people in waiting situations was previously described mainly in the domain of marketing (Maister, 1985; Larson, 1987; Katz et al., 1991; Hui and Tse, 1996). Providing feedback significantly reduces anxiety and uncertainty about the situation, and creates an impression of having cognitive control over a waiting situation (Hui and Bateson, 1991; Averill, 1973; Folkman, 1984). These by-products should, in turn, have favorable effects on attitudes and performance, therefore:

> H2a: *A Web site that provides feedback to users while the pages are loading will result in more favorable user attitudes than a Web site that withholds feedback.*
> H2b: *A Web site that provides feedback to users while the pages are loading will result in higher user performance than a Web site that withholds feedback.*

Delay Length and Delay Variability

When mean delay length is low, there is not much room for visible effects of variability. With low delay, even a high level of variability produces relatively small changes in absolute terms for users to notice. On the other hand, when delay is long, variability in its length will be more perceivable by the users. Therefore, it is hypothesized that an interaction between delay mean length and variability exists and results in small variability effects for low levels of delay and high variability effects for high delay levels:

> H3a: *There will be an interaction between delay length and delay variability on user attitudes.*
> H3b: *There will be an interaction between delay length and delay variability on user performance.*

Delay Length and Feedback

A similar argument can be drawn for the interacting effects of delay length and feedback. In situations where the Web pages load very fast (i.e., the delay is low), the manner in which the page loads matters much less than when there is a significant delay involved. Short loading times do not subject users to any significant levels of uncertainty about the delay time. Only a slowly loading page presents an opportunity for users to engage in mental time estimation (Zakay, 1989; Zakay and Hornik, 1991) and the presence or absence of process feedback (e.g., a partially displayed page) could have any effects on them. Therefore, it is hypothesized that presenting users with the partially loaded page (giving them feedback during the waiting situation) should create positive effects on user attitudes and performance only under high-delay conditions:

H4a: *There will be an interaction between delay length and feedback on user attitudes.*
H4b: *There will be an interaction between delay length and feedback on user performance.*

Delay Variability and Feedback

Low variability in delay length affords users the ability to tune in to the timing pattern of the loading Web site because the pages always load in the same predictable amount of time. Thus, the loading pattern with low variability serves as an implicit feedback mechanism because users see page loads when they expect them, in accordance with the observed timing rhythm. Providing the users with partial page displays (explicit process feedback) should bring some benefit to users; however, it should be much lower than in the case of high delay variability when no predictions and estimates can be made. High variability conditions present no common base to the users; page loads occur at random with seemingly large variability in timing. Providing partial page display as the individual page parts load should greatly reduce the uncertainty about the loading process and the waiting situation in which the users find themselves. Thus, it is hypothesized that the benefit of providing feedback to users will be much greater in the case of high variability than in situations with low variability (and therefore, to some extent, high predictability):

H5a: *There will be an interaction between delay variability and feedback on user attitudes.*
H5b: *There will be an interaction between delay variability and feedback on user performance.*

Delay Length, Delay Variability, and Feedback

Finally, building on the previous arguments, an overall prediction incorporating all three factors can be stated. Given the combinations of delay length, variability, and feedback, it is hypothesized that the users will find most benefits provided by process feedback in situations of high mean delay and high delay variability. It is when the variability is perceivable (high delay) and is also high (thus preventing timing predictability and tuning in to the timing of the environment's events) that the presence of feedback will be most pronounced in reducing the negative effects of delay and uncertainty in the waiting context:

H6a: *There will be an interaction among delay length, delay variability, and feedback on user attitudes.*
H6b: *There will be an interaction among delay length, delay variability, and feedback on user performance.*

Behavioral Intentions

Intentions to revisit a Web site can serve as an excellent summary variable that indicates users' overall level of contentment with the site. The theory of reasoned action, and its successor, the theory of planned behavior, have proposed attitudes as the main antecedent of behavioral intentions.

However, research shows that performance is also a significant antecedent of intentions (Compeau et al., 1999). Therefore, we hypothesize that both attitudes and performance will have an effect on intentions to return to the Web site:

> H7a: *More favorable user attitudes will lead to more favorable behavioral intentions about the site.*
> H7b: *Higher user performance will lead to more favorable behavioral intentions about the site.*

Methodology

Materials, Subjects, and Procedure

The study was conducted as a laboratory experiment. The research model was implemented as a between-subjects $2 \times 2 \times 2$ fully factorial design with random assignment of subjects to treatment conditions. Subjects for the study were 152 undergraduate business students enrolled in an upper-division management course. Incentives for participation were provided in the form of extra credit toward a final course grade.

Experimental materials consisted of a fictional Web site representing an online art gallery. The Web site followed a hierarchical structure similar to that of the other experiments in this paper. Besides the home page (the starting location for all experimental tasks), the site was composed of a tree structure containing four levels of categories and one final level of product pages. It used a deep $3 \times 3 \times 3 \times 3$ design (four category levels; each category page had three links to subcategories/products). The site contained a total of 121 Web pages, of which eighty-one were product pages.

Individual category pages contained descriptions that classified art by age, by style, by region, and so forth, and included links to further subcategories. Product pages contained samples of art with descriptions, images, and pricing.

Experimental tasks consisted of ten searches for specific art samples throughout the Web site. Subjects were given the name of a painting (with less specific indication of its location in the Web site as the tasks progressed), for which they were asked to find pricing information. Upon completion of the ten tasks, the subjects were asked to complete a post-experiment survey.

Operationalization of Variables

Delay Length. Delay length factor could not be manipulated as zero and eight seconds as before because it was impossible to provide variability to a zero-second treatment. A pilot study used two and eight seconds, but the results indicated that eight seconds was very likely to be slightly too fast. Therefore, main data collection used a "low" average level of two seconds from the user's click on the hyperlink to the complete load and display of the Web page, and a "high" level of ten seconds. Even though the previous study found a "spike" at ten seconds, there are still very strong main effects of delay on all outcomes at ten seconds. To prevent subjects from leaving a page before experiencing the full delay, the most important piece of information that the subject was looking for (either the links to lower categories on category pages or the table with the pricing information on the product pages) was loaded and displayed last, only after the full expiration of the designated delay time.

Delay Variability. The variability factor also assumed two levels. The low variability treatment was designed as a zero percent variability condition, that is, no variability was built into the delays. In this treatment, subjects always experienced a two- or ten-second delay, depending on their delay treatment. The high delay variability level simulated a $+/-60$ percent variability in delay length. Thus, in the low delay, high variability condition the subjects were exposed to randomly chosen delays of 0.8, 2.0, and 2.8 seconds (each chosen with the probability of 33 percent, thus preserving the mean of 2.0 seconds). In the high delay, high variability condition the delays took on a value of four, ten, and sixteen seconds, at random (again, keeping the mean delay at ten seconds).

Feedback. In accordance with the design, the feedback factor had also two levels. Feedback was either absent or present during the delay when the page was loading. An absent feedback treatment was simply a blank page after the user clicked on a hyperlink; the page remained blank for the complete delay length, depending on the delay/variability combination. Only at the conclusion of the full delay was the user presented with the completely loaded page with all page elements displayed. This treatment simulated a dynamically built page when table data must be completely retrieved from databases and tables must be fully built in order for the browser to display them to the end users.

A "feedback" treatment was implemented by showing the user a continuously loading screen while the delay was in progress. Each individual Web page consisted of several elements, for example, the company logo, page title, main page image, lengthy description, category links or product pricing information. Feedback was provided by progressively displaying all elements but the one containing the information sought. The user therefore had an indication that the page was loading; however, skipping to another page was not possible before the user had fully experienced the delay because the necessary information for that step remained hidden until the delay period elapsed.

Time was divided into units, and loading of the page followed a predetermined script and order. The low-delay treatments followed the same time proportions as the high-delay treatments for loading objects; they were broken into "beats," but the units were compressed.

Attitudes and Behavioral Intentions. Attitudes toward the Web site and intentions to return were measured as specified earlier. Reliability analysis revealed Cronbach's alpha of .89 for attitudes and .84 for intentions.

Performance. The performance measure consisted of three separate measures. Success rate measured the average number of correctly completed tasks of the ten assigned, ranging from zero to ten. Software automatically logged the subjects' browsing activity, and thus provided two more measures: the number of clicks executed by the subjects, and the amount of time they spent browsing the Web site. The time value was deflated for each subject in accordance with the treatment condition and the amount of page loads, resulting in the performance measure net time, which is comparable across all subjects regardless of the delay experienced.

Manipulation Checks and Control Variables. Manipulation checks on all three factors were employed to assess subjects' perceived levels of the treatments. In addition, several control and demographic variables were included in the survey so that randomization checks could be performed. Some of these variables were also entered as potential covariates in the analysis.

Results

The analysis was performed by using a multivariate ANCOVA due to a high level of correlation among the dependent variables. In addition, one of the control variables (art quiz) was highly

Table 3.8

MANCOVA for Performance and Attitudes

Effect	F	Sig.	Eta Squared
ART QUIZ-covariate	6.232	.000	.151
DELAY	22.322	.000	.389
VAR	.634	.639	.018
FEED	3.307	.013	.086
DELAY * VAR	.556	.695	.016
DELAY * FEED	.695	.597	.019
VAR * FEED	.338	.852	.010
DELAY * VAR * FEED	.125	.973	.004

Table 3.9

ANCOVA for Attitudes

Source	Type III Sum of Squares	df	Mean Square	F	Sig.
Corrected Model	64.278	8	8.035	3.170	.002
Intercept	1481.782	1	1481.782	584.609	.000
ART QUIZ	13.072	1	13.072	5.157	.025
DELAY	39.690	1	39.690	15.659	.000
VAR	.0921	1	.0921	.036	.849
FEED	12.837	1	12.837	5.064	.026
DELAY * VAR	.423	1	.423	.167	.684
DELAY * FEED	.401	1	.401	.158	.691
VAR * FEED	.0019	1	.0019	.001	.978
DELAY * VAR * FEED	.0218	1	.0218	.009	.926
Error	362.456	143	2.535		
Total	3707.245	152			
Corrected Total	426.733	151			

R Squared = .151 (Adjusted R Squared = .103)

correlated with all dependent variables, making it a good candidate as a covariate. The results of the MANCOVA are presented in Table 3.8.

Multivariate analysis revealed that only delay and feedback main effects were statistically significant at the .05 level. Further analysis focused on univariate tests for each of the dependent variables.

Attitudes

The results of an ANCOVA for attitudes are presented in Table 3.9. Strong support was found for delay (p = .000). Subjects in the low-delay condition felt more positive about the site (5.15) than the subjects in the high-delay condition (4.14). Support was found for H2a (p = .026), stating that more positive attitudes (4.90) will be obtained by subjects with feedback than those without

Table 3.10

ANCOVA for Performance

Source	Type III Sum of Squares	df	Mean Square	F	Sig.
Corrected Model	.331	8	.0413	2.072	.042
Intercept	41.439	1	41.439	2078.083	.000
ART QUIZ	.0716	1	.07158	3.590	.060
DELAY	.137	1	.137	6.893	.010
VAR	.0014	1	.0014	.067	.795
FEED	.0304	1	.0304	1.525	.219
DELAY * VAR	.0188	1	.0188	.945	.333
DELAY * FEED	.0453	1	.0453	2.271	.134
VAR * FEED	.0003	1	.0003	.017	.896
DELAY * VAR * FEED	.0002	1	.0002	.009	.923
Error	2.852	143	.01994		
Total	117.120	152			
Corrected Total	3.182	151			

R Squared = .104 (Adjusted R Squared = .054)

feedback (4.39). No support was found for the variability factor (H1a), nor for any of the interaction effects (H3a-6a).

Performance

The results for performance were conducted individually for each of the three performance sub-measures. Table 3.10 depicts the ANCOVA results for performance, Table 3.4 for net time, and Table 3.5 for clicks.

The results suggest that the only significant factor influencing performance was the level of delay (p = .010). Subjects in the low-delay condition were successful in finding the answers on average 89.61 percent of the time, while the subjects in the high-delay condition were successful 83.55 percent of the time. Although the largest difference in cell means occurred between feedback and no feedback conditions in the high-delay subset, testing for a feedback effect with a one-way ANOVA does not produce significant results (F = 3.286, df = 1,74, p = .074) at the α = .05 level.

The only effect found for success rate was that of delay. No other factors were supported. The longer the pages of a Web site take to load, the lower the success rate in finding information on the Web site. No effects were found for variability or feedback while loading pages, or for any of the proposed interactions. The research model explains 5.4 percent of the variance in success rate.

In a similar fashion, the results of the ANCOVA in Table 3.11 point out that the only significant factor influencing the time to complete the experiment was the level of delay (p = .000). However, the directionality of the effect is the opposite of what was predicted. Subjects in the low-delay condition took on average 823 seconds to complete the tasks, while the subjects in the high-delay condition completed the tasks on average in 655 seconds. This is consistent with the findings that people develop more careful strategies when response time is long (Grossberg et al., 1976).

The differences in means for the feedback factor are significant (p = .094) only at α = .1 level when performing an ANCOVA test with art quiz as a covariate. However, removing the covariate and testing for effects with ANOVA moves the significance level to p = .046. Subjects with

Table 3.11

ANCOVA for Net Time

Source	Type III Sum of Squares	df	Mean Square	F	Sig.
Corrected Model	1719457	8	214932.1	4.440	.000
Intercept	37664296	1	37664296.2	778.110	.000
ART QUIZ	352349	1	352348.6	7.279	.008
DELAY	1076274	1	1076274.3	22.235	.000
VAR	50705	1	50704.5	1.048	.308
FEED	137287	1	137286.5	2.836	.094
DELAY * VAR	9634	1	9633.9	.199	.656
DELAY * FEED	172	1	171.6	.004	.953
VAR * FEED	24273	1	24272.6	.501	.480
DELAY * VAR * FEED	22941	1	22940.8	.474	.492
Error	6921891	143	48404.8		
Total	91632527	152			
Corrected Total	8641348	151			

R Squared = .119 (Adjusted R Squared = .154)

feedback completed the tasks in 702 seconds, while those with no feedback took 775 seconds. This result is consistent with the expected direction, that is, the participants with feedback would perform better than those with no feedback. Due to the significance levels and explained variance, it is difficult to discern whether removing the covariate shifted explained variance in a desirable way or simply provided an increase in degrees of freedom.

No hypotheses were supported for net time. Although H2b was supported (the feedback factor), its support at $\alpha = .05$ level is conditional upon the removal of the covariate from the analysis. A strong effect was found for the delay factor but in the opposite direction than hypothesized. The higher the delay of a Web site, the less time subjects took to complete the experiment. No effects were found for the variability factor or any of the proposed interactions. The research model explains 15.4 percent of the variance in net time.

The results of the test in Table 3.12 show that only delay has a significant effect on clicks (p = .000). Following the pattern of net time, clicks also exhibits directionality that is contrary to what was predicted. Participants in the low-delay condition browsed through, on average, 166 Web pages, while individuals in the high-delay condition loaded 107 Web pages.

To summarize, no hypotheses were supported for clicks. A strong effect was found for the delay factor, but in the opposite direction than hypothesized. The higher the delay, the less browsing subjects performed. No effects were found for the variability and feedback factors, or any of the proposed interactions. The research model explains 34.6 percent of the variance in clicks.

Behavioral Intentions

Multiple regression analysis was used to test the strength of the relationship among attitudes, performance measures, and behavioral intentions.

A significant regression model was achieved with success rate, net time, clicks, and attitudes included in the model as predictors of intentions (F = 22.0, p = .000). The explained variance reached 35.8 percent of variance in behavioral intentions. However, it was found that the performance

Table 3.12

ANCOVA for Clicks

Source	Type III Sum of Squares	df	Mean Square	F	Sig.
Corrected Model	7.979	8	.997	10.981	.000
Intercept	1432.239	1	1432.239	15768.042	.000
ART QUIZ	.656	1	.656	7.225	.008
DELAY	6.959	1	6.959	76.618	.000
VAR	.201	1	.201	2.212	.139
FEED	.156	1	.156	1.717	.192
DELAY * VAR	.0935	1	.0935	1.029	.312
DELAY * FEED	.0777	1	.07.77	.855	.357
VAR * FEED	.0242	1	.02.42	.267	.606
DELAY * VAR * FEED	.0180	1	.01.80	.198	.657
Error	12.989	143	.0908		
Total	3592.075	152			
Corrected Total	20.968	151			

R Squared = .381 (Adjusted R Squared = .346)

Table 3.13

Regression Analysis with Attitudes

Model	Sum of Squares	df	Mean Square	F	Sig.
Regression	114.094	1	114.094	83.945	.000
Residual	203.873	150	1.359		
Total	317.967	151			

R Squared = .359 (Adjusted R Squared = .355)

variables were not significant predictors of intentions (Success Rate: ß = .136, t = 1.862, p = .065; Net Time: ß = .077, t = .955, p = .341; Clicks: ß = −.080, t = −.936, p = .351) and were therefore excluded from the model. Instead, a modified model that includes only attitudes was fitted and is shown in Table 3.13.

Attitudes are a very strong predictor of behavioral intentions, solidly supporting H7a. On the other hand, performance and behavioral intentions share only a weak relationship, primarily driven by the success rate on the search task. The association does not reach significance at $\alpha = .05$ level, thus failing to support H7b.

The summary results for all hypotheses are presented in Table 3.14.

Conclusions

Delay in loading Web pages remains a significant problem, even with the recent, rapid proliferation of high-speed access in offices and homes. Studies declare that computer response times should not exceed a variety of limits, commonly from two to twelve seconds and everywhere in between. One of the most consistent findings of previous research was that complex tasks allow

Table 3.14

Summary of Findings

H	Expectation	Effect	Result
H_{1a}	Attitudes: Low Variability > High Variability	Main	Not Supported
H_{1b}	Performance: Low Variability > High Variability	Main	Not Supported
H_{2a}	Attitudes: Feedback > No Feedback	Main	**Supported**
H_{2b}	Performance: Feedback > No Feedback	Main	**Mixed***
H_{3a}	Attitudes: Interaction between Delay and Variability	2-way	Not Supported
H_{3b}	Performance: Interaction between Delay and Variability	2-way	Not Supported
H_{4a}	Attitudes: Interaction between Delay and Feedback	2-way	Not Supported
H_{4b}	Performance Interaction between Delay and Feedback	2-way	Not Supported
H_{5a}	Attitudes: Interaction between Variability and Feedback	2-way	Not Supported
H_{5b}	Performance: Interaction between Variability and Feedback	2-way	Not Supported
H_{6a}	Attitudes: Interaction between Delay, Variability, and Feedback	3-way	Not Supported
H_{6b}	Performance: Interaction between Delay, Variability, and Feedback	3-way	Not Supported
H_{7a}	Attitudes as an Antecedent of Behavioral Intentions	–	**Supported**
H_{7b}	Performance as an Antecedent of Behavioral Intentions	–	Not Supported

*Supported: *Net Time*, Not supported: *Success rate, Clicks*

longer response times. Other design factors have been examined in isolation, but not as interactions between delay and those factors.

This study examined a variety of delay times of zero, two, four, six, eight, ten, and twelve seconds in two experiments, and used "fast" (zero or two seconds) and "slow" (eight or ten seconds) treatments in the other two. Subjects assigned randomly to treatments were asked to complete several search tasks, causing them to experience those delays in significant quantity.

Extent of Delay

As delay increases, performance, attitudes, and intentions to return to a site suffer. As the delay increases to two seconds, performance on a task (approximating the capacity of users to stick to their task on the site) ceases to decline further. As the delay increases to four seconds, attitudes and intentions cease to decline further. When considering only a site that is familiar to subjects, attitudes do not bottom out until the delay reaches eight seconds and intentions do not bottom out until the delay reaches six seconds. It is clear that using familiar terminology "buys" a site a few seconds.

Performance, attitudes, and behavioral intentions were predicted marginally better using nonlinear regression, and the explained variance was about 2 percent, 5 percent, and 7 percent, respectively. Explained variance was highest in the familiar site, at about 16 percent.

Cultural Factors

Volunteers in Mexico were solicited and invited to participate in an examination of whether or not cultural variables show promise in accounting for variation. In spite of an expectation that the Mexican subjects would be less impatient, it was found that their patterns matched those of the subjects from the United States more closely than expected. The Mexican subjects, in general, had more positive performance and attitudes in the fastest treatment (with zero-second delay) than the subjects from the United States. However, when delay was imposed, most of the differences disappeared. Therefore, examining people from different countries might reveal overall differences in performance, attitudes, or intentions. In such studies, the data deserve a close examination to determine whether patterns under changing conditions are different.

Familiarity

Consistent with prior research, ensuring that users are familiar with the terminology used to structure the site (reflected in interpage links) greatly helps them navigate a site without backtracking or becoming lost. Familiarity is an important component of scent, and lack of familiarity raises the cost of browsing.

Depth

Also consistent with prior research, providing more breadth (more links per page and fewer levels) will reduce the number of navigation steps users must complete. If a user is on the wrong path, more links per page will reduce the need for navigation, as the user will have more links to the bottom-level pages available for review. The scent, therefore, is decreased for users when a deep site is constructed.

Interaction: Delay, Familiarity, and Depth

Regarding the three factors, the most interesting finding, not covered in previous research, is that of a significant three-way interaction between delay, familiarity, and depth. This interaction indicates that performance and attitudes are dependent on all three factors together, beyond the simple main effects. Inspection of the means for both performance and attitudes provides some design guidance: If a site will suffer from delay problems, making the terminology familiar and the site broader will greatly alleviate the delay. If a site uses unfamiliar terminology, then making it load quickly and/or broadening the site will be helpful. Also implied is the warning that a site should not at the same time (1) use terminology that will be unfamiliar to its users, (2) have many levels of depth, and (3) have significant delay, as the combination of these three factors appears synergistic.

Feedback

Some of the literature on delay points to user uncertainty and anxiety when delays are long. If the user is provided with reliable feedback and can see the content continuously loading as it arrives, then this uncertainty should be eliminated. We find that feedback does indeed improve user attitudes.

Variability

The literature was rather equivocal about the variability of delay in the context of time-sharing systems. Some practitioners in the past slowed response rates in a highly variable system to a median and relatively constant rate to control user expectations. Constant delay might allow users to estimate computer response timing (as predicted to be desirable by Tuning Theory), and perhaps even allow users to schedule cognitive activities so that they are finished by the time the computer is ready for more input. Unfortunately, the outcome of our experiment is that variability does not seem to have an effect. Perhaps users are simply very accustomed to variability.

Interaction: Delay, Variability, and Feedback

An examination of an interaction among the three delay factors has not been covered before. A MANOVA revealed an interaction among the three factors, but separate ANOVAs failed to determine the reason for the significant interaction. It is possible that Experiment 4 did not have enough statistical power to reveal this interaction. It is also possible that the task was too easy or not interesting enough for users to react with a wide range of responses.

IMPLICATIONS AND CONCLUSION

Practitioners should be advised to pay close attention to delay and related factors. Familiarity, site depth, and delay have strong interactions and at least one of the three can be used to some extent to compensate for the other two. Feedback during the page-loading process can be effective in improving a user's attitude. Variability in page load times, perhaps one of the most common and least controllable factors, fortunately does not seem to be of major concern to users.

Analysis of interactions in these studies provide researchers with deeper understanding of what is "fast" and what is "slow," and how other factors interact with delay. Future work can benefit from refining and extending such interaction models in an attempt to advance theory and practice simultaneously.

Delay, considered universally to be a negative factor in use of the Web, is also enormously difficult to control. It is likely that problems of delay will be with us for many years to come. Therefore, it is important to study delay to understand the levels at which there is concern, whether or not cultural factors can make a difference, and to find out whether related design factors interact with delay.

ACKNOWLEDGMENTS

The authors would like to acknowledge travel funding from the International Business Center at the University of Pittsburgh.

NOTES

1. Although there are no easy ways to calculate the significance of the differences in country scores from the published data, according to Voris (2005), out of 53 countries, ranks for power distance, individualism, uncertainty avoidance, and masculinity were 38, 1, 43, and 15 for the United States and 5, 32, 18, and 6 for Mexico, respectively. On all scales except masculinity, the United States and Mexico are on opposite sides of the mean.

2. The United States ranks first in the world for individualism.

3. Of twenty countries with long-term orientation (LTO) scores, the United States ranks fifteenth. While Asian countries range from 48 to 118, Brazil is 65, and India is 61, the United States has a score of 29. The lowest score in LTO is West Africa at 16, only 13 points lower than the United States.

REFERENCES

Ajzen, I. The theory of planned behavior. *Organizational Behavior and Human Decision Processes*, 50 (1991), 179–211.

Anderson, R.E. Consumer dissatisfaction: the effect of disconfirmed expectancy on perceived product performance. *Journal of Marketing Research*, 10, 1 (1973), 38–44.

Au, N.; Ngai, E.W.T.; and Cheng, T.C.E. A critical review of end-user information system satisfaction research and a new research framework. *OMEGA—International Journal of Management Science*, 30, 6 (2002), 451–478.

Averill, J.R. Personal control over aversive stimuli and its relationship to stress. *Psychological Bulletin*, 80, 4 (1973), 286–303.

Barber, R.E., and Lucas, H.C. System response time, operator productivity, and job satisfaction. *Communications of the ACM*, 26, 11 (1983), 972–986.

Bergman, H.; Brinkman, A.; and Koelega, H.S. System response time and problem solving behavior. In *Proceedings of the Human Factors Society, 25th Annual Meeting*. Rochester, NY: Human Factors Society, 1981, pp. 749–753

Bitner, M.J. Evaluating service encounters: the effects of physical surroundings and employee responses. *Journal of Marketing*, 54, 2 (1990), 69–82.

Boucsein, W.; Greif, S.; and Wittekamp, J. systemresponsezeiten als belastungsfaktor bei bildschirm-dialogtätigkeiten. *Zeitschrift für Arbeitswissenschaft*, 38 (1984), 113–122.

Butler, T.W. Computer response time and user performance. In *Proceedings of the 1983 SIGCHI Conference on Human Factors in Computing Systems*. Boston: ACM Press, 1983, pp. 58–62.

Carbonell, J.R.; Elkind, J.I.; and Nickerson, R.S. On the psychological importance of time in a time-sharing system. *Human Factors*, 10 (1968), 135–142.

Card, S.K.; Moran, T.P.; and Newell, A. *The Psychology of Human-Computer Interaction*. Hillsdale, NJ: Lawrence Erlbaum Associates, 1983.

Card, S.K.; Pirolli, P.; Van Der Wege, M.; Morrison, J.B.; Reeder, R.W.; Schraedley, P.K.; and Boshart, J. Information scent as a driver of web behavior graphs: results of a protocol analysis method for web usability. In *Proceedings of the 2001 SIGCHI Conference on Human Factors in Computing Systems*. Seattle: ACM Press, 2001, pp. 498–505

Chau, P.Y.K.; Au, G.; and Tam, K.Y. Impact of information presentation modes on online shopping: An empirical evaluation of a broadband interactive shopping service. *Journal of Organizational Computing and Electronic Commerce*, 10, 1 (2000), 1–22.

Chi, E.H.; Pirolli, P.; Chen, K.; and Pitkow, J. Using information scent to model user information needs and actions on the web In *Proceedings of the 2001 SIGCHI Conference on Human Factors in Computing Systems*. Seattle: ACM Press, 2001, pp. 490–497.

Chin, J.P.; Diehl, V.A.; and Norman, K.L. Development of an instrument measuring user satisfaction of the human-computer interface. In *Proceedings of the 1988 SIGCHI Conference on Human Factors in Computing Systems*. Washington, DC: ACM Press, 1988, pp. 213–218.

Commerce Department. Retail e-commerce sales, third quarter 2005. Census Bureau Report, November 22, 2005 (available at http://www.census.gov/mrts/www/data/html/05Q3.html, accessed December 8, 2005).

Compeau, D.R.; Higgins, C.A.; and Huff, S. Social cognitive theory and individual reactions to computing technology: a longitudinal study. *MIS Quarterly*, 23, 2 (1999), 145–158.

Dannenbring, G.L. The effects of computer response time on user performance and satisfaction: A preliminary investigation. *Behavior Research Methods and Instrumentation*, 15, 2 (1984), 213–216.

Davis, E.S., and Hantula, D.A. The effects of download delay on performance and end-user satisfaction in an Internet tutorial. *Computers in Human Behavior*, 17 (2001), 249–268.

Davis, F.D. Perceived usefulness, perceived ease of use and user acceptance of information technology. *MIS Quarterly*, 13, 3 (1989), 319–340.

Davis, M.M., and Heineke, J. How disconfirmation, perception and actual waiting times impact customer satisfaction. *International Journal of Service Industry Management*, 9, 1 (1998), 64–73.

Davis, M.M., and Vollmann, T.E. A framework for relating waiting time and customer satisfaction in a service operation. *Journal of Services Marketing*, 4, 1 (1990), 61–69.

Dellaert, B.G.C., and Kahn, B.E. How tolerable is delay? Consumers' evaluations of internet web sites after waiting. *Journal of Interactive Marketing*, 3, 1 (1999), 41–54.

Devaraj, S.; Fan, M.; and Kohli, R. Antecedents of B2C channel satisfaction and preference: validating e-commerce metrics. *Information Systems Research*, 13, 3 (2002), 316–333.

Dubé, L.; Schmitt, B.H.; and Leclerc, F. Consumers' affective response to delays at different phases of a service delivery. *Journal of Applied Social Psychology*, 21, 10 (1991), 810–820.

Dumais, S.T., and Landauer, T.K. Using examples to describe categories. In *Proceedings of the 1983 SIGCHI Conference on Human Factors in Computing Systems*. Boston: ACM Press, 1983, pp. 112–115.

Fishbein, M., and Ajzen, I. *Belief, Attitude, Intention and Behavior: An Introduction to Theory and Research.* Reading, MA: Addison-Wesley, 1975.

Folkman, S. Personal control and stress and coping processes: a theoretical analysis. *Journal of Personality and Social Psychology*, 46, 4 (1984), 839–852.

Folkes, V. Consumer reactions to product failure: an attributional approach. *Journal of Consumer Research*, 10, 4 (1984), 398–409.

Folkes, V. Recent attribution research in consumer behavior: a review and new directions. *Journal of Consumer Research*, 14, 4 (1988), 548–565.

Folkes, V.; Koletsky, S.; and Graham, J.L. A field study of causal inferences and consumer reaction: the view from the airport. *Journal of Consumer Research*, 13, 4 (1987), 534–539.

Forrester Research, Inc. Forrester Online Retail Index, August 2001 (available at http://www.forrester.com/ER/Press/Release/0,1769,621,00.html, accessed December 8, 2005).

Galletta, D.; Henry, R.; McCoy, S.; and Polak, P. When the wait isn't so bad: the interacting effects of web site delay, familiarity, and breadth. *Information Systems Research*, 17, 1 (2006), 20–37.

Galletta, D.; Henry, R.; McCoy, S.; and Polak, P. Web site delays: how tolerant are users? *Journal of AIS*, 5, 1 (2004), article 1 (available at http://jais.isworld.org/authors.asp?auth=273, accessed December 8, 2005).

Gauch, S., and Smith, J.B. Search improvement via automatic query reformulation. *ACM Transactions on Information Systems*, 9, 3 (1991), 249–280.

Gail, T., and Lucey, S. Waiting time delays and customer satisfaction in supermarkets. *Journal of Services Marketing*, 9, 5 (1995), 20–29.

Goodman, T.J., and Spence, R. The effect of computer system response time variability on interactive graphical problem solving. *IEEE Transactions on Systems, Man, and Cybernetics*, 11, 3 (1981), 207–216.

Goodman, T.J., and Spence, R. The effect of system response time on interactive computer-aided problem solving. In *Proceedings of the 5th Annual Conference on Computer Graphics and Interactive Techniques.* New York: ACM Press, 1978, pp. 100–104.

Grossberg, M.; Wiesner, R.A.; and Yntema, D.B. An experiment on problem solving with delayed computer responses. *IEEE Transactions on Systems, Man, and Cybernetics*, 6, 3 (1976), 219–222.

GVU (1999). GVU's tenth world wide web user survey. 1999 (available at http://www.gvu.gatech.edu/user_surveys/survey-1998–10/tenthreport.pdf, accessed December 8, 2005).

Harvey, J.H., and Weary, G. Current issues in attribution theory and research. *Annual Review of Psychology*, 35 (1984), 427–59.

Hilgard, E.R. The trilogy of mind: cognition, affection, and conation. *Journal of the History of the Behavioral Sciences*, 16, 2 (1980), 107–117.

Hofstede, G. *Culture's Consequences: International Differences in Work-Related Values.* Beverly Hills, CA: SAGE Publications, 1980.

Hofstede, G. ITIM: creating cultural competence. 2005 (available at http://www.geert-hofstede.com, accessed on January 15, 2005).

Hofstede, G., and M. Bond. The Confucius connection: from cultural roots to economic growth. *Organization Dynamics*, 16, 4 (1988), 4–21.

Hoxmeier, J.A., and DiCesare, C. System response time and user satisfaction: An experimental study of browser-based applications. *Proceedings of the Association of Information Systems Americas Conference.* Long Beach, CA: Association for Information Systems, 2000, pp. 140–145.

Hui, M.K., and Bateson, J.E.G. Perceived control and the effects of crowding and consumer choice on the service experience. *Journal of Consumer Research*, 18, 2 (1991), 174–184.

Hui, M.K., and Tse, D.K. What to tell consumers in waits of different lengths: an integrative model of service evaluation. *Journal of Marketing*, 60, 2 (1996), 81–90.

Jacko, J.A.; Sears, A.; and Borella, M.S. The effect of network delay and media on user perceptions of web resources. *Behaviour and Information Technology*, 19, 6 (2000), 427–439.

James, W. *Principles of Psychology.* New York: Holt, 1952, p. 410.

Johansson, G., and Aronsson, G. Stress reactions in computerized administrative work. *Journal of Occupational Behaviour*, 5 (1984), 159–181.

Johnson, E.J., and Payne, J.W. Effort and accuracy in choice. *Management Science*, 31, 4 (1985), 395–414.

Kaindl, H.; Kramer, S.; and Afonso, L.M. Combining structure search and content search for the world-wide web. In *Proceedings of the Ninth ACM Conference on Hypertext and Hypermedia.* Pittsburgh, PA: ACM Press, 1998, pp. 217–224.

Katz, K.; Larson, B.; and Larson, R. Prescription for the waiting in line blues: entertain, enlighten and engage. *Sloan Management Review*, 32, 2 (1991), 44–53.

Katz, M.A., and Byrne, M.D. The effect of scent and breadth on use of site-specific search on e-commerce web sites. *ACM Transactions on Human-Computer Interaction*, 10, 3 (2003), 198–220.

Koblentz, E. Web hosting partner keeps stone site rolling. *Eweek*, October 30, 2000, p. 27 (also available at http://www.zdnet.com.au/news/business/0,39023166,20106701,00.htm, accessed December 8, 2005).

Kohlisch, O., and Kuhmann, W. System response time and readiness for task execution—the optimum duration of inter-task delays. *Ergonomics*, 40, 3 (1997), 265–280.

Kuhmann, W. Experimental investigation of stress-inducing properties of system response times. *Ergonomics*, 32, 3 (1989), 271–280.

Langer, E.J. *The Psychology of Control*. Beverly Hills, CA: Sage Publications, 1983.

Larson, R. Perspectives on queues: social justice and the psychology of queuing. *Operations Research*, 35, 6 (1987), 895–905.

Larson, K., and Czerwinski, M. Web page design: implications of memory, structure and scent for information retrieval. In *Proceedings of the 1998 SIGCHI Conference on Human Factors in Computing Systems*. Los Angeles: ACM Press, 1998, pp. 25–31.

Lee, A.T. Web usability: a review of the research. *SIGCHI Bulletin*, 31, 1 (1999), 38–40.

Lohse, G.L., and Spiller, P. Electronic shopping. *Communications of the ACM*, 41, 7 (1998), 81–87.

Maister, D. The psychology of waiting lines. In J. Czepiel, M. Solomon, and C. Suprenant (eds.), *The Service Encounter*. Lexington, MA: Lexington Books, 1985, pp. 113–123.

Miller, R.B. Response time in man-computer conversational transactions. In *AFIPS Proceedings for 1968 Fall Joint Computer Conference*. San Francisco: Thompson, 1968, pp. 267–277.

Muramatsu. J., and Pratt, W. Transparent queries: investigation users' mental models of search engines. In *Proceedings of the 24th Annual International ACM SIGIR Conference on Research and Development in Information Retrieval*. New Orleans: ACM Press, 2001, pp. 217–224.

Nah, F.H. A study on tolerable waiting time: how long are web users willing to wait? In *Proceedings of the 9th Americas Conference on Information Systems*. Tampa, FL: Association for Information Systems, 2003, pp. 2212–2222.

Nielsen, J. User interface directions for the web. *Communications of the ACM*, 42, 1 (1999), 65–72.

Nickerson, R.S. Man-computer interaction: A challenge for human factors research. *IEEE Transactions on Man-Machine Systems*, 10, 4 (1969), 164–180.

Nickerson, R.S. Why interactive computer systems are sometimes not used by people who might benefit from them. *International Journal of Man-Machine Studies*, 15, 4 (1981), 469–483.

Norman, K., and Chin, J. The effect of tree structure on search in a hierarchical menu selection system. *Behaviour and Information Technology*, 7, 1 (1988), 51–65.

Oliver, R.L., and Swan, J.E. Consumer perceptions of interpersonal equity and satisfaction in transactions: a field survey approach. *Journal of Marketing*, 53, 2 (1989), 21–35.

Olston, C., and Chi, E.H. ScentTrails: integrating browsing and searching on the web. *ACM Transactions on Computer-Human Interaction*, 10, 3 (2003), 177–197.

Osuna, E.E. The psychological cost of waiting. *Journal of Mathematical Psychology*, 29, 1 (1985), 82–105.

Otter, M., and Johnson, H. Lost in hyperspace: metrics and mental models. *Interacting with Computers*, 13, 1 (2000), 1–40.

Paap, K.R., and Roske-Hofstrand, R.J. Design of menus. In M. Helander (ed.), *Handbook of Human-Computer Interaction*. Amsterdam: Elsevier, 1988, pp. 205–235.

Palmer, J. Web site usability, design, and performance metrics. *Information Systems Research*, 13, 2 (2002), 155–167.

Parasuraman, A.; Zeithaml, V.A.; and Berry, L.L. Reassessment of expectations as a comparison standard on measuring service quality: implications for further research. *Journal of Marketing*, 58, 1 (1994), 111–124.

Pardu, J.H., and Landry, J. Evaluation of alternative interface designs for e-tail shopping: an empirical study of three generalized hierarchical navigation schemes. In *Proceedings of the 7th Americas Conference on Information Systems*. Boston: Association for Information Systems, 2001, pp. 1335–1337.

Pirolli, P., and Card, S. Information foraging. *Psychological Review*, 106, 4 (1999), 643–675.

Planas, M.A., and Treurniet, W.C. The effects of feedback during delays in simulated teletext reception. *Behaviour and Information Technology*, 7, 2 (1988), 183–191.

Polak, P. *The Direct and Interactive Effects of Web Site Delay Length, Delay Variability, and Feedback on User Attitudes, Performance, and Intentions.* PhD dissertation, University of Pittsburgh, Katz Graduate School of Business, 2002.

Ramsay, J.; Barbesi, A.; and Preece, J. A psychological investigation of long retrieval times on the world wide web. *Interacting with Computers,* 10, 1 (1998), 77–86.

Roast, C. Designing for delay in interactive information retrieval. *Interacting with Computers,* 10, 1 (1998), 87–104.

Robertson, G.; McCracken, D.; and Newell, A. The ZOG approach to man-machine communication. *International Journal of Man-Machine Studies,* 14, 3 (1981), 461–488.

Rose, G.M. The effect of download time on e-commerce: the download time brand impact model. PhD dissertation, Georgia State University, 2000.

Rose, G.M.; Lees, J.; and Meuter, M.A. Refined view of download time impacts on e-consumer attitudes and patronage intentions toward e-retailers. *The International Journal on Media Management,* 3, 2 (2001), 105–111.

Rose, G.M., and Straub, D. The effect of download time on consumer attitude toward the e-service retailer. *e-Service Journal,* 1, 1 (2001), 55–76.

Ross, M., and Fletcher, G.O. Attribution and social perception. In L. Gardner and E. Aronson (eds.), *Handbook of Social Psychology,* Vol. 2. New York: Random House, 1985, pp. 73–122.

Rushinek, A., and Rushinek, S. What makes users happy? *Communications of the ACM,* 29, 7 (1986), 594–598.

Sawrey, J.M., and Telford, C.W. *Psychology of Adjustment,* 3rd ed. Boston: Allyn and Bacon Inc., 1971.

Schwartz, J.P., and Norman, K.L. The importance of item distinctiveness on performance using a menu selection system. *Behaviour and Information Technology,* 5, 2 (1986), 173–182.

Shneiderman, B. *Designing the User Interface: Strategies for Effective Human-Computer Interaction,* 3rd ed. Reading, MA: Addison-Wesley, 1998.

Shneiderman, B. Response time and display rate in human performance with computers. *Computing Surveys,* 16, 3 (1984), 265–285.

Simon, H.A. Reflections on time sharing from a user's point of view. *Computer Science Research Review,* Carnegie Institute of Technology, 1966, 43–51.

Somberg, B., and Picardi, M. Locus of the information familiarity effect in the search of computer menus. In *Proceedings of the Human Factors Society 27th Annual Meeting.* Santa Monica, CA: Human Factors Society, 1983, pp. 826–830.

Song, J., and Zahedi, F. Web design in e-commerce: a theory and empirical analysis. In *Proceedings of the 22nd International Conference on Information Systems.* New Orleans: Association for Information Systems, 2001, pp. 205–220.

Stephens, G.K., and Greer, C.R. Doing business in Mexico: understanding cultural differences, *Organizational Dynamics,* 24, 1 (1995), 34–55.

Swan, J.E.; Trawick, I.F.; and Carrol, M.G. Effect of participation in market research on consumer attitudes towards research and satisfaction with a service. *Journal of Marketing Research,* 18, 3 (1981), 356–363.

Taylor, S. Waiting for service: the relationship between delays and evaluations of service. *Journal of Marketing,* 58, 2 (1994), 56–69.

Taylor, S. The effect of filled waiting time and service provider control over the delay on evaluations of service. *Journal of the Academy of Marketing Science,* 23, 1 (1995), 38–48.

Taylor, S., and Todd, P.A. Understanding information technology usage: a test of competing models. *Information Systems Research,* 6, 2 (1995), 144–176.

Thadhani, A.J. Interactive user productivity. *IBM Systems Journal,* 20, 4 (1981), 407–423.

Thuring, M., Hannemann, J., and Haake, J. M. Hypermedia and cognition: designing for comprehension. *Communications of the ACM,* 38, 8 (1995), 57–66.

Todd, P., and Benbasat, I. Evaluating the impact of DSS, cognitive effort, and incentives on strategy selection. *Information Systems Research,* 10, 4 (1999), 356–374.

Treurniet, W.C.; Hearty, P.J.; and Planas, M.A. Viewers' responses to delays in simulated teletext reception. *Behaviour and Information Technology,* 4, 3 (1985), 177–188.

U.S. Bureau of Economic Analysis. National Income and Product Account, 2001 (available at http://www.bea.doc.gov/bea/dn1.htm#comp, accessed July 1, 2002).

Venkatesh, V.; Morris, M.G.; Davis, G.B.; and Davis, F.D. User acceptance of information technology: toward a unified view. *MIS Quarterly,* 27, 3 (2003), 425–478.

Voris, M. Hofstede's dimension of culture scales, 2005 (available at http://spectrum.troyst.edu/~vorism/hofstede.htm, accessed on January 15, 2005).

Weinberg, B.D. Don't keep your internet customers waiting too long at the (virtual) front door. *Journal of Interactive Marketing*, 14, 1 (2000), 30–39.

Weiner, B. A cognitive (attributional)-emotion-action model of motivated behavior: an analysis of judgments of help-giving. *Journal of Personality and Social Psychology*, 39 (1980), 186–200.

Weiner, B. An attributional theory of achievement, motivation and emotion. *Psychological Review*, 92, 4 (1985), 548–573.

Weiner, B. Attribution, emotion and action. In R.M. Sorrentino and E.T. Higgins (eds.), *Handbook of Motivation and Cognition*. New York: Guilford Press, 1986, pp. 281–312.

Wonnacott, L. When user experience is at risk, Tier 1 providers can help. *Infoworld*, November 6, 2000, p. 76 (available at http://infoworld.com/articles/op/xml/00/11/06/001106opsavvy.html, accessed December 8, 2005).

Woodrow, H. Time perception. In Stevens, S.S. (ed.), *Handbook of Experimental Psychology*. New York: Wiley, 1958, pp. 1224–1236.

Wrightsman, L.S., and Deaux, K. *Social Psychology in the 80's*. Monterey, CA: Brooks/Cole Publishing, 1981.

Zakay, D. An integrated model of time estimation. In I. Levin and D. Zakay (eds.), *Time and Human Cognition: A Life Span Perspective*. Amsterdam: North-Holland, 1989, pp. 365–397.

Zakay, D. and Hornik, J. How much time did you wait in line? A time perception perspective. In J.C. Chebat and V. Venkatesan (eds.), *Time and Consumer Behavior*. Montreal: Université du Québec à Montréal, 1991.

Zona Research Study. The need for speed. 1999 (available at http://www.zonaresearch.com/info/press/99%2Djun30.htm, accessed July 1, 2001).

CHAPTER 4

POP-UP ANIMATIONS

Impacts and Implications for Web Site Design and Online Advertising

PING ZHANG

Abstract: *Owing to the rapid growth of Internet technologies, Web site design, and online adver-tisements, pop-up animations have affected and will continue to affect millions of people. Our under-standing of the effectiveness and the impact of online advertisements on consumers is still limited from a theoretical perspective, and the empirical evidence continues to be scant. This paper syn-thesizes and integrates several lab-controlled experiments conducted by the author over an eight-year period (from 1996 to 2003) on the impact of pop-up animations in the Web environment. Human visual attention literature is used to emphasize human cognitive characteristics that pre-vent or enable us to behave in certain ways when there is animation in our vision field. These studies, together, address the following research questions: (1) As a non-primary information source, does animation decrease viewers' information-seeking performance? (2) If so, do location and timing of pop-up animation matter? (3) As viewers' familiarity with online advertisements increases, do those early animation effects diminish over years? The studies also validate the applicability of visual attention theories in the Web environment and have significant practical implications for online advertising strategies, both for marketers and content providers.*

Keywords: *Animation, Pop-Up, Information Seeking, Online Advertising, Visual Attention, Visual Interference, World Wide Web, Lab-Controlled Experiment*

INTRODUCTION

Animation is a dynamic visual statement, form, and structure evolving through movement over time (Baecker and Small, 1990). Pop-up animation in a Web environment refers to animation that begins or appears on the screen as additions to the original content on the screen. Owing to the advancement of software tools and specialized graphic and animation packages, vivid and wild animations become very easy to produce and have been widely used in the Web environment. Animations are popular objects that users encounter frequently, if not all the time. They have been used for different purposes and can be found in many computing environments, especially Web pages and online advertisements. Some designers use animations to convey messages, believing they are more powerful than text within the limited display area of a computer screen (Gonzalez and Kasper, 1997), although there are cautions regarding animations' efficacy (Tversky et al.,

2002). To online advertisers, pop-up and pop-under (in the background rather than on the surface of the screen) animations are considered great ways of reaching potential consumers and increasing brand awareness, Web traffic, and click-throughs.

The utilization of animations in the computing environment for various purposes is based on the understanding that human beings respond involuntarily to moving objects. This is proven by the experiences of many viewers. To most people and at most times, animations on the Web are disturbing and annoying. Being interrupted or having one's attention involuntarily shifted by animation on a Web page is a typical experience for many Web users. This is especially so when animations carry information that has nothing to do with viewers' tasks and needs at the time. We refer to this type of animation as non-primary information stimulus or secondary stimulus to users (Zhang, 2000). In other words, the animation carries no information for users' information-seeking tasks or immediate informational needs.

Animations as non-primary information stimulus can create visual interference that affects one's information-seeking performance. Extraneous animation that is present continuously or appears suddenly can act as a distraction, interfering with users' concentration on pertinent information. Thus, it disturbs and often annoys people as they search for useful information on the Web, lengthening the time needed to obtain information correctly.

Although visual attention theories may explain certain visual interference phenomena, it is unclear whether we can apply them directly to information-seeking tasks in a computing environment such as the Web. A primary reason for this is that the exposure time of stimuli in traditional visual attention studies is much shorter (milliseconds) than that on the Web (seconds or minutes), and one's visual attention behavior may change during this relatively long exposure time (Zhang, 2000). The second reason is that the experimental environment or setting in visual attention studies is different from that in a computing environment, such as the Web. In visual attention studies, special types of equipment are used to display stimuli and capture responses. To date, few empirical studies report the effects of animation in a Web environment. So the applicability of visual attention studies needs to be tested in the Web environment (Zhang, 2000). It is encouraging that there are compatible models and theories on visual orienting responses and limited capacity (Lang, 2000; Lang et al., 2002; Reeves et al., 1999) that are more relevant to the Web environment and these have found empirical support. They can help augment the traditional cognitive psychology studies to explain animation's effect in the Web environment.

In this paper, we report and synthesize three studies on the effects of pop-up animations in the Web environment. These studies, evolving between 1996 and 2003, consist of a series of lab-controlled experiments to address a set of general research questions that evolved with the research: (1) As a non-primary information source, does animation decrease viewers' information seeking performance? (2) If so, do location and timing of pop-up animations matter? (3) As viewers' familiarity with online advertisements increases, do those early animation effects diminish over years?

The contribution of this research is threefold. First, it sheds light on the applicability of visual attention and perception theories to the Web environment. Visual attention theories have not been extensively applied to IS research and practice in general and the Web environment in particular (Zhang, 2000). Although the Web environment is different from the context within which visual attention theories were developed, it presents a unique opportunity to study the generalizability of research results in human visual attention. Second, this paper demonstrates some aspects of the research process. These aspects include (1) the formation and evolution of specific research questions and the process of searching for answers; (2) the appropriateness of applying theories from other fields to the IT environment, and the search for alternative theoretical support and explanations that better fit the empirical results when necessary; and (3) understanding of possible discrepancies between objective performance measures and subjective perceptions from self-reports. Third, the research has practical value in providing Web page designers with empirical evidence that can replace speculation regarding the effects on user performance of pop-up animations as non-primary information carriers. Such evidence can provide strategic suggestions for the marketers (who want to be "intrusive" and persuasive) and the Internet content providers (who want to make money by providing ad space, but do not want to annoy their customers) to be better informed as they design effective Web pages and online advertisements. As many more people search for information on the Web, conduct business over the Internet, and encounter animations more frequently as advertisers invest heavily in online advertising, research that investigates the real effects of pop-up animations becomes increasingly important (Zhang, 2000).

The rest of the paper is organized as follows. In the section "Theoretical Support," we review relevant theoretical work on visual perception and attention. These works support both the original theoretical understanding when the hypotheses were developed and the later discovery of alternative theories. The next three sections, "Study 1," "Study 2," and "Study 3," describe the three studies in detail, including research questions, hypotheses, experiment design and conduct, data collection and analysis, results, and a summary. To demonstrate some aspects of the research processes, we follow the actual steps through which the research was conducted. The hypotheses are based on the original theoretical understanding. In "Discussions," we review several interesting findings, including some surprising discrepancies between objective performance measures and subjective perception data, a need to search for alternative theoretical explanations of some empirical results, lessons learned about conducting experiments, limitations of the current research, and some future directions. Then we highlight the practical implications of the findings on Web user interface design from both content provider and online advertiser perspectives. The final section, "Conclusions," summarizes and concludes the research.

THEORETICAL SUPPORT

It is widely believed that human attention is limited and allocated selectively to stimuli in the visual field (Lang, 2000; Pashler, 1998). Theoretical work on visual attention and selection has been done primarily in cognitive psychology, but also in a few other disciplines (such as communication) in recent years. This section highlights some of the theories that contribute to our hypotheses development and research question formation.

Visual Attention Theories in Cognitive Psychology

Research results from studies in visual attention and perception can provide a plausible explanation for the disturbance phenomenon. Studies show that, in general, objects in our peripheral vision can capture our attention (Driver and Baylis, 1989; Warden and Brown, 1944). The meaning of a non-attended stimulus is processed to a certain extent (Allport, 1989; Duncan and Humphreys, 1989; Treisman, 1991). Because attention has limited capacity, the resources available to attend to pertinent information are reduced, with the result that information-processing performance, including time and accuracy, deteriorates (Miller, 1991; Spieler et al., 2000; Treisman, 1991).

Since our ability to attend to stimuli is limited, the direction of attention determines how well we perceive, remember, and act on information. Objects or information that do not receive attention usually fall outside our awareness and, hence, have little influence on performance (Proctor and Van Zandt, 1994, p. 187). Perceptual attention is usually studied with two primary themes: selectivity (conscious perception is always selective) and capacity limitations (our limited ability to carry out various mental operations at the same time), although a variety of other notions are also studied (Pashler, 1998). Specifically, attention has been studied from two perspectives in order to understand different aspects of attention: selective attention and divided attention.

Selective attention is also known as "focused attention." It concerns our ability to focus on certain sources of information and ignore others (Proctor and Van Zandt, 1994, p. 187). Usually the criterion of selection is a simple physical attribute such as location or color (Pashler, 1998). It is studied by presenting people with two or more stimuli at the same time, and instructing them to process and respond to only one (Eysenck and Keane, 1995, p. 96). Work on selective attention can tell us how effectively people can select certain inputs rather than others, and it enables us to investigate the nature of the selection process and the fate of unattended stimuli (Eysenck and Keane, 1995, p. 96). Divided attention is also studied by presenting at least two stimulus inputs at the same time, but with instructions that all stimulus inputs must be attended to and responded to (Eysenck and Keane, 1995, p. 96). In divided attention, the question asked of the subject depends on the categorical identity of more than one of the stimuli (Pashler, 1998, p. 29). Studies on divided attention provide useful information about our processing limitations (ability to divide attention among multiple tasks), and tell us something about attentional mechanisms and their capacity (Eysenck and Keane, 1995; Proctor and Van Zandt, 1994).

Pashler (1998) summarizes the discoveries in the visual attention literature. The following is a list of conclusions that are relevant to this study.

1. The to-be-ignored stimuli are analyzed to a semantic level, although "the totality of the evidence does not favor the view that complete analysis takes place on every occasion."
2. Capacity limits are evident when the task requires discriminating targets defined by complex discriminations (e.g., reading a word).
3. More specifically, the capacity limits in perceptual processing of complex discriminations depend on the attended stimulus load and hardly at all on the ignored stimuli.

In summary, "people can usually exercise control over what stimuli undergo extensive perceptual analysis, including, on occasion, selecting multiple stimuli for analysis. When this takes place, the stimuli that are selected compete for limited capacity. If the total load of stimulus processing does not exceed a certain threshold, parallel processing occurs without any detectable reduction in efficiency. Above this threshold, efficiency is reduced by the load of attended stimuli, and processing may sometimes operate sequentially, perhaps as a strategy to minimize loss of accuracy" (Pashler, 1998, p. 226).

The Orienting Response (OR)

The Orienting Response (OR) was first proposed by Pavlov (Pavlov, 1927) and was further developed by a number of scholars (Sokolov et al., 2002). It is an automatic, reflexive physiological and behavioral response that occurs in response to novel or signal stimuli. A novel stimulus is one that represents a change in the environment or an unexpected occurrence (Lang, 2000). The OR has been used for the development of theories of information processing and coding in cognitive science (Sokolov et al., 2002).

Limited Capacity Model of Mediated Communication

In communication research, Lang (2000) proposed the limited-capacity model of mediated message processing in the context of television and radio to explain how messages interact with the human information-processing system. According to this framework, an individual either consciously or subconsciously selects which information in the message to attend to, encode, process, and store. The amount of the selected information is limited by the individual's processing resources. While the individual controls some aspect of the processing resources, the stimulus elicits orienting responses from individuals. Research suggests that the physiological response is associated with attention and stimulus intake (Campbell et al., 1997; Hoffman, 1997). The orienting response causes an automatic allocation of processing resources to encoding the stimulus (Lang, 2000), decreasing the available resources for primary tasks such as information seeking in the Web environment, thus affecting the users' performance.

A plausible note is that these responses occur within seconds, which is more applicable to a Web-based environment. Lang and colleagues (Lang et al., 2002; Reeves et al., 1999) use this model to study the effects of different types of computer-presented messages. In one of their experiments, they investigate whether the presence of Web-based advertisement banners would elicit an orienting response. The results show that Web animated banners elicit an orienting response, whereas static Web advertisement banners do not.

STUDY 1

Research Questions and Hypotheses

This study was designed to answer the following research questions by applying visual attention theories and studies to the Web environment, keeping in mind the potential differences of the environment, and thus the potential problems of the appropriateness of the theories.

RQ1: *As non-primary information stimuli, do animations decrease viewers' information seeking performance?*

RQ2: *If so, what are some characteristics of animations that may have an impact on viewers' information-seeking performance?*

In this study, the primary task for the subjects was information seeking: Subjects were to search for some information (a phrase, word, or term) from a document on a Web page. Animation provided no information for the primary task. In a real-world situation, animation can have different attributes such as size, speed, location, and content design and color. All these factors can have some impact. The effect of the same animation could also depend on the types of user tasks and different individuals. To make this study feasible, we considered some factors as constants—namely size, speed, and location of animations. We treated three factors as independent variables: task difficulty (simple and difficult), animation color (bright colors such as red, green, light blue, and orange, and dull colors such as gray, white, and black), and animation content (task-similar and task-dissimilar). Individual differences were eliminated by the experimental design (within-subject design).

For information-seeking tasks in the Web environment, both target stimulus (information to be searched for) and non-target stimuli are defined by "complex discriminations" and must be identified by the subject before a decision (i.e., whether a stimulus is a target) can be made. In this situation, capacity limits should be evident, as summarized by Pashler (1998). The amount of resources for processing the target stimulus may be affected by the amount of resources used to "attend" to non-target stimuli, either different words in the document or the animation. Given that the number of non-target words in a document was a constant, adding animation to the document may add demand for resources and thus decrease the available amount of resources for processing the target stimulus. Therefore, the subject's information-seeking performance may be affected. It should be noted that we developed hypotheses based on the characteristics of our human visual attention mechanisms, as discovered by visual attention studies. But the experimental settings for the Web environment were different from those in the visual attention studies.

H1. *Animation as a non-primary information stimulus deteriorates subjects' information-seeking performance.*

As indicated in the summary of attention research results, increasing the difficulty of processing the attended items eliminates effects of unattended stimuli (Pashler, 1998, p. 98). Researchers, for example, discovered that a distracter has less impact on a more difficult task (that is, a task with high perceptual load) than on a simple or low-load task (Lavie, 1995; Lavie and Tsal, 1994). In Lavie's study (1995), after a string of one to six letters was exposed to them for 50 ms, participants were asked whether a target letter appeared in the string. The one- or two-letter condition was called a simple task; the six-letter condition was a difficult task. The argument was that a difficult primary task required more cognitive effort from participants; thus their capacity was utilized, leaving less room for processing irrelevant information (i.e., the distracter). We applied the arguments and findings to the Web-based tasks. In order to test this, we divided tasks into simple and difficult ones. The corresponding hypothesis is:

H2. *As the level of task difficulty increases, subjects' performance will be less affected by animation.*

The visual attention literature also indicates that the degree of interference has to do with the physical and/or the semantic relation between the distracter and the target (e.g., Mayor and Gonzalez-Marques, 1994; Miller and Bauer, 1981; Treisman, 1991). The more similar their physical features or semantic meanings, the greater the interference. The basic argument is that visual items that are perceptually grouped (because they are very similar) will tend to be selected together and thus lengthen the time needed to detect the target or attended stimuli. In our case, we compared animation that had physical features and/or content similar to a user's tasks to another type of animation that had no similar physical features/content to the tasks. The corresponding hypothesis is:

H3. *Animation whose content is similar but irrelevant to a task has more negative effect on performance than animation whose content is dissimilar to the task.*

It is well recognized that bright color is an important attribute of annoying animation. Chromatic colors stand out from achromatic ones and become more salient, easily grabbing our visual attention. If targets are in chromatic colors, one can expect to detect them rather easily among all other non-targets. If distracters are in chromatic color, they would compete for visual attention with targets. Viewers have to expend additional effort to find achromatic targets with chromatic distracters around. Thus, we anticipated that brightly colored or chromatic animation is more noticeable, and thus more distracting, than achromatic animation (with dull colors).

H4. *Animation that is brightly colored has a stronger negative effect on subjects' performance than does dully colored animation.*

Table 4.1

Structure of Study 1: Task Settings

	Baseline (no animation)	Task-Similar Animation		Task-Dissimilar Animation	
		Dull Color	Bright Color	Dull Color	Bright Color
Simple Task	1	2	3	4	5
Difficult Task	6	7	8	9	10

Experiment Design and Conduct

The experiment used a within-subject full factorial design in order to reduce error variability and increase statistical test power. Besides the three independent variables (task difficulty, animation color, and animation content), baseline conditions, where no animation was used, were also considered for tasks with two different difficulty levels. The experiment consisted of ten imposed settings, as depicted by Table 4.1. Each subject did a total of twenty tasks, two for each setting. The sequence of the twenty tasks was randomized for each subject in order to reduce the potential order effect.

Subjects worked with a table of strings where some of the strings were target strings and were to be identified and counted. The table, which was designed as ten rows by eight columns, was displayable on one page and big enough to eliminate the one-glance-grabs-all effect (otherwise time spent on the task would not be measurable). The task of identifying target strings (which could be words, abbreviations, or phrases) from other strings is one of the typical information-seeking tasks in the Web environment. It is frequently conducted when viewers use either browsing or analytical information-seeking strategies in the Web environment (Marchionini, 1995). In this study, we defined a string as a random combination of one to four letters in order to eliminate any automatic processing of familiar target strings. Automatic processing is considered nonselective processing, which requires no attention (Pashler, 1998). A target string appeared from one to five times in a table. After some trials, we found that one-letter strings were too easy to count, and any string with more than four letters was extremely difficult to work with. We decided that in this study, a target string with two letters was a simple task, and a target string with four letters was a difficult one.

Each of the twenty tasks was associated with a pre-page and a task page. A pre-page showed the target string that subjects needed to look for. A click on the link of the pre-page loaded the task page. A task page had a no-border table of strings in the middle, a clickable answer section at the bottom, and possibly some animation, depending on the treatment. The subject could select an answer and click the "Submit" button, which led the subject to the next pre-page in the task sequence.

Animation could appear in a random location right outside the table (top, bottom, and side). The content of animation included moving strings (similar to that in tasks) and moving images such as animals, objects, and people. Both types of animation can be found frequently in real Web pages. String animation seemed to fly into a subject's face from deep in the screen, and then receded; this cycle continued for as long as the page was displayed. Figures 4.1a and 4.1b are two snapshots of a task page at different timing or stages of a string animation. The size for all animations remained the same: 110×110 pixels. This arbitrary size was used in this study because there is normally no fixed size of animation in real Web pages. Animation appeared when a task

Figure 4.1 **A Task Page with a Dull Color String Animation at Different Times**

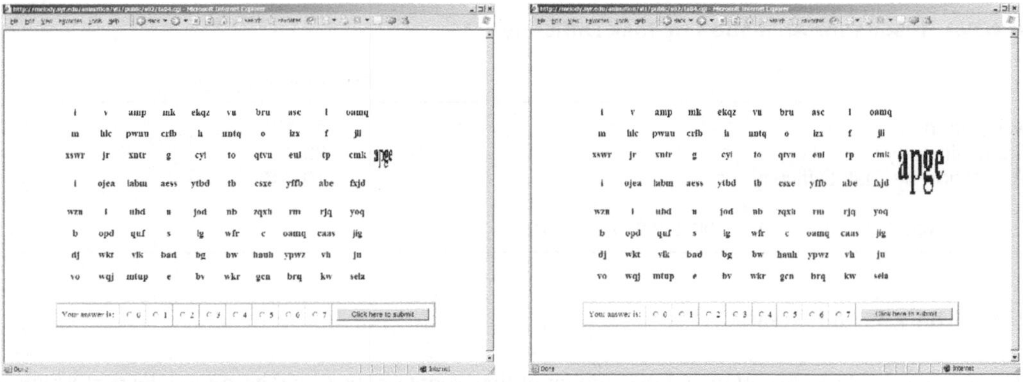

| (a) | (b) |

Microsoft® Internet Explorer screen shots reprinted with permission from Microsoft Corporation.

began and stayed on until the end of the task. This task setting, where subjects need to focus on target strings with animation appearing in the peripheral fields, is very close to—if not exactly—what occurs in the real Web environment.

Both pre-pages and task pages would disappear from the screen within a certain period; a pre-page stayed for ten seconds and a task page for twenty seconds. These pages also allowed subjects to process faster if they wanted, by providing a link to the next page in the sequence.

The experiment was conducted in 1996. The subjects were twenty-four undergraduate students majoring in information management and technology in Syracuse University in the United States. All had experience using the Web and the Netscape Navigator Gold 3.01 browser. Owing to the limited number of computers available, subjects were divided between two sessions. To encourage participation in the study, each subject received a bonus for a course s/he was taking (either substituting an assignment or receiving extra credit). To encourage subjects to do their best during the experiment, prizes of $5, $10, and $30 were offered for best performance in each session.

Subjects were instructed to count as accurately and as quickly as possible how many times a target string appeared in the table. Once finished counting, they clicked the corresponding answer and then the Submit button. They were reminded that "your performance is determined by the correctness of the answers and the time you spend on the task pages; you have only limited time to finish each table." They were also warned that "going back to a previous page will mess up your log and waste your time. Your new answers will not be recorded, and the total amount of time you spend will be increased automatically by a thousand times." At the beginning of the experiment, subjects practiced with four randomly selected tasks (with targets strings different from those used in the competition) to familiarize themselves with the experiment. Following the practice, subjects performed twenty tasks. After finishing the tasks, subjects filled out a questionnaire of demographic data, perceived interference, attitude toward animation used, search strategies, and animation features noticed. When everyone was done, performance scores were calculated, awards were given to the subjects with the best performance scores, and the subjects were dismissed. The entire experimental session lasted less than forty-five minutes. The average length per task was fifteen seconds.

All tasks for all the subjects were located on a computer server and were accessed with the Netscape Navigator browser through a campus local area network. The computer server captured the time spent on and subjects' answers to the tasks.

Table 4.2

ANOVA Results for Animation by Task Difficulty

	Performance $F_{1,23}$
Animation	55.17****
Task Difficulty	00
Animation by Task Difficulty	10.74**

$*p < .05; **p < .01; ***p < .001; ****p < .0001$

Data Analysis and Results

The accuracy of task execution and the amount of time spent on the task determined the performance on the task. Because each task page had a different number of target strings, we used count accuracy to represent errors in a task instead of number of miscounts. The accuracy score should consider that a subject could over-count or under-count the number of targets on a task page. It should also have the property that the higher the score, the higher the accuracy. The following formula, where accuracy is dependent on the difference between reported count and correct count, is thus used to calculate the accuracy score: CA = (1 − absolute(CorrectCount − Reported Count)/CorrectCount).

Time (number of seconds) spent on a task starts when the task page is loaded and ends when the subject submits the answer to the task. The subjects were told that they would be evaluated by a combination of time and accuracy, meaning that they might sacrifice one in order to achieve the other. In order to have a unified performance score for comparison, we used accuracy per unit time as the performance score of a task. That is: p-score = accuracy/time * 1000, where the constant 1000 eliminates the decimal places of the p-scores.

The three factors in Table 4.1 were analyzed at two levels. Level 1 considered a full 2 × 2 factorial repeated measure analysis of animation treatment (baseline and animation) and task difficulty treatment (simple and difficult). This helps us to test the first two hypotheses: whether performance deteriorates with animation, and how animation affects tasks at different difficulty levels. Table 4.2 summarizes the ANOVA results.

Hypothesis 1 is supported by the data. As shown in Table 4.2, animation had a main effect that severely decreased performance from the baseline condition. This was true no matter what the difficulty level of the task. Support for this hypothesis is depicted by Figure 4.2, which displays the group means of the performance scores. Baseline tasks (no animation) had higher performance scores than tasks with animation present.

Hypothesis 2 is supported, as well. The level-1 ANOVA concerned the relationship between animation conditions and task difficulty levels and can be used directly to test this hypothesis. Both Table 4.2 and Figure 4.2 show a significant interaction effect ($p < 0.01$) between animation and task difficulty level. That is, the degree of the animation's effect was related to the task difficulty levels. Specifically, animation affected simple tasks more than it did difficult tasks. Thus, as the level of task difficulty increased, performance was less affected by animation.

The level-2 analysis was within animation conditions. That is, given that all the tasks were done with animation present, we considered a 2 × 2 × 2 full factorial repeated measure analysis on animation content treatment (string and image), task difficulty treatment (simple and difficult), and animation color treatment (dull and bright). This second level analysis helps us to confirm Hypotheses 3 and 4. Table 4.3 exhibits the ANOVA results of this level-2 analysis. The two tasks in each of the ten experimental settings were averaged for the analysis.

Figure 4.2   **Group Means of Animation Effects on Simple and Difficult Tasks**

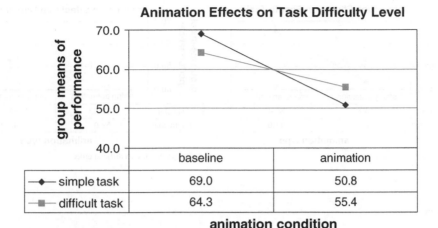

	baseline	animation
◆ simple task	69.0	50.8
■ difficult task	64.3	55.4

animation condition

Table 4.3

ANOVA Results for Task Difficulty by Animation Content by Color

	Performance $F_{1,23}$
Task Difficulty	4.47*
Content	.64
Color	13.41***
Task by Content	10.52**
Task by Color	.48
Content by Color	6.05*
Task by Content by Color	23.68****

*p < .05; **p < .01; ***p < .001; ****p < .0001

The ANOVA results in Table 4.3 indicate that Hypothesis 3 is true under certain conditions. Table 4.3 shows a significant three-way interaction effect (p < 0.0001). This three-way interaction effect can be better depicted by Figures 4.3a and 4.3b. For simple tasks, as in Figure 4.3a, dull color string animation had a more negative effect than dull color image animation; and bright color image animation had a more negative effect than bright color string animation, that is, the effect of string animation that was similar but irrelevant to the tasks was associated with the color of the animation for simple tasks. For difficult tasks, as shown in Figure 4.3b, string animation had a more negative effect than image animation. Color of the animation did not seem to matter.

Table 4.3 shows the significant main effect of color. The group mean for dull color tasks was 57.2 (the average of 43.1, 65.4, 67.5, and 53, which can be obtained from the data tables in Figures 4.3a and 4.3b), compared to the group mean for bright color of 48.9. This shows that dull color animation affected tasks less than bright color animation. The three-way interaction effect shown in Table 4.3 and Figure 4.3, however, indicates that one needs to look at other conditions. For simple tasks as depicted by Figure 4.3a, dull color was worse than bright color when the animation was a string, seemingly refuting Hypothesis 4. For image animation, or for difficult tasks, the hypothesis is supported.

The discussions of the questionnaire responses on perception, attitude and other aspects will be in a later section, together with those in other studies.

Figure 4.3   **Interaction Effect of Color by Relevance by Task Complexity**

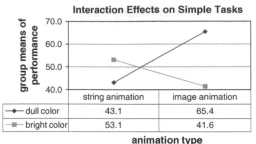

(a) Color by relevance on simple tasks

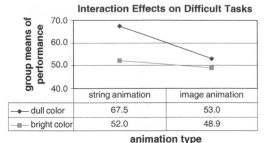

(b) Color by relevance on difficult tasks

Summary

The primary goals of this study were to test the applicability of some visual attention and perception research results to the question of whether animation is a source of visual interference in the Web environment, and to determine under what condition and to what extent animation affects information-seeking performance. In order to achieve these goals, a controlled lab experiment was conducted and many factors were eliminated from this study. For example, in real situations, some animations would have various pop-up or onset timings and could stay or reappear during the period of visual search tasks. Animations could also appear in many potential locations, such as left, right, top, bottom, or in the middle of the screen/document area. There are other factors that were not examined in this particular study, either, such as the size and the speed of animation, or multiple animation images on one page. These animations have become typical in the real Web environment these days.

Overall, as a first empirical test of animation's effect in the Web environment, this study confirmed the appropriateness of applying some visual attention and perception theories and studies to the Web environment. The study supports four hypotheses: (1) animation as a secondary stimulus deteriorates a viewer's information seeking performance; (2) as the difficulty of the task increases, a viewer's performance is less affected by animation; (3) animation that is similar but irrelevant to a task has more negative impact on a viewer's performance than animation that is dissimilar to the task; and (4) animation that is brightly colored has a stronger negative effect on a viewer's performance than dully colored animation.

STUDY 2

Research Questions and Hypotheses

This study was built on the first one to continue exploring potential impacts animations may have in a Web environment. Besides replicating Study 1's findings on pop-up animations' impacts, it was also intended to answer the following research questions:

RQ1: *Does animation's onset timing have an impact on information-seeking performance?*
RQ2: *Does animation's onset location have an impact on information-seeking performance?*

One stream of research in the visual attention and perception literature motivated the first research question. Studies on stimulus onset asynchrony, or SOA (e.g., Mayor and Gonzalez-Marques, 1994; Yantis and Jonides, 1990) report that abrupt visual onsets do not necessarily capture attention in violation of an observer's intention. Interference is dependent on whether a subject's attention is pre-allocated to the focused task before a distracter appears. This means that a subject's attempts can prevent a process from proceeding. In a stimulus onset asynchrony study, Yantis and Jonides (1990, Experiment 2) found that focusing attention in response to a valid and temporally useful cue (-200 ms) virtually eliminated any effect of abrupt onset in the discrimination task. When the attentional cue was not available in advance of the onset of the test (0 ms and 200 ms), attentional resources could not be focused in anticipation of the critical item. Under these circumstances, abrupt onset had a substantial influence on reaction time.

Two cautions exist for applying existing SOA results to this study directly. First, the exposure duration in existing studies for all cues was in milliseconds (e.g., -200 ms, -100 ms, and 200 ms). In this study, subjects were exposed to stimuli that lasted seconds. Whether one can expect similar results remains to be tested. Second, existing studies in stimulus onset asynchrony do not focus on the exposure after a distracter is introduced. They did not consider the change of attention patterns over exposure time.

Nevertheless, we considered pre-allocating a subject's attention to information-seeking tasks by introducing animation in the middle and toward the end of the tasks. Animation onset at the beginning of the task was also considered for comparison purposes.

H1. *Animation that appears at the same time as the task has a larger negative effect than animation that appears in the middle of the task, which in turn has a more negative effect than animation that appears toward the end of the task.*

A related issue to applying SOA in a Web-based computing environment is the duration of animation during a task. Animation could stay on once it is on. The same animation could also appear and disappear repeatedly (on-off-on) during the task. Since the on-off-on animation can be regarded as many abrupt onsets, the performance may be affected by every onset. Thus, we expect that:

H2. *Animation that stays on during the task affects task performance less than animation that appears and disappears repeatedly.*

Animation can be placed at any possible position on a screen. Putting animation (or an online ad) at the top may have a similar effect as animation that appears when the task starts. It could also be regarded as a no-animation condition if viewers scroll down the page to "get rid of" it. It is uncertain, however, whether the animation on the left side of the screen would have an effect similar to the animation on the right side of the screen. Most readers are trained to read from left to right, and most of the time information is presented on the screen from left to right. Our eyes search for the start of a line but don't always look for the end of a line (we often scan or skim over it). If we consider reading one line as a smaller task than reading the entire paragraph, then animation on the left would be similar to animation appearing at the beginning of a task, and animation on the right is similar to animation appearing toward the end of the task. In addition, our eyes take a relatively longer time to "find" the beginning of a line. That is, attention is more demanding when

Table 4.4

Target Item Distribution in Same Paragraph Under Different Conditions

Template 1 (for baseline)	Template 2 (left-right, one position off)	Template 3 (right-left, one position off)
_ _ _ _ _ x _ _ _ x _ _ _ _ _ x _ _ _ _	_ _ _ _ o _ _ _ _ _ o _ _ _ o _ _ _ _ _	_ _ _ _ _ _ f _ f _ _ _ _ _ _ _ f _ _ _
_ _ x _ _ _ _ _ _ _ _ x _ _ _ _ x _ _	_ _ _ o _ _ _ _ _ _ o _ _ _ _ _ _ o _	_ f _ _ _ _ _ _ _ _ _ f _ _ _ f _ _ _
_ _ _ _ x _ _ _ _ _ _ _ _ x _ _ _ _	_ _ _ _ o _ _ _ _ _ _ _ _ o _ _ _	_ _ _ _ _ _ f _ _ _ _ _ _ f _ _ _ _ _
_ _ _ _ _ x _ _ _ _ _ x _ _ _ _ _ _ _ _	_ _ _ _ o _ _ _ _ _ _ _ o _ _ _ _ _	_ _ _ _ _ f _ _ _ f _ _ _ _ _ _ _ _ _

one is looking at the left side. Animation on the left side may thus be exposed longer and have a stronger negative effect than animation on the right side.

H3. *Animation on the left side of the screen has a stronger negative effect on tasks than animation on the right side of the screen.*

Experiment Design and Conduct

Similar to the considerations in Study 1, in order to make the information-seeking tasks closer to reality and eliminate the effect of subjects' prior knowledge of information content on the potential outcome, nonsense words (strings of letters) were used to form a nonsense paragraph. A target word could appear many times in the paragraph. A subject's task was to click all appearances of only the target word. A paragraph template determined the number of total display items, number of targets, and the exact location of each target. In order to make it possible to compare the change in performance over time under different conditions, and to minimize the potential learning effect of target locations, templates with slightly different locations for targets were used in different conditions. For example, given the locations of targets in the baseline, Condition 1 could be that the target is one position to the left from that in baseline position, then one position to the right from the next target position in the baseline, then repeat the left-right order until the end of the paragraph; and Condition 2 could be one position with right then left order. Three different templates were used. Table 4.4 depicts this variation. Each task corresponded to one of the three templates. Order or learning effect was reduced, if not eliminated, by randomly ordering all the nine tasks for each subject.

The experiment was designed as a within-subject factorial 2 × 4 design. The first independent variable was the location or side of the animation on the screen, left or right. The second independent variable was the time at which animation appears. Time 1 means that the animation appeared at the beginning of the task, or when the Web page was loaded. Time 2 was when the animation appeared roughly after the first word in the second half of the paragraph was clicked, Time 3 was the last quarter of the paragraph, and Time 4 was the on-off-on starting at the beginning of the task. A no-animation condition was used as a baseline. Table 4.5 lays out the structure of the design. Each subject would do a total of nine tasks (2 × 4 plus baseline).

Animations in this study had the following characteristics: bright color, fixed size of 200 × 200 pixels, moderate speed, fixed distance from the paragraph, and neutral images that had little

Table 4.5

Structure of Study 2

Task ID	Time 1	Time 2	Time 3	On-Off-On	Baseline
Left	1	2	3	4	0
Right	5	6	7	8	

Figure 4.4   **A Pre-Page and a Task Page for Study 2**

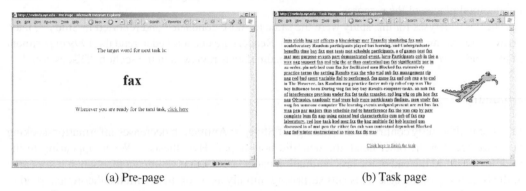

(a) Pre-page   (b) Task page

Microsoft® Internet Explorer screen shots reprinted with permission from Microsoft Corporation.

to do with the content of the tasks. Example animations used were animals, objects such as airplanes and balls, and human faces.

Participants saw three Web pages associated with each of the nine tasks: pre-page, task page, and post-page. A pre-page displayed the target that a subject was to look for in the task page. A post-page gave an indication of task completion and a link leading to the next task. A task page, with or without animation depending on the treatment, had a nonsense paragraph with the target appearing many times in positions determined by a template. Each word (target or non-target) in the paragraph was hyperlinked, and thus clickable, and did not change color after being clicked. The Web page was refreshed after each click, leaving no indication of which word was just clicked. Subjects were thus encouraged to develop a strategy that would help memorize their current position in a task page. Figure 4.4 shows one pre-page and one task page.

Cash prizes were offered to encourage performance during the experiment: one first prize ($30 or $40) for the best performer within a session, and two or four second prizes ($15 each) for the next two or four best performers (the prize amount and numbers were dependent on experiment session sizes). The subjects were twenty-five graduate students from Syracuse University during 1999. They were told to complete each task page as accurately and quickly as possible. They were given the performance and accuracy formula used for data analysis. Subjects practiced with two tasks (not used in the competition) to familiarize themselves with the exercise before the competition started. Each subject then completed a total of nine tasks, followed by a questionnaire that collected data on his or her demographic background, interference perception, and attitude toward animation. When everyone completed the questionnaire, the performance scores were calculated, the best performers identified, and the awards given. A computer server captured the time (the exact click on each word in the task page, and the moment a subject entered a task page and the moment she or he finished) and accuracy data.

Data Analysis and Results

Different tasks could have a different number of targets. Subjects were encouraged to click all the targets, and were told that the number of clicked targets was weighted more heavily (as the square value) than the time spent on the task. They were also told that the number of wrong clicks would affect the accuracy of a task. The following formula, where click accuracy is dependent on the number of correctly clicked targets, the number of wrong clicks, and the total number of targets, was used to calculate the click accuracy of a task: $CA = NumberOfClickedTargets^2 / (NumberOfTargets + NumberOfWrongClicks)$. Performance scores were calculated by the formula similar to that in Study 1: p-score $= 10000 * CA / TimeOnTaskpage$ (the constant 10000 eliminates the decimal places of the p-scores).

The data analyses for this study were the same as those conducted and reported in Study 3, later. To avoid repeating, we omit them in this section. Readers are encouraged to read the 1999 experiment in the Study 3 results. The analysis of questionnaire data is reviewed in the section "Discussions."

Summary

In general, this study confirmed the findings of Study 1: Animation decreases information-seeking performance. On the other hand, the data did not support Hypothesis 1. When appearing in the middle or toward the end of the task, animation had a larger negative impact than when it appeared at the beginning of the task. This was surprising initially as it conflicts with the theoretical prediction. A further analysis of some questionnaire comments revealed that subjects were not expecting to see animation once they started a task without animation at the beginning. Thus animation popping up in the middle of the task turned out to be a surprise. This may help explain the Time 3 condition, where performance was also worse than the Time 1 and the baseline conditions.

Hypothesis 2 about the stability of animation was confirmed for the most part. Repeated onset of animation caused subjects' performance to decrease severely. An interesting fact, though, is that the on-off-on animation caused about the same damage to subjects' performance as the animation that appeared halfway through and stayed until the end of the task. Although there was no hypothesis to compare these two treatments, one would think intuitively that the on-off-on condition would have a much worse effect than the halfway condition. Hypothesis 3 was supported in that animation on the left side had a bigger negative impact than animation on the right side of the screen.

Overall, the fact that the empirical results did not quite support hypotheses 1 and 2 calls for questions regarding the application of some particular visual attention theories such as stimulus onset asynchrony or SOA (Mayor and Gonzalez-Marques, 1994; Yantis and Jonides, 1990) to the Web environment. These theories do not support or cannot explain the onset timing effects obtained in the experiment. Alternative theories are needed. We will discuss theoretical speculations in the later section, in light of more empirical evidence.

STUDY 3

Research Questions and Hypotheses

Results from the two previous studies show that animation as non-primary information significantly reduces information-seeking performance in a Web-based environment—this was also reported by Zhang (1999, 2000, 2001). Animation on the left side of a screen had a higher negative impact on task performance than animation on the right side; animation also had a different impact on task performance, depending on its onset timing.

In general, humans are good at adapting to new environments and can easily "get used to" certain conditions. One would imagine that as the viewers' familiarity with online ads and Web-based animations increases, their familiarity with moving objects on the screen would increase as well, so that animations would eventually have less impact on their information-seeking performance (Zhang and Massad, 2003). Few theoretical explanations and little empirical evidence exist to directly support this speculation.

A multi-year study was conducted to test the speculation. In order to evaluate specific rather than general animation effects, we decided to use Study 2 as the base for Study 3. Specifically, Study 3 is an investigation of whether animation's location and timing impacts have changed over the years, as the Web has become a commodity and people are more used to seeing animated online advertisements. The two research questions are:

RQ1: *As users become more familiar with Web-based animations, does their impact change over time?*

RQ2: *If so, what are the impact patterns in terms of onset timing and location?*

This study collected data from 1999 to 2003, using the same experiment design as the one in Study 2, to test the following hypotheses.

H1. *Animation's timing effects should decrease over the years.*
H2. *Animation's location effect should decrease over the years.*

Experiment Conduct

The same experiment design in Study 2 was conducted four times during the 1999–2003 period. All studies were conducted in campus computer labs with a campus-wide LAN. Within the same experiment, the same setup was used for all participants. A Sun Sparc 5 was used as the server for the first two experiments (1999 and 2001); a Dell computer with a Linux operating system as a server for the last two experiments. Most sessions lasted less than fifty minutes. Netscape Communicator was used as the browser for the 1999 study; Internet Explorer was used for the other three studies. The subjects were students enrolled in Syracuse University. Table 4.6 shows the demographic data of the subjects who participated in these studies. Among the 102 subjects, only two reported red and green color blindness. Their results, however, did not indicate any effects caused by the color blindness.

Data Analysis and Results

To see if subjects in recent years have more experience with the Web than their counterparts in previous years, we compared the number of hours subjects spend on the Web over the years. In addition, we believed that this number can be used as an indication of a subject's exposure opportunities to Web-based advertisements. Thus number of hours on the Web can also be used as a surrogate for subjects' familiarity with online ads. One-way ANOVA analysis of the number of hours per week on the Web showed a non-significant result, indicating that there is no significant difference among the four groups on this variable. A further t-test between 1999 and 2003 groups shows a significant

Table 4.6

Demographic Data of Participants in the Four Studies

Classification

Year	N	Age Mean (std)	Male	Doctoral	Master	Undergraduate	Color-Blind	Hours per Week on Web
1999	25	30.1 (6.8)	32%	24%	76%	0%	0	20.6 (8.5)
2001	37	23.8 (5.2)	54%	0%	14%	62%	2 (R & G)	24.4 (13.5)
2002	27	25.7 (6.5)	59%	0%	56%	44%	0	26.5 (12.0)
2003	32	25.9 (4.3)	50%	25%	63%	13%	0	28.3 (12.4)

Total 121 subjects. Native languages: English (55%), Chinese (16%), Korean (7%), Spanish (4%), other (18%)

Table 4.7

Paired t-test Comparing Baseline and Animation Conditions

Year	df	(t0 t1)	(t0 t2)	(t0 t3)	(t0 t4)	(t0 t5)	(t0 t6)	(t0 t7)	(t0 t8)
1999	24	3.269	5.191	3.969	4.578	1.952	3.918	3.329	4.380
		0.003	*0.000*	*0.001*	*0.000*	0.063	*0.001*	*0.003*	*0.000*
2001	36	5.000	6.417	6.030	7.369	0.857	6.802	3.930	4.925
		0.000	*0.000*	*0.000*	*0.000*	0.397	*0.000*	*0.000*	*0.000*
2002	27	3.906	6.894	4.989	3.927	−0.878	4.933	3.168	2.382
		0.001	*0.000*	*0.000*	*0.001*	0.388	*0.000*	*0.004*	*0.025*
2003	31	3.176	3.779	4.092	3.548	1.027	4.633	2.185	4.165
		0.003	*0.001*	*0.000*	*0.001*	0.312	*0.000*	*0.037*	*0.000*

difference. The subjects in the 2003 group spent a significantly higher number of hours on the Web than did their counterparts five years before.

The performance formula for the visual search tasks is the same as that in Study 2. A paired t-test was conducted to compare the baseline condition with each of the eight animation conditions. This can illustrate whether a particular animation condition affected information-seeking performance. Table 4.7 shows the paired t-test results for two-tail significance at $\alpha = .05$ level (the italic ones are significant). The table shows a consistent pattern over the years, in that all animation conditions affected information-seeking performance except one, in which animation appeared on the right side at the beginning of the task.

A 2×4 full factorial ANOVA for within-subjects repeated measures of side (left and right) and time (beginning, halfway, last quarter, and on-off-on) was conducted for each of the four studies, resulting in Table 4.8. Both side and time consistently had significant main effects. The interaction effects of side and time have not been consistent over the years, with two of the years marginally significant.

Detailed pairwise comparisons on side are shown in Table 4.9, indicating that the left side affected performance more negatively than the right side; this has been consistent over the years. Pairwise comparisons of time treatment are in Table 4.10. There are some slight changes over the years. (1) Performance at Time 1 has consistently outperformed all other timing conditions except Time 3 in 2003 (indicated by shading around 0.272). (2) Performance at Time 3 was

Table 4.8

Tests of Within-Subjects Effects on Performance

Year	Effect	F	df	Sig.	Observed Power
1999	Side	13.463	1	*0.001*	0.940
	Time	17.727	3	*0.000*	1.000
	Side × Time	0.861	3	0.476	0.206
2001	Side	17.64	1	*0.000*	0.983
	Time	15.02	3	*0.000*	1.000
	Side × Time	3.347	3	*0.030*	0.709
2002	Side	18.845	1	*0.000*	0.987
	Time	9.248	3	*0.000*	0.990
	Side × Time	1.656	3	0.203	0.378
2003	Side	7.232	1	*0.011*	0.741
	Time	3.784	3	*0.021*	0.757
	Side × Time	3.219	3	*0.037*	0.680

Table 4.9

Pairwise Comparison of Performance for SIDE Effects

Year	(I) SIDE	(J) SIDE	Mean Diff (I–J)	Std. Error	Sig.
1999	Left	Right	−143.720	39.169	*0.001*
2001	Left	Right	−134.989	32.140	*0.000*
2002	Left	Right	−170.356	39.242	*0.000*
2003	Left	Right	−118.494	44.063	*0.011*

significantly better than Time 4 during the early years (1999 and 2001) but not so during the latter years (2002 and 2003), as indicated by the shading over 0.443 and 0.250. Overall, we can conclude that animation that appeared during the middle of a task had a more negative effect than animation at the beginning or toward the end of the task. Furthermore, animation that appeared toward the end of the task had a more negative effect than animation that appeared at the beginning; and animation that appeared on and off and on again had a similar effect to the animation that appeared during the middle of the task.

The group means of performance under different conditions over the years are plotted in Figure 4.5. It shows some consistent patterns over the years, including the main effect on side (right is better than left), on timing (Time 1 is best, followed by Time 3 most of the time, and Time 2 and Time 4 are similar most of the time), and on animation treatment (that is, performance scores in baseline are better than those in animation conditions).

Summary

Both hypotheses were rejected. The results of Study 3 indicated that over the years, animation's effects have changed very little. Animation affects task performance in all but one condition: when animation appears at the beginning of the task on the right side of the screen.

One way of explaining the consistent side effect is that our habit of reading from left to right requires us to attend to the left side more than to the right side, making the left side more demanding of attention resources. An animation on the left side is closer to the beginning of the line. This

Table 4.10

Pairwise Comparison of Performance for TIME Effects

1999	(I) TIME	(J) TIME	Mean Diff (I–J)	Std. Error	Sig.
	1	2	205.533	33.778	*0.000*
		3	90.600	40.241	*0.034*
		4	225.453	39.504	*0.000*
	2	3	−114.933	29.643	*0.000*
		4	19.920	41.516	0.636
	3	4	134.853	49.105	*0.011*
2001	**(I) TIME**	**(J) TIME**	**Mean Diff (I–J)**	**Std. Error**	**Sig.**
	1	2	228.946	37.541	*0.000*
		3	96.144	32.018	*0.005*
		4	241.802	41.882	*0.000*
	2	3	−132.802	34.894	*0.001*
		4	12.856	39.151	0.745
	3	4	145.658	38.278	*0.001*
2002	**(I) TIME**	**(J) TIME**	**Mean Diff (I–J)**	**Std. Error**	**Sig.**
	1	2	249.025	48.355	*0.000*
		3	110.642	40.294	*0.011*
		4	162.160	55.191	*0.007*
	2	3	−138.383	46.131	*0.006*
		4	−86.864	64.675	0.191
	3	4	51.519	66.116	0.443
2003	**(I) TIME**	**(J) TIME**	**Mean Diff (I–J)**	**Std. Error**	**Sig.**
	1	2	155.740	53.617	*0.007*
		3	62.219	55.621	*0.272*
		4	126.177	49.349	*0.016*
	2	3	−93.521	43.592	*0.040*
		4	−29.563	51.413	0.569
	3	4	63.958	54.581	0.250

proximity increases the interference effect, as evidenced by many visual search studies. This also explains the only animation condition (right side and at the beginning of a task) that did not have a significant impact on search tasks. The animation was on the right side, far away from the visually demanding beginning of each line, and thus was less distracting.

The consistent onset timing effects over the years challenge the original visual attention studies on SOA that we used to predict the onset timing effect. Apparently it does not work in the Web environment. We have cautioned its application due to the dramatic differences between the Web environment and the traditional visual attention experiment environment, and SOA's lack of consideration of after-exposure behavior.

We will explore alternative theoretical explanations for the empirical evidence on timing after we present the analysis of the three studies' subjective perception data.

DISCUSSIONS

Objective Measures vs. Subjective Perceptions

Due to the lack of empirical evidence regarding animation's effect in the Web environment before this stream of studies, we decided from the beginning to collect subjective responses after subjects

Figure 4.5   **Group Means on Performance Under Different Conditions Over the Years**

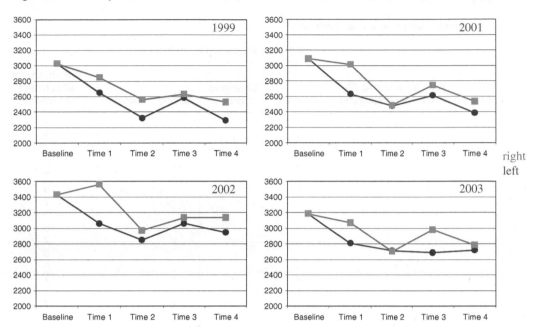

right
left

finished all information-seeking tasks to help gain more insight into the phenomenon. One strik-ing discovery from these studies was the discrepancy between objective performance measures and the subjective perceptions reported by the subjects. In this section, we present the questionnaire data either in a descriptive manner (due to small sample sizes) or in-depth analysis, and discuss the implications of such discrepancies.

In Study 1, subjects were asked to answer questions (either on a seven-point Likert scale or as open-ended comments) on their perceptions of animation's effect and their preferences regarding animation on Web pages. Table 4.11 summarizes the responses on (1) perceived effects of anima-tion and animation's features (columns 2–6) and (2) "How strongly would you agree that you'd rather have no animation while performing this type of task?" (the last column).

When they were asked to describe the most distracting animation, six out of twenty-four sub-jects explicitly mentioned that animation was "not at all" or "not very" distracting. For other subjects, colored animation was explicitly mentioned fourteen times, animation that changed size nine times, word or string animation ten times, and image animation twice. A subject would indicate several animation features, mentioning "brightly colored letters that change size," which includes color, string, and changing size. Two subjects (s08 and s28) did not make any explicit claim about the effects of features but did state that animation distracted them from performing the tasks. It could be that some subjects only mentioned the dominant annoying feature, even though other features were also distracting.

The perceived color effect, exhibited in Table 4.11, is consistent with the performance data. String animation that is similar to tasks is another confirmed distracting feature, with more peo-ple reporting it than image animation. It is, however, difficult to pin down what the changing-size feature actually implies. Among all the animations used in the study, only string animations change size (the way string animation moves makes it look as if it changes its size; see Figure 4.1). Some

Table 4.11

Perceived Animation Effects and Attitude

| Subject ID | Animation Not At All or Not Very Distracting | Tasks Were Distracted by Animation | | | | Preference for Absence of Animation |
		Colored	Changing Size	String	Image	
s01	x					1
s02		x	x			7
s03	x					4
s04		x		x		5
s05		x		x		7
s06		x	x		x	6
s07		x				7
s08						7
s09				x		6
s10		x	x	x		7
s14	x					5
s15	x					6
s17		x	x	x		7
s18		x				7
s19		x	x	x		7
s25				x		6
s26			x			7
s27	x					4
s28						7
s31		x		x		7
s32		x		x		7
s35	x	x				5
s43		x	x	x		5
s44		x			x	5
Total #	6	14	7	10	2	
%	25%	50%	29%	42%	8%	

subjects may use this phrase to describe string animation (as indicated by Table 4.11, some subjects reported either size or string changes, but not both) or the animation that changes its size. This needs to be studied in future research.

The attitude toward animation accompanying information-seeking tasks is shown in column 7 of Table 4.11. When asked "How strongly would you agree that you'd rather have no animation while performing this type of task?" 50 percent of subjects answered "completely agree" (scale 7), 38 percent "strongly or somewhat agree" (scales 6 and 5), 8 percent "neutral" (scale 4), and one subject (4 percent) answered "completely disagree" (scale 1 by s01). Subject s01 further explained that "if a person is looking at a page with a specific goal in mind, such as the task I was given, then any distractions can be easily ignored."

To test whether perceived effects were consistent with the performance data, the data of the six subjects who said animation was not at all or not very distracting were analyzed descriptively. Table 4.12 shows the results. Except for s01 and s27, whose performance was not affected very much by animation, all four other subjects' performance data were substantially decreased (23 percent to 41 percent). Two observations can be drawn from this analysis. First, it seems that perceived effects may not necessarily be the true effects, as indicated by the four subjects whose

Table 4.12

Change in Performance of Those Who Perceived None or Little Animation Effects

	Baseline	Animation	Decrease %
s01	57.0	55.3	−3%
s03	66.3	50.8	−23%
s14	61.6	43.6	−29%
s15	66.7	39.5	−41%
s27	73.4	71.6	−2%
s35	61.6	40.0	−35%
Average	**64.4**	**50.1**	**−22%**

performance dropped when animation was introduced. Second, it could be that animation has little or no effect on some people, such as s01 and s27. This raised a question concerning the conditions under which animation does not interfere with information-seeking tasks.

In Study 3, we continued to gather perception and attitude data using a questionnaire. The following five questions were analyzed using ANOVA on group means.

1. How did you like the animations on the Web pages?
2. Would you rather have no animation while performing this type of task?
3. In general, when you perceived animation, how often were you drawn to look at the animation?
4. In general, did those animations on the task pages distract you from performing the tasks?
5. Comparing the animations that appeared at the beginning of the tasks but (1) stayed on the screen all the time, and (2) appeared intermittently on the screen, which distracted you more? Explain briefly.

None of them showed significance. To examine the data further, a t-test was conducted between each pair of the years for each of the five variables. Only one variable was found to differ significantly for one pair of years: Question 3 "Often Drawn to Animation" for years 1999 and 2003. Subjects in 1999 perceived that they were more often drawn to look at the animation during tasks; however, performance results from 2003 indicated that animation's impact on tasks changed little. Thus, even though subjects thought they could better prevent themselves from looking at animation, their task performance was still affected.

Table 4.13 summarizes the answers to five other relevant questions in the form of the percentage of subjects who responded to a question with a certain answer. Using percentages can facilitate comparisons over all experiments because each experiment had a different number of subjects.

Several interesting observations can be drawn from Table 4.13. First, on-off-on animation was consistently perceived by a majority of subjects to be more distracting than animation that stayed on, which was consistent with performance results. Second, animation that popped up in the middle was consistently perceived to be more distracting than animation that appeared at the beginning or during the third quarter, which also was in agreement with the performance data. Third, more subjects perceived that right-side animation was more distracting than left-side animation, which was in disagreement with the performance data. This may actually provide some strategic

Table 4.13

Answers to Perception Questions in Study 3

Question	Answer	1999	2001	2002	2003	Average
Appearing: Which	On	8%	11%	11%	9%	10%
Is More Distracting	On-off-on	80%	76%	81%	75%	78%
	Equal	4%	0%	0%	6%	2%
	Not sure	8%	14%	7%	9%	10%
Timing: Which	Beginning	12%	11%	4%	16%	11%
Is Most Distracting	Middle	44%	43%	52%	50%	47%
	Third quarter	16%	30%	22%	16%	21%
	Beginning and middle	0%	0%	4%	9%	3%
	Middle and third quarter	4%	8%	4%	0%	4%
	Equal	4%	3%	0%	3%	2%
	Not sure	20%	5%	15%	6%	12%
Side: Which	Left	12%	41%	41%	22%	29%
Is More Distracting	Right	60%	41%	41%	38%	45%
	Equal	24%	19%	11%	25%	20%
	Not sure	4%	0%	7%	16%	7%
Animation Feature:	Move	76%	76%	81%	78%	78%
Which Is Most	Color	60%	57%	70%	69%	64%
Distracting	Size	28%	30%	52%	25%	34%
	Content	20%	24%	22%	19%	21%
Able to Ignore	Yes	68%	86%	67%	78%	75%
	No	32%	14%	33%	22%	25%

suggestions to marketers: putting animation on the left side has the advantage of influencing viewers more (a performance drop means animation received attention) but annoying them less (since subjects perceive them to be less distracting). Fourth, subjects could list multiple features they felt most distracting. Movement dominated all others as the most distracting feature of animation, followed by color, size, and content. Lastly, the majority of subjects admitted that they were not able to ignore animation during tasks.

Comments on Appropriateness of Theories

Overall, the central capacity theory and the limited capacity model seem to work well to predict and explain animation's effect. The theoretical explanations on the side or location effect hold well with the data. There is, however, a need to search for alternative theoretical explanations for the animation onset timing effect.

One explanation of Time 1's smaller impact and the indifference between Time 2 and on-off-on (Time 4) may be the habituation that results from repeated exposure to stimuli (Sokolov et al., 2002). Animation at Time 1 becomes less novel and does not evoke an orienting response once it appears for a while. Thus, a user "gets used to it," in that the impact of such animation decreases over the rest of the task period. It is also possible that since subjects completed a practice session and knew certain animations may come up during tasks, they would anticipate some animation when a task page was loaded. Then they could quickly "selectively habituate" (Sokolov et al., 2002) the animation during the rest of the task. When animation onsets occur during the middle or toward the end of a task, or when on-off-on animation is used, the unexpectedness elicits orienting responses that automatically capture processing resources (Lang, 2000), thus affecting task performance. This explanation seems to be consistent with questionnaire comments revealing that subjects did not expect animation to appear once they started a task. Thus, animation popping up in the middle of the task turned out to be a surprise. Also, some subjects said they would not mind Time 1 animation as they "got used to it" after a while.

Habituation may also explain the indifference between Time 2 (in the middle) and Time 4 (on-off-on) animation conditions. They may have the same or similar initial effects on orienting responses during the first onset, but habituation occurs for the on-off-on condition, diminishing the effects for the rest of the task.

Because the habituation effect seems relatively short and stays within a task, it does not explain why subjects experience interference in each animated condition or across tasks, even when they experienced animations in previous tasks or during the practice sessions.

There have been some changes in animation's timing effect over the years. The noticeable changes were between Times 1 and 3, and between Times 3 and 4. Time 1 had the least negative impact; Time 4 had the most negative impact. Even though Times 1 and 4 are still significantly different, these changes suggests a partial convergence of onset timing effects, that is, the differences between the weakest timing effect and strongest timing effect are getting smaller over the years. This can be depicted roughly by Figure 4.5, although we do not have enough data to empirically test this. Verifying this convergence needs more studies over a longer period of time. Nevertheless, if this convergence is proven to be true, the habituation theory does not seem to explain this change. Thus, it may indicate the limitations of the habituation theory to explain all timing effects.

Comments on Conducting Experiments

Conducting experiments can be both fun and frustrating. Theory is a source of ideas. Thus theory plays an important role both in guiding development of hypotheses and in explaining research results. Finding the appropriate theory can be challenging, as is demonstrated by the studies in this paper.

Conducting the experiment can also be challenging and costly. There are many details that need to be taken care of to ensure successful implementation. For example, the very first experiment for Study 3 was actually conducted in 1997. However, due to a seemingly small error in a seemingly small part of the design, the entire data set had to be thrown away! All animations used in the study were supposed to have the same size so that they could be attached to paragraphs that had a fixed width. Even though we did pilot tests, we did not find out that one of the animations in a Time 4 condition was ten pixels wider than the rest of the animations. Every time this animation popped up during the task, the paragraph would resize to accommodate the ten-pixel-wide space on the screen, making the subjects lose their positions in the paragraph. This affected the performance data completely for this condition. Since the study had a within-subject design counting on all treatments, the lack of performance data for this condition made the entire data set useless.

Limitations and Possible Future Studies

This research suffers all the limitations a lab-controlled experiment would have. In particular, the tasks were artificially designed, many factors were controlled, and the settings were not natural.

Cook and Campbell (1979) consider three factors concerning the external validity of a study: persons or samples, settings, and times. In this study, the intended population was people who may use the Web. These include almost the entire population, with various racial, social, geographical, age, sex, education, and personality groups. The subjects in this study were students in a U.S. university. This non-random sample is not representative of the population. On the other hand, the study was designed to eliminate individual differences by using within-subject measures. From this perspective, the particular sample should not affect the findings. Another benefit of using within-subject measures is the increase in statistical power because of the reduced variability due to individual differences.

The setting of the study was a controlled campus computer lab with performance incentives. This is not a typical setting for Web users. However, viewers often need to find correct information from a Web page, either in a computer lab or at a home computer, within a reasonable—if not the shortest possible—time period. The performance incentives were intended to create pressure similar to that which a Web user might have.

In terms of the external validity factor of time, our findings hold consistent over a period of five years. During the Web's fast development, animation may be used differently on Web pages over time. The effects of animation under the studied conditions, however, should not change much, as our results imply. This can be due to a rather slow process of human evolution. Nevertheless, the findings could be made more robust by further studies.

This research provides a base for future investigations. In the studies described here, the nature of the information-seeking task requires relatively low levels of information processing from respondents. Future studies may investigate how (if at all) animation affects respondents' performance in reading and comprehending a meaningful passage, a task that requires higher levels of information processing. For example, Hong and colleagues (Hong, 2004) studied online shopping tasks that are closer to real tasks in the Web environment. The difference in the nature of the tasks may impose quite different findings. For example, when studying consumers' memory for television advertising, Pieters and Bijmolt (1997) explored the duration and serial position of a commercial and of the number of commercials. They found that placing a commercial first is better than placing it last in achieving the goal of maximizing brand recall. Here the tasks involve memory recall rather than just discrimination at the perception level.

Furthermore, the continual development of sophisticated software has allowed for more aggressive and intrusive advertisements on the Web. Animated online banners used to be restricted to a specific location on a Web page. Current advertisers, however, are increasingly using animations that do not stay in a specific location on a Web page, but instead move from one side to another, demanding more attention from users. Future studies should investigate whether such animations have a greater effect on users' performance on different tasks.

This research considers animation a non-primary information stimulus. Empirical studies on animations that are primary information sources are also limited and deserve much research attention.

Practical Significance and Implications

This stream of research presents theoretical explanations and empirical evidence of animation effects under different conditions and over time. There are few studies of this type. The implications of this research for Web user interface design and online advertising are significant. From either the information-seeking user's perspective or that of companies using the Web to realize both operational and strategic benefits, content providers must understand the potential effects of animation on users.

This study suggests some strategies (Zhang, 1999, 2000, 2001) for both Web site content providers and online advertisers, showing a dichotomy between their very different goals. Content providers want to make money from advertising, but also need to care about the potential side effects of ads on their viewers' information-seeking performance. Given a choice, content providers could prefer ads with a minimum of distracting effects. Results from this research suggest that negative effects should be reduced by (1) raising the perceptual load, that is, making information-seeking tasks more challenging by involving viewers in the content of a Web page; (2) avoiding brightly colored animation; (3) avoiding animation that is semantically similar to the primary tasks; (4) placing ads on the Web page earlier and on the right side; and (5) avoiding on-off-on type of animations.

On the other hand, online advertising is very attractive to marketers, as proven by continued practice since the inception of the Web. Online advertisers or marketers want to continue grabbing viewers' attention, knowing that the ads will be processed, to some extent, involuntarily. Some advice for online advertisers has been provided. For example, some suggest that advertisers should be "negotiating for top of the page for online ads" (Hein, 1997), while others advise that ads should be placed at a place on the page that viewers will reach after they have gained a certain amount of the primary information (Scanlon, 1998). Our findings suggest that marketers may want to take strategies opposite to those used by content providers, that is, they should (1) target pages where audiences tend to have simple tasks; (2) use bright colors when possible; (3) design animation that is semantically similar to the tasks; (4) put ads on the left side of the screen; and (5) use pop-up animations or online ads when the user has already started reading or scanning the Web page. Advertisers may not have to have on-off-on animations on the screen, since they are as "effective" as those that pop up during the tasks. A caution accompanying these suggestions is that they are based on animation's effect on task performance, not on recall of animation content or semantics. Further studies are needed to understand if on-off-on animations enhance recall better than stay-on animations.

CONCLUSIONS

Despite some studies showing that experienced Web users are less likely than novice users to be distracted by competing stimuli on the Web (Bruner and Kumar, 2000; Dahlen, 2001; Diaper and Waelend, 2000), our research indicates that animation's interference effects have not changed much over the years and are still affecting experienced users such as the participants in our research. For the most part, subjects were not able to block the animations, even though they knew animations had little to do with their tasks, and even though some of them thought they were able to ignore the animations. This means that, to some extent, animation is processed involuntarily, a finding supported by major visual attention studies. For example, many researchers (Allport, 1989; Duncan, 1984; Miller, 1991; Yantis and Jonides, 1990) have argued that even though the processing of unattended stimuli can be attenuated with certain manipulations, it cannot be totally ruled out. The meaning of the unattended stimulus must be processed to some extent. Because our attention has a limited capacity, our available resources for attending to pertinent information are reduced, and thus information-processing performance, including speed and accuracy, deteriorates (Driver and Baylis, 1989; Miller, 1991; Treisman, 1991). Our study also supports Lang's limited capacity model (Lang, 2000; Lang et al., 2002), that is, the onset of animation when an individual is performing a task elicits an automatic, reflexive, and attentional response (i.e., orienting response) that affects the individual's task performance. Furthermore, due to this automatic and reflexive nature of responses, it is unlikely that animations as non-primary information have no impact on task performance.

With the rapid evolution of the Internet and the World Wide Web, and as more people use the Web for gathering information, conducting business, and for entertainment, studies on the effect of certain Web features such as animation become timely and important. For a relatively new medium such as the Web, empirical studies are as important as theoretical predictions and implications. Research that tests the applicability of existing theories to new environments has theoretical as well as practical value. In this research, we have tested the applicability of some visual-attention and perception research results to the Web environment by confirming some and ruling out others. The general implication is that human evolution changes our characteristics much more slowly than the environment changes. Certain research results on human characteristics can be applied during a relatively long period. This particular study suggests that designers of any type of user interface should consider possible visual interference sources that may affect an individual's information-seeking performance.

REFERENCES

Allport, A.D. Visual attention. In M.I. Posner (ed.), *Foundations of Cognitive Science.* Cambridge, MA: MIT Press, 1989, pp. 631–682.

Baecker, R., and Small, I. Animation at the interface. In B. Laurel (ed.), *The Art of Human-Computer Interface Design.* Addison-Wesley Publishing Company, 1990, pp. 251–267.

Bruner, G.C., II, and Kumar, A. Web commercials and advertising hierarchy-of-effects. *Journal of Advertising Research*, 40, 1/2 (2000), 35–42.

Campbell, B.A.; Wood, G.; and McBride, T. Origins of orienting and defensive responses: An evolutionary perspective. In P.J. Lang, R.F. Simons, and M. Balaban (ed.), *Attention and Orienting: Sensory and Motivational Processes.* Hillsdale, NJ: Lawrence Erlbaum Associates, 1997, pp. 41–68.

Cook, T.D., and Campbell, D.T. *Quasi-Experimentation: Design and Analysis Issues for Field Settings.* Boston: Houghton Mifflin Company, 1979.

Dahlen, M. Banner advertisements through a new lens. *Journal of Advertising Research*, 41, 4 (2001), 23–30.

Diaper, D., and Waelend, P. World wide web working whilst ignoring graphics: good news for web page designers. *Interacting with Computers*, 13, 2 (2000), 163–181.

Driver, J., and Baylis, G.C. Movement and visual attention: the spotlight metaphor breaks down. *Journal of Experimental Psychology: Human Perception and Performance*, 15, 3 (1989), 448–456.

Duncan, J. Selective attention and the organization of visual information. *Journal of Experimental Psychology: General*, 113, 4 (1984), 501–517.

Duncan, J., and Humphreys, G.W. Visual search and stimulus similarity. *Psychological Review*, 96, 3 (1989), 433–458.

Eysenck, M., and Keane, M. *Cognitive Psychology: A Student's Handbook.* Hove, UK: Psychology Press, 1995.

Gonzalez, C., and Kasper, G.M. Animation in user interfaces designed for decision support systems: the effects of image abstraction, transition, and interactivity on decision quality. *Decision Sciences*, 28, 4 (1997), 793–823.

Hein, K. Improve your online marketing. *Incentive*, New York, November 1997.

Hoffman, H.S. Attention factors in the elicitation and modification of the startle reaction. In P.J. Lang, R.F. Simons, and M. Balaban (eds.), *Attention and Orienting: Sensory and Motivational Processes.* Hillsdale, NJ: Lawrence Erlbaum Associates, 1997, pp. 185–204.

Hong, W. Does animation attract online users' attention? The effects of Flash on information search performance and perceptions. *Information Systems Research*, 15, 1 (2004), 60–86.

Lang, A. The limited capacity model of mediated message processing. *Journal of Communication*, 50, 1 (2000), 46–70.

Lang, A.; Borse, J.; Wise, K.; and David, P. Captured by the world wide web—orienting to structural and content features of computer-presented information. *Communication Research*, 29, 3 (2002), 215–245.

Lavie, N. Perceptual load as a necessary condition for selective attention. *Journal of Experimental Psychology: Human Perception and Performance*, 21, 3 (1995), 451–468.

Lavie, N., and Tsal, Y. Perceptual load as a major determinant of the locus of selection in visual attention. *Perception & Psychophysics*, 56 (1994), 183–197.

Marchionini, G. *Information Seeking in Electronic Environments.* Cambridge: Cambridge University Press, 1995.

Mayor, J., and Gonzalez-Marques, J. Facilitation and interference effects in word and picture processing. In S. Ballesteros (ed.), *Cognitive Approaches to Human Perception.* Hillsdale, NJ: Lawrence Erlbaum Associates, 1994, pp. 155–198.

Miller, J. The flanker compatibility effect as a function of visual angle, attentional focus, visual transients, and perceptual load: a search for boundary conditions. *Perception & Psychophysics,* 49 (1991), 270–288.

Miller, J.O., and Bauer, D.W. Visual similarity and discrimination demands. *Journal of Experimental Psychology: General,* 110 (1981), 39–55.

Pashler, H.E. *The Psychology of Attention.* Cambridge, MA: MIT Press, 1998.

Pavlov, I.P. *Conditional Reflexes: An Investigation of the Physiological Activity of the Cerebral Cortex.* London: Wexford University Press, 1927.

Pieters, R.G.M., and Bijmolt, T.H.A. Consumer memory for television advertising: a field study of duration, serial position, and competition effects. *Journal of Consumer Research,* 23, 4 (1997), 362–372.

Proctor, R., and Van Zandt, T. *Human Factors in Simple and Complex Systems.* Needham Heights, MA: Allyn and Bacon, 1994.

Reeves, B.; Lang, A.; Kim, E.; and Tartar, D. The effects of screen size and message content on attention and arousal. *Media Psychology,* 1 (1999), 49–68.

Scanlon, T. Seductive design for web sites. *Eye for Design,* 1998 (available at http://www.uie.com/articles/seductive_design/, accessed November 20, 2005).

Sokolov, E.N.; Spinks, J.A.; Naatanen, R.; and Lyytinen, H. *The Orienting Response in Information Processing.* Mahwah, NJ: Lawrence Erlbaum Associates, 2002.

Spieler, D.H.; Balota, D.A.; and Faust, M.E. Levels of selective attention revealed through analyses of response time distributions. *Journal of Experimental Psychology: Human Perception and Performance,* 26, 2 (2000), 506–526.

Treisman, A. Search, similarity, and integration of features between and within dimensions. *Journal of Experimental Psychology: Human Perception and Performance,* 17 (1991), 652–676.

Tversky, B.; Morrison, J.B.; and Betrancourt, M. Animation: can it facilitate? *International Journal of Human-Computer Studies,* 57, 4 (2002), 247–262.

Warden, C.T., and Brown, H.C. A preliminary investigation of form and motion acuity at low level of illumination. *Journal of Experimental Psychology,* 34 (1944), 437–449.

Yantis, S., and Jonides, J. Abrupt visual onsets and selective attention: voluntary versus automatic allocation. *Journal of Experimental Psychology: Human Perception and Performance,* 16 (1990), 121–134.

Zhang, P. The effect of animation on information seeking performance on the world wide web: securing attention or interfering with primary tasks. *Journal of Association for Information Systems,* 1, 1 (2000), 1–30

Zhang, P. The impact of animation timing and location on visual search task performance in the web environment. In *Proceedings of the Americas Conference on Information Systems (AMCIS '2001).* Boston, 2001, pp. 1361–1366.

Zhang, P. Will you use animation on your web pages? Experiments of animation's effects and implications for web user interface design and online advertising. In C. Romm and F. Sudweeks (eds.), *Doing Business on the Internet: Opportunities and Pitfalls.* London: Springer-Verlag in conjunction with the British Computer Society, 1999, pp. 35–51.

Zhang, P., and Massad, N. The impact of animation on visual search tasks in a web environment: a multi-year study. In *Proceedings of the Americas Conference on Information Systems (AMCIS 03).* Tampa, FL, 2003, pp. 2265–2272.

PART II

COLLABORATION SUPPORT

CHAPTER 5

BRIDGING DISTANCE
Empirical Studies of Distributed Teams

JUDITH S. OLSON AND GARY M. OLSON

Abstract: *Remote work is acknowledged to have considerable challenges. But, of course, not all remote work is alike. Building on our research into remote work in various types of collaboratories (science collaborations involving many institutions and scientists) and case studies of remote work in corporations, we identify six types of remote work, and then list the challenges shared by all and those that are particular to each type. We then discuss potential solutions to the challenges, best practices noted in our field, and laboratory work. Among the solutions are evenly distributed technology, services for awareness of activity in the remote location, explicit achievement of common ground, trust-building exercises, and incentives designed to encourage collaboration. It is additionally important to design the work so that the remote connections are not tightly coupled, but rather require little interaction to be successful. We additionally acknowledge that the social and technical worlds are evolving, which may make remote work eventually possible and distance matter less.*

Keywords: *Virtual Collocation, Virtual Teams, Collaboration, Collaboratories, Trust, Common Ground*

INTRODUCTION

Recent advances in networking (e.g., Internet2), communication technologies (e.g., AccessGrid multipoint video, voice over IP), and information sharing (e.g., Webex synchronous conferencing and asynchronous information repository) hold the promise that working at a distance can be as effective as working collocated. But our recent review of empirical studies of remote work, both in the field and in the laboratory (Olson and Olson, 2000), showed that distance still matters and may continue to matter forever. In that review we focused on five kinds of challenges:

- *The nature of work*: Tightly coupled work has a number of ambiguities that must be worked out among the team members and lots of interaction and negotiation. It is very difficult to do tightly coupled work at a distance, whereas it is easier to do loosely coupled work, because it is easily divisible and clear, and not as many interactions are needed.
- *The common ground of the team members*: If team members have a lot of shared past experience, have worked together before, share a common vocabulary, and so forth, it is easier for them to work through remote media without a lot of clarification.

- *The competitive/cooperative culture*: If the reward structure or indigenous culture promotes individual competition, team members are less likely to want to share their expertise, cover for each other in times of crises, and so forth. The more naturally cooperative the culture, the easier it is for people to successfully share. This is true of collocated teams as well as distant ones, but an even harder obstacle to overcome at a distance.
- *The level of technology competence of the team members*: If the team members have not adopted common communication technologies (e.g., e-mail) and made them part of their everyday habits, they are unlikely to leap into adopting more sophisticated, complicated technologies, such as real-time sharing of documents and multi-point videoconferencing, often involved in remote collaboration.
- *The level of technical infrastructure in which the work resides*: If neither the networking and computational resources nor the technical support is sufficient to sustain the connectivity, remote work fails. Remote work is hard enough interpersonally without unreliable technology adding to the delays and loss.

There have been a number of advances in our understanding of remote work since 2000 that make a reassessment timely. First, we have been doing a broad analysis of over two hundred organizations that work remotely. In science and engineering these are called collaboratories, laboratories without walls, scientific endeavor that connects people from different universities and institutes (Finholt and Olson, 1997). In our project Science of Collaboratories (www.scienceofcollaboratories.org), we have looked at how the challenges to remote work differ for different kinds of collaborations. Here we will note parallels in the corporate world. Second, we have conducted a series of laboratory studies of two key aspects of remote work: trust and social capital. These studies reveal the costs of remote work (out of sight, out of mind, and loss of trust) and the strength of a variety of remedies.

As a consequence of this new work, to our list of challenges from our earlier review we would add additional challenges that make distance work difficult:

- *Alignment of incentives and goals*: Individuals may have different goals or motives in working on a collaborative project. In addition to being competitive, it may be that some of the people in the collaboration have one set of goals or incentives (such as producing new software), and the others another set (such as conducting science). Incentives and goals are difficult to align when project participants are working at a distance from one another, because alignment is first hard to detect, and then achieving alignment takes a lot of negotiation.
- *Trust is more difficult to establish*: It is harder to establish trust at a distance; lack of trust can erode cooperation and task coordination. Trust seems best established through informal, non-work-related interactions, which are usually less frequent in distance interactions than in collocated ones.
- *Awareness of colleagues and their context*: It is difficult to know what others are doing when they are in a different location. When people are collocated, it is easy to "look over their shoulder" to get a sense of what they are doing and how it is progressing. Distance can lead to frustrating delays in getting collaborative work done.
- *No motivational sense of presence of others*: The physical presence of others has well-documented "social facilitation" effects. People are known to work harder when they are with other people. This sense of presence is more difficult to establish and maintain at a distance.
- *The need for explicit management*: Scientists in particular eschew the need for management, often thinking that science itself is a type of shared understanding of what needs to be done

and by whom. It is difficult to manage collaborative projects in general, especially as the number of participants grows. Geographically distributed projects add additional management challenges, such as ensuring that everyone is heard, and recognizing and overcoming cultural differences. Having these projects led by people trained in project management is becoming essential for success.

These issues have arisen repeatedly in our examination of the two hundred collaboratories, and we have seen correlates in the corporate world as well. Although undoubtedly there are even more challenges than we have identified, we wish to focus on these in this chapter.

In what follows, we first describe the variety of kinds of remote work, with an eye to describing the types of challenges that each type seems to encounter. We then lay out the remedies we have noted, called "bridges," to span collaborative challenges. We continue with a short section on when remote work is better than collocated, describing the unique opportunities afforded by working remotely. We then look ahead, knowing that in the history of the adoption of technology, things evolve. We close with a summary of the challenges and remedies.

KINDS OF REMOTE WORK

There are many kinds of distributed work. Here we illustrate some common types found in the business world. Many of these have analogs in the science and engineering projects we have studied, so these are familiar paradigms for us.

Distributed Project Work

This is work across distance that involves a high degree of communication, data sharing, and facility sharing, if appropriate, while working on a common problem. The idea is to integrate distributed human and physical capital as if it were collocated. In the world of science and engineering, there are a number of such teams. For example, in space physics, scientists come together at various points to view data from instruments around the world while chatting about the unfolding phenomena from solar flares (www.si.umich.edu/sparc/). In the corporate world, we see teams of engineers at the large automotive companies, both design and manufacturing, working out the details of a family of transmissions suitable for various markets and manufacturing facilities. Companies involved in "around the clock, around the world" software development share expertise and the artifacts involved in the development of software (such as architecture diagrams, open-issues lists, bug fixes, and works in process). Even people working on a project where the team members are in the same city but in different buildings, such as corporate campuses, fall into this category of remote work.

Remote Expertise

Remote workers can identify experts in other locations whom they can engage in helpful dialog. In the world of science and engineering, it is common to have a database of experts on various topics (e.g., a particular design of an important component of a linear accelerator) "on call" to others doing integrations of this component for the overall design. In the medical world, there are a number of hospitals that provide remote consultation to rural physicians, reading X-rays and diagnosing from various remotely acquired test results. In the corporate world, we see many instances of at least informal tracking of experts. For example, in a large automotive company, designers of a new transmission in the United States consulted by phone with the designers in Germany who developed the transmission's predecessor. Similarly, sales and customer support are another kind of remote expertise. Catalog and Internet sales are growing rapidly. New tools make it possible to have a salesperson in the loop. For example, it may be possible to have an instant messaging session with a salesperson. Or more sophisticated conferencing tools such as Webex or Centra allow a customer and a salesperson to peruse an online catalog together. Similarly, online help can be available through a variety of mechanisms beyond just a telephone. For instance, a number of academic libraries have people available via instant messaging to help with searches or other issues.

Communities of Interest

Information is shared among people of a particular profession or in related fields not necessarily in support of one project or goal. In science, there are Web sites where a large number of people share job listings, information about conferences, and other information sources. One of the most active is Slashdot (slashdot.org) on which people with technical backgrounds share commentary on various news articles, with a complex system of distributed moderation (involving ratings of each others' contributions and accumulated "karma" points). In the corporate world, a classic example of a community of interest was the Xerox copier repairmen who were given walkie-talkies to share their stories of difficult repairs (Orr, 1996). With the advent of wikis (www.wiki.com), Web sites on which anyone can change anything, add anything, or delete anything, a lightweight mechanism exists to support a wide range of such communities of interest.

Distributed Learning Communities

These communities allow communication among people wanting to learn something esoteric, where the students and experts are likely distant from one another. Similar in flavor to remote expertise collaborations, above, distributed learning communities go one step further. The experts do not stop at consulting, but engage in helping people *learn* remotely. For example, there are some particular skills needed to do mathematical modeling in ecology, with very few experts around the country. They have formed a collaboratory with several interested students who engage in discussion and share information aimed to encourage others to acquire this particular skill set. Training is a major activity for companies. For example, there is opportunity to train automobile service personnel remotely and asynchronously by providing portals to the requisite information, especially for cars that are customized or rapidly changing. Pharmaceutical, medical, biotechnology industries as well as professional societies in particular are ripe for this kind of collaboration.

Federated Data Systems

Federated data systems are information systems that are contributed to as well as used by a wide set of participants. In the sciences, there is a growing need to aggregate data from different laboratories, different facilities, different sources, and sometimes at different scales, so that decisions and discoveries are made on larger, more stable data sets. In science and engineering, for example, the Biomedical Informatics Research Network (BIRN; www.birn.net) is a federation of magnetic resonance images on normal and abnormal brains from many laboratories; the network's goal is to share the work of finding causes and cures for schizophrenia. In the corporate world, there are similar federations sharing financial information from around the world, customer data, research and development data, and so forth. Although many companies will attempt to bring the data under one roof, some have found an advantage to federating the data instead. Federating means leaving the data where it is and in its native format, but providing search and integrating engines that find and translate what is needed with each query. A particular kind of data intensive process in industry is supply chain management. Many industries have complex webs of suppliers that must be managed. New collaboration tools make it possible to manage such relationships more effectively at a distance. Supply-chain relations require the exchange of lots of data, and issues of trust can be daunting. New collaboration technologies make aspects of supply-chain management potentially easier, though the range of technical and organizational problems are daunting (Sengupta, 2004).

Shared Facilities

Large, complex, expensive instruments can now be controlled remotely, and data gathered and transported electronically. This is a common source of collaboration in science and engineering. For example, large electron microscopes can be used remotely (www.emsl.org). Observatories can be accessed remotely (www2.keck.hawaii.edu). Many government sponsored facilities, such as accelerators and colliders in physics and tsunami tanks and shake tables in earthquake engineering, are required by the funders to provide remote access (www.neesgrid.org). This may be a less common source of sharing in industry, although one can imagine allowing remote access to various testing facilities used in manufacturing. For example, in one large automotive company, one major source of delay is the shipping of parts and the design engineers to a single testing facility to set up and watch the test. Other companies control manufacturing remotely (Lian, Moyne, and Tilbury, 2000). There may be good opportunities for the corporate world to take lessons from scientific collaborations with shared instruments.

CHALLENGES TO THE VARIOUS TYPES OF COLLABORATION

Challenges Common to All Kinds of Remote Work

For all the types of remote work outlined above, there is the challenge of the *technology base*. In some cases, individuals lack networking or up-to-date workstations, and so forth, to work well with those who are remote. However, with the increase of voice over IP (VoIP) to connect people without high-bandwidth telephony, and services explicitly programmed for low bandwidth, the product market is beginning to respond to the lower-end user base. For example, Centra is a product that allows the sharing of material such as PowerPoint slides and VoIP for remote presentations and more freeform meetings. They do voice over IP, reassembling the voice at the client end so it is intelligible. In this way, the voice is delayed, but is not broken up into unintelligible fragments.

A related issue to the challenge of technology is the common occurrence of people conversing with uneven capabilities. Many times people are meeting face-to-face with one or more brought in by teleconference—voice only. Because those coming in remotely are invisible, they are quickly out of others' attention. The remote people can neither "see" what is going on to jump in for a turn, nor gauge others' reactions to what they say when they do get a turn. It is a severe case of "out of sight, out of mind." Over time, the remote participants are marginalized unless they take control of the situation. Over time, the collocated people become an in-group, with the natural tendency to categorize the remote person as outside the group, simply because of the connectivity asymmetries (Bos et al., 2004).

As noted in (Olson and Olson, 2000), another related issue is the level of technology "readiness" that the participants have. An early failed science collaboratory, for example, was built on UNIX

workstations, when the scientists themselves were DEC (VMS) based. In order to use the federated data system, they had to move to an unfamiliar platform and learn the interface in order to get
the data. Not only was the interface difficult, but it was not always clear what facilities were available in the system (Star and Ruhleder, 1996). In the beginning of the collaboratory for space physi-
cists, many scientists were not even regular users of e-mail. Early adoption of a remote data viewing
was built on the visual analogy of the instruments they would normally see if they flew to the radar
sites (i.e., similar views of the data sources from the variety of analog displays in the instrument hut
in Greenland). Over time, as the scientists grew more familiar with various office, e-mail, and Web
applications, they even began to demand new integrated displays that allowed them to compare real-
time data streams with the output of super-computer models (Olson et al., 1998).

Challenges to Particular Types of Remote Work

We now turn to some of the specific kinds of collaborations and discuss challenges that are more
peculiar to that form.

Challenges to Distributed Project Work

Corporate work that involves sharing information through artifacts (such as open-issues lists) and
human communication (clarifying conversations as well as presentations of ideas and decision
making) appear in R&D centers, as well as in finance, strategy, and so forth. This kind of collaboration is less successful the more tightly coupled the work is. If the work is ambiguous, ill
formed, or has particular new challenges, it is very difficult to sustain over distance. Many organizations have collocated tightly coupled work and work at a distance on parts that are only loosely
coupled.

Since work involves more than meetings, a lot of information is lost when people are not collocated. It is well known that a lot of communication occurs in informal settings, for example,
before and after meetings, bumping into others in the hall, just passing by people and seeing what
they are working on or with whom they are meeting (Olson et al., 2002; Teasley et al., 2000;
Teasley et al., 2002). Being aware of issues, delays, and so forth and being reminded of things
upon seeing someone are both difficult to support when people are working remotely.

Similarly, the more remote people are, the less common ground they share. If teams are made
up of people with different training (e.g., marketing, software engineering, and user-experience
engineering, a common trio for designing a new digital product), people are sometimes confused
about terminology. For example, software engineers often use the word "system" to refer to the
computer, whereas those in user-experience engineering consider people part of the overall system, including procedures and the roles people play.

Finding common ground is one thing; knowing the particular context of your collaborators'
work or the time at their location is another. Their local situations (e.g., a local snowstorm) can
delay work with the remote people who, unaware of this situation, may interpret the delay as inat-
tention, sloth, or some other personal characteristics (Cramton, 2001). Collocation gives you contextual common ground for free. But as distance increases, it is more and more likely that the
distributed people have different backgrounds and occupy different cultures. In some of our long-
distance videoconferences or audio conferences, people in the United States were insensitive to
the actual time of day in the remote location, ignoring the fact that the speaker had stayed late into
the evening not only to present the talk but to handle a long question-and-answer period, during
which many in the U.S. location were merely talking among themselves.

Of course, the third level of common ground is cultural (both cross-corporate and cross-ethnic cultures). Culture affects what you do and how you interpret the actions of others. With distance technology, however, cultural boundaries are being crossed without them being visible. People who travel *see* that the place is different, including the pace, how people address each other, whose turn it is to say something next, and so forth. But in audio conferencing, these clues to differences are invisible—often even with video. Conference rooms typically all look alike—all modern, and all "locally" familiar. Therefore, specific cultural behaviors may lead to misunderstanding. For example, turn-taking is very slow in China; there are (to Americans anyway) long pauses between utterances so that listeners can take in and understand what was said, and show respect by thoughtful consideration. This long pause is a signal to Americans that the Chinese are finished speaking, and are turning the floor over. Americans then speak; the Chinese interpret this as a sign of shallow understanding and disrespect. As we have said before, "When in Rome, do as the Romans do; but in videoconferencing, where is Rome?"

Another aspect of culture interferes in remote work. People from Western Europe are much more "relationship based" than those in the United States. When meetings happen across U.S. and European cultures, it is often the case that the Americans "get down to business" right away, especially if the work is supported by expensive videoconferencing, whereas Europeans will spend some time at the beginning and the end exchanging pleasantries, personal information, and so forth, to maintain a bond. Mistrust and wrong attributions follow when each culture interprets the others in an "out-group" (less favored) way (Cramton, 2002).

Many collaborations live or die on the implicit culture of competition as opposed to cooperation and sharing. We call this "collaboration readiness." Although one would expect that people working for one company are more cooperative and collaborative than loosely federated scientists in different institutions, this is not always the case. In some large companies, projects requiring a particular skill go to that skill's "cost center," which then charges for its services. In some companies, the services of usability-experience engineers are one such service. We have seen that some collaborations are not efficient (e.g., where low-cost services are not offered) because there is an incentive to get more work, and more money, for the service. Similarly, people within a project may implicitly compete for recognition at the time of performance reviews. If there is no incentive structure in place for collaboration, then perhaps people are not "collaboration ready."

Finally, one of the more insidious challenges to remote work of this type is that "trust needs touch" (Handy, 1995). Remote team members are not seen very often. Lacking personal cues, people tend to mistrust those whom they have not seen. When collocated, we acquire a lot of information that naturally leads to trust. We quickly realize when a person is paying attention to us, and when he or she has things to offer to the common good, two kinds of information that accumulate to engender trust. Of course, this kind of information is hard come by when we are interacting with people over only e-mail or audio conferencing. It is no surprise that trust is slow to form, and in some cases impossible, when we cross distances and have an impoverished medium in which to communicate.

We have experienced this in the field (Rocco et al., 2000) and in laboratory studies (Bos et al., 2002; Zheng et al., 2002). People trust those with whom they have talked about non-work-related issues and shared personal stories, those who respond well to requests, and so forth. Without trust, people have to set up elaborate mechanisms to sign contracts, monitor progress, and punish malfeasance. All this extra work drains resources from getting the work done. So, trust is a major issue when people have to work together, especially across disciplines, across time zones, and across cultures.

Challenges to Collaborations Involving Remote Expertise

When people request help from an expert who is not collocated, there are a number of issues common to those above, but with different instantiations. The person requesting help needs to trust the expert to be truly expert in what is needed. The expert could either adopt the posture of the powerful one or feel like a mere assistant. Thus, the expert and requester will have to show proper respect for the expertise, for timely attention to the request, for the importance of the request, and so forth. Although it is natural to think that this is less a problem when both parties work for the same company, we have seen in a large automotive company some upstart American engineers ignore the expertise of senior German engineers, visibly insulting them. This was seen as a measure of disrespect, engendering in the Germans the attitude that "if they don't want to play, I'll take my toys and go home."

Even when mutual respect is established, issues may still arise in the conversation that ensues. Experts and novices do not speak the same language, and even see the world in different ways (Chase and Simon, 1973; Chi et al., 1981; Reitman, 1976). Therefore, it is important for the two to spend time on establishing common ground, so that each knows what the other knows and can help in efficient and understandable ways. This issue becomes even more important in those collaborations that involve goals of teaching/learning the expertise. It is difficult to mentor someone remotely, not only because of the issue of common ground, but also because it is more difficult to monitor what students do and do not yet understand.

Challenges to Communities of Interest

Although the sharing in communities of interest is less tightly coupled than that in the types of collaborations listed above, there still are social issues. In communities of interest that are built on wikis, there is an element of trust, since anyone can change (even delete) anything. Indeed, in the Wikipedia, a collaborative encyclopedia, an analysis of the growth (and shrinking) of controversial entries, such as that on abortion, shows that there are incidents when entire sections are deleted and restored, back and forth, until there is some agreement to have not just a neutral point of view but a balanced view, covering all major constituencies or values (Viegas et al., 2004).

Of equal importance in communities of interest are the incentives to enter information and keep it up to date. Grudin (1994) correctly pointed out that in many group systems, the people who have to expend effort (e.g., to keep things up to date) are not necessarily the same people who benefit. A team member does not want to keep his calendar and to-do list up to date if someone else will then schedule more meetings and add things to his to-do list. Many Web communities have short lives because of just this issue. Those who originally contribute to and gain from others' sharing later find they are only giving (i.e., to newcomers) and no longer find value themselves (Ackerman and Malone, 1990; Grudin, 1994).

A third issue in communities of interest has to do, once again, with common ground. When multiple people enter information, it must be organized, chunked, and labeled as it grows. People are notoriously bad at agreeing how a collection should be organized (Furnas et al., 1987). The more decentralized the control over organization, the more likely things will be "lost" to some members because they don't recognize how to find things. For example, our own research group abandoned a shared file system, mainly because the folder-naming conventions were incomprehensible to many of the participants. The simpler the scope of the site or the more standardized it is (e.g., a number of communities of interest sites list news items, like upcoming conferences, and job openings), the less this is a problem.

Challenges to Federated Data Systems

Federated data systems have less conversation than distributed project work, and thus have less need for conversational common ground. In addition, the work is by design less tightly coupled. The work of defining what goes into the data system (establishing common ground) is typically done up front, before the data are federated or joined.

The two issues that do loom large in federated data systems are trust and incentives. If data are to be used by others, they must be trustworthy. Procedures have to be in place to vet the contributor, his or her process of gathering data, the accuracy of the entry, and so forth. We have seen in BIRN that the federation of functional MRIs is extremely difficult, because they have to agree on the tasks that the patients will be doing (the "functions") while being scanned, and they have to calibrate the individual instruments to make sure they have the same output for the same input. Indeed, they vet these machines by sending the system support people around to all the sites to be scanned! Testing equipment for automobile design components has to be similarly trusted to give consistent responses to the same input. If data are analyzed and then submitted for common use, then one has to trust the analysis and the analyst (Birnholtz and Bietz, 2003). Because of the old saw "garbage in, garbage out," trust of the people, processes, and instruments in federated data systems is paramount.

Going hand in glove with trust in what people are contributing is the factor of incentives to share. If people don't share their best material, then the shared data will contain only second-rate data/information. In an early study of consultants submitting their best practices into a Lotus Notes database, it was found that the consultants withheld their very best material from the shared database, since that was the information that gave them the competitive edge for promotion (Orlikowski, 1992). In our science collaboratories, we have seen that scientists from those fields where there is high individual recognition (e.g., AIDS researchers, who can get the Nobel prize for their work), do not collaborate well. In space physics, where no work can really get done without a number of people with different instruments and different skill sets cooperating, there is a high degree of collaboration. There seem to be two types of incentives. In one, people want to share because they need the skills and expertise of the others, often dissimilar to their own. In the second, people want to share in order to be a co-author, which then contributes to high performance ratings and personal benefit. The first is inherent in the work; the second can be designed.

Challenges to Shared Facilities Collaborations

Collaborations that involve a shared instrument (e.g., a test facility, a specialized manufacturing facility, a supercomputer for data mining) involve less personal interaction and thus fewer of the delicate issues of trust, common ground, and incentives than the collaborations reviewed thus far. They are not issue free, however. We have seen in scientific collaborations involving high-end systems (e.g., electron microscopes) an issue related to incentives, but better characterized as power and fairness. Typically, an instrument that is shared remotely has a staff and researchers who are on site, who both do the research and maintain the facility. There are very likely issues of priority over who gets to use the facility, both over the number of hours and over flexibility, if there is suddenly open time. There are two possible swings that this could take: either the power is in the hands of the remote people, with the local people feeling like mere servants to their whims, or, more likely, the local people have the power both because they can subtly take priority and because they can capitalize when someone suddenly doesn't require a time slot on the machine (Birnholtz and Horn, 2004).

The issue of fairness is often delicate, because the participants all have to agree on how to divide time at the facility. They have to buy in to an allocation scheme that sometimes might not afford the flexibility to capitalize on found time or to resolve conflicts of priority. The negotiation of the allocation policy and of the moment-by-moment exception handling does require trust.

Summary of Challenges

This review of different kinds of collaborations, in both science and the corporate world, has revealed a series of major issues that have to be addressed in order for remote collaboration to be successful. In all, the technological infrastructure has to exist, that is, both the actual computers and the technical support. When access among participants is uneven, dangers of in-group/out-group dynamics loom. Additionally, the participants have to have enough experience in the technologies to feel comfortable using them. The benefit they get has to be higher than the effort put in.

Many of the collaboratories rely on the participants having and maintaining common ground, trust, and incentives that are aligned with the organization's goals. Success depends on the participants' interpersonal collaboration readiness. Various collaboratories involve uneven power and therefore issues of fairness in the distribution of the benefits. The more loosely coupled the work (e.g., the less dependent people are on understanding each other's ideas and progress), the easier it is to collaborate. Those engaged in tightly coupled work need a fair amount of awareness to gauge the progress and understanding of their collaborators.

In the following section, we outline some possible remedies to these challenges, focusing on the technical (and therefore easier) solutions before the more social.

BRIDGES TO SPAN COLLABORATION CHALLENGES

All solutions to support remote collaboration are socio-technical; they involve both technology adoption and social practices surrounding them. For clarity and simplicity, in the following we group the solutions for whether the primary focus is on the technical or social.

Technical Bridges

Decades of research have confirmed that the important channels for communication among team members who know each other and have worked together before are full-duplex audio (so that backchannel confirmation noises can be heard), and a shared (editable) object to talk about (Finn et al., 1997). Video is very useful, however, when people do *not* know each other and issues of a highly personal nature, such as negotiation and establishing common ground, are the goals of the conversation (Short et al., 1976; Veinott et al., 1999). Video is also useful for supporting the more emotional, subjective elements of collaborations (Daly-Jones et al., 1998; Olson et al., 1995). Of course, many interactions involving people at a distance also involve differential access to high bandwidth and video. To avoid the potential for in-group/out-group bias, it is wise to put everyone on common footing. Webex and Centra are good examples of technologies that allow excellent sharing of the objects of discussion and high-quality audio, even over low-end networks.

Since collaboration involves much more than meetings, it is important to make others involved in tightly coupled work aware of one another's presence and perhaps activities. It is well known that people have a tendency to attribute delays or errors to personal characteristics, such as lower intelligence or sloth, to those who are remote, and situational characteristics, such as an emergency or interruption, to those who are local (Cramton, 2001). Consequently, for those doing tightly coupled work, it is very important to find technical solutions to support awareness. The current lightweight technologies include instant messaging from various vendors, which can signal what the person is doing, where he or she is, and so forth, and a lightweight ephemeral channel with which to chat (Handel and Herbsleb, 2002).

A higher-end solution to awareness involves always-on video connections, more like the channels in the Portland experiment, or those under development in the Connection Project at Michigan (www.connectionproject.org). Here, the video/audio channels are always on, set in some public place like a hallway or lounge, so that remote teammates can get a sense of the activity or issues (like a big snowstorm or a World Cup soccer match) at the remote location that might cause delays or altered attention. CERN has an "always on video" connection between its facility in Switzerland and laboratories at the University of Michigan during hours of work overlap.

Of course, these technologies are no good if people are not able to use them. Many videoconferencing systems have horrendous interfaces, often wasting participants' time at the beginning of the meeting in order to enter the double IP addresses or discover over another phone line why a connection is not being made. Interfaces are becoming more "walk up and use," but they remain a challenge, likely enough of a challenge so that people will choose not to communicate over learning enough to make these connection possibilities common. Much of this is due to the lack of standards and a rapid evolution in the technologies, but these factors impose a definite productivity cost on working remotely.

Social Bridges

As we (Olson and Olson, 2000) and others have pointed out before, many barriers to collaboration are social. This does not mean they are unbridgeable, but that people tend to be less aware of social (as opposed to technical) solutions to problems. For example, we have noted countless times when people were unaware how the height of the monitor affects influence (Huang et al., 2002). Below we list the social bridges we are aware of that will lead to more successful collaboration.

Common Ground

Collaborations are hindered if people have little common ground. In working with people at a distance, it is important to take extra caution and time to establish common ground. One of the most effective business practices that addresses this is called "active listening." When someone has said something important and you need to be clear that you have achieved common ground, you say back what you think you just heard. This allows for explicit acknowledgement of a correct understanding or for opportunities to correct misunderstandings. Of course, this, too, flies in the face of cultures in which people do not want to be very explicit about what they are saying. For instance, China and Japan have cultural expectations that one does not say "too much," is not too explicit. Repeating and clarifying imply that one does not understand what is going on. But if we are to achieve common ground across cultures, all parties are going to have to give a bit.

Similarly, we can achieve a better understanding of the cultural attributes we are dealing with by reading one of the series of books called *Culture Shock.* Written by Americans who have lived for a substantial time in the target country, these books can describe aspects of culture that are invisible to the natives. There are other specific books, too, about particular countries, such as

Brit-Think, Ameri-Think (Walmsley, 1986), and *French or Foe* (Platt, 1998), to name just two that are well written and based on good basic information.

It is important to understand a natural but unfortunate human failing in these situations: We blame failure among our in-group on situational factors; we blame failure among the out-group on their personal characteristics, such as incompetence and their thinking ill of us. We have to repeatedly examine our attributions to bridge this divide.

Trust

As mentioned earlier, "trust needs touch" (Handy, 1995). How can this be bridged? Bos et al. (2002) ran a study recently that bears on this issue. They examined how trust builds over time in a laboratory setting, using the classic "social dilemma" task, which has been used for decades to measure trust and cooperation vs. competition and self-serving attitudes. The task was broken into clusters of rounds, with the ability to "talk" to the partner during various intermissions. Players who "talked" by text chat built no trust; they behaved in very self-serving ways. Those who talked face-to-face cooperated throughout. This is what we expected with "trust needs touch." Those who talked by phone and those who also had video were slower to build trust but they did achieve a level eventually like that of those who met face-to-face. This is important. Trust may not need touch, though it develops fastest that way. Other interactive media with voice intonations and video of the remote person support trust but at a slower rate. It is important to give trust time.

In a second study (Zheng et al., 2002) explored the space of things one could do to prevent the loss of trust when forced to converse only by text chat or e-mail. We confirmed that if people meet face-to-face before working on the task, they build and maintain their trust. If not, they indeed stay mistrustful. But a number of other things were tried: Exchanging pictures, exchanging brief résumés that included their hobbies, and engaging in a social text chat where they were told "to get to know each other." The results were somewhat surprising. The résumés did close to nothing. Both the pictures and the social chat helped engender trust, not as high as meeting face-to-face, but close. This is important. One need not endure the cost of meeting face-to-face to establish trust. If the focus of discussion is less on work-related things and pictures are exchanged, people begin to develop trust. It's not the medium so much as what is done in the medium.

Some of the information that one uses in developing trust is whether the other person takes one's welfare into account, and pays attention. As mentioned above in the section on common ground, delay has particular dangers in remote work. Delay is inherent in remote work, but we have an unfortunate tendency to attribute it not to situational but personal characteristics. Delay, then, also makes people mistrust each other. One remedy is to acknowledge this attribution and to develop what has been called a "communication covenant." This covenant is an agreement made at the beginning of a collaboration that specifies each party's expectations of and commitments to regular communication (e.g., read e-mail every morning and afternoon, respond to voice mails within twenty-four hours, wear and answer a pager, etc.). Covenants often include commitments to communicate about extenuating circumstances, especially if there might be a delay. Some commit to saying "I got your e-mail and will get to it this afternoon," or some equivalent.

If collaboration involves shared use of a scarce resource (like an expensive test instrument or cycles on a supercomputer), trust again comes into play. Trust involves belief that the other person will not take advantage of you when you are vulnerable. When you are remote from the instrument and are repeatedly denied access without explanation, mistrust ensues. Again, open communication, up-front agreements about fair practices, and so forth, can go a long way to bridge this issue.

Incentives for Collaboration

Incentives played the lead in many of the barriers to successful collaboration. When people are not ready for collaboration, the cause is often misaligned incentives. Among those who are competing for recognition or promotion, sharing one's best practices or giving information to other in-house competitors is understandably low. If the culture is one of long-standing cooperation, because no one succeeds without the other, remote collaboration has a higher chance of success. What kinds of incentive structures have we seen that bridged this issue?

In one scientific field, genomics, the accumulation of genetic information is of great value. The Genome DataBank (GenBank) is a very large database of genetic information, useful to others as more is contributed. This field took the idea of incentives head-on. Since publication is the coin of the realm in academics, they declared that in order to publish *any* findings, you had to contribute your raw data to the GenBank. Collaboration is closely tied to institutional practices and existing standards (Knorr-Certina, 1999).

In another scientific collaboratory, the Alliance for Cellular Signaling (ACS), collaboration involves doing a lot of work on a mountain of data, running more analyses, writing the results up in a standard form (called a "molecule page"), and, after review, submitting it to the shared database. Like the GenBank, the rewards for scientists in this field accrue from publications, publishing in A-journals and gaining recognition of their work through authorship. The leaders of ACS arranged a deal with *Nature*, one of the most prestigious journals in the field, to vet molecule pages *as if* they were publications. The molecule pages would undergo peer review, and then be authored so there would be name recognition. One could list these on one's vita and have tenure committees consider them as publications. The editors of *Nature* have been involved in writing tenure letters for those who have contributed molecule pages, as one would do when reviewing someone's journal publication record.

A second successful incentive scheme we have seen has more to do with loyalty and tradition. Those scientists involved in the Zebrafish Information Network (ZFIN), similar to ACS, contribute standardized information on their model organism, the zebrafish. There is no explicit incentive structure in place; instead, the contributors originally came from the same laboratory, and had all been trained by the same professor. As they moved into other organizations, they kept up their contributions in loyalty to this professor. Since his death, they continue ZFIN in his honor. As time goes on and as others get access to their accumulated data, we will see whether this altruism holds up or whether some other mechanism will take its place. In the corporate world, one can imagine internal loyalty, the wish to be externally competitive, and charisma of a lead person keeping contribution levels high.

A third incentive structure has shown up in a large community of practice, Slashdot, whose value as a whole is in keeping activity high. On Slashdot, editors distill various news items about the information technology world ("News for Nerds") and post them on a site that millions of people visit each day. Participants can comment on the articles and on one another's comments. It is hard to monitor comments from so many participants, so that people can see the most interesting contributions. Since single-point moderation is impossible at this scale, the inventors of Slashdot have developed a mechanism of distributed moderation. People who are regular contributors vote on others' contributions; the higher the votes, the higher the item appears in the list of comments. As your contributions are voted higher, you accumulate "karma points" yourself, allowing you to moderate others. So the collective takes pride in making good contributions and monitoring others so that the contributions stay good. Contributors are proud of their "karma points," which offer only a social, not a monetary, incentive. One can imagine this kind of distributed

moderation happening in a corporate setting, sharing news from the outside and advances or challenges from within.

A fourth incentive structure is seen in the BioMedical Informatics Research Network (BIRN),
mentioned above. Here the leaders set up a sharing scheme from the beginning, stating that they
can't get others' data early unless they also contribute. They own their data for a while, keeping
it to themselves for early analysis. They then make it available to others in the BIRN, and, eventually, to anyone. This scheme of not getting until one gives is again applicable in the corporate
world. Sales databases are helpful only inasmuch as others contribute. One can imagine establishing a rule that one cannot see others' data until one makes one's own available.

Coupling of Work

If work that is conducted among remote teams requires a lot of communication because it is
ambiguous or fraught with exceptions, it is best not done remotely. We have seen time and time
again that work that is tightly coupled and done at a distance is eventually reorganized so that the
individual locations have the tightly coupled work and the remote locations need only intermittent
coordination. For example, at a large computer company, the monthly sales and revenue figures
were set up to be "rolled up" by product, coordinating the figures from one product across the
globe. Because local accounting systems were somewhat inconsistent in account numbers and
product identifiers, this work took a great deal of cross-site coordination. After months of hair-
tearing communication and stressful deadlines, the company decided to roll up the numbers by
country first, allowing the tightly coupled disambiguation to happen "locally" before being rolled
up across sites. This greatly reduced the communication needed across sites. Tightly coupled
work should occur locally; loosely coupled work can be accomplished remotely.

Other Remedies

In accessing remote instruments above, we noted the possibility of differences in power. As with
issues of trust, power can be negotiated and made explicit so that people feel included and know
that they are being treated fairly. The same thing appears when people have to communicate over
uneven media. If those with more powerful connections (e.g., face-to-face or open video) recognize their plight and treat them fairly and with proper attention and priority, remote work *can*
work. One bridge to this kind of situation is for *everyone* to experience what it feels like to be in
the less powerful situation, either by being lower-priority users of a shared instrument or living
with more impoverished communication media. This is similar to the benefits of travel in general,
in that one experiences things from another's point of view.

Interestingly, some companies, and our automobile manufacturer in particular, institute a literal rotational scheme. The headquarters are in the United States, but there are major engineering
and manufacturing facilities in both France and Germany. They regularly station an engineer from
France in the United States, and a German in France, to be eyes and ears for things that their
remote location needs to know but that are not being communicated by others. Their "in-group"
of countrymen is their concern, and they look for information the remote people need.

WHEN REMOTE WORK IS BETTER

Being part of a remote post is not all bad. We interviewed the manager of the Shanghai branch of
a large telecommunications company, someone who chose to be remote. He did have constantly

available voice access, e-mail, fax, and so forth, but he used to his advantage the fact that headquarters was *not* aware of all that was going on in China. He had control of what they saw and didn't see, and liked the power to do things his way instead of "by the book." This was not a case of corporate malfeasance, but rather just some flexibility in managing and priorities that he felt fit the country better than "remote control."

We have also seen cases when people communicate over "remote" technologies even when collocated. We had people sitting next to each other in open cubicles communicating to each other about system bugs over Lotus Notes, not by voice. They valued each other's attention to the work at hand (zoning when programming) and put their issues in Lotus Notes, an asynchronous medium, to keep from interrupting each other. Although they recognized that their bug reports were less detailed and clear when typed into Notes than when explained face-to-face, they chose that trade-off to increase their attention to the programming at hand.

The third case where impoverished media are better is that of communicating with those for whom English is not a native language. We had a colleague in Japan whose English was adequate but not swift. Some of our colleagues attributed his errors and delay in speaking to his not being very bright. However, when he communicated over e-mail, he was wonderful! The fact that he could read and re-read our e-mails to understand them, and then take his time to reply greatly increased the bandwidth between us.

As noted in Hollan and Stornetta (1992), with the advent of a greater variety of technologies, we should look for cases where it is *better than being there* (Birnholtz and Horn, 2004).

THE SOCIAL AND TECHNICAL ISSUES ARE EVOLVING

In a classic analysis, Grudin (1994) looked into why so many CSCW applications seem to fail. After examining in detail several companies' failure to adopt group calendars, he pointed out that developers of groupware systems need to be concerned about issues such as (p. 97):

- Disparity in work and benefit. Groupware applications often require additional work from individuals who do not perceive a direct benefit from the use of the application.
- Critical mass and prisoners' dilemma problems. Groupware may not enlist the "critical mass" of users required to be useful, or can fail because it is never to any one individual's advantage to use it.
- Disruption of social processes. Groupware can lead to activity that violates social taboos, threatens existing political structures, or otherwise dissuades users crucial to its success.
- The adoption process. Groupware requires more careful implementation (introduction) in the workplace than product developers have confronted.

In the case of group calendars, having everyone's calendar online may be more valuable to some (such as managers), but all have to do the work of keeping it updated. Group calendars are not very valuable if only a few people use them. Subtle things about how people use their time or who they are willing to schedule are not handled very well. Group calendars, on their first introduction, were quite alien, and were often difficult to use.

This was the situation in the 1980s. More recently, Palen and Grudin (2002) found that organizational conditions in the 1990s became more favorable for the adoption of group tools, with increased "collaboration readiness" and "collaboration technology readiness." Furthermore, the tools themselves had improved in reliability, functionality, and usability. Palen and Grudin found widespread adoption of group calendaring in two large organizations they studied in detail. The lesson here is that broad conclusions about challenges and solutions need to be temporalized. Each successive generation of technologies and users has different properties. For instance, those entering the labor force today have a much greater comfort level with a variety of technologies (e.g., instant messaging, cellular phones) than do those who are in their last decade before retirement.

There can be ups and downs. E-mail is a good example. E-mail is actually a very old technology, first used within computer science research communities in the 1960s. It wasn't until two decades later that it became popular outside of narrow research communities. The explosion of e-mail usage in the 1990s has been hailed as a major success for groupware. But this success in turn led to serious problems. Today we have an explosion of spam, as well as e-mail serving as a conduit for viruses and worms. These are fundamentally social problems that were made possible by advances in the technologies. A variety of technical and social means of dealing with these problems are being explored.

SUMMARY AND CONCLUSIONS

From the above discussion, it is first important to acknowledge that not all collaborations are the same. Some involve casually interacting participants sharing things of use to the field as a whole, whereas some involve people tightly coupled in their project goals and their day-to-day activities. Some share only the use of a facility, some share data, and others share everything. But we have also noted that technical and social issues loom large. On the technical side, having a good technical and support infrastructure is the basis for connectivity; without such an infrastructure, you have haves and have-nots and run the risk of having in-groups and out-groups. People also differ in experience, and, because of personal costs, may make different judgments about the costs/benefits of collaborating. On the social side, we have issues of common ground, trust, and incentives, as well as the difficulty of doing work that is truly tightly coupled.

What do we suggest to bridge distance? On the technical side, bridges include evenly distributed communication capabilities, with good access to shared objects and full duplex audio. When people are not familiar with each other, having video helps. If work is tightly coupled, instant messaging and open video connections greatly help with awareness and attributions for delays.

On the social side, common ground can be achieved if attention and time is paid to it. Active listening helps establish common ground. People from different cultures should talk or read about what cultural differences mean to their interaction styles. People can achieve trust even if they never meet, as long as they have time for non-work interaction and evidence that they are considering each other's interests. Video and audio help create trust in a negotiation (e.g., for the rules for use of a shared instrument, or agreeing on the format for a shared database). But even simple social chats or jokes help establish and maintain trust, even without actual touch. It is possible to "touch" another through media.

One of the most powerful bridges to collaboration is the explicit analysis of the incentives to share. Incentives can come from the sharing culture of the organization, from explicit sharing incentives in performance evaluations, or the underscoring of already extant loyalties within and competition outside the corporation. Also, one can help the success of remote work by requiring very little work that is tightly coupled. The design of what work is done at which site is certainly under control of the managers at some level, and can have a great deal to do with the success of the whole endeavor.

We do not mean to imply that collocated work is the gold standard. Although "radical collocation" has been shown to be powerful, not all work can be collocated, and in some cases the expertise is distributed and unwilling to relocate. So, remote work will be with us. We have even seen some cases where remoteness was preferred: Remoteness allowed managerial freedom, and in some cases the use of remote technologies reduced interruptions and allowed those with less facility with the language flourish with technologies that required less real-time speed.

This field is evolving. Corporate culture is changing to expect people to have facility with remote and sharing technologies. And the technology itself is getting better with higher bandwidth and more reliability. Perhaps in the near future we will see changes in the norms of incentive structures to favor sharing, and a greater understanding of and accommodation to others' native cultures. We may even mature to understand that remote partners' delays are not necessarily their fault, but are perhaps caused by circumstances similar to those in our own lives. Distance will still matter, but it will matter less.

ACKNOWLEDGMENTS

This chapter is supported in part by National Science Foundation Grants IIS-0085951 and IIS-0308009. We are grateful for assistance on earlier drafts by Nathan Bos, Dan Horn, Jeremy Birnholtz, and Cliff Lampe.

REFERENCES

Ackerman, M.S., and Malone, T.W. Answer garden: a tool for growing organizational memory. *Proceedings of the Conference on Office Information Systems.* New York: ACM, 1990, pp. 31–39.

Birnholtz, J., and Bietz, M.J. Data at work: Supporting sharing in science and engineering. Paper presented at *Group 2003: International Conference on Supporting Group Work.* New York: ACM, 2003, p. 20.

Birnholtz, J., and Horn, D. Shake, rattle and role: design implications from experimental earthquake engineering. Paper presented at the Academy of Management conference, New Orleans, LA, 2004.

Bos, N.; Olson, J.S.; Gergle, D.; Olson, G.M.; and Wright, Z. Effects of four computer-mediated communication channels on trust development. In *Conference on Human Factors in Computing Systems, CHI 2002.* New York: ACM, 2002, pp. 135–140.

Bos, N.; Olson, J.S.; Shami, S.; Chesin, A.; and Nan, N. In-group/out-group effects in distributed teams: An experimental simulation. In *Proceedings of the Conference on Computer Supported Cooperative Work, CSCW 2004.* New York: ACM, 2004, pp. 429–436.

Chase, W.G., and Simon, H.A. The mind's eye in chess. In W.G. Chase (ed.), *Visual Information Processing.* New York: Academic Press, 1973, pp. 215–281.

Chi, M.T.H.; Feltovich, P.J.; and Glaser, R. Categorization and representation of physics problems by experts and novices. *Cognitive Science,* 5 (1981), 121–152.

Cramton, C.D. The mutual knowledge problem and its consequences in geographically dispersed teams. *Organizational Science,* 12 (2001), 346–371.

Cramton, C.D. Attribution in distributed work groups. In P. J. Hinds and S. Kiesler (eds.), *Distributed Work: New Ways of Working Across Distance Using Technology.* Cambridge, MA: MIT Press, 2002, pp. 191–212.

Daly-Jones, O.; Monk, A.; and Watts, L. Some advantages of video conferencing over high-quality audio conferencing: fluency and awareness of attentional focus. *International Journal of Human-Computer Studies,* 49, 1 (1998), 21–58.

Finholt, T.A., and Olson, G.M. From laboratories to collaboratories: a new organizational form for scientific collaboration. *Psychological Science,* 8 (1997), 28–36.

Finn, K.E.; Sellen, A.J.; and Wilbur, S. (eds.) *Video-Mediated Communication.* Hillsdale, NJ: Lawrence Erlbaum Associates, 1997.

Furnas, G.W.; Landauer, T.K.; Gomez, L.M.; and Dumais, S.T. The vocabulary problem in human-system communication. *Communications of the ACM,* 30, 11 (1987), 964–971.

Grudin, J. Groupware and social dynamics: eight challenges for developers. *Communications of the ACM,* 37, 1 (1994), 93–104.

Handel, M., and Herbsleb, J.D. What is chat doing in the workplace? *Proceedings of the Conference on Computer Supported Cooperative Work, CSCW 2002.* New York: ACM, 2002, pp. 1–10.

Handy, C. Trust and the virtual organization. *Harvard Business Review*, 73, May–June (1995), 40–50.

Hollan, J., and Stornetta, S. Beyond being there. In *Conference on Human Factors in Computing Systems, CHI 1992*. New York: ACM, 1992, pp. 119–125.

Huang, W.; Olson, J.S.; and Olson, G.M. Camera angle affects dominance in video-mediated communication. In *Conference on Human Factors in Computing Systems, CHI 2002*. New York: ACM, 2002, pp. 716–717.

Knorr-Certina, K. *Epistemic Cultures*. Cambridge, MA: Harvard University Press, 1999.

Lian, F.L.; Moyne, J.R.; and Tilbury, D.M. Implementation of networked machine tools in reconfigurable manufacturing systems. In *Proceedings of the 2000 Japan-USA Symposium on Flexible Automation, July 2000*. Ann Arbor, MI: ASME, 2000.

Olson, G.M.; Atkins, D.E.; Clauer, R.; Finholt, T.A.; Jahanian, F.; Killeen, T.L.; et al. The upper atmospheric research collaboratory. *Interactions*, 5, 3 (1998), 48–55.

Olson, G.M., and Olson, J.S. Distance matters. *Human-Computer Interaction*, 15 (2000), 139–179.

Olson, J.S.; Olson, G.M.; and Meader, D.K. What mix of video and audio is useful for remote real-time work? In *Conference on Human Factors in Computing Systems, CHI 1995*. New York: ACM, 1995, pp. 362–368.

Olson, J.S.; Teasley, S.D.; Covi, L.; and Olson, G.M. The (currently) unique advantages of collocated work. In P.J. Hinds and S. Kiesler (eds.), *Distributed Work*. Cambridge, MA: MIT Press, 2002, pp. 113–135.

Orlikowski, W.J. Learning from Notes: organizational issues in groupware implementation. In *Proceedings of CSCW '92*. New York: ACM Press, 1992, pp. 362–369.

Orr, J. *Talking about Machines: An Ethnography of a Modern Job*. Ithaca, NY: Cornell University Press, 1996.

Palen, L., and Grudin, J. Discretionary adoption of group support software. In B.E. Munkvold (ed.), *Organizational Implementation of Collaboration Technology*. London: Springer-Verlag, 2002, pp. 159–180.

Platt, P. *French or foe?* 2nd ed. Skokie, IL: Distribooks, 1998.

Reitman, J. Skilled perception in GO: deducing memory structures from interresponse times. *Cognitive Psychology*, 8 (1976), 336–356.

Rocco, E.; Finholt, T.A.; Hofer, E.C., and Herbsleb, J.D. Designing as if trust mattered. Technical Report Number: CREW-00-05. Ann Arbor, MI: University of Michigan, 2000.

Sengupta, S. The top ten supply chain mistakes. *Supply Chain Management Review*, 8, July–August (2004), 42–49.

Short, J.; Williams, E.; and Christie, B. *The Social Psychology of Telecommunications*. New York: John Wiley & Sons, 1976.

Star, L.S., and Ruhleder, K. Steps toward an ecology of infrastructure: complex problems in design and access for large-scale collaborative systems. *Information Systems Research*, 7, 1 (1996), 111–134.

Teasley, S.D.; Covi, L.; Krishnan, M.S.; and Olson, J.S. What does radical collocation give a team? In *Conference on Computer Supported Cooperative Work, CSCW 2000*. New York: ACM, 2000, pp. 339–346.

Teasley, S.D.; Covi, L.A.; Krishnan, M.S.; and Olson, J.S. Rapid software development through team collocation. *IEEE Transactions on Software Engineering*, 28 (2002), 671–683.

Veinott, E.S.; Olson, J.S.; Olson, G.M.; and Fu, X. Video helps remote work: speakers who need to negotiate common ground benefit from seeing each other. In *Conference on Human Factors in Computing Systems, CHI 1999*. New York: ACM, 1999, pp. 302–309.

Viegas, F.; Wattenberg, M.; and Kushal, D. Studying cooperation and conflict between authors with history flow visualizations. In *Conference on Human Factors in Computing Systems, CHI 2004*. New York: ACM, 2004, pp. 575–582.

Walmsley, J. *Brit-think Ameri-think: A Transatlantic Survival Guide*. London: Harrap, 1986.

Zheng, J.; Veinott, B.; Bos, N.; Olson, J.S.; and Olson, G.M. Trust without touch: jumpstarting long-distance trust with initial social activities. In *Conference on Human Factors in Computing Systems, CHI 2002*. New York: ACM, 2002, pp. 141–146.

CHAPTER 6

ASYNCHRONOUS VIRTUAL TEAMS

Can Software Tools and Structuring of Social Processes Enhance Performance?

STARR ROXANNE HILTZ, JERRY FJERMESTAD,
ROSALIE J. OCKER, AND MURRAY TUROFF

Abstract: *The virtual teams studied in NJIT's program of research are task-oriented groups, dispersed in time and space, that work together using computer-mediated communication (CMC) to produce a product such as the design and implementation of a software artifact. There are two basic ways of providing support or structure for virtual teams' interaction: construct or use special software (or hardware) tools that support and guide the groups, or impose interaction processes (e.g., leadership roles, schedules of deliverables, rules of interaction) designed to enhance process gains and decrease process losses. Which approach performs better under which conditions is still a major research question. This chapter briefly reviews the literature on virtual teams, describes the evolution of a long-term series of studies on distributed teams using asynchronous computer-mediated communication, and then reports the results of several recent field experiments conducted at NJIT. These experiments included two studies of ways to provide support for large teams: One provided sophisticated listing and voting tools, and the other imposed a Delphi type process. The results were not always as hypothesized. We describe how some independent variables were dropped from subsequent studies or raised issues for future research.*

Keywords: *Virtual Teams, Computer-Mediated Communication, Social Process Structuring*

INTRODUCTION: LITERATURE REVIEW ON GSS AND VIRTUAL TEAMS

For over twenty years, a team of researchers centered at NJIT has conducted experiments and field studies designed to improve the effectiveness of group support systems for distributed groups communicating via asynchronous computer-mediated communication. In this chapter, we describe the persistence and evolution of interest in different independent variables, as well as of methods of inquiry, since each study or series of studies suggested additional research questions and issues. Many other technologies can help distributed teams—synchronous tools such as NetMeeting or a shared editor (Olson et al., 1993); awareness tools such as Instant Messenger; calendaring tools to help schedule meetings; and so forth. However, this chapter reviews a program of studies on asynchronous teams at NJIT, rather than the entire field of research on virtual teams and group support systems in general.

At NJIT we have been pursuing the broad research question of task-technology-group "fit" (Rana et al., 1997). Technology includes, of course, the medium or media mix used; but when the medium is computer-mediated, it also includes tools, structures, and interface. Many studies have asked, "Can software tools or group process structuring help distributed groups to coordinate their interaction and improve their effectiveness?" As noted in the GSS research framework provided by DeSanctis and Gallupe (1987), different types of tasks (e.g., idea generating, idea evaluation) will require different types of tools and structures for optimal performance. Important group characteristics include its size and its degree of heterogeneity (cultural or otherwise). Thus, recent research has studied culturally heterogeneous teams, and larger groups or teams than the 3–5 members used in most experiments on group support systems. In particular, we have begun asking how we can best construct "social decision support systems" for very large groups.

By software "tools" we mean the use of the computer to collect, process, and display data to the group; the most frequent type of software tool is a voting or preference tool. As a "tool," the software plays an automated and active role in guiding or supporting the interaction among group members. By "structure" we mean norms, roles, and procedures that are meant to guide group interaction. "Structure" has been something of a holy grail to the NJIT team for a long time; seeking structures that "make a difference" in helping online groups to coordinate and be more effective. For example, Hiltz and Turoff (1978, p. 287) wrote:

> The fragrance of the future of computerized conferencing emanates from its ability to provide structure to enhance the human communication process. Specification of such factors as the number of participants; the roles that they play; who may communicate with whom, how when and under what conditions, are aspects of structure. Even when a structure is not explicitly designed and imposed on a group, there will be an implicit or emergent structure . . . There exists an obvious need for structure as the size of a group increases; hence we have evolved highly structured parliamentary systems for large face-to-face groups.

What is the difference between CMC (computer-mediated communication), GDSS (group decision support systems), DGSS (distributed group support systems), and virtual teams? The terms overlap a great deal, but we have used the following definitions in our research. By computer-mediated communication systems, the most general term, we mean any use of the computer to support, structure, store, process, and distribute human communications or information (Hiltz and Turoff, 1978; Kerr and Hiltz, 1982; Hiltz and Turoff, 1985). Thus, besides providing the communication medium for decision support or virtual teams, CMC includes instant messaging; Web-based audio conferences or videoconferences; asynchronous, primarily text-based systems, such as e-mail or computer conferencing, and so forth. CMC may be used for any purpose, from electioneering (e.g., the Howard Dean presidential campaign) to e-commerce applications such as commercial Web sites, to looking for a date.

GDSS's were defined in the classic DeSanctis and Gallupe (1987) paper as systems that combine communication, computer, and decision support tools and processes to support problem formulation and solution. For example, GDSSs usually include various kinds of voting tools, and may support processes similar to brainstorming, nominal group technique, or stakeholder analysis. GDSS research usually brings people together in "decision rooms," but they may be distributed in space, with their computers and displays linked together via a computer network. Thus, GDSSs are usually used for a short, defined meeting period and for one or two kinds of tasks in a session (e.g., brainstorming followed by evaluation of alternatives).

In a previous paper (Turoff et al., 1993) we defined the general term group support systems as combining the characteristics of computer-mediated communication systems with the specialized tools and processes developed in the context of group decision support systems to provide communications, a group memory, and tools and structures to coordinate the group process and analyze data. Within this general category, distributed GSS use primarily asynchronous communication; in other words, the group members are distributed in time as well as in space.

Virtual teams can be considered one type of application of distributed GSS. They have been defined as a "group of geographically dispersed individuals who are assembled via technology to accomplish an organizational task"; most often they are "project teams, which are time-limited, non-repetitive groups charged with producing a one-time output" (Massey, Montoya-Weiss, and Hung, 2003, p. 130). (Of course, some primarily "virtual" teams may mix face-to-face meetings with technology-mediated meetings, and/or may persist beyond a single project.) A recent literature review of forty-three empirical studies of virtual teams published between 1991 and February 2002 (Powell et al., 2004, p. 7) defined virtual teams more precisely as "groups of geographically, organizationally and/or time dispersed workers brought together by information and telecommunication technologies to accomplish one or more organizational tasks . . ." As Olson and Olson (2000) emphasize, "distance matters"; when group members are not gathered face-to-face, coordination becomes problematical. Coordination mechanisms and tools that "work" or "don't work" in other media tend to have very different effects in the distributed environment.

As Walther, Boos, and Jonas (2002, p. 1) point out, "virtual teams are becoming increasingly common in dispersed organizations, educational settings, and other ventures." They may or may not be "global" (spread over more than one nation) or part of a single permanent organization. In this application of CMC, a group consists of people in different locations working together to complete a joint project, with the time frame usually varying from weeks to months.

Because successful teamwork requires coordination and cooperation, virtual teams need tools and interaction structures that will help them develop and build trust (Jarvenpaa and Leidner, 1999), as well as to work together on several phases or types of tasks from project definition to completion. This might be referred to as the "design" of virtual teams: the provision of various hardware and software tools, and the structuring of their interactions by suggested or enforced processes. The design of virtual team processes is the key research issue that has driven the recent program of NJIT experimental studies, and which will be described in the section of this chapter titled "Overview of Recent Experiments at NJIT." In particular, as Powell, Piccoli, and Ives (2004, p. 9) point out, "designs that foster knowledge sharing . . . benefit the team by ensuring that a common understanding and language is established. Once a shared language is instituted, the members of the virtual team appear to be able to complete ambiguous tasks relying on electronic communication."

Among the other factors that have been found to strongly affect the success of virtual teams are duration (time), size, and leadership. Walther, Boos, and Jonas (2002) point out that the duration of virtual teams has significant effects on how their members relate to and work with one another: Groups that are afforded extended periods have been shown to establish more positive relationships over time, whereas online groups who experience time pressure respond with fewer affective statements, harsher conflict management, and poorer argumentation strategies.

Bradner, Mark, and Hertel (2003) surveyed members of eighteen virtual teams in an international organization, of which some were in relatively small teams of four to nine members, and others in larger teams of fourteen to eighteen members. They found that compared to members of larger teams, members of smaller teams participated more actively, were more committed to their team members and more aware of the team's goals, were better acquainted with other team members' characteristics, and reported higher levels of rapport. This suggests that larger virtual teams will face problems if they use "plain vanilla" CMC without any special tools or procedures. However, whereas experiments with students in virtual teams usually use small groups (e.g., between three and eight members), actual virtual teams in industry have mostly been larger, with all of the published studies having more than eight members, and the average in field studies being twelve to thirteen members. But as Powell et al. (2002, p. 14) point out, "no study [published before 2002] has explicitly examined virtual team size as a variable controlled during the team design phase." As we will see below, one of the recent NJIT studies (Cho, 2004) compares teams of different group size, explicitly examining how team size interacts with the structuring of the team process.

Kayworth and Leidner (2002) studied thirteen culturally diverse global teams, each of which had a project team leader. They observed that highly effective virtual team leaders act in a mentoring role, exhibit a high degree of empathy, and are able to assert their authority without being perceived as overbearing. In addition, effective leaders provided regular, detailed, and prompt communication that coordinated group efforts by articulating the relationships among and the responsibilities of various roles.

The method used to assess the effectiveness of a group support system of any type also seems to be related to whether or not one will obtain significant results. Fjermestad and Hiltz (1999, 2000) analyzed the methods and findings of experimental studies of GSS, and of case and field studies. In examining over one hundred experimental studies, they found that using a GSS usually did not produce statistically significant improvements over unsupported face-to-face meetings. By contrast, the results of fifty-four case and field studies show that the modal outcome for a GSS in field settings is to improve performance relative to manual or other methods (as measured by effectiveness, efficiency, consensus, usability, and satisfaction) in 86.5 percent of the cases. These are much more positive results than have been obtained in laboratory experiments. Among the reasons for this difference are that field studies use participants who are normally engaged in the type of task being performed and who are doing their "real" work, thus providing participants who are motivated to achieve a positive group product, and prepared to participate in its creation. Secondly, field studies do not usually severely constrain the time given to the group, whereas experiments often do. It may take considerable time for group members to become familiar and comfortable with a new set of tools, and thus in a short time frame, they may represent a hindrance rather than a help to the group.

HIGHLIGHTS FROM PRIOR NJIT RESEARCH ON VIRTUAL TEAMS

During the 1980s and early 1990s, a group of NJIT faculty and PhD students began a series of experiments and field studies exploring how best to use computer-mediated communication to provide support for distributed groups interacting primarily asynchronously over the Internet or its predecessors.

NJIT CMC Research Feedback Loop

Over the years our efforts at NJIT have followed the cycle of investigation shown in Figure 6.1.

The hypotheses we developed come from a variety of theories and a recognition of a wide variety of external influencing factors, process-structuring and software-supported tools and roles. To a large degree each investigation followed in the footsteps of earlier efforts; there were a number of underlying themes that remained consistent through all the efforts.

Overview of the First and Second Series of NJIT Studies

The initial series of controlled experiments in the 1980s, conducted before widespread availability of the Internet or PCs, focused on comparing face-to-face with computer-mediated communication,

Figure 6.1   **General Theoretical Model**

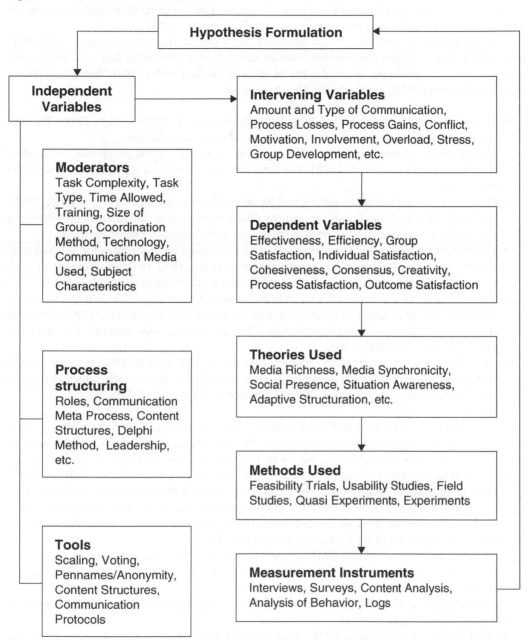

but actually used groups communicating from different rooms in the same building at the same time, because one could not simply give groups a few weeks to interact asynchronously and assume that they could find the equipment or the access. This initial series of three experiments is described in Turoff and Hiltz (1982); Hiltz, Turoff, and Johnson (1986); Hiltz, Johnson, and Turoff (1991); and Hiltz, Turoff, and Johnson (1991). Field studies were the only really possible way of empirically studying asynchronous CMC, since we could make sure in a longer-term field study that the participants had the needed equipment and network access. The extensive field studies included in the first series of NJIT studies were summarized in Turoff et al. (1993).

The second series of studies, which consisted solely of experiments, was reviewed in Hiltz et al. (2001). Each of the second series of studies represented an attempt to find appropriate tools and processes to coordinate different types of tasks in the McGrath (1984) "task circumplex," within a distributed CMC environment. They examined:

- Voting tools and sequential procedures for a preference task (Dufner et al., 1994). The voting tools improved group outcomes but sequential procedures did not.
- Conflict vs. consensus structures, plus experience (first vs. second group task) for a planning task (Fjermestad et al., 1995). The structures did not make a significant difference on effectiveness.
- Question-response tool and a polling tool for an intellective task (peer review) (Rana, 1995). Although these tools produced few positive effects, on the whole, the mode of appropriation by the group was more important than the presence or absence of one of the tools.
- Designated leadership and sequential vs. parallel coordination procedures for a mixed task, that is, choosing a stock portfolio (Kim, 1996; Kim et al., 2002). In terms of quality of decision, parallel communication mode was more effective than sequential mode.
- The effects of face-to-face (FtF) vs. distributed asynchronous CMC as it interacts with a structured design procedure, for software requirements design (Ocker et al., 1995). Although there was no difference in quality of design, CMC groups were more creative; the structured procedures made no difference.
- In a follow-up experiment on the software requirements task, we found that combined media (FtF plus CMC) are more effective than asynchronous CMC alone, which in turn tends to be more effective than synchronous CMC or FtF alone (Ocker et al., 1996).

Most scholars who have spent time developing and studying CMC as a medium for group interaction share the assumption that it can be an effective and sociable form of communication, but they differ on how this can best come about. One group views such systems essentially as a technological mechanism, feeling that effective CMC must be built into a feature-rich and highly structured and restricted environment. The technology can force the group to behave in what are seen as effective ways to use the medium, in order to minimize process losses and maximize process gains, for example, the coordinator (Flores, 1988), or software to force a completely sequential mode of coordination of interaction (Johnson-Lenz, 1991).

A second approach to building CMC systems conceives of them as a context for interaction, "containers" so to speak, just as rooms are. This conception is based on a social theory that human systems are self-organizing and arise out of the unrestricted interaction of autonomous individuals. From this perspective, the role of the computer system is to provide a place for people to meet and self-organize (Johnson-Lenz, 1991).

Regardless of one's leanings, CMC differs greatly from face-to-face communication—for example, see media synchronicity theory (Dennis and Valacich, 1999)—and it takes some time for individuals to effectively learn the mechanics of the system and adjust to the social dynamics of this form of interaction. In an attempt to allow for a period of adjustment, all of our experiments included at least one condition in which groups used asynchronous CMC without time pressure. Asynchronous groups had adequate training and at least a week to complete their discussions and produce their group product or decision.

Conclusions from the Second Series of Experiments

We came away from our second series of experiments with several key realizations, not the least of which was that, with only one exception (Kim, 1996), our attempts at structuring the group interaction process had no significant positive effects on outcomes.

On the other hand, the presence of software tools available for groups' discretionary use did seem to improve the perceived richness of CMC, group processes and the resulting group outcomes.[1] The tools we developed for various experiments in the second series included the ability to build a common list, a set of voting options, a "question-response activity" that structured the exchange of ideas and opinions similarly to nominal group process, the possibility of anonymity, and a "polling" tool that allowed a group to construct any sort of questionnaire type item and display results of the polling.

Experimental results indicated that coordination mechanisms and tools that "work" (or "don't work") in one medium tend to have very different effects in the distributed environment. For example, although Watson (1987) did not find any significant benefits for listing and voting tools in a decision room, Dufner (1995) and Rana (1995) did observe enhancement of results associated with the use of these tools in the distributed mode. We have also consistently found that designated leaders and/or technical facilitators are crucial for coordination in the asynchronous environment, and, as a result, we always provide groups with one or both of these supports.

Given the aforementioned conditions (i.e., small groups given adequate time, training, and designated leaders), it appears that groups do not need a restrictive, "mechanistic" approach to coordinate their efforts. They are capable of organizing themselves. Because of this ability, structures and procedures designed to enhance group performance are often, in actuality, overly restrictive and result in inefficient and frustrating group interaction processes. However, we felt that the situation might be quite different for larger groups.

OVERVIEW OF RECENT EXPERIMENTS AT NJIT

In preparing for the third series of studies, we had to build new software tools, because the CMC software world had changed with the spread of the World Wide Web and full-screen browsers. Given the results from our second series of experiments, we decided to focus on integrating tools and the structuring of interaction processes instead of treating them as two separate approaches. In particular, since virtual teams in real organizations are usually much larger than the four- or five-person groups we had used in the preceding experiments, we planned to use some larger groups and to examine whether structure becomes more helpful as group size increases. The goal was to develop and study some tools and structures that could be used for very large groups or even "publics" (large categories of people with no regular interaction, for example, all the people interested in a particular topic, such as whether the United States should adopt national identity cards); a concept we labeled as "social decision support systems." We also wanted to advance our use of CMC by exploring new possibilities for multimedia communication via the Web and wireless devices, and to examine the effects of cultural heterogeneity on virtual teams.

A summary of the methodology and results of NJIT's 1998–2003 series of five published studies is presented in Tables 6.1 and 6.2. The following sections will explain and discuss selected aspects of these studies in more detail, and will also comment on where we might like to take each line of research in the future, based on the results we obtained. However, before reviewing these published studies, we will describe an experiment that did not work out as anticipated and that forced us to redirect our efforts.

Table 6.1

Methodology, Third Series of Studies

Authors	Technology	Experimental Design	Group Subject Variables and Incentives	TASK/Type	Number of Sessions/ Session Length
Anderson and Hiltz (2001)	CMC: Web-EIES, Level 2, asynchronous, no tools, training—yes.	2 × 2 factorial; communication mode: asynchronous, FtF; group composition: culturally homogeneous, culturally heterogeneous	46 groups; 10 to 15 groups per cell; 5 or 6 subjects per group; 268 total subjects; undergraduates; ad hoc; course credit	Noble industries task; cognitive conflict; Type 5	Asynchronous; 10 days
Li (2003); Wang (2003)	CMC: WebBoard, Level 2, asynchronous, tools: dynamic voting, list; training: online.	2 × 2 factorial; process support—dynamic voting, manual; process support—list tool, manual	33 groups; 8 groups per cell; 4 to 6 subjects per group; 178 total subjects; graduate and undergraduate; ad hoc; 15% course credit	Computer purchasing task; Type 4	Asynchronous sessions; 10 days
Li (2003); Wang (2003) field study	CMC: WebBoard, Level 2, asynchronous, tools: dynamic voting, list; training online.	Field study evaluating the effectiveness of the SDSS toolkit in four online classes	79 total students; graduate students	Course evaluation using SDSS toolkit	Two weeks
Han (2004)	CMC: WebBoard & iPAQ mobile PDA; Level 2; asynchronous and synchronous, tools: IM and chat; training: online and 30 min for PDA	3 × 1; communication mode: asynchronous; combined desktop (asynch/ synch); combined mobile (asynch/synch)	36 groups; 14, 13, 9 groups per cell; 4 or 5 subjects per group; 159 total subjects; graduate and undergraduates; course credit; ad hoc	Exchange student service center; Type 4	Asynchronous: 10 days
Cho et al. (2003); Cho (2004)	CMC: WebBoard; Level 2; asynchronous, pen names; tools: Delphi and no tool; training: Yes	2 × 2 factorial; process structure: Delphi-structure, no-structure; group size: large (12), small (6)	44 groups; 11 per cell; 6 or 12 subjects per group; 396 total subjects; undergraduates; ad hoc; 10% to 20% course credit	Computer chip case; Types 2 & 4	Asynchronous: 17 days

Table 6.2

Results, Third Series of Studies

Authors	Dependent Measures—Outcomes			Comments—Group Process Adaptation	Conclusions
Anderson and Hiltz (2001)		Comm Mode	Group Composition	In terms of influence equality no differences were found based on the cultural composition of the group. It is suggested that since ad hoc culturally heterogeneous groups do not share the same history and values, status differences are minimal and so conformance pressure and evaluation apprehension are less likely to occur. Consequently, it appears that an asynchronous communication system can be used effectively for both culturally homogeneous and culturally heterogeneous ad hoc groups.	The results of this study suggest that mixed cultural groups facing a value-based cognitive conflict (negotiation) may effectively use task-distributed, asynchronous GSS. Finally, on each of the three dependent variables reported in this study, culturally mixed groups equaled U.S. groups, in the asynchronous as well as face-to-face condition. Thus, the practical results of this research are that multicultural groups can succeed online in decision making, at least as well as homogeneous U.S. groups.
	Influence equality:	Ns	Ns		
	Post-meeting consensus:	Ns	Ns		
	Consensus change:	FtF > Asyn	Ns		
Li (2003); Wang (2003)		Process support-Voting	Process support-List	SDSS toolkit was somewhat complex and not very easy to understand, given a relatively short period of time. Since most of the students were already very familiar with the WebBoard conferencing system, which they frequently use for their regular courses, their mental models were more likely to accept the structures of that system. The SDSS toolkit designed and developed by the researchers was not exactly the same as the one in their mental model, and it might take a longer time for subjects to adapt this system.	The results suggest that the Voting and List tool did not improve the overall quality of decision making. However, there was significantly less communication comments (average comment lines) required by the groups using the Voting and List tools.
	Decision quality	Ns	LT > Manual		
	Average Comment Length	VT < Manual	LT < Manual		
	Average comments by leaders	VT < Manual	LT < Manual		
	Participation	Ns	Ns		
	Perceived quality				
	Task effort of decision making	VT < Manual	LT < Manual		
	Solution satisfaction	Ns	Ns		
	Process satisfaction	Ns	Ns		

(continued)

Table 6.2

(continued)

Authors	Dependent Measures—Outcomes	Comments—Group Process Adaptation	Conclusions
Li (2003); Wang (2003)	Each student was asked to suggest only the most important item he or she learned in this course, provided it was different from the items already entered by the other students. The top-rated item is more than two times the scale strength of the second item (16.5:6.78) and the next three items are essentially at the same scaling point, showing an equal rating for the group as a whole for all three items. This demonstrates the power of a good scaling method to provide significant visualization results that aid the group to interpret and understand what their votes means.	The faculty involved felt that this method of evaluating the outcome of a course is far more informative for improving a course than the standard university "student satisfaction" survey. The faculty member finally realized from the discussion that, although the course had devoted only an hour's lecture to the topic of runaways, many students were using it as an organizational framework for the other material in the course. This led to moving the topic up to an earlier part of the course, pointing out some of the relationships to later topics, and referring back to it when discussing other topics in the course.	The results show how one can utilize the new SDSS Toolkit to enhance learning for both face-to-face and distance-learning classes. Assessing the achieved course objectives helps not only the students to review what they have learned, but also the instructors to improve their future teaching.
Han (2004)	Communication Mode Total communication: M > DT, A Creativity: Ns Quality: Ns Perceived media richness: Ns Cue variety: Ns Feedback: Ns Parallelism: Ns Reprocessability: Ns Social presence: Ns Awareness: Ns Group development: Ns Decision satisfaction: Ns Process satisfaction: Ns	Members in the Mobile Chat groups chatted more often than Desktop Chat group members, but their conversations were often not related to work. The Mobile Chat group members had rather short chat sessions but chatted more frequently due to their easy access to MSN Messenger. They spent more time to get to know one another and were less focused on the task.	The major findings were that Mobile Chat groups did have more comments than other conditions, were more highly developed, and had higher social presence as well. Groups with more interaction showed higher social presence and group development. However, the most important practical finding was that mobile groups with higher social presence whose members spent more time interacting performed very poorly on their group decision-making tasks.

	Process structure	Group
Size		
Participation (total):	Ns	M > S
Participation equality:	D > U	M > S
Decision quality (total raw ideas)	D > U	M > S
Total unique ideas	D > U	M > S
Unique ideas (per person):	D > U	S > M
Creativity	Ns	Ns
Quality-report	Ns	Ns
Process satisfaction	Ns	Ns
Cohesiveness:	Ns	Ns

D: Delphi; U: Unstructured; M: Group size 12; S: group size 6

Cho et al. (2003); Cho (2004)

The formal facilitation using Delphi structure effectively improved the productivity of asynchronous groups by helping them generate more ideas. However, informal leadership by group coordinators seems to have played a more important role in helping the groups produce better reports. In terms of per person reports, small-sized groups were more productive, even though medium-sized groups produced more total ideas than small-sized groups. The superiority of Delphi groups and small-sized groups is related to their higher equality of participation. This result suggests that in asynchronous meetings, equal participation of group members in discussion is important in improving idea-generation productivity while in synchronous meetings, the process loss of production blocking plays a crucial role.

Delphi small-sized groups produced significantly more per person rare ideas than the unstructured small-sized groups and the unstructured medium-sized groups produced significantly more per person rare ideas than the unstructured small-sized groups. These interaction effects were also found in terms of the efficiency of rare idea production; in producing rare ideas, the Delphi small-sized groups were significantly more efficient than the unstructured small-sized groups and the unstructured medium-sized groups were significantly more efficient than the unstructured small-sized groups.

Delphi structure is effective in producing more ideas in asynchronous meetings. In asynchronous group communication environments, the groups facilitated by Delphi structure produced significantly more total unique ideas and more total rare ideas than unstructured groups having no facilitation supports. The members of the medium-sized groups participated in discussion more equally than the members of the small-sized groups. The evaluation of the quality/creativity of ideas and quality of report found no significant differences between the small-sized groups and the medium-sized groups. There was no difference on process satisfaction and cohesiveness between the small-sized and medium-sized groups.

The members of Delphi groups participated in discussion more equally than did those in unstructured groups. There were significant positive correlations between the equality of participation and the total number of raw ideas or the total number of unique ideas in discussion.

Table 6.3

Multimedia Experimental Design

Condition	Number of Groups	1-Hour Synchronous Meeting	14 Days of Asynchronous Discussions
Desktop Video Conferencing	5	Distributed Audio and Video	WebBoard
Audio	5	Distributed Audio	WebBoard
Face-to-Face	7	Face-to-Face	WebBoard
Asynchronous Only	7	No Meeting	WebBoard

An Aborted Experiment on Multimedia

In 1998, when we received funding for a new series of studies, we were enthusiastic about building on our prior studies of media mixes for distributed groups by replacing virtual teams' initial face-to-face meetings with newly developed Web-based audio conferences and video conferences. However, our results were not at all what we had expected. When we checked them midway through the planned experiment, we decided to abort this line of study and concentrate on other issues.

The experiment employed a single factor design consisting of four levels (Table 6.3). The independent variable, communication mode, had three conditions: an initial meeting via distributed audio conferencing, distributed video conferencing or synchronous face-to-face, each combined with subsequent asynchronous CMC Web-based conferencing. The fourth condition (control) was asynchronous CMC Web-based conferencing without any initial synchronous session. We replicated the group size (5) and the task that had been used in Ocker et al. (1996), a modified version of development of software requirements for a computerized post office that had previously used by Olson et al. (1993), so that the results would be comparable.

Hypotheses

Based on media richness theory (Daft and Lengel, 1986) and our previous experiments on mixes of face-to-face and asynchronous meetings, we expected:

- Decision quality will be higher in the lower-bandwidth conditions (initial meeting: audio or asynchronous CMC alone) than for the high-bandwidth conditions (initial meeting: face-to-face or desktop video conferencing).
- Group development will be higher in the higher-bandwidth conditions (initial meeting face-to-face or desktop video conferencing) than for the lower-bandwidth conditions (initial meeting audio or asynchronous CMC alone).
- Process satisfaction will be higher in the higher-bandwidth conditions (initial meeting face-to-face or desktop video conferencing) than for the lower bandwidth conditions (initial meeting audio or asynchronous CMC alone).

However, we observed tremendous variance in the quality and reliability of the Web-based audio and video conditions. In particular, the Web often seemed to "slow down," and the audio track skipped sound segments or became distorted. There seemed to be even more variance in groups' willingness or ability to deal with technical shortcomings. Some groups cheerfully worked around the difficulties and carried on as some of their members temporarily dropped out and reconnected. Others were very intolerant of any degradation in audio quality, taking off their earphones, complaining that "this does not work," and refusing to continue. What individual differences in physiology or personality account for this difference in tolerance for "less than (hard wired) telephone quality" audio signals is an interesting question, which we did not anticipate. There were also some cultural differences; people of some nationalities tend to talk very quickly or very softly, and their speech was more likely to be difficult to understand when digitized over the Internet.

When we paused the experiment midway through the planned number of groups to see what the data were showing us, we found that there was indeed large statistical variance within conditions, and no significant differences among conditions. Thus, we concluded that, as of the year 2000 at least, desktop Web-based audio conferencing for medium- or large-sized groups was "not yet ready for prime time," and we dropped further experimentation with such conditions until such time as Internet2 and other technical advances may give distributed users reliable service with few technical difficulties. (Given the improvements in Web-based digital audio or video meeting systems since 2000, groups probably could manage to succeed more consistently with them now, especially if they have "back-up" technologies such as conference calls; this would be worth studying again).

Cultural Heterogeneity in Virtual Teams

As Watson, Ho, and Raman (1994, p. 54) note, "Cross-cultural studies of GSS technology are highly relevant to a post-industrial society in which managerial teams, often composed of individuals from different national cultures, will make extensive use of information technology to support group decision-making." Jessup and Valacich (1993) recommended that the future GSS research should focus primarily on issues related to the group, rather than the technology, such as the impact of cultural norms, values, and processes. Despite the potential importance of cultural composition to the process and outcomes of groups using group support systems, very few studies have focused on this variable. The review by Fjermestad and Hiltz (1999) of approximately two hundred published GSS experiments identified only six studies where either ethnic diversity or culture was used as an independent variable. All six of these studies involved the use of synchronous (decision room) systems, and none of them compared culturally homogeneous to culturally heterogeneous groups.

The experiment conducted by Anderson (2000; see also Anderson and Hiltz, 2001) had a 2 × 2 design, comparing culturally homogeneous (all U.S. citizens) teams with culturally heterogeneous teams, in face-to-face vs. asynchronous CMC meetings. Classification as a "non-American" was done based on cultural identity (place of birth, number of years living in the United States, and cultural self-identification). The heterogeneous groups were designed to be as mixed as possible, representing individuals from many different national and cultural backgrounds; some of the heterogeneous groups included Americans. The group size was six, but some of the asynchronous groups lost one member during the period of online group work. The subjects, consisting of a total of 175 subjects from thirty-nine countries, were NJIT undergraduates, mainly majoring in information systems, computer science, or management.

The task was specifically designed for the study. Called "Noble Industries," it was a value-laden cognitive conflict task specifically designed to elicit diverse opinions from subjects based on their cultural backgrounds. The scenario described an IS division in a medium-sized company facing the possibility of downsizing; subjects individually decided the rank order in which ten employees would be laid off, if necessary, and then the group was required to try to reach consensus on the rank order of firing. The hypothetical supervisor's descriptions of each employee presented five employees described at one pole of Hofstede's (1980) and Bond's (1988) five dimensions of culture (individualism/collectivism, power distance, uncertainty avoidance, masculinity/femininity, and Confucian dynamism), while the other five employees were described as being at the other pole. Basic demographic information about each employee (job title, years of service, education, and number of dependents) was also included. The purpose of the task was to force subjects to make a judgment based on their cultural values and also create an environment where value-based cultural differences would serve as the basis for conflict.

Generally, no statistically significant differences were found among conditions in the major dependent variables—that is, influence equality within the groups, post-meeting consensus, and consensus change—except that asynchronous groups did have a lower amount of consensus change than FtF groups. A pessimistic interpretation of these results is that despite a relatively large number of subjects, there was not enough statistical power to obtain significant results. The optimistic interpretation of the results is that asynchronous CMC can be used by culturally heterogeneous teams just as effectively as by culturally homogeneous teams.

As for following up on this experiment: Due to the questionable validity of using undergraduate students to represent members of Global Virtual Teams, we would like to replicate the study of culturally heterogeneous vs. culturally homogenous teams in a field study, should we find the opportunity to do so.

Social Decision Support Systems (SDSS)

Turoff et al. (2002) proposed the concept of a social decision support system as an instrument to promote a large-scale consensus, or at least an understanding by a populace of the complex problems facing post-industrial society. It is a type of inquiry system that supports the investigation of complex topics by large groups that hold many diverse and opposing views. The objective of such a system is to facilitate the integration of diverse views into an evolving, collaborative knowledge base.

The SDSS toolkit contains the initial set of collaborative tools developed to enhance the group process so that:

- All participants can come to respect and understand the differences caused by diverse values and interests of the contributing population
- There can be a movement towards consensus on at least some of the issues involved
- There is limited need for human facilitation of the meta-process of communication, which is replaced by dynamic voting processes

As stated in adaptive structuration theory (AST; DeSanctis and Poole, 1991), groups will not always use coordination structures designed with a deterministic view in ways intended by system designers. They will actively choose appropriate (or inappropriate) technology to fit their own needs. The SDSS toolkit is flexible enough for groups easily to adjust their contributions and indicate relationships among them. The SDSS toolkit, designed and developed as a collaborative effort by Li and Wang (2003) has two major parts to support two processes: a list-gathering tool for collecting all the options or actions that may be available (Wang, 2003) and the dynamic voting tool (Li, 2003).

Design and Experimentation on the List-Gathering and Dynamic-Voting Tools

The main objective of this controlled experiment was to examine the ability of two group process support tools to enhance the effectiveness of group decision making. The list-gathering tool was designed to help a group of users to collaboratively pull their ideas together and organize those ideas into a common list, which produces a group view or perspective. Groups can build several related lists (e.g., a list of tasks to accomplish, a list of goals to achieve, and so forth). Within each list, group members can also vote on items in the list. The dynamic voting tool was designed to solicit individual preferences on the formed lists, and then help form group preferences. Rather than a simple tool that provides majority voting or simple ranking, the dynamic voting tool integrates several major voting and scaling methods. It supports "yes/no," rank order, Likert scales, semantic differential scaling methods, and different voting methods such as plurality voting and approval voting. During a group process, members can repeatedly alter their votes (which represents their current mind-set/understanding at a particular point in time). Dynamic voting is designed to improve the group process by providing a feedback mechanism on group preferences.

Procedures and Experimental Design. A field experiment used a 2 × 2 factorial design (vote tool, no tool; list tool, no list tool). The experiment included thirty-three groups (eight groups per cell) with between five and seven subjects per group randomly assigned to each condition. The 178 student subjects were a combination of graduate and undergraduate students. All groups were ad hoc and received 15 percent course credit for participation. All subjects completed an asynchronous, Web-based training exercise prior to participating in the experiment.

A computer-purchasing task was used in this experiment. This was a decision-making task (type 4) (McGrath, 1984), where groups are to develop consensus on issues that do not have correct answers. The answers are open-ended and the quality of the decision making has to be judged by experts in the field. The task took ten business days to complete.

Selected Hypotheses. The basic hypotheses fall into three categories: decision quality (perceived and judged), satisfaction, and communication (comments). It was hypothesized that:

- The decision quality and satisfaction of groups supported by either tool would be higher than groups not using a tool
- There would be an interaction effect such that groups using both tools would be disproportionately higher in terms of both quality and satisfaction
- The amount of communication among groups supported by either tool would be less than groups not using a tool

Results. Contrary to many of these expectations, there were very few differences between the conditions. Teams using the list tool had significantly better decision quality, as measured by the expert judges, than the teams with only manual support. There were no differences related to the voting tool. As predicted, communication (as measured by average comment length) was significantly less for the SDSS toolkit teams than manual teams. There were no interaction effects.

After obtaining these somewhat disappointing results, we discussed the possible reasons. Even though the task had been rated in pilots as "interesting," students had not seemed very motivated. In addition, the overhead of learning new tools did not seem to be "worth it" or necessarily helpful for groups of only five to seven. We thus decided to conduct field trials with larger groups engaged in a task that was more "real" and relevant to them.

Field Studies of the SDSS System

The SDSS system has been used in a field study mode in five different graduate courses to allow students to propose the important things they have learned in a course and to rank order them

(Wang et al., 2003). Thurstone's law of comparative judgment can then be used to translate rank orders into a single group interval scale for the group as a whole (Li et al., 2001; Thurstone 1927).

In all the case studies of this type, most of the students participated actively and enthusiastically, since the task related to the work they had been doing in their course. This field trial produced unanticipated results: In all five cases, the students ranked things highly that the faculty member teaching the course did not expect. For example in CIS 679 (management of information systems) the highest-ranking item was "runaway projects," to which the faculty member had devoted only one hour in the course lectures. The Thurstone scale showed this topic to be more than twice as important as the second most important item. It took the review of the student discussion about this item to determine that the students had adopted it as a framework for classifying problems discussed in the course. This has caused the faculty member to change when and how this subject is now introduced in the course.

The faculty members involved felt that these evaluations helped them improve their courses much more than the standard "student satisfaction" surveys that universities now commonly use. We were generally encouraged by the results of these field trials and hope to study some more applications of the SDSS to groups sized twenty to approximately two hundred in the future.

The Impacts of Delphi Communication Structure on Small and Medium-Sized Asynchronous Virtual Teams

The Delphi method was created in the 1950s at the RAND Corporation to allow large groups of experts to collectively examine complex problems (Linstone and Turoff, 1975). It was named after the Greek oracle at Delphi because it was often used to predict future technological break-throughs. The technique structures and facilitates written, asynchronous communication among a large problem-solving group so that it is tailored to the nature of the problem, the characteristics of the group, and the objectives of the problem-solving exercise.

The Delphi technique has been employed to obtain physically dispersed experts' judgments or opinions on a particular topic by combining a set of carefully designed sequential questionnaires with summarized information and opinions derived from earlier responses (Turoff, 1970). Delphi achieves consistency by using feedback, anonymity, and iteration to reduce biases of individual and group intuitions (Linstone and Turoff, 1975).

Participants conduct controlled discussions by means of Delphi's group feedback mechanism. Previous literature introduced two kinds of feedback: outcome feedback providing the result of a group decision-making process, and cognitive feedback clarifying the decision maker's intentions. In general, previous research showed that outcome feedback did not help GSS groups achieve better outcomes, although cognitive feedback did (Bose and Paradice, 1999; Hiltz et al., 1991; Harmon and Rohrbaugh, 1990; Sengupta and Te'eni, 1993). This suggests that the true benefit of the Delphi technique may come from qualitative comments reflecting the insights of group members, combined with quantitative judgments.

Experimental Design and Procedures

The main objective of this experiment, conducted by Cho (2003), was to examine the interaction of group size with the effectiveness of a Delphi structure (Cho, 2004). The experiment used a 2×2 factorial design, which crossed process structure (Delphi structure, no imposed structure) with group size (small groups with five or six members, medium groups with ten to twelve members). In total, 396 subjects (eleven groups per condition) were recruited from undergraduate level courses. Their incentive to participate in the experiment was 10 to 20 percent of the course grade; an alternative assignment was offered. The experiment lasted two and a half weeks.

The task was the Special Technology, Inc., case, which presented a scenario involving a computer chip manufacturing company that had just developed a pill-sized object-tracking device. Groups were asked to generate as many possible applications of such a device as they could, to develop the positive and negative consequences of each application, and to rank on a three-point scale each application's potential impact on U.S. society. This task corresponds to the combination of a creativity task (Type 2) and a decision-making task (Type 4) of McGrath's Task circumplex (McGrath, 1984).

A WebBoard asynchronous group communication discussion board was assigned to each group. Before the task was posted, group members were instructed to log in to the discussion board and select a group coordinator. The group coordinator was responsible for distributing the workload of writing a group report to every member and ensuring that the group report was submitted on time. Pen names allowed members in both the Delphi and the unstructured conditions to remain anonymous.

The Delphi process as instantiated in this experiment is as follows:

- Anonymity: This study uses pen names.
- Facilitation: A human facilitator designs the procedure and instructions, and aggregates responses. Automated facilitation functions support nominal idea generation, group feedback, and controlled discussion (e.g., only when all group members had posted their initial ideas could other participants view them.).
- Delivery: A combination of an asynchronous CMC (WebBoard) and survey software (Survey Tracker) is used.
- Nominal idea generation: Participants post their ideas in a moderated asynchronous conference.
- The group feedback facilitator approves and reveals the list of items group members generate. The facilitator generates a report of voting results using SurveyTracker and posts the URL of the report in the WebBoard; participants comment on others' ideas.
- Iteration: A sequence of instructions is posted in a conference. Two rounds of voting are used.

Hypotheses and Results

Due to the enforced individual initial contribution, members of Delphi groups are expected to participate more in group discussion regardless of their status or personal predispositions, because this structure provides equal opportunity for every member to express his or her opinion on the issue. Since small groups tend to have less free riding than medium-sized groups, the members in a small group are expected to participate more equally, even without Delphi structuring. However, the individual idea generation phase of Delphi should make members in medium-sized or large groups participate much more equally than members of small groups, who might feel a greater commitment to their efforts. From the above reasoning, hypotheses included:

- The unstructured asynchronous groups will participate in discussion less equally than the Delphi groups.
- Medium-sized groups will participate in discussion less equally than small groups.
- Delphi will have a greater impact on equality in medium-sized groups than in small groups.

Van de Ven and Delbecq (1971) stated that based on three measures of performance (the number of unique ideas per person, the mean total number of ideas, and the quality of ideas produced), nominal groups (groups wherein each member generates ideas alone without interacting with other members, as in the initial phase of this Delphi structure) have been found to be significantly superior to interacting groups. Therefore, it was hypothesized that:

- The Delphi groups will produce more raw ideas, more unique ideas per group, more raw ideas per person, and more rare (i.e., creative, occurring only in one or two groups) ideas than the unstructured asynchronous groups.
- The medium-sized groups will produce more raw ideas and more unique ideas, but fewer unique ideas per person and fewer rare ideas per person than the small groups.
- Communication structure interacts with group size so that the medium-sized Delphi groups will produce disproportionately more rare ideas per person than the small Delphi groups.

The results support the majority of the hypotheses in that Delphi teams demonstrated significantly greater participation equality than the unstructured teams. Surprisingly, the medium-sized teams (12 members) had greater participation equality than did the smaller teams (6 members). In terms of decision quality, as measured by the number of raw ideas, unique ideas, and unique ideas per person, the Delphi teams outperformed the unstructured teams and the medium-sized teams outperformed the smaller teams. There were no significant differences observed for creativity, quality of the report, process satisfaction, or cohesiveness.

In the future, we would like to apply the online Delphi techniques used in this study to some very large groups of people, perhaps in combination with the listing and voting tools described in the preceding section. There is still much to be learned about how to effectively structure and support the interaction process among groups consisting of hundreds or even thousands of participants.

Virtual Teams Combining Mobile Devices with Web-Based Communication on Group Decision Making

This was a study of a new technology, a mobile device with a wireless Internet connection, combined with the use of asynchronous and/or synchronous CMC by virtual teams (Han, 2004). The main research question investigated whether teams that can communicate "anytime, anywhere" using small devices with wireless Internet connections perform better than those restricted to desktops using wired Internet service. A second, related question focused on how groups using only the asynchronous communication mode differ from groups using both asynchronous and synchronous modes, when all communication is text based.

This experiment looked at how different communication devices and modes affect the process and outcome of distributed group work, investigating efficiency, productivity, interaction, and satisfaction, particularly as related to pervasive computing technologies.

The basic model is shown in Figure 6.2. In addition, theories related to media richness, media synchronicity, social presence, and awareness were adopted to test whether there is any difference among different communication devices and modes.

Experimental Design

The two independent variables are (1) communication mode (asynchronous only or asynchronous and synchronous combined) and (2) communication devices (desktop condition only or desktop and mobile combined). There are three different treatments for groups: (1) groups without mobile devices using asynchronous communication only, called "asynchronous" in this study; (2) groups

Figure 6.2   **Research Framework for the Study of Mobile Device Use by Virtual Teams**

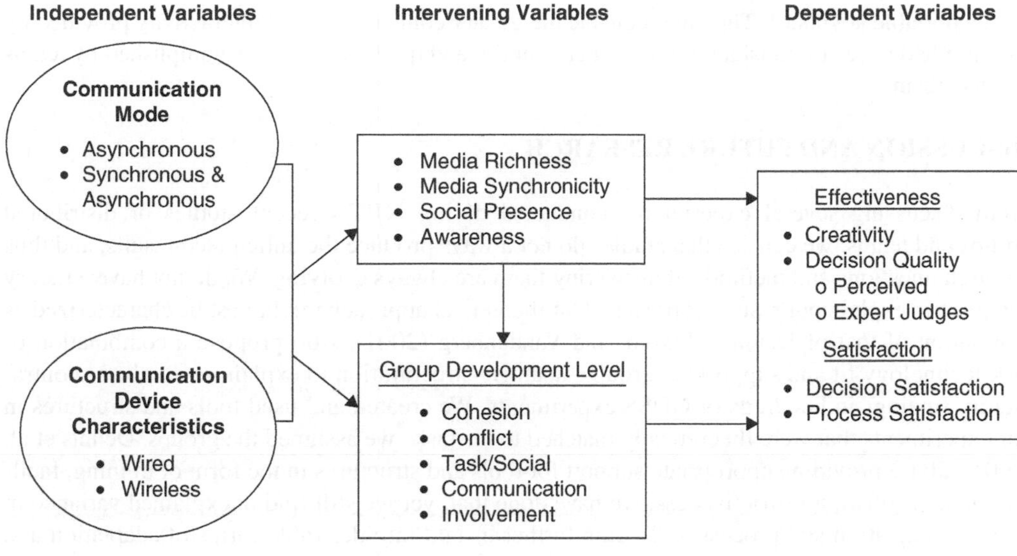

Source: Han, 2004.

without mobile devices using both asynchronous and synchronous communication, called "desktop chat"; and (3) groups with mobile devices using both asynchronous and synchronous communication, called "mobile chat."

A total of 159 graduate and undergraduate students in information systems were assigned to thirty-six groups consisting of either four or five subjects per team. The students received course credit for their participation in this ten-day experiment. The experimental task was called "Exchange Student Service Center," for which the subjects had to design a Web site and deliver a final report. The deliverables included (1) requirement specifications, (2) user interface design, (3) business case analyses, and (4) priority strategies.

The technology used by all groups for their asynchronous communications was WebBoard, and all groups had access to desktop PCs. Compaq iPAQ pocket PCs were used for mobile communication with either AT&T's or Verizon's wireless service. Microsoft Networking (MSN) was the instant messaging feature used in the experiment.

The basic hypotheses were derived from media richness theory (Daft and Lengel, 1986) which suggests that the richer medium—in this case, mobile chat—will significantly improve levels of the dependent variables compared to the less rich media—here, desktop chat and asynchronous discussion only. The results (see Table 6.2) suggest that that are no significant differences among these three levels of the independent variables for most of the dependent variables, including quality of the team product and subjective satisfaction. The one significant difference is in total communication, where mobile chat outperformed desktop chat and asynchronous-only teams. Mobile chat groups did have more comments than other conditions, were more highly developed, and had higher social presence. However, looking at the content of their chat sessions (which they were required to record), we found that social conversation dominated the interaction when mobile devices were used for chat. We speculate that this is because the tiny display and keyboard on the devices makes it difficult to do anything "serious" or lengthy. In future studies, we plan to replace the small iPAQs with light tablet PCs that are wireless and Web-enabled for portable use, but also have a portable keyboard. This might enable the greater connectivity and interactivity provided by the mobile devices to translate into a greater quantity and quality of work accomplished by teams that use them.

DISCUSSION AND FUTURE RESEARCH

From discussing several experiments conducted during NJIT's recent studies of distributed groups and teams, we can see that studies do not always produce the anticipated results, and thus research questions and methods of answering them are always evolving. We do not have a theory adequate to explain our results at present. Our theoretical approach might best be characterized as a variation of that of Dennis, Wixom, and Vandenberg (2001), who propose a combination of task-technology fit and support for groups' adaptive structuration to explain researchers' contradictory findings in hundreds of GDSS experiments. We created and used tools and structures in our experiments that were theoretically matched to the tasks we assigned the groups. Dennis et al. (2001) advise providing appropriate support for tools and structures in the form of training, facilitation, and software restrictiveness; we have done that, yet we still find unexplained variance in groups' adaptation and processes. To gain further insight into desirable forms of adaptation and structuration, we are qualitatively analyzing virtual team transcripts. We expect that by delving into the heretofore black box of team interaction, rich insight can be gained (cf. Ocker's 2005 interpretive study on creativity in virtual teams). By comparing and contrasting the interaction process of teams that had different performance outcomes (e.g., high, medium, and low), we hope to discern patterns of interaction and appropriation that inform our understanding beyond that obtained from a strict reliance on quantitative analysis.

To obtain sufficient participants for our controlled experiments, we had to use students as subjects. In the near future we plan to return to field studies, where we can address issues of the generalizability of the results of our experiments. More importantly, we suspect that many of our inconsistent results are due to many of our experimental groups' lack of motivation to do a good job. Subjects often seemed to do just enough to obtain a good grade for their participation, on tasks that were not "real" for them. We also plan to do more studies on medium- to large-sized groups, since they seem to benefit most from tools and structures. These methodological changes are related, since if one is going to use groups of, say, ten to one hundred, it is not practical to obtain enough of them to conduct controlled experiments.

We are also considering what kinds of tools and support structures we would like to try to create in the future, and how to study and improve their effectiveness. Much literature on computer-mediated communications, even some of our own, has utilized the morphology of same time/different time and same place/different place. This gives the impression that we are talking about four different technologies. There are a number of reasons why this is a mistake in terms of guiding research:

- In the real world, teams will not use four different technologies to carry out their communications about a task. They wish to have a system, an interface, and a technology that can service any of these modes. It should not matter if they are in a single room or dispersed around the world, or if they are there at the same time or interacting asynchronously. They want a system that will serve any of these modes of communication.
- CMC users will also demand a system that integrates all of the group's work materials. As part of their ongoing discussions, they will want to link dynamically to databases, digitized

drawings, or any other computer-stored knowledge and resources, and they will want to see current data displayed when links are triggered within comments. People will not want to interrupt their review of the ongoing discussion to obtain separately the relevant organizational data.

- Users will expect to be able to use decision support tools such as scaling methods to improve group understanding. Voting to guide the discussion should work in a similar dynamic manner, where participants may change their votes in response to the ongoing communication process (Turoff, 1990; Turoff et al. 2001).
- Support tools will include forms of content organization that provide numerous nonlinear options that diverge from the current discussion thread. These will allow people to use shared cognitive maps of a problem area to organize and filter their presentation and comprehension of the discussion (Catanio et al., 2003).

Technology is evolving to accommodate these requirements. CMC systems are becoming fully Web compatible and allow for embedded functionality via object-oriented development environments. To date, many research efforts have ignored the supporting and inference processes that accompany the real-world mix of communications and data that can support a task group.

The same sort of division takes place in task classifications, where we study different communication process objectives, such as creativity or negotiation, in an isolated manner, without recognizing that real group problem solving involves a host of different communication objectives mixed together as one holistic process. Future research is needed that situates technological understanding in the context of realistic problem solving by real groups; this applies for the whole "life cycle" of a project conducted by a virtual team or virtual organization.

ACKNOWLEDGMENTS

The recent (third) series of studies described in this chapter were partially supported by the National Science Foundation (CISE–ITO 9732354 and 9818309) and the New Jersey Commission on Science and Technology, through the New Jersey Center for Pervasive Information Technology; the opinions are solely those of the authors and do not necessarily represent those of the sponsors.

The research reported in the section titled "Overview of Recent Experiments at NJIT" was carried out by our PhD students (for whom the authors served as advisors and committee members): William Anderson (currently acting vice president for Academic and Student Services at NJIT), Hee-Kyung Cho (currently assistant professor at Fairleigh Dickinson University), Hyo-Joo Han (now at the University of Southern Georgia), Zheng Li (now at Pace University), and Yuanquiong Wang (now at Towson State University). It should be noted that prior to 2001, all of our PhD students were part of the joint Rutgers-NJIT PhD program in management of information systems, a long-standing and fruitful partnership for which we are grateful. We also thank our reviewers, who made many excellent suggestions to help improve this chapter.

NOTE

1. A theoretical premise was that one must select the tools made available to the group very carefully, matching them to the nature of the task and the size and characteristics of the group.

REFERENCES

Anderson, W.N. *Cultural Values and Communication Mode: A Study of Culturally Homogeneous and Culturally Heterogeneous Groups*. PhD dissertation, Rutgers University, Newark NJ, 2000.

Anderson, W.N., and Hiltz, S.R. Culturally heterogeneous vs. culturally homogeneous groups in distributed group support systems: effects on group process and consensus. In *Proceedings of the 34th Hawaii International Conference on Systems Sciences*. CD-ROM. Los Alamitos, CA: IEEE Computer Society Press, 2001.

Anson, R.; Bostrom, R.; and Wynne, B. An experiment assessing GSS and facilitator effects on meeting outcomes. *Management Science,* 41, 2 (1995), 189–208.

Bond, M.H. Finding universal dimensions of variation in multicultural studies of values: the Rokeach and Chinese value surveys. *Journal of Personality and Social Psychology,* 55, 6 (1988), 1009–1015.

Bose, U., and Paradice, D. The effects of integrating cognitive feedback and multi-attribute utility-based multicriteria decision-making methods in GDSS. *Group Decision and Negotiation,* 8, (1999), 554–571.

Bradner, E.; Mark, G.; and Hertel, T.D. Effects of team size on participation, awareness and technology choice in geographically distributed teams. In *Proceedings of the Thirty-Sixth Hawaii International Conference on System Sciences*. CD-ROM. Los Alamitos, CA: IEEE Computer Society Press, 2003.

Catanio, J.; Bieber, M.; Im, I.; Paul, R.; Yoo, J.; Ghoda, A.; Pal, A.; and Yetim, F. Relationship analysis: a research plan for enhancing systems analysis for web development. In *Proceedings of the 36th Hawaii International Conference on System Sciences*. CD-ROM. Los Alamitos, CA: IEEE Computer Society Press, 2003.

Cho, H. Delphi structure and group size in asynchronous computer mediated communications. In *Proceedings of the Americas Conference on Information Systems*. CD-ROM. Atlanta, GA: The Association for Information Systems, 2003.

Cho, H. The effect of Delphi structure on small and medium-sized asynchronous groups. PhD dissertation, New Jersey Institute of Technology, 2004 (available at http://www.library.njit.edu/etd/index.cfm, accessed on November 20, 2005).

Daft, R.L., and Lengel, R.H. Organizational information requirements, media richness and structural design. *Management Science,* 32, (1986), 554–571.

Dennis, A.R., and Valacich, J.S. Rethinking media richness: towards a theory of synchronicity. In *Proceedings of the Thirty-Second Hawaii International Conference on Systems Sciences*. CD-ROM. Los Alamitos, CA: IEEE Computer Society Press, 1999.

Dennis, A.R.; Wixom, B.H.; and Vandenberg, R.J. Understanding fit and appropriation effects in group support systems via meta-analysis. *MIS Quarterly,* 25, 2 (2001), 167–194.

DeSanctis, G., and Gallupe, R.B. A foundation for the study of group decision support systems. *Management Science,* 33, 5 (1987), 589–609.

DeSanctis, G., and Poole, S. Understanding the difference in collaborative systems use through appropriation analysis. In *Proceedings of the Twenty Fourth Hawaii International Conference on System Sciences,* Los Alamitos, CA: IEEE Computer Society Press, 1991, pp. 547–553.

Dickson, G.; Partridge, J.; and Robinson, L. Exploring modes of facilitative support for GDSS technology. *MIS Quarterly,* 17, 2 (1993), 173–192.

Dufner, D.K. *The Effects of Group Support (Listing and Voting Tools) and Sequential Procedures on Group Decision Making Using Asynchronous Computer Conferencing*. PhD dissertation, Rutgers University, Newark NJ, 1995.

Dufner, D.; Hiltz, S.R.; and Turoff, M. Distributed group support: a preliminary analysis of the effects of the use of voting tools and sequential procedures. In *Proceedings of the Twenty-Seventh Hawaii International Conference on System Sciences,* Vol. IV. Washington, DC: IEEE Computer Society Press, 1994, pp. 114–123.

Fjermestad, J.; Hiltz, S.R.; Turoff, M.; Ford, C.; Johnson, K.; Czech, R.M.; Ocker, R.; Ferront, F.; and Worrell, M. Distributed computer supported cooperative strategic decision making using structured conflict and consensus approaches. In *Proceedings of the Twenty-Eighth Hawaii International Conference on Systems Sciences*. CD-ROM. Washington, DC: IEEE Computer Society Press, 1995.

Fjermestad, J., and Hiltz, S.R. An assessment of group support systems experimental research: methodology and results. *Journal of Management Information Systems,* 15, 3 (Winter 1998–99), 7–149.

Fjermestad, J., and Hiltz, S.R. Group support systems: a descriptive evaluation of case and field studies. *Journal of Management Information Systems,* 17, 3 (2000), 112–157.

Han, H.-J. *Virtual Teams Combining Mobile Devices with Web-Based Communication for Group Decision Making*. PhD dissertation, NJIT, Newark, NJ. 2004.

Harmon, J., and Rohrbaugh, J. Social judgment analysis and small group decision making: cognitive feedback effects on Individual and collective performance. *Organizational Behavior and Human Decision Processes,* 46, (1990), 34–54.

Hiltz, S.R.; Johnson, K., and Turoff, M. Group decision support: the effect of a designated leader and statistical feedback in computerized conferences. *Journal of Management Information Systems,* 8, 2 (1991), 81–108.

Hiltz, S.R.; Turoff, M., and Johnson, K.J. Experiments in group communication via computer, 1: face-to-face vs. computer conferences. *Human Communication Research,* 13, 2 (1986), 225–252.

Hiltz, S.R., and Turoff, M., *The Network Nation: Human Communication via Computer.* Revised ed. Cambridge, MA: MIT Press, 1992.

Hiltz, S.R., and Turoff, M. Structuring computer-mediated communication systems to avoid information overload. *Communications of the ACM,* 28, 7 (1985), 680–689.

Hofstede, G. *Culture's Consequences: International Differences In Work-Related Values,* Beverly Hills, CA: Sage, 1980.

Jarvenpaa, S., and Leidner, D. Communication and trust in global virtual teams. *Organization Science,* 10, 6 (1999), 791–815.

Jessup, L.M., and J.S. Valacich, Future directions and challenges in the evolution of group support systems. In L.M. Jessup and J.S. Valacich (eds.), *Group Support Systems, New Perspectives.* New York: Macmillan, 1993, pp. 311–318.

Johnson-Lenz, P., and Johnson-Lenz, T. Post mechanistic groupware primitives: Rhythms, boundaries and containers. *International Journal of Man-Machine Studies,* 34, (1991), 395–417.

Kayworth, T. R., and Leidner, D.E. Leadership effectiveness in global virtual teams. *Journal of Management Information Systems,* 18, 3 (2001–2002), 7–40.

Kerr, E.B., and Hiltz, S.R. *Computer-Mediated Communication Systems: Status and Evaluation.* New York, NY: Academic Press, 1982.

Kim, Y.J. *Coordination in Distributed Group Support Systems: A Controlled Experiment Comparing Parallel and Sequential Processes.* PhD dissertation, Rutgers University, 1996.

Kim, Y.; Hiltz, S.R.; and Turoff, M. Coordination structures and system restrictiveness in distributed group support systems. *Group Decision and Negotiation,* 11, 5 (2002), 379–404.

Li, Z. *Design and Evaluation of a Voting Tool in a Collaborative Environment,* PhD dissertation, New Jersey Institute of Technology 2003 (available at http://www.library.njit.edu/etd/index.cfm, accessed on November 20, 2005).

Li, Z.; Cheng, K.; Wang, Y.; Hiltz, S.R.; and Turoff, M. Thurston's law of comparative judgment for group support. In *Proceedings of the Americas Conference on Information Systems.* CD-ROM. Atlanta, GA: The Association for Information Systems, 2001.

Linstone, H., and Turoff, M. *The Delphi Method: Techniques and Applications.* Reading MA: Addison-Wesley Advanced Book Program, 1975 (available at http://is.nit.edu/turoff/#db, accessed November 20, 2005).

Massey, A.P.; Montoya-Weiss, M.M.; and Hung, Y.T. Because time matters: temporal coordination in global virtual project teams. *Journal of Management Information Systems,* 19, 4 (2003), 129–156.

McGrath, J.E. *Groups: Interaction and Performance.* Englewood Cliffs, NJ: Prentice-Hall, 1984.

Ocker, R. *Requirements Definition Using a Distributed Asynchronous Group Support System: Experimental Results on Quality, Creativity and Satisfaction.* PhD dissertation, Rutgers University, 1995.

Ocker, R.J. Influences on creativity in asynchronous virtual teams: a qualitative analysis of experimental teams, *IEEE Transactions on Professional Communication,* 48, 1 (2005), 22–39.

Ocker, R.; Hiltz, S.R.; Turoff, M.; and Fjermestad, J. The effects of distributed group support and process structuring on software requirements development teams. *Journal of Management Information Systems,* 12, 3 (1996), 127–153.

Ocker, R.J.; Fjermestad, J.; Hiltz, S.R.; and Johnson, K. Effects of four modes of group communication on the outcomes of software requirements determination. *Journal of Management Information Systems,* 15, 1 (1998), 99–118.

Olson, G.M., and Olson, J.S. Distance matters. *Human-Computer Interaction,* 15 (2000), 139–179.

Olson, J.S.; Olson, G.M.; Storrøsten, M.; and Carter, M. Group work close up: a comparison of the group design process with and without a simple group editor. *ACM: Transactions on Information Systems,* 11 (1993), 321–348.

Powell, A.; Piccoli, G.; and Ives, B. Virtual teams: A review of current literature and directions for future research. *The DATA BASE for Advances in Information Systems,* 35, 1 (2004), 6–36.

Rana, A.R. *Peer Review Processes and Group Support Systems: Theory Development and Experimental Validation.* PhD dissertation, Rutgers University. 1995.

Rana, A.R.; Turoff, M.; and Hiltz, S.R. Task and technology interaction (TTI): a theory of technological support for group tasks. In *Proceedings, Hawaii International Conference on Systems Sciences.* Los Alamitos, CA: IEEE Computer Society Press, 1997, pp. 66–75.

Sengupta, K., and Te'eni, D. Cognitive feedback in GDSS: improving control and convergence. *MIS Quarterly,* 17, 1 (1993), 87–113.

Thurstone, L.L. A law of comparative judgment. *Psychological Review,* 34 (1927), 273–286.

Turoff, M. The design of a policy Delphi. *Technological Forecasting and Social Change,* 2, (1970), 149–171.

Turoff, M. Computer-mediated communication requirements for group support. *Journal of Organizational Computing,* 1, 1 (1990), 85–113.

Turoff, M., and Hiltz, S.R. Computer support for group versus individual decisions. *IEEE Transactions on Communications,* Com-30, 1 (1982), 82–90.

Turoff, M.; Hiltz, S.R.; Bahgat, A.N.F.; and Rana, A. Distributed group support systems. *MIS Quarterly,* 17, 4 (1993), 399–417.

Turoff, M.; Hiltz, S.R.; Fjermestad, J.; Bieber, M.; and Whitworth, B. Computer mediated communications for group support: past and future. In J.M. Carroll (ed.), *Human Computer Interaction in the New Millennium.* New York: ACM Press and Addison-Wesley, 2001, 279–302.

Turoff, M.; Hiltz, S.R.; Cho, H.; Li, Z.; and Wang, Y. Social decision support systems (SDSS). In *Proceedings of the 35th Hawaii International Conference on Systems Sciences.* CD-ROM. Los Alamitos, CA: IEEE Computer Society Press, 2002.

Van de Ven, A.H.; and Delbecq, A.L. Nominal versus interacting group processes for committee decision-making effectiveness. *Academy of Management Journal,* 14 (1971), 203–212.

Wang, Y. *Design and Evaluation of a List Gathering Tool in a Web-Based Collaborative Environment.* PhD dissertation, NJIT, Newark, 2003 (available at http://www.library.njit.edu/etd/index.cfm, accessed November 20, 2005).

Wang, Y.; Li, Z.; Turoff, M.; and Hiltz, S.R. Using a social decision support system toolkit to evaluate achieved course objectives. In *Proceedings of the Americas Conference on Information Systems.* CD-ROM. Atlanta, GA: The Association for Information Systems, 2003.

Watson, R.T. *A Study of Group Decision Support Systems Use in Three and Four Person Groups for a Preference Allocation Task.* PhD dissertation, University of Minnesota. 1987.

Watson, R.T.; Ho, T.H.; and Raman, K.S. Culture: the fourth dimension of group support systems. *Communications of the ACM,* 37, 10 (1994), 45–55.

Walther, J.B.; Boos, M.; and Jonas, K.J. Misattribution and attributional redirection in distributed virtual groups. In *Proceedings of the 35th Hawaii International Conference on Systems Sciences.* CD-ROM. Los Alamitos, CA: IEEE Computer Society Press, 2002.

Wheeler, B.C., and Valacich, J.S. Facilitation, GSS, and Training as sources of process restrictiveness and guidance for structured group decision making: an empirical assessment. *Information Systems Research,* 7, 4 (1996), 429–450.

CHAPTER 7

COLLABORATION TECHNOLOGIES, TASKS, AND CONTEXTS

Evolution and Opportunity

ILZE ZIGURS AND BJØRN ERIK MUNKVOLD

Abstract: *From the early days of computer conferencing, through the heyday of group decision support systems, to the current profusion of communication technologies, the elusive goal of effective collaboration has been examined from a variety of perspectives. Three important themes recur in this ongoing search: collaboration technologies, collaboration tasks, and the contexts in which they come together and are used. Collaboration technologies have been characterized in a variety of ways, at the same time that radical changes continue to occur in their capabilities. Collaboration tasks have also been defined in a variety of ways and their fit with specific technologies remains a complex issue. Technologies and tasks are brought together in use contexts that range from face-to-face settings to virtual spaces, and many issues raised by differences in use context remain unresolved. This paper examines our evolving understanding of collaboration technologies, tasks, and contexts. The changing characterization of each of these concepts is described. Key research findings are summarized, and opportunities for future research are discussed. The main contribution of this paper is to provide a summary analysis of how collaboration technologies, tasks, and contexts have been treated in information systems research, along with recommendations for future research on unresolved issues.*

Keywords: *Collaboration Technology, Collaboration Task, Virtual Teams, Group Support Systems*

INTRODUCTION

Collaboration is embedded in the world of work today, and the technology that makes new forms of collaboration possible has evolved rapidly. The relatively short but remarkable history of collaboration technology presents challenges for understanding the difference between ephemeral and lasting phenomena. The "e-rooms" of today look nothing like the computer conferences of the 1970s—or do they? Have changes in technology brought about any fundamental changes in how we approach collaboration, or the types of activities that we engage in through the technology? These are all interesting questions for speculation. But the starting point for exploration of these issues must be a clear understanding of the fundamental concepts.

Collaboration technology has been viewed from a wide variety of perspectives in the decades since the idea was first born. Different reference disciplines have contributed to that variety, including group communication, management and organizational behavior, sociology, psychology, decision making, computer science, human-computer interaction (HCI), and software engineering, to name a few. Indeed, the first conference on computer-supported cooperative work (CSCW), held in 1986 in Austin, Texas, declared itself a unique confluence of people from widely varied disciplines, working together in a new way to achieve a truly interdisciplinary field (Greif, 1986). Since then, this community of researchers and industry practitioners has grown to attract large audiences at the international CSCW conferences and workshops held regularly. Yet the diversity of backgrounds and interests in this forum has led it to be characterized as "an *un*disciplined marketplace of ideas, observations, issues, and technologies" (Grudin and Poltrock, 1997) rather than a distinct academic field or discipline. We also see broad regional variations in the focus of research. For example, CSCW research in the United States and Japan has focused primarily on design and product development of small-group applications, while European researchers have tended to focus more on organizational issues (Grudin, 1994a).

In addition to the diversity of perspectives on collaboration technology, collaboration tasks also have a challenging history. Decades of research on the nature of group tasks have resulted in several well-known frameworks and theories, with some identifiable common themes. Complexity, for example, is a key characteristic of tasks that is the foundation of several frameworks. But tasks are carried out in different contexts, by people of different skill levels, and through different interpretive lenses; thus, the challenge is in conceptualizing the nature of these relationships. Bringing tasks together with technology also results in interesting questions about the nature of fit, and how task-technology fit can help us achieve a higher level of understanding of these issues.

We have no all-encompassing, unified theory of either collaboration technology or tasks, nor would we expect one. The interesting thing is to ask how different views of technology, task, and context have contributed to where we are today in our understanding of the intersection of humans with computers in collaborative activity. What have we learned in this area and what remains to be studied? Therein lies the focus of this paper. We examine our evolving understanding of these concepts and their characterization. We provide a summary analysis of how collaboration technologies, tasks, and contexts have been treated in various research traditions, and we identify gaps that provide fruitful ground for further analysis.

The next section of the paper provides a definition of collaboration technology and a review of key typologies. The third section does the same for collaboration tasks. The fourth section brings these two concepts together in a discussion of task-technology fit. The fifth section focuses on different collaboration contexts and the issues associated with each of those contexts. The discussion is organized around four eras—teleconferencing, group support, enterprise applications, and virtuality—and the major research findings of each era that are relevant to the focus of this paper. The sixth section brings these ideas together in an analysis of needs for future research, and the final section concludes the paper.

COLLABORATION TECHNOLOGIES

Definition

A clear definition of collaboration technology is a necessary starting point for setting the scope of this paper. Consider this collection of terms, all of which have been used at various times to describe various facets of the phenomenon: teleconferencing, distributed work, computer-mediated communication, groupware, computer-supported cooperative work, collaborative computing, group decision support, group support system, electronic meeting system, virtual teams, digital collaboration, and e-collaboration. In addition to these generic terms, we could list specific technologies, such as e-mail, computer conferencing, videoconferencing, video walls, Listservs, discussion boards, chat rooms, knowledge repositories, workflow management systems, and so on. Clearly, the technology side provides a wide variety of capabilities and perspectives.

The very concept of collaboration has also been the subject of debate, with the meaning of this term being addressed as a research question in itself (Bannon, 1993; Lyytinen and Ngwenyama, 1992; Schmidt and Bannon, 1992). For example, while the terms "collaboration" and "cooperative work" tend to be used interchangeably, some argue that the term "collaboration" implies a particular "complying spirit" among the cooperators and is thus somewhat different from the more neutral term "cooperative work" (Bannon and Schmidt, 1991). In the formation stage of the CSCW community, several perspectives were suggested for describing and modeling various aspects of collaboration, including coordination theory (Malone and Crowston, 1990), language/action perspective (Winograd, 1987–1988), activity-based theory (Kuutti, 1991), structuration theory (Lyytinen and Ngwenyama, 1992), transaction cost perspective (Ciborra and Olson, 1988), and social network theory (Pickering and King, 1992). In line with the focus of this paper, we apply a task-oriented perspective in discussing collaboration and related technology support. This perspective is discussed in depth in the third section.

For the purposes of this paper, we define collaboration itself as the process of two or more people working together on a common task. Accordingly, we define collaboration technology as *comprising one or more computer-based tools that support the communication, coordination, and/or information processing needs of two or more people working together on a common task.* Our definition highlights the communication, coordination, and information-processing aspects of supporting collaborative work, as well as allowing for either a single tool or an integrated set of tools for the technology. The definition also provides for a broad-ranging analysis of the research that takes us all the way from dyads to organization-wide and cross-organizational systems.

Considerable debate has occurred on the question of which specific technologies "pass the test" for being included in the collaboration technology domain. Some authors have argued for a restricted perspective that includes only applications designed explicitly for supporting collaborative work through offering mechanisms such as awareness and multi-user support, for example, shared whiteboards. Others have taken a broader perspective that also includes basic communication and infrastructure technologies such as e-mail and network file servers (Grudin, 1994a). Ellis, Gibbs, and Rein (1991) argued for a groupware spectrum that comprised the two dimensions of a common task and a shared environment. Systems would then be placed at different points in this spectrum, depending on the degree of support offered within each dimension. While the debate has not been resolved, most researchers and practitioners today tend to imply a broad spectrum of tools and services when speaking about collaboration technology. We concur with this broader view, arguing for a contextual perspective where a technology's *potential* for being used to support different forms of collaborative work is of primary interest, rather than whether it simply meets a set of functional criteria.

Typologies of Collaboration Technology

The challenge in characterizing collaboration technology has always been about choosing relevant factors or dimensions for highlighting differences. Frameworks and typologies have been developed from such varying perspectives as information exchange, communication and group process, time/place configuration, underlying technology, and functionality. We address exemplars of these perspectives below.

The information-exchange perspective focuses on the extent to which collaboration technology supports the group in the critical task of exchanging information for group decision making. This perspective is grounded in the literature of group communication and decision making. The exemplary

Figure 7.1   **Time/Place Typology of Collaborative Systems**

	Same Time	**Different Time**
Same Place	Group support system Electronic meeting system	E-mail Document management system Calendar and scheduling system Workflow management system Electronic bulletin board Collaboration product suite
Different Place	Audio conferencing Videoconferencing Data conferencing Instant messaging/Chat room Integrated team support technology E-learning system	E-mail Distributed group support system Document management system Calendar and scheduling system Workflow management system Electronic bulletin board Collaboration product suite Web-based team/project room Integrated team support technology E-learning system

and widely cited typology of this type is the Level 1–2–3 framework (DeSanctis and Gallupe, 1987). Three levels of collaborative systems are defined, each representing progressively more support for the group. Level 1 systems remove common communication barriers by providing such features as anonymous communication, simultaneous communication, and easy capture and display of each person's ideas and comments. Level 2 systems address decision-making needs by providing modeling and idea-structuring tools. Level 3 systems provide expert advice and computer-based guidance and design of the group process—a concept that was quite rare when the typology was originally developed—thus going beyond simple information exchange to process intervention.

Several typologies have been founded in the communication and group process perspective. Initially, the differentiation was between supporting the collection of information and structuring of group process (Pinsonneault and Kraemer, 1989). Later typologies of this type provided finer distinctions between communication, internal information support, external information support, and group performance support (McGrath and Hollingshead, 1994). The themes of communication, information, and process structure recur in several other typologies in various forms (e.g., Nunamaker et al., 1991; Zigurs and Buckland, 1998).

A different approach for categorization of technologies is by time/place configuration. Figure 7.1 shows the popular 2 × 2 framework, which represents four modes of group interaction with current examples of technologies listed in each cell (Johansen, 1988; Munkvold, 2003).

The time/place framework provides a very concrete view of the capabilities of certain tools. However, organizational work is seldom restricted to one of these cells, but rather involves combinations of different time/place interactions (Grudin and Poltrock, 1997). The evolution of technology has been toward increased flexibility and Web-based options, thus making "any time, any place" a common goal of most tools. This trend is reflected in Figure 7.1 by the appearance of some technologies in more than one cell, for example, integrated team support technology and collaboration product suites that support both synchronous and asynchronous interaction. Clearly,

Table 7.1

Functional Typology of Collaboration Technologies

Functional Category	Examples of Technologies
Communication Technologies	E-mail Instant messaging/Chat room Audio and videoconferencing
Information-Sharing Technologies	Document management system Data conferencing Electronic bulletin board
Process-Support Technologies	Group support system (GSS)/Distributed GSS Electronic meeting system
Coordination Technologies	Workflow management system Calendar and scheduling system
Integrated Technologies Across Functional Categories	Collaboration product suite Web-based team/project room Integrated team support technology E-learning system

typologies based on underlying technology are difficult to keep current, given the rapid developments of the last few years. For example, collaboration support is becoming increasingly embedded as part of traditional office support tools.

An alternative to technology-based typologies is a *functional* typology, which classifies technologies based on the types of tasks or activities they support. Although characterizations of technologies along functional dimensions do vary, there are four consistent broad group tasks or activities that can be identified: communication, information sharing, process support, and coordination (Grudin and Poltrock, 1997; Zigurs and Buckland, 1998). The trend towards integration of features for supporting different collaborative tasks complicates this classification. As illustrated in Figure 7.1, one technology may support various forms of interaction and tasks. Yet, it is normally possible to identify which dominating feature serves as the core functionality of a product, and then classify according to this feature (Grudin and Poltrock, 1997). Table 7.1 shows a functional categorization of technologies (Munkvold, 2003).

Clearly, there are common themes across the typologies that we have discussed in terms of the kinds of group activities that are candidates for enhancement through technology. Furthermore, with the move toward integration and "collaboration suites" that cross functional categories, it might be tempting to say that typologies have outlived their usefulness. We argue otherwise. Decisions about matching tools to tasks are still made at fairly detailed levels; therefore characterizations of technology are important for assessing the match for a particular task. Table 7.1 represents our recommended categorization, given that it builds on group process as well as technology characteristics. The next section shifts to a focus on collaboration tasks.

COLLABORATION TASKS

Definition

The nature of a collaborative group's task has long been recognized to have a profound effect on group interaction (Poole et al., 1985; Shaw, 1981). Groups and group process have been subjects

Table 7.2

Key Findings with Respect to Task Circumplex

Task Type	Task Definition	Finding (Fjermestad and Hiltz [1998–99])
Planning	Generate plans	GSS groups did better than non-GSS groups, but based on few studies
Creativity	Generate ideas	GSS groups outperformed non-GSS groups by a ratio of 2.8 to 1
Intellective	Solve problems with correct answers	GSS groups generally did worse than non-GSS groups
Decision-Making	Decide issues with no right answer	GSS groups outperformed non-GSS groups by a small margin
Mixed-Motive	Resolve conflicts of interest	GSS groups were generally equivalent to non-GSS groups

of research for well over half a century and, in that time, no unified theory of task has emerged as dominant. Over the years, task has been defined from the perspective of a behavior description, as ability requirements, as behavior requirements, and as the set of instructions provided to the group (Hackman, 1969). More recent views have attempted to account for adaptation of tasks over time through the process of group interaction (DeSanctis and Poole, 1994; McGrath and Hollingshead, 1994).

For the purposes of this paper, and with reference to collaborative activity in particular, we define a group's task as *a set of behavior requirements for accomplishing both explicit and emergent goals via a process that uses available resources and techniques.* This broad perspective includes what a group does as well as the means and process by which the group carries out its objectives. Within this broad view, we can now examine the variety of task typologies that might be useful for characterizing group tasks.

Typologies of Tasks

The most popular task classification scheme in the literature of group support has been McGrath's task circumplex (McGrath, 1984). The circumplex defines what a group is expected to do, which means it is a behavior approach to task classification. Four quadrants are defined, with two types of tasks in each quadrant: Generate (planning and creativity tasks); Choose (intellective and decision-making tasks); Negotiate (cognitive conflict and mixed-motive tasks); and Execute (contexts/battles and performances/psychomotor tasks). The first three quadrants, with their six different types of tasks, are the most relevant for group decision making and collaboration.

The task circumplex was an essential part of the heyday of research in technology for same-time, same-place groups—what we define as the group support era. The period of the late 1980s and early 1990s experienced a surge of studies that examined various kinds of tasks with different technologies. Much of the research had a positivist orientation with an emphasis on identifying factors and their impact on group functioning. The group's task tended to be viewed as one bundle of factors that contributed to how process unfolded and how well a group could ultimately perform. Key findings with respect to collaboration tasks from the perspective of the circumplex are summarized in Table 7.2. These findings are from a summary of two hundred experiments that had been conducted up through the late 1990s (Fjermestad and Hiltz, 1998–99).

Table 7.3

Key Findings with Respect to Complexity Typology

Task Type	Key Characteristics and Example of Task	Findings (Zigurs et al. [1999])
Simple	Single desired outcome and single solution scheme, e.g., brainstorm ideas for improving tourism	GSS generally better than non-GSS with groups that used appropriate technology (emphasizing communication support over process structure and information processing)
Problem	Single desired outcome, but multiple solution schemes, e.g., develop the most efficient sequence of activities for carrying out a project	GSS better than non-GSS in one study with group that used appropriate technology (emphasizing information processing over communication and process support)
Decision	Multiple outcomes, with single solution scheme, e.g., choose the best person for a specific job from a pool of applicants	No difference between GSS and non-GSS groups in one study that had mismatched fit profile for task and technology
Judgment	Conflicting interdependence or uncertainty, e.g., assign sales territories	Not tested by existing studies
Fuzzy	Multiple outcomes, multiple solutions schemes, and potential for conflicting interdependence and uncertainty, e.g., develop a strategic plan for a university	GSS better than non-GSS with groups that used appropriate technology (emphasizing communication and information processing support, with medium process structure); and GSS generally no better than or worse than non-GSS groups with mismatched fit profile

The findings based on the task circumplex were mixed, and it was difficult to draw consistent conclusions about GSS effects from a task perspective. An alternative perspective was developed based on the concept of task complexity. The complexity typology views tasks in terms of behavior requirements while recognizing that there are some essential elements that can be generalized in terms of how a task is presented to the group (Zigurs and Buckland, 1998). The typology defines five task types in the context of group support, based on earlier work by Campbell (1988), who defined the dimensions by which the tasks vary. These dimensions are outcome multiplicity (more than one desired outcome), solution scheme multiplicity (more than one possible course of action to attain a goal), conflicting interdependence (conflict between possible outcomes or possible solution schemes), and solution-scheme/outcome uncertainty (uncertainty about whether a given solution scheme will lead to the desired outcome). Table 7.3 shows key findings related to task types from the perspective of the complexity typology, stated in terms of the fit between the different task types and collaboration technology (Zigurs et al., 1999).

Clearly, there are potential problems with any task typology. First, is it really possible to develop task categories that are mutually exclusive? For example, it is difficult to separate the generate aspects of a task from the choice aspects. Second, at what level of granularity should a task be defined? Tasks may consist of sub-tasks, and sub-tasks may include activities or steps. Such differences in terminology are common and they create a challenge for consistency in analysis. Furthermore, both of the typologies presented above are open to criticism for their somewhat deterministic approach and relative simplicity when compared to the complexity of tasks found in business environments (Saunders, 2000). These issues come together in the challenge of specifying the fit of tasks with technologies. The next section presents different views of this problem.

TASK-TECHNOLOGY FIT

In the previous two sections, we examined technology and task separately. Here, we bring the two concepts together and look more closely at the issue of fit of technology with task. As noted in the previous sections, there is no dearth of typologies of technology and tasks, each of which treats those concepts in terms of different dimensions or characteristics. What is new when combining them is the issue of how to characterize fit itself—a concept that is often assumed to be understood but in fact is rather complex. Fit as a construct has been analyzed in some depth in the literature of strategic management (Drazin and Van de Ven, 1985; Venkatraman, 1989). The concept of fit has been characterized in terms of matching theoretically related variables; showing internal consistency among a set of variables; defining internal congruence or gestalt of attributes; showing interaction through a moderating variable; defining intervention of a mediating variable, and specifying profiles of related variables (Venkatraman, 1989). Each of these perspectives implies a different type of proposition about effects and different measurement and analysis issues.

Table 7.4 summarizes different perspectives that have been taken on the fit of task with technology. The table reinforces what was just discussed, namely that task and technology have been defined in a wide variety of ways. The table also reveals that very few of these theories have been explicit in terms of the precise nature of the fit construct. Instead, their focus tends to be on defining tasks and technologies, while leaving fit as an assumed matching process. Without an explicit characterization of the nature of fit, it can be quite difficult to examine it empirically (Venkatraman, 1989). A second major challenge with respect to fit is how to account for emergent properties of collaborative interaction and potential feedback effects. Each theory has a different worldview, ranging from relatively prescriptive or deterministic to more open in terms of a variety of paths through the collaboration process. The synopsis of each perspective provides a glimpse into the different philosophical underpinnings of each theory.

The evolution of fit perspectives that is shown in Table 7.4 can be characterized as moving toward a richer and more complex view of the fit issue. Straightforward contingencies based on objective characterizations of task have given way to explicit recognition of an appropriation and feedback process that occurs through group interaction. The key to managing that complexity is in a clear understanding of the contexts in which collaboration unfolds. Deterministic perspectives can be criticized for not taking into account the diversity and complexity of different contexts in which collaboration occurs, yet purely adaptive or emergent perspectives are sometimes criticized for being capable only of *post hoc* description. We lay the groundwork for our analysis of this issue through a more thorough examination of different collaboration contexts that we present in terms of four eras. In each era, we discuss key research findings and summarize the major themes, relating them to the theories and concepts from the earlier sections of the paper.

COLLABORATION CONTEXTS

Up to this point, we have defined collaboration technologies and tasks, described different typologies, and reviewed several theories of task-technology fit. In this section, we address different contexts in which collaborative activity occurs. Clearly, the range of settings for collaboration has become very diverse, as new application areas emerge and new technologies are developed and diffused. There is also a growing diversity in the different types of users of collaboration technology, for example, knowledge workers, engineers, health-care professionals, software developers, educators, and government workers, just to name a few. New technologies redefine context on a regular basis. Further evolution of the Web, wireless devices, mobility, and multimedia applications

Table 7.4

Perspectives on Task-Technology Fit in Group Collaboration

Theory/Framework	Synopsis	Reference
Contingency Approach	Different task types from McGrath circumplex are best associated with different characteristics of group support, e.g., a Choose task requires tools for aiding selection.	DeSanctis and Gallupe (1987)
Adaptive Structuration Theory	Task is a key source of structure that combines with other sources, such as technology, to affect social interaction. Though not a fit theory per se, AST does address how resources and rules are combined, adapted, and used for task performance.	DeSanctis and Poole (1994)
Flow of Effects Model	Task is a key input variable that combines with other input variables, such as technology, to set up conditions that result in different patterns of group interaction.	Hollingshead and McGrath (1995)
Task-Technology Interaction (TTI)	Tasks are defined on dimensions of complexity, validation, and coordination. Technology dimensions are individual support, process support, and meta-process support. Each task dimension is matched with prescribed, best-fit technology dimension.	Rana et al. (1997)
Task-Technology Fit Theory (TTF)	Tasks are defined on the basis of complexity attributes as five types: simple, problem, decision, judgment, and fuzzy. Technology is defined in terms of dimensions: communication support, process structuring, and information processing. Fit is defined as ideal profiles composed of matching task environments with technology support.	Zigurs and Buckland (1998)
Media Synchronicity Theory (MST)	Fit is the congruence of communication support capabilities of the technology with the needs of the task. Two communication processes are defined: conveyance and convergence, and different tools are appropriate for each process.	Dennis and Valacich (1999)
Fit-Appropriation Model (FAM)	Fit is affected by (1) fit between task and technology structure, and (2) the appropriation support provided to the group, e.g., training, facilitation, software restrictiveness. Technology structures are from TTF theory of Zigurs and Buckland, which is integrated with adaptive structuration theory.	Dennis et al. (2001)

are just a few examples of how rapidly context can change (Munkvold, 2003). We present key findings in the evolution of collaboration technology in various contexts, starting with early studies in teleconferencing, to the surge of face-to-face group support, through an emphasis on organizational applications, and ending with virtual settings.

Early Research in Computer Conferencing: Teleconferencing Era

During the 1960s and '70s, developments in teleconferencing systems and services opened up new and exciting possibilities for human communication. Defined as *the use of electronic telecommunications to enable people to meet in spite of physical separation* (Egido, 1990), the term teleconferencing comprised a range of different media, including videoconferencing, computer conferencing, and audio conferencing. While the developments in audio conferencing and videoconferencing had been driven by large telecommunications companies such as Bell and AT&T, university research groups were more central in the development of computer conferencing systems, defined as "any system that uses the computer to mediate communication among human beings" (Hiltz and Turoff, 1978, p. 30).

Douglas Englebart and his group at Stanford Institute were among the pioneers in this era. They ran a data conferencing facility, operated by a mouse and pen-based interface. Although not widely acknowledged, these researchers laid the groundwork for many of the current features of modern computer technology and applications, such as word processing and hypertext. Another influential group was located at the New Jersey Institute of Technology (NJIT). Headed by Murray Turoff and Starr Roxanne Hiltz, this group developed a computer conferencing system called EIES (Electronic Information Exchange System), which was put into operation in 1976 and served as both an R&D platform and a prototyping environment (Turoff et al., 1993). The system was completely centralized and based on a single minicomputer. In 1990, it was replaced by a new version, EIES 2, which was an object-oriented, fully distributed system. Several field studies were conducted of groups ranging from ten to several hundred that used EIES for working asynchronously to solve tasks of varying complexity (Turoff et al., 1993). A contingency framework of communication mode, task type, and group size was used both to inform the design of applications adapted to different task and group combinations, and to evaluate and compare these applications. One conclusion from these studies was that this type of distributed system actually can support large groups working together on ambiguous problems.

The merger of telecommunications and computer technologies represented a radical expansion of the application scope of computers from information processing to human communication. Building on experience from their work with EIES and similar systems, Hiltz and Turoff (1978) presented a vision of how computer-mediated communication would revolutionize social and intellectual life. Introducing the concept of the "network nation," they extended the perspective of the importance of social network relations that had been presented by contemporary sociologists (Craven and Wellman, 1973) to include the new dimensions offered by teleconferencing technologies. Later referred to as the "bible" of computer conferencing, the *Network Nation* book presented a comprehensive analysis of the nature of computer conferencing, related social and psychological processes, and potential applications and impacts for individuals, organizations, and society. To truly appreciate the visionary scope of their scenarios, we need to remember that the book appeared in an era when personal computers, the Internet, and e-mail were still unknown to the general public. In the preface to the 1993 revised edition, the authors admitted to being over-optimistic about the speed of adoption of computer conferencing, but during the last decade the networked society has finally become a reality.

The term computer-mediated communication (CMC) gradually became the unifying label for research related to teleconferencing, which also included e-mail as the most common form of electronic interaction in organizations. Rice (1992) discussed propositional reviews and models in CMC research, thus debunking the myth that CMC lacked a theoretical foundation. Three theoretical models have been particularly influential in this research: social presence theory, media richness theory, and the social influence model of media use.

Social presence theory (Short et al., 1976; Williams, 1977) conceptualizes communication media according to their ability to convey social presence, defined as *the degree to which the medium facilitates awareness of the other person and interpersonal relationships during interaction* (Fulk, Schmitz, and Steinfield, 1990). According to this perspective, face-to-face communication has the greatest social presence, followed by videoconferencing, audio conferencing, and ending with text only. Efficient communication requires matching the social presence level with the level of interpersonal involvement required for the task. The model was tested through several laboratory experiments with different telecommunications technologies and using cooperative vs. conflicting tasks. The experiments provided moderate support for the model (Short et al., 1976; Williams, 1977).

An alternative contingency-based theory is media richness theory, or MRT (Daft and Lengel, 1986), which classifies media according to their capacity to process rich information. Information richness is defined as the *ability of information to change understanding within a time interval* (ibid.). The resulting continuum of communication media follows the same ordering as for social presence theory, with face-to-face as the richest medium. Rich media reduce equivocality, and should thus be selected for ambiguous tasks, while media of low richness (lean media) are effective for processing well-understood messages and standard data. Media richness theory has been widely tested, but there is limited support for the theory with more modern technologies (Markus, 1994; Dennis and Valacich, 1999). For example, in organizations, e-mail has been found to be used more intensively for conveying richer information than would be predicted by the theory (Lee, 1994; Markus, 1994). In addition, channel expansion theory has shown how media perceptions are affected by and change over time as a function of knowledge of the task, the communication partner, the technology itself, and the organizational context (Carlson and Zmud, 1999), thus calling into question MRT's fundamental precept that media characteristics are fixed.

The social influence model of media use (Fulk et al., 1990) challenges the rational assumptions of previous contingency models. According to the social influence model, media perceptions are partly subjective and socially constructed, and will thus vary across individuals and situations. Perceptions are also determined by the social influence exerted by coworkers, through their attitudes, overt statements, and behaviors. This model is thus better able than the rational, deterministic models to explain variation in media perceptions that were observed in similar settings. For example, in a field experiment of the adoption and use of two equivalent video telephone systems in one organization, Kraut et al. (1994) tested media richness theory, critical mass theory, and social influence theory. While the fit between tasks and features of the communication medium was found to influence use to a degree, only social influence mechanisms combined with critical mass theory were able to explain why only one of the systems survived.

Sproull and Kiesler (1991) provided a comprehensive summary of much of the CMC-related research, focusing both on efficiency effects and social system effects. They discussed how various communication technologies such as e-mail, electronic bulletin boards, and teleconferencing systems might affect communication at individual, group, and organizational levels. The need for new social protocols and etiquette related to the use of electronic communication media was acknowledged early. Today, this issue seems more current than ever, as evidenced by the increasing problems of information overload and e-mail misuse.

Not surprisingly, the teleconferencing era was primarily about communication technologies, in terms of our typology from Table 7.1. The characterization of technologies and their fit to tasks was through the lens of media and communication characteristics. Media richness and related theories provided a way of thinking about communication technology that focused attention on technical-level aspects of systems and the extent to which each aspect hindered or promoted communication.

Thus, the nature of fit was the extent to which a communication medium was best matched with the communication needs of a task.

The teleconferencing era provided the essential foundation to move into the next phase of collaboration technology, although some of the early pioneers took a while to be recognized by those "discovering" collaboration systems for the first time. The theories just discussed were a starting point for the communication component of the upcoming group support era, which also brought to the forefront the decision support paradigm, thus broadening the scope of concerns related to collaboration.

Face-to-Face Teams and Group Support Systems: Group Support Era

The group support era was characterized by the growth of studies of collaboration technology for supporting face-to-face teams. Although there was no shortage of typologies and discussion of the concept of "anytime, anywhere" support, clearly the greatest attention was given to same-time, same-place groups. For example, nearly 70 percent of 200 studies reported by mid-1998 were conducted in decision rooms (Fjermestad and Hiltz, 1998–99). An interesting aspect of this era is its initial emphasis on decision making, followed by a gradual shift to a broader support of different types of tasks. This shift is reflected in the move away from the GDSS acronym (group decision support system), to simply GSS (group support system). A GSS can be defined as a combination of communication, process structuring, and information processing technologies to support decision making and other functions of groups (Zigurs and Buckland, 1998). Several reviews of the literature of group support systems (GSS) are notable, and we discuss them below.

Several universities had interdisciplinary teams conducting research during the group support era, both in experimental and field settings (Watson et al., 1992). Early system development and foundational research was summarized in Nunamaker et al. (1991), who describe the development of tools for electronic meeting systems (EMS), summarize the extant research, and describe the input-process-output approach that provided the framework for the research. Steiner's (1972) theory of process gains and losses was used to provide an organized way of thinking about how different characteristics of collaboration technology could affect group process, both negatively and positively. For example, the parallel communication provided by a GSS can help overcome common process losses of airtime fragmentation and attenuation blocking, but it can also increase the process loss of information overload.

A meta-analysis conducted during this same period analyzed thirty-one experimental studies, taking an input-output approach to the existing research, with input variables being task characteristics, group characteristics, contextual factors, and technology factors (Benbasat and Lim, 1993). Interestingly, the only contextual factor that was analyzed across the studies was rewards. Use of a GSS resulted in higher decision quality, more alternatives generated, and greater equality of participation, with effects moderated by task, group, context, and technology variables. A comparison of experimental with field studies from this same period catalogued a list of twenty-four potentially important differences in contexts for the research that were likely to account for variations in findings between experimental and field studies (Dennis et al., 1990–91). The contexts were broadly categorized as being related to group characteristics, group size, task, technology tools and environments, and group incentives.

In a later review paper, Nunamaker and Briggs (1996–97) described twelve years of group support research, much of which was conducted in field studies. One important observation from this review was what we might call the field paradox, namely that there was typically considerable initial enthusiasm for GSS and EMS installations in business, but their use was difficult to sustain. The often-cited Boeing study (Post, 1993) is an example of an organization that experienced great gains in efficiency from use of a GSS facility, but that ultimately closed down their facility. That closing, and others like it, was often due to the fact that key champions or trained facilitators moved on to another project and users were not able to continue on their own (Briggs et al., 2003). Other causes of failure in GSS meetings in field studies included problems with the process design, poorly defined goals and expectations of the meeting, failures in or lack of trust of the technology itself, poor choice or inappropriate expertise of participants, and poor facilitation skills (de Vreede et al., 2003).

Two comprehensive reviews of the literature of this era were based on a contingency approach that catalogued studies in terms of contextual factors, intervening factors, adaptation factors, and outcome factors. The review of experimental studies included 230 papers that represented two hundred different studies (Fjermerstad and Hiltz, 1998–99). The percentage of studies that found positive effects for GSS as opposed to traditional groups was less than 20 percent. Larger groups showed somewhat better results on idea-generation tasks in particular. Results were generally moderated by a variety of factors, including the usual task, technology, and group characteristics. A follow-up review included fifty-four case and field studies that were conducted over two decades, through the mid-2000s (Fjermestad and Hiltz, 2000–2001). The majority of these studies showed improved efficiency and effectiveness and high satisfaction with GSS use. What made a difference for positive results was appropriate facilitation, training, use of GSS over multiple sessions, and the ability to combine verbal with computer-based communication.

General conclusions from the group support era are that the use of a GSS can result in significant efficiency gains, enhanced participation, and increased buy-in to group decisions. Key success factors are a structured process, the right training, and the right people as facilitators and as group members. Idea generation tasks may benefit the most from group support, and task structure in decision-making tasks may be what makes the difference rather than the computer support per se (Hollingshead and McGrath, 1995). As for theory, a contingency perspective dominated, based typically on a classic input-process-output approach. Input factors that combined to affect group process were typically organized in terms of the major categories of technology, task, group/individual characteristics, and environment. Output was viewed in terms of effectiveness, efficiency, and member satisfaction, and was measured almost exclusively by member perceptions. Theory can be characterized as being in early developmental stages. Notable theoretical development included the theory of process losses and gains (Nunamaker et al., 1991), adaptive structuration theory (e.g., DeSanctis and Poole, 1994), and time-interaction-performance theory (TIP) (McGrath, 1991).

A significant contribution of the group support era is the expansion of technology functionality to process support, which we identified in Table 7.1 as a category in our functional typology. A natural corollary to the broadened concept of technology is its use across a greater variety of tasks, particularly decision-making tasks. The challenge in terms of fit for group support systems was the lack of application of a shared and consistent characterization of technologies and tasks. But it is unrealistic to expect that such a diverse community would adopt a single perspective; indeed, it may be unproductive to do so. Adaptive structuration theory provides an alternate view—one that allows examination of changes in the role of technology within a group and the very nature of the task itself.

Although we have characterized this era and its heyday from a historical perspective, research on GSS continues in very productive and interesting ways. For example, an interesting question for current study is how to overcome what we called the field paradox by designing and implementing systems that rely less on skilled facilitation and make it easier for any group member to choose appropriate process structures. One stream of this research defines the concept of collaboration engineering and "thinkLets," which are packets of facilitation skills that provide repeatable processes for group tasks (Briggs et al., 2003). A thinkLet specifies a combination of steps in a process, the tool to support each step, and scripted prompts within the tool. This idea, and the broader notion of collaboration engineering, are consistent with a developing theory of "object-oriented teams" that has been proposed in the context of virtual teams (Ramesh and Dennis, 2002). The object-oriented team relies on semantically rich media that make it possible to decouple team members, thus resulting in greater flexibility and adaptability. This greater flexibility and broadening of the concept of GSS is part of the evolution to organization-wide applications.

Organizational Applications of Collaboration Technology: Enterprise Era

During the 1980s, different collaboration technologies for organization-wide use moved out from research labs for pilot testing and field trials in organizations (see Bannon [1993], Bullen and Bennett [1991], Greenberg [1991] for overviews of early systems). Several of these systems were in conflict with local, situated work practices (Suchman, 1987), which exposed a gap between designers' attempts to implement work structure in the technologies and users' actual needs for work support. Thus, we tended to see more failures than successes in these early trials of organizational systems (Carasik and Grantham, 1988; Egido, 1988; Francik et al., 1991).

At the second CSCW conference, Grudin (1988, later published as 1989) presented a seminal analysis of factors contributing to the problems of early organization-wide systems. He compared groupware technologies with the single-user and mainframe systems that were familiar to both designers and users, and showed how the distinguishing characteristics of groupware technologies represented new challenges for adoption. Unlike single-user tools, the benefits and costs of collaboration technologies to one user may be contingent on the behavior of other users. This interdependency can lead to failure in implementation of these technologies, with "free-riding" users in common databases being one example (Markus and Connolly, 1990). As for communication technologies in general, a critical mass of users is often needed for them to be effective, requiring universal access to the technology in the user group (Markus, 1987).

Another potential barrier to adoption of organization-wide systems is that their benefit may not be perceived equally among the different stakeholders. While some users see immediate gains, others may actually perceive the use of such technology only as extra work, for example, in recording and maintaining information. This phenomenon was illustrated by the adoption of automated meeting scheduling, where the immediate beneficiaries were those calling the meetings (manager or secretary), rather than the other group members who were required to maintain their electronic calendars. Later studies have confirmed how this disparity in work and benefit (Grudin, 1989, 1994b) can represent a major barrier in the adoption of collaboration technology, both at the level of individual adopters and organizational units (Bowers, 1994; Munkvold, 2003; Rogers, 1994).

An extensive study of the use of eight groupware products in different organizations showed that intuitive tools paralleling non-electronic activities were perceived to be of most value, thus explaining the universal success of e-mail (Bullen and Bennett, 1991). Tools without clear benefits were perceived by users to require extra efforts, again supporting Grudin's (1989) argument. Lack of integration among different tools was another important barrier for effective use. Organizational factors identified as important were champions, creating realistic expectations, providing adequate training and evolutionary support, and a need for process redesign.

At this stage in time, groupware had become generally accepted as the term denoting the technology component within CSCW research. However, the term was still used only for applications supporting groups that were "either small to moderate in size or narrowly focused" (Grudin, 1989). The launching of Lotus Notes in 1989 expanded this groupware focus to also include organizational applications at the enterprise level (King, 1996). Lotus Notes offered an integrated set of collaborative applications (e-mail, online calendars and scheduling, threaded discussions, document management, and workflow capability), as well as an application development environment based on a scripting language. Thus, it was characterized more as a platform for developing collaborative applications, rather than an off-the-shelf collaborative product.

The rapid diffusion of Lotus Notes was also fueled by the increasing arguments made in both the academic and practitioner press about the need for new, flexible organizational forms that were based on process organization, flattened hierarchies, and teamwork (Drucker, 1988; Galbraith and Lawler, 1993; Scott Morton, 1991). With its possibility for fast development of shared databases that could be synchronized across distributed locations, Lotus Notes was marketed as a tool for "transforming" the organization through increased communication and information sharing (Lloyd and Whitehead, 1996). Referred to as the "groupware standard" (Bate and Travell, 1994), Lotus Notes became the market leader and still holds a strong position based on millions of users worldwide.

Despite the potential of this technology, however, many organizations failed to gain the expected benefits of increased collaboration, communication, service, and productivity (Downing and Clark, 1999; Vandenbosch and Ginzberg, 1996–97). Rather than becoming the intended forum for knowledge sharing and experience transfer, the e-mail functionality in Notes became the main work tool in many companies (Munkvold, 2003; Orlikowski, 1992). Thus, the inherent flexibility of this technology came with a price, in the form of increased complexity for organizations in defining its use. A review of eighteen case studies of Lotus Notes implementation identified three stages of Notes use (Karsten, 1999), and found that only four cases were in the most advanced stage where users took an active role in integrating Notes applications into their work, thus changing the nature and amount of collaboration. It appears that the ability of Lotus Notes to contribute to an increasing level of collaboration is highly contextual and depends on conscious and continued efforts to change work processes and not just the technology.

The challenges involved in deployment and use of Lotus Notes spurred a rich body of research identifying barriers at various levels. At the level of the individual adopter, the flexible nature of this technology, combined with limited information and insufficient training for users, led to confusion and highly varied understanding of the nature of the technology (Karsten, 1995; Orlikowski, 1992; Orlikowski and Gash, 1994). Building on the concepts of mental models and frames from cognitive psychology, these studies illustrate how users establish "technological frames" in the form of shared cognitive structures that influence their understanding and use of the technology.

At the organizational level, structural elements such as reward systems and policies were found to influence adoption and diffusion. A competitive organizational culture, manifested by reward and incentive systems that focus on individual achievements, may be counterproductive to stimulating new collaborative work practices that require sharing information and competence with fellow employees (Orlikowski, 1992). This finding led to a common perception of a collaborative culture as a necessary prerequisite for successful adoption and use of collaboration technology (Bate and Travell, 1994; Downing and Clarke, 1999; Vandenbosch and Ginzberg, 1996–97). If such a culture did not exist prior to implementation, the assumption was that it had to be created. However, later studies challenged this notion of the role of culture. First, the very notion of a collaborative culture is problematic. In most organizations there is no single and distinct culture, but rather several sub-cultures of a more transient nature (Karsten, 1999). Second, in several situations, the adoption of collaboration technology is the first step towards establishing new collaborative work practices, such as global virtual teams or inter-organizational projects, for which there is no preexisting history or culture in the organization (Munkvold, 2000). In these cases, the need for overcoming geographical barriers may itself be sufficient grounds for adoption, regardless of culture. Third, other aspects of organizational context such as economic recession, management style, and changes in roles and work practices have been shown to exert stronger influence on the implementation of collaboration technology than the existence of a collaborative culture (Karsten and Jones, 1998).

Several longitudinal studies of organizational implementation of Lotus Notes have illustrated the complexity of organizational change processes and described the development and use of this technology as "variable, context specific and drifting" (Ciborra, 1996). This complexity is ascribed both to the flexibility of this type of technology and to the improvisational nature of the type of work supported. Rather than seeking to pre-plan and control these processes in detail, managers need a situated change perspective (Orlikowski, 1996) that encourages local improvisations and creates organizational arenas and roles that allow for continuous reflection on the change process and identification of emergent opportunities (Orlikowski and Hofman, 1997). Typically, these evolutionary implementation processes span several years.

In addition to Lotus Notes, other technologies that can be classified as organization-wide collaboration technologies include workflow management systems and knowledge management systems. Workflow management systems have often been implemented as part of process reengineering projects (Stohr and Zhao, 2001). A major factor affecting the success of these projects is the extent to which the workflow model built into the system corresponds to the users' model of work. In cases where there is a good fit between these models, workflow management functionality has resulted in successful improvement of work processes and in satisfied users (Grinter, 2000). In other cases, the systems have been disruptive, resulting in failed adoption or workarounds (Bowers, Button, and Sharrock, 1995). A challenge for designers and implementers is that internalized work practices are often of a tacit nature that cannot be captured from manuals or written procedures. Other challenges are integration with legacy systems and the potential risk of misuse for control purposes.

Knowledge management (KM) became a major movement in the 1990s, with a variety of infrastructures that provided the enabling technologies (Borghoff and Pareschi, 1998). Collaboration technologies constitute an important part of these KM infrastructures in the form of knowledge repositories and electronic forums for knowledge networking (Alavi and Leidner, 2001). Many of the challenges for development and implementation of these systems are similar to issues in research on groupware—in fact, many organizations implemented Lotus Notes as the basis for their KM applications. Examples of such issues include how to capture and explicate tacit knowledge for knowledge repositories, how to develop incentives for information sharing and building a critical mass of users, and how to define new roles responsible for information quality. A concept closely related to the knowledge repository is that of *organizational memory,* studied both in MIS and CSCW research (Ackerman, 1996; Stein and Zwass, 1995). Examples of challenges related to establishing this type of system include developing effective mechanisms for search and retrieval and providing the right level of contextual information to enable effective future use of the memory contents.

In general, the research on enterprise-wide collaboration technology can be characterized as rather diverse and heterogeneous, with few unifying theoretical frameworks or models. Examples of theoretical perspectives that have been applied include diffusion of innovation theory, socio-technical systems theory, social-cognitive perspectives, and structuration theory. Several broad frameworks have been developed, some with a focus on typologies and others on implementation. For example, Applegate (1991) presented a framework for introduction and assimilation of collaboration technologies in organizations, based on exploratory fieldwork in ten companies. Building on innovation research, this framework viewed the assimilation of collaboration technology as alignment of group, task, and technology within a given organizational and environmental context. A similar framework by Sanderson (1992) comprised a set of classes of implementation activities (initiation, definition of technology, decision making, installation, etc.) that interacted reciprocally with four types of contextual forces (organization, technology, users, and work task).

These frameworks are very similar in their categories to the early frameworks of the group support era. They are useful as general tools for analyzing implementation of collaboration technologies, but fail to provide an integrated analysis of how characteristics of different types of collaboration technologies influence their assimilation or use in organizations. All too often, collaboration technology is treated as a unified, single concept, rather than comprising the wide range of technologies that we outlined earlier in this paper. In an attempt to bring together the findings from the many organizational implementation studies, while also acknowledging the variation in technology focus, Munkvold (2003) developed a taxonomy of implementation factors, including factors related to organizational context (external and internal), implementation project, technology (general and related to each type of collaboration technology), and process-related factors. But there is still work to be done in providing an integrated analysis of the many contextual factors identified in the organizational research. The field studies to date represent a broad variation in company size, sector, industry, and application area. While acknowledging the importance of local context and use situations, we clearly see the need for a broad knowledge base that could be utilized more effectively for informing future design and use of organization-wide systems. In addition, attention must be paid to how organizational contexts change over time, with new "behavioral infrastructures" (Palen and Grudin, 2003) developing as both technologies and users mature.

Overall, from the perspective of our typology of collaboration technologies, organization-wide systems bring into the picture the information sharing and coordination functions. In general, the research in organization-wide systems has not been very explicit about the nature of task and fit, at least not in relation to any established typology. That may be partly because the studies are typically field-based rather than experimental. But it may also be that fit in an organizational context needs to focus more on organizational-level phenomena, for example, culture, structure, or reward systems.

Virtual Teams and Global Collaboration: Virtuality Era

Growing capabilities of collaborative technology made the virtuality era possible, even though interest in distributed groups goes back all the way to the teleconferencing era. The late 1990s and early 2000s saw an upsurge in studies of virtual teams. Researchers began in university settings, with students from all over the world engaged in projects to learn about virtual team processes and technologies. These quasi-experimental, quasi–field studies tended to enforce communication through technology only, viewing face-to-face communication as a "contamination" of the virtual nature of a team. But increasing field work showed that most virtual teams also include occasional periods of face-to-face work, whether to initiate strangers or provide crucial "touchpoints" for sustaining team effectiveness (Maznevski and Chudoba, 2000; Dubé and Paré, 2004). The field studies have addressed a wide range of important issues, including technology appropriation and adaptation (Maznevski and Chudoba, 2000; Sarker and Sahay, 2003), best practices in global virtual teams (Lurey and Raisinghani, 2001; Qureshi and Zigurs, 2001); and building of trust (Tucker and Pantelli, 2003).

Naturally, the very definition of virtuality has been a subject of lively discussion. Most researchers define it in terms of dispersion on various dimensions, at a minimum across time and space, but also on organizational affiliation, culture, work group membership, or permanency of the group (Watson-Manheim et al., 2002). An interesting alternative is the definition of virtuality as a bundle of resources and problems that are switched quickly according to explicit criteria (Mowshowitz, 1997). This latter definition highlights the role of technology in providing rapid switching capability, to the point where a virtual entity becomes qualitatively different from a non-virtual one. Indeed, the view that social systems can be created and easily experimented with through technology is a logical extension of this idea (Turoff, 1997). These different views reflect the sometimes confusing use of virtuality on different levels, namely, team, work group, or organization. Thus, one challenge is in being clear on the level and scope of analysis.

Two recent reviews of the research on virtual teams provide useful perspectives on our understanding of this area. The first review identifies forty-nine empirical studies of virtual teams in both laboratory and field settings, in addition to reporting the results of numerous interviews of virtual teams that were conducted by the authors themselves (Dubé and Paré, 2004). Rather than simply cataloguing the findings, however, these authors focus on the need to identify key characteristics that differentiate virtual teams from one another. The paper is a useful definitional piece that makes sense of the great variation in a concept that is clearly not a monolithic one. Virtual teams are characterized on two dimensions: (1) characteristics related to the basics of virtual teamwork, and (2) characteristics that make virtual teamwork more complex, namely size, dispersion, task duration, shared work experience, full- or part-time membership, stability of membership, task interdependence, and cultural diversity. The authors view the defining characteristic of virtuality to be the degree of reliance on information and communication technologies, as opposed to the more common notion of degree of time or space dispersion. This single construct is useful as a more direct measure of virtuality than assumptions about the extent to which a variety of dispersion conditions exist.

The second recent review of virtual teams categorizes existing findings and provides a useful snapshot in time of what has become a rather large body of literature (Powell, Piccoli, and Ives, 2004). The authors, like those of most other reviews, take an input-process-output view for their organizing structure. Input factors are design, culture, technical issues, and training. Process factors fall into the two categories of socio-emotional (including relationship building, cohesion, and trust), and task processes (including communication, coordination, and task-technology-structure fit). Output factors are performance and satisfaction. It is interesting to note the difference in input factors from the group support era, with an explicit emphasis here on culture. A positive aspect of this most recent review is the greater evidence of theory in the virtual team studies as opposed to the group support era. Slightly over 60 percent of the papers reviewed used one or more theories, the most popular being adaptive structuration theory, followed by social information processing theory, social presence theory, and various forms of media richness theory. Other theories were related to such concepts as communication, trust, leadership, conflict, and learning. The scope and diversity of theory reflects the broad palette of factors that affect virtual teams.

The research from the virtuality era reveals a host of difficulties that virtual teams experience, including inefficient information exchange, confusing and lengthy discussion and interaction, unevenly distributed information, misinterpretation of silence, misattribution of team member action, coordination difficulty, cultural barriers, lack of norm development, weak or problematic relational links, and obstacles to trust (Powell et al., 2004). Interestingly, while the research from the group support era started with an enthusiasm about how technology could change group interaction from a positive frame, the virtuality era seems to be more focused on obstacles. We see study after study about coordination, communication, and information exchange difficulties, and little in the way of testing of interventions that might overcome these difficulties. Creative thinking about such interventions is clearly needed.

A second major conclusion from the research in this era is that context is increasingly important, even fundamental. The substitution of "space" for "place" means that the usual physical signals of context are entirely missing, which leads to such problems as misattribution and difficulty with developing common norms. For example, virtual teams are surprisingly quick to conclude that distant members lack motivation but painfully slow to reconsider their attitudes even in the face of evidence to the contrary (Cramton, 2001). Without context cues to create a "sense of place" in cyberspace, virtual teams struggle and often fail. Technology and well-developed process interventions can provide a powerful combination, but the right combinations have yet to be tested.

The collaboration technology of the virtuality era runs the entire gamut of the functions from our typology. Indeed, the ideal for this era would be the integrated suites that offer full collaboration support across all functional categories. But the research on such integrated technologies is in its infancy, and we do not have good models for how we might approach the task and fit issues for integrated systems. A key contribution of the virtuality era in terms of definitional typologies has been the concept of dispersion. As virtual teams and organizations become more dispersed on a greater number of dimensions, their reliance on collaboration technology for supporting a variety of functions becomes greater. But even more fundamental is their need to have the technology create a shared space. These issues create unique opportunities for creative research.

OPPORTUNITIES FOR FUTURE RESEARCH

Extending Current Knowledge to Emerging Contexts

The previous sections have ranged over a wide variety of issues and shown how collaboration technologies, tasks, and contexts have evolved over time. The trend today is toward increasing embeddedness of collaborative functionality in enterprise systems, corporate portals, virtual communities, and just about every aspect of organizational life. This "ubiquity era"—which is the name we give to the current time and near future—challenges us to extend what we know to yet another new context. We return to the question that we posed at the beginning: What is new and what remains the same? This question needs to be addressed from different perspectives, since the changes implied are of more than just a technological nature. In fact, it could be argued that the basic functionality provided in today's products has not changed much from the features of the pioneering collaboration technologies in the early eras. What has changed is the "packaging" of these services, in the form of user interface devices, connectivity, mobility, and so on. Combined with the integration of several services within a single product, these changes create new application areas and use contexts. The question then becomes: Can we transfer what we have learned to these multi-modal, flexible-use contexts?

There are other aspects of change that challenge our existing understanding of phenomena related to collaboration technologies. First, the new generations of users of these technologies are very different from the users studied in most of the empirical research on collaboration technology to date. In less than a decade, the advent of the Internet, powerful and networked PCs in every home, and mobile phones with SMS and chat services have totally redefined the level of technological proficiency and attitudes towards technology for individuals in large parts of the world. While the adoption of Internet services also includes an older generation, the biggest potential change comes from younger generations. For our youth, not being constantly connected through their mobile phones and chat services has already been defined as an abnormal situation, leading to abstinence symptoms. With such technology-comfortable people as the future adopters of collaboration technologies in the workplace, we may need to revise our former theories and knowledge of user characteristics and appropriation effects.

In addition, the world of organizations as we know it is also changing. Virtuality and global-ization are becoming the norm. The concept of the "global village" is at the heart of the ubiquity era. Vendors, business organizations, and governments are all seeking ways to make ubiquitous access both easy and affordable, and the opportunities for research are exciting.

Impact of Technological Developments on Research

Advances in technological developments are part and parcel of advances in research, but there is also a delicate balancing act between the two. Our research creates new technologies at the same time that it tests the environments in which we use them. While we are urged to conduct research at the leading edge of technology, we find that organizational practices vary widely and often lag far behind. For example, even with the astounding technical advances of the last decade, e-mail is still often the technology of choice for collaboration (Bajwa and Lewis, 2002; Watson-Manheim and Belanger, 2002). Group members have difficulty overcoming inertia with respect to estab-lished use of technology, and a collaboration tool has to be perceived as clearly superior to exist-ing practice in order to overcome the effort of learning and using a new technology (Majchrzak et al., 2000; Wierba et al., 2002). In organization-wide systems, the value and spirit of collabora-tion technologies must be made explicit before widespread benefits can be realized (Grudin, 1994b; Orlikowski, 1992).

An important trend with respect to technological developments is the integration of collabora-tion technologies, involving combinations of different interaction modes, media and structural support (Mandviwalla and Khan, 1999). This trend creates new behavioral and organizational research issues related to the development of procedural guidance and appropriation support for these technologies, as well as opportunities to study new, integrated behavioral patterns related to their use (Munkvold and Zigurs, 2005). The development of collaborative portals that offer inte-grated support for collaboration and information management is also a trend that bears watching.

Technology both drives and is driven by changing research agendas. Ubiquitous computing, mobility, multi-modality, new interfaces, and a host of other phenomena are changing the context in which collaboration takes place. Theory needs to evolve alongside the technical changes, as do the methods for developing and testing that theory.

Methodological Issues and Opportunities

As our discussion of eras has shown, a wide variety of methods are used in the research on col-laboration technology, and we continue to have difficulty aggregating findings. The eras highlight one of the key challenges in this research, and that is the level of analysis. As we go from indi-vidual, to group, to organizational level, what measures and instruments are appropriate? The least well developed is the organizational level, where we find few studies that provide measures of effects of the use of collaboration technology on an organizational scale. Group measures are often taken as averages of individual members, but how does such a measure reflect the character of a group as a whole (Zigurs, 1993)? Thus, one opportunity in terms of methods is to develop ways to assess different levels of meaning.

A second issue, and one that remains a continuing subject of debate, is differences in underly-ing philosophies of research. Fortunately, we are seeing a broader range of acceptance of differ-ent worldviews in information systems in general, and perhaps more so in collaboration research, given its extensive interdisciplinary reach. Examples of perspectives other than the traditional positivist perspective (traditional mostly to North American research) include critical social theory (Ngwenyama and Lee, 1997) and hermeneutics (Lee, 1994). There also exist good examples of studies that compare different views or use a multi-methodological lens (e.g., Trauth and Jessup, 2000). Finally, although guidelines for qualitative research have existed in our reference disciplines for years, we now see their emergence in the mainstream MIS journals (e.g., Lee, 1989; Myers, 1997; Klein and Myers, 1999), which is a good sign of maturity in the field.

A related debate that exists in the research of collaboration technology is the role of design versus evaluation methodologies. In the group support era, an early article argued for the importance of systems development as a research method (Nunamaker et al., 1991). Design and development also have a long and important tradition in the CSCW community. Questions seem to arise at the intersection of different disciplines as to the standard for what constitutes a contribution, but proof-of-concept and design methodologies are essential to advancement of research in collaboration technologies. Hevner et al. (2004) summarize this debate nicely in their discussion of behavioral versus design science in information systems research, and they provide a useful set of guidelines for the rigorous conduct of design studies.

As collaboration technology becomes more embedded in everyday applications, questions arise about protection of user privacy, for example, automated logging as a method for recording system usage. New mobile devices that easily capture and send pictures are already raising questions about privacy. Anonymity in group support systems was a popular topic of study in the group support era, but users can be suspicious about the extent to which that anonymity is really guaranteed. Such issues are a matter for review boards that govern research, although the nature and power of such boards varies widely across the world. That variety makes it especially challenging to conduct research in virtual teams, where research partners from different countries have to coordinate the requirements of the differing entities that govern the protection of human subjects.

We have highlighted only a few of the methodological issues that are particularly important in collaboration technology. Clearly, several opportunities exist. Our methods need to provide a balance between contextual sensitivity and control in research design. We need more examples of how to study collaboration technologies that cross organizational and cultural boundaries, with techniques that capture differences while allowing for the emergence of common themes. And, the tools by which we capture data and the very nature of data itself need to evolve, as we experience ever greater variation in the contexts and subjects of our research.

Toward an Integrated Perspective on Technology, Task, and Context

Table 7.5 summarizes the eras and issues that we have discussed in this paper, and notes some of the theoretical advances that have occurred as we go through the eras. The table also shows the ubiquity era that we have labeled as our current and near-future era. The table provides a view of how these issues have evolved that allows us to speculate on how they might relate to one another.

Clearly, one of the challenges is to make sense of the research that has been conducted so that we can identify meaningful directions for the future. In any field of endeavor, there are periodic calls for such sense-making and the identification of a common foundation for the field. Strong theoretical development is one of the ways in which sense-making can occur, and the research in collaboration technology has no shortage of calls for better theoretical development. For example, in a review of case and field studies of group support conducted over the two decades ending in mid-2000, less than 20 percent used or specified a specific theory (Fjermestad and Hiltz, 2000–2001). Fortunately, the use of theory is growing. As noted earlier, 60 percent of the studies of virtual teams between 1991 and 2002 involved one or more theories (Powell et al., 2004).

Table 7.5

Tasks, Technologies, Contexts, and Theory Over the Eras

	Teleconferencing Era	Group Support Era	Enterprise Era	Virtuality Era	Ubiquity Era
Example Systems	Text, audio, videoconferencing, e-mail	Group support system, Electronic meeting system	Collaboration suite, Workflow management system, Knowledge management system	Distributed GSS, Web-based team/project room	Collaboration portal, Embedded collaboration tools
Technology Focus	Communication	Process	Information sharing and coordination	Telepresence	Attention
Task Perspective	Communication	Decision making	Cross-organizational, Knowledge	Modular, rapid switching	Integrative
Contextual Issues	Technology constraints	Team structure, Facilitation	Organization structure, Control, Rewards	Culture, Diversity, Norms, Leadership	Engagement
Theoretical Advances	Social presence, Media richness, Social influence, Critical mass	Process losses and gains, Task-technology fit, AST, TIP, Channel expansion theory	Technological frames, Benefit asymmetry, Situated change, Technological drift, Knowledge management	Swift trust, AST, Social information processing, Duality/discontinuity	?

For the most part, we have taken theory from our reference disciplines and extended or repositioned it, but there are also a few examples of new theories, for example, AST and TIP, that have been developed specifically in the context of collaboration technology. What matters, whether the theories are new or reconditioned, is that we develop clear and consistent constructs and an understanding of their network of relationships. Both deductive and inductive efforts are required, in the wide variety of contexts represented in the eras. Although we have used eras as a way to organize this discussion, clearly there is overlap among the issues and technologies discussed.

What can we conclude from this discussion in terms of a coherent view of technologies, tasks, and contexts? First, a functional typology like that of Table 7.1 provides reasonable support for understanding the key issues in the evolution of technology in different contexts. A matching typology of tasks is less manageable, however, given the different contexts and levels of analysis in which collaboration technology might be used. Our argument is that theoretical advances are the best driver for making sense of this domain. A rich and coherent body of constructs can serve to unify the field as well as account for its complexity.

CONCLUSION

We have presented different views of collaboration technologies, tasks, and contexts from the perspective of eras and the themes that predominated during each era. The paper began with the broader question of whether collaboration has fundamentally changed with changes in technology and the kind of interaction that is possible through that technology. Further, as collaboration functionality becomes embedded in every technology, what will these shifts mean for this area as a research discipline and its relationship to other disciplines?

The evolution of this field is one of increasing theoretical strength and methodological pluralism, both of which are good signs of health. Rapid technology changes only bring greater opportunity, both to examine existing theory in new contexts and create new theory, as we have suggested in the previous section. If we can combine a clear understanding of the fundamental concepts of collaboration technologies and tasks with an appreciation of the evolving nature of the contexts in which they occur, then we are poised to take full advantage of what the future may bring or what we ourselves might create.

REFERENCES

Ackerman, M.S. Definitional and contextual issues in organizational and group memories. *Information Technology & People,* 9, 1 (1996), 10–24.

Alavi, M., and Leidner, D.E. Review: knowledge management and knowledge management systems: conceptual foundations and research issues. *MIS Quarterly,* 25, 1 (2001), 107–135.

Applegate, L.M. Technology support for cooperative work: a framework for studying introduction and assimilation in organizations. *Journal of Organizational Computing,* 1 (1991), 11–39.

Bajwa, D.S., and Lewis, L.F. Current status of information technologies used in support of task-oriented collaboration. In *Proceedings of the 35th Annual Hawaii International Conference on System Sciences.* Washington, DC: IEEE Press, 2002, 28.

Bannon, L.J. CSCW: an initial exploration. *Scandinavian Journal of Information Systems,* 5 (1993), 3–24.

Bannon, L.J., and Schmidt, K. CSCW: four characters in search of a context. In J.M. Bowers and S.D. Benford (eds.), *Studies in Computer Supported Cooperative Work: Theory, Practice and Design.* Amsterdam: North-Holland, 1991, pp. 3–16.

Bate, J., and Travell, N. *Groupware.* Henley on Thames, Oxfordshire: Alfred Waller, 1994.

Benbasat, I., and Lim, L-H. The effects of group, task, context, and technology variables on the usefulness of group support systems: a meta-analysis of experimental studies. *Small Group Research,* 24, 4 (1993), 430–462.

Borghoff, U., and Pareschi, R. (eds.), *Information Technology for Knowledge Management.* London: Springer-Verlag, 1998.

Bowers, J. The work to make a network work: studying CSCW in action. In *Proceedings of CSCW '94.* Chapel Hill, NC: ACM Press, 1994, pp. 287–299.

Bowers, J.; Button, G.; and Sharrock, W. Workflow from within and without: technology and cooperative work on the print industry shopfloor. In *Proceedings of ECSCW '95.* Stockholm: Kluwer Academic Publishers, 1995, pp. 51–66.

Briggs, R.O.; de Vreede, G-J.; and Nunamaker, J.F., Jr. Collaboration engineering with ThinkLets to pursue sustained success with group support systems. *Journal of Management Information Systems,* 19, 4 (2003), 31–64.

Bullen, C.V., and Bennett, J.L. Groupware in practice: an interpretation of work experience. In C. Dunlop and R. Kling (eds.), *Computerization and Controversy: Value Conflicts and Social Choices.* Boston: Academic Press, 1991, pp. 257–287.

Campbell, D.J. Task complexity: A review and analysis. *Academy of Management Review,* 13, 1 (1988), 40–52.

Carasik, R.P., and Grantham, C.E. A case study of CSCW in a dispersed organization. In *Proceedings of CHI '88.* New York: ACM, 1988, pp. 61–65.

Carlson, J.R., and Zmud, R.W. Channel expansion theory and the experiential nature of media richness perceptions. *Academy of Management Journal,* 42, 2 (1999), pp. 153–170.

Ciborra, C.U. (ed.) *Groupware & Teamwork. Invisible Aid or Technical Hindrance?* Chichester: John Wiley & Sons, 1996.

Ciborra, C., and Olson, M.H. Encountering electronic work groups: a transaction costs perspective. In *Proceedings of CSCW '88.* New York: ACM Press, 1988, pp. 94–101.

Cramton, C.D. The mutual knowledge problem and its consequences for dispersed collaboration. *Organization Science,* 12, 3 (2001), 346–371.

Craven, P., and Wellman, B. The network city. *Sociological Inquiry,* 43 (1973), 57–88.

Daft, R.L., and Lengel, R.H. Organizational information requirements, media richness and structural design. *Management Science,* 32, 5 (1986), 554–571.

Dennis, A.R.; Nunamaker, J.F.; and Vogel, D.R. A comparison of laboratory and field research in the study of electronic meeting systems. *Journal of Management Information Systems,* 7, 3 (1990–91), 107–135.

Dennis, A.R., and Valacich, J.S. Rethinking media richness: towards a theory of media synchronicity. In *Proceedings of the Thirty-Second Annual Hawaii International Conference on System Sciences,* 1. Washington, DC: IEEE Computer Society, 1999, p. 1017.

Dennis, A.R.; Wixom, B.H.; and Vandenberg, R.J. Understanding fit and appropriation effects in group support systems via meta-analysis. *MIS Quarterly,* 25 (2001), 167–193.

DeSanctis, G., and Gallupe, R.B. A foundation for the study of group decision support systems. *Management Science,* 33, 5 (1987), 589–609.

DeSanctis, G., and Poole, M.S. Capturing the complexity in advanced technology use: adaptive structuration theory. *Organization Science,* 5, 2 (1994), 121–147.

de Vreede, G.-J.; Davison, R.M.; and Briggs, R.O. How a silver bullet may lose its shine. *Communications of the ACM,* 46, 8 (2003), 96–101.

Downing, C.E., and Clark, A.S. Groupware in practice. Expected and realized benefits. *Information Systems Management,* 16, 2 (1999), 25–31.

Drazin, R., and Van de Ven, A.H. Alternative forms of fit in contingency theory. *Administrative Science Quarterly,* 30 (1985), 514–539.

Drucker, P.F. The coming of the new organization. *Harvard Business Review,* 66, 1 (January–February, 1988), 45–53.

Dubé, L., and Paré, G. The multi-faceted nature of virtual teams. In D.J. Pauleen (ed.), *Virtual Teams: Projects, Protocols, and Processes.* Hershey, PA: Idea Group Publishing, 2004.

Egido, C. Videoconferencing as a technology to support group work: a review of its failure. In *Proceedings of CSCW '88.* Portland, OR: ACM Press, 1988, pp. 13–23.

Egido, C. Teleconferencing as a technology to support cooperative work: its possibilities and limitations. In J. Galegher, R.E. Kraut, and C. Egido (eds.), *Intellectual and Technological Foundations of Cooperative Work.* Mahwah, NJ: Lawrence Erlbaum Associates, 1990, pp. 351–371.

Ellis, C.A.; Gibbs, S.J.; and Rein, G.L. Groupware: Some issues and experiences. *Communications of the ACM,* 34, 1 (1991), 39–58.

Fjermestad, J., and Hiltz, S.R. An assessment of group support systems experimental research: methodology and results. *Journal of Management Information Systems,* 15, 3 (1998–99), 7–149.

Fjermestad, J., and Hiltz, S.R. Group support systems: a descriptive evaluation of case and field studies. *Journal of Management Information Systems,* 17, 3 (2000–2001), 115–159.

Francik, E.; Rudman, S.E.; Cooper, D.; and Levine, S. Putting innovation to work: adoption strategies for multimedia communication systems. *Communications of the ACM,* 34, 12 (1991), 52–63.

Fulk, J.; Schmitz, J.; and Steinfield, C.W. A social influence model of technology use. In J. Fulk and C.W. Steinfield (eds.), *Organizations and Communication Technology.* Newbury Park, CA: Sage, 1990, pp. 117–140.

Galbraith, J.R., and Lawler, E.E., III. *Organizing for the Future. The New Logic for Managing Complex Organizations.* San Francisco: Jossey-Bass Publishers, 1993.

Greenberg, S. (ed.) *Computer-Supported Cooperative Work and Groupware.* London: Academic Press, 1991.

Greif, I. Program chair's message. In *Proceedings of the 1986 ACM Conference on Computer-Supported Cooperative Work.* Austin, TX: ACM Press, 1986.

Grinter, B. Workflow systems. Occasions for success and failure. *Computer-Supported Cooperative Work (CSCW),* 9, 2 (2000), 189–214.

Grudin, J. Why CSCW applications fail: problems in the design and evaluation of organizational interfaces. In *Proceedings of CSCW '88.* New York: ACM Press, 1988, pp. 85–93.

Grudin, J. Why groupware applications fail: problems in design and evaluation. *Office: Technology and People,* 4, 3 (1989), 245–264.

Grudin, J. Computer-supported cooperative work—history and focus. *IEEE Computer,* 27, 5 (1994a), 19–25.

Grudin, J. Groupware and social dynamics: eight challenges for developers. *Communications of the ACM,* 37, 1 (1994b), 92–105.

Grudin, J., and Poltrock, S.E. Computer-supported cooperative work and groupware. *Advances in Computers,* 45 (1997), 269–320.

Hackman, J.R. Toward understanding the role of tasks in behavioral research. *Acta Psychologica,* 31 (1969), 97–128.

Hevner, A.R.; March, S.T.; Park, J.; and Ram, S. Design science in information systems research. *MIS Quarterly,* 28, 1 (2004), 75–105.

Hiltz, S.R., and Turoff, M. *The Network Nation: Human Communication Via Computer.* Reading, MA: Addison-Wesley, 1978.

Hollingshead, A.B., and McGrath, J.E. Computer-assisted groups: a critical review of the empirical research. In R.A. Guzzo, E. Salas, and associates (eds.), *Team Effectiveness and Decision Making in Organizations.* San Francisco: Jossey-Bass, 1995, pp. 46–78.

Johansen, R. *Groupware: Computer Support for Business Teams,* New York: Macmillan, 1988.

Karsten, H. "It's like everyone working around the same desk": organisational readings of Lotus Notes. *Scandinavian Journal of Information Systems,* 7, 1 (1995), 3–32.

Karsten, H. Collaboration and collaborative information technologies: a review of the evidence. *The DATA BASE for Advances in Information Systems,* 30, 2 (1999), 44–65.

Karsten, H., and Jones, M. The long and winding road: collaborative IT and organisational change. In *Proceedings of CSCW '98.* New York: ACM Press, 1998, pp. 29–38.

King, W.R. Strategic issues in groupware. *Information Systems Management,* 13, 2 (1996), 73–75.

Klein, H.K., and Myers, M.D. A set of principles for conducting and evaluating interpretive field studies in information systems. *MIS Quarterly,* 23, 1 (1999), 67–93.

Kraut, R.E.; Rice, R.E.; Cool. C.; and Fish, R.S. Life and death of new technology: task, utility and social influences on the use of a communication medium. In *Proceedings of CSCW '94.* New York: ACM Press, 1994, pp. 13–21.

Kuutti, K. The concept of activity as a basic unit of analysis for CSCW research. In *Proceedings of ECSCW '91.* Amsterdam: Kluwer, 1991, pp. 249–264.

Lee, A.S. A scientific methodology for MIS case studies. *MIS Quarterly,* 13, 1 (1989), 33–50.

Lee, A.S. Electronic mail as a medium for rich communication: an empirical investigation using hermeneutic interpretation. *MIS Quarterly,* 18, 2 (1994), 143–157.

Lloyd, P., and Whitehead, R. *Transforming Organizations Through Groupware: Lotus Notes in Action.* London: Springer, 1996.

Lurey, J.S., and Raisinghani, M.S. An empirical study of best practices in virtual teams. *Information & Management,* 38 (2001), 523–544.

Lyytinen, K.J., and Ngwenyama, O.K. What does computer-support for cooperative work mean? A structurational analysis of computer-supported cooperative work. *Accounting, Management & Information Technology,* 2, 1 (1992), 19–37.

Majchrzak, A.; Rice, R.E.; King, N.; Malhotra, A.; and Ba, S. Computer-mediated inter-organizational knowledge-sharing: insights from a virtual team innovating using a collaborative tool. *Information Resources Management Journal,* 13, 1 (2000), 44–53.

Malone, T.W., and Crowston, K. What is coordination theory and how can it help design cooperative work systems? In *Proceedings of CSCW '90.* New York: ACM Press, 1990, pp. 357–369.

Mandviwalla, M., and Khan, S. Collaborative object workspaces (COWS): exploring the integration of collaboration technology. *Decision Support Systems,* 27, 3 (1999), 241–254.

Markus, M.L. Toward a "critical mass" theory of interactive media, universal access, interdependence and diffusion. *Communication Research,* 14, 5 (1987), 491–511.

Markus, M.L. Electronic mail as the medium of managerial choice. *Organization Science,* 5, 4 (1994), 502–527.

Markus, M.L., and Connolly, T. Why CSCW applications fail: problems in the adoption of interdependent work tools. In *Proceedings of CSCW '90.* Los Angeles: ACM Press, 1990, pp. 371–380.

Maznevski, M.L., and Chudoba, K.M. Bridging space over time: global virtual team dynamics and effectiveness. *Organization Science,* 11, 5 (2000), 473–492.

McGrath, J.E. *Groups: Interaction and Performance.* Englewood Cliffs, NJ: Prentice-Hall, 1984.

McGrath, J.E. Time, interaction, and performance (TIP): a theory of groups. *Small Group Research,* 22, 2 (1991), 147–174.

McGrath, J.E., and Hollingshead, A.B. *Groups Interacting with Technology: Ideas, Evidence, Issues, and an Agenda.* Thousand Oaks, CA: Sage Publications, 1994.

Mowshowitz, A. Virtual organization. *Communications of the ACM,* 40, 9 (1997), 30–37.

Munkvold, B.E. Alignment of collaboration technology adoption and organizational change: findings from five case studies. In M. Khosrowpour (ed.), *Challenges of Information Technology Management in the 21st Century.* Hershey, PA: Idea Group Publishing, 2000, pp. 601–604.

Munkvold, B.E. *Implementing Collaboration Technologies in Industry: Case Examples and Lessons Learned.* London: Springer-Verlag, 2003.

Munkvold, B.E., and Zigurs, I. Integration of e-collaboration technologies: research opportunities and challenges. *International Journal of E-Collaboration,* 1, 2 (2005), 1–24.

Myers, M.D. Qualitative research in information systems. *MIS Quarterly,* 21, 2 (1997), 241–242.

Ngwenyama, O.K., and Lee, A.S. Communicating richness in electronic mail: critical social theory and the contextuality of meaning. *MIS Quarterly,* 21, 2 (1997), 145–167.

Nunamaker, J.F., and Briggs, R.O. Lessons from a dozen years of group support systems research: a discussion of lab and field findings. *Journal of Management Information Systems,* 13, 3 (1996–97), 163–205.

Nunamaker, J.F.; Chen, M.; and Purdin, T.D.M. Systems development in information systems research. *Journal of Management Information Systems,* 7, 3 (1991), 89–106.

Nunamaker, J.F.; Dennis, A.R.; Valacich, J.S.; Vogel, D.R.; and George, J.F. Electronic meeting systems to support group work. *Communications of the ACM,* 34, 7 (1991), 40–61.

Orlikowski, W.J. Learning from Notes: organizational issues in groupware implementation. In *Proceedings of CSCW '92.* New York: ACM Press, 1992, pp. 362–369.

Orlikowski, W.J. Improvising organizational transformation over time: a situated change perspective. *Information Systems Research,* 7, 1 (1996), 63–92.

Orlikowski, W.J., and Gash, D.G. Technological frames: making sense of information technology in organizations. *ACM Transactions of Information Systems,* 12, 2 (1994), 174–207.

Orlikowski, W.J., and Hofman, J.D. An improvisational model for change management: the case of groupware technologies. *Sloan Management Review,* 28, 2, (Winter 1997), 11–21.

Palen, L., and Grudin, J. Discretionary adoption of group support software: lessons from calendar applications. In B.E. Munkvold (ed.), *Implementing Collaboration Technologies in Industry: Case Examples and Lessons Learned.* London: Springer-Verlag, 2003, pp. 159–180.

Pickering, J.M., and King, J.L. Hardwiring weak ties: individual and institutional issues in computer mediated communication. In *Proceedings of CSCW '92.* New York: ACM Press, 1992, pp. 356–361.

Pinsonnault, A., and Kraemer, K.L. The impact of technological support on groups: an assessment of the empirical research. *Decision Support Systems,* 5 (1989), 197–216.

Poole, M.S.; Siebold, D.R.; and McPhee, R.D. Group decision-making as a structurational process. *Quarterly Journal of Speech,* 71 (1985), 74–102.

Post, B.Q. A business case framework for group support technology. *Journal of Management Information Systems,* 9, 3 (1993), 7–26.

Powell, A.; Piccoli, G.; and Ives, B. Virtual teams: a review of current literature and directions for future research. *The Data Base for Advances in Information Systems,* 35, 1 (2004), 6–36.

Qureshi, S., and Zigurs, I. Paradoxes and prerogatives in global virtual collaboration. *Communications of the ACM,* 44, 12 (2001), 85–88.

Ramesh, V., and Dennis, A.R. The object-oriented team: lessons for virtual teams from global software development. In *Proceedings of the 35th Hawaii International Conference on System Sciences.* Washington, DC: IEEE Computer Society Press, 2002, p. 18.1.

Rana, A.; Turoff, M.; and Hiltz, S.R. Task and technology interaction (TTI): a theory of technological support for group tasks. In *Proceedings of the Thirtieth Annual Hawaii International Conference on System Sciences,* II. 1997, pp. 66–76.

Rice, R.E. Contexts of research on organizational computer-mediated communication. A recursive review. In M. Lea (ed.), *Contexts of Computer-Mediated Communication.* Hemel Hempstead, UK: Harvester Wheatsheaf, 1992.

Rogers, Y. Exploring obstacles: integrating CSCW in evolving organizations. In *Proceedings of CSCW '94.* Chapel Hill, NC: ACM Press, 1994, 67–79.

Sanderson, D. The CSCW implementation process: an interpretative model and case study of the implementation of a videoconference system. In *Proceedings of CSCW '92.* New York: ACM Press, 1992, pp. 370–377.

Sarker, S., and Sahay, S. Understanding virtual team development: an interpretive study. *Journal of the Association for Information Systems,* 4 (2003), 1–38.

Saunders, C.S. Virtual teams: piecing together the puzzle. In R.W. Zmud, (ed.), *Framing the Domains of IT Management: Projecting the Future . . . Through the Past.* Cincinnati, OH: Pinnaflex Educational Resources, Inc., 2000, pp. 29–50.

Schmidt, K., and Bannon, L. Taking CSCW seriously. Supporting articulation work. *Computer Supported Cooperative Work (CSCW),* 1, (1992), 7–40.

Scott Morton, M.S. (ed.) *The Corporation of the 1990s. Information Technology and Organizational Transformation.* New York: Oxford University Press, 1991.

Shaw, M.E. *Group Dynamics: The Psychology of Small Group Behavior,* 3rd ed. New York: McGraw-Hill, 1981.

Short, J.; Williams, E.; and Christie, B. *The Social Psychology of Telecommunications.* New York: Wiley, 1976.

Sproull, L., and Kiesler, S. *Connections: New Ways of Working in the Networked Organization.* Cambridge, MA: MIT Press, 1991.

Stein, E.W., and Zwass, V. Actualizing organizational memory with information systems. *Information Systems Research,* 6, 2 (1995), 85–117.

Steiner, I.D. *Group Process and Productivity,* New York: Academic Press, 1972.

Stohr, E.A., and Zhao, J.L. Workflow automation: overview and research issues. *Information Systems Frontiers,* 3, 3 (2001), 281–296.

Suchman, L. *Plans and Situated Action.* Cambridge: Cambridge University Press, 1987.

Trauth, E.M., and Jessup, L.M. Understanding computer-mediated discussions: positivist and interpretive analyses of group support system use. *MIS Quarterly,* 24, 1 (2000), 43–79.

Tucker, R., and Panteli, N. Back to basics: sharing goals and developing trust in global virtual teams. In *Proceedings of IFIP WG 8.2/9.4,* Boston: Kluwer Academic Publishers, 2003, pp. 85–98.

Turoff, M. Virtuality. *Communications of the ACM,* 40, 9 (1997), 38–43.

Turoff, M.; Hiltz, S.R.; Bahgat, A.N.F.; and Rana, A.R. Distributed group support systems. *MIS Quarterly,* 17, 4, (December 1993), 399–417.

Vandenbosch, B., and Ginzberg, M.J. Lotus Notes® and collaboration: plus ça change . . . *Journal of Management Information Systems,* 13, 3 (1996–97), 65–81.

Venkatraman, N. The concept of fit in strategy research: toward verbal and statistical correspondence. *Academy of Management Review,* 14, 3 (1989), 423–444.

Watson, R.T.; Bostrom, R.P.; and Kinney, S.T. (eds.), *Computer Augmented Teamwork.* New York: Van Nostrand Reinhold, 1992.

Watson-Manheim, M.B., and Belanger, F. Exploring communication-based work processes in virtual environments. In *Proceedings of the 35th Annual Hawaii International Conference on System Sciences.* Washington, DC: IEEE Press, 2002, p. 272.2.

Watson-Manheim, M.B.; Chudoba, K.M.; and Crowston, K. Discontinuities and continuities: a new way to understand virtual work. *Information Technology & People,* 15, 3 (2002), 191–209.

Wierba, E.E.; Finholt, T.A.; and Steves, M.P. Challenges to collaborative tool adoption in a manufacturing engineering setting: a case study. In *Proceedings of the 35th Annual Hawaii International Conference on System Sciences.* Washington, DC: IEEE Press, 2002, 272.

Williams, E. Experimental comparisons of face-to-face and mediated communication: a review. *Psychological Bulletin,* 84, 5 (1977), 963–976.

Winograd, T. A language/action perspective on the design of cooperative work. *Human-Computer Interaction,* 3, 30 (1987–1988), 3–30.

Zigurs, I. Methodological and measurement issues in group support systems research. In L.M. Jessup and J.S. Valacich (eds.), *Group Support Systems: New Perspectives.* New York: Macmillan, 1993, 112–122.

Zigurs, I., and Buckland, B. A theory of task/technology fit and group support systems effectiveness. *MIS Quarterly,* 22, 3 (1998), 313–334.

Zigurs, I.; Buckland, B.; Connolly, J.; and Wilson, E.V. A test of task-technology fit theory for group support systems. *The DATA BASE for Advances in Information Systems,* 30, 3–4 (1999), 34–50.

PART III

CULTURE AND GLOBALIZATION

CHAPTER 8

TOWARD RELIABLE METRICS FOR CULTURAL ASPECTS OF HUMAN-COMPUTER INTERACTION

Focusing on the Mobile Internet in Three Asian Countries

JINWOO KIM, INSEONG LEE, BOREUM CHOI, SE-JOON HONG, KAR YAN TAM, AND KAZUAKI NARUSE

Abstract: Mobile Internet is defined as mobile access to the Internet through handheld devices such as mobile phones and PDAs. Popular mobile Internet services differ from country to country, as do usage patterns. In fact, mobile Internet usage patterns may differ more profoundly across countries than traditional stationary Internet usage patterns. This is because mobile devices, which operate only within local areas, access wireless networks, whereas globally uniform devices access the stationary Internet. Although numerous factors might explain the different mobile Internet usage patterns across different countries, this study primarily focuses on cultural differences, since culture profoundly affects the use of localized information technology. Despite the importance of cultural differences, little research has been performed on cross-cultural issues affecting information technologies in general, let alone on the specific case of mobile Internet use. This paucity of research is a consequence of the difficulties in reliably or validly measuring cultural aspects of information technology usage. Based on prior studies of culture, this paper proposes a set of metrics that can measure cultural aspects of mobile Internet usage. We also provide empirical evidence about the reliability and validity of the proposed metrics using survey data collected simultaneously in three Asian countries with the same questionnaire.

Keywords: Culture, Mobile Internet, Metrics

INTRODUCTION

As software products and Web applications are used more and more outside the countries that they have been developed in and designed for, there is a growing interest in the effects of national differences in the area of human-computer interaction (HCI). In the increasingly global market, many HCI practitioners are also faced with the challenge of offering usable products and services to the local users (Khaslavsky, 1998). Numerous factors contribute to national differences, including economies, physical environments, infrastructures, and cultures, encompassing values and norms (Ford et al., 2003). Cultural aspects influence the typical ways in which software products and online services are used within a country, above and beyond economic and environmental factors (Ford et al., 2003; Zakaria and Stanton, 2003). This is because a country's tangible, observable aspects are only the tips of the iceberg in relation to its cultural aspects (Hoft, 1995; Trompenaars, 1993). Moreover, culture has a strong effect on how users interpret a system's interface (Hiltunen et al., 2002). Therefore, user interface (UI) elements that are appropriate for one culture may not be appropriate for others, and this requires localized designs of user interfaces for each cultural group (Badre, 2001; Zakaria and Stanton, 2003).

As mobile Internet—wireless access to the Internet's digitalized content via mobile devices (Francis, 1997)—spreads globally, local cultures can have a strong effect on how mobile Internet services are used. This is demonstrated through the national variance in usage patterns and popular services. For example, 46 percent of Japanese users regularly use an e-mail service via the mobile Internet, while 65 percent of American users are not interested in mobile e-mail services at all (InfoCom Research Inc., 2002). Furthermore, while SMS (Short Message Service) is a popular service in Europe, Americans hardly use it (Urbaczewski et al., 2002). The differences of usage across different countries or regions may be more substantial for the mobile Internet than the traditional stationary Internet. A possible explanation might be that mobile devices, which operate only within local areas, access the wireless network, whereas globally uniform devices access the stationary Internet.

However, despite the importance of the cultural aspects, little research has been performed on cross-cultural issues in information technologies, including the mobile Internet (Okazaki, 2004). This is because such studies have always been confronted with difficulties in explicitly defining and measuring the intangible concept of culture (Ford et al., 2003; Henry, 1976; Straub et al., 2002). In other words, culture is a more difficult concept to define and measure than economic and environmental factors. The dearth of clear concepts and measurements for culture can explain why cross-cultural research has been so difficult to conduct (Straub et al., 2002). Although a few endeavors in the field of HCI consider the cultural aspects of system development, most do so on a superficial level and concentrate on language and image, making the implicit assumption that user needs and requirements are the same across different cultures (De Angeli et al., 2004). According to this assumption, software products and online services can be localized by translating text from one language into another. However, creating truly effective interfaces for an international user base requires more than mere translation of text because of the multidimensional and layered characteristics of culture (Russo and Boor, 1993). Simply translating messages and online documents is not enough to localize online services because the services are cultural amplifiers, which should be designed according to specific cultures (Nakakoji, 1996). Therefore, we should consider deeper levels of localization by incorporating cultural and social aspects of the locale where the technologies and services will be used.

Before we assess cultural differences across different countries, we require valid and reliable measurement that will permit sufficiently sensitive systematic comparisons to disclose such differences (Munson and McIntyre, 1979). If culture is an important determinant of users' behavior or preference, and if culture can be adequately measured, it would be advantageous to use culture as a basis for segmentation techniques (Munson and McIntyre, 1979). In other words, UI designers and content developers can use an approach that segments international markets based on the characteristics of culture to localize mobile Internet services for local users. But first we need to develop a valid and reliable measurement of the cultural aspects of mobile Internet services.

This study proposes a new set of metrics to measure the cultural aspects of mobile Internet usage. In order to develop a set of metrics based on cultural dimensions, we have conducted a literature review of existing studies of culture in the diverse fields of anthropology, psychology, management information systems, marketing, and human-computer interaction. Afterwards, eighteen survey questions were compiled, reflecting the cultural dimensions of Hofstede (1980) and Hall (1976, 1959).

However, unlike preceding research that uncritically accepted either Hofstede's metrics or Hall's subdivision of countries into cultural dimensions, this research has developed a new set of metrics that is better suited to the new mobile Internet environment. Because Hofstede's (1980) cultural dimensions had been developed to measure work-related value, his measurements are not applicable to the current environment of the mobile Internet, which is mainly used to achieve personal goals (Furrer et al., 2000). Similarly, Hall relied on observations and interviews to subdivide the countries into three cultural dimensions without any direct survey measurements (Hoft, 1996). This technique does not provide sufficient empirical evidence to form a foundation for a set of metrics; therefore, a new questionnaire is needed.

This study provides empirical results about the reliability and validity of the proposed metrics, using survey data conducted in three Asian countries—Korea, Hong Kong, and Japan. With regard to mobile Internet services, Korea, Hong Kong, and Japan are considered mature or advanced markets, due to their early adoption of mobile Internet services and the rapid increase in the number of mobile Internet users (Lee and Kim, 2003). Moreover, despite their geographical proximity, the cultures of the three countries are substantially different (Hofstede, 1980), which enabled us to explicate the impact of different cultures on the mobile Internet.

The next section reviews important concepts relating to culture, and reviews empirical cross-cultural studies in various research fields. The following section reviews some of the most important work in cultural dimensions and identifies critical cultural dimensions for the mobile Internet. The next section explains the process of measurement development and the survey method, and presents results from the survey. The final section discusses this study's limitations and the implications of its results.

CULTURE

Culture has been defined in a number of different, but related ways. Kroeber (1952, p. 157) defined culture as "the historically differentiated and variable mass of customary ways of functioning of human societies." Kroeber and Parsons (1958, p. 583) arrived at a cross-disciplinary definition of culture as "transmitted and created content and patterns of value, ideas, and other symbolic-meaningful systems as factors in the shaping of human behavior and the artifacts produced through behavior." For Hofstede (1980, p. 25), culture is "the collective programming of the mind that distinguishes the members of one group or category of people from another." In order to clearly define the concept of culture, he introduces three levels of human mental programming in his pyramid model: individual, collective, and universal. Through this, he attempts to discern the origin of culture and to explain why it is unique in human mental programming. For him, the individual level is the unique part of each person, the collective is shared with some but not all people, and the universal is shared by all humanity. Similarly, Ferraro (1998) defines culture, using three verbs, as everything that people have, think, and do as members of their society.

In summary, culture cannot be understood by studying the individual; rather, culture must be read as a set of shared characteristics within a group of people, which affects the behaviors of individual members by providing norms. Culture can be understood through the limited frame of tangible aspects but, instead, encompasses numerous intangible aspects including human thoughts, norms, and behaviors. Thus, an organization that provides an identical service to users in different countries assumes that these users share common behaviors, customs, and values. However, there are many diverse cultures, and different cultures will not converge in a short time frame (de Mooij, 1998). Thus, the localization of a service is essential to construct a close relationship between the users and the service providers (de Mooij, 1998).

Researchers studying the influence of culture on human life attempt to schematize its multiple affects through a notion of "layering" that, in turn, is proposed through two representative models: the iceberg model and the onion model. The iceberg model, suggested by Hoft (1995), is a popular meta-model that cross-cultural communication consultants often use, since it provides a useful metaphor for describing the layers of culture and how aware we are of their influence on our lives. The analogy drawn in the iceberg model is that just as 10 percent of an iceberg is visible above the surface of the water, only 10 percent of the cultural characteristics of a target audience are easily visible to an observer. It follows that the remaining 90 percent of cultural characteristics are hidden from view and are, therefore, more difficult to identify and study. Hoft's model identifies three metaphorical layers of culture:

- Layer of surface: visible and obvious rules such as number system, currency, and time and date formats
- Layer of unspoken rules: obscured rules that can only be understood through context-specific experiences
- Layer of unconscious rules: rules that fall beyond conscious awareness and are difficult to observe

Alternatively, Trompenaars (1993) metaphorically illustrates culture as an onion. He, too, divides culture into three layers. The outer layer comprises what people principally associate with culture, such as its tangible products and artifacts. This explicit culture is represented by, for example, clothes, food, language, and housing. Secondly, the middle layer of culture refers to the norms and values shared by a community. Norms, shared principles of right and wrong, give a person an idea of how one should behave in a culture. Values define the culture's ideas about what is good and bad, as well as desirable and undesirable. The deepest level, or core, of the onion is implicit culture, which comprises underlying and basic assumptions. Understanding the core of the onion is the key for successfully working with other cultures.

When a service is being transformed for use in multiple markets, there are visible or surface issues for localization (just like the tip of the iceberg model or the external layer of the onion model), such as text that requires translation or unit measurements that must be converted. Once this is accomplished, we can say that the service has been localized to the minimum level.

This will not, however, be enough if the service does not match local users' expectations or understandings about what the service should or might do. A more adequate localization enables users to feel that the service was intended for them, even though they are very distant (culturally or geographically) from the place where the product was originally developed. In this instance, the user experience may need to be radically localized to incorporate unspoken or even subconscious characteristics or rules that are specific to a country or market segment. A radical localization takes into consideration how users from a given locale think, feel, and act in their contextual environment.

In summary, culture has multiple layers and we can explicitly observe only the outmost layer. There are much more profound cultural influences that are not easily discernible. Thus, in order to maximize effective localization, we should investigate the implicit levels, such as norms, values, and symbols, in conjunction with explicit ones. Most researchers have relied on a particular assessment method such as observation and focus groups (e.g., Hall, 1976; Hall, 1959), or questionnaires and interviews (e.g., Hofstede, 1980; Trompenaars, 1993) to investigate the implicit levels. Of all the traditional assessment methods, questionnaires are used frequently to identify the implicit levels (Hoft, 1996). This is because questionnaires are probably the only method that makes such extensive coverage feasible, with the ensuing possibility of discovering differences between various users from different cultures (Nielsen, 1993).

THE CROSS-CULTURAL RESEARCH ENDEAVORS

Prior studies on cultural differences among countries have been conducted in the diverse fields of anthropology (e.g., Hall, 1976; Hall, 1959), psychology (e.g., Basabe et al., 2002; Bond and Smith, 1996; Schwartz, 1994; Triandis, 1990), management information systems (e.g., Garfield and Watson, 1998; Huang et al., 2003; Igbaria and Zviran, 1996; Kedia and Bhagat, 1988; Lim, 2004), marketing (e.g., Chang and Ding, 1995; Cho et al., 1999; Clark, 1990; Donthu and Yoo, 1998; Douglas and Craig, 1997), and human-computer interaction (e.g., Choong and Salvendy, 1998; Evers, 1997; Marcus and Gould, 2000). The recent research endeavors in the fields of marketing, management information systems (MIS), and human-computer interaction (HCI) are of particular interest to our study because they are closely related to metrics for cross-cultural aspects of the mobile Internet.

Cross-Cultural Studies in the Field of Service Marketing

Since mobile Internet services can be considered as a specific type of service, prior studies on culture in the field of service marketing are reviewed first. Service marketing theorists generally accept culture as one of the underlying determinants of consumer behavior (Henry, 1976).

Having adopted Hofstede's (1980) proposition of the concept of cultural dimensions, Donthu and Yoo (1998) found that customers' cultural orientations affect their service quality expectation (SERVQUAL) both generally and in the five service quality dimensions. Furthermore, Furrer et al. (2000) demonstrated a correlation between the dimensions of SERVQUAL and Hofstede's cultural dimensions. Based on this, they have subdivided the world market for services into culturally homogeneous groups, and have provided the Cultural Service Quality Index (CSQI), in an effort to allocate resources and localize the provision of services according to the subdivided market.

Also, Mattila (1999) has argued that customers from a Western cultural background and customers from an Asian background differ in which attributes of a service they deem important, such as in the context of hotel services. According to the study, customers from a Western cultural background place more emphasis on concrete conditions such as the physical environment, and they cherish the hedonic dimension of consumption more than their Asian counterparts do.

Finally, Liu et al. (2001) analyzed the services marketing and cross-cultural psychology literature to study how culture influences behavioral intentions toward services. They found that customers from cultures characterized by lower individualism or higher uncertainty avoidance tend to have a higher intention to praise if they receive superior service. The same groups tend not to switch services, give negative word of mouth, or complain even if they received poor service. These effects are reversed for customers from cultures characterized by higher individualism or lower uncertainty avoidance.

In summary, prior research in the marketing field suggests the importance of culture in shaping customers' attitudes and preferences. Customers from different cultures have been found to form different perceptions of service quality, either because of differences in expectations or inclinations towards different service quality criteria (Liu et al., 2001). However, most of the prior research has categorized subject countries based on Hofstede's (1980) or other researchers' descriptions, and attribute observed differences in dimensions of interest to the cultural tendencies of the countries (Kim et al., 1998). Before we can accept these results, we need to explore, empirically, whether a country that Hofstede (1980) or other researchers have categorized really exhibits tendencies consistent with their findings in the area of the mobile Internet.

Cross-Cultural Studies in the Field of Management Information Systems

An increasing number of information systems (IS) applications are implemented across national and cultural boundaries. As a result, much work has been done in the MIS field to gauge the effects of cultural aspects on IS usage, adoption, or diffusion patterns (e.g., Straub, 1994).

For example, after a cross-cultural study involving the United States and Japan, Straub (1994) asserted that cultural differences were important in IT diffusion. He reasoned that Japanese respondents would value e-mail lower than other communication media since they tended to eagerly avoid uncertainty (Hofstede, 1980). Furthermore, he proposed that because of their tendency to avoid uncertainty in communication, Japanese knowledge workers would be more likely to choose information-rich (e.g., body language, facial expression, and tone of voice), socially present (e.g., face-to-face meeting, telephone) communication methods over systems such as e-mail. He found that this tendency on the part of the Japanese translated into lower perceptions of usefulness and lower usage of e-mail in comparison with U.S. workers, suggesting that the technology adoption model may be influenced by cultural differences. Straub concluded by calling for research that includes culture as a key variable in IT diffusion (Straub, 1994).

A number of studies have been conducted on the use of group support systems (GSS) involving culture. For example, Watson, Ho, and Raman (1994) investigated the impact of culture on the change in consensus resulting from GSS. Singaporean groups were found to have higher pre-meeting consensus and less change in consensus than U.S. groups. According to their research, this is because Singaporean groups are more likely to be collectivists than U.S. groups and collectivists value consensus more highly and strive for it independent of GSS use. Therefore, the value of GSS to increase consensus will be diminished when it is employed by collectivists. Also, in a cultural model used to examine GSS participation, Robichaux and Cooper (1998) concluded that the level of cultural values a group held had significant impact on the ability of GSS to increase participation. They called for additional research propositions to be developed to explore cultural influences, as these would affect TAM components. Also, they suggested that because GSS and e-mail have some important similarities in terms of computer keyboard input, and parallel and anonymous entry, Hofstede's cultural theory could be applied to both technologies.

In addition, Leidner, Carlsson, and Elam (1995) proved the hypothesis that cultural factors affected the use of executive information systems (EIS) in different countries. Their findings suggested that U.S. executives use EIS primarily for monitoring and achieving benefits in the areas of speedy problem identification and decision making, whereas Swedish executives use EIS primarily for a more thorough and analytical decision-making process.

Kankanhalli et al. (2004) examined the relationship between cultural dimensions (individualism vs. collectivism and masculinity vs. femininity) and three development values (technical, economic, and socio-political) of IS developers through a field survey in Singapore and the United States. According to the findings, individualism-collectivism and masculinity-femininity had significant impacts on the economic, technical, and socio-political values of IS developers. Notably, IS developers with individualistic inclinations appear to have higher economic, technical, and socio-political values than IS developers with collectivistic inclinations. IS developers with masculine inclinations also seem to have higher economic, technical, and socio-political values than IS developers with feminine inclinations.

Meanwhile, having adopted Hofstede's (1980) proposition of the concept of cultural dimension, Png, Tan, and Wee (2001) demonstrated that businesses from higher uncertainty avoidance countries were less likely to adopt IT infrastructure, while power distance was not significantly correlated with adoption of the IT infrastructure. Based on these results, they suggested that it is not appropriate to apply the same strategy to promote adoption of IT infrastructure for all businesses.

Also, Vishwanath (2003) investigated the effects of differing information on participants within a standardized Web site (eBay) across three countries (Germany, Japan, and the United States). The study found a significant interaction among culture, information, and uncertainty avoidance. According to the study, in high uncertainty avoidance cultures such as Japan, participants in an online auction may exhibit drastic behavioral changes (e.g., lower valuation and reduced participation) when they are faced with limited information within an ambiguous decision-making context. This contrasts with the behavior of participants in Germany and the United States.

Finally, through content analysis of eighty U.S. domestic and Chinese Web sites, Singh, Zho, and Hu (2003) have shown that the Web is not a culturally neutral medium, but replete with cultural markers that give country-specific Web sites a look and feel unique to the local culture. For example, according to their research, the high uncertainty avoidance nature of Chinese people is responsible for Chinese Web sites providing more uncertainty avoidance features, such as secure payment and free trials, than did U.S. Web sites. Similarly, Robbins and Stylianou (2001) argued that differences in national culture are evident in the Web sites of global corporations. Through content analysis of ninety global corporations' Web sites, they concluded that multinationals should continue to explore methods to develop Web sites that will be tailored to the cultures of the major countries in which they are conducting business.

In summary, MIS researchers have investigated how national culture affects a wide variety of IT-related issues. However, as with marketing research, most of the cross-cultural research in the MIS field simply categorized countries based on prior researchers' findings (e.g., Hofstede, 1980) without reexamining the cultural characteristics of the countries in terms of the target IT. Also, because the MIS field tends to focus on business or government use of IS instead of personal goals, prior cross-cultural researches in the MIS field have focused mostly on users who intend to achieve work-related goals in an organization, rather than users who intend to achieve personal goals in various contexts. Although little research has been performed on the relationship between culture and the behavior or preference of users who intend to use IT for personal purposes, adoption and diffusion of information technologies have been studied at the individual level in the MIS field. In this instance, Venkatesh and Brown (2001) argued that the factors affecting household PC adoption decisions are somewhat different from those affecting workplace decisions, due to the personal goals for technology use and the personal nature of the expense. Also, Chae and Kim (2001) proved the hypotheses that four major dimensions of information quality in mobile Internet services are positively related to user satisfaction and customer loyalty, and that their relative importance varies according to users' personal goals. Thus, we need to examine the relationship between culture and the behavior or preference of users who intend to use IT for personal purposes.

Cultural Consideration in HCI studies

Under the assumption that culture plays a key role in the interaction between human and computer, cultural studies are appearing in the field of HCI (Hoft, 1996). Choong and Salvendy (1998) have conducted an experiment, presenting alphanumeric icons and pictorial icons, respectively, to

American and Chinese participants to show that the users' reactions and the time taken to perform the tasks differed according to their cultural inclinations. They found that Chinese users performed tasks faster, with fewer errors, when presented with pictorial icons, whereas American users excelled when offered alphanumeric ones. Similarly, through focused group interview (FGI), survey, and usability testing, Honold (1999) found that German cellular phone users prioritized clearly written and comprehensive user manuals, whereas Chinese cellular phone users demanded more pictorial information.

Meanwhile, Marcus and Gould (2000) analyzed the relationships of intangible cultural dimensions, as postulated by Hofstede (1980), to Web site design. They found that cultural elements are embedded in user interfaces as a set of contextual and social cues for effective use. They also proposed that Hofstede's cultural dimensions are mapped to the design of user interface components, such as metaphors, mental models, navigation, interaction, and appearance. For example, combining uncertainty avoidance and navigation, they suggested that high uncertainty avoidance countries prefer limited options and simple controls, whereas low uncertainty avoidance countries prefer multiple options and complex controls. As a result, they proposed the design guidelines of user interface for Web sites according to Hofstede's cultural dimensions.

From observations and interviews in India, Honold (2000) identified factors that influence the use of products in foreign cultures. He suggested that eight factors—namely, objectives of the users, characteristics of the users, environment, infrastructure, division of labor, organization of work, mental models based on previous experience, and tools—should be considered when defining requirements in different cultures.

Similarly, based on the results of an ethnographic study aimed at building an understanding of Indian ATM users, De Angeli et al. (2004) demonstrated the cultural context's unique role in affecting users' expectations of and behavioral possibilities with the ATM machine. They concluded that an understanding of metaphors and cultural bias can facilitate technology diffusion and acceptance since localized designs help motivate and train users.

In summary, culture has been considered as an important research topic because it represents a variable that widely affects the behavior and preferences of people. However, most research on cultural issues in the HCI field outlines very limited techniques for improving localization, usually through superficial adaptations like language translation and icon transformation (Khaslavsky, 1998). Such tangible, or explicit, level approaches to localization may miss fundamental differences in user requirements. Similarly, literature that recommends design guidelines for successful localization does not provide extensive information about how cultural factors and cultural differences can be applied in a meaningful way to a system design. We should, therefore, conduct more in-depth studies to discover the cultural factors and differences that may affect the systems' usability.

CULTURAL DIMENSION

There is no denying that culture influences human computer interaction (Hoft, 1996). However, in practice, there are still difficulties in describing and capturing cultural influences to create a basis for localization of software design (Honold, 1999). This is because we lack a robust measure of culture to use as a starting point for comparing different cultures. To resolve this problem, researchers have attempted to define cultural aspects in a set of dimensions (Straub et al., 2002). Cultural dimensions provide excellent variables that can be employed to analyze cross-cultural user behavior (de Mooij, 2003). Some of the most important work in cultural dimensions has been undertaken by Parsons and Shils (1951), Kluckhohn and Strodtbeck (1961), Hall (1976, 1959),

Hofstede (1980), Trompenaars (1993), and Schwartz (1994). In this section, we review six popular models of cultural dimensions that identify cultural variables at deeper levels of localization.

Parsons and Shils (1951) suggested that culture is defined by the unique combination of cultural dimensions. They distinguished five cultural dimensions on which people have to make choices in everyday life: affectivity vs. affectivity neutrality, self-orientation vs. collectivity orientation, universalism vs. particularism, ascription vs. achievement, and specificity vs. diffuseness.

Kluckhohn and Strodtbeck (1961), on the other hand, suggested that each of the dimensions can be meaningfully viewed separately. They developed four basic dimensions: humans' relation to nature (subjugation, harmony, mastery), time dimension (past, present, future), personal activity (being, containing, doing), and humans' relation to others (lineal, collateral, individualistic).

Hall (1976, 1959), an anthropologist and cross-cultural communication researcher, developed his model of cultural dimensions based on years of observation and extensive interviewing throughout the world. He distinguishes cultures according to two dimensions: context (high context vs. low context) and time perception (polychromic time vs. monochromic time).

Meanwhile, Hofstede (1980) conducted a survey of IBM employees in forty different countries to measure his four dimensions of national culture. His model distinguishes culture according to four dimensions: uncertainty avoidance, individualism vs. collectivism, masculinity vs. femininity, and power distance. In addition to these four dimensions, Hofstede and Bond (1988) subsequently defined a fifth dimension, long-term orientation vs. short-term orientation.

On the other hand, Trompenaars (1993) developed a set of seven cultural dimensions based on a study involving thirty companies in fifty nations. His cultural dimensions were based on Parsons and Shils's (1951), and can be described as conceptually related to some of Hofstede's dimensions. The seven dimensions of culture identified by Trompenaars are universalism vs. particularism, individualism vs. collectivism, affective vs. affective-neutral communication style, specific vs. diffuse relationships, ascription vs. achievement, time orientation, and nature orientation.

Lastly, Schwartz (1994) presented an alternative conceptual and operational approach for deriving cultural dimensions of work-related values. Drawing on findings from his individual-level study of the content and structure of values, Schwartz distinguished seven cultural value types: conservatism, intellectual and affective autonomy, hierarchy, mastery, egalitarian commitment, and harmony. His model was based partly on Hofstede's (1980) and Kluckhohn and Strodtbeck's (1961) work and was tested using data collected between 1988 and 1992 from respondents in forty-eight cultural groups across thirty-eight nations.

Table 8.1 contains a summary of the most commonly cited cultural dimensions, which will be explained in detail in the following subsections.

Individualism vs. Collectivism (Conservatism vs. Autonomy)

Individualism vs. collectivism has been suggested as the most important cultural dimension through numerous studies (Cho et al., 1999; Triandis, 1990). Individualism represents a preference for a loosely knit social framework in a society where people are supposed to take care of themselves and look after their own interests, whereas collectivism signals a preference for a tightly knit social framework where people expect their comrades to look after them and where personal goals are subordinated to those of the group (Hofstede, 1980). Similar to Hofstede (1980), Parsons and Shils (1951) and Trompenaars (1993) describe individualism as a primary orientation to the self and collectivism as a primary orientation to common goals and objectives.

Meanwhile, Schwartz (1994) identified two distinct notions, conservatism and autonomism, that may be understood as similar to individualism and collectivism. He defines conservatism as placing

Table 8.1

Cultural Dimensions

Cultural Dimension	Citation
Individualism vs. Collectivism, Conservatism vs. Autonomy, or Relation Orientation	Parsons and Shils (1951), Hofstede (1980), Trompenaars (1993), Schwartz (1994), Kluckhohn and Strodtbeck (1961)
Uncertainty Avoidance	Hofstede (1980)
Masculinity vs. Femininity	Hofstede (1980)
Power Distance or Hierarchy vs. Egalitarianism	Hofstede (1980), Schwartz (1994)
Context	Hall (1976)
Notions of Time	Hall (1959), Kluckhohn and Strodtbeck (1961), Trompenaars (1993), Hofstede and Bond (1988)
Affectivity vs. Affectivity Neutrality	Parsons and Shils (1951), Trompenaars (1993)
Universalism vs. Particularism	Parsons and Shils (1951), Trompenaars (1993)
Ascription vs. Achievement or Activity Orientation	Parsons and Shils (1951), Trompenaars (1993), Kluckhohn and Strodtbeck (1961)
Specificity vs. Diffuseness	Parsons and Shils (1951), Trompenaars (1993)
Humans' Relation to Natural and Social World	Kluckhohn and Strodtbeck (1961), Trompenaars (1993), Schwartz (1994)

a cultural emphasis on the maintenance of the status quo, the protection of property, and the restraint of actions or inclinations that might disrupt the group solidarity or the traditional order. Social order, respect for tradition, family security, wisdom, preserving public image, and self-discipline are important values in conservative cultures. Conservatism is similar to collectivism, as both conceive of a person as an entity embedded in the collective who finds meaning in life largely through social relationships (Schwartz, 1994). Autonomy, the other end of this dyad, characterizes cultures in which the person is viewed as an autonomous entity entitled to pursue his or her individual, independent interests and desires, who relates to others in terms of self-interest and negotiated agreements (Schwartz, 1994). In this, autonomy resembles Hofstede's individualism. Schwartz (1994) divides autonomy into (1) intellectual autonomy, stressing that individuals will independently pursue their own ideas and intellectual directions, and (2) affective autonomy, stating that individuals will independently pursue affective positive experiences, for example, pleasure, or a varied and exciting life.

Lastly, Kluckhohn and Strodtbeck (1961) divide a person's relation to others into three distinct notions: linearity, co-laterality, and individualism. These, too, are closely linked to Hofstede's individualism vs. collectivism. In Kluckhohn and Strodtbeck's model, if individualism dominates, personal goals and interests have primacy over the goals of the groups to which a person belongs. In linearity and co-laterality, group goals are dominant. The difference between the two is in application. In the case of linearity, an older person decides what is best for the group, whereas in co-lateral cultures, group goals are determined through a consensus among its members.

Uncertainty Avoidance

Uncertainty avoidance can be defined as "the extent to which the members of a culture feel threatened by uncertain or unknown situations" (Hofstede, 1980, p. 161). People in high uncertainty avoidance cultures accept uncertainty uncomfortably and show a low tolerance for risk. They try to avoid these situations by believing in absolute truths and expertise, providing greater stability, establishing more formal rules, and rejecting deviant ideas and behaviors. By contrast, people in low uncertainty avoidance cultures deal well with uncertainty and can be characterized as risk-takers.

Masculinity vs. Femininity

Masculinity vs. femininity is another dimension that describes what is valued and how one relates to others (Hofstede, 1980). The construct is defined as the degree to which a society is characterized by assertiveness (masculinity) vs. nurturance (femininity). People in masculine cultures place greater value on achievement, tasks, money, and performance, whereas people in feminine cultures place greater emphasize on people, the quality of life, helping others, and tenderness. Furthermore, masculinity pertains to societies in which gender roles are clearly distinct, while femininity pertains to societies in which gender roles overlap.

Power Distance (Hierarchy vs. Egalitarianism)

Hofstede (1980) defines power distance as the extent to which the members of society accept unequal distributions of power. People in cultures with a large power distance accept hierarchical orders and do not question power inequalities. By contrast, people in cultures with a small power distance do not feel comfortable when operating in hierarchical situations.

In line with Hofstede, Schwartz (1994) contrasts hierarchical and egalitarian cultures. The first emphasizes the chain of authority and hierarchical structures. An unequal distribution of power and status is legitimate and expected. By contrast, people in egalitarian cultures view one another as equal.

Context

Context is defined by Hall (1976) as the information that surrounds an event. In high context cultures, information is either conveyed contextually or implicitly assumed. Low context cultures can be characterized by explicit messages and direct communications. People in high context cultures tend to rely on visual elements and symbols, while people in low context cultures tend to rely on hard facts, data, and statistics.

Notions of Time

Time is one of the fundamental bases for all cultures; all activities revolve around it (Hall, 1959). Hall (1959) identified two distinct notions of time: monochronic and polychronic. People in monochronic cultures focus on and perform only one task at a time, proceeding in a sequential or linear manner. They are task-oriented, emphasize promptness, and stick to their plans. By contrast, people in polychronic cultures can act in parallel modes, doing many things at once and proceeding in a simultaneous or concurrent manner. They tend to change plans and emphasize relationships rather than tasks.

Meanwhile, both Kluckhohn and Strodtbeck (1961) and Trompenaars (1993) proposed three distinct notions of time: past-, present-, and future-orientation. People from past-oriented cultures like to preserve traditions and talk about history or the origins of families. By contrast, people from present-oriented cultures prefer to think in terms of the present and value spontaneity. Finally, people from future-oriented cultures are interested in youthful and future potentials. Elsewhere, Hofstede and Bond (1988) identified two major orientations towards time: short-term orientation and long-term orientation. Short-term orientation stands for the fostering of virtues related to the past and present. By contrast, long-term orientation cultures value virtues orientated toward future rewards.

Affectivity vs. Affectivity Neutrality

This dimension, suggested by Parsons and Shils (1951) and Trompenaars (1993), is best described as the range of feelings and emotions expressed in public. Reason and emotion both play a role in affectivity, and which of these dominates depends upon whether people are affective or affective neutral. People in affective cultures show their feelings plainly by language, smiling, grimacing, and gesturing. On the other hand, people in affective-neutral cultures do not telegraph their feelings but keep them carefully subdued and controlled (Trompenaars, 1993).

Universalism vs. Particularism

This dimension, suggested by Parsons and Shils (1951) and Trompenaars (1993), describes the degree of adhering to agreed standards. Universalists are rules-based. Rules define morality, ethics, or what is good and right. In a serious situation involving another person, universalists tend to apply these rules regardless of their relationship with the other person. Particularists are relationship-based. In a serious situation involving another person, particularists base their solution to the problem on the relationship that they have with the other person and will break the rules if necessary.

Ascription vs. Achievement or Activity Orientation

According to Parsons and Shils (1951), ascription refers to the normative pattern that prescribes that actors in a given type of situation should, in deciding upon differential treatment of social objects, give priority to certain attributes that they possess over any specific performances. Achievement refers to the normative pattern that prescribes that actors in a given type of situation should give priority to their specific performances over their given attributes. Similarly, Trompenaars (1993) defines this dimension as the method of according status to others. While some societies accord status to people on the basis of their achievements, others ascribe it to them by virtue of age, class, gender, education, and so on (Trompenaars, 1993). The former is called achieved status; the latter is ascribed status.

Meanwhile, activity orientation, suggested by Kluckhohn and Strodtbeck (1961), is related to what Parsons and Shils (1951) and Trompenaars (1993) refer to as ascription vs. achievement. This dimension is made up of doing, being, and "being-in-becoming" (Kluckhohn and Strodtbeck, 1961). A "doing" orientation implies that a person is judged on his accomplishments. In such cultures, obtaining results and working hard are particularly important. In case of a "being" orientation, the emphasis is placed on the person as a social human being. In such a society, personal characteristics and enjoyment of life are more important than achievements or working hard to obtain results. The "being-in-becoming" orientation stresses the development of the individual and may be understood as an intermediary between being and doing.

Specificity vs. Diffuseness

This dimension, suggested by Parsons and Shils (1951) and Trompenaars (1993), refers to how closely involved people get with one another. People in specific cultures easily make close contacts without involving privacy in relationships, whereas people in diffuse cultures begin from a foundation of great privacy and take a long time to build personal relationships (Trompenaars, 1993). For example, in extremely specific cultures it is rare to have colleagues who are close friends as well, because work and social life are largely separated from each other. However, in more diffused cultures it is common to spend time (e.g., having a drink) with colleagues after working hours.

Human's Relation to Natural and Social World

This dimension refers to the relationship of humans to the natural and social world (Schwartz, 1994). One response is to master and change the world actively, to assert control over it, and to exploit it in order to further personal or group interests. An opposite resolution is to accept the world as it is and try to fit into it rather than to change or exploit it. The former is labeled as mastery and the latter as harmony (Schwartz, 1994). Similarly, Kluckhohn and Strodtbeck (1961) classified humans' relation to nature into three distinct notions: subjugation, harmony, and mastery. Trompenaars (1993) returns to the binary and identifies two major orientations towards nature: control and subjugation.

CULTURAL DIMENSIONS AND MOBILE INTERNET

Among the various cultural dimensions detailed, this study adopts the four dimensions proposed by Hofstede (1980) and the two dimensions proposed by Hall (1976, 1959). Hofstede's extensive number of surveys in forty countries enables comparisons among cultures and is complemented by Hall's work, which concentrates on the communication patterns in various countries.

There are four reasons why we have selected the six cultural dimensions for our study. First, the six dimensions proposed by Hofstede and Hall have been considered as the most general ones in studying cross-cultural issues (de Mooij, 1998; Hoft, 1995; Singh et al., 2003; Strauss and Mang, 1999). Second, many researchers have already tested the validity of the dimensions (de Mooij, 1998; Hoft, 1995; Nakata and Sivakumar, 1996; Singh et al., 2003; Tan et al., 1998). Third, Hofstede and Hall's models of cultural dimensions are also perceived to have great relevance to the study of marketing and consumer behavior (de Mooij, 1998; Lee and Hong, 2001). That Hall's model classified cultural dimensions through communication patterns makes it relevant to studies of mobile Internet services, which are also tools for communication. Finally, Hofstede and Hall's models of cultural dimensions are the theories most often quoted both in general cross-cultural studies (e.g., Cho et al., 1999; Hasan and Ditsa, 1999; Singh et al., 2003; Strauss and Mang, 1999; Zakaria and Stanton, 2003) and in usability studies in HCI fields (e.g., Choong and Salvendy, 1998; De Angeli et al., 2004; Gould et al., 2000; Marcus and Gould, 2000; Smith et al., 2004; Zahedi et al., 2001). Hofstede's model has been quoted over one hundred times in MIS journals, proving that it is empirically well verified (Ford et al., 2003). Therefore, the six cultural dimensions may be relevant to cross-cultural issues of the mobile Internet. More specific reasons why we have selected each of the six cultural dimensions to measure cultural aspects of mobile Internet follow.

Uncertainty Avoidance

The uncertainty avoidance dimension may have substantial impacts on the usage of mobile Internet services. Users from countries with a high uncertainty avoidance culture feel threatened by uncertain or ambiguous situations and are likely to refrain from using contents and information that are of uncertain quality. They may also refrain from using a new service before others.

These users might also feel uncomfortable in a situation where they are faced with an unusual interface or feedback during the use of the mobile Internet (Evers, 1997).

In terms of usability, uncertainty avoidance may also influence the design of mobile Internet interfaces. For example, because high uncertainty avoidance cultures emphasize the predictability of user actions before they actually occur, mobile Internet users within that culture should be provided with a more predictable interface and with limited options (Marcus and Gould, 2000).

Individualism vs. Collectivism

An individualistic propensity may also have significant impacts on the usage of mobile Internet services. It could be inferred that users from a country with high individualistic tendencies will use the mobile Internet to showcase their individuality and opt to use services that are more personalized, since such users base decisions on personalized objectives. Meanwhile, people with a higher collectivistic propensity may tend to use services that will enable them to feel better connected to other people, since they place a priority on the group's objectives.

In terms of usability, individualism may also influence users' preference for mobile Internet interfaces. For example, because highly individualistic cultures would emphasize individualistic objectives (Cho et al., 1999), its mobile Internet users may prefer an interface that can be customized by them.

Masculinity vs. Femininity

Different masculinity characteristics can also be important in the mobile Internet environment. Strauss and Mang (1999) have shown that consumers from societies with high masculinity have a strict expectation of gender roles. A user from such countries will use services that better characterize his or her gender, differentiating the objective of a female user from that of a male. Moreover, they will feel uncomfortable when they are provided with services opposed to their expectations.

Dormann and Chisalita (2002) found one practical instance of the effects of masculinity vs. femininity in a study of Dutch and Austrian subjects. After exposing their participants to a Web site that stressed feminine values such as good relationships, quality of life, and tenderness, Dormann and Chisalita concluded that the Dutch participants who had higher femininity tendencies exhibited greater concordance than their Austrian counterparts with higher masculine tendencies.

Mobile Internet users from high masculinity cultures may focus on navigation that is oriented towards exploration and control (Marcus and Gould, 2000). Therefore, mobile Internet users from high masculinity cultures may be provided with relatively more navigation tools and cues, in order to prevent the users from becoming "lost in space."

Power Distance

Power distance may play an important role in the usage of the mobile Internet. Because authority, status, and legitimacy are emphasized in societies with greater power distance (Singh et al., 2003), the reputation of the mobile Internet service provider may be considered very important. For example, Zahedi, van Pelt, and Song (2001) proposed that people from societies that have greater power distance will prefer Web sites emphasizing authority, power, expertise, and wealth.

Power distance may also influence usability. For example, in cultures with greater power distance, users' mental models have many levels of depth and breadth (Marcus and Gould, 2000) and, therefore, mobile Internet users may prefer deep hierarchical menu structures.

Context

Context can also play an important role in mobile Internet usage. Users in low context cultures crave information in the form of explanatory texts, while users in high context cultures prefer symbolic and animated forms of information (Evers, 1997). Communications in high context cultures tend to be more implicative, underlying, and indirect. Users of the mobile Internet in such a cultural context may enjoy implicative and indirect expression in their use of e-mail and chat rooms.

Also, in terms of usability, users of the mobile Internet from a society with high context culture will prefer implicative menus with icons or animations to text-based explanatory menus. For example, Choong and Salvendy (1998) conducted a comparative study between Chinese software developers, whom Hall thought carried high context cultural backgrounds and American software developers, whom Hall thought to be from low context cultural backgrounds. It was found that Chinese software developers performed better in an iconic or pictorial environment, while their American counterparts excelled in alphanumerical mode. Likewise, Evers (1997) argued that users from low context cultures tend to prefer explicit and detailed information from a system, while users from high context cultures prefer pictorial or symbolic expressions. Thus, depending on users' contextual inclinations, the mobile Internet may require different menus or representational designs. For example, users from low context cultures may be provided with textual menus or clearly written representations, while users from high context cultures may be provided with iconic menus or pictorial representations.

Time Perception

Time perception may also influence how people use mobile Internet services. Since people from polychronic cultures tend to engage in multiple tasks simultaneously and be less organized (Hoft, 1996), these users will tend to use the mobile Internet not only for its intended purposes but also for other unexpected services. These users will also try to search for the necessary information immediately.

In terms of usability, time perception may also influence users' perceived waiting time. Rose, Evaristo, and Straub (2002) conducted an experiment with participants from four continents and found that participants from polychronic societies were less bothered by download delays and perceived the delays to be shorter. Therefore, when mobile Internet users perform a task with a given time delay, polychronic users will be more comfortable than monochromic users.

The Necessity for a New Questionnaire

Although the six dimensions proposed by Hofstede and Hall have been considered as the most general ones in studying cross-cultural issues, the dimensions may be criticized for a number of reasons. In particular, Hofstede's work has received considerable criticism regarding the sample data, the internal validity of the dimensions, and the assumption of equating country with culture. Hofstede collected the survey data from forty organizations across forty different countries. However, the organizations were subsidiaries of the same multinational organization (IBM). Thus, because the respondents had been trained by IBM and shared the IBM corporate culture, the sample data were not representative of people in the respective countries, and all respondents may represent the work-related values in business organization (Fernandez et al., 1997; Myers and Tan, 2002). Further, many items in Hofstede's study had significant cross-loading on more than one factor (Fernandez et al., 1997). Lastly, Hofstede's dimensions raise issues such as the problem of equating countries with cultures (Baskerville, 2003; Ford et al., 2003; Myers and Tan, 2002; Tung and Quaddus, 2002). That is, cultures may not be countries, and there may be more than one culture in a country at any one time.

Therefore, unlike preceding research, which unconditionally referred to Hofstede's metrics or Hofstede and Hall's subdivision of countries into cultural dimensions, this research developed a new set of metrics better suited to the characteristics of the mobile Internet. The necessity for a new questionnaire is predicated on Hofstede's focus on work-related value. His measurements are not applicable to the current environment of the mobile Internet, which is mainly used to achieve personal goals (Furrer et al., 2000; Nakata and Sivakumar, 1996). For example, it is difficult to apply Hofstede's original questions—such as "How frequently, in your experience, are subordinates afraid to express disagreement with their superiors?"—to the context of the mobile Internet. Hall, on the other hand, had relied on observations and interviews, without any direct survey questions, to subdivide the countries into two cultural dimensions (Hoft, 1996). The absence of any previous survey means that a new questionnaire is required anyway; this research fills these gaps through the methodology of an online survey.

RESEARCH METHODOLOGY

Measurement Development and Pilot Test

For this study, we have developed a new questionnaire that is better suited to the new mobile Internet environment. The initial twenty-four questions were developed in Korean. Questions for all the cultural dimensions were adapted from related prior studies. To make them more relevant to the mobile Internet environment and to increase the content validity of the empirical data, they were then modified based on in-depth interviews with experts in the field of mobile Internet services in Korea. The interviews started by explaining to the experts in twelve mobile Internet-related Korean companies (e.g., SK Telecom, KTF, LG Telecom, Samsung Electronics, and Yahoo! Korea) about which cultural dimension each question was trying to measure; they ended with feedback from the experts.

The modified twenty-four questions were pilot-tested again in Korea in order to identify the problems the questionnaire might imply and to test reliability and validity. This test was done through the mall intercept method, in which visitors to a multiplex movie theater were randomly selected for the test. A total of 256 people, who had prior experience in using the mobile Internet, participated in the test. Through data gathered by such pilot-testing, six questions were dropped for not meeting the validity and reliability criteria.[1]

The final questionnaire, which consists of eighteen questions, was then translated into English to facilitate the communication among researchers in Korea, Hong Kong, and Japan. To obtain language equivalence, the back translation method was used. The questionnaire was translated from each country's native language into English and vice versa by two independent translators separately. Any discrepancies among the translated questions were reconciled with discussions. The final questions are listed in Appendix 1.

Data Collection

Large-scale online surveys were conducted simultaneously in Korea, Hong Kong, and Japan with the same survey questions. Respondents were solicited via banner advertisements on the Web sites of several popular portals, and one hundred respondents won a free gift in the lottery. Survey

Table 8.2

Demographic Information

		Korea	Hong Kong	Japan
Average Age		26.2	27.6	36.8
Gender	Male	47.4%	48.6%	50.6%
	Female	52.6%	51.4%	49.4%

data were collected as follows. Before asking the questions, we emphasized that only those who had used mobile Internet services at least once were eligible to respond. We also made sure that only those who allowed us to check their usage log data participated in the survey. We then asked the respondents to provide their mobile phone numbers, which the telecommunication companies would use to verify some responses from the users, such as prior experience with the mobile Internet. We enforced accurate reporting of phone numbers by sending the lottery prizes for their participation to the billing addresses of the reported phone numbers. Then, respondents went on to answer each of the survey questions shown in Appendix 1 on a seven-point Likert type scale ranging from strongly disagree (1) to strongly agree (7). They finished the survey by providing demographic information.

A total of 532 people participated in Korea, 437 in Hong Kong, and 423 in Japan. Once they had finished the survey, their phone numbers and survey responses were sent to the telecommunication companies for data verification. The companies checked whether the phone numbers reported were legitimately registered, and whether the owners of the phone numbers had used the mobile Internet at least once in the past. Those who did not pass the test were deleted from the data set. As a result, the number of the final effective respondents was 368 in Korea, 379 in Hong Kong, and 328 in Japan. Demographic profiles of the respondents in the three countries are shown in Table 8.2.

Respondents were balanced in terms of gender in the three countries. However, the three countries were different in terms of the age distribution of respondents. Respondents in Japan were older on average than respondents in Korea and Hong Kong.

MEASUREMENT VALIDATION

The survey questionnaire consisted of eighteen questions about cultural dimensions in the mobile Internet environment as shown in Appendix 1. Validity and reliability of the measurements were tested as follows:

Exploratory Factor Analysis

Using data from the entire sample (n = 1,075), we first conducted exploratory factor analysis. The 18 items were subjected to exploratory factor analysis with the Varimax rotation method. The results are summarized in Table 8.3.

All eighteen questions converged into their corresponding factors. For example, the three questions for uncertainty avoidance (UA1, UA2, and UA3) were converged into a single factor across the three countries. The cumulative variances explained were high, 76.73 percent, and the Eigenvalues of all the six dimensions exceeded 1.0.

Table 8.3

Exploratory Factor Analysis

	ID	PD	CT	TP	UA	MA
ID1	.897	.022	.050	.132	.083	.092
ID2	.896	.012	.035	.158	.102	.065
ID3	.859	.048	.039	.128	.159	.074
PD2	.026	.922	.021	.081	.093	.128
PD1	.028	.905	.016	.105	.120	.087
PD3	.029	.770	.091	.159	.033	.176
UA3	.034	.061	.867	.055	.068	.061
UA1	−.030	.080	.853	−.005	.067	.100
UA2	.118	−.022	.851	.016	.137	.104
CT1	.100	.171	−.017	.865	−.002	.133
CT2	.258	.084	.026	.823	.087	.117
CT3	.087	.100	.107	.800	.102	.160
MA3	.220	.056	.055	.093	.845	.019
MA1	.122	.028	.154	.033	.823	.054
MA2	.004	.151	.065	.050	.803	.112
TP2	.043	.142	.037	.093	.087	.837
TP1	.031	.139	.136	.091	.117	.817
TP3	.173	.112	.119	.252	−.015	.773
Cumulative %	**14.140**	**27.483**	**40.231**	**52.801**	**64.853**	**76.726**
Eigenvalue	**4.835**	**2.325**	**2.256**	**1.759**	**1.346**	**1.289**

Index: UA = Uncertainty Avoidance, ID = Individualism, MA = Masculinity, PD = Power Distance, CT = Context, TP = Time Perception

Confirmatory Factor Analysis

Confirmatory factor analysis for the six cultural dimensions was conducted using LISREL 8.50. To conduct confirmatory factor analysis, we first examined model fit for the entire sample (n = 1,075). The results are shown at the top row of Table 8.4. With the entire sample, the measurement model has a chi-square of 494.17 for 120 degrees of freedom (p = .0000). Inspection of model fit revealed indices that were well above the acceptable thresholds (Doll et al., 1998; Hair Jr. et al., 1998). The GFI and AGFI are well above 0.90, the NFI and NNFI are higher than 0.90, and finally RMSEA and SRMR are lower than 0.05. The results indicate that the measurement model is specified appropriately (Doll et al., 1998).[2]

We then conducted subgroup analyses of model fit for the three countries, respectively. For each of the three subgroups, Korea, Hong Kong, and Japan, the bottom three rows of Table 8.4 report goodness of fit indices. Inspection of model fit for each of the three countries revealed indices that are considered to be reasonable model fit.

Convergent Validity

Convergent validity examines the magnitude of correlation between item measures of a construct across multiple methods of measurement (Gefen, 2003). Evidence of the convergent validity of the measure is provided by the extent to which it correlates highly with other questions designed

Table 8.4

Confirmatory Factor Analysis

Subgroup	Size	Chi-square	df	p-values	GFI	AGFI	CFI	NFI	NNFI	SRMR	RMSEA
Recommended		Non-Significant			Close to 1	>0.90	>0.90	>0.90	>0.90		<0.08
Korea, Hong Kong, and Japan	1075	494.17	120	0.0000	0.95	0.93	0.96	0.95	0.95	0.044	0.054
Combined											
Korea	368	151.24	120	0.0283	0.96	0.94	0.99	0.96	0.99	0.035	0.027
Hong Kong	379	291.51	120	0.0000	0.92	0.90	0.96	0.93	0.95	0.059	0.061
Japan	328	209.22	120	0.0000	0.94	0.91	0.95	0.90	0.94	0.058	0.048

Table 8.5

Convergent Validity

	UA	ID	MA	PD	CT	TP
UA1	0.81					
UA2	0.81					
UA3	0.77					
ID1		0.88				
ID2		0.89				
ID3		0.81				
MA1			0.85			
MA2			0.68			
MA3			0.75			
PD1				0.90		
PD2				0.95		
PD3				0.66		
CT1					0.83	
CT2					0.83	
CT3					0.71	
TP1						0.75
TP2						0.74
TP3						0.77

to measure the same construct (Churchill Jr., 1979). It can also be assessed from the measurement model by determining whether each indicator's estimated maximum likelihood loading on the underlying construct is significant (Arnold and Reynolds, 2003).

As illustrated in Table 8.5, completely standardized factor loadings for the six constructs exceed .66, and all are significant with their t values. Thus, the completely standardized factor loadings indicate that we have evidence of convergent validity for the proposed eighteen questions.

Table 8.6

Discriminant Validity

Dimension	UA	ID	MA	PD	CT	TP
UA	**0.80**					
ID	0.14	**0.86**				
MA	0.26	0.35	**0.76**			
PD	0.11	0.10	0.22	**0.85**		
CT	0.09	0.40	0.22	0.30	**0.79**	
TP	0.29	0.26	0.22	0.35	0.44	**0.75**

Table 8.7

Reliability

Dimension	Coefficient Alpha	Composite Reliability	Average Variance Extracted
UA	0.84	0.84	0.64
ID	0.90	0.90	0.74
MA	0.80	0.81	0.58
PD	0.87	0.88	0.72
CT	0.83	0.83	0.63
TP	0.80	0.80	0.57

Discriminant Validity

Discriminant validity is the extent to which the measure is indeed unique and not simply a reflection of some other variables (Churchill, 1979). For discriminant validity, Fornell and Larcker's (1981) test was conducted. This test requires that the AVE (Average Variance Extracted) for each construct should be greater than the squared correlation between the construct and other constructs in the model. Table 8.6 lists the correlation matrix, with correlations among constructs and the square root of AVE on the diagonal. The six diagonal elements are all larger than their corresponding correlation coefficients, which indicates that the metrics have appropriate discriminant validity.

Reliability

Reliability can be measured by coefficient alpha estimates, the composite reliability and AVE (Fornell and Larcker, 1981; Hair Jr. et al., 1998). Coefficient alpha is the basic statistic for determining the reliability of a measure based on internal consistency and a lower threshold of 0.70 is used (Churchill, 1979; Hair et al., 1998). Composite reliability assesses whether the items are sufficient in representing their respective construct and a common lower threshold of 0.70 is used (Hair et al., 1998). AVE indicates the amount of variance that is captured by the construct. Thus, if AVE is less than 0.50, the variance due to measurement error is larger than the variance captured by the construct, and the validity of the individual items, as well as the construct, is questionable (Fornell and Larcker, 1981). As illustrated in Table 8.7, all estimates exceed the recommended thresholds.

In summary, the eighteen questions we developed for the six cultural dimensions for the mobile Internet were found to have an appropriate level of convergent and discriminant validities, as well as reliability for the three countries.

Table 8.8

Invariance Analysis

Model Test	Chi-square	df	Change in Chi-square	Change in df	Significance Level	CFI	NNFI	RMSEA
All λ's Unconstrained	651.98	360				0.970	0.961	0.048
Only UA Constrained	672.90	364	20.92	4	$P < .05$	0.968	0.960	0.049
Only ID Constrained	668.82	364	16.84	4	$P < .05$	0.968	0.960	0.048
Only MA Constrained	672.39	364	20.41	4	$P < .05$	0.968	0.960	0.049
Only PD Constrained	672.49	364	20.51	4	$P < .05$	0.968	0.959	0.049
Only CT Constrained	680.22	364	28.24	4	$P < .05$	0.968	0.959	0.049
Only TP Constrained	654.87	364	2.89	4	$P > .05$	0.970	0.962	0.047
All λ's Constrained	762.46	384	110.48	24	$P < .05$	0.962	0.955	0.053

Invariance Analysis

Multi-group invariance analysis is used to test whether these instruments provide equivalent measurement across different cultures (Doll et al., 1998). In this study, the equivalence of factor loading across three countries in each dimension was tested. Factor loadings should be examined because the equivalence of factor loadings is the minimal condition for factorial invariance (Doll et al., 1998). In addition, the equality of factor loadings is generally of a higher priority than the equality of other parameters (Bollen, 1989). To test for equal factor loadings, an equal factor loading constraint is added to the baseline model, creating a nested or more restrictive model that is a subset of the baseline model. For this step in testing equivalence, Little (1997) and Doll et al. (1998) suggested examining differences in the fit indices, such as CFI, NNFI, and RMSEA, between the constrained versus unconstrained model rather than using the changes in chi-square, because the chi-square statistic is sensitive to sample size.

Although no absolute threshold levels for acceptability have been established, a difference of less than .05 between the values of the fit indices for the constrained vs. unconstrained models indicates equivalence of the measurement models across the groups (Deci et al., 2001; Little, 1997). As shown in Table 8.8, the CFI, NNFI, and RMSEA scores show changes of less than 0.05 between the constrained and unconstrained models. These minor changes in fit indices suggest that, while the chi-square difference in factor loadings for six instruments is statistically significant, it does not appear to be substantial throughout the samples of the three countries (Doll et al., 1998). Thus, the results indicate equivalence of the six instruments measured by eighteen questions across three countries.

DISCUSSION AND IMPLICATIONS

The intention of this paper was, firstly, to discuss some important contributions to the concepts of culture and cultural dimensions, and to review prior cross-cultural endeavors in various research fields. This study proposed a set of metrics to measure cultural dimensions of mobile Internet usage. Lastly, this study provided empirical results concerning the reliability and validity of the proposed metrics, using preliminary survey data conducted in Asia—Korea, Hong Kong, and Japan.

However, this study has several limitations. Firstly, although we developed a new metrics of the six cultural dimensions, culture may not be the only reason for mobile Internet usage differences across countries; we must also consider factors such as infrastructure, economic situation, physical environment, and language. Thus, future research is necessary to prove a causal relationship between different cultural dimensions and different mobile Internet usage patterns. Secondly, it is difficult to extend this study's results to countries in other continents. In other words, an instrument that is invariant across three Asian countries may not be so across other countries in other continents. Consequently, we are planning to extend the survey to other countries in Europe and North America. Finally, it suffers from a methodological limitation, in that it relies on an online survey. The online survey method involves a random sampling error and a self-selection bias (Kehoe and Pitkow, 1996; Pitkow and Kehoe, 1996). That is, when people decide to participate in the online survey, they select themselves. For example, although we announced that one hundred respondents would win a free prize in the lottery, people who have higher uncertainty avoidance may doubt the truth of what we announced. As a result, we may get respondents who have low uncertainty avoidance, relatively. Hence, alternative data collection methods, such as stratified random sampling with an e-mail survey, should be used in order to increase the reliability of study results in future research.

Despite these limitations, this study has several theoretical and practical implications.

On the theoretical side, this study may extend our knowledge of culture in the field of HCI, by discussing some important contributions to the concepts of culture and cultural dimensions in the usage and interface of the mobile Internet. Furthermore, we developed, and empirically validated, the metrics of cultural dimensions, which are better suited to the characteristics of the new mobile Internet environment. Developing a valid and reliable measurement for cultural aspects of mobile Internet usage is theoretically meaningful.

On the practical side, this study can provide valuable information to companies that are considering importing or exporting mobile Internet services. The metrics suggested here can be a useful tool for understanding the impact of culture on mobile Internet users in target countries.

Furthermore, the metrics help practitioners directly to segment the international mobile Internet markets and to develop strategies for new mobile Internet contents. Because it is difficult to localize contents for each country, practitioners can classify multiple countries into a relatively homogeneous cultural group by measuring the cultural dimensions. Based on the cultural groups, they can also conduct different strategies for new content development or UI design. That is, the metrics help developers or designers to develop localization strategies for target cultural groups and to provide local users with culture-specific mobile Internet content. For instance, if mobile Internet users in a country show high uncertainty avoidance, content developers may design mobile Internet services with limited options or, alternatively, marketers may provide free trials. Similarly, if users in a country show individualistic tendencies, companies may provide personalized content and functions such as bookmarks. Furthermore, for mobile Internet uses in feminine countries, UI designers may use "warm" colors, which feminine users were found to favor. As a result, the proposed metrics can lead mobile Internet content developers or UI designers to envision a cultural UI or usability framework, based on cultural dimensions, that provides fundamental understanding about target countries (Kim et al., 2003). UI design or usability engineering, grounded upon the framework, can cover a wider range of unknown cultural issues beyond simple language translation.

In conclusion, we believe this study will help not only HCI or MIS researchers but also UI designers in mobile Internet-related companies. This study can also serve as a starting point for future study in the field of cultural user interface or cultural usability.

ACKNOWLEDGMENTS

This research was funded by the Korea Research Foundation (KRF-2003–042-B00045).

NOTES

1. Results from pre and pilot tests are available from the authors upon request.

2. The chi-square statistic is significant because it is highly sensitive when the number of respondents are bigger than 300. Since all other model fit indices are well above the threshold figure, we have decided to proceed to further analysis regardless of the high chi-square statistic.

APPENDIX 8.1

SURVEY QUESTIONNAIRE

Cultural Dimension	Item Code	Questionnaire
Uncertainty Avoidance	UA1	I am reluctant to use mobile Internet services if the security of operations is compromised for any reason.
	UA2	I get very upset when a mobile Internet service does something strange.
	UA3	I do not use mobile Internet content when I am unsure of its quality.
Individualism	ID1	I frequently use mobile Internet services that can bring out my personality.
	ID2	I do not want to feel that using a mobile Internet service makes me part of a homogeneous group.
	ID3	I frequently use mobile Internet services that can differentiate me from other people.
Masculinity	MA1	Males and females may have different goals in using mobile Internet services.
	MA2	I usually use mobile Internet services that are oriented to my gender.
	MA3	I think that most mobile Internet services are male-oriented.
Power Distance	PD1	Mobile Internet services provided by small companies need to be more beneficial than those provided by big or well-known companies (e.g., high level of service, reasonable price, free prizes).
	PD2	I trust mobile Internet services provided by big or well-known companies more than those provided by small companies.
	PD3	I think that mobile Internet services provided by big or well-known companies are better than those provided by small ones.
Context	CT1	When I use e-mail or chatting services, I prefer to use implicit expressions rather than explicit expressions.
	CT2	When I use e-mail or chatting services, I prefer indirect expressions rather than direct expressions.
	CT3	When I am searching for information, symbolic iconic representation is more convenient than detailed textual information.
Time Perception	TP1	When I have to search large amounts of information, I usually search information line by line.
	TP2	Before connecting to the mobile Internet, I usually decide which service I am going to use.
	TP3	When I use mobile Internet services, I use only the services I planned to use beforehand.

REFERENCES

Arnold, M.J., and Reynolds, K.E. Hedonic shopping motivation. *Journal of Retailing*, 79, 2 (2003), 77–95.

Badre, A.N. *Shaping Web Usability*. Boston: Pears Education, 2001.

Basabe, N.; Paez, D.; Valencia, J.; Gonzalez, J.L.; Rime, B.; and Diener, E. Cultural dimensions, socio-economic development, climate, and emotional hedonic level. *Cognition and Emotion*, 16, 1 (2002), 103–125.

Baskerville, R.F. Hofstede never studied culture. *Accounting, Organizations and Society*, 28, 1 (2003), 1–14.

Bollen, K.A. *Structural Equations with Latent Variables*. New York: John Wiley and Sons, 1989.

Bond, M.H., and Smith, P.B. Cross-cultural social and organizational psychology. *Annual Review of Psychology*, 29 (1996), 32–62.

Chae, M., and Kim, J. Information quality for mobile internet services: a theoretical model with empirical validation. In *Proceedings of the 22th International Conference on Information Systems*. New Orleans, LA: IEEE Computer Society Press, 2001, pp. 43–54.

Chang, K., and Ding, C.G. The influence of culture on industrial buying selection criteria in Taiwan and mainland China. *Industrial Marketing Management*, 24, 4 (1995), 277–284.

Cho, B.; Kwon, U.; Gentry, J.W.; Jun, S.; and Kropp, F. Cultural values reflected in theme and execution: a comparative study of U.S. and Korean television commercials. *Journal of Advertising*, 28, 4 (1999), 59–73.

Choong, Y.Y., and Salvendy, G. Design of icons for use by Chinese in mainland China. *Interacting with Computers*, 9, 4 (1998), 417–430.

Churchill, G.A., Jr. A paradigm for developing better measures of marketing constructs. *Journal of Marketing Research*, 16, 1 (1979), 64–73.

Clark, T. International marketing and national character: a review and proposal for an integrative theory. *Journal of Marketing*, 54, 4 (1990), 66–79.

De Angeli, A.; Athavankar, U.; Joshi, A.; Coventry, L.; and Johnson, G.I. Introducing ATMs in India: a contextual inquiry. *Interacting with Computers*, 16, 1 (2004), 29–44.

de Mooij, M. *Consumer Behavior and Culture: Consequences for Global Marketing and Advertising*. Thousand Oaks, CA: Sage Publications, 2003.

de Mooij, M. *Global Marketing and Advertising: Understanding Cultural Paradoxes*. Beverly Hills, CA: Sage Publications, 1998.

Deci, E.L.; Ryan, R.M.; Gagne, M.; Leone, D.R.; Usunov, J.; and Kornazheva, B.P. Need satisfaction, motivation, and well-being in the work organizations of a former eastern bloc country: a cross-cultural study of self-determination. *Personality and Social Psychology Bulletin*, 27, 8 (2001), 930–942.

Doll, W.J.; Hendrickson, A.; and Deng, X. Using Davis's perceived usefulness and ease-of-use instruments for decision making: a confirmatory and multigroup invariance analysis. *Decision Sciences*, 29, 4 (1998), 839–869.

Donthu, N., and Yoo, B. Cultural influences on service quality expectations. *Journal of Service Research*, 1, 2 (1998), 178–186.

Dormann, C., and Chisalita, C. Cultural values in web site design. In *Proceedings of the 11th European Conference on Cognitive Ergonomics*. Catania, Italy: European Association of Cognitive Ergonomics, 2002, pp. 63–71.

Douglas, S.P., and Craig, C.S. The changing dynamic of consumer behavior: implications for cross-cultural research. *International Journal of Research in Marketing*, 14, 4 (1997), 379–395.

Evers, V. *Human-Computer Interfaces: Designing for Culture*. Master's thesis, Information Systems, University of Amsterdam, Amsterdam, 1997.

Fernandez, D.R.; Carlson, D.S.; Stepina, L.P.; and Nicholson, J.D. Hofstede's country classification: 25 years later. *Journal of Social Psychology*, 137, 1 (1997), 43–54.

Ferraro, G.P. *The Cultural Dimensions of International Business*. Englewood Cliffs, NJ: Prentice Hall, 1998.

Ford, D.P.; Connelly, C.E.; and Meister, D.B. Information systems research and Hofstede's culture's consequences: an uneasy and incomplete partnership. *IEEE Transactions on Engineering Management*, 50, 1 (2003), 8–25.

Fornell, C., and Larcker, D. Evaluating structural equation models with unobservable variables and measurement error. *Journal of Marketing Research*, 18, 1 (1981), 39–50.

Francis, L. Mobile computing: a fact in your future. In *Proceedings of the 15th Annual International Conference on Computer Documentation*. Salt Lake City, UT: ACM Press, 1997, pp. 63–67.

Furrer, O.; Liu, S.C.B.; and Sudharshan, D. The relationships between culture and service quality percep-tions: basis for cross-cultural market segmentation and resource allocation. *Journal of Service Research*, 2, 4 (2000), 355–371.

Garfield, M.T., and Watson, R.T. Differences in national information infrastructures: the reflection of national cultures. *Journal of Strategic Information Systems*, 6, 4 (1998), 313–337.

Gefen, D. Assessing unidimensionality through LISREL: an explanation and example. *Communications of Association for Information Systems*, 2 (2003), 23–47.

Gould, E.W.; Zakaria, N.; and Yusof, S.A.M. Applying culture to website design: a comparison of Malaysian and US websites. In *Proceedings of the 18th Annual ACM International Conference on Computer Documentation: Technology & Teamwork*. Cambridge, MA: IEEE Educational Activities Department, 2000, pp. 161–171.

Hair, Jr., J.F.; Anderson, R.E.; Tatham, R.L.; and Black, W.C. *Multivariate Data Analysis*. Upper Saddle River, NJ: Prentice Hall, 1998.

Hall, E.T. *Beyond Culture*. Garden City, NY: Anchor Doubleday Press, 1976.

Hall, E.T. *The Silent Language*. Garden City, NY: Anchor Doubleday Press, 1959.

Hasan, H., and Ditsa, G. The impact of culture on the adoption of IT: an interpretive study. *Journal of Global Information Management*, 7, 1 (1999), 5–15.

Henry, W.A. Cultural values do correlate with customer behavior. *Journal of Marketing Research*, 13, 2 (1976), 121–127.

Hiltunen, M.; Laukka, M.; and Luomala, J. *Professional Mobile User Experience*. Edita, Finland: IT Press, 2002.

Hofstede, G. *Culture's Consequences: International Differences in Work-Related Values*. Beverly Hills, CA: Sage Publications, 1980.

Hofstede, G., and Bond, M.H. The Confucius connection: from cultural roots to economic growth. *Organizational Dynamics*, 16, 4 (1988), 5–24.

Hoft, N. Developing a cultural model. In E.M. del Galdo and J. Nielsen (eds.), *International User Interfaces*. New York: John Wiley & Sons, 1996, pp. 41–73.

Hoft, N.L. *International Technical Communication*. New York: John Wiley & Sons, 1995.

Honold, P. Culture and Context: An Empirical Study for the Development of a Framework for the Elicitation of Cultural Influence in Product Usage. *International Journal of Human-Computer Interaction*, 12, 3 & 4 (2000), 327–345.

Honold, P. Learning how to use a cellular phone: comparison between German and Chinese users. *Technical Communication*, 46, 2 (1999), 196–205.

Huang, L.; Lu, M.T.; and Wong, B.K. The impact of power distance on email acceptance: evidence from the PRC. *Journal of Computer Information Systems*, 44, 1 (2003), 93–101.

Igbaria, M., and Zviran, M. Comparison of end-user computing characteristics in the U.S., Israel and Taiwan. *Information & Management*, 30, 1 (1996), 1–13.

InfoCom Research, Inc. *Information & Communications in Japan 2002*. Tokyo, Japan: InfoCom Research, 2002.

Kankanhalli, A.; Tan, B.C.Y.; Wei, K.K.; and Holmes, M.C. Cross-cultural differences and information sys-tems developer values. *Decision Support Systems*, 38, 2 (2004), 183–195.

Kedia, B.L., and Bhagat, R.S. Cultural constraints on transfer of technology across nations: implications for research in international and comparative management. *Academy of Management Review*, 13, 4 (1988), 559–571.

Kehoe, C.M., and Pitkow, J.E. Surveying the territory: GVU's five WWW user surveys. *The World Wide Web Journal*, 1, 3 (1996), 77–84.

Khaslavsky, J. Integrating culture into interface design. In *Proceedings of the CHI '98 Conference Summary on Human Factors in Computing Systems*. Los Angeles, CA: ACM Press, 1998, pp. 365–366.

Kim, D.; Pan, Y.; and Park, H.S. High- versus low-context culture: a comparison of Chinese, Korea, and American cultures. *Psychology & Marketing*, 15, 6 (1998), 507–521.

Kim, S.; Choo, M.J.; Kim, H.; Kang, S.H.; and Joo, H. Cultural issues in handheld usability: are cultural models effective for interpreting unique use patterns of Korean mobile phone users? In *Proceedings of the 12th UPA Conference*. Scottsdale, AZ: Usability Professionals' Association, 2003, pp. 1–5.

Kluckhohn, F.R., and Strodtbeck, F.L. *Variations in Value Orientations*. Westport, CT: Greenwood Press, 1961.

Kroeber, A.L. *The Nature of Culture*. Chicago: University of Chicago Press, 1952.

Kroeber, A.L., and Parsons, T. The concept of culture and of social system. *American Sociological Review*, 23, 5 (1958), 582–583.

Lee, M., and Hong, S. *Consumer Behavior*. Seoul, Korea: Bobmunsa, 2001.

Lee, Y., and Kim, J. What is the mobile Internet for? A cross-national study on the value structure of the mobile internet. In *Proceedings of the 9th Americas Conference on Information Systems*. Tampa, FL: Association for Information Systems, 2003, pp. 93–102.

Leidner, D.E.; Carlsson, S.; and Elam, J.J. A cross-cultural study of executive information systems. In *Proceedings of the 28th Annual Hawaii International Conference on System Sciences*. Maui, HI: IEEE Computer Society Press, 1995, pp. 91–100.

Lim, J. The role of power distance and explanation facility in online bargaining utilizing software agents. *Journal of Global Information Management*, 12, 2 (2004), 27–43.

Little, T.D. Mean and covariance structures (MACS) analyses of cross-cultural data: practical and theoretical issues. *Multivariate Behavioral Research*, 32, 1 (1997), 53–76.

Liu, B.S.C.; Furrer, O.; and Sudharshan, D. The relationships between culture and behavioral intentions toward services. *Journal of Service Research*, 4, 2 (2001), 118–129.

Marcus, A., and Gould, E.W. Crosscurrents: cultural dimensions and global web user-interface design. *Interactions*, 7, 4 (2000), 32–46.

Mattila, A.S. The role of culture and purchase motivation in service encounter evaluations. *Journal of Service Marketing*, 13, 4/5 (1999), 376–389.

Munson, J.M., and McIntyre, S.H. Developing practical procedures for the measurement of personal values in cross-cultural marketing. *Journal of Marketing Research*, 16, 1 (1979), 48–52.

Myers, M.D., and Tan, F.B. Beyond models of national culture in information systems research. *Journal of Global Information Management*, 10, 1 (2002), 24–32.

Nakakoji, K. Beyond language translation: crossing the cultural divide. *IEEE Software*, 13, 6 (1996), 42–46.

Nakata, C., and Sivakumar, K. National culture and new product development: an integrative review. *Journal of Marketing*, 60, 1 (1996), 61–72.

Nielsen, J. *Usability Engineering*. San Francisco, CA: Morgan Kaufmann, 1993.

Okazaki, S. Does culture matter? Identifying cross-national dimensions in Japanese multinationals' product-based websites. *Electronic Markets*, 14, 1 (2004), 58–69.

Parsons, T., and Shils, E.A. *Toward a General Theory of Action*. Cambridge, MA: Harvard University Press, 1951.

Pitkow, J.E., and Kehoe, C.M. Emerging trends in the WWW user population. *Communications of ACM*, 39, 6 (1996), 106–108.

Png, I.P.L.; Tan, B.C.Y.; and Wee, K.L. Dimensions of national culture and corporate adoption of IT infrastructure. *IEEE Transactions on Engineering Management*, 48, 1 (2001), 36–45.

Robbins, S.S., and Stylianou, A.C. A study of cultural differences in global corporate web sites. *Journal of Computer Information Systems*, 42, 2 (2001), 3–9.

Robichaux, B.P., and Cooper, R.B. GSS participation: a cultural examination. *Information & Management*, 33, 6 (1998), 287–300.

Rose, G.M.; Evaristo, R.; and Straub, D. Culture and consumer responses to web download time: a four-continent study of mono- and polychronism. *IEEE Transactions on Engineering Management*, 50, 1 (2002), 31–44.

Russo, P., and Boor, S. How fluent is your interface? Designing for international users. In *Proceedings of the SIGCHI Conference on Human Factors in Computing Systems*. Amsterdam: ACM Press, 1993, pp. 342–347.

Schwartz, S.H. Beyond individualism-collectivism: new cultural dimensions of values. In C. Kagitcibasi, S.C. Choi, G. Yoon, U. Kim, and H. Triandis (eds.), *Individualism and Collectivism: Theory, Method, and Applications*. Thousand Oaks, CA: Sage Publications, 1994, pp. 85–119.

Singh, N.; Zho, H.; and Hu, X. Cultural adaptation on the web: a study of American companies' domestic and Chinese websites. *Journal of Global Information Management*, 11, 3 (2003), 63–81.

Smith, A.; Dunckley, L.; French, T.; Minocha, S.; and Chang, Y. A process model for developing usable cross-cultural websites. *Interacting with Computers*, 16, 1 (2004), 63–91.

Straub, D.W. The effect of culture on IT diffusion: e-mail and fax in Japan and U.S. *Information Systems Research*, 5, 1 (1994), 23–47.

Straub, D.W.; Loch, W.; Aristo, R.; Karahanna, E.; and Strite, M. Toward a theory-based measurement of culture. *Journal of Global Information Management*, 10, 1 (2002), 13–23.

Strauss, B., and Mang, P. "Culture shocks" in inter-cultural service encounters? *Journal of Service Marketing*, 13, 4/5 (1999), 329–346.

Tan, B.C.Y.; Wei, K.K.; Watson, R.T.; Clapper, D.L.; and McLean, E.R. Computer-mediated communication and majority influence: assessing the impact in an individualistic and a collectivistic culture. *Management Science*, 44, 9 (1998), 1263–1278.

Triandis, H.C. Cross-cultural studies of individualism-collectivism. In *Proceedings of the Nebraska Symposium on Motivation*. Lincoln, NE: University of Nebraska Press, 1990, pp. 44–133.

Trompenaars, F. *Riding the Waves of Culture: Understanding Diversity in Global Business*. London: Economist Books, 1993.

Tung, L.L., and Quaddus, M.A. Cultural differences explaining the differences in results in GSS: implications for the next decade. *Decision Support Systems*, 33, 2 (2002), 177–199.

Urbaczewski, A.; Wells, J.; Sarker, S.; and Koivisto, M. Exploring cultural difference as a means for understanding the global mobile Internet: a theoretical basis and program of research. In *Proceedings of the 35th Hawaii International Conference on System Science*. Big Island, HI: IEEE Computer Society Press, 2002, pp. 654–663.

Venkatesh, V., and Brown, S.A. A longitudinal investigation of personal computers in homes: adoption determinants and emerging challenges. *MIS Quarterly*, 25, 1 (2001), 71–102.

Vishwanath, A. Comparing online information effect: a cross-cultural comparison of online information and uncertainty avoidance. *Communication Research*, 30, 6 (2003), 579–598.

Watson, R.T.; Ho, T.H.; and Raman, K.S. Culture: a fourth dimension of group support systems. *Communications of the ACM*, 37, 10 (1994), 44–55.

Zahedi, F.M.; van Pelt, W.V.; and Song, J. A Conceptual framework for international web design. *IEEE Transactions on Professional Communication*, 44, 2 (2001), 83–103.

Zakaria, N., and Stanton, J.M. Designing and implementing culturally-sensitive IT applications. *Information Technology & People*, 16, 1 (2003), 49–75.

CHAPTER 9

CULTURAL AND GLOBALIZATION ISSUES IMPACTING THE ORGANIZATIONAL USE OF INFORMATION TECHNOLOGY

GEOFFREY S. HUBONA, DUANE TRUEX III, JIJIE WANG,
AND DETMAR W. STRAUB

Abstract: *Cultural and globalization issues are known to affect the organizational use of information technology (IT). In particular, studies have indicated that a variety of cultural and globalization factors affect the organizational adoption and diffusion of IT. Among sociocultural factors, the differing effects of gender, social norms, beliefs and values, technological acculturation, and degree of technological advancement have all been shown to impact the transfer and use of technology in organizations. Globalization issues also have ramifications with respect to differences in government policy, environmental factors, structural language features, and national economic and IT policies. We sample from the voluminous published literature that reports on cultural and global factors that impact the organizational use of IT. Organizational impacts examined include technology transfer, IT use, adoption and diffusion, systems development, the creation and evolution of standards, and employment practices. Field studies include IT applications in Switzerland, Japan, Egypt, Jordan, Saudi Arabia, Lebanon, the Sudan, Canada, Denmark, Hong Kong, the United Kingdom, and France, as well as other countries, largely as compared with the United States. Some of the specific IT applications examined include the Internet, e-mail, fax, electronic communications media, personal computing, electronic data interchange (EDI) standards, and systems development methods and approaches. Implications for relevant theory and practice are discussed, as are suggestions for future research directions in this domain.*

Keywords: *Cultural Impacts of Technology, Globalization Issues, Organizational Adoption of IT, Use of IT*

INTRODUCTION

Factors and issues that affect the organizational adoption, diffusion, and use of information technology (IT) have been widely studied for the past three decades. However, in the 1970s and 1980s these studies were largely based in North America, particularly in the United States. With the advent of organizational globalization and an increased number of transnational firms using IT in non-Western cultures, researchers have increasingly focused on sociocultural issues and factors that were heretofore overlooked in this domain. Specifically, an increasing number of studies published since 1995 have examined cultural issues affecting the organizational adoption and use of

IT in countries in Europe, in the Middle East, and in the Far East. A number of these studies have also focused on developing and lesser developed countries and cultures.

Recent studies on this topic have been conducted in European countries, including Switzerland, Denmark, France, and the United Kingdom. Furthermore, studies have been conducted recently in the Middle Eastern countries of Egypt, Jordan, Saudi Arabia, Lebanon, and the Sudan. Studies have also been conducted in the Far East, in Hong Kong, and in Japan. By contrast with earlier studies that focused exclusively on North America, many of these studies conducted in non–North American cultures have discovered additional nuances and issues that impinge on technology acceptance and diffusion. It is important to consider this broader range of cultural and sociocultural factors that influence the adoption and use of IT.

Interestingly, one of those studies was conducted by the son of Gert Hofstede, whose early studies of the influence of national culture (Hofstede, 1981; Hofstede, 1983; Hofstede, 1985) have informed generations of research in the fields of international studies, organization theory and design, management, and information technologies. His son's work is not country specific, in that it takes data from sixty countries and demonstrates how an understanding of the countries' cultures better explains differences in technology adoption. More precisely, it considers the rate of adoption and penetration of several major IT technologies, taking into account national GNP and adjusting for national culture (Hofstede, 2001).

The purpose of this paper is to examine cultural and globalization issues known to affect the organizational adoption, diffusion, and use of IT in a multicultural and international context. We examine specific selected factors and explanatory models that have been empirically tested in the MIS literature and shown to affect the organizational use and adoption of IT. The goal is to sample from, review, and synthesize frameworks, models, and theories that have been examined in this domain, so as to highlight some cultural and globalization factors that affect organizational IT outcomes in an international domain.

BACKGROUND AND RELATED WORK

Voluminous published studies have examined various sociocultural and globalization issues impacting multicultural organizational outcomes relating to the adoption and use of IT. Given that a single paper cannot conceivably do justice to the full set of possibilities, our objective here is to highlight frameworks and theories that provide theoretical bases and research guidance for empirical studies in this area. For each framework and theory, we sample, select, and review one or a few related empirical studies to illustrate what has been done. Our primary focus is positivistic empirical research, both qualitative and quantitative. Other empirical approaches, including interpretative and postmodern deconstructive research, do not fall within the scope of this paper.

Figure 9.1 represents our conceptual framework of the impacts of sociocultural and globalization factors on the adoption and use of IT at the individual, organizational, and national levels. Particular sociocultural factors that we consider include gender, worker motivation, social norms, beliefs and values, technological acculturation, and the degree of technological advancement. Globalization factors that we consider include governmental policy differences, environmental factors, structural language features, national economics, and IT policies. The impacts of these factors on the adoption and use of IT are considered in different countries and regions of the world. Table 9.1 positions a representative sample of the studies in the context of the applicable level of analysis (individual, organizational, or national), the theory base, and that study's respective contribution to the literature.

At the individual and organizational level of analyses (see next section, "Cultural IT Adoption Studies at Individual and/or Organizational Level"), we largely review studies relating to three

Figure 9.1 **Framework of Sociocultural and Globalization Factors on Adoption and Diffusion of IT**

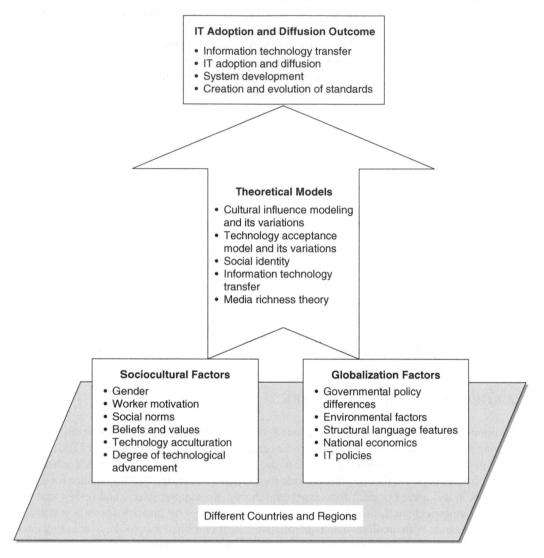

theories or frameworks—cultural influence modeling, the technology acceptance model, and media richness theory—and related empirical studies. Culture influence modeling (CIM) is a methodological approach that posits that certain features of a culture can predict the success or failure of IT transfer and other systems outcomes (Hill, 1998). Variations of the CIM model have been used to study the impact of technological acculturation, beliefs and values, and IT policies on IT adoption at different levels (Loch et al., 2003; Loch et al., 2000; Checchi et al., 2002). The technology acceptance model (TAM) predicts and explains the adoption and use of information technologies, based on users' beliefs and attitudes regarding the use of that technology (Davis, 1989). Modified TAM models using additional culture-specific constructs have been proposed and tested to explain differences in IT adoption within different cultural contexts (Straub, 1997; Rose and Straub, 1998;

Straub, 1994; Gefen and Straub, 1997; Huang et al., 2003). Media richness theory (also known as information richness theory) proposes that task performances will be enhanced when task requirements are matched to a medium's ability to convey information. Row et al. (1999) used information richness theory to explain the choice of telecommunications media in different cultures.

In the section "Cross-culture Comparative Studies on IT Diffusion at National Level," we review four studies that examine the impact of sociocultural and globalization factors on IT diffusion at the national level of analysis. Checchi et al. (2003) developed an integrative framework for positioning the impact of future public IT policy implementation on the adoption and diffusion of IT. Gibbs et al. (2003) developed and tested a framework of factors shaping global e-commerce diffusion. Damsgaard and Truex (2000) drew on theories of evolutionary and culturally mediated exchange to illustrate how national and organizational cultural differences affect the emergence of e-business standards. Based on Hofstede's (1991) four distinct organizational models, Garfield et al. (1998) studied the reflection of national cultures on national information infrastructure.

Cultural IT Adoption Studies at Individual and/or Organizational Level

Cultural Influence Modeling

Cultural influence modeling is a methodological approach that has been used to predict successful IT transfer and other system outcomes in single cultures. Hill et al. (1998) first presented this conceptual approach by asserting that an examination of the features of single cultures can lead to predictions, even in the absence of comparative cultural data. The model that was initially used to test this approach involved three constructs: national IT policies and infrastructure, technological acculturation, and culture-specific beliefs and values. Each of the three constructs potentially influences IT transfer and systems outcomes. Figure 9.2—reproduced from Loch et al. (2003)—enumerates the various original elements of the theoretical base for the first empirical test of cultural influence modeling.

In Figure 9.2, the construct *National IT Policies and Infrastructure* refers to national information technology policies that, together with the existing structure of computing and telecommunication capabilities, enable and guide the cumulative ability of the population to utilize these capabilities (Hill et al., 1994). The extent of public and private IT industries and initiatives, the support of governmental tax benefits and/or tariffs to encourage IT use or to discourage IT imports, and the public perception of the current supply and demand of IT, are all candidate factors that comprise national IT policies and infrastructure.

Technological Acculturation relates to the degree of cultural exposure and to the extent of explicit experiences that individuals in one culture have with technology developed in other countries. According to Straub et al. (2001), technology is a non-neutral cultural agent, one that intrinsically reflects the culture-specific beliefs and values embedded in its country of origin. The greater the degree of technological acculturation, the more likely is a new technology to be accepted, even in the presence of cultural barriers. Factors that can enhance technological acculturation include the degree of computer literacy in the adopting culture; the extent of individual travel to other technically advanced cultures; exposure to IT in TV, films, and other media; and exposure to IT through social contacts.

Culture-Specific Beliefs and Values are artifacts of a culture as demonstrated through social actions that typically become ingrained in social institutions via the creation of social norms (Ajzen et al., 1980; Hofstede, 1980; Hofstede, 1981; Hofstede, 1983; Hofstede, 1985; Hofstede, 2001; Loch et al., 2003). Loch et al. (2003) argue that the more general social norms construct can

Table 9.1

Summaries of IT Adoption and Diffusion Studies at the Individual, Organizational, and National Levels

Level of Analysis	Theoretical Lens	Studies	Contributions
Studies of IT Adoption and Diffusion at Individual and/or Organizational Level	Culture Influence Modeling	Hill et al. (1998)	The paper proposed a methodological approach using features of single culture to predict success of IT transfer and other system outcomes
		Loch et al. (2003)	Adapt culture influence modeling to study Internet usage in Arab world and conclude that technological acculturation and social norms affect individual system usage and technological acculturation affects the organizational system usage.
		Loch (2000), Checchi et al. (2002)	Posit positive influence of national ICT policies and technology infrastructure on ITT/ICT system outcomes
	Technology Acceptance Model	Straub (1997)	Cultural dimensions identified by Hofstede have impact on IT adoption
		Rose and Straub (1998)	Originated in the developed world, TAM also applies to the developing countries
		Straub (1994)	Propose a cross-cultural IT diffusion process model based on TAM and social presence/information richness
		Gefen and Straub (1997)	Explore the role of gender on the cross-cultural IT diffusion of e-mail
		Huang et al. (2003)	Examine the moderator effect of power distance on the relationship between subjective norm and IT adoption
	Media Richness Theory	Rowe et al. (1999)	Technologies features/factors are interpreted through the lens of cultural values.
Studies of IT Adoption and Diffusion at National Level	Culture Influence Modeling	Checchi et al. (2003)	Develop an integrative framework for positioning the impact of public policy implementation on the adoption and diffusion of IT
	Divergence Theory, Convergence Theory, and Transformation Theory	Gibbs et al. (2003)	Develop a framework to understand global, environmental, and policy factors that determine B2B and B2C e-commerce diffusion
	Evolutionary and Culturally Mediated Exchanges Theory	Damsgaard and Truex (2000)	Illustrate how national and organizational cultural differences impact IT standards' emergence
	Hofstede's Organizational Model	Garfield et al. (1998)	Examine the role of national culture on IT policy decisions and the formation of national information infrastructure

Sociocultural Factors	Globalization Factors	Organizational Outcomes	Specific Technology Examined	Countries or Regions
Social Norms, technology culturation		Technology transfer, IT adoption and diffusion	Development and implementations of information systems	Jordan, Egypt, Saudi Arabia, Lebanon, and the Sudan
Social norms, technology culturation		Technology transfer, IT adoption and diffusion	Internet	Egypt, Kuwait, Lebanon, Saudi Arabia
Beliefs and values, technology acculturation	Governmental policy differences	Technology transfer, IT adoption and diffusion	PC, PDA, E-mail	US, Egypt
Hofstede dimension (PDI, UAI, IDV, MAS)		IT adoption and diffusion	E-mail, fax and communication media	US, Switzerland, and Japan
	Generalizability of TAM in less developed countries	IT adoption and diffusion	Personal computing	Egypt, Saudi Arabia, Lebanon, the Sudan
	Structural language features	Technology transfer	E-mail, fax, and communication media	Japan
Gender, social norms, beliefs and values		IT adoption and diffusion	Email, fax and communication media	Japan
Subjective norms, power distance		IT adoption and diffusion	E-mail	China
Reactivity, entrepreneurship, individualism flexibility, innovation, task orientation, power distance		IT adoption and diffusion	E-mail, fax and communication media	France
	Environmental factors, IT policies	IT adoption and diffusion		
	Global environment, national environment, and national policy	E-commerce diffusion	B2B and B2C e-commerce diffusion	Brazil, China, Denmark, France, Germany, Mexico, Japan, Taiwan, United States.
Beliefs and values, languages		Creation of IT standards	EDI	Hong Kong, Finland, Denmark
Power distance, uncertainty avoidance		Technology transfer	National information infrastructure	China, Singapore, France, Japan, United Kingdom, United States, Finland, Germany

Figure 9.2   **Cultural Influence Modeling and IT Transfer**

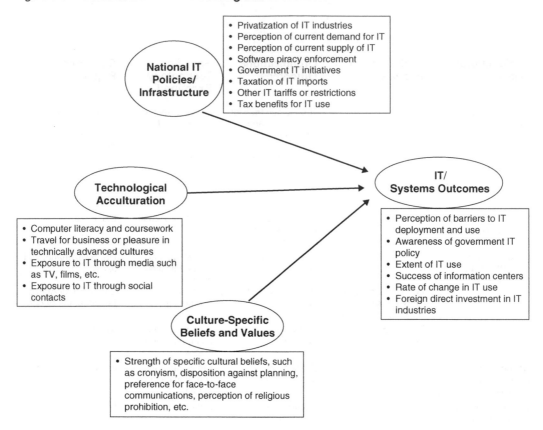

National IT
Policies/
Infrastructure

- Privatization of IT industries
- Perception of current demand for IT
- Perception of current supply of IT
- Software piracy enforcement
- Government IT initiatives
- Taxation of IT imports
- Other IT tariffs or restrictions
- Tax benefits for IT use

Technological
Acculturation

- Computer literacy and coursework
- Travel for business or pleasure in technically advanced cultures
- Exposure to IT through media such as TV, films, etc.
- Exposure to IT through social contacts

IT/
Systems Outcomes

- Perception of barriers to IT deployment and use
- Awareness of government IT policy
- Extent of IT use
- Success of information centers
- Rate of change in IT use
- Foreign direct investment in IT industries

Culture-Specific
Beliefs and Values

- Strength of specific cultural beliefs, such as cronyism, disposition against planning, preference for face-to-face communications, perception of religious prohibition, etc.

Source: Based on Loch et al. (2004).

complement the culture-specific beliefs and values construct in Figure 9.2. Social norms can be defined as social pressure to perform, or not to perform, some behavior (Azjen et al., 1980). Typically, there is an important reference group of persons that the individual identifies with and uses as a benchmark to evaluate "appropriate" socially normative behavior. These norms become reified and develop the character of social structures that may even make it difficult, if not impossible, to fold certain technologies into the worldview of an individual, a family, or even a whole community of people.

In general, *IT Transfer and Systems Outcomes* refers to the actual or intended uses of new technologies within the institutions and organizations of a country. It also refers to the success and failure of adopting and diffusing new technologies, including system development processes—for example, a particular system development methodology or another paradigmatic approach to specifying, designing, or implementing new systems.

Adapting and Testing the Cultural Influence Model to Study Internet Usage in a Single Culture. Loch et al. (2003) extended the cultural influence modeling theory base, as depicted in Figure 9.2, to examine culture-specific enablers and impediments to the adoption and use of the Internet in the Arab world. Specifically, they adapted the model to examine: (1) the impact of both technological

Figure 9.3 **Model Predicting Individual Internet Acceptance**

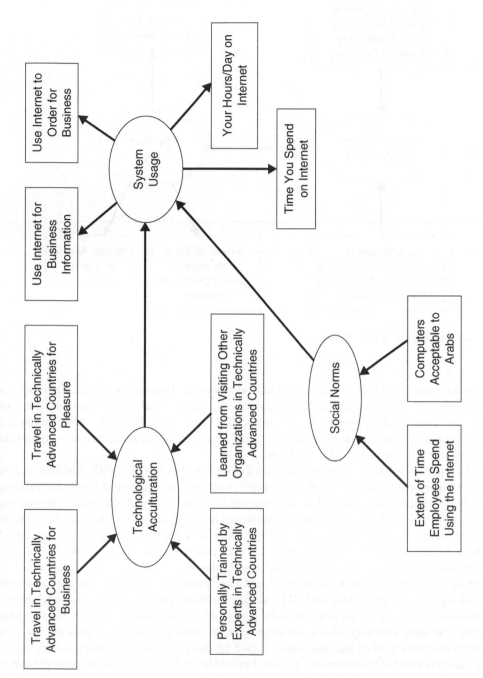

Source: Based on Loch et al. (2003).

Figure 9.4   **Model Predicting Organizational Internet Acceptance**

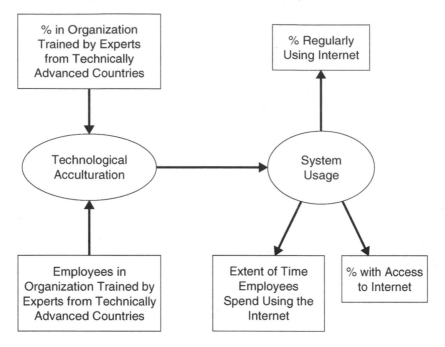

Source: Based on Loch et al. (2003).

acculturation and social norms constructs on individual system (Internet) usage (see Figure 9.3); and (2) the impact of technological acculturation alone on organizational system (Internet) usage (see Figure 9.4). They cited previous empirical studies (Hill et al., 1994; Hill et al., 1998; Straub et al., 2001) supporting the notion that both cultural beliefs and technological acculturation significantly impact the transference of IT to Arab cultures.

With respect to individual system usage (see Figure 9.3), Loch et al. (2003) reasoned that both technological acculturation and social norms would predict individual Internet usage. Technological acculturation occurs when people become educated or informed about advanced computer technologies from other cultures, particularly technologies not presently assimilated into their own culture. Technological acculturation can stem from extensive education or training in a technically advanced culture or from less formal experiences such as travel abroad. Their technological acculturation construct was comprised of four measures: the degree of (1) business travel and/or (2) pleasure travel to technologically advanced non-Arabic countries; and the amount of learning (3) resulting from expert training and (4) by visiting businesses in more technologically advanced non-Arabic countries. They argued that social norms are a critical driver of likely Internet usage, since an individual's affinity with a particular referent group that highly regards the use of the Internet will similarly affect that individual's regard for using the Internet. Their social norms construct was comprised of two measures. The first targeted the individual's group of peers in the workplace as a referent group and asked about the amount of time these peer employees spent using the Internet. The second measure targeted Arab society as a referent group and asked if the individual believed that computers were acceptable to Arabs. The dependent variable, individual system

Figure 9.5   **Results of PLS Analysis for Individual Internet Acceptance**

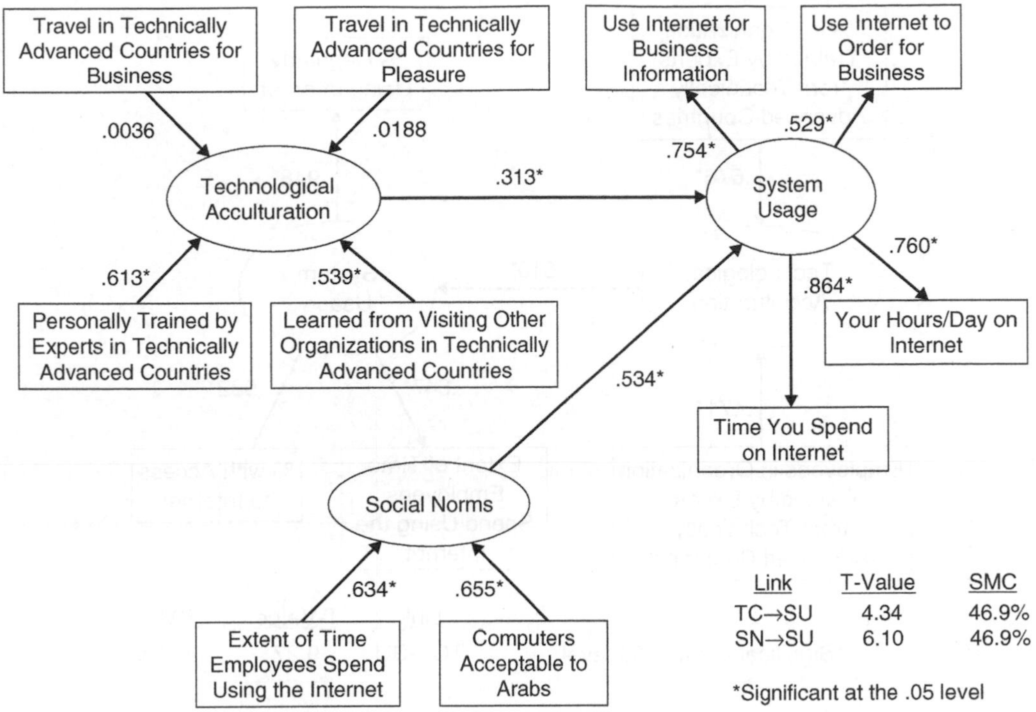

Source: Based on Loch et al. (2003).

(Internet) usage, was formative and comprised of four measures: (1) the percentage of usage hours per day, (2) the perceived degree of time that an individual reported using the Internet; and the amount of Internet usage for (3) business purchasing, and for (4) gathering business information.

With respect to the organizational usage of the Internet in the Arab world (see Figure 9.4), Loch et al. (2003) reasoned that unlike social norms that affect the individual's behavior, technological acculturation should impact the acceptance and use of IT in the organization as a whole. Specifically, the greater the employees' exposure to information technology through, for example, frequent training sessions on technology developed in another culture, the more they should be positively influenced to use that technology. Their technological acculturation construct was comprised of two factors: (1) the percentage of employees, and (2) the perceived extent that experts from technically advanced countries had trained employees. The predicted construct, organizational system (Internet) usage, was comprised of three measures: (1) the average amount of time employees spent using the Internet; and the percentage of employees who (2) regularly use the Internet, and (3) have access to the Internet. The complete instrument used to assess the Arabic organizational usage of the Internet is presented as Appendix 9.1.

Figure 9.5 displays the PLS path coefficients for the model predicting individual system (Internet) usage in the Arab world. Despite the non-significant loadings on two of the travel-related technological acculturation indicators, there were strong predictive relationships between technological acculturation and individual Internet usage, and between social norms and individual Internet usage.

Figure 9.6   **Findings of PLS Analysis for Organizational Internet Acceptance**

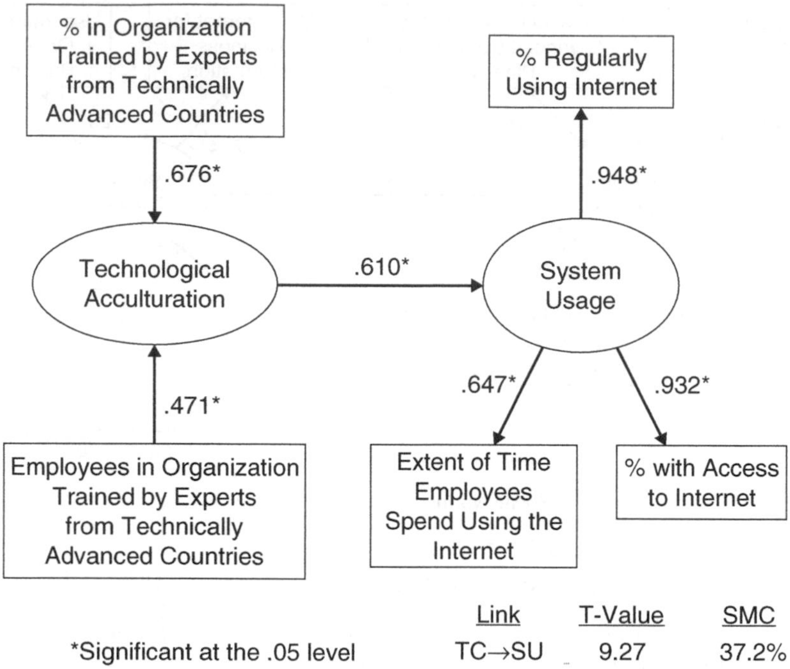

	Link	T-Value	SMC
*Significant at the .05 level	TC→SU	9.27	37.2%

Source: Based on Loch et al. (2003).

Both of the social norms construct factors were significant, as were all four of the individual system (Internet) usage construct factors. The model explained 47 percent of the variance in individual Internet usage among Arabs.

Figure 9.6 shows the PLS path coefficients for the model predicting organizational Internet usage in the Arab world. The respondents, who were mostly managers and knowledge workers, were significantly affected by both measures of training from experts from other cultures. All three of the organizational system (Internet) usage factors were significant. The model explained 37 percent of the variance in organizational Internet usage.

Extending CIM to Study Impact of Government IT Policy on the Diffusing of Computing. Loch, Sevcik, and Straub (2000) extended the theory base first examined through cultural influence modeling depicted as Figure 9.2, with the support of U.S. National Science Foundation funding. Checchi, Sevcik, Loch, and Straub (2002) discuss the instrumentation developed to measure the effects of culture on information and communication technologies (ICT) government policy on the diffusion of computing hardware, software, telecommunications, and applications in Egypt. The dependent variables relate to information technology transfer (ITT) and ICT outcomes. The Checchi et al. (2002) research model, which indicates both positive and negative influences among the constructs, is presented as Figure 9.7; construct definitions are shown in Table 9.2.

Although previous research had explored the influence of culture-specific beliefs and values and technological acculturation on IT outcomes, Checchi et al. (2002) extended this thread of research to include national IT policies and IT transfer implementation factors. As reflected in their research

Figure 9.7   **Model Predicting ICT/ITT Outcomes**

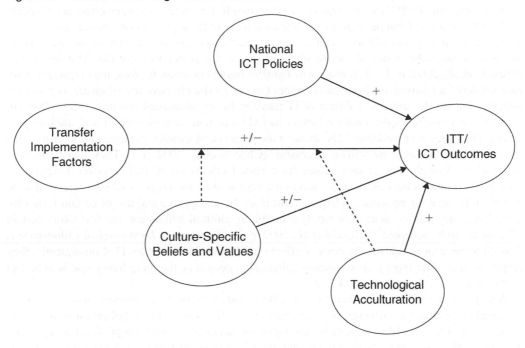

Source: Based on Loch et al. (2000) and published in Checchi et al. (2002).

Table 9.2

Construct Definitions

Construct	Description
National ICT policies/technological infrastructure	Status of the technology infrastructure of the nation. Policies aimed at encouraging or impeding ICT
Transfer implementation factors	Factors that influence the success or failure of the deployment of a technology or technologies
Culture-specific beliefs and values	Cultural and social responses of individuals and groups; beliefs and values; socioculturally influenced motivations. This set is limited to those beliefs and values that are expected to have an influence on the adoption of ICT and specific to the culture or ethnic group being studied
Technological culturation	Influence of external, technologically advanced cultures (such as Western industrialized cultures, former Soviets, Japan, Turks, etc.) on individual/ group/culture as a whole
Information technology transfer (ITT)/ICT outcomes	Measures of outcomes include prediction of success; actual use; intention to use; diffusion; success of system development

Source: Based on Checchi et al. (2002).

model (Figure 9.7), they posited a strong positive influence of *National ICT Policies & Technological Infrastructure* on *ITT/ICT (System) Outcomes.* Viewing ICT policies as a social construct, Checchi et al. (2002) reasoned that the degree of public awareness of these policies serves as a surrogate for the reality of these policies in the social context. Thus, they proposed that: "The more aware a person is of a particular policy, the more s/he will expect the policy to favor the diffusion of IT" (Checchi et al., 2002, p. 7). With respect to *Transfer Implementation Factors,* they argued that for national-level initiatives, environmental factors (including the effective use of media to publicize policies) impact the success or failure of IT transfer. In organizational systems, it is well documented that transfer implementation factors include top management support and training programs. Thus, they proposed that: "The stronger the presence of transfer implementation factors, the more likely the ITT outcome will be successful" (Checchi et al., 2002, p. 7). They also maintained that *Culture-Specific Beliefs and Values* have varied effects on ICT/ITT (system) outcomes. Inhibiting cultural beliefs and values, such as the degree of hierarchical social structures and individual preference for personal contact, can diminish the acceptance and use of certain technologies. Thus, they posited that: "The stronger inhibiting cultural beliefs are, the less likely certain systems are to be accepted." (Checchi et al., 2002, p. 7). By contrast, *Technological Culturation* is thought to have an unequivocally positive effect on diffusion outcomes for IT. Consequently, they proposed that: "The more technologically culturated a person is, the more likely s/he is to accept certain systems" (Checchi et al. 2002, p. 7).

A major contribution of the Checchi et al. (2002) study was the development of instrumentation designed to measure the influence of government ICT policies and cultural beliefs on systems outcomes. A sample of the illustrative items developed for this instrumentation is provided as Appendix 9.2. To identify categories of relevant government ICT policies that affect system outcomes, CEOs and top managers of multinational corporations and leading Egyptian firms were interviewed. Twelve categories of relevant ICT policies were identified, presented in Appendix 9.3.

The Checchi et al. (2002) study reported the progress of the first phase of a multi-phased study designed to assess the effects of culture and ICT government policy on the diffusion of computing. Data analysis and publishing of results of Phases 2, 3 and 4 are currently under way. The purpose of Phase 1 was to develop instrumentation and to identify relevant ICT policies. Phase 2 tests the importance of these policies by assessing top managers' awareness of the policies, their perception of the policies' completeness, and their evaluation of the policies' relative merit. Through large-scale sampling via semi-structured interviews and Web surveys, Phases 3 and 4 validate the final instrumentation and assess the influences of the constructs in the research model on ICT/ITT system outcomes.

Culture-Related Modified Technology Acceptance Models

Modified versions of the technology acceptance model (TAM) have been applied to assess cross-cultural technology acceptance and diffusion. Modifications to TAM to address multicultural nuances have included testing TAM in non–North American cultures, using TAM to assess IT diffusion in less developed cultures (LDCs), adding social presence/information richness constructs to TAM, assessing the influence of gender on TAM, and assessing the moderate effect of power distance on relationship between subjective norms and IT adoption.

Testing IT Adoption and Use in Non–North American Cultures. Straub, Keil, and Brenner (1997) comprised one of the first research teams to apply TAM to understand the adoption and use of IT in non–North American nations. Using employees of three airline companies engaged in the use of

Table 9.3

Hofstede's Four Cultural Dimensions

Hofstede Dimension	Abbreviation	Description
Power Distance	PDI	Degree of inequality among people which the population of a culture considers normal
Uncertainty Avoidance	UAI	Degree to which people in a culture feel uncomfortable with uncertainty and ambiguity
Individualism	IDV	Degree to which people in a culture prefer to act as individuals rather than as members of groups
Masculinity	MAS	Degree to which values like assertiveness, performance, success, and competition prevail among people of a culture over gentler values like the quality of life, maintaining warm personal relationships, service, care for the weak, etc.

Source: Based on Straub et al. (1997).

e-mail, they applied TAM across three countries: Japan, Switzerland, and the United States. Their results indicated that TAM was validated in the United States and Switzerland, but not in Japan. They theorized that Japan and the United States would differ markedly on certain cultural dimensions defined by Hofstede (1980), thus explaining the disparity. They constructed a computer-based media support index (CBMSI) for each country, a composite measure based on four of Hofstede's dimensions. Japan ranked highest on this CBMSI value; the United States ranked lowest. Switzerland, on the other hand, ranked in between the United States and Japan on this CBMSI measure of cultural values, but was not ranked significantly different from the United States.

Drawing on Hofstede's research on cultural dimensions (1980) and on social presence theory, Straub et al. (1997) maintained that the cultural dimensions identified by Hofstede would have a specific cross-cultural bearing on technology acceptance, particularly for communications support technologies including groupware, e-mail, voice mail, and videoconferencing. Hofstede's four cultural dimensions are presented in Table 9.3.

Straub et al. (1997) argued that in societies where managers and knowledge workers are separated by a large *power distance* (PDI), the equalizing effect of computer-based media is not regarded as a desirable feature. Thus, in relatively high PDI cultures, such as Japan, lower-echelon workers will defer to authority figures by abstaining from using technology-based media that disallows face-to-face contact. Accordingly, the use of e-mail and other electronic media may be restrained by social norms. With respect to *uncertainty avoidance* (UAI), both information richness and social presence theories suggest that individuals choose media related to how well such media reduce uncertainty. Rich media, including face-to-face communication, use multiple visual and auditory channels; consequently, they support tasks in which uncertainty is high. Computer-based media such as e-mail are leaner channels with respect to cues, and thus do not support tasks that involve a high degree of uncertainty. Consequently, for cultures in which individuals avoid uncertainty (such as Japan), electronic media should be used less often than face-to-face media or other rich channels (see also Straub, 1994). Knowledge workers in high UAI cultures (for example, Japan) should therefore perceive computer-based media to be less useful and harder to use than workers in low UAI cultures (such as the United States and Switzerland). Moreover, low individualism (IDV) should mute the use of computer-based communications in collectivist or group-effect cultures such as Japan, since workers using this technology fail to recognize details about the social situation, as compared to workers engaged in face-to-face communication. Finally, assertiveness (MAS) relates to interpersonal presence. Assertive cultures that value masculinity (such as Japan) would not favor media such as e-mail that do not convey the social presence of the communicator. Conversely, in less assertive cultures (such as the United States and Switzerland), face-to-face communication, and other media rich in interactional cues, should neither be as necessary nor as valued. Rather, media that are less socially present should be more acceptable in assertive cultures.

Testing Technology Adoption in Less Developed Countries. Rose and Straub (1998) conducted one of the first comprehensive studies on how technology adoption differs between less developed countries (LDCs) and more highly industrialized nations. Applying TAM to assess the diffusion of personal computing in five Arab nations in the Middle East (Egypt, Jordan, Saudi Arabia, Lebanon, and the Sudan), Rose and Straub utilized a cross-sectional survey of knowledge workers in these countries. Their basic research question asked whether TAM (i.e., the technology acceptance model) applies to developing countries. To address this question, they proposed three hypotheses, framed within the setting of LDCs: (1) the more a system is perceived to be useful, the more it will be used; (2) the more a system is perceived to be easy to use, the more it will be used; and (3) perceived usefulness mediates the effects of perceptions of ease of system use on actual use.

Using questionnaires to assess modified versions of the TAM perceived usefulness (PU), perceived ease-of-use (PEOU), and system usage (System Use) constructs, the researchers sampled 274 respondents: 121 from Jordan, 45 from Egypt, 28 from Saudi Arabia, 35 from Lebanon, and 45 from the Sudan. They drew samples from a wide variety of organizations, including public, private, and health-care sectors within the respective LDC nations. Using partial least squares (PLS) analyses of the collected data, they found that each of the three hypotheses was supported by the data. The PLS findings in Figure 9.8 show that the path coefficients for each of the TAM constructs were positive and highly significant. Further, the model explained 19.6 percent of the variance in PU and 40.4 percent of the variance in System Use. This study provided one of the early insights into the adoption and use of IT outside of the technologically advanced world.

A Cross-Cultural IT Diffusion Process Model. Drawing again from Hofstede's (1980) seminal work on dimensions of cultural difference among countries, Straub (1994) added a social presence/information richness (SPIR) factor to existing TAM constructs to propose a cross-cultural IT diffusion process model (depicted as Figure 9.9). He used this model to test whether cultural differences in the perception of social presence and information richness characteristics of communications media play a role in predispositions to use e-mail and fax. Testing this model with Japanese knowledge workers, Straub (1994) reasoned that in Diffusion Phase I, individuals assess the SPIR characteristics of a communication medium to judge how well it "fits" a particular task. They then form perceptions about the usefulness (PU) of the medium in Diffusion Stage 2. Combined with their perception of the ease of use (PEOU) of the medium, individuals make choices and enact a pattern of usage (USE) in Diffusion Stage III. Finally, in Diffusion Stage IV, use of the chosen medium is associated with work productivity benefits (or decrements).

Largely due to greater Japanese uncertainty avoidance and to structural language differences between Japanese and U.S. knowledge workers, Straub (1994) found that Japanese knowledge workers perceive e-mail to be lower in medium SPIR, and perceive fax to be higher in medium SPIR, than do U.S. workers. He also found that Japanese knowledge workers perceive e-mail to

Figure 9.8 **PLS Findings for LDC Arab Region Sample**

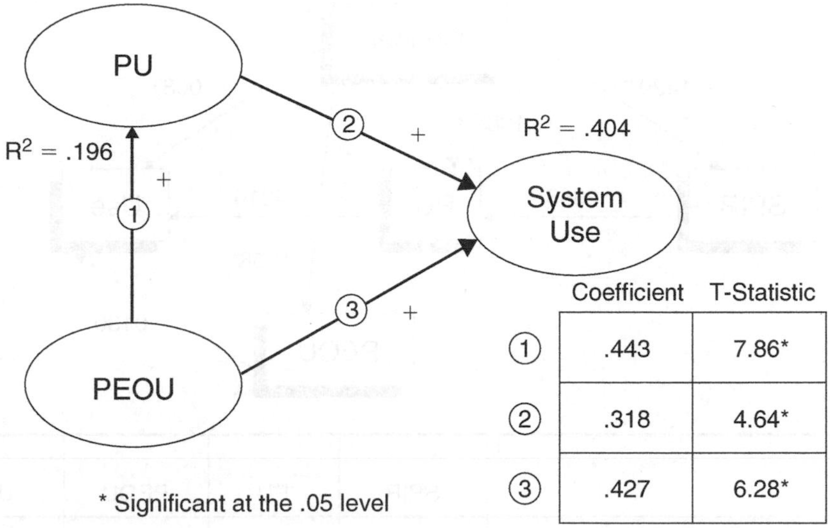

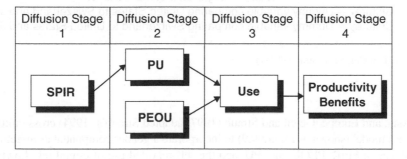

PU
R2 = .196
+
1
2
+
R2 = .404
System Use
3
+
PEOU
Coefficient
T-Statistic
1 .443 7.86*
2 .318 4.64*
3 .427 6.28*
* Significant at the .05 level

Source: Based on Rose and Straub (1998).

Figure 9.9 **Cross-Cultural IT Diffusion Process Model**

Diffusion Stage 1
Diffusion Stage 2
Diffusion Stage 3
Diffusion Stage 4
SPIR
PU
PEOU
Use
Productivity Benefits

Source: Based on Straub (1994).

be less useful than do U.S. workers, use e-mail less than their U.S. counterparts, and rate the productivity benefits of e-mail lower than U.S. workers. However, the Japanese perceive fax to be more useful and rate the productivity benefits of fax higher than U.S. workers. There was little difference between the two cultures in their perceptions and use of traditional media, such as face-to-face conversations and telephones.

The Role of Gender on the Cross-Culture IT Diffusion of E-mail. In another TAM study, Gefen and Straub (1997) focused on the role of gender on the cross-cultural IT diffusion of e-mail. Examining comparable groups of knowledge workers using e-mail systems in the airline industry in North

Figure 9.10   **Gender Effects on TAM Variables**

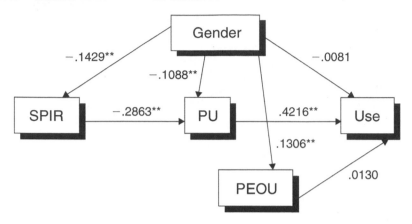

	SPIR	PU	PEOU	Use
Covariate Culture$_1$ on...	.5464**	.3073**	.9606**	.4381**
Covariate Culture$_2$ on...	.1475**	.0546	.3145**	.3322**
Overall R^2 (including the effects of culture)	.37	.59	.53	.34

Note:** = Significant at the .05 level
Culture$_1$ = Dummy variable comparing United States to Switzerland and Japan
Culture$_2$ = Dummy variable comparing Switzerland to United States and Japan

Source: Based on Gefen and Straub (1997).

America, Asia, and Europe, Gefen and Straub (1997) adapted Straub's (1994) cross-cultural IT diffusion process model (shown as Figure 9.9) to incorporate a gender component as affecting the perceived attributes of SPIR, PEOU, and PU, and the self-reported use of e-mail (as shown in Figure 9.10). Citing Hofstede's (1980) extensive work on cultural dimensions, they argued that gender roles are transferred through socialization, and represent an important sociocultural factor that influences perceptions and behaviors, particularly with respect to language. They hypothesized that men and women would exhibit different perceptual and usage patterns in adapting respective discourse patterns as well as in their tendencies to use e-mail, an electronic form of discourse. Gefen and Straub (1997) cite previous research showing that men tend to adopt a pattern of oral communication based on social hierarchy and competition, whereas women prefer a networking approach that uses discourse to achieve intimacy, support, consensus, rapport, and cooperative behavior. Arguing that these gender-disparate communication patterns imply radically different values for the need for social presence, Gefen and Straub (1997) hypothesized that: (1) women would perceive the social presence of e-mail to be higher than men would; (2) women would rate the perceived usefulness of e-mail higher than men would; (3) women's rating of the perceived ease of use of e-mail would be higher than men's; and (4) women's use of e-mail would be greater than that of men.

Their results are presented as Figure 9.10. In addition to the gender variable, the analysis used covariate dummy variables (Culture$_1$ and Culture$_2$) representing surrogates for culture (specifically, the countries of the United States and Switzerland, respectively) to account for the effect of culture in the variance of the dependent variables. Gender did have a significant impact on SPIR ($\beta1 = -0.1429$), on PU ($\beta2 = -0.1088$), and on PEOU ($\beta3 = 0.1306$). The effect of gender on use was insignificant ($\beta4 = -0.0081$). Gender and the covariate culture accounted for 37 percent of the variance in SPIR, 59 percent of the variance in PU, 53 percent of the variance in PEOU, and 34 percent of the variance in Use. These results clearly suggest that gender does have an effect on the IT diffusion process.

The Moderator Effect of Power Distance on E-mail Acceptance. (Huang et al., 2003) studied the acceptance of e-mail in PRC by incorporating power distance (PD) into an extended TAM model. Prior research on TAM found that subjective norm (SN) directly affects perceived usefulness of a technology (PU), which in turn affects people's intention to use a technology. Subjective norm (SD) is defined as a person's perception that most people who are important to him or her think he or she should or should not perform the behavior in question. Since power distance (PD) has been found to be important in determining an individual's reactions in the workplace by affecting interaction and association among individuals, Huang et al. (2003) assert that influence of SN on PU could be moderated by PD perception in the context of e-mail diffusion in an organization.

The direction of moderator effect is controversial. On one hand, because individuals with higher PD perception tend to perceive the views of higher-status individuals to be superior to their own, they will be more influenced by their supervisors' opinions, indicating a positive moderator effect of PD on the relation between SN and PU of e-mail. On the other hand, individuals with higher PD value are sensitive to power status or power position and use social cues to express their respect for social hierarchy. The relative inability of e-mail to deliver "rich" information narrows down social status and results in the equalizing effect that, in turn, may reduce the perceived usefulness of e-mail, indicating a negative moderator effect of PD on the relation between SN and PU of e-mail.

Huang et al. (2003) conducted a survey study with an organization in mainland China. In this study, they measured PN, SD, PEOU, PU, and intention to use e-mail at the individual level. The data were analyzed using structural equation modeling. The model and results of this study are shown in Figure 9.11.

The findings show that, contrary to some beliefs, the influence of subjective norms on perceived usefulness is stronger among individuals with lower power distance than among those with higher power distance. The negative moderation effect reported in this study might be explained by the fact that individuals tend to shun activities that are deemed as inappropriate in regard to their power and status in a group, even if they are persuaded to believe that the activities are useful to them.

Culture, Media Richness Theory, and Related Empirical Research

One study comparing the impact of cell phones and portable computers on sales forces in different industries in France and the United States was not successful in explaining differences in use (Carson, Kahn, and Rowe, 2002). It was, however, able to provide rich, descriptive examples of technology use in companies in the two cultures. Specifically, it described the relative speed of decision making, standardization on certain technologies, and the formalization of work. The research employed a survey of large firms in which users, IT managers, and the managers in charge of organizing the workforce were asked to describe IT use in their own work settings.

Figure 9.11   **Results of the LISREL Analysis of the Path Model**

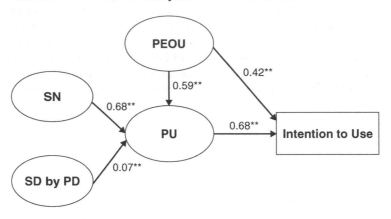

Source: Based on Huang et al. (2003).

In a French field study, Rowe et al. (1999) examined the relationship between cultures and media use and related the relationship among e-mail, voice mail, and telephone use to Hofstede's "task orientation" scales. They conclude that although the technologies' features/factors are important, they are always interpreted through the lens of cultural values. Using media richness theory, Rowe et al. (1999) demonstrate empirically the relationship between the individual's preference for organizational cultures and his or her telecommunication use (fax, e-mail, voice mail, and telephone). They measured cultural values of 223 individuals in a French company using a Q-sort balance block design, coupled with diaries, to record telecommunications use from nearly 800 communications by 145 individuals using four or more communications media. They found that the use of new media was more related to an orientation towards innovation, reactivity, or entrepreneurship than was telephone use. E-mail appeared to be associated with relation-oriented rather than task-oriented cultural values, suggesting that the amount of feedback plays a role in the process of telecommunications media choice. They found culture to be an interesting complementary approach to information richness theory for understanding telecommunication choices.

Their research method is illustrated in Table 9.4 and Figure 9.12.

Cross-Culture Comparative Studies on IT Diffusion at National Level

A Meta-Framework of Public IT Policies

Focusing on the role of public IT policies, Checchi, Hsieh, and Straub (2003) explored how well existing diffusion models originating from developed countries explain the adoption of IT in less developed countries. Conducted as a meta-analysis of existing studies in mainstream IS and internationally oriented journals, Checchi et al. (2003) surveyed articles that focus on public IT policies with a view towards developing an integrative framework for positioning the impact of future public IT policy implementation on the adoption and diffusion of IT.

Checchi et al. (2003) noted that the governments of industrialized countries not only participate actively in the development of information capabilities—they also invest heavily in

Table 9.4

Q-Sort Procedure

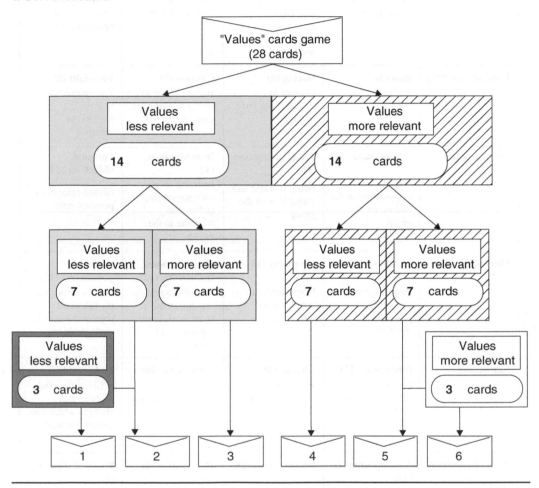

IT-related research (see Table 9.5). Furthermore, with respect to the role of governments in formulating public IT policies, they noted that governments of developed nations take more proactive positions in creating environments that efficiently promote economic development, whereas governments from less developed countries play a more passive or reactive role and rely more on regional or international agencies for this purpose.

Checchi et al. (2003) examined existing literature for characteristics of IT policies in less developed countries that are (or are not) successful in promoting economic development (see Table 9.6). Specifically, case studies of successful examples of economic development in less developed countries (notably including Ireland, China, and Singapore) were typified by building capacity through their national IT policies (Checchi et al., 2003). These countries often developed policies that transferred IT capability from more advanced countries by importing foreign resources, and by building human resources and infrastructure for IT adoption and diffusion.

Figure 9.12　**Set of Cards Describing Cultural Values**

Reactivity	Action (1)	Speedy decision making (2)	Reflecting (4)	Analyzing (3)
	Preferring action; acting quickly	Being quick to take advantage of an opportunity that presents itself	Not leaping in without thought	Analyzing the situation before taking action
Entrepreneurship	Risk (5)	Daring (6)	Caution (7)	Foresight (8)
	Willing to take risks	In order to succeed, you have to dare	Being careful and trying to minimize exposure to risk	Taking precautions to avoid unpleasant surprises
Individualism	Compromise (15)	Social interaction (16)	Individualism (13)	Personal objectives (14)
	Seeking a compromise in the interest of the group	Being sociable and fitting in with the group	Insisting on your own personality rather than adapting to the group	Giving priority to personal goals
Flexibility	Flexibility (9)	Simplicity (10)	Organizational framework (12)	Rules and procedures (11)
	Being able to adapt the procedures to the situation	Doing without ceremony and formality	A well-thought-out organizational framework ensures a good use of resources	Strictly respecting the rules and regulations avoids many problems
Innovation	Innovation (17)	Change (18)	Continuity (20)	Stability (19)
	Looking for progress and new ideas	Welcoming change favorably	Wishing to preserve what is, as it has always worked	Wishing to avoid ruptures and changes which can disturb the work process
Task Orientation	Accomplishment (25)	Recompenses (28)	Recognition (26)	Personal dignity (27)
	Working hard and achieving set targets is an essential source of well-being	A financial reward is preferable to an increase in leisure time	Valuing the contributions and the qualities of each individual and never ignoring the human factor	Respecting the rights of the individual and his or her personal dignity
Power Distance	Conflict (21)	Equality (22)	Subordination (23)	Differentials (24)
	Not avoiding conflicts with superiors in the hierarchy	Everybody has the same rights without regard to their position	Conforming to the point of view of a superior in order to avoid conflict	Those who have more responsibility have the right to certain advantages

Table 9.5

Differences in IT Policy Setting

Policy Intervention Component	Developed Countries	Less Developed Countries
Initiator for policy making (mostly)	Domestic government	Regional or international agencies
Attitude of the government	Proactive	Passive or reactive
Investment purpose	Invest in both research knowledge and IT infrastructure	Invest mostly in IT infrastructure
Typical capabilities of the government	Has both technical and financial capabilities	Lack of technical skills, financial limitations
Position with respect to standards	Standard setting	Standard following

Source: Based on Checchi et al. (2003).

Table 9.6

Success Factors in IT Policies of Less Developed Countries

Successful IT Policies	Unsuccessful IT Policies
Long-term-oriented	Short-term-oriented
Capability-building	Resource-consumption
Adaptive	Less responsive
Collaborative	Noncollaborative

Source: Based on Checchi et al. (2003).

By contrast, less developed countries with less successful public IT policies typically relied on short-term, consumption-oriented (as opposed to production-oriented) IT policies that relied on foreign resources and assistance for additional future development. In addition, governments of less developed countries that were more flexible in adapting their IT policies to shifting environmental conditions led to more successful IT adoption. Finally, countries such as Ireland, Singapore, Korea, Costa Rica, and Taiwan that related their IT policies to other government policies—such as construction and education programs, and other economic development projects—were more successful in promoting economic development. Cases of unsuccessful IT policy implementation, including the Ukraine and many African countries, characteristically had IT policies that were disconnected from other governmental activities.

Noting that existing research exploring the effects of public IT policies had produced a disjointed set of propositions and elements, Checchi et al. (2003) developed a meta-framework of IT policies (shown as Figure 9.13) that considers the interactive nature of the process, the networks and actors involved, and other relevant constructs. Business and governments are the principal actors in their model, although other institutions also assume stakeholder roles. Central to their meta-framework are the public environmental characteristics that typically vary across more and less developed countries. Table 9.7 summarizes these public environment characteristics and indicates how they vary.

Figure 9.13 **Meta-framework of IT Policies**

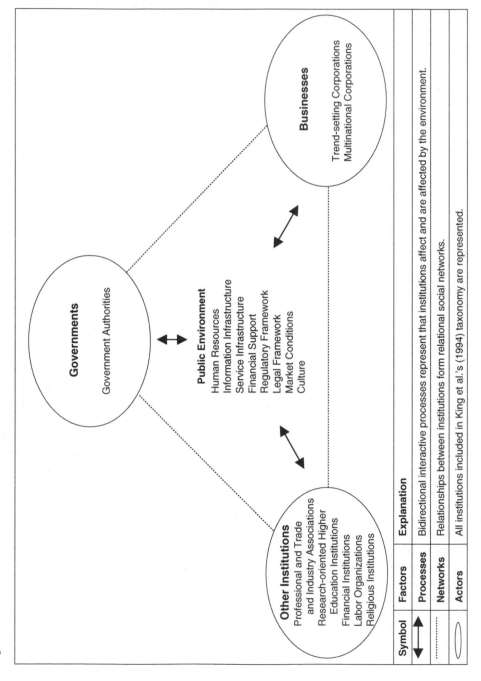

Governments

Government Authorities

Businesses

Trend-setting Corporations
Multinational Corporations

Other Institutions

Professional and Trade
and Industry Associations
Research-oriented Higher
Education Institutions
Financial Institutions
Labor Organizations
Religious Institutions

Public Environment

Human Resources
Information Infrastructure
Service Infrastructure
Financial Support
Regulatory Framework
Legal Framework
Market Conditions
Culture

Symbol	Factors	Explanation
↕	Processes	Bidirectional interactive processes represent that institutions affect and are affected by the environment.
⋯⋯	Networks	Relationships between institutions form relational social networks.
◯	Actors	All institutions included in King et al.'s (1994) taxonomy are represented.

Table 9.7

Summary of Public Environmental Characteristics on IT Policies

Public Environment Characteristics	Summary of Public Environment Characteristics for Less Developed Countries
Human Resources	Lower supply of knowledge workers due to more restrictive educational opportunities. Demand is also lower due to lower economic activity.
Information Infrastructure	Low teledensity, poor connection quality, and insufficient power supply. These lead to low economies of scale and negatively affect national adoption of IT.
Services Infrastructure	Inferior services infrastructure.
Financial Support	More developed countries have technology research programs with technologies developed spilling into the private sector. IT diffusion in less developed countries have fewer investments in research and is mostly subsidized by international agencies.
Regulatory Framework	More restrictive and more highly regulated contexts, including state-owned communication services monopolies and high import costs.
Legal Framework	Incomplete laws and legal structures, and unwillingness to enforce laws relating to intellectual property, resulting in higher levels of software piracy.
Market Conditions	Lower purchasing power and lower customer readiness to adopt IT innovation.
Culture	Non-Western cultures typify most less developed countries, creating conflicts adopting and using Western features embedded in the adopted technologies.

Source: Based on Checchi et al. (2003).

The primary contribution of the Checchi et al. (2003) study is to better explain the role of government IT policies in promoting the successful adoption and diffusion of IT in less developed countries. This study is one of the first to focus on this critically important element with underpinnings in cultural influence modeling (see Figure 9.2). Their meta-framework suggests fruitful areas for additional empirical testing to provide more insights for policy makers to formulate IT policies that efficiently and effectively promote the adoption and diffusion of IT, particularly in less developed, non-Western nations.

Environment and Policy Factors Shaping Global E-Commerce Diffusion

Trade, political openness, and advances in information technology facilitate the worldwide flow of information, capital, and people, thus accelerating the process of globalization. One of the most significant economic trends of the past decade is the growing use of the Internet for conducting business. Gibbs et al. (2003) examined the key factors shaping e-commerce diffusion among different countries. Specifically, they asked: What global and national environmental and policy forces affect the adoption of e-commerce across counties? Which factors are drivers or enablers

Table 9.8

Conceptual Framework of Factors Shaping Global E-Commerce Diffusion

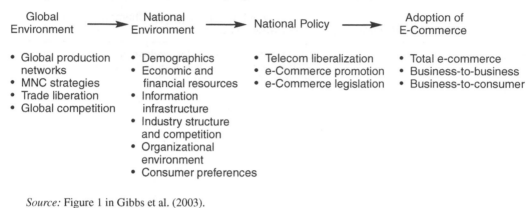

Source: Figure 1 in Gibbs et al. (2003).

and which are barriers or inhibitors; and how do they influence business-to-business (B2B) and business-to-consumer (B2C) e-commerce adoption?

Gibbs et al. (2003) posited that factors in the global environment as well as infrastructural and policy lead to adoption. At the global environment level, globalization of production and markets, multinational corporation (MNC) strategies, and open trade regimes commonly drive countries and industry sectors to adopt e-commerce. At the national level, key factors were classified into two categories. National environmental factors include a country's demographics, economic and financial resources, information infrastructure, industry structure and competition, organizational environment, and social and cultural factors such as consumer preferences. National policy factors include liberalization of telecommunications and IT markets, government promotion initiatives for e-commerce and IT in general, and e-commerce legislation (as shown in Table 9.8).

The researchers commissioned detailed case studies by scholars and experts in ten countries. The countries in the study—Brazil, China, Denmark, France, Germany, Mexico, Japan, Singapore, Taiwan, and the United States—were selected to include developed, newly industrializing, and developing nations, and to represent each major region of the world. Two types of data related to the countries are discussed in the article: (1) qualitative data, or findings, from the in-depth case studies prepared by scholars and experts in each country, and (2) statistical data compiled from the cases and secondary sources (IDC, ITU, UNDP, OECD) that enable cross-country comparison. The researchers conducted cross-case analysis and identified commonalities and differences of key factors impacting e-commerce diffusion among the countries, and they assessed whether these findings pointed to convergence or divergence in the factors shaping diffusion. The results are shown in Table 9.9.

The researchers reported that B2B e-commerce is driven by global forces, whereas B2C is more of a local phenomenon. The preliminary explanation for this difference is that B2B is driven by global competition and MNCs that "push" e-commerce to stay competitive, while B2C is "pulled" by consumer markets, which are mainly local and therefore divergent. Although all consumers desire convenience and low prices, consumer preferences and values, national culture, and distribution systems differ markedly across countries, and define differences in local consumer markets. These findings support the perspective of transformation theorists, who regard globalization as an

Table 9.9

Overall Determinants of E-Commerce

	B2B	B2C
Drivers (D) and enablers (E)	(D) International competitive pressure due to globalization	(D) Consumer desire for convenience, lifestyle enhancements, and greater product/service selection, especially among younger generation
	(D) Pressure for cost reduction	(D) Business desire to research new markets or protect existing markets
	(D) Government procurement	(E) Consumer purchasing power
	(E) Opening of economy, market liberalization	(E) Rapid Internet diffusion: High IT literacy, strong IT infrastructure
	(E) Government promotion and investment	(E) Government promotion
Barriers (B) and inhibitors (I)	(I) Business environment and culture: risk aversion, difficulty changing organizational processes, lack of resources and skills in businesses, especially SMEs	(B) Lack of valuable and useful content for consumers
	(I) National culture: lack of innovation, slow change, cautious imitator mentality, lack of service mentality	(B) Inequality in socioeconomic levels
	(I) Limited scope of e-commerce, local/regional focus	(B) Consumer reluctance to buy online and lack of trust due to security/privacy concerns
	(I) Education and tax system	(I) Consumer reluctance to buy online due to preferences for in-store shopping
	(I) Political concerns and instability, short-term focus	(I) Existence of viable alternatives, such as dense retail networks, convenience stores
		(I) Lack of online payment mechanisms
		(I) Lack of customer service
		(I) Language difference

Source: Table 9.8 in Gibbs et al. (2003).

uneven process that incorporates elements of both convergence and divergence. In terms of policy, the case studies suggest that liberalizing trade and telecommunications is likely to have the biggest impact on e-commerce, both by making ICT and Internet access more affordable to firms and consumers, and by pressuring firms to adopt e-commerce to stay competitive. Specific e-commerce legislation appears not to have as large an impact, although inadequate protection for both buyers and sellers in some countries suggest that mechanisms need to be developed to ensure greater confidence in conducting business online.

EDI Standards as Evolutionary and Culturally Mediated Exchanges

In the realm of exchange of business documents and data, the goal of creating a stable set of technical and linguistic standards governing computer-mediated exchanges has long been considered essential to successful B2B e-commerce. This concern has fostered the development of elaborate ANSI X12 standards in the United States and UN/EDIFACT standards in Europe. Yet the goal of creating stable standards has been elusive and has contributed in part to the attempt to use XML to resolve certain failings of the ANSI and UN standards. Even so, the goal remains elusive and the task remains formidable. Damsgaard and Truex (2000) posited that the notion of a standard, although typically celebrated as an advance over a nonstandard, is nevertheless still problematic in interorganizational communication. "whilst typically celebrated as an advance over a nonstandard, still represents a problem in interorganizational communication." They illustrate how the problems in creating a stable grammar and language set are consistent with those in any language system: Structures may exhibit forms of temporal regularity, but that they are not "stable"; they are emergent, subtly but constantly adjusting and changing. The core force behind the process is in the praxis of the interorganizational exchange, for example, in refining and redefining a set of documents or specific format to enable an exchange between two binary trading partners, meaning specific to that exchange and to the two partners must be negotiated. In the negotiation, subtle changes lead to the emergence of new ways to deploy and interpret the standard. After many successive such binary exchanges, the standard itself undergoes an adjustment to compensate for "nonstandard use," and so a whole new standard set emerges.

Using a set of cases from Hong Kong, Finland, and Denmark, Damsgaard and Truex illustrated how both national and organizational cultural differences exacerbate the problem and may hasten standards emergence. Cultural assumptions and values are embedded in language, in work processes, and in the manner in which individuals and organizations interrelate. Accordingly, in order to establish successful EDI exchange, in the performative sense, those differences have to be understood and then negotiated. This process may be trivial or complex. But it is always confounded when there are deeply embedded, and hence unquestioned, cultural differences that may not even rise to the level of the speaker's awareness.

Such differences may often go undetected in research settings that do not surface important emic versus etic differences in the linguistic, hence cultural, exchange. Some of the traditional empirical research can be justly criticized because it takes an etic approach wherein categories and constructs are given by the researcher, rather than being taken from within the value set and culture of the people and entities being studied. This emic approach is, in fact, the stance taken by the Hill et al. (1998) cultural influence modeling discussed earlier.

One such critique has been leveled at Hofstede's classic typology of cultural differences (Hofstede, 1980; Hofstede, 1981). In a country-specific study, D'Iribarne (1997) critiqued the etic view as being unable to grasp the complexity of culture and the concepts used by Hofstede the younger in the case of France, the Netherlands, and Germany. Sharing this concern, other researchers will hopefully undertake research sensitive to linguistic cultural differences using anthropological, ethnographic, or highly mixed intensive field study approaches to their research.

Reflections of National Cultures on National Information Infrastructure

Garfield et al. (1998) conducted a content analysis of descriptive cases regarding eight countries' National Information Infrastructure (NII) formation and found that national cultures play a pervasive role in the development of NII. Hofstede (1991) identified four distinct organizational models using the dimensions of power distance and uncertainty avoidance (shown in Figure 9.14). In the village-market type of organization, market conditions, rather than people or formal rules, dictate what should take place. In the family structure, power is unevenly distributed but people in the dominant position operate within a certain set of rules or boundaries based on interpersonal relationships. In

Figure 9.14   **Organizational Models of Different Cultures**

High	Family *China, Singapore*	Pyramid of people *France, Japan*
Power Distance		
Low	Village market *United Kingdom, United States*	Well-oiled machine *Finland, Germany*

Low   Uncertainty
                               Avoidance

Source: Figure 3 in Garfield et al. (1998).

Figure 9.15   **NII Component**

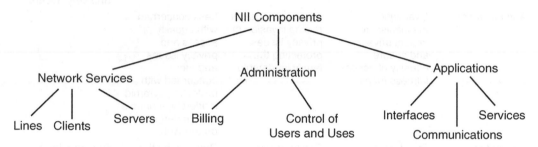

Source: Figure 2 in Garfield et al. (1998).

the pyramid-of-people type of organization, personal power and formal rules are very important. Leaders in this culture have authority and deploy formal rules and regulations to guide others. "Well-oiled machines" are organizations in which the real authority lies within rules, not in people. Garfield et al. (1998) use Hofstede's four models to categorize national ideologies. The specific countries of China, Singapore, France, Japan, the United Kingdom, the United States, Finland, and Germany were categorized according to their national cultural characteristics.

The researchers integrated prior models of NII and looked at NII at two levels: at a higher level with three layers (network services, administration, and applications) and at a more refined level by examining the specific components within each of the three broad categories (see Figure 9.15). Network services describe the physical connection between servers and clients. The administrative level controls the customers and uses of the network, including the method for billing and access control. The applications component includes all services offered on the NII.

Garfield et al. (1998) proposed that each type of culture will support different formations of the NII and that cultural differences will reflect on single NII components. For example, the village market typically assumes a hands-off approach in the formation of any projects that are driven by the larger marketplace. Governments and organizations that are more family oriented tend to be very centralized and guided by visions rather than rules. In the pyramid-of-people type of country, NII is fully controlled by the government, which sets rules for NII implementation and use. The NII in "well-oiled machine" countries may be designed to be the ultimate machine, with superior engineering. See Table 9.10 for a detailed analysis.

Collecting descriptive cases about formation of NII in China, Singapore, France, Japan, the United Kingdom, the United States, Finland, and Germany, these researchers conducted a content

Table 9.10

NII Components and Organizational Models

NII Components	Village Market	Family	Pyramid of People	Well-Oiled Machine
Network services	Encouragement of a competitive environment—a market pull	Regulated competition and use	Hierarchical-government sponsored development of a network—a push approach	Hierarchical-government sponsored development of a network with concerns for quality engineering—over-engineered and very secure
Administration	Oversight mechanism to protect privacy and ensure equality of access-fairness for all	Intrusive oversight raising invasion of privacy issues-protecting the family leadership	Less concerned with equality of access and privacy issues and more concerned with protecting pyramid leadership-controls over material on the Web	
Application	Freedom of speech can override other issues; created by the market for the market (e.g., entertainment and pornography)	Group values are important—maintain harmony; seeded by the government for the public (e.g., health)	Provided by the government for the public good	Provided by the government to improve economic performance

Source: Table 9.2 in Garfield et al. (1998).

analysis based on their conceptual framework, and identified the characteristics of NII components of each country. The detailed results are shown in Table 9.11.

The findings of this research show that culture seems to play a significant role in the development of an NII. Countries that design NII policies that are appropriate for their cultures are likely to be more successful in the creation of an NII. Countries creating an NII should first learn what has been successful in culturally similar cultures. Mimicking the successful NII policies of a culturally dissimilar country may result in policies that are culturally inappropriate and doomed to failure.

DISCUSSION AND CONCLUSIONS

Theory

In summary, these studies affirm that cultural effects can and do directly influence or moderate theoretical relationships in models predicting IT adoption and use in an international arena.

Table 9.11

Country NII Component Summary

NII Components	United Kingdom	United States	Germany	France	Japan	Singapore	China
Network Service	A deregulated marketplace. (Note: Prestel was designed when the market was not deregulated.)	Slowly deregulating networks. Government does not own networks but regulates the companies that do.	Government-owned centralized network.	Government designed and controlled network. Client market is becoming more open to competition.	Government orchestrates the implementation of the network by private industry.	Government currently owns networks but plans to partner with industry in the future.	Government will control networks but may contract with vendors to provide services.
Administration	Government oversees major policy decisions. Private industry vies for business.	Government protects public interest and promotes private competition.	Government regulates billing though does not levy it. Government nonintrusive in terms of privacy.	Government actively trying to make network access equal to all. It oversees billing, though private industry is given some latitude on the fees they can charge.	Attempting to design network that will allow equal access to different geographic locations.	Government encourages the use of network by all. Government retains control over the use of the network. The good of the country outweighs the right to individual privacy.	Government is very invasive. Its goal is to protect citizens and the government. The good of the country outweighs the right to individual privacy. Access to the network is restricted.
Applications	Private businesses design applications, marketplace determines if they will succeed.	Private businesses design applications, marketplace determines if they will succeed.	Private industry designs applications.	Government designed and implemented first application. It then allowed market to determine all other applications.	Government provides seed applications. It then works with private sector to develop future applications.	Applications will be designed by the government and developed jointly by public and private entities.	Government not actively involved in the design of applications but is restricting the availability of some.

Source: Table 3 in Garfield et al. (1998).

Among the many studies that examine sociocultural factors that impact the adoption, diffusion, and use of IT in an international context, one of the most useful and versatile emic epistemological approaches could be cultural influence modeling (Hill et al., 1998). Variations (Checchi et al., 2002; Hill et al., 1994; Loch et al., 2003; Straub, 2001) on the Hill et al. (1998) model have effectively applied a number of antecedent constructs to predict a variety of international IT system outcomes. Original and alternative antecedent constructs in the model have included national IT policies and technological infrastructure; technological acculturation; culture-specific beliefs and values; social norms; IT transfer implementation factors; and traditional IT implementation factors such as system pricing, top management support, and system implementation staff time. Some of the IT system outcome variables that have been examined with this model include the international perception of barriers to IT deployment and use, awareness of government IT policy, the success of IT policy in promoting IT-driven economic development, the success of IT diffusion, the success of system development, intention to use IT, the extent of IT use, the success of information centers, the rate of change in IT use, the amount of foreign direct investment in IT industries, and the degree of individual and organizational Internet usage.

Another model that has been applied a number of times to assess the multinational adoption and use of IT is Davis's technology acceptance model. However, the application of TAM in a multicultural setting has been adjusted to accommodate nuances tied to culture-specific perceptions of the usefulness of different types of IT. Specifically, the cultural dimensions of Hofstede (1980) and social presence theory have been used to modify TAM to predict the adoption and use of IT in non-Western countries.

Practice

As the trend towards globalization continues, firms expanding into new international arenas need to understand how cultural factors potentially affect the organization's likely success or failure in adopting and utilizing IT. A different culture need not be viewed as a barrier obstructing the transfer of IT. The successful transfer of IT into new workplaces residing in culturally diverse regions of the world requires "an understanding of micro-level beliefs, norms, and actions within the framework of national and international macrostructures" (Straub et al., 2001, p. 33). Managers need to acknowledge cultural differences and need to adapt newly introduced technologies to the cultural context. In dealing with new workers who are not technologically acculturated, managers should work with, rather than against, prevailing cultural patterns. Technological acculturation has been shown to be rooted in experience, education, and training (Loch et al., 2003). Consequently, firms that are expanding into new countries and cultures should expose new employees from those countries to cultural experiences in more technologically oriented cultures. In this regard, Straub et al. (2001) reported that informally derived acculturation experiences, such as travel, contact with family members abroad, and reading foreign technology journals, were more effective than formal acculturation activities such as foreign-based education and training. However, this finding was contravened by the later work of Loch et al. (2003), so managers might be advised to adopt all forms of exposure and persuasion.

Future Research

Cultural influence modeling has proved useful for investigating how to overcome cultural differences, partly because it advocates that cultural beliefs do not have to be measured in the aggregate (i.e., through emic forms of measurement). Instead, cultural beliefs can be examined individually, and in their respective cultural contexts. Consequently, knowledge in this domain will grow through an accumulation of studies that examine a variety of specific beliefs in different cultural contexts.

Furthermore, it has been demonstrated that there are at least three separate levels of culture, relating to ethnicity (often overlapping with national cultures), organizations, and functions (which includes IT). Consequently, future research on the effects of culture-specific beliefs, values, and social norms on organizational IT outcomes should be studied within this tri-level context.

Where should cross-cultural and globalization researchers specializing in information systems go next to further this vibrant, cumulative tradition that is extending our understanding of how cultural and national associations impact the use of information systems? There are at least two aspects of this discussion. First are the research connections that can be leveraged to incorporate new insights into international IT studies. Second are theoretical directions in which we should be moving.

Research Connections

International IT research has been very insular. IT scholars have not generally formed associations and connections with international business researchers, published in their favored journals, or attended their conferences. The top-ranked journal in this arena is the *Journal of International Business (JIBS)*, and it would be extremely useful for IS researchers to begin submitting their best work here. Other highly rated journals such as the *Journal of International Management* can also be considered, and IT scholars need to familiarize themselves with the review procedures of these alternative venues. In order to ensure proper inducements to publish in this venue, scholars need to lobby business and information schools to include a reasonable set of international business journals on P&T target journal lists. In this way, journal standards both inculcate and reify the behaviors that would be most beneficial. For templates of such lists, see the list at the Robinson College of Business, Georgia State University (URL: http://www.robinson.gsu.edu/facultyresearch/journals/index.html). Washington State University also has target journal lists that include international business journals.

Attending conferences focusing on international business issues is also desirable. The International Academy of Business (IAB) holds annual conferences, mostly in international destinations (the cities for the last four conferences have been Stockholm, Sweden; Monterey, California, United States; San Juan, Puerto Rico; and Sydney, Australia). These conferences are a primary means by which faculty working on international business issues can meet with like-minded scholars, hear the latest research going on in the larger domain of study, and become socialized within this community. Groups such as the Global ITM Association or GITMA (in Anchorage, Alaska, in 2005) hold conferences that focus on IT issues. Although joining this community has its own distinct advantages, the larger perspective of the IAB could lead to other business disciplines recognizing the value of international IT studies.

Theoretical Advancements

Working in cultures far from one's home is costly. Theoretical advancements can occur in the absence of sufficient funding to support empirical and interpretative work abroad, but testing these theories requires an infrastructure that includes money for travel, outsourced data collection, and translation.

This work cannot conceivably be carried out without new sources of funding from governmental agencies and university research funds. Funding agencies such as the National Science Foundation (NSF) in the United States has shown a greater interest in international work in recent years and we hope this trend continues. The European Union has also allowed certain proportions of its research funding to flow to projects outside of Europe. Once again, it would be highly beneficial if even higher percentages of funds were allocated to projects in the developing world and newly industrialized countries. It is crucial, for example, that more work be done on the tremendous transformations that are taking place in the Chinese economy and its deployment of IT.

Irrespective of new sources of funds to support data-intensive science, what can be done, especially in IT studies? The most crucial theoretical need, in our opinion, is a deeper understanding of culture and what it means. To what extent is culture related to national boundaries, as opposed to ethnicity, race, or gender? How do these cultural identities interact with and relate to organizational and professional cultures? Finally, when looking within such broad cultural categories as ethnicity, what impact do subcultures have? If, for instance, one is a Kurd living in Iraq and also an urbanite and a member of a prominent family, it is probable that this person's subcultures of city-dweller and family heritage are as powerful and influential on behaviors as ethnic and national identity. These are not entirely separable: Family heritage may itself have a strong relationship with one's Kurdish ethnicity.

The need to define culture more precisely and then, subsequently, to measure it is discussed in Straub et al. (2002). A theory offered by these scholars to frame the question of culture is social identity theory (SIT). This theory suggests that individuals are influenced by and establish their own identity according to the groups with which they most identify. In the case of culture, they propose a virtual onion model wherein layers in an onion are similar to an individual's reactions in given situations. Each layer represents a different cultural influence, so that in one circumstance, one's professional culture (as a professor, a surgeon, a laborer, a clerk) is at the core, whereas in another circumstance, something else, such as a religious culture, takes precedence.

This paper is suggestive but does not go very far in developing the theoretical base and the operationalizations that are required for scientific work. Is this even the best theory base? Defining culture is central to generating new insights into how important outcomes are affected by culture. We need to move beyond the hand-waving that has been the de facto standard for work in this arena and wrestle with the hard theoretical conundrum that devolves from work on culture-sans-definition-of-culture.

Cultural anthropology would seem to be a reasonable discipline from which to draw in a quest to define culture. Theoretical development in anthropology takes a form different from other social sciences—the business disciplines in particular—but thoroughly studying relevant portions of this literature should yield working definitions that can then be taken to the next intellectual level. Social psychological theory bases, such as SIT, would seem to be reasonable places to search for viable propositions and theoretical approaches.

It would be helpful if more high-profile IT scholars and junior faculty devoted their talents to exploring international issues. There is no question that the area represents only a niche in overall IT studies, but the millennium drive to globalization means that scholars can no longer focus exclusively only on domestic issues. The need for more involvement by bright and energetic IS scholars is obvious. We most emphatically encourage you to join in this effort.

APPENDIX 9.1

INSTRUMENT TO ASSESS ORGANIZATIONAL USAGE OF THE INTERNET IN THE ARAB WORLD

X INSTITUTE   Y UNIVERSITY
Cairo, Egypt   City, State USA

Research Questionnaire on
Use of the Internet by Organizations in the Arab World

This is a research questionnaire dealing with how people feel about the Internet. Even if you yourself do not use the Internet, we are interested in your responses!

We are studying the use of Internet in Arab businesses and organizations. Please fill out the questionnaire! This is for non-commercial purposes only, and all responses are strictly confidential.

Thank you.

The Research Team

Dr. A   Dr. B
A Department   B Role
A University   B Institute
City, State USA   Cairo, Egypt
A@A.edu   B@b.com.eg

Dr. C   Dr. D
C Dept.   D Dept.
D University   D University
City, State USA   City, State USA
C@c.edu   D@d.edu

Section I. Personal Information

1. How many years of work experience do you have? _____ years

2. Which best describes your current position? *(Please check one)*
_____ Top management   _____ Administrative staff
_____ Middle management   _____ Professional staff
_____ Supervisory management   _____ Other (please specify): _____

3. Your country of birth: _____   4. Current nationality: _____

How many years have you lived in each of the following Arab countries?

	No. of Yrs		*No. of Yrs*		*No. of Yrs*
Algeria	_____	Lebanon	_____	Saudi Arabia	_____
Bahrain	_____	Libya	_____	Sudan	_____
Egypt	_____	Mauritania	_____	Syria	_____
Iraq	_____	Morocco	_____	Tunisia	_____
Jordan	_____	Oman	_____	U.A. Emirates	_____
Kuwait	_____	Qatar	_____	West Bank	_____
Yemen	_____				

6. How many years, in total, have you lived in *non-Arab industrialized countries?* _____ years

7. Age: _____   8. Sex: Male _____ or Female _____

(continued)

APPENDIX 9.1 (*continued*)

9. Education: High school _____ Bachelor's degree _____
                Master's degree _____   Doctorate _____

	A great deal of travel	A fair amount of travel	A small amount of travel	Have not traveled at all
10a. How much do you travel in the *non-Arab industrialized world* for business purposes?	_____	_____	_____	_____
10b. How much do you travel in the *non-Arab industrialized world* for pleasure?	_____	_____	_____	_____

11. On a workday, how much work-related time do you spend on the Internet? _____ Hours _____ Minutes

	A great deal of time	A fair amount of time	A small amount of time	No time at all
12. How much time do…				
12a. people in your organization spend working on the Internet?	_____	_____	_____	_____
12b. you spend on the Internet at work?	_____	_____	_____	_____

13. Please indicate your agreement or disagreement with the following statements about the Internet by checking off the appropriate response:

	Strongly Agree	Agree	Neutral or Not Sure	Disagree	Strongly Disagree
13a. Most people in my organization feel threatened by how the Internet could affect our family and community life.	_____	_____	_____	_____	_____
13b. Most people in my organization believe the Internet relates to how much human interaction takes place.	_____	_____	_____	_____	_____
13c. I use the Internet to order goods and services for business purposes.	_____	_____	_____	_____	_____
13d. The Internet is attractive to most employees of organizations because computers are well accepted in Arab society.	_____	_____	_____	_____	_____
13e. Most people in my organization feel that the amount of face-to-face contact at work and the use of the Internet are related.	_____	_____	_____	_____	_____
13f. I use the Internet very frequently for business information gathering.	_____	_____	_____	_____	_____

14. Please indicate your own experiences and viewpoints by checking the appropriate response.

	Strongly Agree	Agree	Neutral or Not Sure	Disagree	Strongly Disagree
14a. I have learned a great deal about the Internet from experts (Arab or non-Arab) trained in technologically advanced countries.	_____	_____	_____	_____	_____

(*continued*)

APPENDIX 9.1 (*continued*)

14b. Most people in my organization feel   _____   _____   _____   _____   _____
strongly that the Internet will strengthen
Arab family and community ties.
14c. I have learned a great deal about   _____   _____   _____   _____   _____
the Internet by visiting other businesses
in the non-Arab industrialized world.
14d. A company or organization's rules   _____   _____   _____   _____   _____
should not be broken—even when
the employee thinks it is in the
organization's best interests.
14e. The employees in my organization   _____   _____   _____   _____   _____
have learned a great deal about the
Internet from experts (Arab or non-Arab)
trained in technologically advanced
countries.
14f. I plan to continue working for my   _____   _____   _____   _____   _____
organization until I retire.
14g. Given how Arabs feel about   _____   _____   _____   _____   _____
computers, I think most workers
in organizations are going to find
it difficult to accept the Internet.
14h. I feel nervous and tense at   _____   _____   _____   _____   _____
work very often.

15. What percentage of employees in your organization have received training from experts (Arab or non-Arab) trained in technologically advanced countries? _____%

16. What percentage of employees in your organization have access to the Internet? _____%

17. What percentage of employees in your organization use the Internet regularly? _____%

Section II. Feelings About Media

Please indicate your feelings towards the following communication media by marking the appropriate number in each box. *Example:*

1	2	3	4	5	6	7
Costly						Not costly
E-mail	Face-to-face	Telephone		WWW		Fax
6	2	4		1		3

1. Personal/Impersonal

1	2	3	4	5	6	7
Personal						Impersonal
E-mail	Face-to-face	Telephone		WWW		Fax
___	___	___		___		___

2. Unsociable/Sociable

1	2	3	4	5	6	7
Unsociable						Sociable
E-mail	Face-to-face	Telephone		WWW		Fax
___	___	___		___		___

(*continued*)

APPENDIX 9.1 (*continued*)

3. Cold/Warm

1	2	3	4	5	6	7

Cold   Warm

    E-mail   Face-to-face   Telephone   WWW   Fax
    ———   ———   ———   ———   ———

4. Sensitive/Insensitive

1	2	3	4	5	6	7

Sensitive   Insensitive

    E-mail   Face-to-face   Telephone   WWW   Fax
    ———   ———   ———   ———   ———

Section III. Questions About Your Ideal Job

Please think of an ideal job—disregarding your present job. In choosing an ideal job, how important would it be to you to (please circle one answer number in each line across):

	Of Utmost Importance	Very Important	Of Moderate Importance	Of Little Importance	Of Very Little or No Importance
1. Have sufficient time left for your personal or family life?	————	————	————	————	————
2. Have challenging tasks to do, from which you can get a personal sense of accomplishment?	————	————	————	————	————
3. Have good physical working conditions (good ventilation and lighting, adequate workspace, etc.)?	————	————	————	————	————
4. Have considerable freedom to adopt your own approach to the job?	————	————	————	————	————
5. Have training opportunities (to improve your skills or to learn new skills)?	————	————	————	————	————
6. Fully use your skills and abilities on the job?	————	————	————	————	————

Section IV. Free Format Question

On the back of the questionnaire, please answer the following question. Please write as much as you wish.

In your opinion, what factors *encourage* or *discourage* the use of the Internet in organizations in the Arab world?

Thank you very much for your time and participation. Please return to the registration desk.

The Research Team

Source: Adapted from Loch et al. (2003).

APPENDIX 9.2

SELECTED INSTRUMENTATION ITEMS

1. Personal Information (Selection of Demographic Measures)

a. Type of company in terms of "internationalization" (select one)

Egyptian only doing business with Egyptian Companies only ❑
Egyptian only doing business with Arab Companies only ❑
Egyptian only doing business with non-Arab Companies ❑

Egyptian-**transnational** ❑
Arab-**transnational** ❑
Non-Arab **transnational** ❑

b. Have you lived all your life in Egypt?
Yes ❑
No ❑

c. If no, please list the other country or countries in which you have lived

Country	Number of Years Lived	Reason (e.g., work, study, family)
_____	_____	_____
_____	_____	_____

d. Education:

Degree Obtained	Country
_____	_____
_____	_____

Please indicate your level of agreement with the following statement

	Strongly 1	Agree 2	Neutral 3	Strongly 4	Disagree 5
e. I have had extensive exposure to advanced information technologies developed outside the Arab world.	___	___	___	___	___

To *what extent* do you use the following information technologies or ICT applications? (reduced list)

	Not at all	To a small extent	To some extent	To a large extent	To a great extent
f. PC (personal computer—IBM/Windows or Apple)	1	2	3	4	5
g. PDA (handheld devices)	1	2	3	4	5
h. E-mail	1	2	3	4	5

2. Electronic Government (Selection of Questions on ICT Policies)

"There is a government effort [policy] to make government forms, such as tax and driver's license forms, available to citizens on the Internet."

	Not at all	To a small extent	To some extent	To a large extent	To a great extent	No answer given
a. "Using the scale, to what extent are you aware of this effort to make government forms available to citizens via the Web?"	1	2	3	4	5	NA

(*continued*)

APPENDIX 9.2 (*continued*)

b.. "Using the same scale, how much do you think that this effort makes the government more responsive to citizens?"	1	2	3	4	5	NA

c. "Why do you think that?"

_____

_____

_____

Field Notes:

"There is another government effort to computerize the sharing of information between government agencies."

	Not at all	To a small extent	To some extent	To a large extent	To a great extent	No answer given
d. "To what extent are you aware of this effort to computerize the sharing of information between government agencies?"	1	2	3	4	5	NA
e. "How much do you think that this effort increases government efficiency?"	1	2	3	4	5	NA
f. "Why do you think that?"						

_____

_____

_____

Field Notes:

Sample Scenario: Manufacturing Company

Mr. Khaled, the head of information processing in an Egyptian manufacturing company, has decided that the time has come for the firm to take advantage of e-mail. He expects the system to facilitate communication with overseas suppliers and customers.

The firm is a medium-sized firm with 80–100 employees, several departments, and has two locations. No personnel reduction is anticipated due to the implementation of the system. Their information systems capability is about average for a firm of this size and the management is already familiar with the use of computers. The software and hardware for setting up the system have been provided for free by the vendor to induce other sales in Egypt.

To implement the system, each employee will need a workstation or a portable device connected to the Internet. Unless a large percentage of the staff uses the system, the implementation will not succeed. The system has the capacity to work well both in English and in Arabic. The following sequence of messages shows how the system might affect how people communicate.

(*continued*)

APPENDIX 9.2 (*continued*)

E-mail system ....

TO: Sherif El Sawy, Manager, Sales – Cairo Office
FROM: Ahmed Koban, Manager, Production – Alexandria Office
RE: Quarterly presentation
DATE: 1 October 2001, 13:00

Hello Sherif,
Let's set our monthly meeting for October 3. We can review our standard
reports and prepare the quarterly presentation for the senior management team.
Ahmed Koban

E-mail system ....

TO: Ahmed Koban, Manager, Production – Alexandria Office
FROM: Sherif El Sawy, Manager, Sales – Cairo Office
RE: Quarterly presentation
DATE: 1 October 2001, 15:35

Hello Ahmed,
Thanks for your e-mail. I think we can forego the monthly meeting. I will send
you a draft document for the presentation by end of the week. Make your
additions and changes and send it back to me. Will that work for you?
Sherif

E-mail system ....

TO: Sherif El Sawy, Manager, Sales – Cairo Office
FROM: Ahmed Koban, Manager, Production – Alexandria Office
RE: Quarterly presentation
DATE: 2 October 2001, 11:00

Hello Sherif,
I'm not sure I agree. I think it would be better for us to meet in person.
Ahmed.

---

3. IT System Outcomes

a. "Do you think this system will ultimately succeed or fail in this company?"
Succeed   ❏
Fail   ❏

b. "Now, using the scale, how sure are you of your previous answer?"

0%	10%	20%	30%	40%	50%	60%	70%	80%	90%	100%

Pure guess   Absolutely sure

c. "Why do you believe the system will ultimately [succeed/fail]?"

_____

_____

_____

(*continued*)

APPENDIX 9.2 (*continued*)

4. Factors (Gauge the Effect of Cultural Beliefs)

a. For each factor, first check which condition leads to success. Then, rank them in order of importance from 1 to 7, where 1 is the most important.

			First For each factor, <u>choose</u> the condition that leads to <u>success</u>	**Second** <u>Rank</u> as 1 to 7 ("1" is MOST important)
No.	**Factor**	**The condition is that . . .**	**Choose one**	**Rank**
1	Top Management Support	There is top management support. There is not top management support.	❏ ❏	
2	Training	There is sufficient training for employees. There is not sufficient training for employees.	❏ ❏	
3	Accessibility	The system is accessible from outside the workplace. The system is not accessible from outside the workplace.	❏ ❏	
4	Reliability	The system runs well. The system does not run well.	❏ ❏	
5	Personal Contact*	The system leads to less personal contact. The system does not lead to less personal contact.	❏ ❏	
6	Number of Meetings*	The system leads to a reduction in the number of meetings. The system does not lead to a reduction in the number of meetings.	❏ ❏	
7	Length of Meetings*	The system leads to shorter face-to-face interactions. The system does not lead to shorter face-to-face interactions.	❏ ❏	

*Culturally loaded factors.

Source: Based on Checchi et al. (2002).

APPENDIX 9.3

RELEVANT ICT POLICIES IDENTIFIED

Policy		Description
1	MCIT	In October of 1999, the Egyptian government created a separate Ministry of Communications and Information Technology. The purpose of this ministry is to encourage the growth of the telecommunications and IT industries in Egypt. The ministry is acting as an agent for change rather than as an enforcer of change.
2	Custom Duties	The Egyptian government reduced the tax on importation of computer hardware from 15 percent to 5 percent in 2000. This reduced the cost of a 2000LE PC to organizations, for example, by 200LE
3	Computer Literacy	The Egyptian government is working with the private sector to greatly increase public awareness of computers, IT, and the Internet. Training programs under way at the present time have the goal of graduating 100,000 persons per year with heightened computer literacy. A more computer-literate workforce is a goal of the program.
4	Professional IT Training	The Egyptian government is working with the private sector to significantly increase the number of skilled IT professionals, analysts, and programmers in Egypt. Companies involved are ICL and IBM. Presently, 5,000 university graduates per year are being targeted for training in this "professional development program." One goal is to make Egypt the software leader in the region by the year 2010.
5	E-Commerce	The Egyptian government is encouraging e-commerce initiatives within the government itself, In part to stimulate the movement of the entire private sector to e-commerce. The United States Agency for International Development (USAID) has been supporting this initiative with large-scale funding.
6	National Center for the Documentation of Egypt's Cultural and Natural Heritage	The Egyptian government is establishing a National Center for the Documentation of Egypt's Cultural and Natural Heritage. With such accurate databases about many facets of Egyptian heritage, this project will encourage tourism and preserve knowledge about the national archeological treasures.
7	Privatization	The Egyptian government is privatizing the telecommunications industry in Egypt. Begun five years ago, this government policy initiative will lead to government minority ownership of the industry within another five years. The formation of MobiNile, ClickGSM, and EgyNet are all part of this privatization initiative. Made up of private and public sector members, the Telecomm Regulatory Authority (TRA) is a body being formed as part of the transition.
8	Outsourcing	The Egyptian government is encouraging the development of an advanced Egyptian industry for communication and information technology by outsourcing government systems, networks, and applications to the private sector to a much larger extent.
9	Smart Villages	The Egyptian government is granting tax-free status to IT and high-tech firms that locate their operations in incubator cities or villages, known as "Smart Villages." One of these villages will be located near the pyramids. High-speed Internet connections and other high-tech capabilities will be built by the private sector into these villages.
10	Certified Computer Network Engineers	The Egyptian government is working with the private sector to educate and make employable a large number of certified computer network engineers each year. Companies involved are Cisco, Lucent, and Microsoft.
11	Copyright	The Egyptian government is putting in place legislation to support e-commerce and a software industry within Egypt. Copyright laws as well as digital signature and digital certificate laws are part of this initiative.
12	Technology Clubs	The Egyptian government is working with the private sector to increase the knowledge and awareness of young people about computer systems and the Internet. Along with the Egyptian-sponsored "Future Generations Foundation," they have created technology clubs (formerly known as "21st-century kids' clubs") for local communities in order to offer computers and Internet access to young people. Training sessions on computer literacy and on certain computer applications such as spreadsheets and word processing are also offered. Mrs. Suzanna Mubarak is a public spokesperson for these clubs.

Source: Based on Checchi et al. (2002).

REFERENCES

Ajzen, I., and Fishbein, M. *Understanding Attitudes and Predicting Social Behavior.* Englewood Cliffs, NJ: Prentice-Hall, 1980.

Carlson, P.; Kahn, B.; and Rowe, F. Organizational impacts of new communication technology: a comparison of cellular phone adoption in France and United States. *Journal of Global Information Management,* 7, 3 (1999), 19–30.

Checchi, R.M.; Hsieh, J.J.P.-A.; and Straub, D.W. Public IT policies in less developed countries: a critical assessment of the literature and a reference framework for future work. *Journal of Global Information Technology Management,* 6, 4 (2003), 45–64.

Checchi, R.M.; Sevcik, G.R.; Loch, K.D.; and Straub, D.W. An instrumentation process for measuring ICT policies and culture. *Proceedings of the Information and Communications Technologies and Development Conference,* Kathmandu, Nepal, 2002.

D'Iribarne, P. The usefulness of an ethnographic approach to the international comparison of organizations. *International Studies of Management and Organizations,* 26, 4 (1997), 30–47.

Damsgaard, J., and Truex, D.P. Binary trading relations and the limits of EDI standards: the procrustean bed of standards. *European Journal of Information Systems,* 9, 3 (2000), 1–16.

Davis, F. Perceived usefulness, perceived ease of use and user acceptance of information technology. *MIS Quarterly,* 13, 3 (1989), 319–340.

Garfield, M.J., and Watson, R.T. Differences in national information infrastructures: the reflection of national cultures. *Journal of Strategic Information Systems,* 6 (1998), 313–337.

Gefen, D., and Straub, D.W. Gender differences in the perception and use of e-mail: an extension to the technology acceptance model. *MIS Quarterly,* 21, 4 (1997), 389–400.

Gibbs, J.; Kraemer, K.L.; and Dedrick, J. Environment and policy factors shaping global e-commerce diffusion: a cross-country comparison. *The Information Society,* 19, 5 (2003), 5–18.

Hill, C.; Loch, K.; Straub, D.W.; and El-Sheshai, K. A qualitative assessment of Arab culture and information technology transfer. *Journal of Global Information Management,* 6, 3 (1998), 29–38.

Hill, C.E.; Straub, D.W.; Loch, K.D.; Cotterman, W.; and El-Sheshai, K. The impact of Arab culture on the diffusion of information technology: a culture-centered model. *Proceedings of the Impact of Informatics on Society: Key Issues for Developing Countries Conference.* Havana, Cuba: IFIP 9.4, 1994.

Hofstede, G. *Culture's Consequences: International Differences in Work Related Values.* London: Sage Publications, 1980.

Hofstede, G. Do American theories apply abroad? A reply to Goodstein and Hunt. *Organizational Dynamics,* 10, 1 (1981), 63–68.

Hofstede, G. The cultural relativity of organizational practices and theories. *Journal of International Business Studies,* 14, 2 (1983), 75–89.

Hofstede, G. The interaction between national and organizational value systems. *Journal of Management Studies,* 22, 4 (1985), 347–357.

Hofstede, G.J. Adoption of communication technologies and national culture. *Systèmes d'Information et Management,* 6, 3 (2001), 55–74.

Huang, L.; Lu, M-T.; and Wong, B.K. The impact of power distance on email acceptance: evidence from the PRC. *Journal of Computer Information Systems,* 44, 1 (2003), 93–101.

Kvasny, L. A conceptual framework for examining digital inequality. *Proceedings of the Americas Conference on Information Systems.* Dallas, TX, 2002, pp. 1798–1805.

Kvasny, L. Problematizing the digital divide: cultural and social reproduction in a community technology initiative. Dissertation, Department of Computer Information Systems, Robinson College of Business, Georgia State University, Atlanta, 2002.

Kvasny, L., and Truex, D. Information technology and the cultural reproduction of social order: a research program. In R. Baskerville, J. Stage, and J. DeGross (eds.), *Organizational and Social Perspectives on Information Technology.* New York: Kluwer Academic Publishers, 2000, pp. 277–294.

Kvasny, L., and Truex, D. Defining away the digital divide: a content analysis of institutional influences on popular representations of technology. In B. Fitzgerald, N. Russo, and J. DeGross (eds.), *Realigning Research and Practice in IS Development: The Social and Organisational Perspective.* New York: Kluwer Academic Publishers, 2001, pp. 399–414.

Loch, K.; Sevcik, G.; and Straub. D. *IT Transfer to Egypt: A Process Model for Developing Countries,* National Science Foundation Grant Proposal, Funded Grant #DST-0082473, August 2000–August 2003.

Loch, K.; Straub, D.; and Kamel, S. Diffusing the Internet in the Arab world: the role of social norms and technological culturation. *IEEE Transactions on Engineering Management,* 50, 1 (2003), 45–63.

Rose, G., and Straub, D. Predicting general IT use: applying TAM to the Arabic world. *Journal of Global Information Management,* 6, 3 (1998), 39–46.

Rowe, F., and Struck, D. Cultural values, media richness and telecommunication use in an organization. *Accounting Management and Information Technology,* 9, 3 (1999), 161–192.

Straub, D.; Keil, M.; and Brenner, W. Testing the technology acceptance model across cultures: a three country study. *Information & Management,* 31, 1 (1997), 1–11.

Straub, D.W. The effect of culture on it diffusion—e-mail and fax in Japan and the United States. *Information Systems Research,* 5, 1 (1994), 23–47.

Straub, D.W.; Loch, K.; and Hill, C. Transfer of information technology to the Arab world: a test of cultural influence modeling. *Journal of Global Information Management,* 9, 4 (2001), 6–28.

Straub, D.W.; Loch, K.; Evaristo, R.; Karahanna, E.; and Srite, M. Toward a theory-based measurement of culture. *Journal of Global Information Management,* 10, 1 (2002), 13–23.

PART IV

LEARNING AND TRAINING

CHAPTER 10

TECHNOLOGY-BASED TRAINING

Toward a Learner-Centric Research Agenda

SHARATH SASIDHARAN AND RADHIKA SANTHANAM

Abstract: *Technology-based training has the potential to become one of the key tools for knowledge dissemination. Yet, the effectiveness of technology-based training is not fully established. Hence, it will be fruitful to conduct detailed research to identify factors that could enhance the outcomes of technology-based training. Towards this end, we review existing research on this topic. Based on this, we suggest that there be a shift in research focus to dwell more on the learner rather than the technology used in training. We provide suggestions for future research.*

Keywords: *Technology-Based Training, E-Learning, Training Effectiveness*

INTRODUCTION

The use of technology-based training (TBT) methods has become common in many organizations. The potential of such training to become a cost-effective method to transfer knowledge to large numbers of people is obvious. Yet, reports of mixed results on the effectiveness of TBT points to a need to conduct detailed investigations. In this paper, we describe the growth of TBT, identify factors that could influence training outcomes, and provide a framework and some ideas to stimulate future research on TBT.

Scope and Growth of Technology-Based Training

Technology-based training (TBT) refers to a medium that delivers educational content. The American Society for Training and Development (ASTD) describes TBT as "the delivery of content via Internet, LAN or WAN (intranet or extranet), satellite broadcast, audio or videotape, interactive TV or CD-ROM" (Kaplan-Leiserson, 2004). It includes delivery to individual learners via computer-based and Web-based methods, as well as to groups of learners. In universities, the latter is typically referred as distance learning courses. Some universities offer blended learning courses whereby learners, in addition to receiving distance-learning content, also spend some time having face-to-face interaction with instructors and fellow students.

Although TBT delivered via CD-ROM has been around for almost two decades, the growth in telecommunications infrastructure, advances in Web-design technologies, and high-quality streaming media have made TBT appealing to institutions that want to offer real-time, low-cost training content. One of the recent trends is toward reusable digital resources called learning objects (Wiley, 2001). The US corporate e-learning market is projected to have a sustained double-digit expansion reaching nearly $10.6 billion in 2007 (Brennan, 2003). Educational institutions have promoted TBT as a viable learning tool, with 81 percent of all institutions of higher education offering at least one fully online or blended course, and 34 percent offering complete online degree programs, with the numbers being much higher for public and state universities (Allen and Seaman, 2003).

Current Status and the Need to Conduct Research

Despite the obvious advantages and benefits offered by TBT, reports from business organizations state that even dedicated workers sometimes find it difficult to learn from TBT modules, and appear to drop out (Harris, 2002; Rossett and Shafer, 2003). The dropout rate from distance-learning courses in educational institutions is estimated to range from 20 to 50 percent (Carr, 2000). Learners seem to lose the motivation to study in these learning environments (Mayer et al., 2001). Business organizations report that investments in TBT have not provided the anticipated returns, while several major vendors of e-learning packages have withdrawn from the market (Barron, 2001; Harris, 2002). Classroom or instructor-based training still remains the dominant method for transferring knowledge, with only 15 to 25 percent of training delivered via technology-based methods (Sugrue, 2003). This situation is unfortunate, because TBT has immense potential to transfer knowledge to large numbers of people, and become an important educational tool in business and educational institutions (Schank, 2001; Shneiderman et al., 1995; Shneiderman, 1998). Therefore, systematic research must be conducted to identify the cause of these problems, and provide directions to improve the effectiveness and delivery of TBT. Formal research investigating the effectiveness of TBT is scanty, and more comprehensive studies that examine TBT related issues in greater breadth and depth are needed (Alavi and Leidner, 2001).

Patterns of Adoption of TBT

We can explain the current situation facing TBT by using Moore's (1991) concept of a "chasm" within the technology adoption life cycle. Customers who adopt an innovation can be categorized as belonging to one of the following: innovators, early adopters, early majority pragmatists, late majority conservatives, or laggards (Rogers, 1995). Initial adopters of technology—innovators— adopt technology for the sake of technology, rather than for any advantages that technology may offer. They are followed by the early adopters who, in addition to being technically savvy, can appreciate the benefits and future potential of the innovation. These two types of customers constitute the primary drivers of demand in the introductory stages of an innovation. They form a relatively small customer base. However, they are followed by a larger customer base comprising early majority pragmatists and late majority conservatives. These customers are attracted to tried and tested technologies. Finally, a few laggards adopt the technology. Moore (1991) argues that a perceptible chasm exists between the needs of the innovators/early adopters and the early majority pragmatists/late majority conservatives. The smaller former group of customers focus primarily on the novelty of technology; the latter larger group of customers is more driven by the usefulness and conveniences the technology provides (Norman, 1998).

Applying this technology adoption life cycle to TBT (Stacey, 2001), we can say that initial use of CD-ROMs and multimedia to deliver training appealed primarily to innovators. Learners and institutions adopted TBT based on its novelty, and probably paid less attention to its outcomes and effectiveness. With the advent of the Internet as a medium for delivering training, early adopters started using TBT, and they, too, did not pay much attention to training outcomes. Now that early majority pragmatists and late majority conservatives have started to use TBT, questions about its usefulness, effectiveness, and value are surfacing. These two groups potentially represent a large customer base, if they can effectively cross the chasm in the technology adoption life cycle. For them to cross the chasm, ways to increase the usefulness of TBT have to be discovered. This will require a shift in focus: Training providers need to emphasize and understand the learners, their learning styles, their learning needs, and the processes by which they learn from TBT. Hence, research has to more closely examine learners' interactions with TBT environments, and identify ways to improve training outcomes.

FACTORS THAT COULD INFLUENCE TBT OUTCOMES

To identify factors that may influence TBT outcomes, we first examined the large amount of research conducted in traditional training environments (e.g., Bostrom et al., 1990; Santhanam and Sein, 1994; Venkatesh, 1999). We then examined research conducted in TBT environments (e.g., Alavi et al., 1997; Piccoli et al., 2001; Webster and Hackley, 1997). We must emphasize that our search uncovered fewer than a dozen research studies on TBT in mainstream information systems journals. Therefore, in the interests of identifying and including factors that could influence TBT outcomes, we also included journals, such as the *Journal of Asynchronous Learning Networks*, that focus primarily on providing information to practitioners. Based on this review, we summarized and synthesized factors that could potentially influence the outcomes of TBT. We present the results pictorially in Figure 10.1. We describe training outcomes as consisting of cognitive, skill-based, and affective dimensions (Marcolin et al., 2000). Note that Marcolin et al. (2000) gives the term "affective outcome" a much broader scope than it generally has in the information systems literature; they include motivational and other components that denote any change in individual learners' values. Then, based on Webster and Hackley (1997), we categorize factors that can affect these TBT outcomes into one of the following types: learner, instructor, course, and technology. TBT outcomes could be affected by any of these factors, or by an interaction among them, and is mediated by the dominant learning model adopted in designing the TBT package. We now explain these characteristics and their influence.

Learner Characteristics

As shown in Figure 10.1, many learner characteristics play an important role in influencing TBT outcomes. The motivation of an individual in undergoing a TBT program will play a big role in learning outcomes (Schrum and Hong, 2002; Wang and Newlin, 2002). The extent of motivation might depend on whether the TBT course is being taken as a mandatory skills upgrade, as a promotion requirement, as a necessity to change careers, or out of a simple desire to gain knowledge. Another characteristic that could influence learning effects is an individual's self-regulation ability (Pintrich and DeGroot, 1990; Zimmerman and Martinez-Pons, 1986; Zimmerman 1989, 1990). Self-regulation refers to the capability of learners to take charge of their own learning. It includes skills such as the ability to plan and manage time, to attend and concentrate on instruction, and to set performance goals. It also includes the ability to effectively organize, rehearse, and encode information (Vockell, 2004). These skills have increased relevance in the context of TBT due to the absence of direct face-to-face interaction with an instructor who can organize, set goals for the learner, and monitor his or her performance.

250

Figure 10.1   A Consolidation of Research Findings on TBT

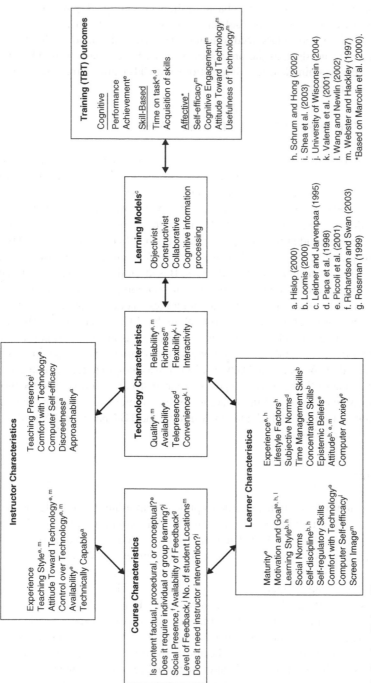

Explanation of Selected Terms

Teaching Presence—The design, facilitation, and direction of cognitive and social processes in the online context.
Discreet—Discreet instructors do not dominate an online session; they know when to comment publicly and when to switch to private communication.
Approachability—Approachable instructors encourage high levels of interactivity.
Telepresence—Shared presence sensation related to the perception of presence of other learners, image quality of the teacher and learner and the overview of the classroom.
Screen Image—Level of comfort when viewing one's image on the screen.
Social Presence—Extent to which individuals (instructor, other students) are interpreted as being "real" in technology-mediated communication.

Another set of learner characteristics emerge from research on technology acceptance, wherein several individual characteristics have been identified as influencing users' acceptance and use of technology. These same factors could also potentially influence the use and outcomes from a TBT program, because TBT involves the use of technology for a learning task. This includes computer self-efficacy, which in this context is the learner's belief regarding his or her ability to perform a learning-related task with a computer (Chau, 2001; Hu et al., 2003; Igbaria and Iivari, 1995; Thong et al., 2002; Venkatesh, 2000), and subjective norms, which is the extent to which learners perceive people important to them think they should be learning (Karahanna and Limayem, 2000; Venkatesh and Davis, 2000; Venkatesh and Morris, 2000). Factors such as computer anxiety (Igbaria, 1993; Igbaria and Iivari, 1995; Venkatesh, 2000), attitude towards computers (Chau, 2001), and personal traits such as playfulness (Moon and Kim, 2001; Venkatesh, 2000) could also influence TBT outcomes. Learners' sense of enjoyment (Heijden, 2003; Venkatesh, 2000) when they are interacting with the TBT, and their level of cognitive absorption in the learning task (Agarwal and Karahanna, 2000), could influence TBT outcomes. Finally, learners' backgrounds, that is, their level of education (Agarwal and Prasad, 1999), prior experiences with technology (Agarwal and Prasad, 1999; Piccoli et al., 2001), and other demographics could play a role in TBT outcomes.

Instructor Characteristics

Instructor characteristics represent an ignored but key factor in determining the effectiveness of TBT. Though TBT implies that human instructors may not be very involved, their participation in the TBT process is essential, as they perform the roles of designer and facilitator, planning and preparing course material and facilitating discourse, thereby conveying a sense of "teaching presence" (Anderson et al., 2001). As in the case of the learner, an individual instructor's characteristics—such as his or her computer self-efficacy and anxiety, level of comfort with technology, and prior experiences—could impact the design of the course and consequently impact training outcomes. Though the interaction between the instructor and the learner is an important issue, very little formal research has been conducted in this area. Some best practices that have been suggested include the need to increase the instructor's visibility (so that the instructor's presence is felt frequently in the online environment), his or her explicitness (so that he or she provides timely, detailed directions), his or her proactivity (so that he or she makes extra efforts to reach out to learners in ways beyond what would be typical in a traditional environment), and his or her approachability (so that learners are encouraged to actively interact with the instructor) (Hislop, 2000; Piccoli et al., 2001).

Technology Characteristics

TBT encompasses a wide range of technologies ranging from simple stand-alone computers to more complex virtual reality systems and synchronous/asynchronous communication classrooms (Leidner and Jarvenpaa, 1995). Though a given technology might have specific requirements and ways to use it, certain features can be generalized across technologies. These include the quality and reliability of technology (Piccoli et al., 2001; Webster and Hackley, 1997), extent of continuous availability of the system (Piccoli et al., 2001), and the flexibility and convenience of TBT (Valenta et al., 2001; Wang and Newlin, 2002). Telepresence is described as a sensation of shared presence brought about by image reproduction quality and visual contact among group members. This has been recognized as an important factor, particularly in collaborative environments (Papa et al., 1998).

Course Characteristics

A key factor influencing course design and consequently TBT outcomes is obviously the nature of knowledge that has to be transferred to the learner. A TBT course on calculus could be presented as factual statements of computations, derivations, and equations. But a course on relational databases will perhaps be more effective if presented in a conceptual mode, followed by hands-on exercises that show how the concepts are implemented in a database software. Essentially, as in a regular training/teaching environment, a good match between the course content and the representations used to convey the content (i.e., course design) will enhance learning outcomes. If course content could benefit from group learning exercises, the course design and technology features must be flexible enough to accommodate interaction and communication among learners.

As suggested by Leidner and Jarvenpaa (1995), we include learning models as a factor in Figure 10.1. When technology is used to help transfer knowledge, implicit in the course design is a dominant learning model that could be an objectivist, constructivist, cooperative, or cognitive information processing model. In objectivist learning models, training is seen as the transfer of knowledge from the instructor to the learner, the former controlling the pace and content of the course, and the latter expected to repeat and memorize the content. By contrast, in the constructivist learning model, the learner is viewed as an active participant in the learning process. Learners are encouraged to experiment and discover new knowledge, control their learning pace, and apply the knowledge gained to real-world situations. A collaborative learning model assumes that learning is maximized when learners work in groups. It is believed that the process of interaction and dissemination of information among participants leads to the creation of new and shared understandings. The cognitive information processing model assumes that learning essentially involves the processing and transfer of new knowledge into long-term memory. Hence, the goal is to improve the learner's cognitive processing abilities to aid recall and retention of material and produce increased learning outcomes.

A learning model is important, and is typically woven into a TBT course design. For example, if a TBT program is designed so that groups of learners from different locations will collaborate, then a collaborative learning model is the underlying learning model. The assumption behind the course design is that learners learn best by collaborating with peers. On the other hand, if a TBT system provides many methods for the learner to simulate scenarios, experiment, and control what he or she learns, the design is built on a constructivist learning model. The role of different factors, particularly the extent to which learner characteristics influence TBT outcomes, will depend on the underlying learning model. For example, a learner's self-regulation may play a greater role when constructivist learning models are integrated into the course design, while social norms may play a greater role when collaborative learning models are integrated into the course design.

In designing a TBT course, the course content will influence the nature of technology (technology characteristics) and the learning model that has to be adopted. For example, if the course content will require experimentation and knowledge discovery on the part of the learner, such as in a course that will train learners to design and develop a tool, the content could be presented using high resolution, multidimensional graphical images and simulations that are generated through sophisticated visualization technologies (e.g., 3-D virtual reality systems). The underlying model could be a constructivist learning model.

TOWARD AN AGENDA FOR RESEARCH

We now integrate the findings listed in Figure 10.1 with existing models to develop a broad framework for research on TBT. We use the model provided by Alavi and Leidner (2001), and develop

Figure 10.2 **A Framework for Research on TBT**

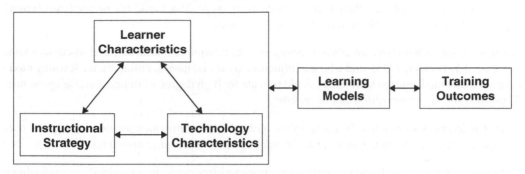

upon it based on: (1) the need to cross the "chasm" and focus on learner requirements and (2) the findings from our survey. Alavi and Leidner (2001) suggest that the mutual interaction among technology features, instructional strategies employed, and psychological learning processes influence learning outcomes. First, instead of focusing solely on learning outcomes, we use the term "training outcomes" to draw attention to several categories of outcomes, because they are all equally important in TBT (Kirkpatrick, 1998; Marcolin et al., 2000). Second, we find that in the limited research on TBT, learner characteristics appears to play a critical role in influencing TBT outcomes, and we therefore explicitly include it in our model. Because one of the primary advantages of TBT is that technology can provide a powerful way to personalize instruction, we propose that every effort should be made to pay attention to individual learner characteristics. Learning models assume a certain type of learning process on the part of the learner, and therefore it is omitted from our model. Note that the instructional strategy shown in our framework is essentially a combination of the course and technology characteristics that were identified in our survey. Our framework is shown in Figure 10.2.

The proposed framework, combined with the list of factors shown in Figure 10.1, provides different avenues to research and find ways to improve the outcomes of TBT. For example, as shown in Figure 10.1, consider the learner's level of self-regulation, which is identified as a key individual characteristic that influences academic performance (Pintrich and DeGroot, 1990; Zimmerman and Martinez-Pons, 1986; Zimmerman, 1989, 1990). As mentioned earlier, self-regulation refers to learners taking control of their own learning, so that they can function with minimal supervision. Self-efficacy is an individual's belief that he or she has the ability to perform a task. Hence, for learners who have high levels of self-regulatory skills or computer self-efficacy, TBT outcomes can be maximized, if constructivist learning models are adopted and the technology provides high levels of interactivity and flexibility. On the other hand, for learners with low levels of self-regulatory skills, or with high levels of computer anxiety, objectivist learning models can be adopted, the technology could provide low levels of flexibility, and the instructional strategy could focus on generating feedback and controlling the learner's learning path. Thus, we can test propositions as follows:

A. *The higher the level of self-regulation (or computer self-efficacy) of the learner, the higher will be the level of training outcomes from TBT programs.*

B. *For learners with high levels of self-regulation (or computer self-efficacy), increasing the levels of interactivity with technology will be associated with enhanced training outcomes.*

C. *For learners with low levels of self-regulation (or high levels of computer anxiety), increased control over their learning path (such as feedback and instructor intervention) will be associated with enhanced training outcomes.*

For those learners who have an active learning style that requires interacting and discussing with other learners (Felder, 1993), and who are influenced by social norms, collaborative learning models can be assumed, and the technology could provide for high degree of richness and telepresence. Thus, the following proposition can be tested:

D. *For learners with active learning styles, technology that provides for networking and collaboration (with other learners) will result in enhanced training outcomes.*

In this manner, the influence of individual characteristics could be examined, and guidelines on how to design appropriate course content can be developed. Current inquiries into effectiveness of TBT courses do not pay enough attention to whether individual learner characteristics and their interaction with technology play a role (Phipps and Merisotis, 1999). We think this needs to change. As TBT customers shift their focus from being captivated with the novelty of technology to evaluating usefulness and value, we believe that a corresponding shift in thinking must take place among researchers and practitioners. We believe that not only do individual characteristics influence TBT outcomes, and therefore they have to be examined to understand why TBT is successful in some groups and not so successful in others; we also believe that TBT provides an excellent opportunity to use the power of technology to fine-tune instruction to suit individual learners' needs. It is conceptually possible to envision the design of a TBT package that checks the learner's profile, identifies personal characteristics, and then offers an instruction sequence that is suited to these characteristics.

Our proposed research framework could be used in multiple ways to investigate research propositions. But in light of the increasing importance of learner characteristics, we suggest that research in this area be learner-centric. We suggest that the primary issue that needs to be examined is the relationship between learner characteristics and training outcomes (e.g., Proposition A) rather than a link between technology and training outcomes. After understanding this relationship, research could examine the interaction of different levels of technology characteristics with learner characteristics and/or instructional strategy (e.g., Propositions B, C, and D). We believe that this approach will ensure that research remains focused on the learner who is the eventual customer.

CONCLUDING REMARKS

TBT has the potential to become a very powerful educational tool in today's knowledge economy. Particularly with the large number of working professionals enrolling in university courses, and with shrinking budgets of universities, TBT might be one way to meet the demands of a growing student population. We found that systematic research has not been conducted in understanding the impact of TBT or on identifying ways to improve the outcomes. Therefore, we synthesized existing knowledge on factors that could influence training outcomes, and presented a framework that can help us conduct systematic investigations on ways to improve TBT effectiveness.

REFERENCES

Agarwal, R., and Prasad, J. Are individual differences germane to the acceptance of new information technologies? *Decision Sciences*, 30, 2 (1999), 361–391.

Agarwal, R., and Karahanna, E. Time flies when you are having fun: cognitive absorption and beliefs about information technology usage. *MIS Quarterly*, 24, 4 (2000), 665–694.

Alavi, M., Yoo, Y., and Vogel, D.R. Using information technology to add value to management education. *Academy of Management Journal*, 40, 6 (1997), 1310–1333.

Alavi, M., and Leidner, D.E. Research commentary: technology-mediated learning—a call for greater depth and breadth of research. *Information Systems Research*, 12, 1 (2001), 1–10.

Allen, I.E., and Seaman, J. Sizing the opportunity: the quality and extent of online education in the United States, 2002 and 2003. The Sloan Consortium, Needham, MA, 2003 (available at www.sloan-c.org/resources/sizing_opportunity.pdf, accessed on April 26, 2004).

Anderson, T., Rourke, L., Garrison, D.R., and Archer, W. Assessing teacher presence in a computer conferencing context. *Journal of Asynchronous Learning Networks*, 5, 2 (2001), 1–17 (available at www.sloan-c.org/publications/jaln/index.asp, accessed on August 5, 2004).

Barron, T. E-learning weathers a bear market. American Society for Training and Development, Alexandria, VA, 2001 (available at www.learningcircuits.org/2001/mar2001/barron.html, accessed on April 28, 2004).

Bostrom, R.P., Olfman, L., and Sein, M.K. The importance of learning style in end-user training. *MIS Quarterly*, 14, 1 (1990), 101–119.

Brennan, M. U.S. corporate and government eLearning forecast, 2002–2007. International Data Corporation, Framingham, MA, 2003 (available at www.idc.com/getdoc.jsp?containerId=fr2003_10_09_163314, accessed on April 18, 2004).

Carr, S. As distance education comes of age, the challenge is keeping the students. *Chronicle of Higher Education*, 46, 23 (2000), 39–41.

Chau, P.Y.K. Influence of computer attitude and self-efficacy on IT usage behavior. *Journal of End User Computing*, 13, 1 (2001), 26–33.

Felder, R. Reaching the second tier: learning and teaching styles in college science education. *Journal of College Science Teaching*, 22, 5 (1993), 286–290.

Harris, P. E-learning: a consolidation update. *Training and Development*, 56, 4 (2002), 27–33.

Heijden, H.v.d. Factors influencing the usage of websites: the case of a generic portal in the Netherlands. *Information & Management*, 40, 6 (2003), 541–549.

Hislop, G. Working professionals as part-time on-line learners. *Journal of Asynchronous Learning Networks*, 4, 2 (2000), 73–89 (available at www.sloan-c.org/publications/jaln/index.asp, accessed on August 5, 2004).

Hu, P.J.H., Clark, T.H.K., and Ma, W. Examining technology acceptance by school teachers: a longitudinal study. *Information & Management*, 41, 2 (2003), 227–241.

Igbaria, M. User acceptance of microcomputer technology: an empirical test. *Omega*, 21, 1 (1993), 73–90.

Igbaria, M., and Iivari, J. The effects of self-efficacy on computer usage. *Omega*, 23, 6 (1995), 587–605.

Kaplan-Leiserson, E. (ed.) Learning circuits glossary. American Society for Training and Development, Alexandria, VA (available at http://www.learningcircuits.org/glossary.htm, accessed on April 28, 2004).

Karahanna, E., and Limayem, M. E-mail and v-mail usage: generalizing across technologies. *Journal of Organizational Computing and Electronic Commerce*, 10, 1 (2000), 49–66.

Kirkpatrick, D.L. *Evaluating Training Programs: The Four Levels.* San Francisco: Berrett-Koehler Publications, 1998.

Leidner, D.E., and Jarvenpaa, S.L. The use of information technology to enhance management school education: a theoretical view. *MIS Quarterly*, 19, 3 (1995), 265–291.

Loomis, K.D. Learning styles and asynchronous learning: comparing the LASSI model to class performance. *Journal of Asynchronous Learning Networks*, 4, 1 (2000), 23–32 (available at www.sloan-c.org/publications/jaln/index.asp, accessed on August 5, 2004).

Marcolin, B.L., Compeau, D.R., Munro, M.C., and Huff, S.L. Assessing user competence: conceptualization and measurement. *Information Systems Research*, 11, 1 (2000), 37–60.

Mayer, R.E., Heiser, J., and Lonn, S. Cognitive constraints on multimedia learning: when presenting more material results in less understanding. *Journal of Educational Technology*, 93, 1 (2001), 187–198.

Moon, J.W., and Kim, Y.G. Extending the TAM for a world-wide-web context. *Information & Management*, 38, 4 (2001), 217–230.

Moore, G.A. *Crossing the chasm: Marketing and Selling High-Tech Goods to Mainstream Customers.* New York: HarperBusiness, 1991.

Norman, D.A. *The Invisible Computer: Why Good Products Can Fail, the Personal Computer Is So Complex, and Information Appliances Are the Solution.* Cambridge: MIT Press, 1998.

Papa, F., Perugini, M., and Spedaletti, S. Psychological factors in virtual classroom situations: a pilot study for a model of learning through technological devices. *Behavior and Information Technology*, 17, 4 (1998), 187–194.

Phipps, R., and Merisotis, J. What's the difference? A review of contemporary research on the effectiveness of distance learning in higher education. The Institute for Higher Education Policy, Washington, DC, 1999 (available at www.ihep.com/Pubs/PDF/Difference.pdf, accessed on April 20, 2004).

Piccoli, G., Ahmad, R., and Ives, B. Web-based virtual learning environments: a research framework and a preliminary assessment of effectiveness in basic IT skills training. *MIS Quarterly*, 25, 4 (2001), 401–426.

Pintrich, P.R., and DeGroot, E.V. Motivational and self-regulated learning components of classroom academic performance. *Journal of Educational Psychology*, 82, 1 (1990), 33–40.

Richardson, J.C., and Swan, K. Examining social presence in online courses in relation to students' perceived learning and satisfaction. *Journal of Asynchronous Learning Networks*, 7, 1 (2003), 68–88 (available at www.sloan-c.org/publications/jaln/index.asp, accessed on August 5, 2004).

Rogers, E.M. *Diffusion of Innovations*. New York: The Free Press, 1995.

Rossett, A., and Schafer, L. What can we do about e-dropouts? *Training and Development*, 57, 6 (2003), 40–46.

Rossman, M.H. Successful online teaching using an asynchronous learner discussion forum. *Journal of Asynchronous Learning Networks*, 3, 2 (1999), 91–97 (available at www.sloan-c.org/publications/jaln/index.asp, accessed on August 5, 2004).

Santhanam, R., and Sein, M.K. Improving end user proficiency: effects of conceptual training and nature of interaction. *Information Systems Research*, 5, 4 (1994), 378–399.

Schank, R.C. Revolutionizing the traditional classroom course. *Communications of the ACM*, 44, 12 (2001), 21–24.

Schrum, L., and Hong, S. Dimensions and strategies for online success: voices from experienced educators. *Journal of Asynchronous Learning Networks*, 6, 1 (2002), 57–67 (available at www.sloan-c.org/publications/jaln/index.asp, accessed on August 5, 2004).

Shea, P., Pickett, A., and Pelz, W. Follow-up investigation of teaching presence in the SUNY learning network. *Journal of Asynchronous Learning Networks*, 7, 2 (2003), 61–80 (available at www.sloan-c.org/publications/jaln/index.asp, accessed on August 5, 2004).

Shneiderman, B., Alavi, M., Norman, K., and Borkowski, E.Y. Windows of opportunity in electronic classrooms. *Communications of the ACM*, 38, 11 (1995), 19–24.

Shneiderman, B. Relate–create–donate: a teaching/learning philosophy for the cyber-generation. *Computers & Education*, 31, 1 (1998), 25–39.

Stacey, P. E-Learning: The second wave. T-Net British Columbia, Vancouver, BC, 2001 (available at www.bctechnology.com/statics/pstacey-feb0201.html, accessed on May 5, 2004).

Sugrue, B. *ASTD 2003 State of the Industry Report*. Alexandria, VA: American Society for Training and Development, 2003.

Thong, J.Y.L., Hong, W.H., and Tam, K. R. Understanding user acceptance of digital libraries: what are the roles of interface characteristics, organizational context, and individual differences? *International Journal of Human-Computer Studies*, 57, 3 (2002), 215–242.

University of Wisconsin–Madison. Designing distance learning courses. (available at www.soemadison.wisc.edu/outreach/deweb/index.html, accessed on April 26, 2004).

Valenta, A., Therriault, D., Dieter, M., and Mrtek, R. Identifying student attitudes and learning styles in distance education. *Journal of Asynchronous Learning Networks*, 5, 2 (2001), 111–127 (available at www.sloan-c.org/publications/jaln/index.asp, accessed on August 5, 2004).

Venkatesh, V. Creation of favorable user perceptions: exploring the role of intrinsic motivation. *MIS Quarterly*, 23, 2 (1999), 239–260.

Venkatesh, V. Determinants of perceived ease of use: integrating perceived behavioral control, computer anxiety and enjoyment into the technology acceptance model. *Information Systems Research*, 11, 4 (2000), 342–365.

Venkatesh, V., and Davis, F.D. A theoretical extension of the technology acceptance model: four longitudinal field studies. *Management Science*, 46, 2 (2000), 186–204.

Venkatesh, V., and Morris, M.G. Why don't men ever stop to ask for directions? Gender, social influence, and their role in technology acceptance and usage behavior. *MIS Quarterly*, 24, 1 (2000), 115–139.

Vockell, E. Educational psychology: a practical approach. (available at http://education.calumet.purdue.edu/vockell/EdPsyBook, accessed on April 5, 2004).

Wang, A.Y., and Newlin, M.H. Predictors of web-student performance: the role of self-efficacy and reasons for taking an on-line class. *Computers in Human Behavior*, 18, 2 (2002), 151–163.

Webster, J., and Hackley, P. Teaching effectiveness in technology-mediated distance learning. *Academy of Management Journal*, 40, 6 (1997), 1271–1281.

Wiley, D.A. Connecting learning objects to instructional design theory: a definition, a metaphor, and a taxonomy. In D.A. Wiley (ed.), *The Instructional Use of Learning Objects*. Bloomington, IN: Agency for Instructional Technology and Association for Educational Communications Technology, 2001, pp. 2–35 (available at http://reusability.org/read/chapters/wiley.doc, accessed on August 5, 2004).

Zimmerman, B.J., and Martinez-Pons, M. Development of a structured interview for assessing student use of self-regulated learning strategies. *American Educational Research Journal*, 23, 4 (1986), 614–628.

Zimmerman, B.J. Models of self-regulated learning and academic achievement. In B.J. Zimmerman and D.H. Schunk (eds.), *Self-Regulated Learning And Academic Achievement: Theory, Research, and Practice*. New York: Springer, 1989, pp. 1–25.

Zimmerman, B.J. Self-regulated learning and academic achievement: an overview. *Educational Psychologist*, 25, 1 (1990), 3–17.

CHAPTER 11

DEVELOPING TRAINING STRATEGIES WITH AN HCI PERSPECTIVE

LORNE OLFMAN, ROBERT P. BOSTROM, AND MAUNG K. SEIN

Abstract: *This chapter outlines a strategic perspective for designing, implementing, and delivering software training with a human-computer interaction (HCI) perspective. The IT training strategy development framework is based on research we have conducted over the past two decades. A comprehensive training strategy is a plan for matching an appropriate training method to the specific type of trainee and the specific IT tool to achieve a desired set of training outcomes. In order to develop a training program it is necessary to know what knowledge trainees must have at the end of the training program. What trainees must know can be mapped into a set of knowledge levels. Knowledge levels comprise an integrated hierarchy of skills that, taken together, form the basis for ensuring the ability to effectively learn either a specific software application or, at the highest level, to be able to learn any application. A training strategy provides a basis for creating a training program that includes activities and methods necessary to move the trainees to the appropriate knowledge level. The strategy is especially important because there is no one training program that can be universally applied. It enables the right approach for the right system for the right trainee. A training strategy is integrated into an organization's learning strategy, which determines how resources are expended on training. The learning strategy is itself in tune with the organization's corporate strategy. Thus, our conceptualization of a training strategy is firmly embedded within the HCI perspective as defined and articulated in this book and reflected in other papers.*

Keywords: *End-User Training, Software Training, Knowledge Levels, Training Strategy, Learning Strategy*

INTRODUCTION

In 1999, we called for a reconceptualization of training, arguing that the traditional view of training that focused almost entirely on the tool and skills required to use the tool was limited and did not meet the requirements for the workforce of the future (Sein et al., 1999). We proposed a knowledge-level framework that listed the knowledge (levels) that trainees must have in order to fully understand the capabilities of a system (or software), and thus use it effectively within an organizational context. In order for trainees to achieve the required knowledge level, we proposed a framework to develop a comprehensive training strategy.

While we believe that this is an innovative approach that takes a much more pervasive view of training than the traditional view, it is still somewhat narrow when considered in the light of the human-computer interaction (HCI) perspective outlined in this book. As the editors, Galletta and

Zhang, stress, an HCI perspective in IS includes much more than a simple interaction between a user and the computer. They stress that environmental issues (organizational, social, and global) as well as job issues (task goals and task characteristics) are equally important in HCI.

We concur. Based on this HCI perspective, we take a critical look at our work in the training area, especially at our reconceptualized view of training articulated in the 1999 article. We quickly realize that, seen in the light of HCI, our framework has some serious shortcomings. For one, it refers to environmental issues, especially organizational issues, only as contextual, and that, too, just in passing. Thus, the vital aspect of placing a training strategy firmly in the context of higher-level organizational strategies was missing. It is apparent that we need to further conceptualize training, especially with respect to formulating strategies.

In this paper, we build on our 1999 framework, incorporate our later work, and propose a training strategy development framework that we believe is more in keeping with the philosophical underpinnings of the HCI perspective that is the theme of this book.

The rest of the chapter is organized as follows. First, we briefly review our 1999 model, especially the knowledge level framework that remains the cornerstone of our conceptualization of training. We also review the various training strategies that have been proposed in the literature. Next, we critique our work based on the view of HCI articulated in this book. We then proceed to present our later work on training and propose a new training framework that comprises training and learning strategy development models. We discuss that framework in detail and present best practices that illustrate it. Finally, we present research questions and directions for future work.

BACKGROUND: EARLIER TRAINING STRATEGY MODEL

In an earlier article (Sein et al., 1999), we argued for a much broader view of training than the prevailing tool-focused view. We cited a story to thrust home our argument. It is worth retelling:

> In a revealing article, Snell (1997) describes the process of how Carnegie Mellon University (CMU) implemented a platform based on client/server (C/S) architecture. The implementation plan was sound, or so it seemed. Intensive training of both the systems employees and the end users preceded the rollout. In developing the training plan, CMU followed the tried and tested traditional pattern. Programmers and developers were trained in C/S tools and the users were trained in the operations of the applications. The result was an almost unmitigated disaster. Programmers, viewing the tools as yet another development platform, refused to move away from the tool set with which they were familiar. Users blamed the applications for every problem, even those caused by the network and the desktops. It was apparent that the training had failed, both for users and the IT staff.

And further on . . .

> Snell (1997) goes on to describe how CMU finally realized that in order to successfully deploy C/S, both IT staff and users needed to be provided with a broad conceptual view of C/S architecture.

We used this example to emphasize that we need a broader reconceptualization of training. We argued that the traditional view of IT training has been to impart skills in the use of the particular target system (the technology in the form of software or hardware), focusing on the system itself. This view is reflected in the training materials, methods, and examples provided for a wide range of software applications. Materials used in IT skills training typically illustrate the syntax and semantics of the system functions. For example, training manuals for a word processing application normally include a description of how to use commands and manipulate icons, and define what these commands and icons mean. Sometimes training materials provide a conceptual model of the system, but the standard objective is training the user in the functions of the system rather than in the concepts underlying it. All of these efforts reflect a particular IT training strategy.

The crucial question a training strategy must address is: Given an IT tool on which a specific type of user needs to be trained, what training approaches and methods should be used to attain the appropriate level of knowledge? An effective strategy will match the appropriate method with the appropriate user for the appropriate tool. The framework we proposed was based on a classification of trainees, specific training approaches for different classes of IT tools, and the knowledge outcome for the trainees. To answer the question of what knowledge the trainees should have, we proposed a knowledge level framework. By discussing the training process, especially its stages, we proposed a training strategy development framework. These two frameworks are described below.

Training Needs/Outcomes: Knowledge Levels

All training starts with identifying training needs or outcomes. Thus, a training strategy framework must start with a good model of training outcomes. Based on prior work, we developed a seven-level knowledge content hierarchy (Sein et al., 1999). We make a major departure from the reviewed research by integrating motivation and meta-cognition as key knowledge components. Figure 11.1 shows the hierarchy. We briefly describe each level of knowledge below.

Command-Based

This is knowledge of the syntax and semantics of IT (software) tools. The syntax of a tool is its set of commands and the command structures. Semantics are the meaning of those commands. Without this level of knowledge, users are unable to recover from errors or transfer knowledge from one system to another. Some training methods and manuals cover semantic knowledge. Generally speaking, end-user training focuses primarily on command-based knowledge.

Tool Procedural

This level refers to grouping individual commands to perform a function such as creating a document. Tool procedural knowledge is needed to synthesize a set of commands into a method for accomplishing a generic task. As with command-based knowledge, most end-user training covers tool procedural knowledge.

Business Procedural

This is knowledge about applying tool procedures to business processes. For example, to prepare letters for a group of people, the "mail merge" function of a typical word processor could be taught in the context of this task. Another term for this level might be task-based knowledge.

Figure 11.1 **Knowledge Levels**

Knowledge Level	ERP System Example
1. Command-Based: syntax and semantics of computer tool*	Mouse click on a button to enter a transaction
2. Tool Procedural: combining commands to do generic tasks	Create a transaction
3. Business Procedural: application of tool to a business process	Query the database for other functional transactions
4. Tool Conceptual: the big picture of what to do with the tool	Workflow tool
5. Business Conceptual: the big picture of where the specific business process fits in the organization	Entry of a transaction affects order processing
6. Motivational: what can the tool do for trainee and organization	Enables consistent transactions across organizational functions
7. Meta-Cognitive: learning to learn	Enhancing participants' self-efficacy and outcome expectations for the training

*Tool is defined as an end-user application that has been developed or purchased.

Business procedural knowledge has recently become of interest to software trainers, especially in the form of electronic performance support or workflow-based learning, which aim to provide just-in-time training on the job.

Tool Conceptual

This level of knowledge focuses on the big picture, that is, the overall purpose and structure of the IT tool. It provides a basis for being able to transfer learning to new situations. For example, a conceptual model of an ERP system is that it acts as a workflow tool. The concept of a workflow would be presented to trainees at the outset of training. Currently, tool conceptual knowledge is rarely provided in traditional training. If it is, it is almost always outlined in terms of command architecture. Providing appropriate tool conceptual knowledge can be expected to facilitate the learning of command-based, tool procedural, and business procedural knowledge because it acts as an "advance organizer" for understanding these knowledge levels.

Business Conceptual

This is knowledge about where the specific business process supported or enabled by the tool fits in the organization's overall processes. This knowledge is required to give the "big picture" of how various processes interface with one another. It is especially vital for ERP systems where an error in one module can propagate across the modules with which it interfaces. Thus, the effect of an error can be felt in a process far removed from the process where the error occurred. Business process modeling tools can be used to impart this level of knowledge.

Motivational

This is knowledge about what the IT tool can do for the trainee, the trainee's job, and the trainee's organization. It focuses on creating knowledge to increase the trainee's motivation to learn. Business motivational knowledge typically requires instructor-led training to show how the software to be learned fits into the overall job function and the organization. One possibility is to have managers be involved in providing this type of knowledge.

Meta-Cognitive

This level of knowledge focuses on learning to learn or self-regulated learning. Meta-cognitive knowledge provides learners with the process skills and beliefs for actively attaining learning outcomes on their own. For example, one belief, self-efficacy, has received a lot of attention in IS training research. One view of meta-cognitive knowledge is that it provides learners with the ability to be successful in any type of learning environment. Another aspect is that learners can generalize what they have learned from a particular training experience to another situation. That is, they gain the ability to transfer their learning to other IT tools. This type of knowledge is important in an environment that stresses continuous learning.

Training literature and practices have almost exclusively stressed command-based and tool procedural knowledge, and, to some extent, business procedural knowledge. These levels define the traditional view of end-user training. In the context of current and future uses of IT, we would argue that training methods need to be extended to include the tool conceptual, business conceptual, motivational and meta-cognitive levels of knowledge. This was the lesson Carnegie Mellon University learned in the client/server architecture implementation discussed earlier (Snell, 1997).

Recent research provides further support for this view. For example, a study conducted by Coulson et al. (2003) was designed to impart specific levels of ERP knowledge to two subject groups in different manners. Both methods followed a traditional ERP procedural training approach, but one method added a conceptual advance organizer. In general, the study found that when a tool conceptual knowledge level was added to the training, the end users developed more accurate mental models. The training results became stronger as time progressed. Even ten days after training ended, end users who received conceptual training continued to evolve their mental models. Coulson et al. propose that by using the knowledge-level framework and incorporating tool conceptual knowledge into an organization's training design, organizations may see an improvement in overall ERP implementation results.

Training Strategy

As we stated earlier, an effective strategy will match the appropriate method with the appropriate user for the appropriate tool. Therefore, our framework (Figure 11.2) is based on a classification of trainees, specific training approaches for different classes of IT tools, and the level of knowledge required for using the tools (Sein et al., 1999). The output of the training process is the level

Figure 11.2   **Training Strategy Framework**

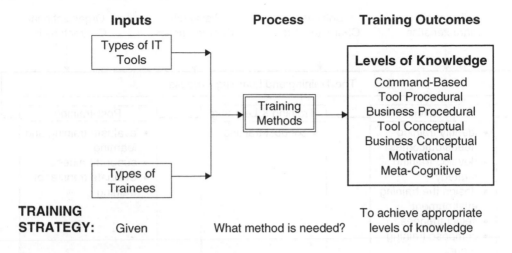

Source: Adapted from Sein et al., 1999.

Figure 11.3   **SAP Training Strategy**

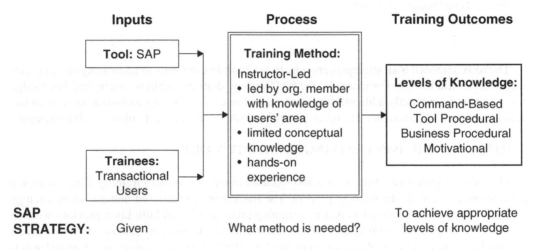

of knowledge discussed earlier. Below, we discuss the other elements of the framework: the input elements of IT tools and trainees, and the process elements of training approaches and methods.

It is heartening to note that some vendors have recognized the need for an integrated strategy and are offering documents to that end. A recent example from SAP illustrates our model (see Figure 11.3). This example outlines the content of recommendations from SAP to one of its clients who recently purchased the software. For example, one training strategy recommended by SAP is:

> Transactional user training should contain a high percentage of hands-on exercises, have limited theoretical discussion about the application, and if possible, the training should be led by a member of the organization who best understands the user work requirements.

Figure 11.4 **The Training and Learning Process**

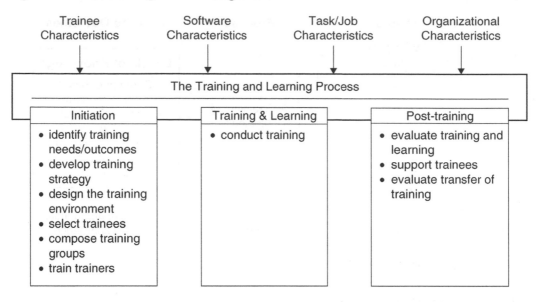

Source: From Compeau et al., 1995.

The recommended SAP strategies are not always complete in terms of addressing all of the elements in our framework. For example, the SAP strategy does not address conceptual knowledge levels, and only indirectly addresses the motivational level by choosing an instructor who understands user work requirements. However, we applaud SAP's efforts to articulate training strategies.

CRITIQUING THE 1999 TRAINING STRATEGY MODEL

Our framework improved on the narrow tool-focused traditional view of training. First, we took a comprehensive view of the training process. The framework emphasized that a training strategy is developed and implemented as part of a training process. We had built upon previous work in end-user training, which emphasizes that the most effective training of software users would be accomplished using a life cycle approach (Sein et al., 1987). The life cycle approach aimed at getting trainers to focus on stages before, during, and after the delivery of training. This approach (see Figure 11.4) was reiterated by Compeau et al. (1995) and by Olfman and Sein (1997).

The initiation phase emphasizes the design of training, matching trainees to appropriate training, and training the trainers. The delivery phase focuses on conducting training. Important rules are to give trainees a strong grounding in conceptual understanding, to emphasize motivation, and to aim at building accurate and flexible mental models. The post-training stage recognizes that learning does not stop at the end of a training session, and points to the need for evaluation and support.

Research in the literature has examined the full range of the training life cycle. This includes work on assessing end-user training needs (e.g., Nelson et al., 1995), assessing training materials (e.g., Carroll and Rosson, 1995), and matching learning styles with training approaches (e.g., Bostrom et al., 1990).

Although this framework, and related research, can serve as part of the context for developing training strategies, the specifics needed for an effective strategy were not addressed. For example, while trainee characteristics, such as cognitive and learning styles, have been proposed to categorize users (e.g., Bostrom et al., 1990), organizational levels, job specificity, and organizational needs have been ignored. Does a clerical user with a concrete learning style require the same training content as a top manager with a concrete learning style? Without a strategy, trainers are left to select the content of training based on personal experience.

Another topic not addressed was matching training methods to specific tools and trainees. A survey of the practitioner literature adds little value. While most training literature explores the potential of computer-based technology (e.g., multimedia presentations, computer-based training), there is very little written on how to train software users, let alone how to train specific groups of users of specific packages. A few topics appear to dominate the trade press training literature, most noticeably multimedia and online training products. The emphasis is on the advantages of these packages, not on how they can be used effectively.

The major change in the last few years has been the huge growth in various forms of computer-supported training approaches, such as learning management systems, virtual/real-time classrooms, simulation, and so forth. Thus, the number of training methods has exploded, and organizations are struggling to blend these different methods into an effective training strategy. Thus, what is needed is not simply matching a single training method to specific tools and trainees, but a blend of training methods.

Our framework explicitly addressed these issues and provided guidelines to develop effective training strategies. By specifically explicating different knowledge levels, the framework showed that methods and approaches to be used in a training initiative depend on the knowledge level that the trainee must attain. That of course depends on the job context of the trainee and her position in the organization. These aspects are key ingredients of the HCI perspective, as defined by the editors of this volume.

Need for Further Reconceptualization

Despite the apparent contribution our framework made to the field of end-user training, it still falls short of encompassing an HCI perspective. As Kutzschan and Webster (2006) emphasize this perspective "take[s] a more contextual view of HCI considering wider task, organizational, and international issues. Thus, MIS researchers view HCI as the interplay between not only the human and the computer, but between other factors such as environmental issues and job characteristics. This results in MIS researchers working at a wide range of levels of analysis, from individual to cross-cultural issues."

Our 1999 framework was more focused on the individual level; although we mentioned organizational issues, they did not form an explicit dimension of the strategy. It is clear that a training strategy cannot be developed in isolation from the organization's "higher" strategies. This implies that an organizational level of analysis and decision making are essential to a comprehensive IT training strategy. Moreover, our framework viewed the training process as linear, with an input-process-output form. On closer examination, we see that the elements of the model are, in reality, interdependent, and cannot be decided upon in isolation.

These issues led us to further reconceptualize training strategy. As stated earlier, an effective training strategy matches a training method appropriate to the specific type of trainee and the specific IT tool to achieve a specific set of training outcomes. These aspects are dependent on the organization's strategies and objectives, which determine how resources are to be spent on training.

Figure 11.5   **The Training Context**

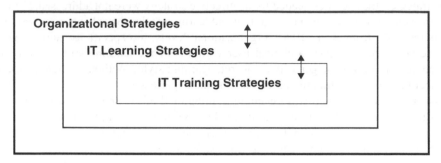

AN HCI-BASED TRAINING STRATEGY DEVELOPMENT FRAMEWORK

The Training Context

Delivering effective training requires an integrative and comprehensive set of strategies. Figure 11.5 presents a layered view of this approach. We use the term "strategy" to denote the pattern of actions for deploying resources to achieve organizational goals. Organizations deploy resources to train a particular set of users on a particular IT tool. These "IT training strategies" provide the basis for selecting the best training methods for a given situation (training session, project, etc.). An "IT learning strategy" determines how training resources are deployed to develop the knowledge and skills in an organization's workforce. As Figure 11.5 shows, the two strategies are related. IT training strategies are defined by and at the same time are a means for attaining the IT learning strategy.

Later in this chapter, we show specific ways in which the two strategies are related (see Figure 11.6). Both strategies should lead to the achievement of organizational strategies and should follow from them. We focus on IT learning, training strategies, and their relationship. Their link to organizational strategies is important, but is beyond the scope of this chapter. If the reader wants to pursue this topic in more detail, we refer to two starting points: Watkins and Marsick (2003) and Rosenburg (2001). Watkins and Marsick stress the importance of technology systems in creating organizational learning strategies. Rosenburg outlines a process for developing an e-learning strategy based on organizational strategies. This type of process could be applied to IT resources in general. Since there is very little research on the link to organizational strategies, this is a rich research area.

The HCI Perspective of Learning and Training Strategies

Essentially, our current framework addresses the shortcomings of our 1999 model by explicitly addressing organizational aspects, interrelationships with higher strategies, and the interdependence of dimensions. Figure 11.6 depicts how specific dimensions of the training strategy are linked to specific dimensions of the learning strategy. Thus, decisions and the focus on the individual level of training strategy are meshed with the organizational focus and level of the learning strategy. The linkages between the two models are described in the next section.

The models and linkages in Figure 11.6 were developed from research we conducted between 1999 and 2002 on best practices in end-user software training in sixteen organizations. Details of

Figure 11.6   Linking IT Learning and Training Strategies

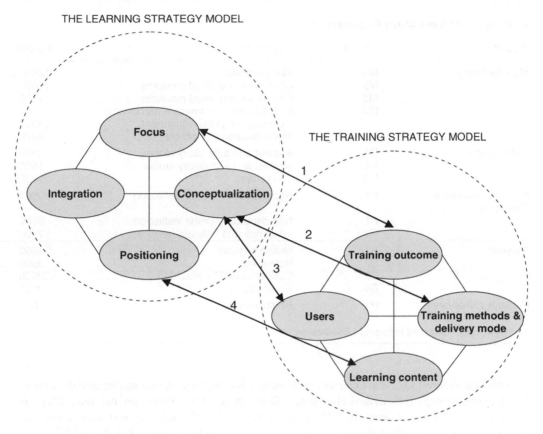

THE LEARNING STRATEGY MODEL

THE TRAINING STRATEGY MODEL

Source: From Simonsen and Sein (2004).

the study are described elsewhere (Olfman et al., 2003; Simonsen and Sein, 2004; and Olfman et al., 2000). We provide a brief overview here and reproduce Table 1 from Olfman et al. (2003) to acquaint the reader with the study.

Our sample was a subset of one hundred companies that we first identified as having successfully implemented innovative best practices in end-user training. The sources of such designation were trade publications, the American Society for Training and Development (ASTD), and word of mouth. Table 11.1 describes the organizations. One organization was based in Norway, one was in Canada, and the rest were based in the United States.

We conducted interviews mainly with training managers and other specialists using a protocol that we developed by identifying patterns of actions for deploying training resources. These trainers concentrated on a variety of software, including "office" packages, groupware, enterprise resource planning systems (ERPs), and sometimes in-house systems.

We analyzed the interview protocols to determine key learning and training strategies. We then developed our learning and training strategy models based on this data analysis. The two strategies

Table 11.1

Description of Case Study Organizations

Industry	Case #	Major Focus (SIC*)	# Users
Manufacturing	M1	Multiple areas	12000
	M2	Chemicals and allied products	15000
	M3	Chemicals and allied products	1500
	M4	Industrial and commercial machinery, including computer equipment	16000
	M5	Transportation equipment	4000
Retail Trade	R1	Apparel and accessory stores	8000
	R2	Apparel and accessory stores	1500
	R3	Food stores	1800
Finance, Insurance, Real Estate	F1	Non-depository credit institution	3600
	F2	Non-depository credit institution	9000
	F3	Insurance and financial services	17900
Services	S1	Motion pictures	2000
	S2	Hotels, etc.	3800
	S3	Business and IT consulting	32000
	S4	IT consulting	8200
Public Administration	P1	Multiple areas	3000

*Note: SIC = Standard Industrial Classification

are shown in Figure 11.6. As we can see, each strategy is composed of four interrelated dimensions. Our learning strategy is described elsewhere (Olfman et al., 2003; Simonsen and Sein, 2004). We summarize the learning strategy in Table 11.2, and briefly describe it in the next section. After this discussion, we describe the training strategy in more detail, and summarize it in Table 11.3.

The Learning Strategy Model

Table 11.2 lists the dimensions of the learning strategy. The leftmost column lists and defines the four dimensions of the strategy model: focus, conceptualization, integration, and positioning. Each dimension can take a spectrum of values. The best practice observed in our study and in the literature is also listed in that column. The middle column lists the components of each dimension. Each component can have subcomponents (e.g., the trainee conceptualization component of conceptualization has an active vs. passive subcomponent and a learning style subcomponent). The rightmost column shows examples of mechanisms that were used to achieve best practices.

We will briefly discuss each dimension outlined in Table 11.2. In this discussion, we refer to the expected, normative, and descriptive best practices for each dimension. Expected best practices are those we thought would emerge based on our reading of the literature and of experiences in the field. Normative best practices are the ones that emerged through theoretical premises and our assessment and integration of case interviews. Descriptive best practices are the ones we found in the organizations we studied. The best practices summarized in Table 11.2 are a combination of normative and descriptive findings. Where an organization will be or is positioned on the learning strategy dimensions is determined by answering key questions, as outlined below.

Table 11.2

Summary of Learning Strategy Model

Dimensions	Components	Example Best Practice Mechanisms
Focus		
Main driver of training being business or technology	• Mission statement	• To identify training needs: Analyze corporate business plans, business processes, and specialized roles such as those of relationship managers
Best Practice: Business	• Determine training needs	• To integrate business procedures into training: Use functional area personnel as trainers
	• Assessment and evaluation	• To address motivation: Use specific business process examples during training
	• Training ownership	• To let functional area own training: Functional areas control training resource allocation
	• The integration of business procedures and tasks into content of training sessions	
Conceptualization		
Conceptualization of training as continuous vs. discrete and viewing trainees as active or passive	Training conceptualization: Continuous or discrete	To implement continuous conceptualization: Use support mechanisms, people networks, business coaches, reward structure
Best Practice: Continuous with active trainees	Trainee conceptualization: Active or passive; same learning style or different	To implement active and different learning style trainee conceptualization: Match trainees to training, offer free choice to trainees to select training
Integration		
Training group is viewed as proactive or reactive and links with related groups such as HR, IS, and functional units	• Proactive or reactive stance	To implement a proactive stance: Establish permanent cross-functional teams, set up work groups for projects
Best Practice: Proactive with strong links	• Links with business units	To implement strong link with business units: Ensure presence of business unit managers in training unit policy-making bodies, develop specific roles such as relationship managers
	• Links with HR	To offer business process training: Embed business process in technical training, use business area personnel as trainers
	• Links with IS group (systems development and infrastructure)	

(continued)

Table 11.2 *(continued)*

Dimensions	Components	Example Best Practice Mechanisms
	• Location of training group • Who offers business process training?	
Positioning Where in the learning supply/value chain the training group positions itself (create, distribute, and deliver training) both in the traditional and the online contexts	Traditional supply chain: create; distribute; deliver	To create, distribute, and deliver in the traditional context
Best Practice: Depends on context	Online supply chain: IT infrastructure; create; distribute; deliver	To create, distribute, and deliver in the online context

Focus Dimension

The focus dimension addresses the vital question: To what extent is IT training based on business needs? Along a continuum, the answer can be "technology" at one end or "business" at the other. The "technology" end implies that training focuses on providing technical skills to employees, while the "business" end implies that the focus is on providing training that helps employees to achieve business outcomes through using technology. For this dimension, the best practice is a business focus. It implies continual aligning of the training efforts with the business objectives of the organization. This is a much-needed conceptualization of training, and is an expressed concern of top management (Masie Center, 2000). We expected to find that the typical best practice organization was somewhere in the middle of the continuum because the literature does not indicate that a business focus is normal. Somewhat surprisingly, fourteen of the sixteen organizations clearly had a business focus. We see this trend being even more dominant today.

Conceptualization Dimension

The conceptualization dimension addresses the question: To what extent is training viewed as a continuous and active process? An organization on the "discrete/passive" end of this continuum considers that training is provided in chunks when it is required (e.g., when a new software package is acquired). An organization on the "continuous/active" end of this continuum believes that training is part of the ongoing learning process. Two key choices confront the training organization. The first is deciding whether to think about training as continuous (which includes discrete offerings as well) or in only a discrete fashion. The second is how to address trainee conceptualization. In this case, it must be determined whether the motivation perspective is for active or passive learners, and whether all learners have the same learning style or if they are different.

The emphasis on organizational learning as a strategic necessity implies that as a best practice, training needs to be viewed as continuous and trainees should be viewed as active. We base this on the tenets of the learning organization (see Robey et al., 2000; Watkins and Marsick, 2003). In the organizations we studied, only one had a "true" continuous conceptualization. However, several were either moving towards it, or were thinking about it. Encouragingly, several companies had already implemented specific mechanisms that could be used to employ a continuous training conceptualization (see Table 11.2). Since our data collection, we have seen a key shift in most major organizations toward a continuous focus. For example, in 2003, IBM conducted 48 percent of its training via the Internet, thus making it available twenty-four hours a day. Learning was under the control of the IBM employee, who, on average, spent 60 percent of her time on the road.

Integration Dimension

The integration dimension addresses the question: To what extent are training stakeholders working together and to what extent technology resources are integrated? An organization on the "reactive" end of this continuum considers that each business and/or support partner is responsible for ensuring its own technology training requirements, and does not have links to other stakeholders. Their technology efforts would obviously not be integrated either. An organization on the "proactive" end of this continuum believes that it is necessary to work closely with all stakeholders to deliver technology training to users, and is closely linked to other stakeholders.

The best practice is a proactive stance with high integration. The IS literature stresses the need for tight linkage between training and human resource functions (e.g., Andrews and Niederman, 1998). This requires the training unit to take the initiative in facilitating functional units to determine their training needs, to tie in with HR policies to implement incentive and reward structures, and to tie in training integrally with new system development and new system rollout. We expected that the typical organization would be somewhere in the middle of the continuum, since both approaches were indicated in the practitioner literature. In our sample, ten out of sixteen companies took a proactive stance.

One of the key business drivers operating very strongly these days is the integration of business processes and the systems that support these processes within the organization and supply/value chain to improve performance. With advances in technology in the last few years, especially service-oriented architectures and Web services, integration efforts have been greatly facilitated. In the learning area, we are seeing the emergence of workflow, workflow-based, or work-embedded learning (Adkins, 2004). Workflow learning is entrenched within work, that is, delivered in real time in the context of the employee's work. This change is the revival of an old research stream, electronic performance support.

We are also seeing trends in integration of key organizational systems: learning, content/knowledge management, business intelligence, and collaboration technology (Bostrom, 2003). The convergence point of these systems is the delivery of information in real time into the employee's workflow to improve performance. It is also predicted that these systems will have common/shared knowledge repositories that contain standardized knowledge objects (Bostrom, 2003). In 2004, we are already seeing this type of integration between content/knowledge and learning systems. Effective integration, both organizationally and technically, is critical to implementation of effective learning strategies.

Positioning Dimension

The positioning dimension addresses the question: To what extent is the training supply/value chain outsourced? An organization on the "outsourcing" end of this continuum considers that training materials should be created, distributed, and delivered by outside entities. An organization on the "insourcing" end of this continuum believes that training materials should be created, distributed, and delivered in-house. This dimension needs to be assessed in two contexts: traditional and online. A traditional context implies either classroom-based, instructor-led training offerings or providing a library of training materials—such as manuals and computer-based training software—at specific places where trainees go. The online context implies computer-based offerings that may or may not include distance learning or Web-based training, but that are under the control of the learner.

This dimension has no ideal best-practice choice. Our research indicated that the choices depend on budgetary and resource constraints and choices in the other strategic dimensions. This contingency perspective is supported in research literature, for example, the concept of "right sourcing" (Lacity et al., 1996) and the importance of organizational context in formulating learning strategies (Compeau et al., 1995). The trend that we observed in our sample companies was that generic and skills training were more likely to be outsourced. More specific training needs were generally met through internally custom-designed material, mostly through purchased content that was modified internally. An important point is that positioning along the supply chain was sometimes course specific, that is, a company may perform all three activities for a specific course, but may only deliver for another course. In addition, outsourcing may be internal, for example, delivery through business coaches. Since we collected our data, the availability of content and training programs, especially technology-enabled ones, has grown substantially. This has made outsourcing of training a very hot issue for companies, making this another rich area for research.

The Training Strategy Model

The model is summarized in Table 11.3 and shown in Figure 11.6. The columns in Table 11.3 are analogous to the columns in Table 11.2. The four dimensions of the model are described below.

Training Outcomes

The Outcome dimension represents the knowledge and skills about a specific IT tool (or tools) that a trainee can achieve at the end of the training. Figure 11.1 shows the seven knowledge levels. It can range from levels 1 to 3 (the bare minimum) to all seven. O is tightly linked to focus of learning strategy (see connecting line 1 in Figure 11.6). A business focus requires that motivational and business procedural levels be covered in training in addition to knowledge levels 1 to 3. Best practice is to achieve levels 1 to 5, and sometimes level 6 (i.e., the motivational level; see Figure 11.1).

Training Method and Delivery Mode

Training method and delivery mode represents how the training material is delivered to the trainees and who delivers it. The methods range from traditional instructor-led to self-based. Instructor-led implies that training is conducted or facilitated by an instructor in a real or virtual classroom. The self-based mode leaves training to the trainee who works at his/her own pace. Delivery mode ranges from traditional to online training. In the traditional mode, training is delivered to the trainee primarily at a fixed time and in a fixed place (e.g., a classroom). The online mode delivers training to the trainee anytime, anyplace via the Internet and intranets, and through desktop applications. T is tightly linked to the training component of conceptualization of learning strategy (see connecting line 2 in Figure 11.6). A continuous training conceptualization requires a multi-method, multi-mode approach. Best practice is to use a mix of instructor-led and self-based multi-method delivery (mix of traditional and online).

Table 11.3

Summary of Training Strategy Model

Dimensions	Components	Example Best-Practice Mechanisms
Training Outcomes		
Knowledge levels addressed	• Knowledge level	Lower levels: Use functional area personnel as trainers
Best Practice: At least up to motivational level	• Assessment and evaluation	Lower levels: Use functional area personnel as trainers Address motivation: Use specific business process examples during training Address business procedural: Including business process training in materials
Training Method and Delivery Mode		
Who trains and how trainees receive training	• Instructor led vs. self-based	Blending of methods and delivery modes to accomplish outcomes
Best Practice: Mix of instructor-led and self-based multi-method delivery (mix of traditional and online)	• Traditional vs. online	Use methods based on proven learning theories, e.g., social cognitive theory
Users		
Classifying users and matching with training method	• Job class	To classify users according to job class: Hold training sessions where all trainees are from the same job class. Tailor outcome level accordingly
Best Practice: Match users to training method by job class and learning style (or free choice)	• Learning style	To classify users according to learning style: Tailor training content according to whether a learner is active or passive learner
Learning Content		
What is conveyed in training and in what chunk size	• Chunk size and combinability	To implement appropriate chunk size: Conduct task and process analysis to determine usable and combinable hunk size. Develop learning object module accordingly.
Best Practice: Smaller learning chunks of material or objects that can be combined	• Training material • Training setting	

Research in end-user training methods has been limited, focused primarily on traditional modes of training (e.g., the classroom), and most of the research is based on established theories in psychology as well as IS. Perhaps the most influential premise has been social cognitive theory. As theorized by Bandura (1977), training methods using observational/behavioral modeling have been found to be more effective than lecture-based training methods (Gist, 1988; Yi et al., 2003). Yi et al. (2001) also showed that the inclusion of retention enhancement mechanisms though symbolic representation also have a significant positive impact on training outcome.

The use of self-paced computer-based training tools provides a rich area of research that has seen little activity. The results in this area have been inconsistent; results have shown better, same as, and worse performance than traditional classroom training (Bowman et al., 1995; Desai 2000).

Limited research using collaboration in end-user training has found both positive and negative results (Davis et al., 2004).

Researchers have also compared exploratory- with instructional-based training methods (Davis and Bostrom, 1993), and conceptual with procedural methods of training (Olfman and Mandviwalla, 1994), but have found no direct impact of these different methods on training outcomes. On the other hand, a comparison of optimistic preview versus realistic preview provided positive support for using optimistic preview to enhance training outcomes (Webster and Martocchio, 1995). Finally, the use of advanced organizers (Sein and Bostrom, 1989) or enhancement of self-ability to achieve (Martocchio, 1994) has a positive impact on training, mediated through individual differences.

User

This dimension represents classifying users based on a variety of factors such as job classes, roles, and learning style. An organization may view all users as the same and adopt the same training method for everyone. At the other end of the continuum, an organization may classify users according to the criteria listed above and then choose either to match users to a specific method or provide a variety of choices in terms of training method. U is linked to the trainee component of conceptualization of learning strategy (see connecting line 3 in Figure 11.6). At the learning strategy level, the emphasis is on whether to allocate resources to adopt a user classification and matching strategy. Should that be the case, user classification at the training strategy level is essential. Best practice is to match users to training method by job class and learning style (or free choice).

Learning Content

Learning content represents the learning objects that combine to form the training materials. At one end of the continuum are large chunks that are difficult to combine for different classes and users. This is the traditional and current form in many organizations. At the other end of the continuum are smaller chunks, mostly in electronic form (database of learning objects), that are easy to reuse and combine for a specific class or individual user. This approach is a future best practice that many organizations are adopting. L is linked to the supply chain positioning of learning strategy in that smaller reusable chunks would be easier to create, distribute, and deliver in an online context (see connecting line 4 in Figure 11.6). The best practice is to provide smaller learning chunks of material or objects that can be combined and reused.

Using the Learning and Training Strategy Models

Management can use our models as tools to audit an organization's existing approach to training. The learning strategy model can be used to create a "strategy profile." We show a sample learning strategy profile in Figure 11.7. The profile will highlight areas where management needs to pay attention. Depending on the nature of the audit, the model can be used to balance an existing approach into a true learning strategy, or to create a new learning strategy. The process of developing a learning strategy is as follows:

1. Pick a dimension.
2. Determine where the organization fits (or should fit) along the continuum that describes this dimension.
3. Repeat Step 2 through the other three dimensions, ensuring that each choice is compatible with the other choices.

Figure 11.7 **Example Learning Strategy Profile**

Dimension	Choice	Components	Choices
Focus	Technology ·········· Business X (Business)	Training needs determination	Training group ········· Functional area X (Functional area)
		Training ownership	Training group ········· Functional area X (Functional area)
		Integration of business tasks into contents of training sessions	Not addressed ········· Addressed X (Addressed)
Conceptualization	Discrete ·········· Continuous X (Continuous)	Trainee conceptualization	Passive learner ········· Active learner X (Active learner) All same ········· Different X (Different)
Integration	Reactive ·········· Proactive X (Proactive)	Links with business areas	Weak ········· Strong X (Strong)
		Links with HR	Weak ········· Strong X (Strong)
		Links with IS group	Weak ········· Strong X (Strong)
		Location of training group	Independent ····· IS ····· HR X (IS)
		Who offers business process training	Training group ········· Functional area X (Functional area)
Positioning	Insourcing ·········· Outsourcing X (Insourcing)	Traditional supply chain	Create → ········· Distribute → Deliver X (Create) ········· X (Deliver)
		Online supply chain	Create → ········· Distribute → Deliver X (Create) ········· X (Deliver)

Once a learning strategy is established, the needed actions, policies, and practices can be implemented to achieve the strategy. Of course, an organization need not position itself on a continuum end point. Major organizational characteristics or areas where resources are allocated to achieve the strategic position determine location on each dimension.

The training strategy model allows management to address any training situation where specific user type(s) need to be trained on a specific IT tool, and select the training method that should be used to attain the appropriate level of knowledge. The best practices developed from research and practice can be used to guide the selection of a training strategy. The linkages to the learning strategy profile (see Figure 11.6) can be evaluated to make sure the training strategy is aligned with the learning strategy.

IMPLICATIONS FOR RESEARCH AND PRACTICE

Clearly, the first research goal is to validate the model. One study carried out two simultaneous evaluations using the strategy models (Simonsen, 2004; Simonsen and Sein, 2004). The summative evaluation used our model to assess an oil company's training initiatives. The goal of the formative evaluation was to validate the model itself. The findings suggested that the models were very useful for evaluating the training function in organizations. The company was able to implement our models to assess whether the training initiatives were achieving their purpose. At the same time, the findings also suggested that the frameworks need further development. For example, the definitions of the dimensions needed to be expanded to capture a greater variety of organizational arrangements. Furthermore, the relationships among dimensions within each model and between models need to be explored in more depth.

Our framework identifies other important research issues. We state them in the following subsections as research questions. For each, we list the guidelines for practice that emerge from current best practice. We then list research issues, that is, what research needs to be carried out to add to the best practice. Our focus will be on key research issues and best practices for the training strategy model. We do not list citations for best practices based on our research. Citations are provided for major claims that are not based on our research.

Research Question #1

What specific methods exist for assessing the training needs and developing training outcomes of different categories of end users?

Guidelines from Best Practice

- There is a real trend today toward embedding learning directly into workflow/business process. Needs-assessment techniques should be integrated into business process analysis. Needs assessment can be accomplished partly through constant analysis of the feedback from users, help desks, and trainers. Some sample needs-assessment methods are cited in Table 11.2 under the focus dimension.
- In developing training outcomes, the knowledge level framework (see Figure 11.1) can be used to ensure that all necessary knowledge levels are being addressed.
- Involving the training manager from the beginning of a new training project is an effective way to identify training needs.

Research Issues

- Although there is evidence that particular need-assessment methods have worked, we need good models for applying specific methods, based on specific job/function categorizations and training outcomes.
- Additional methods of best practice in training needs-assessment need to be identified and studied, especially ones that can be integrated with or derived from business process analysis techniques.
- There is a need to develop new techniques to map current techniques into different knowledge levels.
- Although a trainee's manager's buy-in and support for a training program is essential, very little literature addresses this issue. There is a need for studies that explore it in more depth.

Research Question #2

How do we further refine and develop the knowledge-level framework for categorizing training outcomes? Since training outcomes drive the entire training strategy process, a good framework is very important in this area.

Guidelines from Best Practice

- Training literature and practices have almost exclusively stressed command-based and tool procedural knowledge, and, to some extent, business procedural knowledge (levels 1 to 3). Based on our research, we recommend including the motivational (level 6) and considering including conceptual levels (tool and business, levels 4 and 5).
- Trainers and training materials should aim to assess and, if needed, increase a trainee's beliefs that she or he can master the training. There are two primary beliefs involved: self-efficacy (belief that one is capable of carrying out necessary training behaviors) and outcome expectations (belief that behaviors will produce desired outcomes). In software training, both have been shown to affect learning, especially self-efficacy (Compeau et al., 2006). Both of these beliefs would be considered part of meta-cognitive knowledge. They are both related to the motivation level, which captures the desirability of the training outcomes.

Research Issues

- Each of the levels in the framework needs to be better grounded and linked to needs-assessment techniques for generating specific outcomes and training methods for achieving particular knowledge levels. In addition, developing a map outlining what levels of knowledge are needed for different technologies would be very useful to guide training strategy development.
- Other than the research on self-efficacy (Compeau et al., 2006), the meta-cognitive knowledge level has not received much attention in the end-user training literature. As end-user tools and applications change faster than ever, and as organizations focus more on continuous learning using online technology, learners need to be self-regulated, that is, to have the ability to learn on their own, which requires meta-cognitive knowledge and skills. We do not yet know how to fashion an active/self-regulated computer user, let alone how we use software to support this type of user. This is a rich area of research. Recent papers by Gravill et al. (2002, 2003) provide a good idea of the type of work that needs to be done is this area.

Research Question #3

What specific methods exist to appropriately categorize end users?

Guidelines from Best Practice

- Currently, most companies are using job-role competencies to classify users because training methods and materials are mapped to job-role competencies.
- Trainers should be trained to recognize and utilize individual differences, especially learning styles. An excellent trainer in an instructor-led situation can get learners to understand and use their own learning styles. He/she is also able to design flexible materials to accommodate different types and styles.
- Self-based training packages that accommodate individual differences should be developed or acquired.

Research Issues

- It is not well known how user categorizations are applied, or which specific method of categorizing users has proved to be most useful in practice.
- As stated above, most companies are using job-role competencies. For example, the Ford Learning Network contains (Sketch, 2003): 400,000 titles, including 1500 online courses, 800 classroom courses, 1900 e-books, internal resources, and 48,000 twenty-minute learning objects in various media designed as just-in-time solutions or refreshers. Workers self-assess skills, determine gaps, and find training opportunities. Besides linking methods and materials to job-role competencies, learning management systems capture additional individual characteristics in their user profiles. A user profile can be used to personalize learning content for the trainee. As such, profiling and job-role competencies categorizations need to be studied.
- Although there has been a lot work on learning styles in education in the last few years, we see little of that research applied in IT domains. Some studies were conducted in the early 1990s and there was debate about the usefulness of learning style (Bostrom et al., 1990; Bostrom et al., 1993; Ruble and Stout, 1993). A resurgence of research in this area is needed.
- The trend towards creating small reusable learning objects that can be combined to build training content has made the possibility of personalizing training a reality. A learning object (LO) is a combination of "learning" concept with object concept (borrowed from IS and computer science). It is small/granular (but there are no specific size constraints), self-contained, and self-describing (it contains metadata). An LO is usually complete enough to accomplish one or more learning outcomes. It is reusable, revisable, standards based (e.g., SCORM, XML) and data based (e.g., is part of a scalable repository of objects). An example of an LO might be a single PowerPoint slide or portion of a slide. This slide (or portion) can be easily packaged in other presentations. Shayo and Olfman (chapter 12 in this book) provide an overview of the accomplishments and challenges that lie ahead in the LO area.

  Most learning content is currently developed for a specific purpose, such as a course, and not for the sake of populating an object base. We will see more content developed as LOs that can be deployed in multiple settings and personalized for individual learners. Personalization involves two issues: selection of the right LOs and then packaging them with appropriate context information (Longmire, 2000). Personalization is a rich area of research in training as well as content/knowledge management in general.

- Since almost all uses of categorizations in the past have been linked to instructor-led training, we need to know how to apply user categorizations to self-based training.
- Moreover, the literature does not indicate how to match individual differences with the technology to be learned.

Research Question #4

How do we combine and define training methods?

Guidelines from Best Practice

- As we have discussed, there are many different forms of instructor-led vs. self-based learning approaches. This problem is accentuated in the e-learning area where many different terms are used to describe similar training approaches (see Sasidharan and Santhanam, chapter 10 of this book). For example, virtual learning, distributed learning, and distance learning are all terms for learning at any time, in any place. It seems that best practice is to use a very general framework that accommodates the needs of each organization.
- A major problem for most companies and universities is how to blend or combine different training methods to create an effective approach. There is not a great deal of end-user training research or research in general in this area. The general best practice we have found is to use a mix of instructor-led and self-based methods.

Research Issues

- To create a cumulative body of knowledge, there must be well-understood frameworks for major independent variables, training methods and users (addressed under the previous question). Such a framework is missing for end-user training methods. This problem has worsened with the advent of the new computer-based training approaches generally described as e-learning. There is a need to gain conceptual clarity and develop conceptual frameworks. Sasidharan and Santhanam, chapter 10 of this book) address this issue and suggest such a framework.
- It is not well known how training methods are categorized, or which specific way of categorizing methods has proved to be most useful in practice. Methods used in practice and research need to be investigated to generate useful frameworks to guide both research and practice.
- Blending practices as well as guidelines for combining training methods need to be investigated.
- As we described earlier, there is a strong movement in learning systems toward the use of learning objects. We are now seeing terms such as object-oriented instructional design (OOID) appear in both the educational research and practitioner literatures. The MIS field has a great deal of expertise and experience in object-oriented systems design (OOSD). Much of this knowledge will be applicable to OOID. Research is needed to help guide OOID to create effective training methods. This area, along with many others we have listed, provides a great opportunity for joint research between MIS and educational researchers.

Research Question #5

The overarching question, built upon all of the previous questions, is: What are the most appropriate training methods for specific types of end users and specific IT tools given a set of training outcomes (training strategies)?

Guidelines from Best Practice

- A key best practice is matching training methods to training outcomes (knowledge levels). Online self-based end-user training is better suited for attaining knowledge levels 1 to 3; other levels are currently best obtained through instructor-led training. Advance organizers are particularly useful for developing conceptual knowledge.
- Best practice to achieve accelerated learning is to use methods that focus on conceptual, motivational, and meta-cognitive knowledge levels.
- An effective way to implement a business focus is to break training materials into smaller learning objects/chunks of job-specific/workflow-based learning.
- Self-based training best practice is to integrate learning objects into workflow/business process applications used. As we discussed earlier, workflow learning is becoming an important outcome for organizations. This is a new area that we believe will become the dominant best practice.
- An efficacious way to sequence training is to use behavior modeling followed by hands-on practice. One consistent research finding is that behavior modeling, in which trainees watch a demonstration of computer skills and then trainees reenact the modeled behavior, is more effective than computer-aided instruction, lecture-based instruction, and self-study (Yi and Davis, 2004).
- Using collaborative learning practices with pairs, teams, learning communities, and so forth, can pay handsome dividends. Although there has been no end-user training research on collaborative learning, the research evidence from education clearly demonstrates that learning together is better than competitive or individual learning.

Research Issues

- In general, studies are always needed to compare training methods in terms of their abilities to achieve training outcomes for a specific set of users and IT tools.
- Implementing specific training methods based on specific IT tools and user types given a set of training outcomes is an area that needs to be studied in much more depth. Some key areas are:
  - Online self-paced tools: A great deal of training on end-user tools such as Microsoft Office is being done using online self-paced tools. For example, Drexel University offers 2000 Skillsoft courses for credit (see http://www.drexel.com/skillsoft). A majority of these are IT courses. These tools use a form of behavior modeling with built-in assessments and feedback. There has been minimal research in this area; clearly more is needed.
  - Collaborative learning: There has been only one study (Yi and Davis, 2004) that we could find in end-user training research that investigated collaborative learning. We believe that collaborative learning, especially peer learning, provides rich possibilities to enhance training effectiveness. We are seeing success with peer programming and peer learning of programming. We feel that similar results can be found with end-user tools. For research directions in this area, see Gupta and Bostrom (2004).

- Simulation and simulators: There has been a huge growth in the last few years in the use of simulation and simulators in training. For example, more and more end-user application training is being done using a simulator instead of the actual software. Simulators allow better control and easier assessments with feedback linked to assessments. We have seen no studies in this rich area.

- Workflow learning: Web services foster the integration of enterprise applications into unified real-time systems. This enables organizations to redefine learning as a core business process to be automated like any other process. Thus, companies and vendors are incorporating learning technology into their applications and products. This individualized, small-chunk, immediate, work-driven, relevant learning is commonly referred to as workflow or workflow-based learning. We believe that workflow-based training will be a major source of end-user training in the future. This is a very rich area of research. For a good overview of workflow learning see workflowlearning.com.

• In practice, post-training support appears to be a separate domain from training. There is clearly a need to understand how to integrate the training and ongoing support functions (e.g., help desk, reference materials, and knowledge bases). This issue is related to the workflow learning issue discussed above. In the future, distinctions among "learning," "KM," "EPSS" will become blurred, as the focus will be on workflow and doing the job better. Training will not be treated as a separate event needing followup; learning will be continuous, workflow/job driven, and available on demand. Thus, the training process we outlined in Figure 11.4 will radically change. Research is needed to guide this integrated evolution.

• There is a need to document how organizations are using accelerated training methods in practice.

• There is a need to develop guidelines for trainers and instructional designers that help them break training materials into smaller learning objects/chunks of job-specific/workflow-based learning.

CONCLUSION

Five years ago, we emphasized that it is imperative to take a broader view of computer skills training for the workforce of the future. Based on our research and examples from the field, we argued that it was not enough to emphasize the skills/knowledge outcomes of training. We proposed that training needs to move closer to education and that a comprehensive strategy needs to be developed by organizations to meet this objective. We proposed a framework to develop such a strategy based on a knowledge level framework, which we also developed. Today, the need to take a comprehensive view of training is even more crucial. When viewed in the light of the broad perspective of HCI, as this book does, the need to further enhance the frameworks to provide training strategy guidelines for practice is vital. In this chapter, we have attempted to do so. Based on our work since 1999, we have enhanced our views and frameworks on training. As with any effort in academia, this is very much a work in progress. We invite researchers and practitioners in the training field to continue to work on this vital issue, keeping in mind the ultimate objective of developing workers who will successfully apply what they have learned about IT tools in their work situation.

REFERENCES

Adkins, S. Introduction to workflow learning. Workflow Learning Institute, 2003 (available at http://www.internettime.com/workflow/intro_wfl.htm, accessed on October 23, 2004).

Andrews, A., and Niederman, F. A firm-level model of IT personnel planning. In *Proceedings of the 1998 ACM SIGCPR Conference on Computer Personnel Research.* New York: ACM Press, 1998, pp. 274–285.

Bostrom, R.P. Tutorial: e-learning: facilitating learning through technology. In *Proceedings of the Americas Conference on Information Systems*, Tampa, FL, 2003, 3159–3164.

Bostrom, R.P.; Olfman, L.; and Sein, M.K. Learning styles and end-user training: A first step. *MIS Quarterly*, 17, 1 (1993), 118–120.

Bostrom, R.P.; Olfman, L.; and Sein, M.K. The importance of learning style in end-user training. *MIS Quarterly*, 14, 1 (1990), 101–119.

Carroll, J.M., and Rosson, M.B. Managing evaluation goals for training. *Communications of the ACM*, 38, 7 (1995), 40–48.

Compeau, D.; Gravill, J.; Haggerty, N.; and Kelley, H. Computer self-efficacy: a review. P. Zhang and D. Galletta (eds.), *Human-Computer Interaction in Management Information Systems: Foundations. Advances in Management Information Systems*, Volume 5, Armonk, NY: M.E. Sharpe, 2006.

Compeau, D.; Olfman, L.; Sein, M.; and Webster, J. End-user training and learning. *Communications of the ACM*, 38, 7 (1995), 24–26.

Coulson, T.; Shayo, C.; Olfman, L. and Rohm, C.E.T. ERP training strategies: conceptual training and the formation of accurate mental models. In *2003 ACM SIGMIS CPR Conference*. New York: ACM Press, 2003, pp. 87–97.

Davis, S.A., and Bostrom, R.P. Training end users: an experimental investigation of the roles of the computer interface and training methods. *MIS Quarterly*, 17, 1 (1993), 61–85.

Desai, M.S. A field experiment: Instructor-based training vs. computer-based training. *Journal of Instructional Psychology*, 27, 4 (2000), 239–244.

Gist, M.E. The influence of training method and trainee age on acquisition of computer skills. *Personnel Psychology*, 41, 2 (1988), 255–265.

Gravill, J., and Compeau, D. Self-regulated learning strategies and computer software training. In *Proceedings of the International Conference of Information Systems*, Seattle, WA, 2003, 788–793.

Gravill, J.; Compeau, D.; and Marcolin, B. Metacognition and IT. The influence of self-efficacy on self-awareness. In *Proceedings of the Eighth Americas Conference on Information Systems*, Dallas, TX, 2002, 1055–1064.

Gupta, S., and Bostrom, R.P. Collaborative e-learning: information systems research directions. In *Proceedings of the Tenth Americas Conference on Information Systems*, New York, 2004, 3031–3039.

Kutzschan, A.O., and Webster, J. HCI as MIS. In D. Galletta and P. Zhang (eds.), *Human-Computer Interaction in Management Information Systems: Foundations.* Armonk, NY: M.E. Sharpe, 2006.

Lacity, M.; Willcocks, L.; and Feeny, D. The value of selective IT sourcing. *Sloan Management Review*, 37, 3 (1996), 13–25.

Longmire, W. A primer on learning objects. Learning Circuits (available at http://www.learningcircuits.org/2000/mar2000/longmire.htm, accessed on October 23, 2004).

Martocchio, J.J. Effects of conceptions of ability on anxiety, self-efficacy, and learning in training. *Journal of Applied Psychology*, 79, 6 (1994), 819–826.

Masie Center. Top learning decisions for 2000. *Learning Decisions Interactive Newsletter*, January (2003).

Nelson, R.R.; Whitener, E.M.; and Philcox, H.H. The assessment of end-user training needs. *Communications of the ACM*, 38, 7 (1995), 27–39.

Nilsen, H., and Sein, M.K. Determinants of user satisfaction with the support function. In *Proceedings of the 2002 ACM SIGCPR Conference on Computer Personnel Research*, New York, NY: ACM Press, 2002, pp. 47–51.

Olfman, L., and Mandviwalla, M. Conceptual versus procedural software training for graphical user interfaces: a longitudinal field experiment. *MIS Quarterly*, 18, 4 (1994), 405–426.

Olfman, L.; Bostrom, R.P.; and Sein, M.K. Training with a business focus: a best practice. In *Proceedings of the BITWORLD 2001 Conference*. CD-ROM. 2001.

Olfman, L.; Bostrom, R.P.; and Sein, M.K. A best-practice based model for information technology learning strategy formulation. In *Proceedings of the 2003 ACM SIGMIS Conference on Computer Personnel Research*. New York: ACM Press, 2003, pp. 75–86.

Olfman, L., and Sein, M.K. Ten lessons for end-user trainers. In *Information Systems Management Series*. Boston: Auerbach, 1997, no. 94–00–07, 10 pp.

Robey, D.; Boudreau, M.-C.; and Rose, G.M. Information technology and organizational learning: a review and assessment of research. *Accounting, Management and Information Technologies,* 10, 2 (2000), 125–155.

Rosenberg, M.J. *e-Learning Strategies for Delivering Knowledge in the Digital Age.* New York: McGraw-Hill, 2001.

Ruble, T.L., and Stout, D.E. Learning styles and end-user training: an unwarranted leap of faith. *MIS Quarterly,* 17, 1 (1993), 115–117.

Sein, M.K., and Bostrom, R.P. Individual differences and conceptual models in training novice users. *Human-Computer Interaction,* 4 (1989), 197–229.

Sein, M.K.; Bostrom, R.P.; and Olfman, L. Training end-users to compute: cognitive, motivational and social issues. *INFOR,* 25, 3 (1987), 236–255.

Sein, M.K.; Bostrom, R.P.; and Olfman, L. Rethinking end-user training strategy: applying a hierarchical knowledge-level model. *Journal of End User Computing,* 11, 1 (1999), 32–39.

Simonsen, M. *Conceptual Frameworks in Practice: Evaluating End-User Training Strategy in Baker Hughes.* Master's thesis, University of Bergen, 2003.

Simonsen, M., and Sein, M.K. Conceptual frameworks in practice: evaluating end-user training strategy in an organization. In *Proceedings of the 2004 ACM SIGMIS Conference on Computer Personnel Research.* New York: ACM Press, 2004, pp. 14–24.

Sketch, E. Ford's drive toward quality education. Chief Learning Officer Profile (available at http://www.clomedia.com/content/templates/clo_cloprofile.asp?articleid=180&zoneid=4, accessed on October 23, 2004).

Snell, N. Why Johnny can't do client server. *Inside Technology Training,* 1, 7 (1997), 21–26.

Webster, J., and Martocchio, J.J. The differential effects of software training previews on training outcomes. *Journal of Management,* 21, 4 (1995), 757–788.

CHAPTER 12

THE LEARNING OBJECTS ECONOMY
What Remains to Be Done?

CONRAD SHAYO AND LORNE OLFMAN

Abstract: *Learning objects consist of small chunks of digitized instructional content that can be delivered online. Each small chunk is a self-contained, objective-centered unit whose content helps the learners achieve a demonstrable learning objective. The application of the learning object concept in education and training was borrowed from object-oriented theory, which is used in computer and information science to design and develop high-quality software products more quickly, cheaply, and flexibly. Just as each software object is self-contained and fulfills a single programmed objective, each learning object is self-contained, focuses on a single job task, and fulfills a single learning objective. The idea that learning objects can provide learners with customized, just-in-time instructional content that meets their specific learning needs is compelling. However, despite projections that the corporate e-learning market (outside the school system) would surpass $11.5 billion by 2003, a learning objects economy has remained elusive. The learning object economy infrastructure—national politics and policies, digital learning objects repository, specifications and standards, and so forth—is still evolving. A critical mass of learning object producers, managers, and consumers has yet to materialize. Problems with teachers' resistance to change, lack of clear compensation, and rights management systems still persist. The jury is still out! We review the existing literature on the learning objects economy, focusing on its promises and challenges, on what has been accomplished thus far, and on what remains to be done to make it a reality.*

Keywords: *Learning Object, Learning Objects Economy, Reusable Learning Object, Reusable Information Object, Learning Objects Value Chain, Learning Objects Standards, Learning Object Specifications*

BACKGROUND

Reusing and sharing knowledge has always been at the core of human civilization. Later generations learn and benefit from those who came before. We do not have to reinvent the wheel or repeat the mistakes of our predecessors. Each civilization, in its own way, has tried to develop educational and training systems that ensure the codification and dissemination of knowledge to succeeding generations

Figure 12.1   **Technology Innovation Life Cycle**

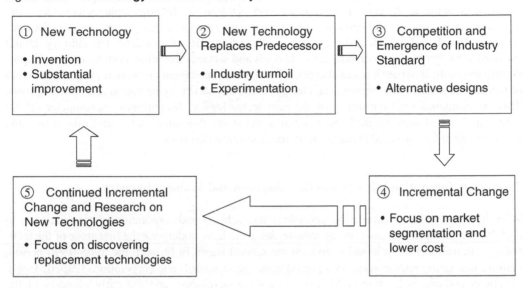

(Houghton and Sheehan, 2002). In this quest, handedness and tool making gave way to language and speech; oral traditions gave way to stylized pictographs, writing, reading, and printing.[1] Then home schools gave way to public schools, colleges, and universities where the instructor was the primary manager of learning and assessor of learners. Publishing companies, bookstores, and libraries (public and private) became sanctuaries for learners and instructors alike. Instructors adopted books or other materials that fit the objectives of their courses. Instructional designers, authors, and experts on particular subject matters wrote content for self- or classroom-based learning. Books were developed in a linear fashion, and consequently took a long time to write or update (Looney and Sheehan, 2001). Once a book is borrowed from a library, it is not possible to share it; you have to buy your own, or initiate a recall for it. But current information and communication technologies (ICTs) will change all that. One person's use of a digital learning resource will not affect someone else's use of the same resource.

ICTs such as the Internet infrastructure are bringing about dramatic changes in the way instructional materials are designed, developed, codified, and delivered. Traditional methods of developing and delivering instructional content are too linear, monolithic, and instructor-centered (Looney and Sheehan, 2001). Content is mass-produced and not customizable to learners' immediate needs. In today's dynamic and competitive learning environment, there is demand for just-in-time instructional content that meets learners' needs, interests, and learning styles. Moreover, any investment in learning should show demonstrable returns. Learners want to learn anytime, anywhere, and at their own pace. The maturing of the ICT infrastructure and its application in learning are bringing about a technological discontinuity in the education and training industry.

Technological discontinuities occur when breakthrough innovations significantly improve the technological state of the art of entire industries (Tushman and Anderson, 1986; Christensen, 1997; Christensen and Ovedorf, 2000). Such technological discontinuities may threaten to upset the mode of doing business in the industry (Ehrnberg and Jacobsson, 1997). According to Anderson and Tushman (1990, 1997), Utterback (1994), and Angle and Van de Ven (2000), technological innovations tend to have a life cycle of their own. As shown in Figure 12.1, the cycle begins with a new technological invention or the arrival of a newer technology that is a substantial improvement on the current state of the art. An era of turmoil then occurs as the new technology replaces its predecessor. In this era, entrepreneurs and innovators experiment with alternative designs and compete for market share. Finally a dominant design emerges as the industry default standard. The industry default standard wins by offering a combination of features and services that allow customers to make productive use of the design at a reasonable price. Then the technological innovation cycle enters an era of incremental change. The incremental changes focus on market segmentation and lowering costs. This era continues until the arrival of the next technological discontinuity. Schumpeter (1942) argues in favor of technological discontinuities and states that unprofitable methods, firms, and industries must be liquidated to release resources for new enterprises.

Technology Innovation Life Cycle in the Education and Training Industry

With the introduction of computing technology into schools and corporations during the early to mid-1960s, the education and training industry seems to have undergone the first stage of the technology innovation life cycle and is now on the second stage. In Phase I, the 1965–1990 period, mainframes, minicomputers, and PCs gained wide use in schools and corporations (Papert, 1980). Computer-assisted instruction (CAI) programs were developed, and the early pioneers in the e-learning market who had developed specifications for learning technologies started experimenting with their proprietary standards (Harel and Papert, 1991; Molnar, 1975; Burg and Thomas, 1998; Gates, 1998). In Phase II, the 1990–2005 period, multimedia PCs were developed, schools and corporations started using CAI programs on videodiscs or CD-ROM disks, object-oriented authoring systems gained wider popularity in schools and businesses, most schools hooked into the Internet, and MP3 technology and Peer to Peer (P2P) networks became popular. We saw the formation of the Advanced Distributed Learning (ADL) initiative, and the emergence of e-learning industry standards and specifications, for example, the shareable content object reference model (SCORM), and Institute of Electrical and Electronic Engineers' learning object meta-data (LOM) standard (IEEE—LOM) (Wiley, 2001; Merrill, 1999; Polsani, 2003). Starting from 2006 and beyond, we will be witnessing the transition from Phase II to Phase III, and then to Phases IV and V.

Although governments' and international organizations' efforts to develop common learning object standards, as well as corporate and academic institutions' development of learning object–based online learning prototypes, provide anecdotal evidence for the future viability of a learning objects economy, only the future will tell exactly when the remaining phases will be attained. In the next section we define what a learning object is.

DEFINITION OF A LEARNING OBJECT

"Learning objects" mean different things to different people. They come in all shapes and formats: large, small, and in between. They could comprise book chapters, journal articles, discussion papers, Web pages, or tutorials. Or they could also be simulations, multimedia exercises, animations, Java applets, PowerPoint presentations, or QuickTime movies (Oliver, 2001). Instructional designers, managers, content developers, trainers, and learners could use a single learning object to meet a range of different purposes. This confusion has even led some learning object proponents to suggest that searching for a single definition of a learning object may be inappropriate at this stage (Higgs et al., 2003).

Figure 12.2   **Components of an RLO**

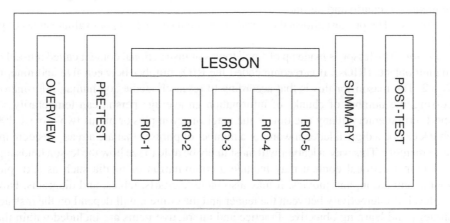

According to IEEE Learning Technology Standards Committee:

> A learning object is any entity, digital or non-digital, that can be used, re-used, or referenced during technology-supported learning. Examples of technology-supported learning include computer-based training systems, interactive learning environments, intelligent computer-aided instruction systems, distance learning systems, and collaborative learning environments. Examples of learning objects include multimedia content, instructional content, learning objectives, instructional software and software tools, and persons, organizations, or events referenced during technology supported learning (IEEE-LTSC-LOM, 2001).

Most scholars of the learning object economy agree that this definition is too broad (Wiley, 2001). Some scholars and practitioners have come up with narrower definitions:

- "The smallest independent structural experience that contains an objective, learning activity and an assessment" (L'Allier, 1997).
- "A learning object contains a learning objective, a unit of instruction that teaches the objective, and a unit of assessment that measures the objective" (Quinn and Hobbs, 2000).
- "Any digital resource that can be used to support learning" (Wiley, 2001, p. 4).
- "A lesson, packaged with an overview, pre-test, summary and post test that is based upon a single job task" (Navy Reusable Learning Object [RLO] Content Development Guidelines, 2003, p. 2).
- "Any non-rival resource, digital or non-digital that can be used, reused or referenced in service of learning activities" (Sloep, 2003, p. 6).

We find the definition provided by the Navy e-learning content development guidelines more precise and comprehensive because it specifies the contents of a learning object. The Navy uses the term "reusable learning objects," or RLOs, instead of "learning objects." They define reusable information objects as smaller components of a lesson.[2] Figure 12.2 shows the components of an RLO according to the Navy e-learning content development guidelines (2003). The components of an RLO are: overview, pre-test, lesson, summary, and post-test.

Overview: The overview section provides the introduction, importance, objective, pre-requisites, scenario and outline.

Pre-test: The pre-test allows the learner to test out of the RLO or evaluate areas of greater focus.

Lesson: The lesson is made up of small topics of instructional content called reusable information objects (RIOs). It is recommended the RIOs number between five and nine, that is, 7 ± 2. The reason for this is that according to research studies on human information processing, the number of chunks of information an average person can temporarily store in short-term memory at any one time is the magical seven plus or minus two (Sousa, 2000). A chunk can be a digit, a letter, a word, or a number of phrases that are already resident in long-term memory. This way, a learner will most likely be able to see how the lesson holds together.

The instructional content may include a combination of media such as text, pictures, sound, animation, and movies. It may also include charts, tables, and diagrams. However, the level of interactivity between the leaner and the content will depend on the instructional strategy and learning objective. Practice and interactive items are included within the content to ensure that at the end the learners are able to fulfill the promise of the learning objective. An example of a learning objective is:

"At the end of this lesson, you will be able to define what a learning object is and what it is not!"

Summary: The summary provides a review, next steps, and additional resources the learner might need if necessary.

Post-test: Finally the post-test allows the learner to assess what has been learned. Note that the RLO overview, pre-test, summary, and post-test sections act as the wrapper for the lesson section.

In summary, reusable learning objects consist of small chunks of digitized instructional content that can be delivered online. Each small chunk is a self-contained, objective-centered unit, whose content helps the learners achieve a demonstrable learning objective. The learning objective focuses on whether learners will be required to recall what was learned or apply the knowledge to perform a task (Clark, 1989; Merrill, 1998). Moreover, the reusable learning objects can also be aggregated into modules, courses, curricula, or entire programs or disciplines. The learning object aggregation hierarchy is presented in Figure 12.3.

Exhibit 12.3 presents an example of the RLO aggregation hierarchy (Navy Reusable Learning Object [RLO] Development Process, 2003). In the example, the curriculum is for a medical assistant certificate. For simplicity we have included two courses: (1) Introduction to Human Anatomy, and (2) Emergency Medical Care Procedures. The latter course is then decomposed into five modules 2.1, 2.2. . . . 2.5. The first module, 2.1: General First Aid, is further decomposed into five RLOs: 2.1.1, 2.1.2 . . . 2.2.5. Then, the third RLO, 2.1.3, is decomposed into five RIOs: 2.1.3.1, 2.1.3.2 . . . 2.1.3.5. As already discussed above, the necessary graphics, animations, text, audio, and illustrations will be used to assemble the RIO content.

Note that each component in the hierarchy is assigned a specific objective that must be accomplished. Each sub-objective fulfils the terminal objective of a higher component in the aggregation hierarchy. For example, each RIO objective described in 2.1.3.1, 2.1.3.2 . . . 2.1.3.5 enables the fulfillment of the single terminal objective for RLO 2.1.3: Non-surgical Methods for Clearing an Airway Obstruction. Similarly, each RLO objective in 2.1.1, 2.1.2 . . . 2.2.5 facilitates the accomplishment of the single terminal objective assigned to Module 2.1: General First Aid and so on. The ultimate objective is to prepare students to take the state medical board medical assistant examination.

Figure 12.3   **The Learning Object Aggregation Hierarchy**

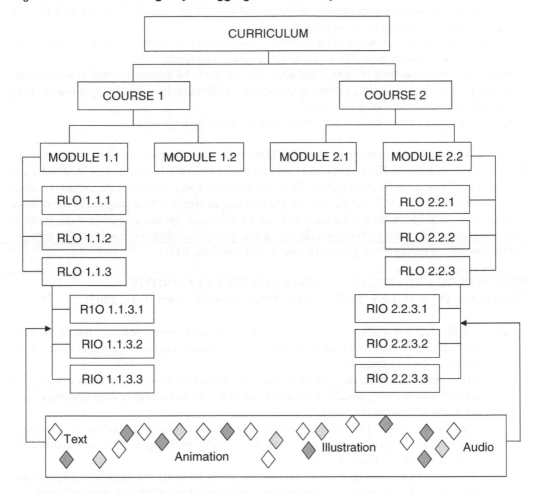

CHARACTERISTICS OF A REUSABLE LEARNING OBJECT

A reusable learning object must:

* Be aware of other learning objects.
* Enable users to have a common method for identifying, searching, and retrieving other learning objects.
* Be aware of the learners—who they are, their proficiency level.
* Recognize who the learner is and record information about the learner's experience.
* Be able to change its behavior based on learner performance—that is, learners might be sent to different places in the content based on test scores, language preferences, learning style inventories, competencies, certifications, organizational roles, and other data.
* Interoperate with other learning objects from multiple sources.
* Be aware of the contexts in which it is used.
* Be able to satisfy a single learning objective.

- Be portable and reusable in other contexts.
- Permit decomposition into smaller self-contained meaningful chunks, each of which plays a special role in instructional design methodology.
- Allow each chunk to communicate with other chunks in other learning content management systems. What happens within a chunk is that chunk's business.
- Conform to overarching standards that allow the content to be aggregated and disaggregated.
- Function as an independent performance support aid that can be called up by a learner who needs a specific piece of information.
- Allow a learner to summon it for a more in-depth learning experience.

Learning content management systems (LCMSs) based on different operating systems (e.g., Windows, UNIX, Mac OS X, Solaris, Linux), and database platforms; using different Web browsers (e.g., Internet Explorer or Firefox) will be able to use common specifications and standards to share data about learners. This will include how the learners access courses, their progress in the course, and their pre-test/post-test scores. Learners will also be able to access learning content using information and communication technologies (ICTs) such as personal digital assistants (PDAs), laptops, cellular phones, or personal computers (Houghton and Sheehan, 2002).

BENEFITS OF CREATING A LEARNING OBJECTS ECONOMY (MERRILL, 1999; WILEY 2001; SLOEP, 2003; MASSIE, 2003; IMS, 2003)

1. Ability to dynamically find, aggregate, or disaggregate learning objects—that is, increasing the value of learning objects by making them easily accessible, reusable, interoperable, durable, and scalable.
2. Make personalized learning "just in time" by decreasing how long it takes a learner to transfer knowledge gained to productive use—that is, increasing human learning transfer at the lowest possible cost.
3. Use of common industry-wide set of specifications and standards to ensure that learning objects are of high quality, easily searched, profitably exchanged, and dynamically configured to satisfy unique needs.
4. Ability to copy learning objects from one repository to another through any delivery system that conforms to the common industry-wide set of specifications and standards.
5. Reduction of effort and time used to create new instructional materials by leveraging and repurposing both internal and external learning objects.
6. Ability to provide secure access to the learning objects and dynamically enforce digital rights through a digital rights management system.
7. Ability to repurpose the content of learning objects to apply to different contexts and be delivered by different learning content management systems via multiple ICT channels, for example, mobile devices, phone, print, laptops, and personal computers.
8. Ability to provide automated security through efficient digital rights management and license tracking.
9. Ability to add, delete, update, or modify a learning object without impacting other learning objects in the repository.

In the next sections we use the value chain concept (Porter, 1990) to help organize and discuss the key drivers in the learning objects economy. For each driver we describe what has been accomplished, and what remains to be done.

THE LEARNING OBJECTS ECONOMY VALUE CHAIN

The learning objects economy can be broken down into a series of value-creating activities that combine to generate profits for firms participating in it. The value-creating activities can be viewed as the building blocks that create learning modules and services valuable to its learners. The value chain consists of primary activities, support activities, and profit margin, as shown in Figure 12.4. Primary activities consist of the physical creation of the reusable learning objects, storage, delivery to the learner, and supporting the learners after signing a learner's contract.

Support activities complement the primary activities by providing the infrastructure support needed. These will include national economies, national policy and politics, standards and specifications, ICTs, and level of technology literacy. Profit margin is the difference between the collective cost of the learning object value-creating activities (primary and support), and the amount the end-user learners are willing to pay to benefit from using the learning objects in their education or training endeavors.

The primary activities in the value chain are:

- *Inbound Logistics*—Receiving and storing of learning objects, instructional content, graphics, and multimedia assets in digital repositories.
- *Transformation*—Analysis, design, and development of RLOs, for example, assembly and packaging of topics, courses, curricula, and programs.
- *Outbound Logistics*—Storing of validated RLOs, and delivery and tracking of customized instruction (topics, courses, curricula, and programs).
- *Sales and Marketing*—Retailers, aggregators, exchanges, and portals bring RLO buyers and sellers to connect, communicate, and transact business.
- *After-Sales Service*—Help desk services, mentorship of learners, evaluations (formative and summative).

Learning objects value creation is made possible by the support of the following secondary activities:

- National economies, politics, policies, and international organizations
- Global economy
- Information and communication technology infrastructure
- Enlightened and technology-literate learners
- Procurement of RLOs from existing digital repository

In the next sections, we briefly discuss each of the items in the learning object economy value chain by identifying the main actors, what has been accomplished, and what remains to be accomplished.

NATIONAL ECONOMIES, POLITICS AND POLICY, AND GLOBAL ORGANIZATIONS

National governments in developed countries such as the United States, Australia, Canada, and Britain continue to fund initiatives that support the development of an infrastructure for a reusable learning object economy concept (Massie, 2003). Exhibit 12.1 shows initiatives from a sample of international Web sites. We will briefly summarize a few of these initiatives here.[3]

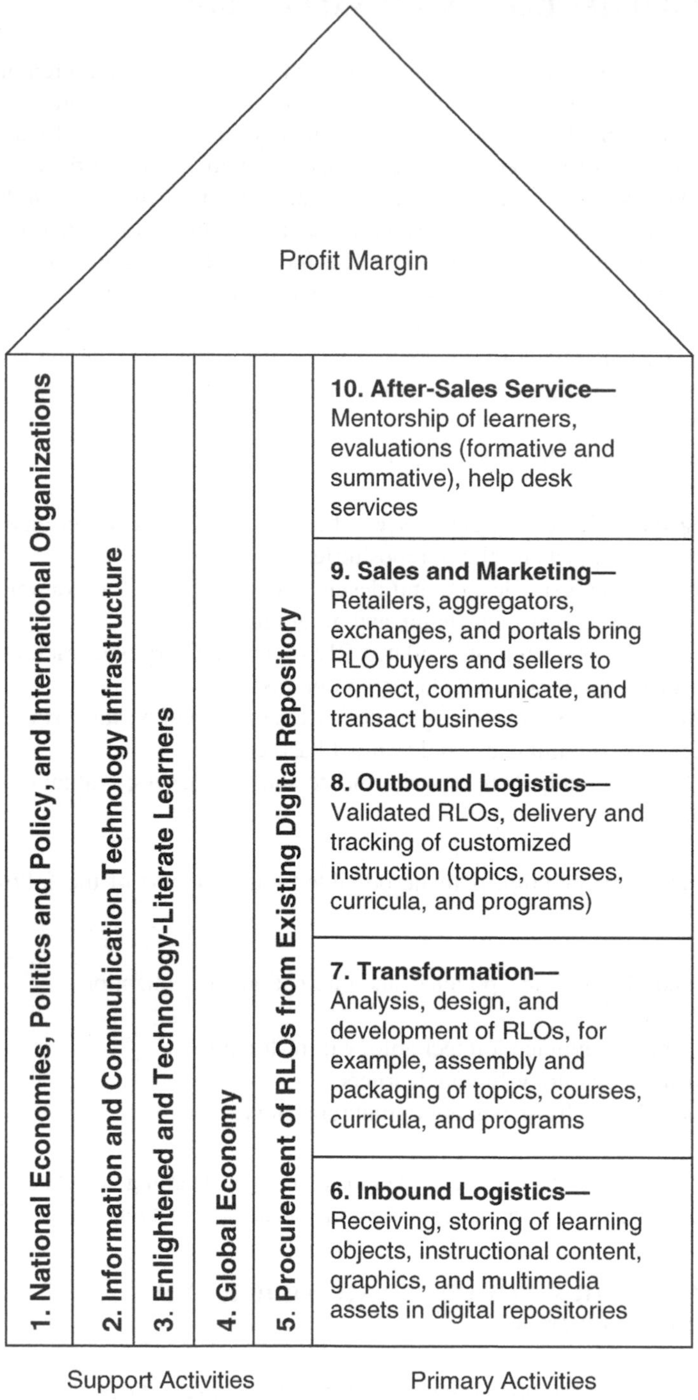

Figure 12.4   The Learning Objects Economy Value Chain

Profit Margin

1. National Economies, Politics and Policy, and International Organizations

2. Information and Communication Technology Infrastructure

3. Enlightened and Technology-Literate Learners

4. Global Economy

5. Procurement of RLOs from Existing Digital Repository

10. After-Sales Service—
Mentorship of learners, evaluations (formative and summative), help desk services

9. Sales and Marketing—
Retailers, aggregators, exchanges, and portals bring RLO buyers and sellers to connect, communicate, and transact business

8. Outbound Logistics—
Validated RLOs, delivery and tracking of customized instruction (topics, courses, curricula, and programs)

7. Transformation—
Analysis, design, and development of RLOs, for example, assembly and packaging of topics, courses, curricula, and programs

6. Inbound Logistics—
Receiving, storing of learning objects, instructional content, graphics, and multimedia assets in digital repositories

Support Activities   Primary Activities

The main initiative in the United States is the Advanced Distributed Learning (ADL) initiative that brought together partners in industry, academia, and government to develop the sharable content object reference model (SCORM)—a common technical framework that will facilitate interoperability of reusable learning objects across computer and Web-based learning courseware. Other initiatives in the United States include the Multimedia Educational Resource for Learning and Online Training (MERLOT), the Open Knowledge Initiative (OKI), and many others. Australia and New Zealand have the Le@rning Federation, which was launched in 2001 to facilitate the breakdown of content into discrete "objects" and their reassembly and repurposing to meet the needs of teachers and students in those countries' schools.

Canadian initiatives include eduSourceCanada, CANARIE, and BELLE. The mission of eduSourceCanada is to create a network of linked and interoperable learning object repositories across Canada. The Canadian Network for the Advancement of Research, Industry, and Education's (CANARIE) mission is to accelerate Canada's advanced Internet development and use. The Broadband Enabled Lifelong Learning Environment (BELLE) has the main responsibility for building object repositories. Other initiatives in Canada include the Campus Alberta Repository of Educational Objects (CAREO) and the Portal for Online Objects in Learning (POOL) project.

Britain has the Center for Technology Interoperability Standards (CETI), formed to advise British universities and colleges on the strategic, technical and pedagogic implications of educational technology standards. The European Union has the Alliance of Remote Instructional Authoring Distribution Networks for Europe (ARIADNE) initiative, which focuses on developing tools and methodologies to produce, manage, and reuse learning objects.

International organizations such as the IMS Global Learning Consortium, the Aviation Industry CBT Committee (AICC), and the Institute of Electrical and Electronics Engineers' Learning Technology Standards Committee (IEEE-LTSC), to mention but a few, have been at the forefront of establishing the framework for the learning objects economy. The IMS Global Learning Consortium was formed in 1997 as part of the National Learning Infrastructure Initiative. Although its initial focus was higher education in the United States, it has since broadened its membership and its scope to include members from educational, commercial, and governmental organizations from all over the world. Its mission is to develop and promote open specifications for e-learning products worldwide. The AICC was formed in 1988 as an international organization to provide guidelines that will facilitate the development, delivery, and evaluation of CBT and related training technologies for the aviation industry. It is now working closely with the IEEE-LTSC, IMS, ADL and others to develop common specifications. The IEEE is an international standards organization for electrical and electronic products, including computing, information, and communication technologies. The IEEE-LTSC is charged with the responsibility of developing accredited technical standards, recommended practices, and guidelines for learning technology. The committee is organized into five working groups. Each group coordinates with other organizations such as the IMS and AICC to produce specifications and standards for the learning objects economy.

Summary

We have seen that efforts are being made by federal and state governments as well as international organizations to make a learning objects economy possible. Most national and international efforts have focused on facilitating the development of standards that will allow interoperability of reusable learning objects across computer and Web-based learning courseware. However, as noted by Sloep (2003) and others, more needs to be done.

What Remains to Be Done

When fifteen renowned world leaders on the learning objects economy met in September 2002 in San Francisco, they concluded that national policy initiatives are still needed to address the issues of digital rights management and intellectual property that continue to discourage the development of electronic commerce. They noted that since most current successful learning object applications have tended to be proprietary, national governments should help in the development of digital learning object repositories by promulgating policies that encourage individuals and institutions to make available their learning objects for free or a fee (Johnson, 2003).

Policies should also be enacted to encourage individuals and educational institutions to join in the creation of the learning objects economy. Nobody will spend time creating learning objects to give them away for free. There is a need to educate learning object designers and developers. One way is to provide public funding targeted at educating a new generation of instructional analysts, designers, and technologists versed in object-oriented analysis and design techniques. MIS departments could seize the opportunity to establish a minor in learning object technology. The current establishment of a special interest group (SIG) on reusable learning objects by the Association of Information Systems (AIS)[4] and the *Interdisciplinary Journal of Knowledge and Learning Objects*[5] are steps in the right direction.

National governments should also create a market for RLOs by consuming RLO-based learning materials themselves. Moreover, organizations that have benefited from using RLO prototypes should be encouraged to provide information on the costs and benefits of using RLO-based instructional strategies instead of traditional strategies. MIS academic researchers should continue to demonstrate where the RLO approach works or does not work (Zhang et al., 2004). Research is also needed to identify the critical national economic, political, and policy-related factors that are needed to support a learning objects economy.

INFORMATION AND COMMUNICATION TECHNOLOGY INFRASTRUCTURE

The information and communication infrastructure is comprised of specifications and standards, and the software tools needed for the analysis, design, authoring, and delivery of the reusable learning objects.

Specifications and Standards

As noted earlier, pioneers in the e-learning market started to develop specifications for learning technologies as early as the mid-1980s. Prominent among the early pioneers were the Alliance for Remote Instructional Authoring and Distribution Networks for Europe (ARIADNE), the Aviation Industry Computer-Based Training Committee (AICC), the Dublin Core, IEEE, and the Instructional Management System (IMS) Global Learning Consortium. The early efforts concentrated on metadata tagging, learner profiling, content sequencing, and computer-managed instruction. Each pioneer worked alone and focused on different areas of the standards.

Lessons learned from standards battles between cellular phone companies, the VHS and Betamax videotape formats, the Microsoft and Linux operating systems, and so forth, called for the need to establish a common set of standards that would allow learning objects to be reusable, interoperable, portable, and accessible using Internet and communication technologies. Many realized that proprietary specifications would stall the creation of the learning objects economy. There was a need to define criteria on how the learning objects will be created, categorized, stored, searched, reused, aggregated, and delivered to individual learners. This caused business, academic, and governmental leaders from different national and global institutions to come together to develop common specifications and standards.

In 1997, the Department of Defense (DOD) and White House Office of Science and Technology Policy (OSTP) launched the Advanced Distributed Learning (ADL) initiative in order to merge the best guidelines and specification ideas from the various organizations and develop a common reference model. In 2000 ADL released the sharable content object reference model (SCORM), consisting of a set of guidelines and specifications that will allow accessibility, interoperability, durability, and reusability of Web-based learning objects, systems, and services. The key players that participated in developing the SCORM include the:

- Advanced Distributed Learning (ADL) Initiative (http://www.adlnet.org)
- Alliance for Remote Instructional Authoring and Distribution Networks for Europe (ARIADNE) (http://www.ariadne-edu.org)
- Institute for Electrical and Electronic Engineers Learning Technology Standards Committee (IEEE-LTSC) (http:/www.ltsc.ieee.org)
- Aviation Industry Computer-Based Training Committee (http://www.aicc.org)
- Instructional Management System (IMS) Global Learning Consortium (http://www. imsproject.org)
- Dublin Core Metadata Initiative (DCMI) (http://dublincore.org)
- World Wide Web Consortium (W3C) (http://www.w3.org)

Each organization above is involved in an aspect of making the learning object economy possible. Some organizations have been tasked to develop functional specifications for certain areas (Massie, 2003). Exhibit 12.2 provides a brief summary of the main standards and specifications and the involvement of each key player. Some of the common specifications that have already been developed include:

- Learning object metadata—descriptive information about learning objects that allows indexing, storage, searching, and retrieval from a repository.
- Content packaging—defines a standard way to organize and package learning objects so that they can be distributed and exchanged among different systems and tools.
- Learning object sequencing—description of the data that defines the intended sequencing behavior of the learning objects as they interact with the learner.
- Question and test interoperability—definition of an eXtensible Markup Language (XML) that can be used to represent questions and assessments in any vendor platform.
- Metadata XML binding specification—defines specifications that will allow the creation of learning object metadata (LOM) instances in XML. This will facilitate the interoperability and exchange of LOM instances between various systems.
- Run-time interaction—the launching, communicating with, and tracking learning objects in a Web-based environment that takes place between a learning management system and a browser.

Common specifications, once developed, are sent to standards bodies such as IEEE for accreditation. The accredited standards become de facto industry standards once they find wide acceptance in business government and academia. IEEE has already accredited the Learning Object Metadata and Content Packaging.

The standards are supposed to realize the following:

Interoperability: the ability to select and aggregate learning objects from different sources between or within different systems; and the ability of different systems to communicate, exchange, and interact transparently.

Reusability: the ability to aggregate, disaggregate, repurpose, or reuse learning objects quickly and easily; and the ability to use the learning objects in different contexts. Reusability requires learning objects to have the properties of inheritance, encapsulation, aggregation, composition, and polymorphism. These properties are based on object-oriented programming theory.

Manageability: ability of systems to know the learner, track information about the learners' interaction with the learning objects, and manage the selection and aggregation of customized learning objects for the learner.

Accessibility: ability for a learner to access the customized learning objects using appropriate learning technologies.

Durability: ability for buyers to have the flexibility to use learning objects from different vendors, and to benefit from reusability and interoperability properties of learning objects without additional significant investment of time and money.

Scalability: ability to configure learning technologies and expand their functionality, and to leverage learning technologies by expanding their use to other areas.

Affordability: ability to ensure that organizations and individuals can invest in learning technologies that provide demonstrable value.

De Jure and de Facto Standards

When a standards body such as IEE LTSC or the International Standards Organization (ISO) accredits a specification, it becomes a de jure standard. De jure is Latin for "by right," or "of law." A de jure standard may become a de facto standard if it is widely adopted.

A de facto standard is a specification that is widely adopted, for example, TCP/IP, whether it has been accredited or not. The best scenario is when a de jure standard also becomes a de facto standard. De facto is Latin for "existing in fact" or "of fact"—lawfully or not.

As shown in Table 12.1, the standards development process has seven phases, which generally follow the systems development life cycle. Note that the final phase is similar to acceptance testing. Each organization tasked with initiating a specification liaises and seeks input from all other organizations in order to eventually succeed.

Software Tools

Analysis and Design

Since learning objects are meant to behave just like their software programming object counterparts, it is possible to use existing object-oriented computer-assisted software design (CASE) tools (e.g., Rational Rose) to analyze and design learning objects. Unified modeling language (UML) diagrams, such as use cases, sequence diagrams, state and chart diagrams, activity diagrams, and class diagrams, will be useful at the analysis stage. Design class diagrams and interaction diagrams should be used at the design stage. An example of using UML notation to depict the overall learning object design conceptual model is shown in Figure 12.4. (IMS, 2003).

Table 12.1

The Specifications and Standards Development Process

Phase	Activity
1	A learning need that may have a technological solution is identified.
2	A requirements analysis and feasibility study is conducted to identify possible viable solutions.
3	A feasible solution is selected and detailed technical specifications are written for its implementation. Various consortia or working groups such as IMS, Dublin Core, ARIADNE, or AICC may be assigned to develop the technical specifications.
4	The specifications are tested on a pilot basis. A pilot system is developed and used to test the technical specifications under extreme and normal situations. Feedback is sought on what works, problems, and beta tester reactions. The ADL Laboratories are the ones mostly used as test beds.
5	The feedback is used to further improve the specifications and retest them until they are ready for submission to an accrediting standards body.
6	The tested specifications are now submitted to an accrediting body such as the IEEE-LTSC, ISO/IEC JTC1/SC36, or CEN/ISSS/LT-WS for review and development of a working draft.
7	The working draft is taken through an open consensus-based process and officially balloted on. If approved, it becomes a de facto standard.

Authoring and Delivery

There are three different tools available for authoring and delivery of instructional content in the industry: (a) content management systems (CMSs), (b) learning management systems (LMSs), and (c) learning content management systems (LCMSs). CMSs are used for the creation and administration of online content. Macromedia's Dreamweaver is an example of a CMS. LMSs are used to administer education and training programs. Learners can use a LMS to evaluate their learning progress, and to collaborate with their peers. Instructors can use a LMS to target, deliver, track, analyze, and report on the progress of their students. Most LMSs don't have the ability to *create* instructional content. LCMSs are hybrid systems that function both as CMSs and LMSs. They are used to author, approve, publish, and manage learning objects. Currently, the distinction among the three is fading and the term LMS is being used for LCMS.

The LCMS acts as a learner interaction management system. It delivers the learning modules, and monitors, tracks, and scores learner performance. It is the information system that glues the course vendors with the learner and provides the services the learner might need. A learner may sample a course offering before entering into a learning contract with an e-learning provider. Also, a learner may use an LCMS to obtain information about design and course specifications prior to entering a learning contract. Once a learner enters into a learning contract, the LCMS will monitor and provide progress reports to the learner at any time. The LCMS must also have the ability to allow the learner to repudiate a learning contract or transfer to another provider.

Blackboard, WebCt, and IBM's Lotus Workplace Collaborative Learning are the more popular proprietary LCMSs in the industry, but many other open source and free LCMS challengers are emerging and challenging the dominant players. Most of the new LCMSs have adopted SCORM and IMS specifications.[6]

Summary

There are attempts by software vendors to adopt some of the SCORM/IMS specifications. In fact a few software vendors have representatives in the standards and specification organizations. We have also seen attempts by instructional analysts and designers to use existing object-oriented analysis to design CASE tools such as IBM's Rational Rose. LCMSs are still evolving. Proprietary LCMS producers such as Blackboard and WebCt are trying to make their LCMSs less proprietary due to the challenges they are receiving from new vendors.

What Remains to Be Done

Most instructional designers and content authors do not have experience with UML or CASE tools. MIS departments can help in this. Multidisciplinary programs between MIS and Education departments must be initiated to cross-train students who will eventually become future creators of learning objects. MIS departments can also take the lead by establishing a degree minor in learning object technology.

Additionally, LCMS vendors need to adopt more of the SCORM/IMS specifications such as simple sequencing and learner design (Sloep, 2003). The recent emergence of open source and free LCMS vendors that are adopting SCORM/IMS specifications will facilitate quicker standardization.

ENLIGHTENED AND TECHNOLOGY-LITERATE LEARNERS

The success of a learning objects economy depends in part on having people who understand the benefits as well as the challenges posed by such an economy. Virtual learning requires participants who can think fast, type fast, and are not afraid of being tracked by a computer system. The so-called Nintendo generation—kids who grew up playing Nintendo-like object-oriented computer games—may have the necessary computer skills, but older generations will have to take computer literacy courses.

It may therefore be easier to introduce learning objects to the Nintendo generation (younger elementary, secondary, and university student population) than to older learners. This is more so in the workplace where older workers are most likely to be found. Non-computer-literate workers may feel pressure to complete online training programs offered by their organizations if the programs are part of their professional development. Such pressure will be high especially if employers are paying for training or providing company time for employee online training. Pressure will also mount if employees have to complete collaborative learning sessions that involve their peers or members of their communities of practice.

Learner characteristics such as learning styles, self-discipline, and work experience may also influence adoption of learning objects. Similarly, online instructor characteristics such as mentoring or teaching style, teaching experience, attitudes towards instructional technology, computer self-efficacy, and availability will become important factors in a learning objects economy.

A recent study (Griffith, 2003) found that teachers' resistance to RLO adoption was mainly caused by difficulties of integrating learning objects into LCMSs, lack of knowledge about best practices for developing learning objects and development guidelines, and lack of technical knowledge. Administrators in academic and training institutions should be convinced about the value of implementing the RLO approach so that they can provide teachers with the needed resources to migrate from more traditional instructional approaches to the RLO approach (The COHERE Group, 2002).

What Remains to Be Done

Research needs to be conducted to attest to the effectiveness of learning objects as a viable approach to online instruction. For example: will RLOs make it easier to learn from the online modules, and thus reduce the online training drop-out rates noted by Rossett and Shafer (2003) or Mayer et al. (2001)? What levels of learner content customization are needed to facilitate faster RLO adoption? A more comprehensive study on why there is resistance to RLO adoption by some teachers, academic institutions, and corporations is also needed.

There are legal factors as well. Employers may find it easier to track employee online learning performance and the transfer of that learning to the workplace. Legal issues related to promotion, demotion, or firing of employees based on learning transfer would have to be addressed. Federal and state laws and regulations may be necessary.

GLOBAL ECONOMY

The last twenty years have seen an unprecedented expansion of businesses into global markets with value chain activities spread throughout the world. National boundaries are becoming more transparent as trading blocks such as Canada, the United States, and Mexico (formed by the North America Free Trade Agreement [NAFTA]); the European Union (EU); and the Association of Southeast Asian Nations (ASEAN) countries exchange goods and services. Offshore and near-shore outsourcing is becoming a global phenomenon. Outsourcing companies are forced to develop or rely on a well-educated and trained global workforce where pieces of work can be performed across time zones without compromising quality. A learning objects economy would provide the means for offering standardized training across the globe.

The rapid adoption of English as the lingua franca for international commerce and availability of more reliable translation software applications will pave the way for the adoption of a learning objects economy worldwide.

Most learning objects standards and specification groups including the Dublin Core Metadata Initiative, IEEE, IMS Global Learning Consortium, and the International Organization for Standardization (ISO), to mention but a few, have international representation.

What Remains to Be Done

There are research opportunities to investigate the cultural implications of standardized education and training across the globe. Also, despite the rapid adoption of English as the lingua franca for international commerce, RLO content may have to be translated from English to other languages or from other languages to English. The costs and benefits of supporting an RLO global economy where intellectual property rights are enforced still need to be worked out.

PROCUREMENT OF RLOS FROM AN EXISTING DIGITAL REPOSITORY

There is a chicken-and-egg relationship between the availability of learning objects in a digital repository for reuse, and the building and deployment of new learning objects. A good analogy is with being required to write a research paper that depends on journal articles that have not yet been written.

Few object repositories are now available in the public domain. Repositories such as those listed in the Academic ADL Co-lab (http://projects.aadlcolab.org/repository-directory/repository_listing.asp) and the University of Texas (http://elearning.utsa.edu/guides/LO-repositories.htm) are still in their infant stage, and have yet to garner a critical mass of learning objects (Higgs et al., 2003, Sloep, 2003). Educational institutions may have to collaborate by contributing their current digital assets to an initial repository; they may also partner with publishing companies, most of which already have digitized instructional content.

Faculty trained as instructional content analysts and designers should be provided time and money to disaggregate existing content into the appropriate levels of granularity and build the initial learning objects. Contribution of learning objects could also be requested or licensed from commercial ventures, although this will require working out intellectual property, licensing, and quality issues to the satisfaction of all parties.

As noted elsewhere, federal and state governments should continue to provide seed money for the creation, use, and management of learning object digital libraries and help grow the learning objects economy through government, academia, and industry partnerships.

INBOUND LOGISTICS

Instructional analysts and designers should be able to use an LCMS to access learning object digital repositories. As they do so, they must make sure that they adhere to existing licensing or purchase agreements. They should also make sure they have access to other internal resources such as training manuals and standard operating procedures in digital or paper form.

TRANSFORMATION: DEVELOPMENT OF INSTRUCTIONAL MATERIALS, FOR EXAMPLE, TOPICS, COURSES, CURRICULA, AND PROGRAMS

The learning object development life cycle uses the PADDIE model (planning, analysis, design, development, implementation, evaluation) used in software development (Clark, 1989). Cisco[7] and the U.S. Navy[8] have adopted this model as well. What follows is a brief description of the activities involved at each phase.[9]

Planning

At the planning phase, the learning object production manager receives client instructional requirements and performs an initial review. The production manager then assigns resources to the project by designating a project team leader, instructional designers, subject matter experts, multimedia, and quality assurance support. The project team leader determines the scope of the requirement, establishes team roles and responsibilities, and drafts a plan of action and milestones (POA&M).

Analysis

At the analysis phase, the team reviews and familiarizes itself with existing content and determines what will be taught. This includes researching learning object repositories and company education and training assets. The team collects additional information from the client if necessary. It then develops an instructional architecture that resembles the learning object aggregation hierarchy shown in Figure 12.3. Each reusable learning object (RLO) is assigned a single terminal objective that specifies what the learner will be able to do after completing the RLO lesson; and each reusable information object (RIO) is assigned an enabling objective that supports the overall terminal objective of the RLO as demonstrated in Exhibit 12.3. The RLOs are then organized and sequenced.

Additional analysis is carried out to:

- Determine prerequisite knowledge needed for each RLO and RIO.
- Identify RIO types (whether they are concept, fact, procedure, process, principle, or theory types).
- Determine references for each RLO and RIO.
- Organize and sequence the RIOs.
- Search for additional information if necessary.
- Conduct a quality review of the analysis phase using a specific checklist.

Design

This phase provides a framework for the overall development of effective instruction. A comprehensive conceptual model for the reusable learning objects design is shown in Figure 12.5 (IMS, 2003). The model shows that a learner or staff (developer, designer etc.) gets a role in the teaching–learning process, to perform activities that lead to a specific outcome within a learning environment. The environment consists of the required reusable learning objects and services needed to perform the activities. An activity can either be a learning activity, or support activity. Each activity describes precisely what role (a teacher or learner, etc.) should do, and what environment is available to do it within the act. The assignment of roles to activities is determined by a method or by a notification.

A notification is triggered by the outcome of an activity. The method is designed to attain specific learning objectives assuming the learners have the needed prerequisites. A method consists of one or more play(s). In turn a play consists of one or more act(s) and an act consists of one or more role-part(s). The acts in a play follow each other in sequence. A method may contain conditions that further refine the specific activities and environment entities for persons and roles based on their properties.[10]

At the design level, the following activities should be accomplished:

- Design the overview section of the RLO.
- Design all the RIO components by specifying where text content, graphics, video, simulation, and other elements should go.
- Develop or acquire practice items that will evaluate learning within the RIO.
- Develop or acquire assessment items that will be used in the pre-test and post-test.
- Develop or acquire interaction items that will provide opportunity to practiced learned information.
- Develop or acquire graphics and multimedia elements.
- Develop meta-data for each instructional item.
- Develop search keys or keywords that will be used to locate the content and graphic media.
- Review each RLO and its associated RIO for: accuracy, clarity, completeness, and instructional soundness.
- Update the plan of action and milestones.

Instructional designers should also make sure that the instructional content that goes into each RIO is well thought out based on the RIO type (fact, procedure, concept, process, principle, or theory), the desired cognitive level (remember or perform), and instructional strategy (receptive, directive, guided discovery, or exploratory) (Cisco Systems, 2003).

302

Figure 12.5 **Overall Learning Design Conceptual Model**

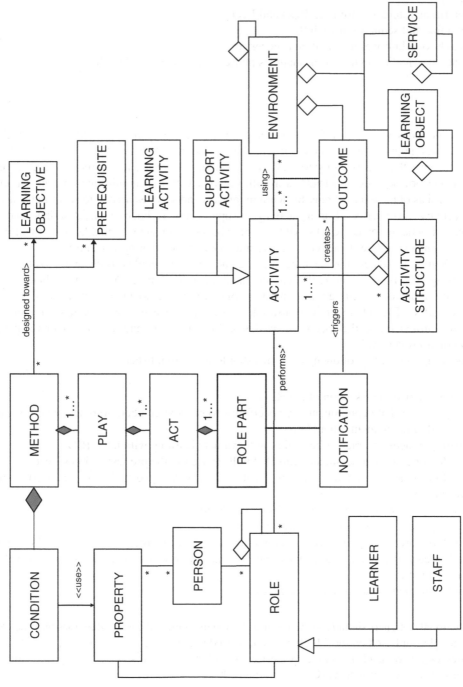

Source: Adopted from IMS *Learning Design Best Practice and Implementation Guide,* version 1.0 (http://www.imsproject.org/learningdesign/). Used with permission from IMS.

Development

At the development phase, the design is implemented by developing the overview, RIOs, and summary. Once each part is developed, subject matter experts, instructional design reviewers, and a quality assurance manager carry out a quality assurance evaluation to make sure that the learning objects fulfill their stated instructional objectives.

What Remains to Be Done

Although existing CASE tools have the potential to ensure robust analysis and design of RIOs and RLOs, we have observed that most people working in this area do not have the necessary background. As already noted this is one area where MIS departments could take the lead by coordinating with education departments and or creating an MIS minor degree in learning object technology.

OUTBOUND LOGISTICS: DEVELOPED MATERIALS, TOPICS, COURSES, CURRICULA, AND PROGRAMS

The developed materials are then packaged and uploaded into a Learning Content Management System (LCMS) for immediate delivery to learners.[11] The Instructional Management System (IMS) Global Learning Consortium has provided a specification for content packaging that specifies how content is imported, stored, managed, and manipulated for instructional purposes. Technical details on content packaging are beyond the scope of this paper.[12]

SALES AND MARKETING

Sales and marketing is where e-learning vendors bring RLO buyers and sellers together to communicate and transact business. Five types of markets seem to be taking shape in the learning objects economy (Johnson, 2003).

Proprietary Exchanges

These are private markets where learning object–based courses are used exclusively on a company's intranet or extranet. The learning object repositories are hidden behind the corporate firewalls. For example, Cisco Systems, Microsoft, and AT&T Business Learning Services have developed and used RLOs for company training, but have decided to keep their repositories private.

Commercial Exchanges

These are commercial markets where end users and aggregators can license learning object repositories. Traditional publishers and new training companies are the candidates for this market. This may be the holy grail of the learning objects economy.

Free Exchanges

These are arrangements similar to MERLOT or EOE where faculty from academic institutions received public funding to develop learning object repositories for public consumption. Faculty members are encouraged to contribute learning objects for peer review for inclusion into a learning object repository.

Shared Exchanges

These are arrangements where high-quality learning objects are developed or purchased using federal or state government funds for inclusion in a repository that is open only to specific groups of people within those countries.

Peer-to-Peer Exchanges

These are markets where end users will use P2P networks to share learning objects, similar to the Kazaa and Napster music-sharing networks.

MENTORSHIP OF LEARNERS, EVALUATIONS (FORMATIVE AND SUMMATIVE)

This is a service function where learners may need a more personalized service from help desk instructors. Trained help desk instructors should be available and distributed across multiple time zones and languages so that they can support learners. Learners may request a variety of services, some of which may not be related to learning. For example, learners may have technical or platform-related problems that need immediate attention.

LCMS should gather statistical data about learners and their performance so that it can suggest other learning opportunities to them. This is analogous to Amazon.com's practice of informing you that people who bought the title you are buying also bought other books that might interest you. Also, it may be possible to suggest alternative career choices to the learners based on their education, training, and experience profile.

Challenges and Opportunities for a Viable Learning Objects Economy

Challenges

Although much has been accomplished in building parts of the learning objects infrastructure, more needs to be done. Mere knowledge and application of robust object-oriented practices to developing instructional content will not get the learning objects economy off the ground. Many complex issues that need immediate attention include creating a critical mass of instructional analysts and designers, developing a critical mass of digital learning object repositories, resolving intellectual property and digital rights management at the national and international levels, and convincing more software vendors to adopt current specifications and standards. National governments should continue to provide public funds and create demand for reusable learning object-based courses.

Moreover, the mental models of traditional instructors schooled in the teacher/manager model that were first implemented in public schools in the 1980s will need to be unfrozen. Traditional instructors should see the usefulness of spending time, money, and energy to develop learning objects and integrate them into their teaching. School administrations should provide the necessary infrastructural support to make it easier for instructors to develop and experiment with learning objects. Instructors should collaborate in research studies that demonstrate the effectiveness of blended or pure online educational solutions.

Our experience also indicates that more needs to be done in educating graphic designers and multimedia technologists in object-oriented theory, object-oriented analysis and design techniques, instructional theory, and cognitive psychology. They will need this knowledge to develop high-quality learning objects. A multidisciplinary approach involving MIS, education and computer science departments may be necessary. Moreover, MIS departments may take the lead by establishing a cognate minor degree in instructional technology.

Opportunities

Online learning using RLOs offers great potential for reinventing education and training (Schank, 2001; Shneiderman, 1998). MIS researchers now have the opportunity to address some questions posed by the RLO economy:

- Why have individuals, groups, and organizations been slow to adopt learning objects? What are the main resistance factors, and what are the possible solutions?
- What is the demonstrable effectiveness of the RLO approach? What are the learning outcomes (learning performance, satisfaction, performance on the job, productivity, mastery) for a variety of job tasks and individual characteristics, for example, learning styles, attitudes towards technology, computer self-efficacy, and so forth?
- How does the RLO approach facilitate transferring learning to the job, as compared to alternative approaches? Why?
- How can different instructional design models be integrated into the RLO approach for given varieties of learning tasks, individual characteristics, teacher characteristics, and Internet technologies?
- Are the research findings reported in the MIS education and training literatures still valid in a reusable learning object environment?

Exhibit 12.1

Sample of Global and National Learning Objects Economy Initiatives

Nations/Global Organizations	Brief Description
Global Organizations	Instructional Management System (IMS) Global Consortium (http:/imsproject.org); New Media Consortium (http://www.nmc.org); AICC: The Aviation Industry CBT (Computer-Based Training) Committee (AICC) (http:www.aicc.org); Dublin Core Metadata Initiative (DCMI) (http://dublincore.org); IEEE-Learning Technology Standards Committee (IEEE-LTSC) (http://ltsc.ieee.org); International Organization for Standardization (ISO) (http://www.iso.org); World Wide Web Consortium (W3C) (http://www.w3.org)
United States	Advanced Distributed Learning (ADL) Initiative (http://adlnet.org); Multimedia Educational Resource for Learning and Online Training (MERLOT) (http://taste. merlot.org); Open Knowledge Initiative (OKI) (http://web.mit.oki/product); Gateway to Educational Materials (GEM) (http://thegateway.org); EDUCAUSE (http://www.educause.edu)
Canada	Canada's Advanced Internet Development Organization (CANARIE) (http://www. canarie.ca); Broadband Enabled Lifelong Learning Environment (BELLE) (http:// belle.netera.ca); Campus Alberta Repository of Educational Objects (CAREO) (http://www.careo.org); LearnCanada (http://www.learncanada.ca); Portal for Online Objects in Learning (POOL) (http://www.edusplash.net); Canadian Core Learning Resource Metadata Application Profile (CANCORE) (http://www.cancore.ca/indexen.html)

(continued)

Exhibit 12.1 (*continued*)

Sample of Global and National Learning Objects Economy Initiatives

Nations/Global Organizations	Brief Description
Australia and New Zealand	Le@rning Federation (http://socci.edna.edu.au/); Education Network Australia (EDNA) (http://www.edna.edu.au/edna/page1.html); Collaborative Online and Information Learning Services (COLIS) (http://www.colis.mq.edu.au); Information and Communication Technologies (ICT) Based Learning Designs (http://www. learning designs.uow.edu.au/index.html)
Britain	The Center for Educational Technology Interoperability Standards (CETIS) (http://www.cetis.ca.uk/static); Union Learning Fund (ULF) (http://www.dfes.gov.uk/index.htm); University for Industry (UFI) (http://www.learndirect.co.uk); SoURCE (http:www.source.ac.uk)
European Union	Promoting Multimedia Access to Education and Training in European Society effort (PROMETEUS) (http://www.prometeus.org); Alliance of Remote Instructional Authoring and Distribution Networks for Europe (ARIADNE) (http://www.ariadne-edu.org/); European Committee for Standardization/Information Society Standardization System (CEN/ISSS) (http://www.cenorm.be/isss).
Holland	Open University of the Netherlands (OUNL) Educational Modeling Language (OUNL/EML) (http://eml.ou.nl)

Exhibit 12.2

Important Standards and Specifications Being Developed to Support a Learning Object Economy

Specifications and Standards	Brief Description of the Specification or Standard
ADL Initiative– Sharable Content Object Reference Model (SCORM)	A model that references a set of technical specifications and standards (mostly taken from other organizations) that aims to foster creation of reusable learning objects for computer and Web-based learning. SCORM describes: (1) a content aggregation model (CAM), (2) a run-time environment (RTE) model, and (3) a sequencing and navigation (SN) model. The CAM has adopted the content packaging from IMS, the learning object metadata specification from IEEE-LTSC, and the metadata XML binding best practice from IMS/IEEE. The run-time environment model has been adopted from the AICC/IEEE specification. The sequencing and navigation model has been adopted from the IMS simple sequencing specification.
IEEE-LTSC Leaning Object Metadata (LOM) Specification	Defines the attributes required to fully and adequately define a learning object. Some of the attributes include type of object, author, owner, terms of distribution, and format. Others are: teaching or interaction style, grade level, mastery level, and prerequisites.
IMS Content Packaging (CP) Specification	Specifies how to describe and package learning materials, such as an individual course or a collection of courses, into interoperable, distributable packages. Will benefit content producers, LCMS vendors, computing platform vendors, and learning service providers.
IMS/IEE Metadata Binding Best Practice Specification	Defines specifications that will allow the creation of learning object metadata (LOM) instances in eXtensible Markup Language (XML). This facilitates the interoperability and exchange of LOM instances between various systems.

(*continued*)

Exhibit 12.2 (*continued*)

Specifications and Standards	Brief Description of the Specification or Standard
IMS Digital Repositories Specification	Provide specifications that will allow the interoperation of the most common repository functions. Those include XML query and simple object access protocol (SOAP) capabilities.
IMS Simple Sequencing Specification	Specifies how learning objects will be sequentially presented by a LCMS to the learner depending on the outcomes of a learner's interactions with the instructional content.
IMS Learning Design Specification	Provides specifications that allow the use of diverse pedagogical approaches in a learning object such as adaptive, blended, directed, or problem-based or competency-based learning.
IMS Learner Information Package Specification	Defines how information about the learner (individual or group of learners) or a producer of content (creators, providers, or vendors) will be shared among various LCMSs. Will benefit learning object creators, publishers and LCMS software vendors.
IMS Question and Test Interoperability Specification	Proposes a standard XML language for describing questions and tests that will allow the interoperability of content within assessment systems. This benefit publishers, certification authorities, teachers, trainers, publishers and creators of assessments, and the software vendors whose tools they use.

Exhibit 12.3

Example of the Reusable Learning Object Hierarchy (adopted from Navy reusable learning object (RLO) development process, Version 1.0, February 28, 2003)

Curriculum Title		Curriculum Objective
Medical assistant certificate		After completing this curriculum, you will be certified by the state medical board as a certified medical assistant

Course Number	Course Title	Course Objective
1	Introduction to Human Anatomy	After completing this course, you will be able to locate the various parts of the human body in detail.
2	Emergency Medical Care Procedures	After completing this course, you will be able to render appropriate emergency aid to victims in the field.

Module Number	Module Title	Module Objective
2.1	General First Aid	After completing this module, you will be able to recall general first aid techniques.
2.2	Patient Assessment in the Field	After completing this module, you will be able to recognize the assessment sequence for emergency medical care in the field.
2.3	Basic Life Support	After completing this module, you will be able to recall basic life support techniques for upper airway obstruction, respiratory failure, and cardiac arrest.
2.4	Injuries	After completing this module, you will be able to recognize types of injuries and determine management and treatment procedures for each type of injury.

(*continued*)

Exhibit 12.3 (*continued*)

Curriculum Title		Curriculum Objective
2.5	Common Medical Emergencies	After completing this module, you will be able to choose the appropriate treatment and management techniques for the common medical emergencies.
RLO Number	**RLO Title**	**RLO Objective**
2.1.1	Assessing Airway Obstructions	After completing this lesson, you will be able to identify the process for assessing an airway obstruction.
2.1.2	Choosing a Non-surgical Method for Clearing an Airway Obstruction	After completing this lesson, you will be able to identify the process for determining the appropriate non-surgical method for clearing an airway obstruction.
2.1.3	Non-surgical Methods for Clearing an Airway Obstruction	After completing this lesson, you will be able to identify the non-surgical methods for clearing an airway obstruction.
2.1.4	Methods of Artificial Ventilation	After completing this lesson, you will be able to recall the steps in the techniques for artificial ventilation.
2.1.5	Cardiopulmonary Resuscitation	After completing this lesson, you will be able to recall the steps involved in one and two rescuer CPR for adults, children and infants.
RIO Number	**RIO Title**	**RIO Objective**
2.1.3.1	How to Reposition a Victim	After completing this lesson, you will be able to identify the process for assessing an airway obstruction.
2.1.3.2	How to Perform the Head Tilt–Chin Lift Maneuver	After completing this lesson, you will be able to identify the process for determining the appropriate non-surgical method for clearing an airway obstruction.
2.1.3.3	How to Perform the Jaw Thrust Maneuver	After completing this lesson, you will be able to identify the non-surgical methods for clearing an airway obstruction.
2.1.3.4	How to Perform an Abdominal Thrust with the Victim Standing or Sitting	After completing this lesson, you will be able to recall the steps in the techniques for artificial ventilation.
2.1.3.5	How to Perform an Abdominal Thrust with the Victim Lying Down	After completing this lesson, you will be able to recall the steps involved in one and two rescuer CPR for adults, children and infants.

NOTES

1. Please note that older technologies still co-exist with the new.

2. We do not distinguish between "learning objects" and "reusable learning objects" since a learning object, by definition, must be reusable.

3. Many more countries in the developed world, such as Switzerland, France, Germany, Ireland, and Italy, are implementing various learning object initiatives.

4. See AIS Newsletter, August 2004 at: http://www.aisnet.org/newsletter/AISNewsletter2004–08.pdf (accessed on September 30, 2004).

5. Visit http://www.ijklo.org (accessed on September 30, 2004).

6. For more information, visit http://www.criticalmethods.org/collab/v.mv?d=1_71 (accessed on May 1, 2004).

7. See Cisco Systems White Paper on Reusable Learning Object Strategy: Designing and Developing Learning Objects for Multiple Learning Approaches, 2003.

8. Navy reusable learning object (RLO) development process; February 28, 2003.

9. The process described here is based on the Cisco/U.S. Navy content development guidelines.

10. For a more detailed description of the model please visit http://www.imsproject.org/learningdesign/index.cfm.

11. Please note that a beta test may need to be carried out to improve the RLOs further.

12. Please visit http://www.imsproject.org/content/packaging/cpv1p1p3/imscp_bestv1p1p3.html for more discussion on the subject.

REFERENCES

Anderson, P.C., and Tushman, M.L. Technological discontinuities and dominant designs: a cyclical model of technological change. *Administrative Science Quarterly,* 35 (1990), 604–633.

Angle, H.L., and Van de Ven, A.H. Suggestions for managing the innovation journey. In A.H. Van de Ven, H.L. Angle, and M. S. Poole (eds.), *Research on the Management of Innovation: The Minnesota Studies.* New York: Oxford University Press, 2000, pp. 663–698.

Association of Information Systems (AIS) Newsletter, August, 2004 (available at http://www.aisnet.org/newsletter/AISNewsletter2004–08.pdf, accessed on January 12, 2005).

Burg, J., and Thomas, S. Computers across campus. *Communications of the ACM,* 41, 1 (1998), 22–25.

Clark, R.C. *Developing Technical Training.* Beverly, MA: Addison-Wesley, 1998.

Christensen, C.M., and Ovedorf, M. Meeting the challenge of disruptive change. *Harvard Business Review,* 78, 2 (2000), 67–76.

Christensen, C.M. *The Innovator's Dilemma: When New Technologies Cause Great Firms to Fail.* Boston: Harvard Business School Press, 1997.

Cisco Systems White Paper: Reusable Learning Object Authoring Guidelines: How to Build Modules, Lessons and Topics (available at http://business.cisco.com/servletw13/FileDownloader/iqprd/104119/104119_kbns.pdf, accessed on January 12, 2005).

Ehrnberg, E., and Jacobsson, S. Technological discontinuities and incumbents' performance: an analytical framework. In C. Edquist (ed.), *Systems of Innovation Technologies, Institutions, and Organizations.* London: Pinter, 1997, pp. 318–341.

Gates, K.F. Should colleges and universities require students to own their own computers? *CAUSE/EFFECT Journal,* 21, 3 (1998), 51–53.

Graham, I. *Object Oriented Methods: Principles and Practice,* 3rd ed. Harlow, England: Addison-Wesley, 2001.

Griffith, R. Learning objects in higher education. report by the academic ADL co-lab with sponsorship by WebCT. 2003 (available at http://www.academiccolab.org/resources/webct_learningobjects.pdf, accessed on January 12, 2005).

Harel, I., and Papert, S. Software design as a learning environment. In I. Harel and S. Papert (eds.), *Constructionism: Research Reports and Essays 1985–1990 by the Epistemology & Learning Research Group.* Norwood, NJ: Ablex Publishing, 1991, pp. 41–84.

Higgs, P.; Meredith, S.; and Hand, T. Technology for Sharing: a research project to inform VET Australia about learning objects and digital rights management including systems and metadata to support them. Flexible Learning Leader 2002 Report, Australian National Training Authority, 2003 (available at http://www.flexiblelearning.net.au/leaders/fl_leaders/fl1102/finalreport/final_hand_higgs_meredith.pdf, accessed on January 12, 2005).

Houghton, J., and Sheehan, P. A primer on the knowledge economy, 2002 (available at http://www.cfses.com/documents/knowledgeeconprimer.pdf, accessed on January 12, 2005).

IEEE Learning Technology Standards Committee Draft Standard for Learning Object Metadata. IEEE Standards Department, Piscataway, NJ, 2002 (available at http://ltsc.ieee.org/wg12/files/LOM_1484_12_1_v1_Final_Draft.pdf, accessed on November 28, 2005).

IMS Learning Design Information Model, Version 1.0 Final Specification. IMS, 2003 (available at http://www.imsproject.org/learning design/ldv1p0/imsld_infov1p0.html, accessed on January 12, 2005).

Johnston, L.F. Elusive vision: challenges impeding the learning object economy. Macromedia White Paper, 2003 (available at http://download.macromedia.com/pub/solutions/downloads/elearning/elusive_vision.pdf, accessed on January 12, 2005).

L'Allier, J.J. Frame of reference: NETg's map to the products, their structure and core beliefs, 1997 (available at http://web.archive.org/web/20010712183454/www.netg.com/research/whitepapers/frameref.asp, accessed on November 28, 2005).

Looney, M.A., and Sheehan, M. Digitizing education: A primer on e-books. *Educause Review,* 36, 4 (2001), 38–46.

Massie, E. Making Sense of Learning Specifications and Standards; A Decision Maker's Guide to their Adoption, 2nd ed. Industry Report, The Masie Center, 2003 (available at http://www.masie.com/standards/S3_Guide.pdf, accessed on November 28, 2005).

McElroy, P., and Beckerman, B. Developing an international learning object economy: a new industry model for the e-learning market. *Leaning Content eXchange, Inc.,* 2002 (available at http://www.learning-contentexchange.com/LearningObjectEconomy.pdf, accessed on January 12, 2005).

Mayer, R.E.; Heiser, J.; and Lonn, S. Cognitive constraints on multimedia learning: when presenting more material results in less understanding. *Journal of Educational Technology,* 93, 1, (2001), 187–198.

Merrill, D. Instructional transaction theory (ITT): instructional design based on knowledge objects. In C.M. Reigeluth (ed.), *Instructional Design Theories and Models, Volume II: A New Paradigm of Instructional Design.* Mahwah, NJ: Lawrence Erlbaum Associates, 1999, pp. 397–424.

Merrill, D. Instructional strategies that teach. *CBT Solutions.* November–December (1998), 1–11.

Molnar, A.R. Visions of a virtual university, 1997 (available at http://www.nyupress.org/professor/webinteaching/chapt6_main2.shtml, accessed on January 12, 2005).

National Center for Educational Statistics, 2002 (available at http://nces.ed.gov/pubsearch/pubsinfo.asp?pubid=2003060, accessed on January 12, 2005).

Navy Reusable Learning Object (RLO) Development Process Version 1.01, February 28, 2003. (available at http://www.navylearning.com and http://www.navylearning.navy.mil, accessed on January 12, 2005).

Navy Reusable Learning Object (RLO) Content Development Guidelines Version 1.1, February 21, 2003 (available at http://www.navylearning.com and http://www.navylearning.navy.mil, accessed on January 12, 2005).

Oliver, R. Seeking best practice in online learning: flexible learning toolboxes in the Australian VET sector. *Australian Journal of Educational Technology,* 17, 2 (2001), 204–222.

Polsani, P.R. Use and abuse of reusable learning objects. *Journal of Digital Information,* 3, 4 (2003) (available at http://jodi.ecs.soton.ac.uk/Articles/v03/i04/Polsani, accessed on January 12, 2005).

Porter, M.E. *The Competitive Advantage of Nations.* New York: The Free Press, 1990.

Quinn, C., and Hobbs, S. Learning objects and instruction components. *Educational Technology and Society,* 3, 2 (2000), 13–20.

Rossett, A., and Schafer, L. What can we do about e-dropouts? *Training and Development,* 57, 6 (2003), 40–46.

Schank, R.C. Revolutionizing the traditional classroom course. *Communications of the ACM,* 44, 12 (2001), 21–24.

Schumpeter, J.A. *Capitalism, Socialism, and Democracy.* New York: Harper and Row, 1942.

Shneiderman, B. Relate–create–donate: a teaching/learning philosophy for the cyber-generation. *Computers & Education,* 31, 1 (1998), 25–39.

Sloep, P.B. (2003). Learning objects: the answer to the knowledge economy's predicaments? 2003 (available at: http://www.ou.nl/open/psl/Publicaties/LOsAndTheKnowledgeEconomy2003.pdf, accessed on January 12, 2005).

Sousa, D.A. *How the Brain Learns.* 2nd ed. Beverly Hills, CA: Sage Publications, 2000.

The Collaboration For Online Higher Education Research (COHERE) Group. The learning objects economy: implications for developing faculty expertise. *Canadian Journal of Learning and Technology,* 28, 3 (2002), 121–134.

Tushman, M.L.; Anderson, P.C.; et al. Technology cycles, innovation streams, and ambidextrous organizations: organizational renewal through innovation streams and strategic change. In M.L. Tushman and P.C. Anderson (eds.), *Managing Strategic Innovation and Change.* New York: Oxford University Press, 1997, pp. 3–23.

Utterback, J.M. *Mastering the Dynamics of Innovation: How Companies Can Seize Opportunities in the Face of Technological Change.* Boston: Harvard Business School Press, 1994.

Wiley, D.A. Connecting leaning objects to instructional design theory: a definition, a metaphor, and a taxonomy. In D.A. Wiley (ed.), *The Instructional Use of Learning Objects.* Bloomington, IN: Agency for Instructional Technology and Association for Educational Communications Technology (2001), pp. 3–24.

Zhang, D.; Zhao, J.L.; Zhou, L.; and Nunamaker, J.F. Can e-learning replace classroom learning? *Communications of the ACM,* 45, 5 (2004), 74–79.

PART V

USER-CENTERED IS
DEVELOPMENT

RESEARCH ISSUES IN INFORMATION REQUIREMENTS DETERMINATION FOR SYSTEMS DEVELOPMENT AND HUMAN-COMPUTER INTERACTION

GLENN J. BROWNE

Abstract: *The most important factors in the development of usable and functional systems are the completeness and accuracy of requirements gathered from users. Information requirements determination is a difficult and complex process that remains one of the major challenges in systems development. This paper reviews recent research in requirements determination, highlighting questions that have been partially answered and questions that still need to be investigated. A detailed framework of the requirements determination environment is presented to organize the research in this critical aspect of systems development and human-computer interaction. The framework includes a model of the requirements determination process, together with influences on the process, including cognitive, motivational, communication, organizational, problem domain, and other issues. Research questions resulting from the requirements determination process and surrounding influences are discussed.*

Keywords: *Information Requirements Determination, Human-Computer Interaction, Systems Development, Pre-Elicitation Conditioning, Cognition, Motivation, Problem Domain*

INTRODUCTION

Information requirements determination (IRD) is the process by which systems analysts build an understanding of users' needs for an information system. Also termed "requirements analy-sis" and "requirements engineering," the process identifies the requirements that underlie the basic usability and functionality of systems, and thus is fundamental to systems development.[1] Researchers in human-computer interaction and information systems development have long recognized the importance of gathering requirements from users. The IRD process is widely regarded as the most crucial and difficult stage in systems development (Brooks, 1987; Dalal and Yadav, 1992; Davis, 1982; Leifer et al., 1994; Teng and Sethi, 1990; Vessey and Conger, 1993; Watson and Frolick, 1993). This paper reviews recent literature in requirements determination and develops a framework for guiding research in this critical aspect of systems development.

Requirements determination will always be a fundamental concern in systems development because it is the upstream activity most crucial to a system's ultimate success. Much has been written about requirements determination over the past thirty years or so. However, because the

IRD process involves several sets of people (analysts, users, and sometimes other stakeholders), typically concerns projects of significant complexity, and requires translations and reductions of human needs, desires, and preferences into models, languages, and symbols, it is inherently difficult (Brooks, 1987). Because the process deals with different sets of people, the challenges of human cognition, motivation, and communication must be addressed using a wide variety of techniques. Complexity and translations of needs and usability criteria must also be managed. Although standard methodologies exist to help analysts with many of these tasks, much anecdotal evidence suggests that the process is often not performed very well. Analysts encounter many assessment challenges and often miss many important requirements (Pitts and Browne, 2004). Many (if not most) systems development failures can be attributed to inadequate or ineffective requirements determination efforts (Byrd et al., 1992; Davis, 1982; Ewusi-Mensah, 1997; Standish Group, 2001; Vessey and Conger, 1993; Watson and Frolick, 1993; Wetherbe, 1991). Although much has been accomplished in past research on requirements determination, the central position of IRD in the systems development process, and the new and continuing challenges in constructing systems, suggests the need for much additional research.

The remainder of this paper is organized as follows. A framework of the requirements determination environment is presented to organize the research in the domain. Important research questions for each aspect of the framework are then discussed.

A FRAMEWORK FOR INFORMATION REQUIREMENTS DETERMINATION

Requirements determination has been conceptualized in many ways. In this paper, IRD will be organized as a process containing four steps: pre-elicitation conditioning, elicitation, representation, and verification (see Browne and Ramesh, 2002; Larsen and Naumann, 1992; Vitalari, 1992; see also Hickey and Davis, 2004, Jarke and Pohl, 1994, and Zave, 1997 for other IRD process models). The last three stages are well known from various past conceptualizations. The first stage is presented here as a stage that has been overlooked in nearly all past research (see also Browne and Ramesh, 2002).

To organize the research, a requirements determination environment framework will be presented using these four stages. The framework brings together perspectives on IRD from management information systems and human-computer interaction research, and is intended to serve as an organizing mechanism for understanding research performed and questions still unanswered. The framework is shown in Figure 13.1. The process of IRD is shown in the center box, with the four activities of pre-elicitation conditioning, elicitation, representation, and verification represented as iterative steps with feedback loops. The results of the elicitation stage yield inputs to representations. The representations are then used to verify the requirements with users and other stakeholders. In each stage, inadequacies in inputs or outputs lead to the need to feed back through the process to prior steps.

Surrounding the IRD process are factors that influence the process. For all these factors, perspectives of both the analysts and the users are relevant. For example, cognitive considerations (e.g., cognitive biases) are important for both users and analysts. Many of the surrounding factors also may affect one another. Although such interactions between the factors are not indicated on the diagram, they are acknowledged to exist. Research issues in IRD will be examined using Figure 13.1 as a guide. The central IRD process will be discussed first, followed by the factors influencing the process.

Although the model in Figure 13.1 attempts to be exhaustive in its coverage, the research issues in the tables are intended to be illustrative only. Space considerations limit the questions posed. Nonetheless, the questions are indicative of the kinds of issues that are important to investigate.

Figure 13.1   **Requirements Determination Environment**

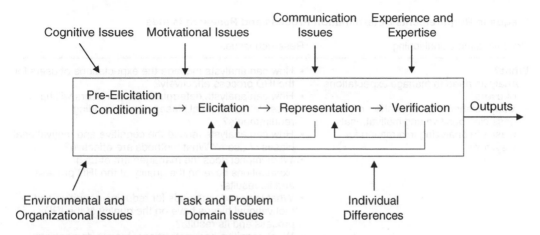

In many cases, questions posed have been answered in part; citations following the questions show illustrative studies. However, additional research into each of the questions would aid our understanding of requirements determination efforts.

REQUIREMENTS DETERMINATION RESEARCH

Research in the Requirements Determination Process

Research in the four stages of the IRD process can be organized by addressing five interrogatories: What? Where? How? How much? With whom? These questions and research related to answering them are shown in Table 13.1. I will now summarize the research in each stage and suggest places where gaps exist in the research and/or the research could be extended.

Pre-Elicitation Conditioning

The first stage of the process, pre-elicitation conditioning, is largely a blank slate in terms of research in requirements determination. Pre-elicitation conditioning is familiar to decision analysts, who consider pre-elicitation discussions with decision makers critical to useful and productive elicitation efforts (Spetzler and Stael von Holstein, 1975; von Winterfeldt and Edwards, 1986). However, surveys of requirements determination process models by Browne and Ramesh (2002) and Hickey and Davis (2004) failed to find any such models that explicitly include conditioning of users prior to elicitation. Pre-elicitation conditioning is important as a unique stage of IRD because it can set the tone for the entire IRD effort by setting and managing users' expectations for the process. Pre-elicitation conditioning consists of discussions, workshops, or other communications between analysts and users prior to the elicitation of requirements. During these discussions, analysts explain the purpose and goals of the system and of the elicitation procedures to the users, attempt to foresee and mitigate any cognitive and motivational biases that might exist for the users, and generally manage users' expectations for the elicitation effort (Browne and Ramesh, 2002). Such discussions can aid significantly in securing user cooperation and buy-in for the requirements determination effort. As noted, such sessions are regarded as critical in decision

Table 13.1

Stages in Requirements Determination Process and Research Issues

Pre-Elicitation Conditioning	Research Issues
What? • Analysts need to manage expectations of users • Analysts should consider their own possible cognitive and motivational biases in analyzing information for a system	• How can analysts manage the expectations of users for the IRD process effectively? • How can analysts determine whether users will have possible motivational biases when providing requirements? • How can analysts reduce the cognitive and motivational biases of users? What methods are effective? • What impact does the management of user expectations have on the quality of the IRD process and its results? • What impact do methods for reducing cognitive and motivational biases have on the quality of the IRD process and its results? • What cognitive and motivational biases do analysts have when approaching systems development efforts? Can these biases be identified and mitigated? • Can analysts be trained to recognize potential biases in users and themselves? Can they be trained to offer strategies for reducing biases?
Where? • Face-to-face meetings	• How can meetings with users be organized or structured to be most effective in pre-elicitation conditioning? • Can pre-elicitation conditioning be accomplished using other communication media?
How? • Discussions with users	• What are the best methods to use for pre-elicitation conditioning? For example, in addition to simply providing users with information about what to expect, analysts might use various questioning and probing techniques to discover potential cognitive and motivational biases.
How Much? • Stopping rules	• How can analysts determine when users are adequately prepared for the requirements elicitation efforts?
With Whom? • Users • Other stakeholders	• Who are the appropriate stakeholders to include in pre-elicitation conditioning sessions?
	Elicitation
What? • Documents, forms, reports, procedures manuals • Users' observed instances and episodes (scenarios) • Users' preferences • Users' experiential beliefs • Requirements *developed* as part of the IRD process	• How should the analyst balance information gleaned from documents, forms, and procedures manuals with conflicting information elicited from users about how tasks are actually performed? • What other evidence can be examined or developed to provide a richer and more complete understanding of user needs? • How can we measure or document requirements elicited? (Browne and Rogich, 2001; Byrd et al., 1992)

(continued)

Table 13.1 (*continued*)

Elicitation

- How can we develop requirements more effectively through reflection, sense-making, socio-cognitive frames (Davidson, 2002), individual reasoning and articulation, and/or group discourse?

Where?
- Face-to-face
- Virtually, in distributed environments

- How can requirements be elicited effectively in virtual environments? (Conkar et al., 1999)

How?
- Choosing elicitation methods (Hickey and Davis, 2004; Kaulio and Karlsson, 1998)
- Prompting (Browne and Rogich, 2001)
- Semantic structuring (Marakas and Elam, 1998)
- Observation, silent and interactive
- Surveying
- Prototyping
- Situated action approach (Smith and Dunckley, 2002)
- Scenario-based approaches (Bustard et al., 2000; Carroll, 2000; Maiden et al., 1999; McGraw and Harbison, 1997; Robertson and Robertson, 1999; Rosson and Carroll, 2001)
- Use of metaphors (Boland and Greenberg, 1992; Mason, 1991)
- Joint application development sessions (August, 1991; Davidson, 1999)
- Nominal group technique (Duggan and Thachenkary, 2004; Havelka, 2003)
- Computer-supported cooperative work (CSCW) (Galegher and Kraut, 1994; Kiesler and Sproull, 1992; Ocker et al., 1998)
- Focus groups (Kuhn, 2000; Leifer et al., 1994)
- Collaborative engineering (Grunbacher et al., 2004)
- Card-sorting (Maiden and Hare, 1998)
- Ripple-down rules (Richards and Compton, 1998)
- Error-based approaches (Viller et al., 1999)
- Contradiction approach (Turner and Turner, 2002)

- How can prompting techniques be improved? (Browne and Rogich, 2001; Lauer et al., 1992; Marakas and Elam, 1998)
- How can interviewing techniques be improved? (Moody et al., 2001)
- How can user preferences be assessed accurately?
- How can users be prompted to tell stories about their work?
- How can user stories be interpreted and made sense of? (Davidson, 2002; Dubé and Robey, 1999)
- How should elicitation methods be chosen? (Hickey and Davis, 2004)
- Can task analyses and cognitive task analyses can be applied more fruitfully to systems analysis efforts?
- How can elicitation techniques be combined for more effective requirements gathering? (e.g., observation, prompting, scenario-based approaches)
- Which user/analyst collaboration techniques yield the best results?
- Can anonymity of users during the elicitation process help in the quantity and veracity of requirements elicited?
- How should requirements be elicited for Web-based information systems? (Romano et al., 2003; Yang and Tang, 2003)

How much?
- Stopping rules (Pitts and Browne, 2004)

- Do stopping rules utilized by analysts differ depending on context?
- Do stopping rules utilized by users differ depending on context?
- What stopping rules are used by groups during JAD sessions?

(continued)

Table 13.1 (continued)

	Elicitation
	• Do expert and novice analysts use different stopping rules to terminate information acquisition? • Can prescriptive stopping rules be developed to mitigate under-acquisition and over-acquisition of requirements?
With Whom? • Importance of involving users (e.g., Damodaran, 1996; Doll and Torkzadeh, 1989, 1991; McGraw and Harbison, 1997; Smith and Dunckley, 2002) • Other stakeholders	• How should users be selected for observation and/or interviews? (Damodaran, 1996) • What other organizational stakeholders should be included in requirements elicitation efforts?

	Representation
What? • Traditionally data and processes • Use cases, scenarios, and so forth • Requirements traces	• Are there additional forms of evidence that can be represented for improved systems design? • How can requirements traceability help in IRD and in the overall systems development process? (Jarke, 1998)
Where? • Face-to-face • Virtually, in distributed environments	• How can representations be created effectively when analysts are in different locations?
How? • Informal diagrams (Browne and Ramesh, 2002; Montazemi and Conrath, 1986; Robertson and Robertson, 1999) • Use cases, scenarios, storyboards, information displays (Klein et al., 1997; Robertson and Robertson, 1999; Sutcliffe, 1997) • Semi-formal diagrams (ERDs, DFDs, object-oriented diagrams, UML) (Bolloju, 2004; Mylopoulos et al., 1999)	• Can new informal diagrams be created that help in the initial representation of requirements? • Can rules be created for transferring information from informal diagrams to semi-formal diagrams? • Do users understand semi-formal representations? (Browne et al., 1997) • What additional refinements can be made to semi-formal diagrams to make them more accessible to users? • How can various diagrams be integrated? (Hahn and Kim, 1999; Kim et al., 2000) • Which diagrams are most effective at representing user requirements? (Yadav et al., 1988)
How much? • Stopping rules	• How do analysts stop their requirements representation efforts? • Can analysts' stopping rules be improved to prevent under-specification and over-specification of requirements?
With Whom? • Other analysts • Users	• Would representations be created more effectively and efficiently if done by groups of analysts or by analysts alone? • Would representations be better if users were included in every step of the representation process?
What? • Diagrams • Scenarios • Use cases	• Are informal diagrams or semi-formal diagrams more effective in verifying requirements with users? (Browne et al., 1997) • Can users understand semi-formal diagrams?

(*continued*)

Table 13.1 (*continued*)

	Verification
Where? • Face-to-face • Virtually	• Can requirements verification be accomplished successfully in virtual environments? If so, how would that be done?
How? • User sign-off	• How can requirements be verified with users? (Plant and Preece, 1996; Maiden et al., 1999; Sakthivel and Tanniru, 1989) • How meaningful is user sign-off? • Do differing views of data aid in verification of requirements? (Parsons, 2002)
How much? • Stopping rules	• How do analysts stop with the verification process? • Can prescriptive rules be developed for stopping the verification process?
With Whom? • Users • Other stakeholders	• With whom should analysts verify requirements?

analysis practice and therefore are likely to be crucial in IRD practice as well. Some analysts undoubtedly employ practices akin to those described, but systematic research into how such sessions might work in IRD could provide significant improvements to the overall success of requirements determination efforts. Users should be more likely to provide complete and truthful information, and to cooperate more fully, if they understand what is expected of them and have bought in to the process.[2]

Elicitation

The elicitation of information stage of IRD has received considerable attention in the systems development and HCI literature. The question of what to elicit is standard material in most systems analysis and design books. For example, checking forms and reports is crucial for understanding the inputs and outputs of processes, and the importance of eliciting requirements from users is universally recognized. Elicitation issues that have received less attention include requirements that are developed by users and analysts through sense-making activities (Davidson, 2002) and other sources of rich interpretive data. Elicitation has traditionally been performed in face-to-face meetings with users, and on-site for analysis of documents, but new communication media such as the Internet are now enabling off-site interactions (Conkar, Noyes, and Kimble, 1999). Whether requirements can be gathered effectively in virtual environments is currently an important research question.

The majority of research concerning the elicitation of requirements has been concerned with *how* elicitation should be accomplished. Table 13.1 lists a large number of methods that have been used with varying degrees of success. Commonly used methods such as prompting (asking) and observing users and employing joint application development (JAD) sessions and prototyping have been supplemented by numerous other methods. Recently, Hickey and Davis (2004) have provided a methodology for helping select elicitation methods. Eliciting information from users and interpreting their statements is enormously complex, and despite all the methods available, much more research needs to be performed in this area. For example, although user preferences are obviously key to much of systems development, decision theoretic approaches to eliciting user preferences have long been neglected. Further, story- and scenario-based approaches hold much promise for yielding a rich understanding of user performance and the task environment, and additional research along these lines would be very useful. In the HCI literature, researchers have introduced task analyses and cognitive task analyses to help analysts understand organizational tasks that need to be performed and how users perform them (e.g., Fleishman and Quaintance, 1984; Klein et al., 1997; McGraw and Harbison, 1997; Richardson et al., 1998). Task analyses have proven to be critical in several aspects of systems development, such as interface design, but their importance has not perhaps been recognized fully in the MIS literature.

The question of *how much* information should be gathered during IRD has received little attention until recently. Pitts and Browne (2004) have investigated cognitive stopping rules that analysts use in terminating the elicitation process, finding that the use of certain stopping rules yields greater quality and quantity of requirements. Much more research in this area remains to be performed, including investigations of motivational stopping rules. The whole question of when requirements gathered are sufficient for proceeding to the next step in systems development is a critical one that has long been overlooked.

The question of *with whom* requirements should be elicited has received some attention in the literature, although the assumption that users should be the primary focus of elicitation efforts is largely ingrained. This focus is appropriate, although other stakeholders, such as managers and executives, should be included at various times to ensure that requirements are consistent with larger organizational goals and system architectures (Wetherbe, 1991). Additionally, the question of how to sample users for requirements determination efforts remains an important one that is often not addressed.

Representation

Representation of information has a relatively long history in systems analysis. Early diagramming methods such as entity relationship diagrams (representing data), data-flow diagrams (representing processes), and class diagrams were enormously important in advancing systems development. More recently, diagrams from object-oriented analysis and the unified modeling language (UML) have proven useful (Bolloju, 2004; Mylopoulos et al., 1999). In addition to these semi-formal diagrams, task analyses have allowed researchers to develop informal representational techniques such as scenarios, storyboards, and information displays (Klein et al., 1997; McGraw and Harbison, 1997; Sutcliffe, 1997). Other informal representational devices have also been proposed, such as evocative knowledge maps, influence diagrams, decision maps, context diagrams, business event patterns, and affinity diagrams (Browne and Ramesh, 2002; Robertson and Robertson, 1999; see also Brassard, 1989; Howard, 1989; Ramaprasad and Poon, 1985). Research questions concerning representations remain, however. For example, systematic investigations of which diagrams best capture user requirements are few. Whether analysts should attempt to capture requirements first using informal diagrams, and then translate those diagrams into semi-formal diagrams, is also an important research question (Browne et al., 1997; Browne and Ramesh, 2002; see also Potts et al., 1994).

Requirements tracing is another very interesting and potentially useful area for research (Jarke, 1998). Requirements tracing attempts to capture the origins of requirements and to document those origins, resulting in requirements that are well defined and well documented. Such documentation can aid the IRD process by facilitating communication between analysts and users, and can help in generating potential design solutions. It can also contribute to a knowledge repository and can protect systems developers from later criticisms over design decisions (Jarke, 1998). Much additional research into requirements tracing is warranted.

In addition to what requirements to represent and how to represent them, there is also the question of how much to represent. As in the case of elicitation, little is known about how analysts stop the representation process. How much is enough? How much is too much? How do analysts decide to stop representing? Because the mapping between informal requirements representations (e.g., notes, sketches, informal diagrams) and semi-formal diagrams such as DFDs is obviously not one-to-one, information is lost in the translation process. What information should be disregarded? How many layers should DFDs contain? Systems analysis textbooks generally attempt to answer these questions in some fashion, but researchers have not fully addressed such issues.

The final issues regarding representations concern with whom representations should be created. Should analysts work on representations in teams or alone? Should users participate in the creation of the diagrams? Would this increase both buy-in and the legitimacy of the user sign-off during verification? Some studies have addressed these issues, but more research in a variety of contexts would be very valuable.

Verification

Verification of requirements concerns analysts' efforts to ensure that the requirements captured and represented in fact reflect users' needs and preferences. Verification has received less attention in the literature than elicitation or representation. One important research question is whether users understand the materials (e.g., ERDs and DFDs) shown to them during the verification process. If they do not, then the usual user sign-off is obviously not very meaningful. Whether there are better methods for accomplishing verification would be a useful area of inquiry. Another important question is whether verification can be accomplished in virtual settings, when the geographic dispersion of users and analysts prevents face-to-face meetings.

As with the prior two stages, when and how analysts stop verification are also unanswered questions. Verification may be halted primarily for motivational reasons, such as time schedules, rather than after ensuring user understanding. This is a potentially fruitful area for further research. Finally, the question of with whom analysts should verify requirements is important. It is arguable that in addition to users, other organizational stakeholders charged with seeing that the larger project goals are met should be present to verify the requirements. Additional research into this question would be worthwhile.

PROCESS INFLUENCES

In addition to the research issues addressing aspects of the IRD process, there are numerous factors that influence the process (as shown in Figure 13.1). These process influences will be discussed next.

Cognitive Issues in IRD

Cognitive issues in requirements determination have received a reasonable amount of attention from researchers. Davis's (1982) seminal article outlined many of the cognitive issues in IRD, and various researchers have since explored some of the important topics (e.g., Agarwal and Sinha, 1996; Davidson, 2002; Holtzblatt and Beyer, 1995; Kim et al., 2000; Roast, 1997; Stary

Table 13.2

Cognitive Issues in IRD

Cognitive Issues	Research Issues
Cognitive heuristics	• How does the use of general cognitive heuristics, such as availability and anchoring and adjustment, affect the answers users give to questions and the questions analysts ask? • What specific cognitive heuristics do users utilize in performing tasks, and how do these affect the requirements they give? • What specific cognitive heuristics do analysts use, and how do these heuristics affect the questions analysts ask and the IRD methods they employ?
Cognitive biases in judgment	• How do cognitive biases in judgment (e.g., ease of recall, misconceptions of chance, overconfidence) affect requirements gathered from users, questions asked by analysts, and analysts' interpretations of users' responses? (Browne and Ramesh, 2002; Holtzblatt and Beyer, 1995; Stacy and Macmillan, 1995) • What methods can help overcome cognitive biases?
Automaticity	• How does users' automaticity of steps in tasks affect the requirements determination effort? (Browne and Ramesh, 2002) • What tools can help overcome this problem?
Problems in recall	• How can analysts help overcome forgetting of information by users? (Fisher and Geiselman, 1992; Moody et al., 2001) • How can analysts overcome their own forgetting?
Understanding users' mental models of tasks	• Can a better understanding of users' mental models of tasks help with developing usability criteria? (Stary and Peschl, 1998) • How do users' mental models adjust dynamically to changes in context?
Creativity in IRD	• How can creativity be developed and encouraged in systems analysts and users? (Couger, 1996; Zmud et al., 1993)

Note: See also Browne and Ramesh, 2002.

and Peschl, 1998; Sutcliffe and Maiden, 1992). Table 13.2 lists important cognitive issues in IRD. For example, Browne and Ramesh (2002) examined the role of heuristics and cognitive biases in requirements determination. Stacy and Macmillan (1995) also documented several cognitive biases that occur in software development. Findings across a variety of domains have shown that the application of sub-optimal heuristics leads to poor task performance and systematic biases in judgment and reasoning (Bazerman, 2002; Tversky and Kahneman, 1974), which in turn can lead to the elicitation and representation of inappropriate requirements and poor systems design. The ubiquity of cognitive biases in human decision making suggests that such biases are prevalent in both analysts and users, and much more research on this topic is warranted.

Another potential cognitive problem in the evocation of information by users is automaticity. During task performance, procedures for accomplishing steps quickly become routinized, and the performer loses conscious access to the procedures in memory (Leifer et al., 1994; Simon, 1979). Therefore, when asked how a task is performed, users will typically leave out those steps that have been automated. This is a significant hindrance to the systems analyst attempting to understand how the task is performed. To overcome this problem, analysts generally utilize both silent and interactive observation. However, while observation typically helps the analyst understand *what* the users are doing (the behaviors), it is less helpful for understanding *how* and *why* the task is being performed (the cognition). Thus, additional methods for helping users "re-discover" these process steps, and helping the analyst understand them (such as tracing users' responses to scenarios and "garden path tasks"), hold much promise for improving IRD (Browne and Ramesh, 2002; Johnson et al., 1991).

Additionally, problems in recall are always present for users in IRD. Users simply forget important information. Prompting methods can obviously help in the recall of information (Browne and Rogich, 2001), but specialized forms of interviews can also be very useful (Fisher and Geiselman, 1991; Moody et al., 1998). Additional important questions concern how analysts can prevent their own forgetting. For questions to ask, analysts can obviously use mental or physical lists of items. For what users say, analysts use various representational devices such as note-taking and diagrams. However, much information is clearly lost, and analysts sometimes videotape sessions to avoid losing information.

Finally, understanding users' mental models of tasks is certainly an important goal in interpreting user needs. Understanding how a user performs a task is critical to designing appropriate process steps and knowing what information the user will need while performing the task. Although some research has been devoted to this topic (e.g., Stary and Peschl, 1998), much more is needed. For example, there is still a need to know how users' mental models adjust dynamically to changes in context.

Motivational Issues in IRD

Another important set of issues in IRD is motivational issues (shown in Table 13.3). Motivational issues concern internal or external influences that cause people to alter their behaviors in some way. Internal motivational issues include such phenomena as unrealistically positive views of self, the illusion of control, egocentrism, and self-serving attributions and the motivational biases that result (Bazerman, 2002). Little research has addressed the impact of such factors on the IRD process. However, the potential payoff from such research is likely to be huge. Motivational biases play a major role in decision making generally (Bazerman, 2002), and there is no reason to believe that requirements determination settings will be any different. If motivational factors cause people to report judgments, preferences, or data that do not reflect their true beliefs, the result is likely to be incorrect requirements that lead to poorly functioning systems.

Externally driven issues include organizational incentive systems and political systems and power structures that cause users to give safe, conservative, subservient, and politically and socially correct answers to analysts' questions (Bazerman, 2002). While such answers are perfectly rational from the user's point of view, deviations from the truth are obviously not ideal for the system developers. As noted in Table 13.3, some research has addressed the impact of power and politics in requirements determination efforts (e.g., Davidson, 2002; Markus, 1983), but much more research could be performed. In terms of variance explained, it is likely that motivational factors have even more impact on requirements determination outcomes than cognitive issues.

Communication Issues in IRD

Communication issues (Table 13.4) refer primarily to the communication between analysts and users during IRD, but can also be concerned with communication between analysts or between

Table 13.3

Motivational Issues in IRD

Motivational Issue	Research Issues
Incentive systems	• How do incentive systems affect analysts' judgments concerning cost and quality of system requirements? • How do incentive systems affect analysts' judgments of when to stop eliciting, representing, and verifying requirements? (See Pitts and Browne, 2004) • How do incentives in the organizational environment affect the quality/time trade-off in software development? (Austin, 2001)
Internally driven motivational issues, such as unrealistically positive views of self, the illusion of control, egocentrism, self-serving attributions (Bazerman, 2002)	• How do internally driven motivations of users affect the requirements elicitation and verification processes? • How do internally driven motivations of analysts affect all stages of the IRD process? • How do internally driven motivations affect the veracity of requirements evoked by users? • What techniques can be used to overcome problems in IRD caused by internal motivations of users and analysts?
Motivational biases	• How do motivational biases affect the answers given by users to analysts' questions? • How do motivational biases affect the questions that analysts ask?
Politics and power	• How do political considerations by users and analysts affect the requirements determination process? (Davidson, 2002; Markus, 1983) • How do powerful individuals in group and project settings affect the requirements determination process? (Dhillon, 2004; Markus and Bjørn-Andersen, 1987; Robey and Newman, 1996)

users. The general problem arises because analysts and users have different training and backgrounds, and thus speak in some sense different "languages" (Bostrom, 1989; Britten and Jones, 1999). Analysts are trained in MIS, computer science, and allied fields, while users are trained in functional areas such as accounting or marketing or in specialized operational areas such as customer service. The frames of reference and the terms or art used by the two groups of people are thus quite different (Browne and Ramesh, 2002). Furthermore, the goals of the two groups are generally different. Users are focused on maximum functionality and ease of use, while analysts are focused on ease of design, upgradeability, and ease of maintenance. Thus, misunderstandings and misinterpretations of information are inevitable. Research into how to minimize misunderstandings is therefore crucial. Finally, users are understandably wary of analysts at times, because many systems are designed to replace human workers. For all these reasons, managing users' expectations during the pre-elicitation conditioning stage of IRD, discussed above, is critical.

Another communication issue, also discussed above, concerns whether analysts and users communicate effectively when verifying requirements. In particular, the question of whether diagrams created during the representation stage of IRD are effective for verifying requirements with users bears further investigation (see O'Neill et al., 1999; Parsons, 2002).

Table 13.4

Communication Issues in IRD

Communication Issue	Research Issues
Differing backgrounds of users and analysts	• How do differing backgrounds and resulting different "languages" of users and analysts affect the quality and quantity of requirements elicited? How do they affect the verification process? (Bostrom, 1989; Britton and Jones, 1999; Coughlan and Macredie, 2002; Kaiser and Srinivasan, 1984; Keil and Carmel, 1995; Tan, 1994)
Modes of communication	• How do differing modes of communication affect the requirements determination process? (Ocker et al., 1998)
IRD representations	• Are analysts able to communicate systems requirements to users using representational devices? If so, which representations work best? (O'Neill et al., 1999; Parsons, 2002)
Gathering requirements from distributed users, and gathering requirements from users in ways other than in person.	• What are the special issues encountered when gathering requirements from users dispersed across geographical areas? • IRD has traditionally been performed in face-to-face interviews or JAD sessions. What issues (quantity and quality of requirements) arise when in-person contact is not feasible? • In distributed environments, are there computer-mediation processes or tools that can facilitate communication between analysts and users? Can models of distributed cognition help in these situations? (See Hollan, Hutchins, and Kirsh, 2000) How can verification be performed under such conditions? (Conkar et al., 1999)

Finally, communication issues will be an increasing challenge as members of systems development teams and users become more geographically dispersed. Systems being developed by teams spread across countries throughout the world are now commonplace. How can analysts communicate with one another effectively in such circumstances? How can analysts communicate with users who may be several continents away? Preliminary answers to these questions are only beginning to appear (Conkar et al., 1999), and much more research is necessary to ensure that systems developed under these conditions are successful.

Experience and Expertise Issues in IRD

Experience and expertise are important considerations in all task performance. Considerations relevant in the present context are shown in Table 13.5. In the case of information requirements determination, and for systems analysis and design generally, it has typically been assumed that experience and expertise improve the success of requirements determination efforts (Schenk et al., 1998; Vitalari, 1992; Walz et al., 1993). Recent findings with practicing systems analysts have suggested, however, that experience is uncorrelated with the quantity and quality of requirements elicited (Pitts and Browne, 2004). Therefore, further research into the role of experience in requirements determination is warranted.

Table 13.5

Experience and Expertise Issues in IRD

Experience and Expertise Issue	Research Issues
Role of experience in IRD	• How do experienced analysts gather requirements? (See Pitts and Browne, 2004; Schenk et al., 1998) • What heuristics are used by experienced analysts in gathering requirements? (See Pitts and Browne, 2004.) Can those heuristics be taught to novices to improve IRD? • How does experience affect the quality and quantity of requirements for design? (Pitts and Browne, 2004; Schenk et al., 1998; Vitalari, 1992; Walz et al., 1993)
Role of expertise in IRD	• What is "expertise" in IRD? (Schenk et al., 1998; Sutcliffe and Maiden, 1992) • What is the best way to acquire expertise in IRD? • How does experience correlate with expertise? • What happens when there is conflict between expertise and motivations? (Austin, 2001)
Analyst familiarity with task domain	• How does the analyst's familiarity with the task domain of the system affect the strategies he employs for IRD? • Does familiarity with a task domain lead to better questions from the analyst and better interpretation of users' responses? Does it lead to a better shared understanding with the users of the system's requirements?
User familiarity with task domain	• If the user has little experience in the task domain, or if the system is a new one (and thus no one has any real experience with it), how should the analyst gather requirements? • If the user is familiar with the task domain, does this enhance his ability to provide more precise answers to the analyst's questions concerning the system?
Knowledge levels of analyst concerning systems development and business goals	• How does the knowledge level of the analyst affect the methods and tools he uses in IRD? Are some methods more appropriate in certain contexts than others?
Knowledge levels of users concerning systems development and business goals	• How do differing knowledge levels of users affect the methods an analyst employs in IRD? • Do high levels of knowledge by both analysts and users lead to more efficient and effective requirements determination efforts?

The role of expertise in IRD is also an important research area (Austin, 2001; Schenk et al., 1998; Sutcliffe and Maiden, 1992). One important preliminary question is simply, What is expertise in requirements determination? That is, what do expert analysts do, and how and why are they successful? (Schenk et al., 1998) These questions can be partially answered by documenting the heuristics used by expert analysts in the various stages of the IRD process. Such heuristics are important both to establish best practices and to train novices. Another question of interest concerns what happens when expertise and motivation collide (Austin, 2001). For example, if an analyst's expertise suggests a particular behavior, but motivational forces (particularly those external to the analyst) require a different behavior, what is the result? If motivations overrule expertise, the consequences pose potential hazards for an organization.

Other issues of importance include the analysts' and users' familiarity with the task domain, their knowledge about systems development, and, more generally, their knowledge of the company's business. Familiarity with the task domain (e.g., detecting fraud in accounting reports) should have an impact on the requirements determination effort. If the analyst understands the task domain, he or she should have a better idea of what questions to ask and how to interpret answers. Furthermore, an analyst's familiarity with the task domain should allow him to choose IRD elicitation and representation strategies that are appropriate for the task. If the user has a good understanding of the domain, she should be able to provide more precise answers to questions. The better the knowledge of the participants, the better they should be at building a shared understanding of the needs for the system.

Similarly, if the user has knowledge of systems development, the requirements determination process is likely to be much more efficient and effective. Furthermore, if the analyst has knowledge of the business goals for building a system, he is likely to be more effective in designing appropriate strategies for eliciting requirements and for asking questions that more directly address system needs.

Environmental and Organizational Issues in IRD

Environmental and organizational impacts on the IRD process is a vast class of issues, and I will touch on only a subset here. Important factors in this category are shown in Table 13.6. Project management is one factor that has a critical impact on requirements determination efforts. If the project is well organized and planned, with sufficient time and resources devoted to the requirements determination effort, then the likelihood of success for IRD and the project as a whole are obviously increased (Ewusi-Mensah, 1997; Walz et al., 1993). If, on the other hand, the scope of the project is ill-defined or the scope begins to drift (either becoming larger or shifting to a different focus), then IRD becomes exponentially more difficult. Conflicts regarding priorities (e.g., quality vs. cost) can also affect IRD efforts (see Austin, 2001). The impact of project management factors on the IRD process is a fruitful area for further investigations.

The measurement mechanisms available to the project team can also affect the requirements determination effort. For example, if teams can measure the quantity and quality of requirements elicited, they may be able to determine when they have enough (Pitts and Browne, 2004). Further, an understanding of factors that impact the IRD process, and the ability to measure those factors, are likely to significantly improve the quality of the IRD effort (Havelka, 2003).

The organizational environment and culture includes many issues, and only a fraction can be discussed here. For example, numerous types of company cultures have been successful over the long run. For instance, Intel has long embraced a culture of "constructive confrontation," while Hewlett-Packard has always relied on a consensus-building environment (Hamilton, 2001). Both companies have been hugely successful. For requirements determination, which of these environments is more effective, or can they both be effective under certain circumstances? Does it depend on the individuals involved? Is the organizational culture one that attempts to develop managers through continuous learning and improvement and is tolerant of their mistakes along the way? Or is the culture one in which the methods are left to the individual manager and only the results count? Which of these types of cultures results in more effective and efficient requirements determination efforts? These and many other issues are important areas for research.

Relatedly, are certain organizational structures better for requirements determination? For example, are project-oriented organizations, in which the focus of the enterprise is on project performance,

Table 13.6

Environmental and Organizational Issues in IRD

Environmental/Organizational Issue	Research Issues
Project management	• How do characteristics of the management of an IS development project affect the results of requirements determination? (Walz et al., 1993)
Measurement capabilities	• How do measurement capabilities of the organization and team affect the quality of the IRD effort? • Does the ability to measure quantity and quality of requirements affect the overall IRD effort and ultimate system success? (Pitts and Browne, 2004) • Does an understanding of the factors important to IRD process quality, and an ability to measure those factors, impact overall IRD efforts? (Havelka, 2003)
Changing requirements	• How do shifting requirements over time affect the IRD process? (Davidson, 2002; Galal and Paul, 1999; Patel, 1999)
Scope creep	• How do changes in project scope (typically enlargement) affect analysts' abilities to gather and manage the IRD process? (Berry, 1998)
Organizational environment and culture	• How do characteristics of the organizational environment and culture enhance or inhibit the IRD process? • How does an organization's capability maturity affect its ability to determine requirements effectively? (Jiang et al., 2004)
Change management	• How do organizational changes (e.g., to operating procedures) suggested by a proposed system affect analysts' abilities to elicit requirements from users? (Jiang et al., 2000)
Organizational structure	• Does the structure of an organization (e.g., project-oriented vs. functional-area-oriented) affect analysts' abilities to perform IRD effectively? • How does the structure of the organization affect the accessibility of users? • How does the structure enhance or inhibit user participation in the IRD process?
Team structure, support for teams, and social networks in organizations	• Do organizations that provide good support for teams have more success in IRD efforts? • Does the structure of teams have an impact on IRD? (Borovits et al., 1990; Curtis et al., 1988; Guinan et al., 1998; Walz et al., 1993; Yang and Tang, 2004) • How does the structure and maturity of the social networks in the organization affect the IRD process? (Yang and Tang, 2004)

more effective in requirements determination and systems development efforts than traditional functional organizations? The assumption is probably that project-oriented organizations are generally more effective, but companies such as General Electric, which in many cases operates using a hybrid organizational structure, have been enormously successful in cross-functional projects (Brady, 2004).

Change management is another factor that may impact IRD efforts. Information systems are nearly always built to automate processes and/or support decision making in some way. Systems thus intervene in an organizational process and change the way people perform their work. Since it is cognitively difficult to change the way one performs a task, people generally do not like to change and resist it. For requirements determination, users *anticipate* change because of the planned information system, and therefore may be reluctant to participate in the process and be motivated to provide the least information possible. For these reasons, careful change management is critical for IRD to be successful (Jiang et al., 2000).

A factor of the organizational environment that has received a great deal of attention in the literature is the effect of teams and team structure on systems development efforts. Teams have been shown to help in requirements determination efforts, and the structure of teams has an impact on firms' IRD success (Borovits et al., 1990; Curtis et al., 1988; Guinan et al., 1998; Walz et al., 1993; Yang and Tang, 2004). In a particularly interesting vein, Yang and Tang (2004) recently investigated the impact of social networks on the relationship between teamwork and software development performance, finding that group cohesion and having a strong central leader in the group were the best predictors of performance. A strong leader was also critical for success in eliciting user requirements. Additional inquiry into the importance of social networks on requirements determination efforts may be quite useful.

Task and Problem Domain Issues in IRD

Task and problem domain issues are concerned with aspects of the domain or software development task that affect requirements determination efforts (see Table 13.7). One important factor can be labeled variety and complexity of requirements (following Davis, 1982). Variety in requirements is caused by several factors, including the fact that different users perform the same task using different heuristics, the same user may perform the task differently at different points in time, and user preferences are not stable (Browne and Ramesh, 2002). Variety and complexity of requirements may be increased for analysts when system requirements change during the course of the project or when the system being contemplated is a new one (not simply the automation of an existing system) and thus no one knows exactly what the requirements should be a priori. For these reasons, variety and complexity of requirements have a significant impact on the IRD process.

One of the most fundamental questions concerning variety and complexity is how they should be measured (see Mennecke et al., 2000; Wood, 1986). Another important question concerns how requirements differ across development domains. It is also of interest to consider what elicitation strategies should be used for different levels of variety and complexity. Finally, finding ways to reduce variety and complexity is perhaps the most crucial problem of all. When analysts observe, survey, or interview users, they must translate what they find into external representations, such as notes or diagrams. This translation process involves a reduction and simplification of information. When the analyst later translates his notes and informal diagrams into more formal representations, he again reduces and simplifies information. How these translations occur, and what knowledge is omitted or lost, is a crucial issue in requirements determination.

Problem affordances refer to options enabled by various alternatives or design options (Gibson, 1977; Norman, 1990). For example, Norman (1990) notes that knobs on doors naturally afford pulling or turning, depending on their design. Steel plates on doors afford pushing. Doors with steel plates that require pulling confuse people. Many design difficulties with consumer products result from missing the natural mappings between human perceptions and what an object affords. Problem affordances have been considered by HCI researchers (notably Norman himself while at

Table 13.7

Task and Problem Domain Issues in IRD

Task/Problem Domain Issue	Research Issues
Variety and complexity of requirements (Davis, 1982)	• How should variety and complexity be measured? (Mennecke et al., 2000; Wood, 1986) • How do the variety and complexity of requirements differ across development contexts? • What types of variety and complexity exist? • How do analysts' perceptions of variability affect the IRD process? For example, perceiving variation when none exists, or perceiving no variation when in fact there is variation in task performance (see Browne and Curley, 1998). • If requirements have considerable variety and/or complexity, what strategies should be used to elicit, represent, and verify them? • How do variety and complexity affect user participation, which and how many users should be involved in the IRD process, and so forth? • How can variety and complexity be reasonably reduced and/or simplified?
Task type	• What is the impact of task types and characteristics on the methods that should be used for modeling requirements? (Agarwal and Sinha, 1996)
Problem affordances	• How can the identification of problem affordances be used to suggest promising opportunities for reengineering processes and/or adding improvements to existing processes? (Norman, 1990) • How can task analyses and cognitive task analyses be used to supplement user responses in IRD? How can such analyses be used to help prompt users? How can such analyses help identify usability criteria? (Mayhew, 1999; Nielsen, 1993)

Apple Computer), but less so by MIS researchers. Yet understanding users' needs and mapping them to what the task domain affords is most likely to yield effective system design (Baecker et al., 1995). Thus, an analysis of the task domain, using task analysis and cognitive task analysis techniques, is critical to determining problem affordances.

Individual Difference Issues in IRD

Individual differences have been investigated in some IRD research (see Table 13.8). Although individual differences typically account for less variance in task performance than elements of the task environment (Simon, 1981), they are becoming more important as the ability to customize interfaces, databases, and so forth, grows. Individual customization presents new problems for requirements determination, including the obvious need to elicit and assess individuating information. At the very least, this will require additional time. It may also require new techniques, templates, and categorization schemes for users. Among individual differences that are potentially important are cultural and demographic differences and work styles, and personal preferences about screen design and various usability criteria (e.g., Mayhew, 1999; Mills, 2000; Nielsen, 1993; Parker et al., 1997; Roast, 1997; Rosson and Carroll, 2001; Sutcliffe et al., 2000). Eliciting user preferences in a rigorous way has not been a strength of traditional MIS, and improvements may be necessary to provide customization options that users desire.

Table 13.8

Individual Difference Issues in IRD

Individual Difference Issue	Research Issues
Work styles	• Do different work styles of users require that analysts use different IRD methods and tools to be effective?
Preferences	• How should user preferences be elicited? • How should different user preferences be integrated and/or combined? • How does an analyst decide what user needs, desires, and preferences to include in a system? • How much should individual preferences be supported in a particular system?
Cultural differences in users and/or analysts	• Do cultural differences affect IRD? If so, how? (Honold, 2000)
Demographic differences in users and/or analysts	• Do demographic differences (e.g., gender, ethnicity) affect IRD? If so, how?

CONCLUSION

This paper has reviewed research issues in information requirements determination for systems development and human-computer interaction. The purpose of the paper has been to build a framework for organizing the IRD process and to describe research issues within the framework. The framework highlights issues of theoretical and practical importance in requirements determination and sets a broad agenda for research in this critical stage of systems development.

One important contribution of the paper has been to identify pre-elicitation conditioning as a critical stage in the IRD process. This stage helps users understand the IRD process and their role in it, aids analysts in managing users' expectations, and can help ensure more thorough and successful requirements determination outcomes. Prior conceptualizations of the IRD process have not included pre-elicitation conditioning as a stage, but there are significant potential benefits to preparing users adequately for their role in determining requirements for a system.

As the review of the literature demonstrates, requirements determination has been investigated in a wide variety of contexts, reflecting its central importance to the success of users' interactions with computers. Despite the large amount of research, however, many fundamental issues and problems remain to be resolved. Although more research into all the elements on the framework would be worthwhile, some topics seem more crucial than others. In particular, the pre-elicitation conditioning and verification stages of the IRD process need much more attention by researchers. Additional research into these stages holds much promise for improving the effectiveness of IRD. Although elicitation and representation are also critical, they have been the focus of the vast majority of studies. Additionally, the literature would benefit from a greater focus on the cognitive, motivational, and communication influences on the IRD process. Although all influences are important, these three influences are probably the most fundamental. A better understanding of cognition and motivation can help ensure that the information evoked by users is accurate and complete, and improved communication can help analysts gain a full understanding of that information.

Research in IRD will be of continuing importance to systems development and human-computer interaction. Improvements in requirements determination are likely to have a more significant impact on the quality of systems than any other factor. Thus, further research in requirements determination is critical for the continued advancement of the information systems field.[3]

NOTES

1. Subtle distinctions are sometimes made between processes variously termed "information requirements determination," "requirements analysis," "requirements engineering," (and others), depending largely on the domain and research traditions of the researchers. While recognizing that such distinctions exist, I do not address them in this paper. Instead, I attempt to focus on processes that exist regardless of the context of the research.

2. Although users may be uncooperative during elicitation, or may not understand the process, it is unlikely that analysts would repeat the pre-elicitation conditioning stage. Thus, there is no feedback loop from elicitation to pre-elicitation conditioning. In such cases, the analyst may remind the user of information from pre-elicitation conditioning or may simply dismiss that particular user.

3. The author thanks Radha Appan, Vidhya Mellarkod, and an anonymous reviewer for their helpful comments on previous versions of this paper.

REFERENCES

Agarwal, R., and Sinha, A.P. Cognitive fit in requirements modeling: a study of object and process methodologies. *Journal of Management Information Systems,* 13, 2 (1996), 137–162.

August, J.H. *Joint Application Design: The Group Session Approach to Systems Design.* Englewood Cliffs, NJ: Prentice-Hall, 1991.

Austin, R.D. The effects of time pressure on quality in software development: an agency model. *Information Systems Research,* 12, 2 (2001), 195–207.

Baecker, R.M.; Grudin, J.; Buxton, W.A.S.; and Greenburg, S. *Readings in Human-Computer Interaction: Toward the Year 2000.* San Francisco: Morgan Kaufmann Publishers, 1995.

Bazerman, M.H. *Judgment in Managerial Decision Making.* New York: John Wiley and Sons, 2002.

Berry, D.M. Software and house requirements engineering: lessons learned in combating requirements creep. *Requirements Engineering,* 3, 3 (1998), 242–244.

Boland, R., and Greenberg, R. Method and metaphor in organizational analysis. *Accounting, Management, and Information Technology,* 2, 2 (1992), 117–141.

Bolloju, N. Improving the quality of business object models using collaboration patterns. *Communications of the ACM,* 47, 7 (2004), 81–86.

Borovits, I.; Ellis, S.; and Yeheskel, O. Group processes and the development of information systems. *Information and Management,* 19 (1990), 65–72.

Bostrom, R.P. Successful application of communication techniques to improve the systems development process. *Information & Management,* 16 (1989), 279–295.

Brady, D. Reaping the wind. *BusinessWeek,* October 11, 2004, 201–202.

Brassard, M. *The Memory Jogger Plus+.* Methuen, MA: GOAL/QPC, 1989.

Britton, C., and Jones, S. The untrained eye: how languages for software specification support understanding in untrained users. *Human-Computer Interaction,* 14, 1 (1999), 191–244.

Brooks, F.P. No silver bullet: essence and accidents of software engineering. *Computer,* 20, 4 (1987), 10–19.

Browne, G.J., and Curley, S.P. Reasoning with category knowledge in probability forecasting: Typicality and perceived variability effects. In G. Wright and P. Goodwin (eds.), *Forecasting with Judgment.* Chichester: John Wiley and Sons, 1998, pp. 169–200.

Browne, G.J., and Ramesh, V. Improving information requirements determination: a cognitive perspective. *Information & Management,* 39 (2002), 625–645.

Browne, G. J.; Ramesh, V.; Pitts, M. G.; Rogich, M.B. Representing user requirements: an empirical investigation of formality in modeling tools. In *Proceedings of the Americas Conference on Information Systems,* 1997 (available at http://aisel.isworld.org/Publications/AMCIS/1997/browne.htm, accessed on January 4, 2006).

Browne, G.J., and Rogich M.B. An empirical investigation of user requirements elicitation: Comparing the effectiveness of prompting techniques. *Journal of Management Information Systems*, 17 (2001), 223–249.

Bustard, D.W.; He, Z.; and Wilkie, F.G. Linking soft systems and use-case modelling through scenarios. *Interacting with Computers*, 13, 1 (2000), 97–110.

Byrd, T.A.; Cossick K.L.; and Zmud, R.W. A synthesis of research on requirements analysis and knowledge acquisition techniques. *MIS Quarterly*, 16 (1992), 117–138.

Carroll, J.M. *Making Use: Scenario-Based Design of Human-Computer Interactions*. Cambridge, MA: MIT Press, 2000.

Conkar, T.; Noyes, J.M.; and Kimble, C. CLIMATE: A framework for developing holistic requirements analysis in virtual environments. *Interacting with Computers*, 11, 4 (1999), 387–402.

Couger, J.D. *Creativity and Innovation in Information Systems Organizations*. Danvers, MA: Boyd and Fraser Publishing Co., 1996.

Coughlan, J., and Macredie, R.D. Effective communication in requirements elicitation: A comparison of methodologies. *Requirements Engineering*, 7, 2 (2002), 47–60.

Curtis, B.; Krasner, H.; and Iscoe, N. A field study of the software design process for large systems. *Communications of the ACM*, 31, 11 (1988), 1268–1287.

Dalal, N.P., and Yadav, S.B. The design of a knowledge-based decision support system to support the information analyst in determining requirements. *Decision Sciences*, 23, (1992), 1373–1388.

Damodaran, L. User involvement in the systems design process—a practical guide for users. *Behaviour and Information Technology*, 15, 6 (1996), 363–377.

Davidson, E.J. Joint application design (JAD) in practice. *Journal of Systems and Software*, 45, 3 (1999), 215–223.

Davidson, E.J. Technology frames and framing: a socio-cognitive investigation of requirements determination. *MIS Quarterly*, 26, 4 (2002), 329–358.

Davis, G.B. Strategies for information requirements determination. *IBM Systems Journal*, 21, 1 (1982), 4–30.

Dhillon, G. Dimensions of power and IS implementation. *Information & Management*, 41 (2004), 635–644.

Doll, W.J., and Torkzadeh, G. A discrepancy model of end-user computing involvement. *Management Science*, 35, 10 (1989), 1151–1171.

Doll, W.J., and Torkzadeh, G. A congruence construct of user involvement. *Decision Sciences*, 22, 2 (1991), 443–453.

Dubé, L., and Robey, D. Software stories: three cultural perspectives on the organizational practices of software development. *Accounting, Management, and Information Technology*, 9 (1999), 223–259.

Duggan, E.W., and C.S. Thachenkary. Integrating nominal group technique and joint application development for improved systems requirements determination. *Information & Management*, 41 (2004), 399–411.

Ewusi-Mensah, K. Critical issues in abandoned information systems projects. *Communications of the ACM*, 40 (1997), 74–80.

Fisher, R., and Geiselman, R. *Memory Enhancing Techniques for Investigative Interviewing*. Springfield, IL: Charles Thomas Publishers, 1992.

Fleishman, E.A., and Quaintance, M.K. *Taxonomies of Human Performance: The Description of Human Tasks*. New York: Academic Press, 1984.

Galal, G.H., and Paul, R.J. A qualitative scenario approach to managing evolving requirements. *Requirements Engineering*, 4, 2 (1999), 92–102.

Galegher, J., and Kraut, R. Computer-mediated communication for intellectual teamwork: An experiment in group writing. *Information Systems Research*, 5, 2 (1994), 110–138.

Gibson, J.J. The theory of affordances. In R.E. Shaw and J. Bransford (eds.), *Perceiving, Acting, and Knowing*. Hillsdale, NJ: Lawrence Erlbaum Associates, 1977, pp. 62–82.

Grünbacher, P.; Halling, M.; Biffl, S.; Kitapci, H.; and Boehm, B.W. Integrating collaborative processes and quality assurance techniques: experiences from requirements negotiation. *Journal of Management Information Systems*, 20, 4 (2004), 9–29.

Guinan, P.J.; Cooprider, J.G.; and Faraj, S. Enabling software development team performance during requirements definition: a behavioral versus technical approach. *Information Systems Research*, 9, 2 (1998), 101–125.

Hahn, J. and Kim, J. Why are some diagrams easier to work with? Effects of diagrammatic representation on the cognitive integration process of systems analysis and design. *ACM SIGCHI Bulletin*, 6, 3 (1999), 181–213.

Hamilton, D.P. Gambling it can move beyond PC, Intel offers a new processor. *The Wall Street Journal*, May 29, 2001, 1.

Havelka, D.A user-oriented model of factors that affect information requirements determination process quality. *Information Resources Management Journal,* 16, 4 (2003), 15–32.

Hickey, A.M., and Davis, A.M. A unified model of requirements elicitation. *Journal of Management Information Systems,* 20, 4 (2004), 65–84.

Hollan, J.; Hutchins, E.; and Kirsh, D. Distributed cognition: toward a new foundation for human-computer interaction research. *ACM Transactions on Computer-Human Interaction,* 7, 2 (2000), 174–196.

Holtzblatt, K., and Beyer, H.R. Requirements gathering: the human factor. *Communications of the ACM,* 38 (1995), 31–32.

Honold, P. Culture and context: an empirical study for the development of a framework for the elicitation of cultural influence in product usage. *International Journal of Human-Computer Interaction,* 12, 3/4 (2000), 327–346.

Howard, R.A. Knowledge maps. *Management Science,* 35 (1989), 903–922.

Jarke, M. Requirements tracing. *Communications of the ACM,* 41, 12 (1998), 32–36.

Jarke, M., and Pohl, K. Requirements engineering in 2001: (virtually) managing a changing reality. *Software Engineering Journal,* 9, 6 (1994), 257–266.

Jiang, J.J.; Klein, G.; Hwang, H-G.; Huang, J.; Hung, S-Y. An exploration of the relationship between software development process maturity and project performance. *Information & Management,* 41 (2004), 279–288.

Jiang, J.J.; Muhanna, W.; and Klein, G. User resistance and strategies for promoting acceptance across system types. *Information & Management,* 37 (2000), 25–36.

Johnson, P.E.; Jamal, K.; and Berryman, R.G. Effects of framing on auditor decisions. *Organizational Behavior and Human Decision Processes,* 50 (1991), 75–105.

Kaiser, K.M., and Srinivasan, A. User-analyst differences: an empirical investigation of attitudes related to systems development. *Academy of Management Journal,* 25, 3 (1982), 630–646.

Kaulio, M.A., and Karlsson, I.C.M. Triangulation strategies in user requirements investigations: a case study on the development of an IT-mediated service. *Behaviour and Information Technology,* 17, 2 (1998), 103–112.

Keil, M., and Carmel, E. Customer-developer links in software development. *Communications of the ACM,* 38, 5 (1995), 33–44.

Kiesler, S., and Sproull, L. Group decision making and communication technology. *Organizational Behavior and Human Decision Processes,* 52 (1992), 96–123.

Kim, J.; Hahn, J.; and Hahn, H. How do we understand a system with (so) many diagrams? Cognitive integration processes in diagrammatic reasoning. *Information Systems Research,* 11, 3 (2000), 284–303.

Klein, G.; Kaempf, G.L.; Wolf, S.; Thorsden, M.; and Miller, T. Applying decision requirements to user-centered design. *International Journal of Human-Computer Studies,* 46, 1 (1997), 1–15.

Kuhn, K. Problems and benefits of requirements gathering with focus groups: a case study. *International Journal of Human-Computer Interaction,* 12, 3/4 (2000), 309–325.

Larsen, T.J., and Naumann, J.D. An experimental comparison of abstract and concrete representations in systems analysis. *Information & Management,* 22 (1992), 29–40.

Lauer, T.W.; Peacock, E.; and Jacobs, S.M. Question generation and the systems analysis process. In T.W. Lauer, E. Peacock, and A.C. Graesser (eds.), *Questions and Information Systems.* Hillsdale, NJ: Lawrence Erlbaum, 1992, pp. 47–61.

Leifer, R.; Lee, S.; and Durgee, J. Deep structures: real information requirements determination. *Information and Management,* 27 (1994), 275–285.

Maiden, N.; Minocha, S.; Sutcliffe, A.; Manuel. D; and Ryan, M. A co-operative scenario based approach to acquisition and validation of system requirements: how exceptions can help! *Interacting with Computers,* 11, 6 (1999), 645–664.

Maiden, N.A.M., and M. Hare. Problem domain categories in requirements engineering. *International Journal of Human-Computer Studies,* 49, 3 (1998), 281–304.

Marakas, G.M., and Elam, J.J. Semantic structuring in analyst acquisition and representation of facts in requirements analysis. *Information Systems Research,* 9, 1 (1998), 37–63.

Markus, M.L. Power, politics, and MIS implementation. *Communications of the ACM,* 26 (1983), 430–444.

Markus, M.L., and Bjørn-Andersen, N. Power over users: its exercise by system professionals. *Communications of the ACM,* 30, 6 (1987), 498–504.

Mason, R. The role of metaphors in strategic information systems planning. *Journal of Management Information Systems,* 9, 2 (1991), 11–30.

Mayhew, D.J. *The Usability Engineering Lifecycle: A Practitioner's Guide to User Interface Design.* San Francisco: Morgan Kaufmann Publishers, 1999.

McGraw, K.L., and Harbison, K. *User-Centered Requirements: The Scenario-Based Engineering Process Approach.* Hillsdale, NJ: Lawrence Erlbaum Associates, 1997.

Mennecke, B.E.; Crossland, M.D.; and Killingsworth, B.L. Is a map more than a picture: the role of SDSS technology, subject characteristics, and problem complexity on map reading and problem solving. *MIS Quarterly,* 24, 4 (2000), 601–629.

Mills, S. The importance of task analysis in usability context analysis—designing for fitness for purpose. *Behaviour and Information Technology,* 19, 1 (2000), 57–68.

Montazemi, A.R., and Conrath, D.W. The use of cognitive mapping for information requirements analysis. *MIS Quarterly,* 10 (1986), 45–55.

Moody, J.W.; Blanton, J.E.; and Cheney, P.H. A theoretically grounded approach to assist memory recall during information requirements determination. *Journal of Management Information Systems,* 15, 1 (1998), 79–98.

Mylopoulos, J.; Chung, L.; and Yu, E. From object-oriented to goal-oriented requirements analysis. *Communications of the ACM,* 42, 1 (1999), 31–37.

Nielsen, J. *Usability Engineering.* London: Academic Press, 1993.

Norman, D.A. *The Design of Everyday Things.* New York: Basic Books, 1990.

O'Neill, E.; Johnson, P.; Johnson, H. Representations and user-developer interaction in cooperative analysis and design. *Human-Computer Interaction,* 14, 1 (1999), 43–91.

Ocker, R.; Fjermestad, J.; Hiltz, S.R.; and Johnson, K. Effects of four modes of group communication on the outcomes of software requirements determination. *Journal of Management Information Systems,* 15, 1 (1998), 99–118.

Parker, H.; Roast, C.; and Siddiqi, J. Towards a framework for investigating temporal properties in interaction. *ACM SIGCHI Bulletin,* 29, 1 (1997), 56–60.

Parsons, J. Effects of local versus global schema diagrams on verification and communication in conceptual data modeling. *Journal of Management Information Systems,* 19, 3 (2002), 155–183.

Patel, N.V. The spiral change model for coping with changing and ongoing requirements. *Requirements Engineering,* 4, 2 (1999), 77–84.

Pitts, M.G., and Browne, G.J. Stopping behavior of systems analysts during information requirements elicitation. *Journal of Management Information Systems,* 21 (2004), 213–236.

Plant, R., and A.D. Preece. Editorial special issue on verification and validation. *International Journal of Human-Computer Studies,* 44, 2 (1996), 123–125.

Potts, C.; Takahashi, K.; Anton, A.I. Inquiry-based requirement analysis. *IEEE Software,* 11, 2 (1994), 21–32.

Ramaprasad, A., and Poon, E.A. A computerized interactive technique for mapping influence diagrams (MIND). *Strategic Management Journal,* 6 (1985), 377–392.

Richards, D., and Compton, P. Taking up the situated cognition challenge with ripple down rules. *International Journal of Human-Computer Studies,* 49, 6 (1998), 895–926.

Richardson, J.; Ormerod, T.C.; and Shepherd, A. The role of task analysis in capturing requirements for interface design. *Interacting with Computers,* 9, 4 (1998), 367–384.

Roast, C. Specifying cognitive interface requirements. *ACM SIGCHI Bulletin,* 29, 1 (1997), 66–67.

Robertson, S., and Robertson, J. *Mastering the Requirements Process.* Harlow, England: ACM Press, Addison-Wesley, 1999.

Robey, D., and Newman, M. Sequential patterns in information systems development: an application of a social process model. *ACM Transactions on Information Systems,* 14, 1 (1996), 30–63.

Romano, N.C.; Donovan, C.; Chen, H.; and Nunamaker, J.F. A methodology for analyzing web-based qualitative data. *Journal of Management Information Systems,* 19, 4 (2003), 213–246.

Rosson, M.B., and Carroll, J.M. *Usability Engineering: Scenario-Based Development of Human Computer Interaction.* San Francisco: Morgan Kaufmann Publishers, 2001.

Sakthivel, S., and Tanniru, M.R. Information system verification and validation during requirement analysis using petri nets. *Journal of Management Information Systems,* 5, 3 (1989), 33–52.

Schenk, K.D.; Vitalari, N.P.; and Davis, K.S. Differences between novice and expert systems analysts: what do we know and what do we do? *Journal of Management Information Systems,* 15, 1 (1998), 9–50.

Simon, H.A. Information processing models of cognition. *Annual Review of Psychology,* 30, (1979), 363–396.

Simon, H.A. *The Sciences of the Artificial.* Cambridge, MA: MIT Press, 1981.

Smith, A., and Dunckley, L. Prototype evaluation and redesign: structuring the design space through contextual techniques. *Interacting with Computers,* 14, 6 (2002), 821–843.

Spetzler, C.S., and Stael von Holstein, C.S. Probability encoding in decision analysis. *Management Science,* 22, 3 (1975), 340–358.

Stacy, W., and Macmillan J. Cognitive bias in software engineering. *Communications of the ACM,* 38 (1995), 57–63.

Standish Group. Extreme chaos. (2001) (available at http://www.standishgroup.com/sample_research/PDFpages/extreme_chaos.pdf, accessed on January 4, 2006).

Stary, C., and Peschl, M.F. Representation still matters: cognitive engineering and user interface design. *Behaviour and Information Technology,* 17, 6 (1998), 338–360.

Sutcliffe, A. Task-related information analysis. *International Journal of Human-Computer Studies,* 47, 2 (1997), 223–257.

Sutcliffe, A.; Ryan, M.; Doubleday, A.; and Springett, M. Model mismatch analysis: towards a deeper explanation of users' usability problems. *Behaviour and Information Technology,* 19, 1 (2000) 43–55.

Sutcliffe, A.G., and Maiden, N.A.M. Analysing the novice analyst: cognitive models in software engineering. *International Journal of Man-Machine Studies,* 36, 5 (1992), 719–740.

Tan, M. Establishing mutual understanding in systems design: an empirical study. *Journal of Management Information Systems,* 10, 4 (1994), 159–182.

Teng, J.T.C., and Sethi, V. A comparison of information requirements analysis methods: an experimental study. *Data Base,* 20, 4 (1990), 27–39.

Turner, P., and Turner, S. A web of contradictions. *Interacting with Computers,* 14, 1 (2002), 1–14.

Tversky, A., and Kahneman, D. Judgment under uncertainty: heuristics and biases. *Science,* 185 (1974), 1124–1131.

Vessey, I., and Conger, S. Learning to specify information requirements: the relationship between application and methodology. *Journal of Management Information Systems,* 10, 2 (1993), 177–201.

Viller, S.; Bowers, J.; and Rodden, T. Human factors in requirements engineering: A survey of human sciences literature relevant to the improvement of dependable systems development processes. *Interacting with Computers,* 11, 6 (1999), 665–698.

Vitalari, N.P. Structuring the requirements analysis process for information systems: a propositional viewpoint. In W.W. Cotterman and J.A. Senn (eds.), *Challenges and Strategies for Research in Systems Development.* New York: John Wiley and Sons, 1992, pp. 163–179.

von Winterfeldt, D., and Edwards, W. *Decision Analysis and Behavioral Research.* Cambridge: Cambridge University Press, 1986.

Walz, D.B.; Elam, J.J.; and Curtis, B. Inside a software design team: knowledge acquisition, sharing, and integration. *Communications of the ACM,* 36, 10 (1993), 63–77.

Watson, H.J., and Frolick, M.N. Determining information requirements for an EIS. *MIS Quarterly,* 17 (1993), 255–269.

Wetherbe, J.C. Executive information requirements: getting it right. *MIS Quarterly,* 15 (1991), 51–65.

Wood, R.E. Task complexity: definition of the construct. *Organizational Behavior and Human Decision Processes,* 37 (1986), 60–82.

Yadav, S.B.; Bravoco, R.R.; Chatfield, A.T.; and Rajkumar, T.M. Comparison of analysis techniques for information requirement determination. *Communications of the ACM,* 31 (1988), 1090–1097.

Yang, H-L., and Tang, J-H. A three-stage model of requirements elicitation for web-based information systems. *Industrial Management and Data Systems,* 103, 6 (2003), 398–409.

Yang, H-L., and Tang, J-H. Team structure and team performance in IS development: a social network perspective. *Information and Management,* 41 (2004), 335–349.

Zave, P. Classification of research efforts in requirements engineering. *ACM Computing Surveys,* 29, 4,(1997), 315–321.

Zmud, R.W.; Anthony, W.P.; and Stair, R.M, Jr. The use of mental imagery to facilitate information identification in requirements analysis, *Journal of Management Information Systems,* 9, 4 (1993), 175–191.

CHAPTER 14

DIMENSIONS OF PARTICIPATION IN INFORMATION SYSTEMS DESIGN

JOHN M. CARROLL AND MARY BETH ROSSON

Abstract: Only twenty years ago, participatory design (PD) seemed to North Americans a curious Scandinavian perspective. Today, it is widely employed in community informatics, and increasingly in commercial development practices as well. We survey PD from the standpoint of six dimensions of participation: participatory impetus, ownership, scope of design, nature of the participatory process, scope of cooperation, and expectations about learning and human development. Using these dimensions as a framework, we analyze several traditional and emerging models for PD: the original European model (illustrated by the Utopia project); the early North American model (illustrated by the PICTIVE method), and recent variations involving long-term participatory interactions oriented to role development; and an embedded participant model emphasizing facilitation of user initiatives. We discuss when and how various PD approaches are most useful.

Keywords: Participatory Design, Cooperative Design, User-Centered Design

INTRODUCTION

One of the chief lessons learned from the past thirty years of design studies is the recognition of the range and amount of knowledge involved in design. This lesson was not the discrete result of a research program that determined the scope and nature of design knowledge. Indeed, one can see the "new" design methods of the 1970s as a rather concerted effort to push toward a general (that is, domain knowledge free) kit of techniques (Jones, 1970). Nonetheless, the lesson has crept up on us over the years. No longer are customer interviews and focus groups regarded as a comprehensive method for gathering design requirements. Concepts such as stakeholders, trade-offs, design rationale, emergent requirements, design patterns, tacit knowledge, and invisible work have increasingly complicated the picture. Theoretical perspectives such as situated action (Suchman, 1987), activity theory (Nardi, 1996), distributed cognition (Hutchins, 1995), and sociotechnical systems theory (Eason, 1988) have called attention to the critical role of context in design. These perspectives have promoted a broadening of the design problem to include a variety of mediating artifacts, social networks and communities, norms, division of labor, and roles. Today, users are conceptualized as embedded in communities of practice whose knowledge, including self-knowledge, is enacted rather than effable, in the traditional sense of requirements. What are we to do?

An increasingly common response to the complexity and context-laden trade-offs in design is to engage users (and the communities to which they belong) in a participatory process. By bringing the users themselves into the process, participatory design (PD) facilitates the sharing of tacit knowledge. Even if a user-participant cannot explicitly describe a specific work process contingency, his or her knowledge could still enter into the design deliberation through expressed preferences, design visions and other shared construction activities, and through linked discussions. Moreover, incorporating the users, as well as their knowledge, into the process does something more. It re-allocates power in technology development and adoption.

Participatory design covers all design methods in which users (and other stakeholders) are independent actors in designs. It overlaps with joint application design (JAD; Wood and Silver, 1989) to the extent that representative end users are invited and engaged in JAD sessions. However, JAD sessions tend to be structured as business focus groups, with the user representatives drawn from middle management (Carmet et al., 1993). Participatory design that focuses on end users is an obvious way to bring more knowledge into the design process. It allows the intended users of a system to bring their work-domain knowledge to the decision making about designed systems that ultimately will impact their practices and communities.

In this paper, we survey PD from the standpoint of six dimensions of participation: participatory impetus, ownership, scope of design, nature of the participatory process, scope of cooperation, and expectations about learning and development. Using these dimensions as a framework, we analyze several traditional and emerging models for PD: the original European model, the North American model, and recent variations involving long-term participatory interactions oriented to role development, and an embedded participant model emphasizing facilitation of user initiatives. We discuss when and how various PD approaches are most useful.

DIMENSIONS OF PARTICIPATION

Broadening participation by users and other stakeholders in design is not a monolithic intervention. PD is best conceived as a space of related methods, rather than a single approach. Muller and his colleagues (Muller et al., 1993; see also Muller et al., 1997) offer one view of this space, classifying PD methods according to their position in the product development life cycle, the extent to which designers participate in the users' world (or vice versa), and the size of the groups who work together. For example, ethnographic field studies of workplace practices are often carried out early in a product lifecycle and involve the immersion of one to several analysts into a workplace. In contrast, collaborative low-fidelity prototyping, in which designers and potential users work together with simple materials to create user interface mock-ups, is likely to occur in later phases of development and in the developer's laboratory. Collaborative prototyping usually involves a rather small group of users and designers.

A complementary approach to classifying PD methods highlights the social and organizational context in which PD takes place—for example how participation is initiated and managed, and the consequences for stakeholders of what is created or learned through the process. Clement and van den Besselaar (1993) analyzed a collection of PD projects from the 1970s and '80s. They described how participation took different forms across this sample of projects. In some, users became involved in the development of technology assessment criteria and guidelines. In others, users helped to create new organizational forms including support infrastructure. In half of the projects studied, users were participating in the development of participatory practices.

Our view expands on the distinctions made by Clement and van den Besselaar (1993). Like these researchers, we consider *participatory impetus* to be a critical factor, but we also identify several other dimensions of the PD context (Table 14.1). Borrowing from soft systems theory (Checkland, 1981; Checkland and Scholes, 1990) we see *ownership* as an essential feature; the

Table 14.1

Six Dimensions that Define a Space of Participatory Design Methods

Dimension	Defining Question	Possibilities
Participatory Impetus	Whose initiative led to adopting a participatory approach?	External agents (e.g., university researchers); technology developers; the workers/users; other stakeholders
Ownership	Who controls the work activity being supported? Who authorized the project? Who else participates?	Management in a customer organization; technology developers; workers/users; external parties; some mixture of the above
Scope of Design Concerns	What is the design discussion about? What is being produced?	User interface; UI plus software functionality; sociotechnical work system; new PD practices or other infrastructure
Scope of Cooperative Process	When and how long is the cooperative relationship? How is it interleaved with other design activities?	Single workshop or session; multiple workshops on single development phase (e.g., requirements); workshops spanning two or more phases (e.g., requirements and design); workshops spanning entire life cycle; pervasive work collaboration
Nature of the Participatory Interaction	How do participants interact? What analysis and design activities do they share?	Discussion; task/scenario analysis or envisionment; role-playing; creating storyboards, mock-ups or prototypes; design walkthroughs
Expectations about Learning and Development	What do participants (including designers) expect as outcomes beyond the specific work product?	Nothing; designers learn about users' task domain; users learn about technology; users assume responsibility for maintenance and further design

people or groups who own the process determine its character and outcomes whether or not they are the ultimate users.

Two important constraints on the PD process are the scope of design concerns and the scope of the cooperative process. A PD process addressing a narrow or well-understood problem domain (e.g., a Web system for travel reservations) or a well-defined piece of a design endeavor (e.g., the user interface) is likely to be easier, more structured, and more likely to have a good outcome than one aimed at a broad or exploratory problem (e.g., a knowledge management system). Similarly, a PD engagement that is relatively brief and modular (e.g., a single workshop) will have less impact on the overall design than one that involves continuous fieldwork and formative evaluation extending over weeks or months.

Clearly the nature of the participatory interaction has many consequences, as suggested by the taxonomy of Muller et al. (1997)—for example, the collaborative construction of a prototype produces very different experiences and outcomes than a group discussion about the priority of requirements. Finally, every PD process includes (often implicit) expectations about learning and development. From the outside, PD is about facilitating the analysis of requirements and iterative development. But users and their managers may also expect to learn about technology; developers may expect to learn more about work practices. Some users may even transition into a technology position after enough PD activities; developers may become more interested and attuned to the problems of user support.

One reason to construct an analysis of participation into separate dimensions is to articulate participatory design beyond the general concept of designers and users interacting directly. This is likely to be a progressive endeavor for the field. Clement and Van den Besselaar (1993) enumerated what they called "ingredients" for participation: (1) workers must have access to relevant information; (2) workers must have the opportunity to take independent positions on issues; (3) workers must be included in the processes of decision making; (4) appropriate participatory methods must be available; and (5) the process must include sufficient organizational and technological flexibility. The six dimensions articulate a more refined view of participation than these five guidelines. Nonetheless they are also just a partial view, and we expect that others will build from these dimensions to an even more comprehensive and specific enumeration of ways that stakeholders can become involved in participatory endeavors, the ways these joint projects can be organized and managed, the types of design concerns they can address, and the kinds of outcomes they can aspire to and achieve.

Through these dimensions of participation we can reflect more systematically on the differences among alternative approaches to participatory design. The dimensions provide a practical framework for thinking about a range of PD methods, emphasizing how they are conducted and experienced in the context of different PD settings. Note that the six dimensions and associated questions are not mutually exclusive. It is certainly possible that there is a shared impetus for initiating a PD process, that the scope is multi-faceted or evolutionary, and so on. Our argument is simply that these dimensions capture important social and organizational aspects of the PD process and thus are useful in contrasting, discussing, and integrating different approaches to PD.

In the balance of this paper, we use the six dimensions to compare and contrast four paradigms of PD—the cooperative design of work, collaborative prototyping of user interface, long-term participatory design, and embedded design within communities.

COOPERATIVE DESIGN OF WORK: UTOPIA

Participatory design of information systems and technology originated in Scandinavia. At the heart of the early efforts was a commitment to workplace democracy, to enhancing the voice of employees in determining their work practices and their use of information technologies (Bjerknes and Bratteteig, 1995; Ehn and Kyng, 1987). A corollary was the goal of increasing workers' understanding and competence with respect to technology, so that they could better contribute to the process of envisioning its application to their practices. The overall participatory process is sometimes summarized as one of mutual learning, where designers and end users cooperate to understand more about their differing backgrounds and expectations (Kensing and Madsen, 1993).

Project Summary

A classic example of PD in the Scandinavian tradition is the UTOPIA project (Bødker et al., 1987). In this project, researchers from Danish and Swedish universities collaborated with newspaper journalists and graphic workers to develop computer-based tools for reporting and publishing activities. A key stakeholder in the project was the Nordic Graphic Worker's Union; indeed, one motivation for the project was to study ways for giving trade unions a more proactive influence on technology in the workplace. Midway through the project the trade union introduced a technology partner (Liber) interested in a specific aspect of newspaper publishing—page layout and image processing. This relationship led to a narrowing of the project's scope but also resulted in broader support from other national agencies with the mission of facilitating technological development.

The UTOPIA project began with a study of existing technology, work practices, and training, including those prevalent in American newspapers at the time. These investigations were used to develop alternative scenarios for design, including analysis of the challenges inherent in existing practices (e.g., demand for rapid feedback, integration of different technologies). After Liber joined the team and the scope was narrowed to layout and graphics, the trade union provided access to a series of worker representatives who collaborated with the researchers to develop a requirements specification. An innovative aspect of the project was a "technology laboratory" where workers could try out simulations and mock-ups of a variety of tools.

Ultimately the long-term goals of UTOPIA were difficult to realize, to a large part because of conflicting values amongst the diverse stakeholders. Once a pilot system was available, the university researchers wanted to continue their investigation, now focusing on how the pilot system helped (or did not help) graphic workers and journalists to find new ways to collaborate. However the national technology board and hosting newspapers were eager to simply adopt the (prototype) technology; the journalists' trade union was also opposed to an organized experiment. Thus the project concluded with the installation and evaluation of what the team had intended as a pilot system.

Dimensions of Participation

A critical feature of UTOPIA was that its participatory rationale emerged from a history of political and social action on the part of (and for the benefits of) workers. The researchers on the design team were specifically interested in whether and how trade unions and the workers they represent could have a more effective voice in the development and adoption of technology in the workplace and they used this interest to attract other stakeholders. Thus while the impetus for the project came from the university researchers, they were motivated by a combination of scientific goals (design methods) and sociopolitical concerns.

Project ownership started out in the hands of the research team. However, it shifted as the project transpired—after the newspaper publishers and trade unions became involved, the project became more real, and both prospered and suffered as a result. More attention and resources became available (e.g., a real-world software development company and a federal agency joined the collaboration), but at the same time the scope of the design effort was narrowed to coincide with the software company's interest, and ownership and control gradually shifted to the outside organizations. From the research team's view the project ended prematurely: after developing a prototype, the newspapers and trade unions demonstrated ownership by declining to participate in further analysis and design efforts.

The nature of the participation was quite varied. Indeed the methods innovated and demonstrated in this project have had long-lasting effects on PD both in Scandinavia and elsewhere (Madsen, 1999; Muller et al., 1997; Kyng, 1995). Ethnographic field studies, problem analysis workshops, end-user interaction with mock-ups varying in fidelity, and future workshops have become commonplace in usability labs worldwide, and many of these modern techniques were modeled on those explored by the UTOPIA researchers.

The scope of the cooperative process was several years, beginning with the detailed field studies and concluding with the development of an initial prototype. The research team was in place throughout this period to invent, organize, and facilitate the diverse PD interactions. The other participants varied according to the phase of the project (e.g., observing graphics workers on the job; bringing in trade union members for analysis sessions or to work with mock-ups as the design ideas became more concrete). Of course not all stakeholders participated in the same fashion—the federal agency helped in obtaining resources and served as a reviewer or consultant, but was not concretely involved in the PD interactions.

The social and political history leading to UTOPIA meant that the team expected not just a concrete outcome (i.e., newspaper publishing software) but also mutual learning outcomes in which end users learned more about technology options and the designers learned more about newspaper publishing. However, the emphasis was clearly more on the former than the latter, with much effort spent on training that would raise the literacy and further empower graphic workers in Scandinavia.

An evocative metaphor for summarizing PD interactions in the UTOPIA project is that of a *movie or play producer.* The vision of the design team was to create for the graphics workers a meaningful and engaging process of technology learning and application. They documented the current practices and preferences of these workers, then developed carefully scripted interactions with them that built gradually toward a climax, in this case the delivery of a prototype system that the workers could understand and apply in their own work contexts.

COLLABORATIVE PROTOTYPING OF USER INTERFACES: PICTIVE

The American approach to PD has a different emphasis than the Scandinavian. As discussed in the May 1999 special section of *Communications of the ACM* (Madsen, 1999), many of the U.S. companies that pioneered PD methods were developing these methods in concert with professional usability labs. The focus of these labs was on the iterative design of user interfaces (UIs); in a typical lab study, representative users would attempt tasks on a prototype UI, and the evaluators would generate a report of usability problems that could be addressed to improve ease of learning and use. Usability testing methods such as these were given a PD component by asking users to collaborate in design of the UI prototypes.

Project Summary

An early and well-known example of collaborative prototyping is the PICTIVE method (plastic interface for collaborative technology initiatives through video exploration; Muller, 1992). The method includes techniques for participatory creation of low-fidelity UI mock-ups—using paper, scissors, colored pens, and other generic office supplies—relatively early in a design life cycle; it was inspired by the experiences with mock-ups in the UTOPIA project. Similar techniques are used to review or analyze existing software and tasks, but in this case the source materials for the mock-ups may include screen shots or UI components from an installed system. The intent is to de-mystify the analysis and prototyping process, making it more accessible to non-technical participants through the use of informal and familiar construction materials. The participatory process is videotaped to document the design process and outcomes as an informal video design specification.

According to Muller et al. (1995), the strongest cases for PICTIVE methods are found in iterative design efforts. For instance, when designing the TelePICTIVE groupware application (a collaborative system for conducting PICTIVE-like methods via software), the design team met every few weeks to review progress on design and development. Based on their meeting results, they would schedule a PICTIVE session to collaboratively extend the prototype design with low-fidelity mock-ups. The paper and video records would then serve as input for the next few weeks of implementation. As the project progressed, the PICTIVE materials became more and more

Figure 14.1   **Physical Materials and Mock-up Created During a Collaborative Prototyping Session with Community Members Envisioning a Virtual Science Fair**

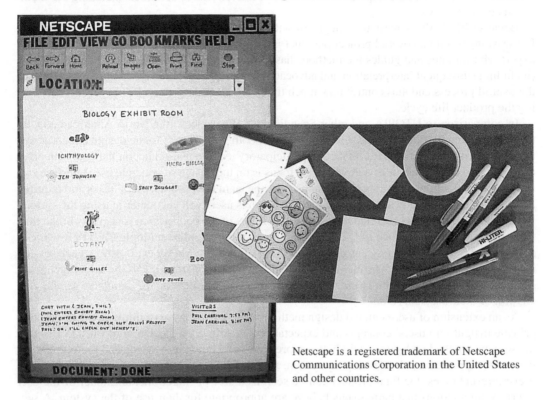

Netscape is a registered trademark of Netscape Communications Corporation in the United States and other countries.

customized for the state of the prototype (e.g., specific questions concerning interaction were explored using partial screen shots, dialog boxes, etc.).

The experience and results of collaborative prototyping sessions depend very much on what is offered as starting materials. For example, in PICTIVE sessions that we conducted with community members designing a "virtual science fair," we provided a felt board constructed to look like a Netscape® Web browser as a base for screen mock-ups (Rosson and Carroll, 2002; see Figure 14.1). We worked with groups of 3–4 older adults across several sessions in which scenarios were envisioned and then illustrated with the materials provided. During these PICTIVE sessions, we noticed that users who were already familiar with Web browsing were more confident and specific in their suggestions; they were clearly recruiting their experiences with other virtual spaces to think about how the science fair should be presented and navigated. Offering an overarching metaphor such as a Web browser is a powerful technique, both in activating participants' prior knowledge and in simplifying the design space.

Dimensions of Participation

When PICTIVE was invented at Bell Labs in the early 1990s (Muller, 1991), its underlying rationale was that of usability engineering. At the time, North American information technology industries were still learning how best to attend to usability concerns, and Muller's methods were developed as part of an industry research group exploring a range of methods for improving product usability. Product design teams increasingly had usability experts as members, and it was these members who provided the impetus for many user-centered design activities, including PD methods such as PICTIVE.

Because PICTIVE is normally integrated with a product's usability engineering process, the PD sessions fit into an overall project plan that is owned by the development team. The usability expert who initiates and guides the methods has a direct responsibility for their implementation (including subsequent interpretation and advocacy) but the product manager would typically own the overall process and thus control how much time and effort is spent on PICTIVE sessions during the product life cycle.

In comparison to UTOPIA and other Scandinavian PD projects, the North American adaptation represented by PICTIVE has a narrower scope, both with respect to the design concerns and the cooperative interactions. PICTIVE is a participatory technique used in conjunction with other user-centered design activities, but where the focus is on the design of concrete user interface elements and interactions. The approach assumes that the team understands users' tasks and required functionality, and is ready to lay out the specific features users will encounter in using the system. Because the design goals are relatively narrow, the scope of the cooperation is also less broad than that observed in projects such as UTOPIA—although there might be multiple PICTIVE sessions supporting iterative design (e.g., as in the TelePICTIVE project; Muller et al., 1995), each session is an hour or two in length. The interactions are deliberately concrete, involving selection among source materials, construction of user interface elements, placement on the simulated screen, discussion of their use, and so on.

As an extension of user-centered design methods (e.g., card-sorting or think-aloud studies that provide insight into users' concepts and expectations), a primary expectation of PICTIVE is that the screens mocked up by users will better express and meet their own needs and preferences for the tasks supported by the developing system. By inviting and merging the efforts of multiple user-representatives, the final product can be seen as a sort of shared mental model of the user interface interactions that participants believe are appropriate for their use of the system. A secondary expectation is that participants would feel a sense of empowerment or contribution—when they see what they can achieve with common office supplies, they should come to understand that they are capable of making substantive contributions to technical design. Of course, in many cases the final system is intended for a much larger group of users, but even this larger group of users may feel more empowered if they know that people like them helped to design the final system's user interface.

As a summary of the PICTIVE approach we offer the *player* metaphor. Muller (1991) has described PICTIVE as providing an "equal opportunity surface" where end users can become active and engaged in selecting, positioning, and refining UI objects and actions. This physical activity can be seen like a design game (i.e., where the underlying goal is design rather than recreation), and the designers seek to become peers with the end users in playing this game.

LONG-TERM PARTICIPATORY DESIGN OF EDUCATIONAL TECHNOLOGY: LiNC

Participatory design requires that users be included as independent agents in design decision (Clement and van den Besselaar, 1993), but often participation is limited to a relatively small number of intensive analysis or design interactions, after which the designers take charge more or less as usual. Scheduled contact with participants is not a bad thing, but it is quite different from a participatory engagement that takes place in the context of ongoing work activities taking place

Figure 14.2 **A Collaborative Environment—the Virtual School—for Science Learning Activities Developed in the LiNC Project. On the left is a session window providing access to partners, applications, and status information. In the center is a multimedia notebook; a text annotation is being added. In the upper right is a video connection**

over months or years. The UTOPIA project occurred over several years, but the only continuous participants in the collaboration were the university researchers; the other partners were institutions (trade unions, publishers, agencies, etc.) who provided representatives for participation at various points of interest to them. An alternate model is to work extensively with a *single set* of participants in a longitudinal fashion, engaging them from the start in an iterative participatory analysis and design process.

Project Summary

During 1995–2001 our research team worked with a group of six middle and high school science teachers to develop computer support and curricular activities for collaborative classroom learning. Our project was embedded in the broader context of the Blacksburg Electronic Village, a leading community network project (Carroll and Rosson, 1996). We called the project Learning in a Networked Community, or LiNC. Our central concept was to allow the teachers to participate fully in the project, from requirements analysis and conceptual design through to evaluation, to successively discover and refine a model for collaborative science learning and to develop software infrastructure that could support that model. Major outcomes of the project included an environment for synchronous and asynchronous collaboration (Figure 14.2; Isenhour, Rosson, and Carroll, 2000), the analysis and design of collaborative science learning activities (Carroll, Chin, Rosson, and Neale, 2002; Chin, 2004; Dunlap, Neale, and Carroll, 2000), and the development of scenario-based participatory design methods (Carroll, Chin, Rosson, and Koenemann, 1998; Chin, 2004).

A premise of LiNC was that teacher participation would improve our chances of developing effective software for students; however the learning and development of the *teachers* became increasingly important to this work as the project transpired. This is not surprising. The history of classroom technology is a history of failure, a repeating pattern in which new technological ideas are developed outside the classroom, oversold as panaceas, and then delivered to the schools, at which point the teachers quietly set them aside to continue teaching (Tyack and Cuban, 2000). Indeed our use of participatory design was an effort to try to break this pattern.

Throughout the LiNC project we interacted extensively with the teachers, in their classrooms and planning areas and in our university research setting. We observed classroom layouts and practices; they visited our labs and meeting rooms to observe technology demonstrations and participate in research discussions. The regular teacher-researcher interactions helped us to focus on the larger context surrounding the project: we explicitly discussed training, logistical, and organizational exigencies and constraints for new classroom technology; we discussed what might be lost pedagogically in remote collaborations; and we discussed impacts on the job role of classroom teachers.

In retrospect, we observed that our extended relationship with LiNC teachers had four distinct stages; evolution through these stages was developmental in the sense that it resolved manifest conflicts in activity through the assumption of greater responsibility and scope of action (Piaget and Inhelder, 1969; Vygotsky, 1978). Each successive stage was a relatively stable organization of knowledge, skills, and attitudes that resolved the instigating conflict. The teachers were initially practitioner-informants; we observed their classroom practices and we interviewed them. Subsequently, they became analysts who were directly and actively involved in requirements analysis and development. Approximately two and half years into the project, the teachers became designers for key aspects of LiNC. During the final two years, the teachers were coaches of their own peers. (This summary focuses on the teachers' development, though we believe a complementary analysis could be constructed for our own development.)

An illustrative example of cognitive conflict and corresponding development is the teachers' transition from informants to analysts. Early in the project we visited classrooms, videotaping small group activities and discussion, and talking with teachers and students. A few months later, we organized a two-week all-hands workshop, where as a group we viewed and discussed video-clips of classroom activity (selected to illustrate themes identified via ethnographic analysis; see Chin, 2004). We used the ideas of scenario-based development (Carroll, 2000; Rosson and Carroll, 2003) in which current practices are analyzed to identify trade-offs that hypothesize and contrast a mix of positive and negative consequences for specific features of a situation (e.g., the observed or likely consequences of allowing students to self-organize into project groups). Up to this point, LiNC teachers had listened and reacted to our ideas, but as they reviewed and discussed *examples of their own practices* their participation became much more active and pointed. Indeed, when we analyzed a videotape of the workshop discussion, we determined that the teachers proposed as many features and trade-offs as the researchers did, despite the fact that we were using analysis methods developed by our research group, and there were twice as many researchers as teachers.

In our analysis the teachers faced a developmental conflict. We had collected field data and were moving to construct a list of requirements for software that would be implemented that summer. They had committed to using the software in their classrooms in the following year. The stakes were too high for them to sit back, observe, and answer questions posed by us. Moreover by seeing their work in action and by activating their everyday skills of trade-off analysis, they were able to see a more ambitious role for themselves in the group, a role that might help to ensure the right system would be built. The transition is best conceived as a developmental stage because after their behavior in the workshops the teachers never returned to their earlier classroom informant role.

Dimensions of Participation

Like the UTOPIA project, LiNC was initiated as a research project by university faculty and students. Thus the impetus came from the researchers' interest in questions related to the possibilities and consequences of online collaboration in science learning, and the efficacy of scenario-based design methods in the design of educational technology. The researchers were also the owners of the project, in the sense that they had won a grant to sponsor the research (ultimately it was the U.S. National Science Foundation that controlled these funds). However, in contrast to many educational research projects, the local school system was formally a full partner in the process—one of the grant's co–principal investigators was the school district's technology coordinator. Within the school system, the teachers reported to the technology coordinator with respect to their own innovative use of technology in the classroom. The technology coordinator formally recruited the teachers into the project, arranged for their research stipends, and so on. As the project continued, it became clear that the school really did control significant facets of the project, for instance school-related pragmatics such as arranging for network connections, installing and managing network firewalls, coordinating teaching schedules, and so on.

At the start of LiNC, the scope of the design concerns was collaborative learning activities in science that could be supported across classrooms using network-based software. As the project continued, the scope expanded to include the design of software supporting specific learning activities that might be part of such interactions (e.g., science simulations, analysis and reporting tools). As the teacher-participants evolved to become a more coherent sub-constituency, the design scope also expanded to include tools that would support their own shared planning and cooperation (e.g., outlines, schedules, grading rubrics, discussions about classroom experiences).

The participatory interactions in LiNC were frequent and varied over a period of approximately six years. During most of the project there were all-hands meetings every two weeks; the location of the meetings alternated between the university and one of the teachers' classrooms. These meetings were used to report progress and problems, as well as to share new tools or to carry out design brainstorming activities. In between these regular meetings, many other interactions took place, for example visits to classrooms to observe, videotape, and interview teachers and students, participatory analysis and design sessions with teachers and students, PICTIVE sessions with mock-ups at varying levels of fidelity, and rapid feedback collection and iterative design once prototype software was installed.

The teachers and the three principal university faculty remained involved throughout the six years. Three key graduate student researchers were each involved continuously for more than three years. Most of the interactions included at least one university researcher and at least one teacher, with the larger sessions also including school administration and a larger set of researchers. In the second half of the project, as the teachers cohered into a strong sub-group, they began meeting for teacher-only analysis and design sessions, enabling them to bring more specific and refined contributions to the all-hands meetings (Dunlap, Neale, and Carroll, 2000).

The expectations of the LiNC participants were for mutual learning—that the teachers would learn more about computer technology and its possibilities for enhancing science learning, and that the researchers would learn more about the practices and workplace culture of classroom teachers. As the project continued and we observed the teachers developing through several stages as collaborators (from informant, to analyst, to designer, to coach; see Carroll et al., 2000), we elaborated our expectations about the extent to which teachers could assume control for developing and disseminating LiNC or similar technologies.

An apt metaphor for summarizing participation in the LiNC project is that of co-worker. The project began by instantiating the teachers and school administration as equal partners on the design team: They attended and hosted meetings, and contributed to all phases of analysis and design. However, we discovered that despite our intentions, the teachers' initial view was that they were more passive participants, largely responsible for informing the rest of the team about classroom practices and requirements. Only after many sessions of practice in activity analysis and design were these teachers able to accept and flourish in the role of equal collaborators.

EMBEDDED DESIGN OF SUSTAINABLE TECHNOLOGY: CIVIC NEXUS

Most design methods—and studies thereof—focus on a design *product*, for example, digital tools for newspaper workers or collaborative systems for cooperative science learning. These methods are appropriate for situations where there is a specific known need (or a specific known technology that stakeholders wish to leverage [Woodward, 1965]). Most design methods thus seek to increase the chances that a designed solution will address the needs and preferences of its intended users, while of course also meeting the needs and preferences of other stakeholders such as managers, software developers, marketers, and so on. Recently, however, we have been studying a different design situation, one in which the end goal is not a particular technology solution but rather a sustainable process of technology learning and application.

Project Summary

In 2003, we initiated a participatory project with a diverse set of community partners in the Centre County region of Pennsylvania (United States) to help them as they learned about and used technology to pursue existing goals, and as they envisioned new directions for their organizations. We have used ethnographic fieldwork to understand the factors that influence technology use, adoption, and decision making in these community groups, and to identify collaborative projects and to develop strategies for working with our community partners in ways that encourage sustainable models of technology use, planning, and learning. Our goal is for the groups to direct the design process itself by choosing what should be done and by taking a central role in the doing of the project. In negotiating our role with these groups, we have minimized our role as experts, instead acting as facilitators and collaborators in technology projects. Our plan is to deliberately fade from the partnerships, with the participants maintaining and continuing to develop the achievement that is produced.

One of our community partnerships has been with the Spring Creek Watershed Community (SCWC), a nonprofit organization concerned with regional environmental and economic planning. Through outreach activities such as their Web site and newsletters, SCWC seeks to shape public policy by influencing decision makers and stakeholders about local watershed issues. In 2002, they hired a commercial vendor to develop their Web site. However, they were unhappy with the result; it depicted SCWC as a generic environmental group interested in preserving watersheds ("tree huggers," as they put it). The Web site failed to convey the local character of SCWC, the concept of sustainable development, and the need to balance environmental issues with economic development. The group was unable to negotiate changes with the vendor, who continued to assert that the design was fine. This breakdown led to a severing of the relationship with vendor, and a struggle over the group's Web content.

This experience was formative for SCWC. They decided to redesign the Web site themselves. A committee of technically proficient volunteers was charged with revamping the Web site and we joined their meetings. A major topic of conversation was how to organize the main page of the Web site to accurately reflect the group's mission. Several organizational schemes for the site were created and their trade-offs were discussed. Through this design process, the lead coordinator of SCWC became more proficient in basic Web technologies (e.g., HTML, SQL, etc.) as well the process of Web site design. The more technically proficient volunteers have learned about SCWC goals, and have thought more about how to translate the mission of the organization into the design of the site.

Our work with SCWC has focused on helping them to make better-informed technological decisions and to initiate a sustainable process for managing technology in their organization. Although the members of the group knew that we had a variety of technical skills, we carefully managed our role to avoid becoming the creators of the new Web site or even the directors of the Web design process. In this negotiation process, we always qualified our involvement as facilitators and peripheral contributors. At first, we took more of an observational role in the meetings as we learned more about the issues that were important to the group. As the design process continued, we took on a slightly more active role, suggesting some design techniques and ways of looking at the process that they could use to address concerns raised in the meeting. For example, success with scenario-based methods in the LiNC project encouraged us to introduce similar techniques to this group. As before, we observed that scenario-based design was accessible and effective—for instance the group coordinator (with no technical background) wrote a scenario to envision how to meet the interests of specific site visitors. The Web site design and implementation process is far from over, but the process of informal learning is well under way.

Dimensions of Participation

Because the goal of Civic Nexus is to instigate and nurture a sustainable design and development *process*, it is essential that each partner organization provide its own design impetus and motivation. The high-level goal for the researchers on the various design teams is to detect, uncover, and reflect back to the group its own information technology development goals, and to facilitate pursuit of these goals in whatever manner suits their organizational context. The challenge has been to do this in as unobtrusive and integrated a fashion as possible, so that the members of the community group believe that they are the ones envisioning and implementing the technology projects (Merkel et al., 2004).

Another important contribution to sustainability is that the receiving organization takes ownership of the project(s). They must be prepared to spend the time, money, or other resources to acquire the new technology and, conversely, to reject ideas that are not possible with the resources available. Of course this does not mean that they must have all of these resources at hand, but rather that they are willing to investigate and leverage opportunities as they arise, taking responsibility for selecting goals and the means for pursuing them.

Because the PD impetus and ownership is wholly within the community group, the scope of the design concerns and cooperation has been customized to the needs of the group. Some groups have specific applications or improvements in mind; others are simply looking for ways to enhance their technology practices. Thus the scope of Civic Nexus design concerns has ranged from changes in organizational practices related to technology (e.g., formation of new committees, volunteer training and recruitment), to the discovery and installation of online data or software (e.g., Web content and authoring tools), to specific analysis and design projects (e.g., the redesign of a Web site). In all cases, the scope of the cooperation has been regular and extended, merging the methods of ethnographic analysis and study with those of participatory development. This is in keeping with the focus on initiation of a sustainable learning process.

The PD interactions have also been quite varied, depending on the group composition, skills, and time available. In most cases the projects began with a serious of interviews of the major stakeholders, aimed at uncovering goals and concerns related to information technology. These interviews were used as a guide in subsequent interactions. In one case, the group was very specific in its goals for developing online educational materials, so the PD interactions included introduction to relevant technology, group design and development workshops, group troubleshooting, and project presentations and evaluation. By contrast, another group had no specific design goal, so the design interactions have been much more indirect, largely comprising a series of ongoing discussions about future directions and resources (including pointers to other potential volunteers) that might be useful. In all of the projects, the main PD interactions have been with a small, relatively stable core of staff or volunteers, with more peripheral members also participating on occasion.

The expectations for the PD process have evolved for both the researchers and the community groups. The researchers expected the groups to share their goals for information technology solutions that they would be able to facilitate, with informal learning occurring along the way. However, most community groups must first better understand technology before they can envision what it is they want to do—this learning must precede the design-solution phase. The community groups expected the researchers to take an active role in proposing and implementing a project; the researchers found themselves often reminding the group (and themselves) that they were there simply to facilitate the activities of the organization. The mutual adjustment of expectations is natural when PD participants include regular users and technologists, but it is important to allow time and energy for the co-evolution of expectations.

Unlike in a PD workshop involving an opportunity sample of workers, PD in a community computing context includes some, or possibly all of the members of a real community—a social network of individuals with a collective identity inhering in shared interests and practices. It is not plausible for the developer to enter into this community on a casual or short-term basis. The community is not constituted to accommodate this. As a result, the developer will tend to stand at the periphery.

We suggest the metaphor of *bard* to summarize this role in PD. Bards—the fellows with lutes and plumed hats, roaming about singing ballads in medieval courts—were not knights, chancellors, or bishops; they were not even blacksmiths, tailors, or farmers. They were not core members of the medieval community at any stratum. However, their songs reminded the community of collective past exploits, of folkways and mores that regulate and sustain them, and of future objectives and visions. Their songs inspired community members to undertake great quests, to defend their comrades, or just to be a bit more creative and daring in their farming or whatever else they did. The bard's tools are unthreatening to the interests and practices of others, and at the same time participatory in the sense that a familiar or rousing ballad asks for sing-along (see Carroll, 2004).

THE FUTURE OF PARTICIPATION

The early discussions of participatory design often stressed design ethics; the argument that users have a right to be involved in the development of technologies that will change their work and their lives. Twenty years on, we can add to this the argument that direct user participation in information systems design is also a technically effective strategy. Users understand their work in ways that designers do not, and they can bring this knowledge into the design process. And this is more than a simple matter of more information or of more information sources. Users who are collaborators will provide better information than users who are merely surveyed or interviewed in the traditional sense of requirements gathering. This is because they understand what the issues are, what information might bear on these issues, and how.

Later on in the design process, users who are real collaborators will provide better formative evaluation feedback, better summative walkthrough feedback, better maintenance feedback. Their involvement will enhance their own learning about the technology being developed, and about all related technologies bearing on it. They will be more advanced, smarter, and more pointedly critical adopters of the technology. And of course, this in turn will help the developers learn more about the critical requirements for their project; about the ways their technology really can be and will be used; and about the ways that technology interacts with the dynamics of human activity.

In the past two decades we have come to better recognize one of the most central conundrums of design, namely, that there are limits to how well we can ever pursue human-centered design without directly involving users in design. In all but the most trivial cases, users comprise communities of practice. They are members of groups bound together by shared concepts, norms of conduct, and values. Only some of this knowledge can feasibly be externalized in representations such as requirements, user models, and work flows. Much of what communities of practice know, and of what allows their members to be effective and productive, is tacit knowledge, shared among members by being enacted in their work activity (Nonaka, 1994; Wenger, McDermott, and Snyder, 2002).

The implication of acknowledging that users are typically members of communities of practice, and that they share critical tacit knowledge about their work practices through enactment, is straightforward: Users must be directly involved in design activity if its outcomes are to accurately and appropriately support them. They must be involved in design activity contexts that permit them to enact what they tacitly know. To the extent that they are not, the design will fail.

In this paper we have explored six possible dimensions of participatory involvement in design. Our motivation for this exploration was our recognition that the participatory relationships we were becoming involved in seemed different in some respects from those we read about and discussed with colleagues. We used the six dimensions to reconstruct these felt differences and to suggest consequences. However, we are far from confident that any firm contrasts or conclusions can be drawn now. It seems likely that more dimensions can be identified, and that perhaps those we have suggested will need to be re-factored. Nevertheless, this is an important direction in which to proceed, especially so given the growing importance of participatory design through the past twenty years, and the likelihood that this trend will continue.

To make these dimensions more vivid and applicable to other PD settings, we contrasted four PD projects, using metaphors to suggest how variations along the six dimensions might lead to rather different PD projects (Table 14.2). Projects such as UTOPIA and LiNC both take users' work contexts and activities as the focus of design, but vary in the extent to which the users are invited in to explore ideas in concert with designers or join the team to work side by side throughout the development process. The PICTIVE method has more narrow and concrete scope, while Civic Nexus has a completely open-ended scope that emerges as the views and goals of the participants develop.

An open question concerns the trajectory of participatory design. Traditionally, PD methods have been viewed as a way for software developers to invite users into the design process, to probe and respond to their domain-specific understandings and practices. The Civic Nexus project shifts

Table 14.2

Relationships of the Four Metaphors and Associated Examples with the Six Dimensions for Participatory Design

Metaphor (example)	Connections to the six dimensions of participatory design
Movie or Play Producer (UTOPIA)	A design team initiates and motivates the process; project is owned by this outside team, perhaps with contributions from other external sponsors; focus of design concerns is on the experiences and empowerment of workers; the process is extended in time as a series of scripted encounters; there is an expectation of co-adaptation and learning through these episodes
Player (PICTIVE)	A usability team within a software development company initiates the process; the development organization is the owner, perhaps in conjunction with the workers' organization; the design focus is on shared construction of user interface ideas using physical materials; expectation is that developers will learn about workers' mental models and workers will feel empowered by their input
Co-worker (LiNC)	Design team initiates the process but co-owns it with workers' organization; scope of design concerns evolved from worker activities to supporting tools and user interfaces details; process involved a variety of interactions over a long period of time, many integrated into workers' lives; expectations for mutual learning, especially regarding the personal development of the workers
Bard (Civic Nexus)	Process triggered by design team but co-initiated by the team and partner organization with ownership explicitly ceded to the partner group; design scope and style of interaction are emergent, evolving as IT needs, goals, and skills of partner organization are "mirrored" back to them; explicit assumption of long term engagement, with expectations shifting as process becomes sustainable

the balance of power; designers are given the role of observing, highlighting, and facilitating technology goals that are owned by the user community. In such a project the PD engagement is contingent on users inviting software designers into *their* context. But how essential is the designer's help? Research in end-user development seeks to enable users to build information systems for themselves, their organizations, or their communities (Lieberman, 2001; Rode and Rosson, 2003; Rosson et al., 2004). If such tools become effective enough, transparent enough, users may be able to help themselves. Perhaps the PD ideal is a participatory process conducted by users for users.

ACKNOWLEDGMENTS

This work was supported by the U.S. National Science Foundation (CNS-0353309, CCF-0405612, IIS-0342547, REC-9554206, REC-0106552, REC-0353101, and RED-9454803), the Office of Naval Research (N00014–00–1-0549), and the Hitachi Foundation.

REFERENCES

Bjerknes, G., and Bratteteig, T. User participation and democracy: A discussion of Scandinavian research on system development. *Scandinavian Journal of Information Systems, 7,* 1 (1995), 73–98.

Bødker, S.; Ehn, P.; Kammersgaard, J.; Kyng, M.; and Sundblad, Y. A utopian experience. In G. Bjerknes, P. Ehn, and M. Kyng (eds.), *Computers and Democracy: A Scandinavian Challenge*. Brookfield, VT: Avebury, 1987, pp. 251–278.

Carmel, E., White, R.D., and George, J.F. PD and joint application design: a transatlantic comparison. *Communications of the ACM*, 36, 4 (1993), 40–48.

Carroll, J.M. *Making Use: Scenario-based Design of Human-Computer Interactions*. Cambridge, MA: MIT Press, 2000.

Carroll, J.M.; Rosson, M.B.; Chin, G.; and Koenemann, J. 1998. Requirements development in scenario-based design. *IEEE Transactions on Software Engineering*, 24, 12 (1998), pp. 1–15.

Carroll, J.M.; Chin, G.; Rosson, M.B.; and Neale, D.C. The development of cooperation: five years of participatory design in the virtual school. In D. Boyarski and W. Kellogg (eds.), *Proceedings of Designing Interactive Systems 2000*. New York: Association for Computing Machinery, 2000, pp. 239–251.

Carroll, J.M.; Chin, G.; Rosson, M.B.; Neale, D.C.; Dunlap, D.R.; and Isenhour, P.L. Building educational technology partnerships through participatory design. In J. Lazar (ed.), *Managing IT/Community Partnerships in the 21st Century*. Hershey, PA: Idea Group Publishing, 2002, pp. 88–115.

Carroll, J.M., and Rosson, M.B. Developing the Blacksburg Electronic Village. *Communications of the ACM*, 39, 12 (1996), 69–74.

Checkland, P.B. *Systems Thinking, Systems Practice*. Chichester: John Wiley, 1981.

Checkland, P.B., and Scholes, J. *Soft Systems Methodology in Action*. Chichester: John Wiley, 1990.

Chin, G. *A Case Study in the Participatory Design of a Collaborative Science-Based Learning Environment*. Doctoral dissertation, Department of Computer Science, Virginia Tech, Blacksburg, VA, 2004.

Clement, A., and Van den Besselaar, P. A retrospective look at PD projects. Communications of the ACM, 36, 4 (1993), 29–37.

Dunlap, D.R.; Neale, D.C.; and Carroll, J.M. Teacher collaboration in a networked community. *Educational Technology and Society*, 3, 3 (2000), 442–454.

Eason, K.D. *Information Technology and Organizational Change*. London: Taylor & Francis, 1988.

Ehn, P., and Kyng, M. The collective resource approach to systems design. In G. Bjerknes, P. Ehn, and M. Kyng (eds.), *Computers and Democracy: A Scandinavian Challenge*. Brookfield, VT: Avebury, 1987, pp. 17–58.

Hutchins, E. *Distributed Cognition*. Cambridge, MA: MIT Press, 1995.

Isenhour, P.L.; Carroll, J.M.; Neale, D.C.; Rosson, M.B.; and Dunlap, D.R. The virtual school: an integrated collaborative environment for the classroom. *Educational Technology and Society*, 3, 3 (2000), 74–86.

Jones, J.C. *Design Methods: Seeds Human Futures*. New York: John Wiley, 1970.

Kensing, F., and Madsen, K.H. PD: structure in the toolbox. *Communications of the ACM*, 36, 6 (1993), 78–85.

Kyng, M. Creating contexts for design. In J.M. Carroll (ed.), *Scenario-based design: Envisioning work and technology in system development*. New York: John Wiley, 1995, pp. 85–107.

Lierberman, H. (ed.) *Your Wish Is My Command: Programming by Example*. San Francisco: Morgan Kaufmann, 2001.

Madsen, K.H. The diversity of usability practices. *Communications of the ACM*, 42, 5 (1999), 61–62.

Merkel, C.B.; Xiao, L.; Farooq, U.; Ganoe, C.H.; Lee, R.; Carroll, J.M.; and Rosson, M.B. Participatory design in community computing contexts: tales from the field. In *Proceedings of the 2004 Participatory Design Conference*. New York: ACM, 2004, pp. 1–10.

Muller, M.J. PICTIVE—an exploration in participatory design. In *Proceedings of CHI '91*. New York: ACM, 1991, pp. 225–231.

Muller, M.J. Retrospective on a year of participatory design using the PICTIVE technique. In *Proceedings of CHI '92*. New York: ACM, 1992, pp. 445–461.

Muller, M.J.; Haslwanter, J.H.; and Dayton, T. Participatory practices in the software lifecycle. In M. Helander, T.K. Landauer, and P. Prabhu (eds.), *Handbook of Human-Computer Interaction, Second Edition*. Amsterdam: Elsevier, 1997, pp. 255–297.

Muller, M.J.; White, E.A.; and Wideman, D.M. Taxonomy of PD practices: a brief practitioner's guide. *Communications of the ACM*, 36, 6 (1993), 26–28.

Muller, M.J.; Tudor, L.G.; Wildman, D.M.; White, E.A.; Root, R.A.; Dayton, T.; Carr, R.; Diekmann, B.; and Dystra-Erickson, E. Bifocal tools for scenarios and representations in participatory activities with users. In J.M. Carroll (ed.), *Scenario-based Design: Envisioning Work and Technology in System Development*. New York: John Wiley, 1995, pp. 135–163.

Nardi, B.A. Some reflections on scenarios. In J.M. Carroll (ed.), *Scenario-based Design: Envisioning Work and Technology in System Development.* New York: John Wiley, 1995, pp. 387–399.

Nardi, B.A. (ed.) *Context and Consciousness: Activity Theory and Human-Computer Interaction.* Cambridge, MA: MIT Press, 1996.

Nonaka, I. A dynamic theory of organizational knowledge creation. *Organization Science,* 5, 1 (1994), 14–37.

Piaget, J., and Inhelder, B. *The Psychology of the Child.* New York: Basic Books, 1969.

Rode, J., and Rosson, M.B. Programming at Runtime: Requirements and paradigms for nonprogrammer web application development. In *IEEE 2003 Symposium on Human-Centric Computing Languages and Environments.* New York: IEEE, 2003, pp. 23–30.

Rosson, M.B.; Ballin, J.; and Nash, H. Everyday programming: challenges and opportunities for informal web development. In *Visual Languages and Human-Centric Computing 2004.* New York: IEEE Press, 2004, pp. 123–130.

Rosson, M.B., and Carroll, J.M. *Usability Engineering: Scenario-Based Development of Human-Computer Interaction.* San Francisco: Morgan Kaufmann, 2002.

Robertson, T.J.; Prabhakararao, S.; Burnett, M.; Cook, C.; Ruthruff, J.R.; Beckwith, L.; and Phalgune, A. Impact of interruption style on end-user debugging. *Proceedings of CHI 2004.* New York: ACM, 2004, pp. 287–294.

Suchman, L.A. *Plans and Situated Actions: The Problem of Human-Machine Communication.* New York: Cambridge University Press, 1987.

Tyack, D., and Cuban, L. *Tinkering Toward Utopia: A Century of Public School Reform.* Cambridge, MA: Harvard University Press, 1995.

Vygotsky, L.S. *Mind in Society.* Cambridge, MA: Harvard University Press, 1978.

Wenger, E.; McDermott, R.; and Snyder, W.M. *Cultivating Communities of Practice: A Guide to Managing Knowledge.* Cambridge, MA: Harvard Business School Press, 2002.

Wood, J., and Silver, D. *Joint Application Design: How to Design Quality Systems in 40% Less Time.* New York: John Wiley, 1989.

Woodward, J. *Industrial Organization: Theory and Practice.* London: Oxford University Press, 1965.

PART VI

HEALTH CARE/HEALTH INFORMATICS

CHAPTER 15

TECHNOLOGY-ENABLED TRANSFORMATIONS IN U.S. HEALTH CARE

Early Findings on Personal Health Records and Individual Use

RITU AGARWAL AND COREY M. ANGST

Abstract: *Information-intensive industries, such as health care, rely extensively on the ability to store, process, analyze, and use data. Although other information-intensive industries have adopted information technology aggressively and reaped the benefits that result from usage, the health care industry has been notoriously slow to implement information systems, with some researchers suggesting that health care is ten to fifteen years behind other industries. Recognizing the critical importance of decision quality in the health care sector, together with the need to improve the speed and efficiency of operations, many have called for the transformation of the health care industry through widespread adoption and usage of information technology (IT). In this paper, we define and discuss health information technology (HIT) and the extensive opportunities for IS research in this field. In particular, we direct our attention to the electronic personal health record (PHR) and investigate the justification for adopting a class of software that we label a discretionary application. Finally, we report findings from an empirical investigation of PHR usage; we show that specific demographic and health conditions drive value for PHRs and ultimately usage intentions.*

Keywords: *Health Information Technology, Personal Health Records, Electronic Health Records, Electronic Medical Records, HIT, PHR, EHR, EMR, eHealth*

INTRODUCTION

"Implementing a computerized record system . . . could save 60,000 lives, prevent 500,000 serious medication errors, and save $9.7 billion each year."

—Leapfrog, 2004

"Existing technology can transform health care. . . . If all Americans' electronic health records were connected in secure computer networks . . . providers would have complete records for their patients, so they would no longer have to re-order tests."

—Gingrich and Kennedy, 2004

The transformational power of information technology in altering the nature of competition in an industry and creating value for both firms and consumers has long been acknowledged in diverse industry sectors such as airlines, financial services, and retailing (Copeland and McKenney, 1988; Lucas, 1999). A common characteristic among industries that have experienced such transformations is that they are *information intensive*—that is, a significant proportion of their value-creation activities occurs through the storage, processing, and analysis of data. The transformation has typically been attributed to specific software applications—for example, the Sabre system in the airline industry and Merrill Lynch's cash management system in the brokerage industry—that trigger far-reaching changes. In this paper we explore an emergent IT application—the electronic personal health record (PHR) that arguably offers the same potential for revolutionary, discontinuous change in the health care sector. In very general terms, an electronic PHR is a software program that an individual uses to manage his or her health information. It can either be a Web-based ASP (application service provider) model, or a stand-alone PC-based platform. Later in this paper we provide a more elaborate, descriptive explanation of PHRs.

Health care accounts for nearly 15 percent of GDP in most industrialized nations (*National Health Care Expenditures: Historical Overview,* 2004). It also represents a sector with significant consequential outcomes—the quality of care delivered often makes the difference between life and death. Thus, it is not surprising that governments, policy makers, and other stakeholders in this sector place considerable emphasis on better understanding how the delivery of care can be improved. Human capital in the form of knowledge and skills is doubtless a critical input factor for the quality of health care; however, to the extent that health care is an information-intensive, knowledge-based activity that requires high reliability in operations, another important input is technology that helps transfer critical information.

Software innovations such as the electronic PHR are an inevitable outcome of developments in information technology. Although the past fifty years of IT innovation suggests that such developments occur with some regularity, research in the adoption, diffusion, and utilization of innovations shows that such innovations are "absorbed" by the intended users at a considerably slower rate. Individual users are socialized with IT both in the workplace, through business information processing applications that are required on the job, and in their personal spheres, through applications they use at home. Indeed, home use information technologies are proliferating both in terms of the range and variety of applications and in revenue opportunities. Some have estimated consumer software to be a $2 billion market (Bear, 2000). Generally, the demarcation between these two classes of systems is fairly straightforward in that use of workplace applications is typically mandated, while home use of applications is volitional. The electronic PHR is somewhat unique in that although the ultimate users of this technology are individual home users, there are systemic, sector-wide implications of its adoption for the cost and quality of health care. Some would argue that most PC- or Web-based software applications that are used at home fall into this category. However, we believe that electronic PHRs differ from other home-use examples because individuals' use of health care management software can actually drive *organizational* adoption of electronic medical record systems among hospitals and other health care institutions. In essence, we are describing a "trickle-up" phenomenon. The more traditional "trickle-down" approach to diffusing the technology is not entirely feasible because the ultimate success of the technology depends on the individual user.

The human issues surrounding electronic PHRs are numerous. First, the IT captures and stores highly personal, sensitive medical information, thereby introducing increased personal vulnerability to privacy and security violations. Second, to the extent that treatment and diagnosis decisions are based on the data captured in the PHR, data quality is of paramount importance. Finally, applications such as the PHR are particularly challenging, since they require users to expend significant effort on data entry. To the degree that anticipated benefits to the health care sector through such applications are predicated on individual use of these systems, questions about individuals' attitudes towards electronic PHRs, and about what will motivate them to accept and use them, are important to address.

In this paper we introduce the emerging technology of the personal health record and situate it within the broader context of technology-led transformations in the health care sector. We identify the roadblocks and obstacles that the technology is likely to face, and illuminate through empirical data, aspects of individuals' adoption and use of this technology. Particularly, we highlight the types of value the technology generates for users and its relationship with intended technology use in the future. Because our data were gathered at an early stage of the diffusion curve for this new technology, the findings are likely to be useful for policy makers and others concerned with successfully diffusing electronic PHRs more widely.

We also feel it is necessary to elaborate upon the terminology used here. The term "health information technology" or HIT, is widely used in the medical informatics field and in government publications. In other disciplines and most practitioner literature, the more general term "eHealth" is typically used. While often used interchangeably, the terms are not synonymous. There are no standard or universally accepted definitions for either term, but the following captures their essence:

> eHealth—the use of emerging technologies, especially the Internet, to improve or enable health and healthcare (eHealth Institute, 2004)

> HIT—information technology [used] to improve the quality, efficiency, and safety of health care (Office of the NCHIT, 2004).

Although the definitions are very similar, the primary difference as we interpret and use them in this paper is that HIT refers directly to the technological artifacts and eHealth describes the use of technology in the health care field. It could be argued that eHealth is the use and application of HIT. Since we are primarily focused on technological artifacts in this paper, we will almost exclusively use the term HIT.

HEALTH INFORMATION TECHNOLOGY

> "Despite more than thirty years of exploratory work and millions of dollars in research and implementation of computer systems in health-care provider institutions, patient records today are still predominantly paper records."
>
> —Dick, Steen, and Detmer, 1997

The State of the Problem

Notwithstanding the focus of the above quotation on electronic health records, a similar observation can be made for the use of information technology in the health care industry in general. Disturbingly, although the quotation dates back over seven years, the situation today is not very different. According to a recent report from the Department of Health and Human Services, only 13 percent of the nation's hospitals and 14–28 percent of physicians' offices used electronic medical records in 2002 (Thompson and Brailer, 2004, p. 10). As recently as 2001, only 6 percent of prescriptions were written electronically (Chin, 2002b; Papshev and Peterson, 2001). Critics of health information technology may argue that medicine has been practiced for centuries without the use of IT, so why is the twenty-first century any different from earlier centuries? The answer is simple: Today, *multiple actors* have to manage the knowledge accumulated over centuries. The emphasis on "multiple" is key, as it is important to recognize that it is not just doctors and medical staff who have knowledge (as was typically the case in the past), but increasingly the patients themselves are conducting searches on their own and informing their health care providers about the most up-to-date treatments and technologies. A recent study showed that about 20 percent of adults in the United States use the Internet to access health information (Baker et al., 2003), while another study reported that 70 percent of health-information seekers use the information retrieved on the Web to make health care decisions (Brodie et al., 2000). This amounts to millions of people seeking health information and providing knowledge to their health care providers. It is, therefore, reasonable to state that HIT is becoming mandatory for managing, retrieving, and storing medical knowledge in a useful manner.

In addition to progressive involvement by patients, health information technology has become increasingly important because Americans' lifestyles have changed so dramatically in recent decades and because the health care system itself has gone through major policy transformations. For example, Kim and Johnson (2002) observe that the increased mobility of people and the provider-specific requirements of managed care insurance have forced people to seek care from several different providers, resulting in a highly decentralized information source for individual health information. This decentralization of data and current inability of sources to communicate with one another has resulted in catastrophic quality-of-care consequences. The Institute of Medicine, in a 1999 report, reported that between 44,000 and 98,000 Americans die in hospitals each year as a result of medical errors (Kohn et al., 1999). Other studies have shown that various forms of HIT could prevent 28–56 percent of adverse drug events (Bates et al., 1998; Bates et al., 1997; Classen et al., 1997). One form of HIT that is slowly gaining acceptance and is viewed as offering significant benefits is the enterprise-wide, electronic medical record (EMR), sometimes known as an electronic health record (EHR). Although many doctors and health systems have embraced this technology, which gives practitioners access to patients' medical records, medication information, and other medical knowledge from any computer connected to the system, others have been slow to adopt or downright resistant. Some feel that using EMRs takes time away from direct interaction with patients and negatively affects the doctor-patient relationship. In addition, many health systems have allowed patients to access portions of the EMR through portals or direct downloads to storage devices, creating in essence, a personal health record with only their health information contained in it. Of course this has also created uncertainty amongst some practitioners, with opinions ranging from highly positive, for example, "The most profound influence of EMRs may lie in their ability to encourage patients' involvement in their own care" (Tsai and Starren, 2001, p. 1765), to highly negative, for example, "Patients will be confused or misled by their record . . . [they] may object to information contained in it . . . [they will] quiz their caregivers incessantly about the meaning of test results and reports [contained in it]" (Cimino et al., 2002, p. 114).

Another solution that is gaining momentum is for patients themselves to collect and manage their health information in an electronic personal health record. Software is currently available that can provide this application service. Some of these packages provide links to health system EMRs, while others are stand-alone applications that reside only on the patient's personal computer. This technology is the focus of this paper and is discussed in great depth in the following sections.

Medical Informatics and Proposed Classification of Health Information Technology (HIT)

We begin by providing a brief introduction to medical informatics and reflect on the opportunities for information systems research in this domain. IS research, specifically in the health care field, is not without precedence (see Devaraj and Kohli, 2003; Kim and Michelman, 1990; Raghupathi, 2002). Although the health care setting is not typical of a traditional firm, there are numerous similarities between health care information systems and business information systems. For example, issues related to integration, implementation, interoperability, and adoption of systems are congruent in business firms or hospitals. As pointed out by Hersh (2002), the delivery of health care is an information-based science. As such, information scientists in the medical field have created their own discipline, known as *medical informatics,* that is specifically focused on using IT in a health care setting. The development of this field was due in part to the exponential improvements in computer technology in recent years, the glaring inadequacies of paper-based information, and the growing awareness that the knowledge was becoming unmanageable through traditional means.

Although several definitions of medical informatics exist, a commonly shared characterization is that the medical informatics field is concerned with the management and use of information in health and biomedicine and the core theories, concepts, and techniques used in the application of information (Hersh, 2002). Others have expanded the medical informatics field to include the application of information in the problem-solving and decision-making process conducted by medical practitioners (Greenes and Shortliffe, 1990). Health care informaticians note that the medical informatics field is closely related to modern information systems research, specifically in the areas of computing and communication systems (Greenes and Shortliffe, 1990). For these reasons, it is apparent that IS scholars should be conducting research in this area and raising awareness amongst students that the health care field is a burgeoning market for IS graduates.

Given the bewildering range of IT applications in health care, it is important to structure and organize the systems used so that research opportunities and gaps can be identified. Figure 15.1 shows a taxonomy of the systems used in the delivery of health care. This diagram describes two distinct technological categories: administrative and clinical. From these two primary branches, several department- and job-specific information systems emerge. For example, on the left of the diagram, one will see administrative information systems such as imaging systems that are used by the administrative staff for operational-level functions, such as retrieving an "Explanation of Benefits" insurance form. On the right of the diagram are clinical information systems that are typically populated by technicians, such as an X-ray technician, but accessed by several interested actors including various clinicians. Some systems, such as the electronic medical record, span both the clinical and administrative branches. Clinicians use medical records for reviewing patient history and other details and the administrative systems are often directly linked to certain portions of the patient record that provide the permanent record for the patient.

Although other classifications exist, none that we are aware of are as comprehensive as the taxonomy proposed here. For instance, Degoulet and Fieschi (1997) classified key areas of medical informatics, but they did not explicitly identify the systems present in a typical health care setting. Others have attempted to classify the type of information that HIT yields. For example, Hersh (2002) identified two types of information used in clinical informatics: (1) patient-specific information, which is generated by and used in the care of patients in the clinical setting, and (2) knowledge-based information that comprises the scientific basis for health care. While our focus in this study is specifically on electronic medical records that span the administrative and clinical types, research into the other information systems is also warranted and lacking. An electronic personal health record, as described in the next section, incorporates both patient-specific and knowledge-based information in that it provides a synopsis of patient information to the practitioner while enabling knowledge-based discovery through links to clinical health information. Our study focuses on this artifact as one of many systems present in a typical HIT environment.

362

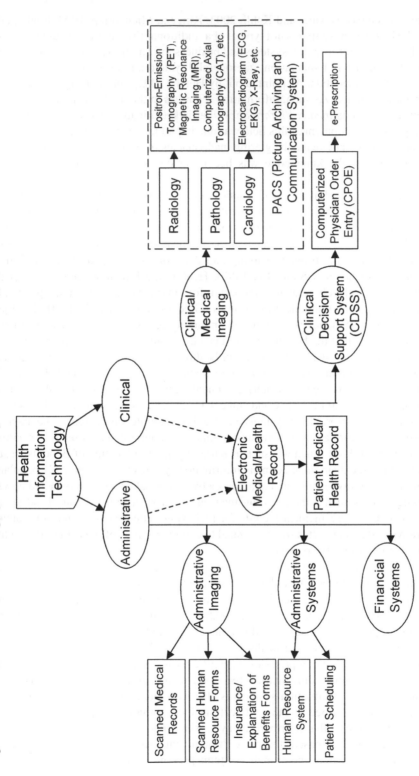

Figure 15.1 Health Information Technology (HIT) Taxonomy

ELECTRONIC PERSONAL HEALTH RECORD (PHR)

Description of the Technology

A patient's medical record is a record used by health care professionals while providing patient care—it is sometimes known as a chart or patient-chart. It is typically used as a means of reviewing patient data and documenting observations. With an electronic medical record, some or all of the data contained in a typical paper-based record would be available in a computerized, electronic form. This type of record is maintained by the provider (doctor, hospital, clinic, etc.), but in some institutions, patients can also add information through a secure Internet portal.

Health care providers across the country are adopting this new class of information system, the electronic medical record (EMR), albeit at a very slow pace. While adoption statistics of EMRs in the United States vary (Cain and Mittman, 2002; Goldsmith et al., 2003; Von Knoop et al., 2003)—with some estimates as low as 13 percent and some as high as 30 percent—the one reality is that the United States is far behind such European counterparts as the United Kingdom, which has a 58 percent adoption rate, and Sweden, which has an adoption rate of almost 90 percent (Chin, 2002a). Today, adoption of EMRs in the United States is just beginning to creep up the steep portion of the S-shaped diffusion of technology curve (Rogers, 1983). Some of the reasons underlying the sluggish acceptance rates for EMRs are the lack of one standardized clinical terminology (more accurately, the multitude of various classifications, nomenclatures, dictionary codes, and standards [Orthner, 1997, p. xi], which essentially results in an unstandardized approach); slow and varied levels of standards adoption (*Data Standards,* 2003, p. 21); concerns about data privacy, confidentiality, and security; physician data entry challenges, and the difficulty associated with the integration of record systems with other information resources in the health care setting (Shortliffe, 1999).

On the other hand, the potential advantages of capturing patient information in an electronic record are numerous. First, because of the need to apply guidelines accurately and consistently, complete and up-to-date patient information, such as that stored in the electronic record, is essential (Elson and Connelly, 1995; Elson et al., 1997). Second, having information easily accessible reduces the cognitive burden on the care provider (e.g., doctor), thereby facilitating higher-quality decisions (Benbasat and Nault, 1989). Finally, the cognitive resources released as a result of not having to search for information can be devoted to better information interpretation (Elson and Connelly, 1997).

For this study, we are particularly focused on the intent to use electronic *personal* health records, which suffer from some of the same barriers, and reap some of the same benefits as EMRs. A personal health record (PHR) is slightly different from a doctor's EMR. A PHR is a document containing health information that is stored and maintained by the patient and typically includes features such as self-tracking and -monitoring of health information and self-entry of information related to diagnoses, medications, laboratory tests, and immunizations (see Figure 15.2, Table 15.1). It usually has the ability to receive and store information from a doctor's electronic medical record or other electronic data source. Some PHRs include features that notify the user of drug-to-drug interactions and dosage warnings.

As a means of further clarifying the concept of a PHR, it may be helpful to draw a connection between a PHR and a personal financial management software package such as Quicken®. With Quicken, an individual can track her finances by monitoring personal checks, logging ATM transactions, and tracking deposits, to name but a few features. Then, at the end of the month, the individual can compare the previous-month's transactions with those on file at the defined bank. This process could be labeled as dissociative, since both "systems" operate in isolation. On the other

Figure 15.2a   **Screen Shot of a Typical PHR**

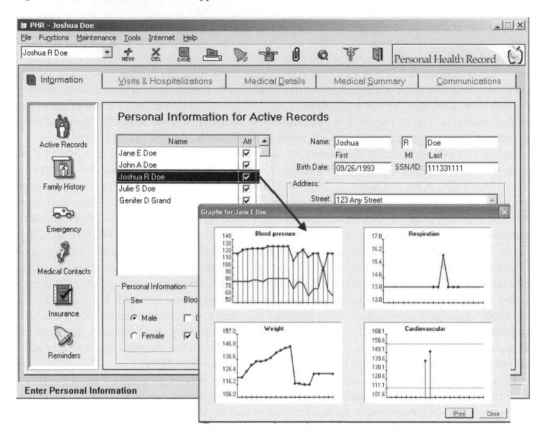

hand, Quicken offers a feature that allows the user to continue to maintain her private banking information on her personal computer, but also gives the option of downloading data directly from the participating bank as a means of reconciling the account.

A PHR is similar in this respect. A user can maintain all health information on her personal computer, entering data from doctor visits as they occur and tracking medications and dosages. In this case, two separate databases (in actuality, several databases are maintained, as it is very common for people to see multiple health providers and it is typical that each maintains its own isolated medical database record) are managed independently. There is, however, technology that allows a user/patient to have a direct link through the Internet—or a portable device such as a USB-flash drive—to participating providers' electronic health record systems. In most cases, information is only made available for download to the patient's personal record, but in some systems, such as one run by Brigham and Women's Hospital in Boston, patients can upload notes and data into their permanent medical record, schedule appointments, and e-mail doctors, to name a few features.

Discretionary Application Software

Application software is defined as a program that performs useful functions in the processing or manipulation of data. This type of software is written for a specific application to perform functions

Figure 15.2b **Screen Shot of a Web-Based PHR**

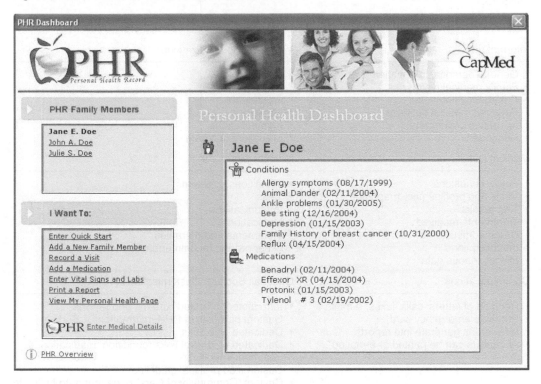

by end users. There are different types of application software, such as database managers, word processors, spreadsheets, and other programs that enable the useful manipulation of data (Laudon and Laudon, 2004). The use of application software in a business setting is normally considered to be mandatory. In addition, the choice of application software is not often left to the users; it is typically dictated by corporate directive. On the other hand, software that is used primarily outside of a work context is most often volitional. Such is the case with PHRs. We take this one step further and identify and classify PHR software as a discretionary application (Grudin and Palen, 1995). In our operationalization, we define a discretionary application as, 1) Software that is typically used outside of a work context with no agency issues associated with its use, and 2) Software for which usage is associated with increased cognitive load and volitional work.

Elaborating on the first point, there are no compensatory rewards associated with usage of discretionary applications. In a work setting, software usage is typically rewarded by management in the form of a salary and job security. If employees choose not to use software, strict punishments such as discipline, demotion, or severance can result. We know from prior work that software use at home is volitional and hedonically driven, which makes it different from use in an office setting, where it is often mandated (Venkatesh and Brown, 2001). Therefore, the first part of the definition should not be too surprising. The second part of the definition may not seem initially as intuitive. An example here may provide the best explanatory power. Approximately 40 percent of the U.S. population keeps track of their personal or family medical history and only 13 percent track their medical information using a computer program ("Harris Interactive: Two in Five Adults," 2004). However, there is a growing group of special-interest users who choose to use a program such as a PHR, even though it generates work

Table 15.1

Typical PHR Functionality

Information	Visits and Hospitalizations
• General personal information • Family medical history • Emergency contacts • Personal medical contacts • Insurance coverage(s) • Reminders	• Conditions • Tests • Treatments • Medicines • Immunizations • Miscellaneous data

Medical Details	Medical Summary
• Active conditions • Vitals and profiles (incl. graphing) • Test results • Treatments received • Drugs administered • Immunizations • Miscellaneous data	• Conditions, problems • Tests • Immunizations • Medications • Treatments and therapies • Other orders, recommendations

Communications	Optional: Sponsor Customization
• Records of letters, calls, faxes, e-mails • Printable emergency card • All screens generate into reports • All reports can be printed or e-mailed	• Introductory branded screens and reports • Custom pick-lists of PHR information • Dedicated web links • Dedicated field-level links (condition, medication, treatment-specific) • Customized profiles, guidelines • Custom "Community of Care" page that auto-builds to user's needs based on sponsor-selected information

beyond that which is necessary. So why would anyone choose to use a discretionary application that can actually be burdensome? The answer is that the application fulfills some real or perceived need, which is likely to differ among individual users of the technology. Some may choose to use the application because it provides structure and organization, others because they enjoy it, and still others because it provides features not readily available through substitutes, for example, electronically searching versus physically searching through filing cabinets of paper. Potential examples of other types of discretionary applications are "living-will" software, "résumé-making" software, "home-and-landscape-architecture" software, and "family-tree" software.

Empirical Studies of Electronic Health Records

There are very few studies that have focused directly on PHRs, and even fewer that examine the impact PHRs have on health outcomes, compliance, or convenience. A few recent studies have investigated the perceived value that people receive from PHRs (Angst, 2004), the receptiveness of patients to accessing a doctor's electronic health record (Masys et al., 2002), and the usability of a patient-interface with an EMR (ibid.). These studies all found that respondents rated usability and functionality quite favorably, and valued having their records available electronically.

Some recent non-empirical studies of electronic record use by patients have speculated that access will contribute to avoiding repeated or unnecessary tests, providing better comparison with existing data from earlier examinations, reducing the number of ineffective treatments, increasing patients' compliance with clinical care processes, reducing length of stay within hospitals, and providing a lifelong health record across institutional boundaries (Ueckert et al., 2003).

Currently, two ongoing projects are investigating patient usage of electronic medical record systems. Tsai and Starren (2001) briefly discuss two patient involvement projects: PATCIS (Patient Clinical Information System), which provides patients with the ability to view lab results and text reports via a Web interface and enter such data as vital signs (Cimino, 2000) and IDEATel (Information for Diabetes Education and Telemedicine), a four-year, $28 million randomized clinical trial enabling diabetes patients to connect to their providers (*IDEATel,* 2004). Finally, Kim and Johnson (2002) provide a review of state-of-the-art PHRs that highlights the functionality of several PHRs currently on the market.

The apparent lack of empirical studies of PHRs does not reflect patients' interest in using them. In a May 2001 survey, Fowles and colleagues (2004) conducted a study that randomly sampled 4,500 adults who had had a recent clinic visit, asking whether they had any interest in reading their medical records. Of the 81 percent who responded to the survey, 36 percent were very interested in reading their medical record. The primary reasons for their interest were being very concerned about errors in care, lacking trust in their physician, seeing what their physician said about them, increasing their involvement in their health care, and understanding their condition better.

In contrast to PHR studies, several studies have investigated EMR adoption and use. Safran (2001) claims that electronic records have already made a direct impact on the practice of medicine and he offers as evidence, studies that show marked improvements in quality of care and medication errors (Safran et al., 1995), reductions in physician and nurse time (Safran et al., 1999), and improvements in practical experience and training for new physicians and medical students (Patel et al., 2000).

Barriers to Adoption and Use of PHRs

In previous sections we identified key barriers to adoption of EMRs in a clinical setting. Although some of these issues are unique to the EMR, others cross over into the PHR spectrum. For example, privacy concerns are a major challenge to widespread adoption. Data accuracy and integrity also greatly impact diffusion. Are the challenges to diffusion unique in this setting relative to other industries in which technology is used? We believe the answer to this question is both yes and no. We are still confronted with people's reluctance to use any system that is not easy to use or useful to them (Davis, 1989), but acceptance is also confounded by high levels of uncertainty about information security, privacy, and the relative importance of the information contained in a health record—after all, the ramifications of using erroneous information can result in adverse health outcomes or even death.

Privacy Concerns

Due in large part to forward-looking policy makers, individuals should feel some degree of relief regarding the security and privacy of their personal health information. HIPAA, the Health Insurance Portability and Accountability Act, is the first federal law that addresses health privacy in a comprehensive way. It requires all "covered entities"—health care providers, plans, and clearinghouses—to protect individually identifiable health information. Personal health information (PHI) includes any information relating to the physical or mental health of the individual, the provision of health care, or payments for health care, and information that could be used to identify an individual (Swartz, 2003).

HIPAA gives patients more control over their health information, and gives them certain rights to privacy and confidentiality. In addition, it establishes appropriate safeguards that health care providers and others must implement to protect the privacy of patients' health information. Most importantly, it holds violators accountable by imposing civil and criminal penalties with fines up to $250,000 and prison terms up to ten years (HIPAA Privacy Implementation Guide, 2002). One of the primary goals of HIPAA is to simply improve quality of care in the United States by restoring trust in the health care system (HIPAA Privacy Essentials, 2002).

Data Accuracy and Reliability

A second significant barrier to diffusion of PHRs is the quality of the information that is contained in the program. That patients themselves maintain PHRs—even though the information is often entered by or downloaded from providers—raises the question of the accuracy and reliability of the information they contain. Of course these issues are not unique to health care systems. They can, however, lead to more catastrophic results than incorrectly recording a number in a financial spreadsheet. There have been no studies of which we are aware that investigate the accuracy or reliability of information in a PHR. There has been extensive work investigating this phenomenon as it relates to paper records and EMRs (Aronsky and Haug, 2000; Brennan and Stead, 2000; Elson and Connelly, 1997; Logan, Gorman, and Middleton, 2001; Stausberg et al., 2003; Stein et al., 2000). In a study conducted by Hogan and Wagner (1997), the accuracy of data in a computerized patient record is assessed using correctness (the proportion of recorded observations in the system that are correct) and completeness (the proportion of observations that are actually recorded in the system). These authors propose methodological guidelines for studying accuracy after reviewing 235 papers discussing data accuracy (among which they found only twenty relevant articles). A common theme underlying research in this area is that computerized health records should be better than paper-based records because of validity checks and usage of standards. Many researchers agree that computerized systems can be an efficient way of reducing errors of omissions and improving adherence (Overhage et al., 1997). However, it should be acknowledged here that regardless of the accuracy and reliability of the information in a medical record—whether paper or electronic—the condition of the patient can only be approximated through a patient record. The only true indicator of the condition of the patient is the actual state of the patient (Hogan and Wagner, 1997).

In summary, although electronic PHRs offer patients greater control over the storage, management, and dissemination of their personal medical information, they are not without challenges. In the next section, we investigate the phenomenon of usage of this discretionary software application and explore the antecedents of its use related to PHR adoption. We embarked on this study because we anticipate a rapidly growing user base for this technology as government agencies and health systems begin to push for increased adherence. President Bush, in his Health Information Technology Plan, has created a strategy to ensure that most Americans have electronic health records within the next ten years (Bush, 2004), and others in top federal government positions have given bipartisan support to this directive (Gingrich and Kennedy, 2004). Thus, it is important to understand the characteristics and concerns of potential users at an early stage of the diffusion cycle, so that appropriate implementation strategies can be crafted.

EARLY ADOPTERS OF PHR: WHO ARE THEY AND WHAT DO THEY VALUE?

In order to understand the characteristics of individuals who are early adopters of PHR software, we conducted an exploratory empirical study. An additional goal of the study was to examine, in

Figure 15.3   **Conceptual Model**

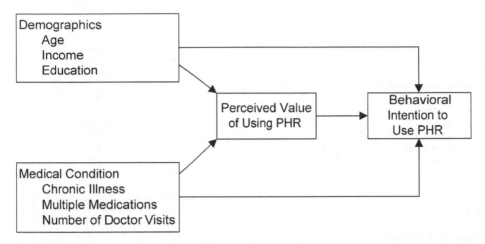

general, the drivers of usage intentions of discretionary software applications. Following from the theory of reasoned action (Ajzen and Fishbein, 1980), the conceptual model underlying the study, shown in Figure 15.3, suggests that individual characteristics of two varieties—demographics, and those related specifically to the individual's medical condition—predict the value cognitions individuals possess in regard to using the software. These cognitions, in turn, drive their usage intentions. Additionally, we allow for the possibility that individual characteristics exhibit direct effects on usage intentions, over and above their mediated influence via perceived value.

The demographic variables included in the study were age, education, and income. The medical condition–related variables were the existence of a chronic health condition in the individual's circle of care, whether or not multiple medications whether required for this chronic condition, and the total number of doctor visits. Our *a priori* expectation was that—as with most other software innovations—income, and education would be positively associated with perceived value (Rogers, 1995). The relationship of age to perceived value, however, is somewhat less clear. In general, empirical evidence across numerous software innovations suggests that younger people tend to view such technologies in a more positive light (Rogers, 1995). On the other hand, to the extent that an individual's health condition tends to decline with age, the value of a PHR may become more evident with increasing age.

As in the case of age, the relationship between variables that describe the individual's health and perceived value is less straightforward. A more severe medical condition could be associated with lower perceived value because of the perception that the PHR distances the individual user from the human care provider (e.g., a doctor). Alternatively, insofar as the PHR allows for better recording and sharing of information between patient and care provider, a positive relationship is also plausible. We tested this model using data gathered through a field study. The study context and our findings are described below.

Study Context and Sample

We mailed a survey to 813 purchasers of an electronic personal health record. These 813 users represent people who had purchased the software through the company's Web site, ordered it over

Table 15.2

Sample Description

Description	Value
Surveys sent	813
Unusable or undeliverable	47
Usable surveys	190
Response Rate	24.8%
Male/Female	72/28
% of users with chronic illness	63%
Average number visits to doctor/year	7.1
Average years of computer experience	15.3

Table 15.3

Descriptive Statistics

	N	Minimum	Maximum	Mean	Std. Deviation
DEM_AGE	190	1	8	5.06	1.267
DEM_EDUC	190	1	6	5.01	1.291
DEM_INC	157	2	10	5.91	2.588
DEM_ILL	192	0	1	.59	.492
DEM_MED	186	0	1	.75	.433
DEM_DOC	190	2	8	3.02	.951
PVA_AVG	190	1	5	2.84	1.023
PVB_AVG	188	1	5	3.35	.937
PVC_AVG	193	1	5	4.22	.738
BI_AVG	190	1	5	3.96	.904
Valid N (listwise)	145				

the telephone, or through a third-party distributor in the three-month period just prior to our study. There were forty-seven unusable or undeliverable surveys and 190 complete surveys, representing a 24.8 percent response rate. Descriptive statistics are shown in Tables 15.2 and 15.3. In other work (Angst, 2004), we found that individuals' beliefs with regard to the value of PHRs consisted of three distinct dimensions: "structure, organization and compliance (PVa)," "relationship and connectedness with one's health care provider (PVb)," and "convenience and empowerment" (PVc; see Appendix 15.1 for scales). Individual characteristics were measured using the scales shown in Appendix 15.1, while the behavioral intention construct was adapted from Davis (1989).

Data Analysis, Results, and Discussion

We used structural equation modeling techniques with the EQS computer program to perform all confirmatory factor and structural analyses (Bentler, 1985). The psychometric properties of the variables are acceptable and the reliability of the constructs is adequate (Cronbach Alpha, BI = .85, PVa = .93, PVb = .92, and PVc = .75). We first tested the relationship between the demographic and medical condition variables and behavioral intention (see Figure 15.4) and found only DEM_AGE (the age of the subject) and DEM_ED (the education level of the subject) to be significant predictors of intention to use. These results showed that younger and less educated

Figure 15.4   Direct Path Analysis—Demographics

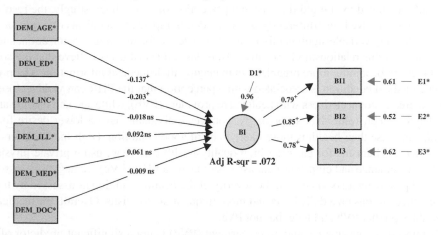

Figure 15.5   Direct Path Analysis with Mediators

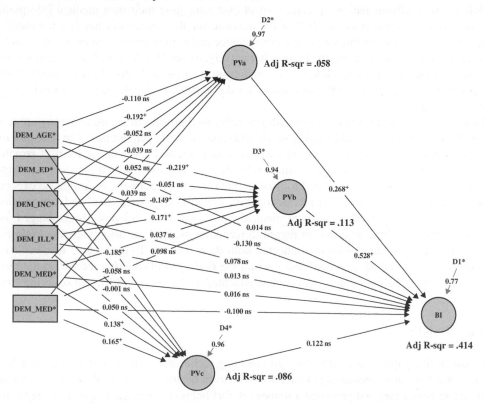

users have greater intentions for future use. Our next step was to test a mediated model with the perceived value constructs acting as mediators. When we introduced the mediators, both age and education became non-significant and PVa and PVb emerged as significant predictors of BI, collectively explaining over 40 percent of the variance in usage intentions (see Figure 15.5).

Our findings show that the effects of individual characteristics on usage intentions for PHR software are fully mediated by a multi-dimensional perception of value. Interestingly, the results suggest that value is perceived very differently across the demographic and medical condition variables. Education is the only variable significantly related to the desire for structure, organization, and compliance (PVa), and this relationship is negative. Thus, less educated users believe that the software will assist them in becoming more organized in managing their medical information. The presence of a chronic medical condition is associated with a perception that the PHR can yield a closer relationship and greater connectedness with health care providers (PVb), while age and income are negatively related to such value. Not surprisingly, younger individuals have a lower desire for close relationships because their health is more likely to be in good condition. High-income users possibly have other mechanisms for ensuring high-quality health care (e.g., using private physicians). Finally, the convenience and empowerment aspects of using a PHR (PVc) are negatively associated with age, and positively associated with the severity of the health condition as assessed by the need for multiple medications on a daily basis and more frequent doctor visits. Overall, the medical condition variables predict PVb and PVc, but not PVa.

We also find that convenience and empowerment (PVc) is not a significant predictor of usage intentions. This finding is somewhat surprising as an important aspect of the value proposition of a PHR is that it affords patients greater control over managing their own medical information. One potential explanation is simply that the measure for this dimension needs refinement: As opposed to the other two dimensions, the convenience and empowerment dimension does not tap into perceptions related to using the PHR. Alternatively, it could be the case that, contrary to what is commonly claimed, patients do not desire such control and would rather have a trained medical professional manage their health information for them. Both explanations point to the need for further investigation.

In summary, the pattern of results reveals that individual profiles in regard to demographic and medical condition factors yield varying levels and types of value perceptions. The lack of a relationship between the medical condition variables and perceived value in the form of structure, compliance, and organization suggests that such value is likely to be salient for most users, independent of whether they have a need to manage their health proactively. As might be expected, value perceptions related to closer interaction with a health care professional and empowerment are amplified in the presence of severe medical conditions. Economically disadvantaged users who may otherwise be challenged in regard to receiving medical attention view the PHR as an important means for staying more connected with their doctors. To the degree that behavioral intentions drive actual adoption and use, overall the findings indicate that the early adopters of PHRs are likely to be individuals who are less educated, older, less wealthy, and suffering from a chronic illness.

CONCLUSION

Our goal in this paper was to introduce an emerging technology—the electronic personal health record—that has transformational potential for the critical health care sector. We examined the state of IT use in health care and proposed a framework that helps organize the range of IT applications used by hospitals, physicians, and other medical professionals. We described the functionality of the PHR application, together with the issues surrounding its adoption and use. Finally, we presented empirical data demonstrating that individuals with different demographic and medical condition characteristics perceive different types of value in the PHR, and that two dimensions of such value are significant predictors of future use intentions. Our data offer some useful insights into the acceptance of this technology at a very early stage of the diffusion curve and provide a glimpse into the profiles of individuals who are likely to be among its early adopters.

The motivation for this study, as articulated earlier in this paper, is the pressing need to contain burgeoning health care costs while simultaneously ensuring that medical errors are reduced and patient safety is enhanced. Technologies such as the PHR can assist in these endeavors by both providing a repository of critical data for use by clinicians, and by aiding patients in becoming more proactive in the management of their health. These technologies, however, are only the tip of the iceberg. There are a host of other areas where HIT, by virtue of its ability to increase the velocity and availability of accurate and reliable information flows, has an important role to play. Mobile technologies such as handheld devices can aid in the distribution of medical expertise by providing clinicians with easy access to needed data on drug interactions at the point of patient care. Likewise, systems such as computerized prescription order entry (CPOE) offer the capability of reducing medication errors (Bates, 2000; Bates et al., 1998; Bates et al., 1999). The transformation of the health care sector is dependent on the ongoing and persistent diffusion of these technologies.

Much more research remains to be done. Technology artifacts such as the PHR create new vulnerabilities for users in regard to privacy and security. Indeed, most "discretionary" software applications for home use give rise to such concerns. How do such concerns inhibit the acceptance of these technologies? How may they be mitigated? These questions are worthy of investigation. The health care system has been slow to adopt information technologies that have provided considerable value to other industry sectors, both in terms of achieving operational excellence and in improving the quality and effectiveness of business processes. To the extent that such gains in the health care sector are contingent upon the willingness of individuals to adopt and use technologies such as the PHR, ongoing research that can aid in developing adoption strategies is critical.

APPENDIX 15.1. SURVEY INSTRUMENT

Value: Structure, Organization, and Compliance (PVa)

- Using the PHR helps me to perform my health care activities (by reminding me to make and keep my appointments, etc.)
- Using the PHR helps me to stay on schedule with my health care activities (such as getting my regular checkup)
- Using the PHR helps me perform my health care activities at the appropriate times (such as refilling prescriptions)
- Using the PHR helps me remember to perform my health care activities (like testing my blood sugar)
- Using the PHR allows me to accomplish more of my health care objectives (such as losing weight)

Value: Relationship and Connectedness (PVb)

- Using the PHR improves communications between my care providers and me
- Using the PHR improves my relationship with my care providers
- Reducing the number of forms to fill out during registration by having the information available on my PHR is valuable to me

Value: Convenience and Empowerment (PVc)

- It would be valuable to have my health information available at all times
- It would be valuable to have my complete medical record with me at all times
- It is critical to have my emergency medical information with me at all times
- It would be valuable to have all of my health care information located in one place

Behavioral Intention to Use

- I intend to use the PHR in the near term
- I believe my use of the PHR will be more extensive in the future
- I intend to use the PHR more frequently in the future

DEM_AGE

What is your age?

1. <20   ___
2. 21–30   ___
3. 31–40   ___
4. 41–50   ___
5. 51–60   ___
6. 61–70   ___
7. 71–80   ___
8. 81+   ___

DEM_ED

Level of Education:

1. Some High School   ___
2. Completed High School   ___
3. Associates Degree   ___
4. Some college   ___
5. Undergrad/Bachelor's degree   ___
6. Post-graduate study   ___

DEM_INC

Household Income (Annual before tax):

1. Less than $20,000   ___
2. $20,000–$29,999   ___
3. $30,000–$49,999   ___
4. $50,000–$69,999   ___
5. $70,000–$89,999   ___
6. $90,000–$109,999   ___

7. $110,000–$129,999   ___
8. $130,000–$149,999   ___
9. $150,000–$174,999   ___
10. $175,000 or more   ___

DEM_ILL

Does anyone in my care have a chronic health condition?

1. No   ___
2. Yes   ___

DEM_MED

Does anyone in my care take multiple medications on a daily basis?

1. No   ___
2. Yes   ___

DEM_DOC

Estimate the total number of doctors that those under my care (including myself) would see in an average year (including dentists, family practitioners, specialists, eye doctors, OB/GYN, Psyc/Soc, etc.):

1. 0   ___
2. 1–4   ___
3. 5–10   ___
4. 11–20 ___
5. 21–30 ___
6. 31–40 ___
7. 41–50 ___
8. 51+   ___

ACKNOWLEDGMENTS

We thank an anonymous reviewer for suggesting that we use the term "discretionary application" as opposed to the term we had chosen. We also acknowledge the support and assistance of CapMed, a division of Bio-Imaging Technologies, Inc., for access to their databases and for allowing us to survey their users.

REFERENCES

Ajzen, I., and Fishbein, M. *Understanding Attitudes and Predicting Social Behavior.* Englewood Cliffs, NJ: Prentice Hall, 1980.
Angst, C.M. Patients' perceived value of using a personal health record. Paper presented at the TEPR— Toward an Electronic Patient Record Conference, Ft. Lauderdale, FL, 2004.

Aronsky, D., and Haug, P.J. Assessing the quality of clinical data in a computer-based record for calculating the pneumonia severity index. *Journal of the American Medical Informatics Association,* 7, 1 (2000), 55–65.

Baker, L.; Wagner, T.H.; Singer, S.; and Bundorf, M.K. Use of the internet and e-mail for health care information. *Journal of the American Medical Association,* 289 (2003), 2400–2406.

Bates, D.W. Using information technology to reduce rates of medication errors in hospitals. *BMJ,* 320 (2000), 788–791.

Bates, D.W.; Leape, L.L.; Cullen, D.J.; Laird, N.; Petersen, L.A.; Teich, J.M.; et al. Effect of computerized physician order entry and a team intervention on prevention of serious medication errors. *Journal of the American Medical Association,* 280, 15 (1998), 1311–1316.

Bates, D.W.; Spell, N.; Cullen, D.J.; Burdick, E.; Laird, N.; Petersen, L.A.; et al. The costs of adverse drug events in hospitalized patients. *Journal of the American Medical Association,* 227 (1997), 307–311.

Bates, D.W.; Teich, J.M.; Lee, J.; Seger, D.L.; Kuperman, G.J.; Boyle, D.; et al. The impact of computerized physician order entry on medication error prevention. *Journal of the American Medical Informatics Association,* 6 (1999), 313–321.

Bear, J.H. (2000). *Desktop Publishing Giants: Software Leaders by the Numbers.* 2000 (available at http://desktoppub.about.com/library/weekly/aa012600c.htm, accessed on October 10, 2004).

Benbasat, I., and Nault, B.R. *Laboratory Experiments in Information Systems Studies with a Focus on Individuals: A Critical Appraisal.* Paper presented at the Harvard Business School Research Colloquium, Boston, MA, 1989, pp. 33–47.

Bentler, P. Theory and implementation of EQS: a structural equations program (Version 6.0). Software program. Los Angeles: BMDP Statistical Software, Inc., 1985.

Brennan, P.F., and Stead, W.W. Assessing data quality: from concordance, through correctness and completeness, to valid manipulatable representations. *Journal of the American Medical Informatics Association,* 7, 1 (2000), 106–107.

Brodie, M.; Flournoy, R.E.; Altman, D.E.; et al. Health information, the internet, and the digital divide. *Health Affiliate (Millwood),* 19 (2000), 255–265.

Bush, G.W. *Transforming Health Care: The President's Health Information Technology Plan.* Executive Order 13335: Incentives for the Use of Health Information Technology and Establishing the Position of the National Health Information Technology Coordinator. Washington, DC: Office of the Press Secretary, 2004.

Cain, M., and Mittman, R. *Diffusion of Innovation in Health Care.* Palo Alto, CA: Institute for the Future—California Health Care Foundation, 2002.

Chin, T. Americans trail much of Europe in adopting EMRs. *American Medical News.* September 2, 2002a. 34.

Chin, T. New players in electronic prescribing. *American Medical News.* February 25, 2002b, 27–30.

Cimino, J.J. *Patient Access to Clinical Information: The PatCIS Project* (No. National Information Infrastructure Contract N01-LM-6–3542): National Library of Medicine Final Report, 2000.

Cimino, J.J.; Patel, V.L.; and Kushniruk, A.W. The patient clinical information system (PatCIS): Technical solutions for and experience with giving patients access to their electronic medical records. *International Journal of Medical Informatics,* 68, 1–3 (2002), 113–127.

Classen, D.C.; Pestotnik, S.L.; Evans, R.S.; Lloyd, J.F.; and Burke, J.P. Adverse drug events in hospitalized patients. Excess length of stay, extra costs, and attributable mortality. *Journal of the American Medical Association,* 277 (1997), 301–306.

Copeland, D.G., and McKenney, J.L. Airline reservation systems: lessons from history. *MIS Quarterly,* 12 (1988), 353–371.

The Data Standards Working Group: Report and Recommendations. Connecting for health, a program of the Markle Foundation. 2003 (available at http://www.connectingforhealth.org/resources/dswg_report_6.5.03.pdf, accessed on December 16, 2004).

Davis, F.D. Perceived usefulness, perceived ease of use, and user acceptance of information technology. *MIS Quarterly,* 13 (1989), 319–339.

Degoulet, P., and Fieschi, M. Critical dimensions in medical informatics. *International Journal of Medical Informatics,* 44 (1997), 21–26.

Devaraj, S., and Kohli, R. Performance impacts of information technology: is actual usage the missing link? *Management Science,* 49, 3 (2003), 273–299.

Dick, R.S.; Steen, E.B.; and Detmer, D.E. (eds.) *Computer-Based Patient Record: An Essential Technology for Health Care.* Washington, DC: National Academy Press, 1997.

eHealth Institute: A catalyst for access and quality. 2004 (available at http://www.ehealthinstitute.org/Index.aspx, accessed on November 17, 2004).

Elson, R.B., and Connelly, D.P. Computerized patient records in primary care: their role in mediating guideline-driven physician behavior change. *Archives of Family Medicine*, 4 (1995), 698–705.

Elson, R.B., and Connelly, D.P. The impact of anticipatory patient data displays on physician decision making: a pilot study. *Proceedings of the AMIA Annual Fall Symposium*. Washington, DC: Hanley & Belfus, 1997, pp. 233–237.

Elson, R.B., Faughnan, J., and Connelly, D.P. An industrial process view of information delivery to support clinical decision-making: implications for systems design and process measures. *Journal of the American Medical Informatics Association*, 4 (1997), 266–278.

Fowles, J.B.; Kind, A.C.; Craft, C.; Kind, E.A.; Mandel, J.L.; and Adlis, S. Patients' interest in reading their medical record: relation with clinical and sociodemographic characteristics and patients' approach to health care. *Arch Intern Med*, 164, 7 (2004), 793–800.

Gingrich, N., and Kennedy, P. Operating in a Vacuum. *New York Times*, May 3, 2004, p. 23.

Goldsmith, J.; Blumenthal, D.; and Rishel, W. Federal health information policy: a case of arrested development. *Health Affairs*, 22 (2003), 44–55.

Greenes, R.A., and Shortliffe, E.H. (1990). Medical informatics: an emerging discipline with academic and institutional perspectives. *Journal of the American Medical Association*, 263, 8 (1990), 1114–1120.

Grudin, J., and Palen, L. Why groupware succeeds: discretion of mandate? *Proceedings of the ECSCW '95*. Dordrecht: Kluwer, 1995, pp. 263–278.

Harris Interactive. Two in five adults keep personal or family health records and almost everybody thinks this is a good idea: electronic health records likely to grow rapidly. *Harris Interactive Health Care News*, 4 (2004), 1–5.

Hersh, W.R. Medical informatics: improving health care through information. *Journal of the American Medical Association*, 288, 16 (2002), 1955–1958.

HIPAA Privacy Essentials. Richardson, TX: Privacy Council, 2002.

HIPAA Privacy Implementation Guide. Richardson, TX: Privacy Council, 2002.

Hogan, W.R., and Wagner, M.M. Accuracy of data in computer-based patient records. *Journal of the American Medical Informatics Association*, 4, 5 (1997), 342–355.

Informatics for Diabetes Education and Telemedicine-IDEATel. 2004 (available at http://www.ideatel.com, accessed on June 14, 2004).

Kim, K.K., and Michelman, J.E. An examination of factors for the strategic use of information systems in the health care industry. *MIS Quarterly*, 14, 2 (1990), 201–215.

Kim, M.I., and Johnson, K.B. Personal health records: evaluation of functionality and utility. *Journal of the American Medical Informatics Association*, 9, 2 (2002), 171–179.

Kohn, L.T.; Corrigan, J.M.; and Donaldson, M. (eds.) *To Err Is Human: Building a Safer Health System*. Washington, DC: Institute of Medicine, 1999.

Laudon, K.C., and Laudon, J.P. *Management Information Systems: Managing the Digital Firm*, 8th ed. Upper Saddle River, NJ: Pearson Education, Inc., 2004.

The Leapfrog Group Fact Sheet. 2004 (available at http://www.leapfroggroup.org/FactSheets/LF_FactSheet.pdf, accessed on June 15, 2003).

Logan, J.R.; Gorman, P.N.; and Middleton, B. Measuring the quality of medical records: a method for comparing completeness and correctness of clinical encounter data. In S. Bakken (ed.), *A Medical Odyssey: Visions of the Future and Lessons from the Past. AMIA 2001 Annual Symposium*. Washington, DC: Hanley & Belfus, 2001, pp. 408–412.

Lucas, H.C. *Information Technology and the Productivity Paradox: Assessing the Value of Investing in IT*. New York: Oxford University Press, 1999.

Masys, D.; Baker, D.; Butros, A.; and Cowles, K.E. Giving patients access to their medical records via the internet: the PCASSO experience. *Journal of American Medical Informatics Association*, 9, 2 (2002), 181–191.

National Health Care Expenditures: Historical Overview. 2004 (available at http://www.cms.hhs.gov/publications/overview-medicare-medicaid/default2.asp, accessed on October 10, 2004).

Office of the National Health Information Technology Coordinator (ONCHIT): Mission. 2004 (available at http://www.hhs.gov/healthit/mission.html#, accessed on November 17, 2004).

Orthner, H.F. Series preface. In C.P. Friedman, J.C. Wyatt, A.C. Smith, and B. Kaplan (eds.), *Evaluation Methods in Medical Informatics*. New York: Springer-Verlag, 1997, i–xii.

Overhage, J.M.; Tierney, W.M.; Zhou, X.-H.; and McDonald, C.J. A randomized trial of "corollary orders" to prevent errors of omission. *Journal of the American Medical Informatics Association*, 4 (1997), 364–375.

Papshev, D., and Peterson, A.M. Electronic prescribing in ambulatory practice: promises, pitfalls, and potential solutions. *American Journal of Managed Care,* 7 (2001), 725–736.

Patel, V.L.; Cytryn, K.N.; Shortliffe, E.H.; and Safran, C. The collaborative health care team: the role of individual and group expertise. *Teaching and Learning in Medicine,* 12, 3 (2000), 117–132.

Raghupathi, W. Strategic IT applications in health care. *Communications of the ACM,* 45, 12 (2002), 56–61.

Rogers, E.M. *Diffusion of Innovations,* 3rd ed. New York: Free Press, 1983.

Rogers, E.M. *Diffusion of Innovations,* 4th ed. New York: Free Press, 1995.

Safran, C. Electronic medical records: a decade of experience. *Journal of the American Medical Association,* 285, 13 (2001), 1766.

Safran, C.; Rind, D.M.; Davis, R.B.; Ives, D.; Sands, D.Z.; Currier, J.; et al. Guidelines for management of HIV infection with computer-based patient's record. *The Lancet,* 346, 8971 (1995), 341–346.

Safran, C.; Sands, D.Z.; and Rind, D.M. Online medical records: a decade of experience. *Methods of Information in Medicine,* 28, 4–5 (1999), 308–312.

Shortliffe, E.H. The evolution of electronic medical records. *Academy of Medicine,* 74, 4 (1999), 414–419.

Stausberg, J.; Koch, D.; Ingenerf, J.; and Betzler, M. Comparing paper-based with electronic patient records: lessons learned during a study on diagnosis and procedure codes. *Journal of the American Medical Informatics Association,* 10, 5 (2003), 470–477.

Stein, H.D.; Nadkarni, P.; Erdos, J.; and Miller, P.L. Exploring the degree of concordance of coded and textual data in answering clinical queries from a clinical data repository. *Journal of the American Medical Informatics Association,* 7, 1 (2000), 42–54.

Swartz, N. What every business needs to know about HIPAA. *Information Management Journal,* 37, 2 (2003), 26–34.

Thompson, T.G., and Brailer, D.J. *The Decade of Health Information Technology: Delivering Consumer-centric and Information-rich Health Care. Framework for Strategic Action.* Washington, DC: Office for the National Coordinator for Health Information Technology (ONCHIT), Department of Health and Human Services, and the United States Federal Government, 2004, pp. 1–38 (available at http://www.hhs.gov/news/, accessed on November 16, 2004).

Tsai, C.C., and Starren, J. Patient participation in electronic medical records. *Journal of the American Medical Association,* 285, 13 (2001), 1765.

Ueckert, F.; Goerz, M.; Ataian, M.; Tessmann, S.; and Prokosch, H.-U. Empowerment of patients and communication with health care professionals through an electronic health record. *International Journal of Medical Informatics,* 70, 2–3 (2003), 99–108.

Venkatesh, V., and Brown, S.A. A longitudinal investigation of personal computers in homes: Adoption determinants and emerging challenges. *MIS Quarterly,* 25, 1 (2001), 71–102.

Von Knoop, C.; Lovich, D.; Silverstein, M.B.; and Tutty, M. *Vital Signs: E-health in the United States.* Boston: Boston Consulting Group, 2003.

CHAPTER 16

ORGANIZATIONAL AND INDIVIDUAL ACCEPTANCE OF ASSISTIVE INTERFACES AND TECHNOLOGIES

ADRIANE B. RANDOLPH AND GEOFFREY S. HUBONA

Abstract: Much of the management information systems literature focuses on organizational and individual technology acceptance for conventional, non-impaired users. However, little of this literature considers the range of users' cognitive and physical differences and the implications on prevailing theories of technology acceptance and use. Individuals with disabilities have unique requirements with respect to using and interfacing with conventional and assistive technologies. For example, many individuals with impaired motor functions cannot effectively use conventional mouse and keyboard interfaces. It is particularly important to understand the impact as affecting the organizational adoption and diffusion of these technologies. We describe important considerations for the acceptance and use of assistive interfaces and new technologies while focusing on both organizational and individual considerations. At the individual level, we investigate how a person's ability affects technology acceptance and usage, and we illustrate this with two novel interface technology case studies. At the organizational level, we consider factors for the diffusion of assistive technologies. It is important that the management information systems and assistive technology research communities share knowledge to ensure that disabled users have adequate technical access and support in organizations.

Keywords: Assistive Technology, Technology Acceptance, Diffusion of Technology, Disabled Users, Alternative Input Devices

INTRODUCTION

A disability is a long-lasting impairment that prohibits what society considers normal activity. The unique concerns of users with disabilities have largely been unrecognized in management information systems (MIS) literature. With greater public awareness, research in the MIS field could help resolve some disturbing statistics. According to the U.S. Census Bureau's 2000 statistics (Waldrop and Stern, 2003), there were over 33 million Americans of working age living with a disability, representing 18 percent of the U.S. working-age population.[1] Also reported in the Census 2000 Brief, 39.9 percent of working-age men with a disability were unemployed while only 20.1 percent of able-bodied men were unemployed. Among women of working age with a disability, 48.6 percent were unemployed, whereas 32.7 percent of those without a disability were unemployed. Despite the passage of legislation designed to increase public awareness and to

379

provide technical assistance, people with disabilities were found less likely to be employed, and more likely to live in poverty, than their able-bodied counterparts.

One factor promoting this disparity may relate to a lack of understanding about how organizations can evaluate and adjust their technological infrastructures so as to productively accommodate the needs of individuals with disabilities. Users with disabilities have different needs and perspectives for evaluating, adopting, and using new technologies. These perspectives should be absorbed into mainstream practices for enabling the organizational adoption of new technologies. Failure to do so may result in an unnecessarily low acceptance rate of new technologies by disabled users, thus further impeding their assimilation into the workforce.

In the MIS literature, prevailing theories and models of technology acceptance and diffusion presume an able-bodied user population, and typically do not account for unique nuances that are characteristic of the substantial numbers in the user population with disabilities. Such able-bodied users typically access computer systems through point-and-click selections and enter information using a keyboard. Most computer systems are designed with this paradigm for input and interactive use. However, users with physical limitations may be encumbered by these input devices and labor-intensive approaches for interacting with computers, and may improve their productivity using alternative, assistive technology input devices. For example, a user may not have the full range of motion and control over his or her hands and fingers and may be more productive employing alternative means for interfacing with the computer, such as by using his or her feet, head, mouth, breath, or even a solitary finger. Furthermore, there exists a population of users who have such severe limitations in mobility that they require even more novel interfaces, such as utilizing input from their eyes, skin conductivity, blood flow, or even directly from their brain signals.

An objective of this chapter is to explore prevailing theories of technology acceptance and diffusion through a methodological analysis and to examine the implications of such theories for individuals and organizations when considering users with disabilities and their special needs. In the following sections, we explore popular technology acceptance models, consider the particular challenges faced by users with physical disabilities, and share some proposed solutions to those challenges. Then, we investigate how factors such as physical disability moderate the acceptance of technology through two case studies of user adoption of systems with novel interfaces: (1) an Internet browser controlled by neural input; and (2) a communications system controlled by galvanic skin response (GSR). Finally, we conclude with discussion about the unique challenges and needs of disabled users and how organizations can better understand and accommodate these users.

BACKGROUND AND RELATED WORK

Users with Disabilities

Disabilities differ in their causes and severity. An individual possessing a physical or mental limitation may be described as having a disability if the condition results in a long-lasting impairment or prohibits what is characterized as "activity in the manner or within the range considered normal for a human being" (World Health Organization, 1980). We can easily describe the normal abilities of a person but not his or her normal skill. Ability is distinguished from skill in that it is a basic trait that can be easily assessed whereas a skill describes how well someone can perform a task and is difficult to predict (Cook and Hussey, 2002).

Ability encompasses both type and degree, since there are various ways in which someone can be able. For example, physical ability can range from being able-bodied and having fine motor control, to someone who has complete loss of voluntary motor control, sometimes referred to as locked-in syndrome. Physical ability may be regarded separately from cognitive ability. Usually, locked-in individuals who lack physical ability nevertheless remain cognitively intact (Ariniello, 1999).

From an analysis of the word, we can say that the absence of ability is *dis*ability. The 2000 Census (Waldrop and Stern, 2003) categorized six types of disability resulting from a physical, mental, or emotional condition. Moreover, these six disability categories could be experienced concurrently and at varying degrees of severity. The six categories of disability include: (1) sensory; (2) physical; (3) mental; (4) self-care; (5) difficulty going outside the home; and (6) employment disability.

A *sensory disability* involves prolonged loss of vision or hearing; a *physical disability* results in physical limitations such as an inability to walk or climb stairs; and a *mental disability* is characterized as having difficulty performing cognitive tasks such as remembering, concentrating, and learning. When someone has difficulty with personal tasks such as bathing and feeding himself or herself, this is categorized as a *self-care disability*. A person could experience great trouble leaving home to run errands or visit the doctor resulting in a *difficulty going outside the home*. Furthermore, he or she could have difficulty working at a job or a business, which is described as an *employment disability*. One group of individuals requiring technical assistance for access to employment typically suffers from spinal cord injury, arthritis, cerebral palsy, visual impairment, or hearing impairment. Another group needing this technical assistance for reemployment comprises those who have suffered a job-related injury (Cook and Hussey 2002). In fact, a twenty-year-old person has a 30 percent chance of becoming disabled before reaching retirement age (Social Security Administration, 2003).

This chapter considers the range of disabilities possessed by users that all have a common consequence: a disabled user is going to filter his or her use of technology by the limitations imposed by his or her disability. This filter constitutes a "cultural screen" (Krefting and Krefting, 1991) since it results from the user's experiences and relationships. Their filtration of the use of technology has significant implications with respect to technology adoption, acceptance, and ultimate usage patterns.

Assistive Technology

Assistive technology refers to devices that seek to "increase, maintain, or improve the functional capabilities of individuals with disabilities" (U.S. Congress, 1998b). There has been an increasing awareness that the challenges faced by people with disabilities are not the result of the impairment itself but rather a combination of the impairment and the context in which that individual operates (Pope and Brandt, 1997). This context includes considerations for: (1) setting; (2) social context; (3) cultural context; and (4) physical context (Cook and Hussey, 2002). *Setting* includes location and characteristics of the environment, such as the task to be accomplished and rules surrounding accomplishment of that task. *Social context* may be the most important for use of assistive technology because it governs what is considered "normal" or "expected." *Cultural context* relates to concepts of shared patterns of behavior and how individuals interact with others and the environment. Finally, *physical context* describes the environmental conditions where the system is situated, and commonly includes measures for heat, light, and sound.

There is a balance between context and three other components that together make up the human activity assistive technology (HAAT) model (Cook and Hussey, 2002), modified from a general model for human performance. The four components include the individual, the activity he or she wishes to perform, and the technology assisting him or her in that activity within a particular context. Studies in MIS have shown that a combination of user characteristics, as well as

Figure 16.1 **Components of the HAAT Model and System Effectiveness**

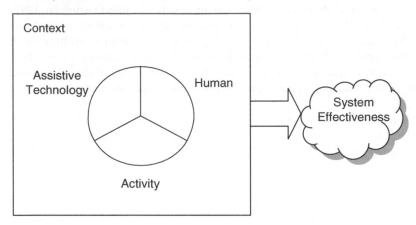

characteristics of the technology, affect system usage (Benbasat et al., 1981). Therefore, when measuring system effectiveness, it is necessary to consider the components of the HAAT model as illustrated in Figure 16.1.

Use of Novel Interfaces

The type and severity of a person's disability directly relate to the challenges faced when interfacing with information technology. For example, individuals considered physically disabled by societal standards may still have reliable control of some muscular activity, as compared with someone suffering from total paralysis. Furthermore, these users may be considered able with respect to other disability classifications, for example, by not having a mental disability. Consequently, the various disability classifications have differing impacts on the types and characteristics of user interfaces that are effective for use with different technologies.

Users retaining limited control over voluntary movement, such as control of a finger or eye movement, have an advantage over those without such reliable channels for control. These users are able to utilize slightly altered, conventional technology interfaces, such as modified keyboards and mice, or eye-gaze control devices, to accomplish a task. Users who experience total paralysis resulting from an injury, stroke, or neurological disease, such as Lou Gehrig's disease, have what is termed *locked-in syndrome.* They must rely on alternative means for input to computers through biometric channels such as skin conductivity and neural signals.

The meaning of the term "biometrics" has evolved over time. Originally relating to the mathematical and statistical analysis of agricultural and atmospheric effects on humans, the term has more recently been used in reference to the identification of humans using biological traits (International Biometric Society, 2002). For our purposes, we will define biometrics and biometric channels as a variation of this latter meaning. Biometrics and biometric channels refer to the use of physical characteristics such as retinal changes and changes in other internal bodily functions (Haag et al., 2004). These characteristics exhibit varying degrees of motor control and, accordingly, can achieve different purposes as input to computers.

Performing a task using these various biometric channels is extremely tedious and time-consuming. For example, spelling with a brain-computer interface takes one minute for every three letters (Wolpaw et al., 2002). Furthermore, the special equipment needed for these novel interfaces is not widely available and is currently built to customized specifications for each user. Therefore, costs are still relatively high, and their use is still a novelty rather than a norm. The following discussion explores some of the most prominent examples of novel interfaces under development.

Galvanic Skin Response

Galvanic Skin Response (GSR) is a measurable change in electrical skin conductivity caused by increased activity in the sweat glands. This change results from stimulation to the sympathetic nervous system, as when a person is anxious (Abrams, 1973). The GSR procedure was first used for psychiatric evaluation (Jung, 1907), and was later adopted for interrogation purposes by law enforcement officials as a component of polygraph testing (Committee to Review the Scientific Evidence on the Polygraph and National Research Council, 2003). Now, more researchers are investigating uses of GSR for control of computer-based systems such as video games (Sakurazawa et al., 2003) and communications systems (Moore and Dua, 2004).

According to Moore and Dua (2004), a typical configuration for a GSR device includes two electrodes placed on the skin in areas with the most active sweat glands: fingers (most common), feet, and armpits. The device sends an imperceptibly small amount of electrical current through the electrodes to measure the momentary amount of skin conductivity created in response to various stimuli. These stimuli attempt to alter the emotional state of the subject, mainly through visual input. First, a baseline reading is taken. Then, a subject is monitored for significant changes in his/her GSR levels from that baseline according to different stimuli. For example, the subject may be asked to talk about a particular incident or watch different visual stimuli. With computer applications such as video games and communications systems, the associated computer system then analyzes the differences in GSR levels online and provides immediate feedback to the user.

Brain-Computer Interfaces

Brain-computer interfaces (BCIs), also known as direct-brain interfaces (DBIs) and brain-machine interfaces (BMIs), form the next frontier for human-computer interaction. They provide users with an alternative to traditional keyboard and mouse interfaces for controlling a computer. For years, researchers from various fields have been investigating how minute changes in the brain's electrical activity can be mapped and harnessed to direct the control of devices such as computers (Wolpaw et al., 2002). Brain-computer interfaces make use of the fluctuating electrical output from the brain in the form of electroencephalograph (EEG) recordings, but largely do not provide input back to the brain, nor do they allow for outright mind reading.

EEG recordings are conducted either through invasive or non-invasive techniques. With invasive techniques, surgery is used to implant a special electrode on the outer layer of the human brain, the neocortex. This electrode transmits the brain's electrical signals to a nearby receiver for computer processing (Kennedy et al., 2000). However, the quality of these electrodes may erode over time, requiring subsequent implants. By contrast, non-invasive techniques use electrodes placed on the scalp (Peralta et al., 2003). There are disadvantages to non-invasive techniques, as well, since the neural signals are attenuated as they travel through layers of fluid, bone, and skin. Furthermore, signals recorded with non-invasive techniques are more susceptible to noise from other neighboring sources, and from extraneous electrically detected muscular activity, or EMG (Wolpaw et al., 2002).

The greatest potential beneficiaries of BCI research are individuals with severe motor disabilities, such as locked-in users, who cannot effectively operate conventional assistive devices.

Brain-computer interfaces can provide users with a means for communicating and interacting with the external world that does not rely on muscular channels (Wolpaw et al., 2002), and can also be used for restoring motor functions through prosthetic devices controlled by neural input (Moore, 2003). The ultimate goal of the BCI research stream is to impart more, and better control, of computer devices to physically challenged users. A number of clinical teams exist, but it is important that the field advance from clinical and demonstration applications to the development of real-world devices (Moore, 2003). Examples of real-world devices under development include neural spellers (Wolpaw et al., 2002), Internet browsers (Tomori and Moore, 2003), and environmental control units (Adams et al., 2003).

ADAPTING THEORIES OF INDIVIDUAL TECHNOLOGY ACCEPTANCE

A number of existing theories are useful for assessing individuals' technology adoption and acceptance, although none discuss the impacts of a person's ability. When considering the technology adoption and diffusion of innovation at an organizational level, studies have largely looked at characteristics of the individual, and have extrapolated their broader impacts on the organization (Leonard-Barton and Deschamps, 1988; Rogers, 1995; Karahanna et al., 1999). Venkatesh et al. (2003) highlighted eight of the most prominent models that have intention to use and/or usage as the dependent variables for characterizing individual technology acceptance. By synthesizing these models, they proposed a unified theory of acceptance and use of technology (UTAUT). They demonstrated that UTAUT explained a variance in usage that was 17 percent greater than the best single model. The eight models examined included the: (1) theory of reasoned action (TRA); (2) technology acceptance model (TAM); (3) motivational model (MM); (4) theory of planned behavior (TPB); (5) combined TAM and TPB model (C-TAM-TPB); (6) model of PC utilization (MPCU); (7) innovation diffusion theory (IDT); and (8) social cognitive theory (SCT). These models are described in great detail in the Venkatesh et al. (2003) *MIS Quarterly* article and are briefly summarized below. We review the key constructs of these models with respect to the ramifications for people with disabilities, and regarding their acceptance and use of assistive technologies.

To facilitate discussion, we make assumptions about the assistive technology under consideration, and about the varying types and degrees of disabilities under consideration. First, we assume that the assistive technology fulfills an intended purpose for that user, that is, that the assistive technology does not hinder the disabled user's functional capabilities, but rather enhances them. Second, because of space constraints, we do not review all of the types of disabilities and their varying impacts vis-à-vis these technology acceptance models. Instead, we use a limited, running example to illustrate our points. Our aim in this regard is to give readers a broader sense of the influence that a person's abilities have on technology acceptance.

The example we utilize considers three categories of a user's physical ability: (1) an able-bodied user; (2) a person afflicted with cerebral palsy (CP); and (3) a locked-in user. We consider these physical abilities and how they would affect the acceptance and use of an assistive spelling device incorporated into a tablet PC. An "able-bodied" individual would possess fine muscle control; the CP patient typically has medium muscle control; and the locked-in individual would suffer from extreme loss of voluntary muscle movement. In the case of the able-bodied individual, we assume that he or she is able to speak at a typical rate for unassisted conversation of approximately 150–200 words per minute. By contrast, the highest rate that assistive technology devices allow is ten to fifteen words per minute (Copestake, 1996). This rate would apply to the user with cerebral palsy when using the tablet PC spelling device. In contrast, rates for locked-in users of neural spellers are significantly slower, at approximately three letters per minute (Wolpaw et al., 2002).

Table 16.1 summarizes the overall ramifications of disability and assistive technology on each of the core constructs from the eight models of technology acceptance. In the section below, we briefly discuss the foundations of each model. Then we explain the rationale for the impacts of ability on selected core constructs in Table 16.1. Space limitations preclude a complete discussion of the rationale for all twenty-two core constructs.

The Theory of Reasoned Action

The theory of reasoned action (TRA) is a fundamental theory for predicting human behavior. Proposed by Fishbein and Azjen (1975), it analyzes the relationship between various performance criteria and a person's attitudes, intention, and subjective norms (Sheppard et al., 1988).

An individual's attitude about using the assistive technology, and his sense of the subjective norm, or support from the individual's social reference group for doing so, would vary with the severity of the disability. For example, the able-bodied user would likely experience negative attitudes about using the tablet PC spelling device, and perceive a lack of social support for doing so, since the assistive technology would impede his task performance. On the other hand, someone with cerebral palsy can often speak, but is sometimes difficult to understand. For these users, a tablet PC device for spelling out clarifications may be helpful. This person would feel a greater motivation for using the device to facilitate interactions with people. His colleagues would likely encourage the use of the device, as they would better understand the CP user's communications. Unfortunately, this tablet PC device is inappropriate for a locked-in user, who does not possess the degree of motor control required to write the letters. Since this user is unable to use the device, discussion about external negative attitudes is not applicable.

The Technology Acceptance Model

The technology acceptance model (TAM) has received wide attention in the MIS literature for predicting technology acceptance of individuals within organizations. Key TAM constructs include a user's perceived usefulness (PU) and perceived ease of use (PEOU) of the new technology. TAM also considers whether usage is voluntary or mandatory as related to a subjective norm (SN) construct (Davis, 1989; Venkatesh and Davis, 2000).

Regarding PU, an assistive technology can be inherently useful to a person with a disability, but the degree of usefulness depends on both the severity and type of disability. As with TRA, an able-bodied individual would see little need for a communication device such as the tablet PC spelling device; if initially misunderstood, she or he would simply speak clarifying remarks. Moreover, a locked-in user could not use the device because of the severe and limiting nature of his or her disability. However, someone with cerebral palsy would benefit from using such a system since it was designed with both his or her type and degree of ability in mind.

Considering PEOU, an able-bodied individual may view the PC spelling device as extremely easy and effortless to use. However, the perceived effort would increase considerably with the loss of mobility. A person with very limited mobility would see the "ease of use" of the tablet PC device as grossly prohibitive, since its use would require motor control beyond the abilities of that user.

Finally, the severity of the disability would impact whether the use of the technology was voluntary or mandatory. An able-bodied individual would have a clear choice not to use the tablet PC device to clarify his or her speech, whereas the CP user might have little choice but to use whatever technology is available. The locked-in user would have no choice; she or he would simply not be capable of using the device.

Table 16.1

Overall Ramifications of Disability and Assistive Technology

Model or Theory	Core Construct	Impacts of Ability
The Theory of Reasoned Action (TRA)	Attitude Toward Behavior	Negative or positive feelings toward the technology may intensify with the severity of the disability and depend on the associated assistive technology.
	Subjective Norm	Support for use of the technology by key individuals may intensify with the severity of the disability.
The Technology Acceptance Model (TAM)	Perceived Usefulness	Seen as inherently useful because allows access. Degree of usefulness varies with severity of the disability.
	Perceived Ease of Use	Increases or decreases the amount of effort needed to perform a task. Paired effect between the system and the user's ability.
	Subjective Norm	May involve mandatory usage to perform certain tasks for those with severe disabilities.
The Motivational Model (MM)	Extrinsic Motivation (reward)	Gained access through use of assistive technology may result in a sense of personal success, social integration, or some monetary value which holds different weights depending on ability.
	Intrinsic Motivation (goal)	Assistive technology is necessary to achieve the goal of obtaining access to work, a key life role.
The Theory of Planned Behavior (TPB)	Attitude Toward Behavior	See TRA above.
	Subjective Norm	See TRA above.
	Perceived Behavioral Control	Relates to internal and external constraints. A disabled user knows his or her limitations for using particular types of assistive technology. External support from the organization should increase as the severity of the disability increases.
The Combined TAM and TPB Model (C-TAM-TPB)	Attitude Toward Behavior	See TRA/TPB above.
	Subjective Norm	See TRA/TPB above.
	Perceived Behavioral Control	See TRA/TPB above.
	Perceived Usefulness	See TAM above.
The Model of PC Utilization (MPCU)	Job-fit	By the definition, the assistive technology will improve the performance of disabled users.
	Complexity	Varies with the degree and type of disability when using a particular assistive technology.
	Long-term Consequences	Assistive technology affords access to long-term, future payoffs within an organization.
	Affect Toward Use	Affinity felt for the assistive technology may depend on the social climate at an organization.
	Social Factors	How welcomed and supported disabled users feel when using assistive technology.
	Facilitating Conditions	Whether a support structure is in place for the assistive technology.
The Innovation Diffusion Theory (IDT)	Relative Advantage	A disabled person should see a greater advantage resulting from the introduction and use of assistive technology than an able-bodied user.
	Ease of Use	Depending on the interface, the perception of ease may increase or decrease with severity of disability.

(*continued*)

Table 16.1 (*continued*)

Model or Theory	Core Construct	Impacts of Ability
	Image	A disabled person may be more sensitive to how he or she is perceived when using assistive technology.
	Visibility	Perceive the adoption of assistive technology through your own perspective which is colored by ability.
	Compatibility	Ability shapes what a user sees as the company standard. Considers whether the organization has embraced assistive technology.
	Results Demonstrability	Ability to see immediate improvements in the performance of disabled users with assistive technology.
	Voluntariness of Use	Degree of voluntariness varies with the severity of the disability. A user's disability may negate the voluntariness of use of assistive technology.
The Social Cognitive Theory (SCT)	Performance Outcome Expectations	Again, by definition, the assistive technology enhances the performance of disabled users.
	Personal Outcome Expectations	More and greater organizational access achieved by the disabled person's use of assistive technology.
	Self-efficacy	A disabled user may consider the incompatibility of some assistive technology interfaces with their particular disability and calibrate their ability to use the device.
	Affect	The social climate of an organization may affect how positively (or negatively) a disabled user views the introduction of the assistive technology despite the need.
	Anxiety	Disabled uses may feel a greater sense of importance for effectively using the assistive technology.

The Motivational Model

The motivational model (MM) examines the psychological motivations for an individual to elicit certain behavior. It combines behavioral and cognitive theories to describe extrinsic motivations (e.g., rewards), and intrinsic motivations (e.g., goals), respectively and has been adapted for various contexts (Vallerand, 1997).

A disabled user may be denied access to work, a key life role, without assistive technology (Cook and Hussey, 2002). Therefore, the intrinsic motivation of increased access to work opportunities characterizes the disabled user. She or he may also realize an enhanced sense of personal success, opportunities for social integration, and monetary reward (for example, a salary), all examples of extrinsic motivators for using the assistive technology. These extrinsic motivations, or rewards, may have different weights for any particular user according to disability.

The Theory of Planned Behavior

The theory of planned behavior (TPB) is an extension of TRA. It adds a perceived behavioral control as an additional construct that predicts intention and behavior (Azjen, 1991). This construct relates to perceptions about the internal and external constraints on an individual's behavior (Taylor and Todd, 1995).

An internal constraint for a disabled user would relate to his/her perception of his or her limitations in accomplishing a particular task with the assistive technology. An *external constraint* relates to the type of support in place for utilizing the assistive technology. The more severe a person's disability, the greater the assistance needed. Provided the organization is amenable, support would increase according to the severity of the disability.

The Combined TAM and TPB Model

The combined TAM and TPB model (C-TAM-TPB) is a hybrid model that adapts constructs from TAM and TPB (Taylor and Todd, 1995). The impacts of disability will also have a combined effect on this model by taking into account a person's internal and external support environments and the relative effects of the severity and type of disability.

The Model of PC Utilization

The model of PC utilization (MPCU) was modified from Triandis' (1980) model of human behavior to describe the acceptance and usage of information technologies (Thompson et al., 1991). The model distinguishes beliefs about how actions are tied to emotions or future consequences.

This notion of disability impinges on this model as the constructs reflect the core definition and goals of assistive technology. For example, job-fit relates to the enhanced performance of an individual, which is one of the primary goals for assistive technology. Furthermore, if there are strong facilitating conditions in place for use of assistive technologies within an organization, this will affect how they feel about the technology in question, their affect towards use.

The Innovation Diffusion Theory

The innovation diffusion theory (IDT), modified from Rogers' (1995) original sociological model, is concerned with the spread of new information technology through channels within an organization. Moore and Benbasat (1991) modified this theory to study technology acceptance by individuals within an organization.

The introduction of a new assistive technology that benefits a disabled user would affect his/her sense of relative advantage more than that of an able-bodied user. For example, a person with cerebral palsy would perceive a large relative advantage in the organization with the introduction of special tablet PCs for spelling. However, this same innovation would not be perceived as offering the same advantage to an able-bodied user.

The feeling of necessity related to ability also affects other related constructs of IDT. For example, the relative visibility that a user perceives with assistive technology may be colored by his or her own ability. For example, an able-bodied user clearly would not perceive enhanced visibility through the adoption of assistive technology. Furthermore, the notion of compatibility is relevant. The perception among disabled employees that an organization has adopted a policy of technical accommodation towards the disabled as a standard rather than as an exception is important.

The Social Cognitive Theory

The social cognitive theory (SCT) evolved from social learning theories to incorporate a key concept about human self-beliefs. It is a dynamic model that incorporates a balanced relationship

Figure 16.2   **Modified UTAUT Model**

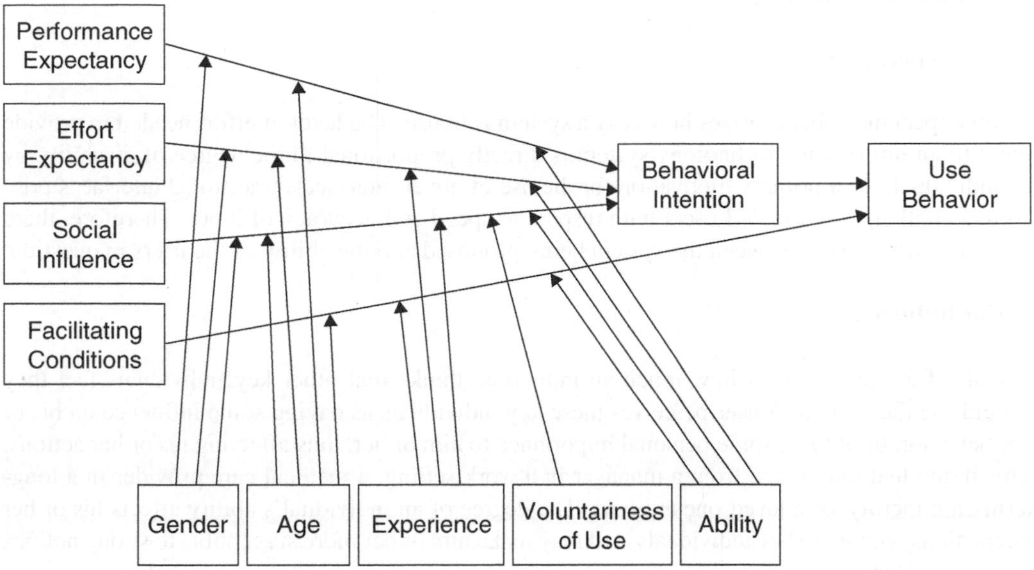

among human behavior, environmental factors, and personal factors (Bandura, 1986). Compeau and Higgins (1995) later expanded this model to apply to an information technology context by exploring computer utilization.

Again, by definition, assistive technology will enable enhanced performance outcome expectations for disabled users, compared to able-bodied users. Moreover, the disabled user would perceive more personal outcome expectations than the able-bodied because of the gains in access within an organization afforded by assistive technologies. A person's disability will also affect the sense of importance placed on being able to effectively utilize the new assistive technology. For example, the new technology interface or device may afford severely disabled users their only opportunity for effective communication, thus magnifying their anxiety toward its use.

From these eight models, UTAUT derived four common, key constructs (see Figure 16.2): (1) performance expectancy; (2) effort expectancy; (3) social influence; and (4) facilitating conditions. However, there is the clear assumption of technology acceptance by able-bodied individuals in UTAUT. Four key moderator variables were formally introduced by UTAUT: (1) age; (2) gender; (3) experience; and (4) voluntariness. The cognitive and physical ability of the individual is not considered by UTAUT.

Work in the field of assistive technology has indicated the necessity for a holistic view of the context for the user that is colored by his/her ability (Cook and Hussey, 2002). Since ability is measurable and directly applicable to the acceptance of assistive technology, we posit that it should be included as a fifth moderating variable in a universal model for technology acceptance. We examine ability as a moderating variable for the four key constructs presented in the UTAUT model. We argue that ability has an effect on each construct, as illustrated in Figure 16.2. At this time our model is purely speculative and remains to be tested.

Performance Expectancy

Performance expectancy is defined as how much an individual thinks that using a particular system will help him or her improve his or her job performance. The inherent nature of technology used by disabled persons is to be assistive. Therefore, there should be a strong effect from ability on performance expectancy.

Effort Expectancy

Effort expectancy characterizes how easy a system is to use. The level of effort needed to provide input to an information technology system is directly proportional to the degree of disability by an individual. As a primary motivation for the use of novel interfaces, traditional interfaces pose a great challenge to disabled users with respect to speed and accuracy of input. Therefore, there is a necessary pairing between the system being proposed and the ability of the users in question.

Social Influence

Social influence considers how much an individual thinks that other key individuals feel they should use the system. A user perceives these key individuals as having some influence on his or her behavior, or holding some personal importance to him or her, thus affecting his or her actions. This individual may range from a manager in a work setting, a medical care provider in a long-term-care facility, or a loved one at home. The degree of an individual's ability affects his or her interactions with these key individuals, and may make him or her more susceptible to strong notions of social influence.

In the HAAT model (see Figure 16.1), the notion of context included social context. Under social context, there is a sensitivity to the stigma that the use of assistive technology may create. Users of assistive technology are sensitive to any potential labeling or isolation resulting from the use of such technology (Cook and Hussey, 2002). The varying degrees of stigmatization are influenced by people important to the user. For example, someone with vision problems may be reluctant to use a screen reader projecting the text through a loudspeaker system at his or her desk, but amenable to using the screen reader with a headphone set.

Facilitating Conditions

There is a direct link between assistive technology and facilitating conditions. Facilitating conditions describe the existing infrastructure in an organization for supporting the use of a system. Recalling the example of a user with impaired vision, it is necessary that some assistive technology be installed, such as the screen reader, to allow that individual to receive the same information as others in an organization. Furthermore, the supporting information technology staff should have knowledge of this application and be able to provide equally effective technical support for disabled and able-bodied members of the organization.

EXPLORING THE USE OF NOVEL INTERFACES

We present two brief case studies of novel interfaces for use by people with disabilities that are under development at the Georgia State University (GSU) BrainLab (see http://www.cis.gsu.edu/brainlab). At the GSU BrainLab, both computer scientists and neuroscientists are working to develop new paradigms for interaction with BCIs and other biometric interfaces. Applications such as a neurally controlled Web browser and a GSR-enabled communications system have been developed and have undergone various levels of testing with able-bodied, as well as with disabled users, to determine their level of acceptance. We investigate the BrainBrowser and extrapolate the results of an initial pilot test with able-bodied users, inferring the greater implications for disabled users. We also investigate a communications system that works with GSR input that a locked-in user had used for more than a year before a formal study was conducted in 2003. Both studies reveal the need to consider ability with technology acceptance; the studies elucidate how a person's ability can color his or her perspective on use, and also discuss the limitations of conventional information technology, especially when considered at the extremes of the ability continuum.

Case 1: Neurally Navigating the Internet

Enabling Internet access for people who suffer from severe motor impairments and who cannot operate conventional keyboard and mouse interfaces has received considerable attention. Unfettered access to the Internet provides an avenue for communication and information, and has the potential for enriching the lives of these individuals. The design and use of conventional Web browsers are prohibitive to users with severe motor disabilities because they require the ability to accurately position and select within a two-dimensional environment using a finely controlled pointing device, such as a mouse. Although BCIs have been used to navigate within a two-dimensional space (e.g., "up and down" and "left and right" on a computer monitor), they are not accurate or consistent enough to allow the fine control needed to select such small items as hyperlinks. Consequently, a novel Web browser, called the "BrainBrowser," is being developed to take advantage of alternative means for computer and Internet interaction afforded by less "finely grained" neural control (Tomori and Moore, 2003).

In contrast to the multi-dimensional input paradigm typified with conventional mouse and keyboard input devices, the BrainBrowser utilizes the paradigm of a one-dimensional (linear) interface that has been found to map well to direct-brain control (Kennedy et al., 2000). This linear interface is implemented through the interpretation of an electrical neural signal from the brain that either exceeds, or does not exceed, a particular threshold.

As illustrated in Figure 16.3, the BrainBrowser is divided into three sections: a "North Panel" on top, a conventional Internet Explorer Web browser in the middle, and a "South Panel" control station on the bottom. The north panel houses an address bar and a Go button. The address bar displays the current Web page URL (and can also be used to type in a Web address by able-bodied users). In the future, this address bar will be integrated with a neural input "virtual" keyboard. The Go button in the north panel activates the Web address currently displayed in the address bar. The middle section houses a working Web browser, which is an instance of the Internet Explorer class embedded in a Java application that implements the BrainBrowser as a whole. The south panel, also known as the control station, houses the navigation buttons that are under neural (electrical signal threshold) control. Some of the buttons in the control station have the same functions as a conventional Internet Explorer application. Other buttons control unique BrainBrowser functionality, as indicated below:

- Home: Navigates to the Web page set as the default homepage in the conventional Internet Explorer settings.
- Back Page: Navigates to the previously visited Web page.
- Forward Page: Navigates to the Web page visited before using the back button.
- Refresh: Refreshes the currently displayed Web page.
- Rest: A "dummy button" that is automatically visited when all other control station button actions are completed.
- Next Link: Sequentially highlights links in the currently displayed Web page.

Figure 16.3   **The BrainBrowser**

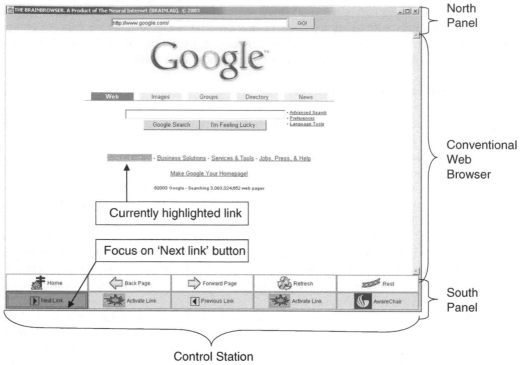

Google™ is a trademark of Google Inc.

- Previous Link: A "reverse function" to the Next Link button. The Previous Link button highlights links on the current page in reverse order (i.e., from the current link "upward").
- Activate Link: Imitates the mouse click function.
- Aware Chair: In the future, this button will house an interface to the "Aware Chair," another GSU BrainLab project (see http://www.cis.gsu.edu/brainlab/ProjectsAwareChair.htm for more information).

The user activates control buttons by invoking an electrical neural signal using their brain that exceeds a certain threshold value. Each button in the Control Station sequentially receives focus for a certain interval of time, a "dwell time" (currently set at three seconds). After three seconds, the focus automatically cycles to the next control button unless the user activates the current button by invoking a brain electrical signal that exceeds the prescribed threshold value. As illustrated in Figure 16.3, the user has scanned from "Home" to the "Next Link" button. They have activated the "Next Link" button by producing an electrical signal exceeding the preset threshold value. Once the "Next Link" button is activated, the system then sequentially scans through each link on the Web page (middle section of the BrainBrowser), dwelling on each link for a preset length of time. Figure 16.3 shows the "Next Link" control button highlighted in red and the "Advertise with Us" link highlighted in magenta, indicating the current Google Web page link that has focus. To activate the "Advertise with Us" Google link, the user would have to invoke a brain signal value above the preset threshold value, causing the control station focus to move to the next control button, which is "Activate Link." The user receives both visual and auditory feedback when he or she makes a selection. (Note: Please contact either author of this chapter for more information about BrainBrowser.)

The BrainBrowser is still in development, but has been tested with able-bodied users. To be sensitive to the health issues that most locked-in users face, the initial testing of the BrainBrowser was done with able-bodied users. Although we infer results for disabled users in this chapter, these results must be confirmed through testing.

Overall, able-bodied users found the BrainBrowser easy to use and understand, thus indicating a low effort expectancy. Simulating the linear neural input signal with pressing a Tab key, one pilot study compared the use of BrainBrowser to the use of a conventional Internet Explorer application in a simple navigation task. Responding to Likert-type survey questions related to the technology acceptance model (TAM) perceived ease-of-use and perceived usefulness constructs, users reported that the BrainBrowser and Internet Explorer were equally easy to use, although they reported that Internet Explorer was more useful for completing simple Web navigation tasks.

Pilot test results also indicate a trade-off in time and performance using the BrainBrowser compared to a standard Internet Explorer Web browser. There was increased time associated with high performance expectancy. We assume that able-bodied users will prefer Internet Explorer because their navigational abilities are unconstrained by the interface. However, disabled users, whose abilities are already constrained, need the access assistance provided by the BrainBrowser interface.

While incurring some trade-offs between performance and flexibility of use, disabled users will nevertheless regain a large measure of control over their environment. Therefore, there is a high social influence for use of the BrainBrowser by a disabled user, but this influence is low for an able-bodied user. Furthermore, the facilitating conditions would vary with the setting for use of the BrainBrowser. In an organizational setting, the information technology staff most likely would not be familiar with the new Web browser and thus be unable to support it, but personal use would more likely elicit support from the research team.

Case 2: Working Up a Sweat to Communicate

Some severely disabled users, such as those with locked-in syndrome, are unable to use traditional assistive technology devices. Without the ability for reliable muscle control needed to operate these devices, AT is largely unavailable to them (Moore and Dua, 2004). Furthermore, due to neural deterioration, some late-stage patients afflicted with amyotrophic lateral sclerosis (ALS) often lose their ability to utilize BCIs (Birbaumer and Hinterberger, 2003). Therefore, GSR represents another sensory modal option for biometric control. At GSU, responses from GSR have been incorporated into systems for responding "yes" and "no," for spelling, for selecting phrases from a chart, and even for playing a chess game. Here we will focus on an application developed for communication with binary (yes/no) responses for a particular locked-in user with late-stage ALS.

Moore and Dua (2004) describe a binary-response GSR system that requires a user to raise and lower his GSR across a calibrated threshold set at the middle point (50 percent) of the GSR's sensitivity range. Using a commercial polygraph system, similar to the ones used by law enforcement officials, the system registers GSR input from the user based on two steel electrodes attached to the user's fingers. The user receives feedback from a visual display of GSR level, desired targets, prompts, and an auditory representation of these same components. In the auditory representations, the GSR level is indicated by emitting a short tone. The pitch of this tone varies according to the GSR signal's amplitude. Figure 16.4 shows the visual control display of the GSR level as it crosses a target threshold. The visual display is projected onto a 72-inch screen at the foot of the user's bed. A large, high-resolution display is needed because this user lost some visual acuity as his

Figure 16.4 **Control Display for GSR System**

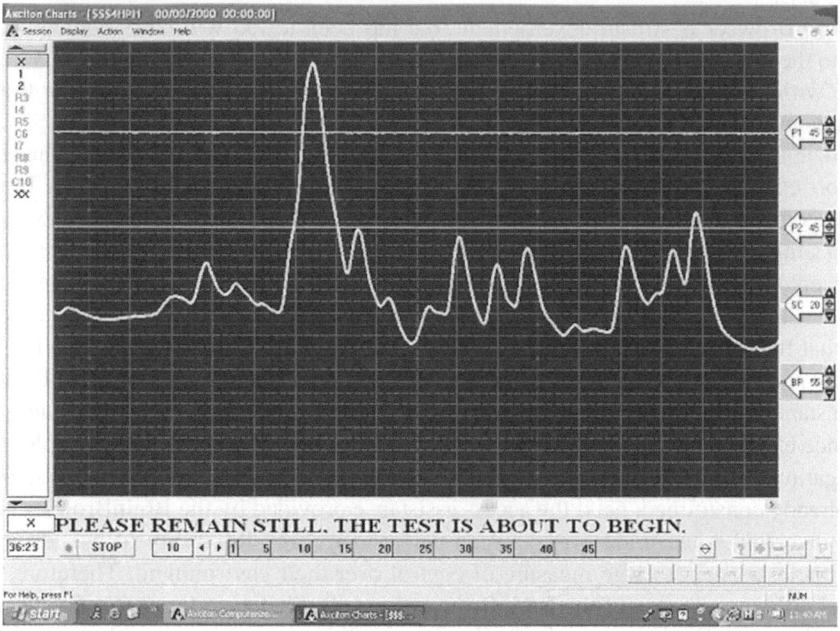

Axciton Polygraph Software for Windows is a product of Axciton Systems, Inc.

disease progressed due to the loss of eye saccades, the rapid movement of the eyes in place as they focus on different visual targets.

The GSR-based binary communication system was tested with the user in thirty independent sessions over a one-year time period. Each session began with the calibration of the GSR device to allow the user to easily obtain the 50 percent threshold. Then, a baseline reading was taken when the user was not trying to influence his GSR. The user then performed a series of three or four runs each consisting of ten trials with a five- to fifteen-minute break in between runs. A single trial lasted between fifteen and sixty seconds to allow various tests of the user's ability to raise and lower his GSR level in response to prompts to generate a "yes" or "no." The user received auditory and visual feedback on his success at generating the desired response.

Overall, the user obtained 62 percent accuracy for generating desired responses. Furthermore, the researchers found that the user's accuracy improved with predicted prompts. For example, if the user knew that the next prompt would be for generating a "yes," then he was more likely to generate a correct yes-response compared to when the next prompt was presented at random. When asked, the user reported feeling a large sense of effort to raise his GSR. Still, the user has continued to use the GSR system since its introduction and also enjoys playing chess on a GSR-based system.

Although a 62 percent accuracy rate and a minimum fifteen-second response time may be disappointing use metrics with more complex communication systems (such as one that incorporates spelling capability), it is a sufficiently high performance expectancy for simple binary communication. Even the ability to accurately communicate "yes" and "no" is a significant improvement over existing communication options for locked-in users. Therefore, locked-in users' reactions to a binary speller have been consistently positive, despite the high effort expectancy to operate the system. Moreover, there is significant social influence on the locked-in user, and on all locked-in users in general, because he has a family around him that includes a wife, children, and mother.

Finally, due to the financial ability of this user to afford round-the-clock assistants and a committed research team, he has excellent facilitating conditions for using this GSR-based assistive technology. So, the intention to use, and the actual usage of this technology should be promoted for this disabled user.

By contrast, able-bodied individuals would be frustrated using this system to communicate, because it would not effectively reflect their abilities for conversation. A GSR-based system with a fifteen-second response latency can only accomplish four responses per minute. Unaided, this would allow for four binary responses per minute to questions posed, and would furthermore not allow sufficient time to narrow down the selection space for multiple conversational phrases, or for selecting a desired letter from twenty-six options.

Therefore, depending on the perspective colored by ability, the influence of the four UTAUT constructs for technology acceptance would have varying effects. A user might perceive various levels of performance expectancy from a reported 62 percent accuracy rate; an able-bodied individual would view this accuracy rate as insufficient, whereas a disabled user might regard it as quite sufficient for his needs. Both able-bodied and disabled users would experience high effort expectancy due to the nature of input to the GSR system, but this feeling may be exacerbated for an able-bodied user who would not need this system to interact with others. An able-bodied individual would likely have a low social influence to use a GSR-based communication system because there would not be a need for its use for interaction with people of importance in his or her life. Finally, the facilitating conditions may also discourage usage for an able-bodied user, since there would likely not be a team in place to support its use.

ORGANIZATIONAL ACCEPTANCE OF TECHNOLOGY

With reference to technology acceptance in organizations, we look to the original diffusion of innovation theory by Rogers (1995) that takes a broader view of the evolution of a new technology, from creation to use. This theory does not limit the view of technology acceptance to an individual's perspective, but rather considers what must happen at the organizational level. According to diffusion of innovation theory, a technological innovation passes through five stages including: (1) knowledge; (2) persuasion; (3) decision; (4) implementation; and (5) confirmation. The following explores factors that may facilitate the organizational diffusion of a technological innovation in the form of assistive technology during each of these five stages.

Knowledge Stage

During the knowledge stage, an organization learns about the existence, and about the functions, of a new technological innovation. For an organization to become aware of newly existing assistive interfaces and technologies, it would be useful to subscribe to a forum that regularly communicates such innovations, such as the Rehabilitation Engineering and Assistive Technology Society of North America (RESNA; http://www.resna.org/). In addition, it would be helpful if key members within the organization received periodic training about disabilities and appropriate job accommodations. For example, there are federally funded Disability and Business Technical Assistance Centers (DBTACs) in every region of the United States, as well as other various regional, state, and local organizations that provide companies with disability training. Finally, a creative medium to involve the organization may be achieved through a mobilized effort to recognize and promote the National Disability Employment Awareness Month (NDEAM) in October. Additional informative and supportive publications are provided by the Office of Disability Employment Policy (ODEP; http://www.dol.gov/odep/) for more information.

Persuasion Stage

During the persuasion stage, widespread members of the organization form a favorable attitude about the adoption and use of a new technology. Again, training would play a large part in educating organizations about disabilities and assistive technologies. From the newfound awareness created, organizations may realize the necessity and benefits of job accommodation for individuals with disabilities. Since work is regarded as one of the three basic performance areas in which people engage on a daily basis (the others being self-care and leisure), organizations may better perceive the need to eliminate barriers for individuals with disabilities so they can better participate in this important life role (Cook and Hussey, 2002).

Decision Stage

At the decision stage, an organization commits to adopting the new technology. At this stage, a strong motivating factor for the adoption of assistive technology should be a concern for legal compliance. The most prominent legislation related to organizational decision making includes the Rehabilitation Act of 1973 (Amended) and the Americans with Disabilities Act (ADA) of 1990. The Rehabilitation Act of 1973 (U.S. Congress, 1973), as amended in 1998, states that any employer or institution of higher education that is receiving federal funding must provide "reasonable accommodation" and a "least restrictive environment" for employees or students with disabilities. Many efforts to provide ramps and curb cuts derived from this Act. The Americans with Disabilities Act (ADA) of 1990 (U.S. Congress, 1990) prohibits employers of more than fifteen people to discriminate against applicants and employees on the basis of disability.

Implementation Stage

During the implementation stage, the organization actually puts the technology to use. Here legislation plays a different role by facilitating ways for organizations to receive technical assistance, as well as training, as they seek to implement assistive technology. The Assistive Technology Act of 1998 (U.S. Congress, 1998b) addresses support options for expanding the availability of assistive technology devices.

Confirmation Stage

In the confirmation stage, an organization receives reinforcement from positive outcomes from using the new technology. Contrary to popular misconceptions that job accommodation costs a great deal and carries few rewards, an organization typically experiences a considerable cost savings because accommodations were made. The incorporation of assistive technology often requires relatively little effort, or spending, by the organization, and can also reduce related costs from worker's compensation and insurance (Job Accommodation Network [JAN], 2002). In fact, 71 percent of job accommodation costs are $500 or less (20 percent of which cost nothing), and have a return of 41 percent in company savings (Job Accommodation Network [JAN], 1999).

Beyond these supportive factors for diffusion of innovation, what may help a new technology be accepted within an organization that is comprised of diverse individuals is to use universal design principles such as those established by North Carolina State University's Center for Universal Design (The Center for Universal Design, 1997). These principles include: (1) creating a system that is equitable in its usefulness and marketability; (2) making sure the system is flexible enough to accommodate a wide range of disabilities; (3) designing something that is simple and intuitive to use; (4) allowing necessary information to be received and understood regardless of filtering conditions; (5) minimizing perilous results from unintended actions; (6) ensuring that low physical effort is required; and (7) making sure the system has the appropriate size and space needed for a user's approach and use of the system. In addition to these design principles, the government has established Section 508 (U.S. Congress, 1998a) guidelines for making all government Web sites and information technology accessible to disabled users. The government has taken the lead on this effort and other organizations have followed suit.

DISCUSSION AND CONCLUSIONS

Organizations must take a proactive stance on expanding their awareness and acceptance of assistive interfaces and technologies or risk excluding a viable sector of the workforce, as well as possibly incurring legal ramifications. Numerous groups offer information and training on job accommodation for people with disabilities; these include the Job Accommodation Network (JAN; http://www.jan.wvu.edu/), the Department of Labor's Office of Disability Employment Policy (ODEP; http://www.dol.gov/odep/), and the Rehabilitation Engineering and Assistive Technology Society of North America (RESNA; see http://www.resna.org/). Contrary to popular belief, there are minimal costs, and usually large monetary benefits in terms of: (1) actual cost-savings to the organization; (2) having a more enabled workforce; and (3) creating a more welcoming atmosphere for diverse individuals (Job Accommodation Network [JAN], 1999; Job Accommodation Network [JAN], 2002).

Organizations can benefit from an increased knowledge about assistive technology, and the MIS community can benefit from recognizing and incorporating ideas about a person's abilities into the models of technology acceptance. As we have discussed, ability colors the way an individual perceives and interacts with technology. Therefore, ability has a moderating effect on performance expectancy, effort expectancy, social influence, and facilitating conditions as described in the unified theory of acceptance and use of technology (UTAUT) (Venkatesh et al., 2003). Similar to gender and age, a person's ability plays a key role in assessing these different factors for individual technology acceptance.

The human-computer interaction (HCI) community has long embraced and promoted the need for universal design and ubiquitous systems (Carroll, 2003). A more encompassing view of technology acceptance will engender an increased understanding and awareness of the needs for disabled computer users in organizations. An understanding of the individual considerations of disabled users may ultimately lead to a better understanding of the organizational impacts when introducing new technological innovations such as assistive interfaces and technologies.

Organizations may help facilitate greater knowledge exchange between the MIS and assistive technology communities. They may support initiatives for MIS researchers to conduct action research in the area of assistive technology. Management information systems researchers may then broaden their focus from just examining able-bodied individuals' acceptance of technology to having a more universal approach that considers ability. It is both possible and necessary to bridge the gap in knowledge between the assistive technology community and MIS research so that we may improve our predictors of technology acceptance and ultimately achieve the goal of making technology accessible to all individuals, regardless of ability.

FUTURE RESEARCH

There is ongoing research in the assistive technology arena to determine the most effective interfaces for various populations of disabled users (Cook and Hussey, 2002). These researchers hope
to ultimately achieve a "curb-cut" effect with these devices, so that they will be used in more
mainstream settings, such as in business organizations, and by more users than just disabled individuals. As organizations adopt more assistive technology practices, these innovations will serve
for more than what may be viewed as novel purposes. To achieve this level of integration, it is necessary to share concepts across the MIS and assistive technology communities.

We suggest a number of areas for productive future research that integrate the domain of assistive technologies with more mainstream organizational MIS research, including: (1) organizational case studies of successful (or failed) assistive technology introductions; and (2) empirical
studies of technology acceptance models and assistive technologies.

There clearly is a need to perform on-site studies examining the success (or failure) of the
introduction of assistive technologies into the workplace. Examining the factors that promote the
success or failure of organizational information system implementations has been a staple in MIS
research over the decades. What unique factors promote or impede the successful implementation
of assistive technologies? What is the relationship between the organizational culture and the success or failure of these assistive technology introductions?

Furthermore, prevailing empirical models of technology acceptance, for example, UTAUT,
should be validated in the domain of assistive technologies. We maintain that ability might prove
to be a fifth moderating variable in the UTAUT model. However, an exploratory study must be
conducted to determine the best way to characterize ability for testing within the proposed model.
Perhaps it would be possible to borrow existing, tested assessments from the physical therapy
community such as the Functional Assessment Inventory (FAI) to determine levels of ability (see
http://uwctds.washington.edu/medaspects/rehab496_protocol.htm). It would then be important
that participants possess a range of ability levels under one disability category and across disabilities. Empirical MIS studies that test this notion would be useful and would inform both the assistive technology and the MIS research communities.

ACKNOWLEDGMENTS

The authors would like to thank two anonymous reviewers for their helpful insights and acknowledge the outstanding efforts of Dr. Melody M. Moore, director of the Georgia State University
BrainLab, who is working to develop real-world applications to aid users with severe disabilities.

NOTE

1. The U.S. Census Bureau defines "working age" as people between the ages of sixteen and sixty-four.
Statistics are reported based on the civilian, non-institutionalized U.S. population in 2000. There were considerable differences between Census 1990 and Census 2000 prohibiting analyses of trends.

REFERENCES

Abrams, S. The polygraph in a psychiatric setting. *American Journal of Psychiatry,* 130, 1 (1973), 94–98.
Adams, L.; Hunt, L.; and Moore, M. The "Aware-System"—prototyping an augmentative communication
    interface. Paper presented during Interactive Poster Sessions of the Rehabilitative Engineering and

Assistive Technology Society of North America's (RESNA) 26th International Conference on Technology and Disability: Research, Design, Practice and Policy. Atlanta, GA, June 19–23, 2003, poster.

Ajzen, I. The theory of planned behavior. *Organizational Behavior and Human Decision Processes,* 50, 2 (1991), 179–211.

Ariniello, L. Unlocking locked-in syndrome. *Brain Briefings,* November 1999.

Bandura, A. *Social Foundations of Thought and Action: A Social Cognitive Theory.* Englewood Cliffs, NJ: Prentice Hall, 1986.

Benbasat, I.; Dexter, A.S.; et al. An experimental study of the human/computer interface. *Communications of the ACM,* 24, 11 (1981), 752–762.

Birbaumer, N., and Hinterberger T. The thought-translation device (TTD): neurobehavioral mechanisms and clinical outcomes. *IEEE Transactions on Neural Systems and Rehabilitation Engineering,* 11, 2 (2003), 190–193.

Carroll, J.M. (ed.), *HCI Models, Theories, and Frameworks: Towards a Multidisciplinary Science.* San Francisco: Morgan Kaufmann Publishers, 2003.

Committee to Review the Scientific Evidence on the Polygraph and National Research Council. *The Polygraph and Lie Detection.* Washington, DC: The National Academies Press, 2003.

Compeau, D.R., and Higgins, C.A. Computer self-efficacy: development of a measure and initial test. *MIS Quarterly* 19, 2 (1995), 189–211.

Cook, A.M., and Hussey, S.M. *Assistive Technology: Principles and Practice.* St. Louis, MO: Mosby, 2002.

Copestake, A. *Applying Natural Language Processing Techniques to Speech Prostheses.* In Working Notes of the AAAI Fall Symposium on Developing Assistive Technology for People with Disabilities. Madrid, Spain, 1996.

Davis, F. Perceived usefulness, perceived ease of use, and user acceptance of information technology. *MIS Quarterly,* 13, 3 (1989), 319–340.

Fishbein, M., and Ajzen, I. *Belief, Attitude, Intention and Behavior: An Introduction to Theory and Research.* Reading, MA: Addison-Wesley, 1975.

Haag, S.; Cummings, M.; et al. *Management Information Systems for the Information Age.* Boston: McGraw-Hill, 2004.

International Biometric Society. Definition of Biometrics, Department of Statistics at Texas A&M University (available at http://tibs.org/biometrics/, accessed on April 24, 2004).

Job Accommodation Network (JAN). Accommodation Benefit/Cost Data, Office of Disability Employment Policy of the U.S. Department of Labor. Report, July 30, 1999 (available at http://www.jan.wvu.edu/media/Stats/BenCosts0799.html, accessed on November 30, 2005).

Job Accommodation Network (JAN) Facts About Job Accommodations (available at http://www.jan.wvu.edu/media/JANFacts.html, accessed on April 26, 2004).

Jung, C.G. On the psychophysical relations of the association experiment. *Journal of Abnormal Psychology,* 1 (1907), 247–255.

Karahanna, E.; Straub, D.W.; et al. Information technology adoption across time: a cross-sectional comparison of pre-adoption and post-adoption beliefs. *MIS Quarterly* 23, 2 (1999), 183–219.

Kennedy, P.R.; Bakay, R.A.E.; et al. Direct control of a computer from the human central nervous system. *IEEE Transactions on Rehabilitation Engineering,* 8, 2 (2000), 198–202.

Khalifa, M. Computer-assisted evaluation of interface designs. *The DATA BASE for Advances in Information Systems,* 29, 1 (1998), 66–81.

Krefting, L.H., and Krefting, D.V. Cultural influences on performance. In C. Christiansen and C. Baum (eds.), *Occupational Therapy.* Thoroughfare, NJ: Slack, 1991, 101–122.

Leonard-Barton, D., and Deschamps, I. Managerial influence in the implementation of new technology. *Management Science,* 34, 10 (1988), 1252–1265.

Moore, G.C., and I. Benbasat. Development of an instrument to measure the perceptions of adopting an information technology innovation. *Information Systems Research,* 2, 3 (1991), 192–223.

Moore, M.M. Real-world applications for brain–computer interface technology. *IEEE Transactions on Neural Systems and Rehabilitation Engineering* 11, 2 (2003), 162–165.

Moore, M.M., and Dua, U. *A Galvanic Skin Response Interface for People with Severe Motor Disabilities.* Sixth International ACM SIGACCESS Conference on Computers and Accessibility (ASSETS), Atlanta, GA, October 18–20, 2004.

Peralta, R.G.d.; González, S.L.; et al. Direct non-invasive brain computer interfaces. In Proceedings of the 9th International Conference on Functional Mapping of the Human Brain, New York, June 18–22, 2003.

Pope, A.M., and Brandt, E.N. (eds.), *Enabling America: Assessing the Role of Rehabilitation Science and Engineering.* Washington, DC: National Academy Press, 1997.

Rogers, E.M. *Diffusion of Innovations.* New York: The Free Press, 1995.

Sakurazawa, S.; Yoshida, N.; et al. A Computer Game Using Galvanic Skin Response. Second International Conference on Entertainment Computing, Pittsburgh, Pennsylvania, Carnegie Mellon University, May 8–10, 2003.

Sheppard, B.H.; Hartwick, J.; et al. The theory of reasoned action: a meta-analysis of past research with recommendations for modifications and future research. *Journal of Consumer Research,* 15, 3 (1988), 325–343.

Social Security Administration. Social Security Online: Social Security Basic Facts. Press Office (available at http://www.socialsecurity.gov/pressoffice/basicfact.htm, accessed on April 20, 2004).

Taylor, S., and Todd, P. Assessing IT Usage: The Role of Prior Experience. *MIS Quarterly* 19, 4 (1995), 561–570.

Taylor, S., and Todd, P. Understanding information technology usage: a test of competing models. *Information Systems Research,* 6, 4 (1995), 144–176.

The Center for Universal Design. Principles of Universal Design. Raleigh, NC: North Carolina State University, April 1, 1997 (available at http://www.design.ncsu.edu:8120/cud/univ_design/princ_overview.htm, accessed on November 30, 2005).

Thompson, R.L.; Higgins, C.A.; et al. Personal computing: toward a conceptual model of utilization. *MIS Quarterly* 15, 1 (1991), 124–143.

Tomori, O., and Moore, M. The neurally controllable internet browser (BrainBrowser). In *CHI 2003 Conference on Human Factors in Computing Systems.* Fort Lauderdale, FL: ACM, 2003, 796–797.

Triandis, H.C. Values, attitudes, and interpersonal behavior. In M.M. Page (ed.), *Nebraska Symposium on Motivation, 1979.* Lincoln, NE: University of Nebraska Press, 1980, pp. 195–259.

U.S. Congress. Rehabilitation Act of 1973 (Amended). *H.R. 8070* (1973).

U.S. Congress. Americans with Disabilities Act of 1990 (1990).

U.S. Congress. 1998 Amendment to Section 508 of the Rehabilitation Act. 29 USC 794d (1998a).

U.S. Congress. Assistive Technology Act of 1998 (1998b).

Vallerand, R.J. Toward a hierarchical model of intrinsic and extrinsic motivation. In M. Zanna (ed.), *Advances in Experimental Social Psychology.* New York: Academic Press, 1997, pp. 271–360.

Venkatesh, V., and Davis, F.D. A Theoretical Extension of the Technology Acceptance Model: Four Longitudinal Field Studies. *Management Science,* 46, 2 (2000), 186–204.

Venkatesh, V.; Morris, M.G.; et al. User acceptance of information technology: toward a unified view. *MIS Quarterly,* 27, 3 (2003), 425–478.

Waldrop, J., and Stern, S.M. *Disability Status: 2000, Census 2000 Brief.* Washington, DC: U.S. Census Bureau, 12, 2003.

Wolpaw, J.R.; Birbaumer, N.; et al. Brain-computer interfaces for communication and control. *Clinical Neurophysiology,* 113, 6 (2002), 767–791.

World Health Organization. *International Classification of Impairments, Disabilities, and Handicaps.* Geneva: WHO, 1980.

PART VII

METHODOLOGICAL ISSUES
AND REFLECTIONS

CHAPTER 17

CONDUCTING EXPERIMENTAL RESEARCH IN HCI

From Topic Selection to Publication

ALAN R. DENNIS, MONICA J. GARFIELD, HEIKKI TOPI,
AND JOSEPH S. VALACICH

Abstract: *Human-computer interaction (HCI) draws on a wide range of academic disciplines and leverages many different theoretical foundations. Identifying the right research projects to pursue in this domain, executing the research, and finding an appropriate outlet for such work is a challenge. This paper presents ways to determine appropriate projects, discuss the role of theory in the formation of a project, analyze issues underlying success in research design, and explore the different models for publishing "relevant" HCI research. Our focus is on laboratory experiments used for theory testing.*

Keywords: *MIS Research, HCI Research, Human-Computer Interaction*

INTRODUCTION

Human-computer interaction (HCI) draws on a wide range of academic disciplines and leverages many different theoretical foundations; as such, it is one of the truly interdisciplinary areas of study. Often, individuals working on comparable HCI issues but from different perspectives are not familiar with one another's work due to the limited cross-fertilization among the various streams of HCI that are building on different reference disciplines (Zhang and Dillon, 2003). Identifying the right research projects to pursue in this domain, crafting the theory, executing the research, and finding an appropriate outlet for such research is a challenge. It is particularly difficult to select projects that can both support knowledge creation in the field and lead to successful publications in top-level journals, either in HCI or in one of its reference disciplines. Despite these difficulties, it is essential that research resources are used effectively (on meaningful and useful projects) and efficiently (so that the selected projects are executed correctly).

This paper presents our thoughts on how to identify interesting projects, discusses the role of theory in the formation of a project, analyzes the issues underlying success in research design, and explores the different models for publishing "relevant" HCI research. Our focus is on laboratory experiments used for theory testing. We believe that case studies and surveys are equally important, but our primary expertise is laboratory research; therefore, we confine our comments to it.

In this paper, we aim to provide our opinions on four critical questions about conducting laboratory research in HCI:

1. How do I find ideas for my research and how do I select ideas worth pursuing?
2. How do I use theory?
3. How do I design laboratory experiments?
4. How do I craft my paper for journal publication?

CREATING INTERESTING PROJECTS

As an HCI researcher, you are faced with many opportunities as well as a seemingly overwhelming number of paths to pursue. Therefore, you have to choose carefully between possible options instead of simply launching projects based on their availability. Researchers in this area should carefully evaluate opportunities and identify those research projects that best fit their interests, long-term goals, and resources. Every research project has both direct costs in the form of time and money, and opportunity costs in the form of the alternative projects that you cannot pursue after selecting a specific path. Because time is the most valuable resource for a researcher, you should decide carefully how to use it.

Given that ideas for research are everywhere, finding ideas, in general, should not be the problem. Finding an idea that matches your interests and that can provide a fruitful path to follow is, however, a more difficult challenge. Life is too short to pursue research topics that you do not find interesting; it is also too short to pursue all of the paths you may find interesting. The trick is to outline a research agenda that will allow you to pursue those areas that are of interest to you and leverage your past work and current resources.

Theory as a Source of Ideas

Most of the time, research is part of an evolving genre that includes a potpourri of previous research. Using previous studies as the foundation for future explorations is critical to extending and building theory. One method of developing theory is to incrementally add one piece to the puzzle at a time to gradually gain a better understanding of the relationships between the theoretical constructs. Another method is to take a revolutionary, instead of evolutionary, approach to theory building. Revolutionary work looks for ways to reconceptualize how we perceive the interrelationships among fundamental constructs within our research theme (Alter and Dennis, 2002).

By looking for anomalies in previous work or synergies between similar projects conducted in different disciplines, you may find insights that enable revolutionary research. Due to the natural interdisciplinary foundation of work in HCI we can learn a great deal from many different disciplines. By embracing the differences between these disciplines and leveraging the synergies, theory can be developed. Furthermore, the use of theories from one discipline may help us understand anomalies in another discipline.

It can be difficult to determine whether or not revolutionary work is possible (Kuhn, 1970). However, there are signs to look for when attempting to identify opportunities for revolutionary research:

*   *Generalize from the bottom.* If many complex theories appear to be interrelated in some way, you may have an opportunity for bottom-up theorizing. Consider ways to generalize from these specialized or complex theories. By doing so you may find a macrolevel answer that simplifies a previously complex problem. For example, Vessey (1991) was able to simplify

the graphs versus tables debate by introducing the cognitive fit theory that explained behavior far more elegantly than the many far more complicated contingency theories then in use.

*   *Identify paradoxical observations.* You can also look for paradoxes in your observations. You might observe a problem that does not appear to make sense; a suggested solution to a problem might also be counter-intuitive. Also, you can look for studies that don't seem to fit with existing theories or seem inconsistent with them. These studies may help you develop new insights into theory and discover new lenses through which you can view a phenomenon. For example, Carlson and Zmud (1999) were able to use paradoxical results to suggest channel expansion theory as an elaboration of media richness theory.

Whether you are more adept at evolutionary or revolutionary work, focusing on fundamental questions means that your research has a longer shelf life. Studying questions that are directly tied to an artifact of today (a specific phenomenon such as SARS or Y2K, or a specific software package such as Lotus Notes or Groove) reduces the likelihood that your work will stand the test of time, unless you use the current phenomena as operationalizations of more fundamental, long-lasting concepts. In fields such as HCI, the physical artifacts repeatedly evolve, but the basic models regarding how humans interact with computers continue to inform practice and theory. At the same time, it is essential that we are able to point out the current implications of the long-term work. As researchers, we need to understand how these fundamental questions impact the world of today. What is it that makes them relevant and newsworthy? It is essential to find a way to express your results that captivates your readers and leads them to recognize the relevance of your work. This is a significant factor affecting the importance of the contribution your research can make. The most relevant research addresses both fundamental theoretical issues of the field and demonstrates what the theoretical findings mean in practice.

You can also use your own prior work as a source of ideas for future projects and as a guide for focusing your efforts. Previous research should enable you to identify the broad theoretical underpinnings that form the foundation for your work and provide it with direction. Identifying an overarching umbrella that organizes your previous work can be helpful in revealing the themes present in your past work. You may find that your previous work (even when various components of it seemingly belong to different streams of research) actually attacks the same fundamental question, such as: How can we increase the chance that a system will be accepted and used by individuals in an organization? When pondering what these themes may be, you can reflect upon the personal experiences that have led you to ask some of the questions your research has revolved around. Another obvious method for helping you focus on the HCI area that best fits your own interests is to read through relevant books and journals and identify what is interesting to you. Once you have a general theme for your work, selecting the specific ideas to pursue is significantly easier.

Organizational Practice as a Source of Ideas

Particularly in HCI, observations regarding the practical use of information technologies can be and should be a very important source of research ideas. Although we do not advocate research that is driven by the latest technological fads, no HCI researcher should close his or her eyes to the current rapid development of interface technologies, or to the practical issues users struggle with in their everyday organizational use of information technology. For a researcher whose main interest is in developing a theoretical understanding of human interaction with information technology, new technical developments provide important new opportunities for testing the boundaries of applicability of existing theories. Identified organizational needs often provide excellent guidance regarding the relative importance of alternative theoretical approaches.

Studying theoretically interesting questions in contexts that have direct practical applicability has the added advantage of increased funding opportunities for research. Many highly successful research programs have served two purposes by helping to solve an organizational problem while simultaneously improving our theoretical understanding of a phenomenon of interest.

Resources as a Source of Ideas

You are, in practice, forced to examine the resources available, both those internal to the researcher and those that are available in their external environment, but you can also turn the process of evaluating these constraints into a useful exploration of the opportunities that are available. If you have strong skills in the use of a particular methodology, you may choose to explore questions that are best answered using that methodology, unless your intention is to use a new project as a way to gain new skills. For instance, if lab studies and positivist quantitative methodologies are your strengths, incremental theory building together with a series of controlled experiments may be a good place to focus. However, if you are stronger as a grounded theory researcher, you may choose to recast the fundamental questions you are pursuing by investigating the phenomena in the field.

Methodological strengths are but one resource you must consider. Others include the breadth and depth of knowledge you have in a specific theoretical area and the external resources available to you. For instance, if a researcher has predominantly utilized traditional IS research in the past, this may be a strength they want to play to. If the fundamental question requires a stronger background in some other reference discipline that informs HCI, one may look to accrue that knowledge by retaining a research team member who has that background; for example, someone trained in cognitive psychology (Dennis and Valacich, 2001). We will discuss the issues related to working as a member of a team later.

External resources necessary for a project may include access to research subjects, financial resources to support the acquisition of participants and the introduction of suitable incentives, contacts with potential research sites, access to various companies, and the existence of a research center within one's work environment. If you decide to pursue a specific research question and as the study design develops it becomes apparent that a lab study would be the most appropriate method for this investigation, you need to decide if you have the resources necessary to run the experiment as well as a sufficient subject pool to draw from. On the other hand, if the optimal study design requires conducting a multiple case study of several large corporations, access to such sites is critical.

Finally, if you have the opportunity to work with an established research center, this may also help define how you pursue your research questions. Even a non-HCI center can enable you to study a specific aspect of HCI more expeditiously. For instance, a center exploring the utilization of ERPs and other enterprise systems may be helpful to you as an HCI researcher if you choose to incorporate ERP as the IS artifact in a study. This is different from studying ERP per se; instead, the focus is on pursuing a fundamental HCI question that happens to use ERP as the technology that enables the specific study.

Conducting high-quality research is an expensive process, and no one should expect that research can be done without resources. This is particularly true if the research includes an emerging technology that isn't widely available, as it normally does in HCI. It is important to be realistic about the resource requirements for particular types of projects and about the level of funding needed to execute high-quality work in HCI.

By first examining your own interests and the research questions you would like to pursue, you can seek to find fit with the resources available to you. By undergoing initial self-examination to identify the research path you want to follow, you will be in a better position to see the opportunities available to you. By taking the extra step to identify the areas in which you may need to incorporate additional resources to enable and enrich your research, you will be able to seek out these resources in a more direct manner. Too often, the path a researcher takes is one that rises before him instead of the one that he creates by selecting the best path to fit his interests, skills, and resources. By wisely selecting the ideas to pursue, you can begin to pave your own road instead of randomly chasing opportunistic research ideas.

Collaboration as a Source of Ideas

In most cases, conducting research as a member of a team is the best way to pursue a project. A team allows you to pool resources, improve participants' ability to generate ideas, and create healthy peer pressure to take projects further faster; collaboration is an excellent source of motivation, particularly if you work with people who are driven by the desire to publish. Working with others in a balanced team makes it possible for each member to use his or her specialized expertise and benefit from the experience and skills of others so that the productivity of the entire team is higher than that of individual researchers working alone. For junior researchers (including doctoral students) collaboration is an outstanding way to learn. For those with more experience, cooperation with more junior people is both a way to give back to the community and to keep one's thinking fresh and exposed to new ideas and perspectives.

Traditionally teams are comprised of a small number of individuals, each of whom possesses complementary skills and backgrounds. There needs to be a balance of diversity within such a group. A highly diverse group may allow the team to study a large range of topics; however, when a group becomes too diverse, managing the dissimilarities can lead to significant process losses. Deciding how big and diverse a team to create is related to the amount of risk and time one can afford while pursing a line of research (Davis, 1992). More modest-sized groups with a strong common background may be more productive in the short term but may not create enough synergies to gain significant long-term payoffs.

From Ideas to Publication Potential

A plan for generating a stream of research should be formulated simultaneously with the set of research ideas. It is much easier to work within a well-defined stream of research rather than to jump from topic to topic over the path of one's career (Watson et al., 1994). This is true for two reasons. First, to gain a rich understanding of any one phenomenon may take many years of accumulating relevant knowledge (via conferences, dialogue with colleagues interested in similar issues, articles, book chapters, conference proceedings, etc.). Secondly, to make significant progress in any one area, a set of research projects needs to be executed. If a single research project is adequate to answer your fundamental research question, then it is likely you have selected a question that is too narrow. This is not to say that a specific project should not attack and answer a smaller question, but there should be an umbrella under which your research falls that allows for synergistic interactions between your previous work and your current work. In other words, your umbrella question intends to answer a relatively broad question (or questions) while a single study focuses on answering a narrow sub-question in a meaningful way. In all likelihood, your research stream will not flow evenly, but it will take on a more organic growth pattern that may lead you to places you did not initially envision. It is, however, in your best interest to have an underlying vision guiding your research.

When deciding which project to select next, you should ask a few questions. First, you should determine whether or not an issue is fundamental to HCI and will continue to be relevant five to ten years from now. Due to the typically long review and publishing cycles, addressing questions that don't have a somewhat lasting impact is a poor strategy. Most journal editors are looking for papers that present results with a lasting impact on the field, and most readers want to read papers that provide lasting insights instead of observations specific to a technology that might already have died. Second, it is essential to find out whether or not the research question is interesting to both the HCI research community and, at least indirectly, to practitioners who want to utilize the results of HCI research. You should ask whether it interests you, and whether you can make it interesting to others. If you don't find a project particularly interesting, you increase the chance that you will not bring it to completion. Also, if you do not find the project interesting the likelihood that you can make it interesting to others also diminishes.

You may also want to consider whether or not a project can result in a contribution to the field regardless of the outcome of the empirical work. You need to determine whether or not your research question is fundamental enough to the field and accompanied with sufficient theory development that the results would be interesting at least to the research community regardless of the outcomes (assuming, of course, that your methodology is strong enough that your readers are willing to accept outcomes with non-significant results). If the hypotheses you set forth are supported, is it newsworthy and does it move the field forward? If not, then there really is little point in pursuing the project. Furthermore, you have to ask whether or not a failure to support a hypothesis is as thought provoking as success in supporting it (see Hayne and Rice, 1997). Not all research questions will lend themselves to all portions of the above criteria for picking a project. It is, however, clear that the more of these things you consider before embarking on a research project, the higher the likelihood that you will succeed in having your results published.

We cannot emphasize enough the need to talk about your research with peers in a number of contexts throughout the research process. Informal discussions with colleagues, talks given at other universities, and workshops and presentations regarding research in progress at conferences are all excellent venues for sharing your research ideas and gaining invaluable feedback that you can use to improve your research. In addition, communicating your ideas regarding research strengthens your position in the network of researchers, which, in turn, creates new opportunities for sharing and collaboration. Researchers and practitioners evaluating your research project from outside often have insights that you might have missed, and the very process of discussing your research with others forces you to think about it, which, in turn, improves it. Don't be afraid of sharing and giving away research ideas; you will get others in return, both directly and through the collaborative process. Also remember that the earlier you find potential problems in your research design, the easier it is fix them—fatal flaws in data collection are impossible to correct without repeating an expensive and time-consuming process. However experienced you are as a researcher, let others evaluate your research idea and design before your data collection efforts take place.

THEORY IS THE HEART AND SOUL OF EXPERIMENTAL RESEARCH

Theory is the primary reason for conducting and publishing experimental laboratory research. Academic laboratory research is seldom intended to produce descriptions of organizational phenomena or direct answers to empirical questions.[1] The purpose of experimental laboratory research is to advance our theoretical understanding of how a set of constructs is related to another set of constructs. Theory explains *how* and *why* one thing influences another. Empirical data collection serves to support or refute our theoretical understanding.

The end result of the theory-development process should be a set of propositions that specify relationships among selected constructs of the theory. The role of the empirical work is to operationalize the propositions, test hypotheses derived from them, and use the results to guide further theory development.

There are many high-quality articles and books that discuss the role of good theories in general (e.g., Dubin, 1978; Van de Ven, 1989; Weick, 1995), and we will not reiterate the key themes of those sources here. Rather we will focus on those areas of theory that we have found to be the most challenging and useful in our work. To illustrate the role of theory in designing and conducting experimental research, we will start with two fictitious examples of projects that vary dramatically in terms of the role theory plays in them (the latter is loosely based on Lightner and Eastman [2002]). After the examples, we will discuss the relationship between prior research and theory, analyze different roles of two major categories of theories, and review the role of theory as a mechanism to build knowledge within the community of scholars.

Vignette 1: Lab Study Lacking in Theory

John is interested in the impact of various features of an online shopping site on user satisfaction. He browses a range of sites and finds a number of dimensions that seem to differ among the sites (use of pictures, size of pictures, use of color, organization of content, etc.). He then designs and implements three different user interfaces so that they vary in some of these specific dimensions. He conducts a lab study and examines the impact of the various features on user satisfaction. John finds that the use of pictures has an impact on user satisfaction, but there is little he can do beyond reporting this empirical finding.

Vignette 2: Theory-Based Lab Study

Sam is interested in the impact of various features of an online shopping site on user satisfaction. She browses a range of sites and finds a number of characteristics that seem to differentiate the sites (such as the existence of pictures, size of pictures, use of color, organization of content, etc.). Instead of jumping directly to the empirical evaluation of the sites, Sam decides to carefully evaluate the factors that might possibly have an impact on user satisfaction in this context. After a careful literature review, Sam concludes that one particular area that presents questions that have not been addressed yet is the differential effects of visual stimuli on different individuals. She feels that this is an area where she can make a contribution; thus, she explores the question further with a focus on what is known about this specific question. Among other things, she finds that prior research has found very significant individual differences in imaginal information processing (Childers et al., 1985) and this, in turn, helps her to formulate theoretical arguments regarding individual differences in how a consumer may react to the visual components of an online store. Sam develops a strong set of theoretical propositions building on prior research and designs a study so that it faithfully operationalizes the relationships among the constructs of the theory. She executes the study, analyzes the statistical results, and then moves on to evaluate and discuss how the empirical findings fit the theoretical expectations and further our understanding of the relationship between the constructs of interest. Because her study is based on a firm theoretical foundation, Sam's study is more focused and produces richer data, and she is also in a significantly better position to explain her findings and what they mean in the broader context.

Theory Is Not Prior Research

The use of theory to build a logical argument that leads to the development of hypotheses goes beyond summarizing past work (Sutton and Staw, 1995). Referring to prior research is necessary but not sufficient for good theory development (in a quantitative positivist study). You need to go beyond what prior research has done and build on it in a logical manner. This should result in the formation of the hypotheses you wish to study. If you are relying only on past research and not moving beyond what has previously been done, the likelihood that your findings will be of sufficient interest to warrant publication in a top journal is low. However, if you do not show clear understanding of previous work and how it relates to your current work, this will also lead to a struggle in publication efforts.

If theory becomes a burden in a research project, it has either been misunderstood or misapplied, because good theory provides conceptual clarity and guidance for research. Theory is what binds a study together and gives the rich context and background to the development of the hypotheses. Regardless of the assumptions underlying theory in a specific study, theory provides explanations regarding the relationships among the constructs of interest in a study. Without explaining and investigating why a specific hypothesis should (or should not) be supported, the meaning of the dependent and independent variables loses its value.

Process Theories vs. Variance Theories

One important conceptual difference is between process theories and variance theories. Process theories attempt to explain how a process operates and how different events induce variables to change states, and often include time-oriented explanations (Markus and Robey, 1988; Mohr, 1982; Sabherwal and Robey, 1995). Process theories focus on the series of steps or events that lead to the outcomes. At the extreme, process theories can be explained with process flow diagrams or state transition diagrams. For example, Simon's (1960) theory of decision making is a classic process theory in that it argues that decision making is composed of three steps: intelligence, design, and choice. Other classic process theories include the garbage can model of organizational decision making (Cohen et al., 1972), the elaboration likelihood model and other dual process models of cognition (Petty and Cacioppo, 1986), and Darwin's theory of evolution.

Variance theories attempt to predict different levels of outcome variables as a function of some input variables (Markus and Robey, 1988; Mohr, 1982; Sabherwal and Robey, 1995). They attempt to explain the variance in outcomes, often as a mathematical function. Variance theories typically use the standard box and line diagrams we've all seen in hundreds of articles. Most laboratory experiments are used to test variance theories because they are the most straightforward to operationalize and measure.

It is also possible to integrate process and variance theories into one overarching theory that is tested in the lab. However, this can be very challenging and may cause more confusion than considering each theory separately (Mohr, 1982). However, if done well, such integration can significantly improve the power of the resulting model (Sabherwal and Robey, 1995).

"Big T" Theories vs. "Little t" Theories

Following Dennis and Valacich (2001), we will discuss the difference between two types of theories, which we label "Big T" and "little t" theories. "Big T" theories are the widely recognized, overarching theories that often have formal names (often abbreviated in capital letters), such as TAM, AST, ACT, TRA, and so forth. Probably the most widely utilized "Big T" theory in IS is

TAM (technology acceptance model), originally introduced in Davis (1989) and Davis et al. (1989), later extended—for example, by Venkatesh and Davis (2000)—and revised under a new name (UTAUT) by Venkatesh et al. (2003). For example, Yi and Hwang (2003) use TAM to guide their investigation of the factors that impact the use of Web-based information systems. Avoiding one of the common problems in developing and presenting theory (Sutton and Staw, 1995), Yi and Hwang go beyond simply referencing prior TAM work. Instead they present the logical arguments (based on TAM) that support their hypotheses.

Many researchers fall into the trap of feeling that they must always work with the overarching "Big T" theories. While these theories may inform your research questions and possibly even organize your stream of research, specific projects may be more manageable if you use the "little t" theories that are more focused, deal with more narrowly defined constructs, and may provide better boundaries for a specific research project. Please note that the difference between these two types of theories is not a value judgment but mostly a reference to the specificity of the theory or a set of theories.

"Little t" theories are the ones that focus on specific issues such as group interfaces, user tailorability, or ubiquitous electronic communications. For example, Speier and Morris (2003) explored the effects of query-interface design on decision-making performance. Specifically, they focused on the differences between text-based and visual-query environments and the interactions between the interface and two additional variables, task complexity and spatial ability (an individual characteristic). Their research is not based on and does not explore one of the "Big T" theories; instead, it carefully identifies the differences between the interface types and then moves on to justify why the two additional constructs of interest should moderate the relationship between the interface and the dependent variables. In this case, the researchers present a number of theoretical arguments in the form of justified statements regarding the relationship between the constructs of interest, specific to this context. The theory they constructed and tested has a more limited context and deals with more narrow constructs than the "Big T" theories do, but this does not mean that this research would be any less valuable than research focusing on a broader theory—its focus simply is different.

An example of a study that utilizes both "Big T" and "little t" theories is Galletta et al. (2004). This study investigated the effects of Web site delays on a number of dependent variables, including performance, satisfaction with the site, and behavioral intentions. Part of the theoretical argumentation in this paper is based on a very well known theory in social psychology, the theory of planned behavior (TPB; e.g., Ajzen, 2001). At the same time, the authors are building their theoretical case on a number of earlier studies on delay and its effects. Thus, the study integrates constructs and their relationships from an overarching "Big T" theory and a number of specific "little t" theories into a theory on the effects of Web site delays on user behavior and attitudes.

The use of "Big T," "little t," or a blend of the two are all equally valuable strategies to follow when designing a research project (Dennis and Valacich, 2001). Fundamentally, the decision comes down to what best fits the current research question and what will enable the research project to move forward and advance current understanding of the phenomena. Strong theorizing is the cornerstone of the research process. Without a strong theoretical foundation research will not stand the test of time and will be vulnerable to the natural erosion of poorly constructed science.

Research as a Community of Scholars

Research does not occur in a vacuum. It needs to breathe the air from other researchers' ideas. Professional groups of like-minded researchers can be established (for example, AIS SIGHCI and

ACM SIGCHI; see, for example, Zhang and Dillon, 2003) to facilitate the exchange of information. These groups can be the basis on which a knowledge community can grow. Furthermore, the exchange of ideas is often accomplished through the absorption of other researchers' work via journal articles and professional conferences. In an optimal world, every research project contributes to our theoretical understanding of the phenomena under investigation. This is not, however, possible without building strong links between research projects and the stream of research to which they belong. This requires not only the study of prior research related to the domain of interest and its theoretical underpinnings but also a conscious effort to use the results of a specific study to develop further the theoretical understanding the community is building through the process of scientific discourse, empirical data collection, and conceptual analysis.

DESIGNING LABORATORY RESEARCH

In this section, we will discuss the process of designing a laboratory study with a focus on research intending to advance our theoretical understanding of a particular HCI phenomenon. For more general information about the design and execution of research, and laboratory experiments specifically, see Kerlinger (1986) and Babbie (1995). The ideas described here have specifically been chosen to apply to empirical work whose primary purpose is theory testing.

In principle, designing a laboratory study is a relatively straightforward process in which the researcher finds feasible ways to operationalize the constructs utilized in the theoretical propositions (which often requires designing or choosing a suitable task, technology, and context combination) and plans for the practical aspects of the data-collection process. This process includes activities such as achieving an acceptance from an internal review board or a similar institutional body, reserving a suitable space, finding funds for the incentives and materials, finding personnel for data collection, recruiting participants for the study, scheduling the data collection sessions, and actually running the experiments. This seeming simplicity is, however, quite misleading and far from the truth.

All research methods can be evaluated on three dimensions (McGrath 1982):

- Generalizability with respect to populations
- Realism for the participants
- Precision in the control and measurement of variables

Generalizability and realism are not as important as the ability of the experimental design to represent the theory in a controlled environment. Laboratory experiments should maximize precision because maintaining control is the main reason to conduct a specific study in a laboratory. In general, experimental work rates low on generalizability and realism, which is acceptable and expected—generalizability in laboratory work is achieved through theory.

It cannot be emphasized enough how important it is to design the study so that various aspects of experimental control can be effectively maintained. The design of the study should include descriptions of the use of the experimental space and equipment during the session, procedures for random allocation of the participants to the various experimental conditions, a detailed script that covers as many aspects of the facilitator's interaction with the participants as possible (including the conditions when a participant's data has to be discarded), and the actions that are needed to ensure that the experimental data is properly captured and secured. Even if data collection is fully automated, it is very important to build in proper mechanisms for backing the data up. Let us reemphasize: the most important issue is to ensure experimental control and reduce unexpected variability in any aspect of the experimental situation; a poorly conducted experimental study is useless.

Designing Valid Operationalizations

One of the most critical issues, if not the most critical issue, in any research design is the faithfulness of the operationalizations to the theoretical constructs they intend to represent. In experimental research, if a treatment is not a valid operationalization of the construct it is supposed to represent, the study is flawed and, consequently, inadequate. This is a fundamental validity issue, and if a researcher cannot be confident that a design adequately represents a theoretical construct, the study should be postponed until a valid treatment is found. Collecting data with a flawed research design is a waste of resources, and the sooner a problem in research design can be captured, the better off the entire research community is. By default, a laboratory study is an artificial situation; in most cases, the only meaningful purpose for lab research is to test theoretical propositions through empirical operationalizations of the constructs. Therefore, ensuring the internal validity of a lab study is very important.

Executing a study with a flawed design will lead to significant waste in several areas. First, the researcher wastes valuable time in data collection, statistical analysis, and reporting the results. Furthermore, the participants' time is wasted (and because access to participants is normally a scarce resource, other research opportunities may be missed as well), as is the space, supplies, incentive money, and so forth. In addition, a flawed design may also waste editors' and reviewers' time, if a manuscript gets past the working-paper stage to the review process. Even worse, if a paper based on a flawed design gets published, it will also waste its readers' time. In the worst case, a flawed design misinforms us about the state of the world and potentially misdirects future research.

Thus, the design is critically important. How does one find out whether a specific design is internally valid and how does one come up with designs in the first place? A strong understanding of prior research is an important first step. Understanding the literature is not only important from the perspective of theory development but also from the perspective of understanding how the key constructs in a specific field have traditionally been operationalized. Constructs and their operationalizations have to be conceptually separated from each other, keeping in mind that in an experimental context, the treatments have no value except as representations of the theoretical constructs. In experimental work, the theory being tested should always drive the design.

Understanding of prior literature and earlier use of various instruments is critical for the design. Particularly if one is conducting a broader research program, maintaining a well-documented inventory of tasks as representations of constructs is important. The use of accepted, carefully validated instruments is advisable, unless the purpose of a project is to study constructs that have not been operationalized before or there is a reason to believe that a particular operationalization is not valid. Even in these cases, the treatments should be carefully linked to prior work in the field, so that a reader can clearly evaluate the effects of the choices made by the researcher.

How can one determine whether or not a particular design is a valid operationalization of the theoretical constructs? There is no magical solution to this important question, but it is possible to provide a set of guidelines. First, as already emphasized above, consistency with work published earlier in the field is very important. The use of established operationalizations is also a safe choice, as long as the study provides enough novelty in other areas. Second, it is essential that several people evaluate the research design before the data collection, however exploratory a study might be. In this process, colleagues interested in similar issues can do each other a great service by maintaining a positive and constructive environment in which it is safe to present research ideas for evaluation at early stages. Third, as will be discussed at a more detailed level later, pilot testing of the operationalizations is essential. Fourth, various manipulation checks are very important in the process of making the case supporting the validity of your results.

Avoiding Confounding Factors

Design is not, however, only about the selection of the operationalization of the constructs; it is also about executing the various components of a study in a way that minimizes the risk of confounding factors affecting the results of the study. The design of a laboratory study has to ensure that the effects that are observed in the study are caused by the experimental treatments and not by any other factors occurring in the experimental situation simultaneously. The most fundamental reason to choose a laboratory study as a method of inquiry is to have the ability to fully control the experimental situation by manipulating specific factors and keeping others constant. If the design does not allow that, it is flawed.

There are multiple excellent resources (e.g., Campbell and Stanley, 1966; Cook and Campbell, 1979) that discuss the threats to internal validity in experimental research, and there is no need to repeat those results at a detailed level here. For example, Campbell and Stanley (1966) identify (1) history, (2) maturation, (3) testing, (4) instrumentation, (5) statistical regression, (6) selection of respondents, (7) experimental mortality, and (8) selection-maturation interaction as possible threats to internal validity. In other words, they remind us to make sure that the intended experimental treatment is the only change that takes place between the pretest and the posttest (assuming both are used). Campbell and Stanley (1966) provide three prototypical "true experimental designs" ("pretest-posttest control group design," "Solomon four-group design," and "posttest-only control group design"), each of which provides protection against the threats listed above. The third one is probably the most common. Unless there is a specific reason why a design that doesn't provide equally good protection against the validity threats should be chosen, these three designs form a good basis for the design selection. A poor design often means that the factors underlying the results of a specific research project remain uncertain because a certain set of outcomes could have been produced by a variety of factors.

Selecting Tasks and Participants

The task used in a study forms the context for any treatments, and the context may determine whether or not the treatments (even though they might appear to be separate from the task) work in the way they were planned. In practice, it is the combination of the task and the treatments that determines whether or not the situation that the participants experience is a valid operationalization of the theoretical constructs. For example, if the purpose of a study is to evaluate the effects of a specific user interface manipulation on a specific aspect of human performance (say, the time it takes to perform the task), it is possible to entirely hide any possible effects of the user interface manipulation by selecting a task that is too complex for the specific participant population. If this happens, the experimental design fails to represent the theoretical constructs and, therefore, the study is flawed.

Selection of the participant population and the recruitment of the participants is another important factor affecting the success of a study, and also another area where a lot has been written (e.g., Gordon et al., 1986). Using an easily accessible student population is usually fine for those research questions where the focus is on fundamental features of human cognition or behavior, but if the intention is to study the effect of, say, a specific technology manipulation on seasoned professionals with expertise in a specific area (e.g., strategic planning, application system development), using college freshmen as the subject population is not usually the right choice.

The selection of the task and participant population is *not* a question of external validity or generalizability of the results. We are *not* concerned about using inexperienced undergraduate students and "toy" tasks; such criticisms of experimental research display a fundamental lack of understanding of research methods. The key issue is whether the selection of the task and partic-ipants operationalizes the theoretical constructs in a meaningful way. It is critical to ensure that the task fits the skills and abilities of the participants and that both the task and participants fit the key aspects of the theory being tested.

Incentives

In recruiting participants for a study (regardless of the population chosen) it is important to pro-vide incentives that motivate them to take the experimental task seriously. This can be in the form of monetary incentives, tasks that create an incentive for the participants to compete, class grade component (naturally following the proper ethical guidelines), or other similar measures. One should not expect that the participants will automatically approach the task enthusiastically; spe-cific mechanisms are important. It is particularly important to understand how the motivation level of the participants affects the study's ability to operationalize the constructs under investi-gation. If, for example, the focus of the study is on the effects of time pressure on various aspects of human performance, no treatment will be valid unless the participants are motivated to perform well in the experimental task and they care about the results. The same incentives do not have the same effect everywhere and for every participant population. The incentives that work for an undergraduate population do not necessarily work for graduate students or professionals; the effects of the incentives depend entirely on how the participants perceive them; therefore, it is essential that this is one of the areas evaluated carefully in pilot testing.

If monetary incentives are used to improve the motivation level of the subjects, it is important that they have a good fit with the treatments. Incentive structures can have hidden effects on per-formance, and thus, they should be evaluated carefully as part of the design of the study. For example, if the experimental task consists of multiple subtasks, the design has to specify whether the incentive compensation should (a) be the same for everybody, (b) vary depending on the over-all performance in the task, or (c) vary depending on the performance in specific subtasks. Also, incentives can be used to direct the participants' focus on specific aspects of performance. For example, there is often a trade-off (at least a perceived trade-off) between quality and time, and particularly in tasks with multiple subtasks it is possible to use the incentive mechanism to guide the participants' focus on either one of these (for example, by rewarding alternatively accuracy at the subtask level or the number of subtasks performed).

Designing for Statistical Analysis

As we develop laboratory experiments, we are sometimes faced with the need to choose between multiple existing operationalizations of the constructs we plan to test. The first and the primary criterion for selecting a method for operationalizing a construct should be the faithful representa-tion of the construct of interest. If the various operationalizations of a construct are equally valid and have good reliability, we have a real opportunity to choose the one to use. In situations such as this, one should pay attention to the issues related to statistical power (Baroudi and Orlikowski, 1989). One of the main selection criteria should then be the ability of the operationalization to demonstrate the differences between the different treatment levels.

In most statistical methods used to analyze results of typical laboratory research designs, the core element is the t-test or one of the related, but more complex analytical approaches such as ANOVA and linear regression. In its simplest form, the very familiar t-test evaluates whether or not we can with a certain probability reject the hypothesis that the means of the populations are the same. The t-value is affected by three components: (a) the difference between the treatment means, (b) the standard deviations of both samples, and (c) the sizes of the populations. The t-value goes up when the difference between the treatment means goes up, when the standard deviation of either sample goes down, and when the sample size is increased.

The ways to have an impact on these three components vary depending on the factor. We can affect the difference between the treatment means by choosing treatments that maximize the effect on the dependent variable while still faithfully capturing the nature of the construct measured with the independent variable. If the nature of the treatment(s) make the experimental results obvious and trivial even though the theory is interesting and worth investigating, it is unlikely that the treatment accurately represents the underlying construct. For instance, if you create a user interface that is extremely difficult to use for one treatment and another that is compatible with most subjects' current mental model of computer interface (a standard GUI), finding that one is more satisfactory to use than the other is not very informative.

We can also affect the sample variances with a careful selection of the population and with careful execution of the study. Homogeneity of the population is important because even though random assignment of subjects to treatments will avoid any systematic biases, large variances within the samples will reduce the experiment's ability to differentiate between the treatment groups. Very careful control over the data collection processes is essential because any operational differences may lead to additional variance which will have a negative impact on the experiment's ability to capture an existing effect. Finally, we can affect the power of the statistical test by increasing the number of participants in the treatments.

Pilot Testing

Pilot testing is an important stage of the research process that should be utilized in every laboratory study. It has two main purposes. First, it allows you to test the experimental procedures, verify that all treatments work the way they were expected to work, test the technology in the real experimental context, verify that your estimates regarding the time required were correct, and so on. This purpose is very important because, as in any other human endeavor, it is, in practice, impossible to fully evaluate how humans and technology will act together in a specific context without verifying the combination in a practical situation. Every pilot test will reveal something about the practical aspects of your experimental design that you had not thought about earlier, and often these are issues that could eventually have a significant impact on the actual data collection.

At least equally important is the second purpose of pilot testing, which is to verify, before the actual high-cost data collection, whether or not the experiment is likely to lead to significant and meaningful results. The number of subjects in a pilot test is normally so low that statistical analysis is not possible, but careful analysis of the pilot results often tells whether or not the full data collection will lead to expected results. If a pilot doesn't provide any indications of differences between the treatments, it is unlikely that the differences would suddenly show up in the actual data collection. In other words, if a pilot test fails to provide any findings in the expected direction, you may want to consider reevaluating various aspects of the study and possibly redesigning it, as discussed below. You can think of a pilot test as the polling surveys done before an election that attempt to predict the outcome; if the results are not what you want, you need to reconsider the study or else you risk "losing" once the data are collected.

What to do if a carefully designed and well-executed pilot study indicates that there will be no results at all or the results are in an unexpected direction? Fundamentally, this may be caused by four different reasons: (1) your theory is incorrect and there simply are no effects to be found;

(2) the operationalization of the constructs you have chosen is invalid and your study is not measuring the intended relationship; (3) the design of your study introduces a confound that hides the expected relationship; or (4) something is wrong with the execution of your study. Whichever option is true, it is very important to find out about the problem as early as possible. The last alternative is the easiest to fix and can lead relatively soon to a new pilot; the second and third alternatives require careful redesign of the experimental study, and the first alternative will force you to go through a careful reconceptualization of the problem domain. Even though you may feel after a failed pilot that you are not any closer to a published study, the pilot has served two very important purposes: it has saved time, human resources, and money; and it has often also advanced our understanding of the field by encouraging either redesign of the study or more focused theorizing. You can do a service to your colleagues by sharing experiences regarding failed studies, too; this will reduce the costs for others, who can learn from your experience.

Data Collection

If your laboratory study is carefully designed and piloted, the actual data collection should be a relatively straightforward process. Things will at times go wrong (Murphy's Law applies in experimental research, too), but careful planning and preparation helps avoid problems that lead to widespread failure. The value of a very detailed experimental script (and adhering to it) cannot be overemphasized; maintaining control and consistency is critically important. It is essential that you document carefully the events during every experimental session, including the timing of the planned events and a description of anything unplanned. Detailed notes can be invaluable in trying to evaluate later the impact of an unexpected event on the execution of the study; in addition, they may lead to insights that guide further theoretical exploration and experimental research.

CRAFTING THE RESEARCH PAPER

Selecting a research project, formulating the theory and executing the design are all vital to high quality research. Once the research has been completed and the data have been collected, preparing the work for publication begins. There are some clear steps that you need to take to bring a study from data collection and analysis to publication. However, the execution of some of these steps is an art, not a science (Peter and Olson, 1983).

Relevance and Rigor

There has been much discussion about the relevance of academic research within the HCI community. Understanding that there are different audiences for our research and that these audiences may perceive relevance very differently is important. The creation of new knowledge (called knowledge exploration by March [1991]) may best fit the needs of the academic community, while the dissemination of knowledge for use (called knowledge exploitation by March [1991]) often has a better fit with the needs and interests of practitioners. While some research is unambiguously targeted to only one of the audiences, we believe that most research projects can be crafted to be relevant to either or both audiences. That is not to say that they will be equally embraced by both audiences, that they will be valued by both audiences at the same time, or that the same paper will serve both audiences. But if we do not strive to find research that has the potential to both move knowledge exploration forward and to be relevant to the practitioners (maybe not immediately but in the future), we are not fully realizing the potential of our work.

While this may be challenging and may not be appropriate for each specific research project, the research path you are exploring and the umbrella of research under which you operate should be relevant for both parties. As academics, our unique contribution to society is knowledge exploration. How we craft our message and interpret our findings may aid practitioners in exploiting the results of our exploration. As a field we need to establish vehicles for exploiting the knowledge that we are creating, making it more accessible to the non-academic world. What those vehicles are is still being debated. Some of the options currently available are journals that target both academic and practitioner markets (e.g., *Communications of the ACM, MIS Quarterly Executive*), the development of joint research activities with private industry or public organizations, presentations at practitioner-oriented conferences (Teradata's Partners conference), and mass media outlets (newspapers, trade magazines, Web sites).

This is not to say that we should focus on these outlets as our primary targets but we may better serve our two target populations by learning to craft our findings for different distribution channels. For junior faculty members, the traditional academic outlets need to be the primary focus. Academia is slow in changing, and tenure-review committees typically rely on traditional academic outlets to measure the quality of faculty members' research efforts. However, if we do not do a better job of embracing practice-oriented research designed to exploit the knowledge we are creating through rigorous research studies, we will miss the opportunity to inform practitioners and empower faculty to be relevant in both the academic and practitioner worlds.

Our discussion in this paper has mostly focused on laboratory experiments; therefore, it is useful to explore the question of relevancy of rigorous research a bit further in this context. Because the main focus of experimental laboratory research is on theory testing in a tightly controlled environment, its external validity is typically weak by design. Attempts to improve the external validity of laboratory studies often lead to violations of internal validity and thus violate the entire idea of conducting a lab study. If this is the case, how can we make a lab study relevant for both academic and practitioner audiences?

There are primarily two ways to make research relevant. First and foremost, lab studies become relevant when they generate knowledge and theory about phenomena that are of interest to the practitioner community. The results of a lab study either support or refute the theory under exploration, and it is the responsibility of the researcher to explain why the theory is relevant and what its practical implications are. The relevancy of lab research results has to be communicated through the relevancy of the theory, not the empirical data. Second, lab studies can produce relevant insights to human behavior when interacting with computing technology through patterns of behavior that are observed in the lab setting. Despite the artificiality of the situation, a detailed analysis of participant behavior in the lab may prove to be highly valuable.

Crafting Your Message

Every article needs a punch line. There needs to be a concrete message that a user can take from each article you write. This message should withstand the "elevator" test: Are you able to express the core idea of your research findings in the time it takes to ride an elevator? If you can't express your punch line in two or three sentences, you will be hard-pressed to capture its relevance and meaning to your target audience in a full-length paper.

Once you have developed your elevator pitch, it is time to craft your paper around it. Make sure that each aspect of the paper is guided by the fundamental message you wish to convey. Logical arguments and theoretical developments that are not directly pertinent to your message should be pruned, and those that directly establish the message you wish to convey should be filled out and expanded upon. There will be time in other articles to discuss other interesting insights you have about your research stream.

Keeping the paper focused on the specific study helps you make the unique message that particular piece of research makes. When other distractions creep into a paper, reviewers and other readers often create an incorrect vision of where they believe your paper is leading and will ultimately be disappointed to find out that that was not the main point of your paper. Finding the unique character and message of each paper is a creative journey built upon the theoretical foundation that guided your research project, fueled by your empirical work. Often, the unique contribution your study makes to the field is not the one you anticipated. Even if this is the case, it is essential that you capture that contribution and convey it as your core message.

Once you have found the punch line for your work, the way you express it has an impact on the paper's survival in the review process. Even when all aspects of the project are executed well and the findings are interesting and insightful, no one may ever know about it if your paper is poorly written. Knowing your audience is essential to writing your paper. What are the expectations of your target audience? What type of language should you use? What is the proper length of an article? What format does your target journal embrace? Find a successful article that utilizes a similar research method to the one you used and study how it is presented. Better yet, see if you can find several published pieces in your target journal that utilize the same methodology you used. Through these papers you can gain insight into the rhythm of the papers of the journal. Style, length, language, and paper structure all become important when you are writing a paper for a specific outlet. The mechanics of the paper are also important. What are the instructions to the author? Does your paper meet the rules set forward by the journal? These are all details in the publishing process that may at first seem irrelevant but are essential to take into account if you want your paper to be seen in the best light possible. By overlooking some basic guidelines you give the impression that you are a novice as a researcher and thus suggest that other areas of your research may be sloppy also.

To further ensure credibility, be clear in your methods section. Provide adequate details so your study can be replicated. Discuss any design decisions you feel are pertinent and let the reviewers and readers know what the limitations of your study are. All studies will have limitations, so expressing the limitations of your study and how you have taken those into account shows that you are aware of them and have done what you can to reduce the impact of them on your findings.

When reporting your results, it is essential to use tables and graphs effectively and provide your readers with both a clear summary of the results and all the necessary details. The styles of reporting the detailed results of statistical analyses vary depending on the journal and the target audience; make sure that you know these conventions before you structure the final format of your submission. Providing descriptive data (e.g., treatment means and standard deviations) in addition to the statistical analysis results is a good idea, because it gives a reader a better opportunity to evaluate what the quantitative results mean (for example, ANOVA analysis might reveal that perceptions regarding satisfaction with a certain interface might be significantly different in two treatments, but it does not tell whether the participants were generally satisfied or unsatisfied with the technologies in question). A summary table is often an excellent way to present the results of the hypothesis tests.

The discussion section is the area in the paper you get to express your insights, explain your findings, make sense of your results, and relate them to prior research. This does not give you license to write a creative novel, but it does give you an opportunity to utilize theory to further illuminate your findings. If you have unexpected findings, this is the place to discuss alternative theoretical explanations to your findings. One of the most important contributions of a good discussion section is to position the findings of the study in a broader context and illustrate how they advance the theoretical understanding in the field. Research is a process of discourse between scholars exploring a specific set of questions, and the discussion section is an excellent place to advance this dialogue.

Here, you can build on the insights gained from the study by discussing what the next possible steps are for future research. Often authors see this as a place to quickly jot down future research that they really do not intend on conducting, and many editors and reviewers have learned to despise this. But with careful thought and a well-designed long-term research plan, this section gives you an opportunity to foreshadow your future work. If you believe that developing a course of research under a unifying umbrella and following a well-defined path for your research are fruitful ways to manage your research career, it naturally follows that speculating on future work should include research that you really are considering doing next. You should not just suggest that it would be nice if this future research was done by someone else (this approach only frustrates your reviewers, editors, and other readers); instead, this section gives you a chance to sit back, think about your findings, strategize your next study in your research path, and foreshadow it in your discussion section.

Finally, relating to making your work relevant to various audiences, you need to include a short tickler (a paragraph or two) on how this research impacts the practitioner community (assuming you are mainly targeting your work to an academic audience). This can also be the beginning of your paper that directly targets practitioners. Boil down the implications for management in two or three sentences and give a few examples of how these implications can enhance practice. For example, think about what you would incorporate into a class based on your research.

Once you have taken the time to understand the message your work offers to management, marketing it to a non-academic audience becomes easier. Make sure that your section on managerial implications is not artificial and forced, and remember that the true managerial implications of most lab studies are indirect and can be found through theory, not from a single study.

It is important to remember that most readers do not read all aspects of all articles. You need to capture their attention and pull them in so they want to read the full article. The conclusion is one place to succinctly state what your research was, what it found, and why anyone should care. Many readers first focus on the abstract and the conclusion, and only then decide whether they will read the full paper. These two portions should convince the reader that the full paper is worthy of his or her time.

Try and Try Again

Once you have completed your research and written the first draft of your study, the journey is far from over. Now is the time to do some trial runs with your work to see how it is accepted by your target audience. Getting the insights and reactions of your colleagues will help you identify those areas that are underdeveloped in your work. What are the things that they seem to question? Are they the things you can do something about by improving the clarity of your own thoughts or by broadening your use of previous theory?

Test-market your paper at a conference to solicit additional feedback from others doing research in your area. Perhaps they see your research topic through a different lens that may enable you to evolve your project to a higher level. Although in the positivist research paradigm we strive to have the front end of our paper written prior to data collection, that is seldom the case in practice (except perhaps in doctoral dissertations). You need to be open to different interpretations of your work; perhaps the lens you were using to design your work is not the lens that brings it into focus for other researchers.

Disentangling your ego and your vision of your work from the work itself helps you be open to new ways of seeing your projects. This makes it possible for you to grow your piece and increase the chances that it will succeed in the review process. As researchers we often become so entangled in our view of the world that we are unable to look at our work from other perspectives (even when they might give additional depth to our project). Discussions with colleagues and the feedback one may get from a conference are two ways to broaden your outlook.

Once you have rewritten the article several times and incorporated feedback from others, it is time to submit your paper. Keep in mind that you should feel that you are submitting your best work each time you submit. However, you need to recognize that your work *will* be modified (and hopefully improved) as it moves through the review process. Handling the review processes is critical to the eventual publication of your paper. Keep in mind that the reviewers are authors, too, and they understand the review process from both sides (Lee, 1999). You need to see the reviewers and editors as part of a team guiding you to develop the best article you can to exhibit your work.

When responding to your reviews, make sure you clearly and specifically address each issue put forward by each reviewer. If the reviewers have not labeled their comments, do it for them, and do whatever else it takes to demonstrate that you have addressed all the points made in the reviews. There is nothing more frustrating for a reviewer than getting a paper to review for the second time and having to hunt through it to see if the authors actually addressed his or her issues, or worse, to try to guess why they decided not to address the issues. Remember that the purpose of these comments was not just to highlight errors but to point out areas for improvement. By not addressing reviewers' comments you run the risk not only of insulting the reviewers but also of not capitalizing on the ideas he or she gave you. If you don't agree with a reviewer, it is acceptable to tell him politely and explicitly why his comments weren't addressed, but don't just avoid responding to his or her thoughts.

Sometimes a reviewer might be wrong. If this is the case, educate him or her in a non-threatening and non-aggressive manner. You should be the authority on your work, but if a reviewer did not understand something, chances are other readers will also not understand it, either. Therefore, you need to figure out a way to express yourself better. Pointing out where you made the changes (by page number or section) helps the reviewer navigate your improvements and increases your chances of satisfying the reviewers' concerns. It is your responsibility to make the reviewer want to accept your paper and not want to reject it!

If the paper is rejected, this does not mean that it is unworthy of publication. It just means it was not a good fit at that particular time, with that particular set of reviewers at that particular journal. Your next step should always be to think about ways to improve your paper and tailor it to another journal. When you do this, make sure you take the time to modify the manuscript (don't just send it out in its last form—you may get some of the same reviewers) and put the manuscript in the target journal's format (this includes your citations). Using EndNote or any other bibliographic software makes reference reformatting easy; it is worth the investment.

When you feel the manuscript is ready to head out the door again to a new journal, submit it. Recall that these reviewers probably have not seen the paper before and they do not know that it has been through a previous review process. It is their first time to tango with the paper. Do not become frustrated if some of the reviewers' comments actually lead you back to an earlier conceptualization of the paper. Crafting a paper is, after all, as much of an art as it is a science. Not all people have the same reaction to all art forms; be ready to remodel your "masterpiece" to impress this particular set of reviewers.

CONCLUSIONS

In this paper, we have discussed the process of successfully producing relevant research in HCI. We have dealt with the issues from the perspective of the research tradition we personally know best, that is, experimental laboratory research based on the positivist research philosophy. Throughout the paper we have emphasized the central role of theory in this type of work: the best use of tightly controlled experimental lab research is to test theory, and the contributions of a lab study can be evaluated through its effect on advancing our theoretical understanding of a phenomenon. "Theoretical" in this context does not mean impractical or void of practical consequences—the practical implications of this type of work become visible through theory. HCI experimental lab research can be relevant for both theoretical development and practice.

No research can be relevant if it is not valid (i.e., if it does not lead to accurate conclusions regarding the state of the world). Conducting poorly designed experiments with inadequate resources is in nobody's interest, and poor-quality research should not be conducted at all. All research is not equally thorough, deep, and broad, and projects may add very incremental steps to the knowledge creation process. Even the smallest projects should, however, be approached with the same criteria of high quality and rigor as the largest projects. In particular in laboratory research, strong focus on internal validity is essential.

We also emphasized the importance of research streams instead of a large number of separate studies. Building a research program and structuring one's work under a thematic umbrella provides structure, leads to more significant contributions, and helps build a deep understanding of a specific area. Institutions of higher education and funding agencies should support efforts to build research programs leading to a deep understanding of essential HCI phenomena.

The paper discussed a number of practical issues related to the process of finding research ideas, designing a study, collecting the data, and reporting the results. Throughout the paper we have emphasized the importance of communicating with the research community, both to provide a quality control mechanism and to find and provide new ideas in a continuous dialogue with one's colleagues. We hope that these ideas will help you be an active participant in this process that will advance our understanding of how humans interact with computing technology.

NOTE

1. We are, naturally, fully aware of the fact that laboratory testing is widely used as an invaluable tool at various stages of product development. This is, however, different from academic research.

REFERENCES

Ajzen, I. Nature and operation of attitudes. *Annual Review of Psychology*, 52 (2001), 27–58.

Alter, S., and Dennis, A.R. Selecting research topics: personal experiences and speculations for the future. *Communications of the AIS*, 8, 21 (2002), 314–329.

Babbie, E. *The Practice of Social Research*. Belmont, CA: Wadsworth, 1995.

Baroudi, J.J., and Orlikowski, W. The problem of statistical power in MIS research. *MIS Quarterly*, 13, 1 (1989), 87–106.

Campbell, D.T., and Stanley, J.C. *Experimental and Quasi-Experimental Designs for Research*. Boston: Houghton Mifflin Company, 1966.

Carlson, J.R., and Zmud, R.W. Channel expansion theory and the experiential nature of media richness perceptions. *Academy of Management Journal*, 42, 2 (1999), 153–170.

Childers, T.L., Houston, M.J., and Heckler, S.E. Measurement of individual differences in visual versus verbal information processing. *Journal of Consumer Research*, 12, 2 (1985), 125–134.

Cohen, M.D., March, J.G., and Olsen, J.P. A garbage can model of organizational choice. *Administrative Science Quarterly*, 17, 1 (1972), 1–25.

Cook, T.D., and Campbell, D.T. *Quasi-Experimentation: Design and Analysis Issues for Field Settings*. New York: The Free Press, 1979.

Davis, F.D. Perceived usefulness, perceived ease of use, and user acceptance of information technology. *MIS Quarterly*, 13, 3 (1989), 319–339.

Davis, F.D., Bagozzi, R.P., and Warshaw, P.R. User acceptance of computer technology: a comparison of two theoretical models. *Management Science*, 35, 8 (1989), 982–1002.

Davis, G.B. An individual and group strategy for research in information systems. In R. Galliers (ed.), *Information Systems Research: Issues, Methods and Practical Guidelines*. Oxford: Blackwell, 1992, pp. 230–252.

Dennis, A.R., and Valacich, J.S. Conducting experimental research in information systems. *Communications of the AIS*, 7, 5 (2001) (available at http://cais.isworld.org./articles/7–5/, accessed on November 22, 2005).

Dubin, R. *Theory Building*. New York: The Free Press, 1978.

Galletta, D.F., Henry, R., McCoy, S., and Polak, P. Web site delays: how tolerant are users? *Journal of the Association for Information Systems*, 5,1 (2004), 1–28.

Gordon, M.E., Slade, L.A., and Schmitt, N. The "science of the sophomore" revisited: from conjecture to empiricism. *Academy of Management Review*, 11, 1 (1986), 191–207.

Hayne, S., and Rice. R. Attribution accuracy when using anonymity in group support systems. *International Journal of Human Computer Studies*, 47, 3 (1997), 429–450.

Kerlinger, F.D. *Foundations of Behavioral Research*. New York: Holt, Rinehart and Winston, 1986.

Kuhn, T.S. *The Structure of Scientific Revolutions*, 2nd ed. Chicago: The University of Chicago Press, 1970.

Lee, A.S. The role of information technology in reviewing and publishing manuscripts at MIS Quarterly. *MIS Quarterly*, 23, 4 (1999), pp. iv–ix.

Lightner, N.J., and Eastman, C. User preference for product information in remove purchase environments. *Journal of Electronic Commerce Research*, 3, 3 (2002), 174–186.

March, J.G. Exploration and exploitation in organizational learning. *Organization Science*, 2, 1 (1991), 71–87.

Markus, L., and Robey, D. Information technology and organizational change: causal structure in theory and research. *Management Science*, 34, 5 (1988), 583–598.

McGrath, J.E. Dilemmatics: the study of research choices and dilemmas. In J.E. McGrath (ed.), *Judgment Calls in Research*. Beverly Hills, CA: Sage, 1982, pp. 69–80.

Mohr, I.B. *Explaining Organizational Behavior*. San Francisco, CA: Jossey-Bass, 1982.

Peter, J.P., and Olson, J.C. Is science marketing? *Journal of Marketing*, 47, 4 (1983), 111–125.

Petty, R.E., and Cacioppo, J.T. *Communication and Persuasion: Central and Peripheral Routes to Attitude Change*. New York: Springer-Verlag, 1986.

Sabherwal, R., and Robey, D. Reconciling variance and process strategies for studying information system development. *Information Systems Research*, 6, 4 (1995), 303–327.

Simon, H.A. *The New Science of Management Decisions*. New York: Harper and Row, 1960.

Speier, C., and Morris, M. The influence of query interface design on decision-making performance. *MIS Quarterly*, 27, 3 (2003), 397–423.

Sutton, R.I., and Staw, B.M. What theory is not. *Administrative Science Quarterly*, 40, 3 (1995), 371–384.

Van de Ven, A.H. Nothing is quite so practical as a good theory. *Academy of Management Review*, 14, 4 (1989), 486–489.

Venkatesh, V., and Davis, F.D. A theoretical extension of the technology acceptance model: four longitudinal field studies. *Management Science*, 46, 2 (2000), 186–204.

Venkatesh, V., Morris, M.G., Davis, G.B., and Davis, F.D. User acceptance of information technology: toward a unified view. *MIS Quarterly*, 27, 3 (2003), 425–478.

Vessey, I. Cognitive fit—a theory-based analysis of the graphs versus tables literature. *Decision Sciences*, 22, 2 (1991), 219–240.

Watson, H.J., Satzinger, J.W., and Singh, S.K. Establishing viable programs of research: the executive information system program at the University of Georgia. *DataBase*, 25, 3 (1994), 40–51.

Weick, K.E. What theory is *not*, theorizing *is*. *Administrative Science Quarterly*, 40, 3 (1995), 385–390.

Yi, M.Y., and Hwang, Y. Predicting the use of web-based information systems: self-efficacy, enjoyment, learning goal orientation, and the technology acceptance model. *International Journal of Human-Computer Studies*, 59, 4 (2003), 431–449.

Zhang, P., and Dillon, A. HCI and MIS: shared concerns. *International Journal of Human-Computer Studies*, 59, 4 (2003), 397–402.

CHAPTER 18

SOFT VERSUS HARD

The Essential Tension

JOHN M. CARROLL

Abstract: *Over the past thirty years, human-computer interaction (HCI) has developed as a strongly theoretical area of interdisciplinary scientific research and technology development. In the mid-1980s, there was a debate in the pages of the journal* Human-Computer Interaction *regarding the nature of science in HCI. Allen Newell and Stuart Card described a "hard science" paradigm for HCI, which they argued would more effectively integrate psychology and computer science as interdisciplinary foundations. Robert Campbell and I questioned this conclusion. Like most significant debates, this discussion is ongoing. This paper summarizes the original debate, and places it in the context of HCI, as this field developed through the ensuing twenty years, and, more generally, in the context of multidisciplinary research visions, which inevitably must wrestle with the tensions between "soft" and "hard" science.*

Keywords: *Science, Theory, Method, Paradigm, Hard Science, Soft Science*

INTRODUCTION

Every field of professional activity analyzes its foundations—assumptions and concepts, methods and practices, and so on. It is no surprise that new areas of endeavor tend to invest more energy in this. Like many longtime participants in the field of human-computer interaction—familiarly known as HCI, I have reflected on the field's foundations throughout the past thirty years.

I am grateful to the editors for inviting me to revisit the mid-1980s debate about "hard science" as a paradigm for human-computer interaction, and in particular for psychology as a part of human-computer interaction. The field has traveled far in the intervening two decades, and the original discussion has lost some of its intelligibility to contemporary reading. However, I think it is worth recalling, as it places contemporary currents of thinking and practice in a more significant context.

Revisiting this debate, and its more recent echoes, suggests to me that interdisciplinary tension has always been a resource to HCI, and an important factor in its success. My own current conclusion is that hang-ups about the differences between soft and hard science have been, and remain, the most significant risk to HCI emerging from this debate.

WHAT IS HCI?

Over the past thirty years, human-computer interaction has developed into a far-flung endeavor incorporating science, engineering, and the arts. It originally formed as a deliberately interdisciplinary area at the periphery of computer science. It was created by software engineers and computer graphics researchers who saw the need to direct more attention to users and user interfaces, and by cognitive scientists and human factors engineers who saw the need for practical behavioral work guided by and contributing to theory.

The vision for HCI, which was pretty explicit from the early 1980s, was not merely a confederation of disciplines, but an *integration* of disciplines. There was a definite edge to this. The vision of HCI implicitly—and sometimes explicitly—criticized the status quo: human factors were criticized for ignoring science and theory, software engineering was criticized for rigid waterfall models of software development that entailed a disregard for usability requirements, computer science was criticized for ignoring the people and organizations that use and are impacted by computer technology, and cognitive science was criticized for ignoring real domains of human activity in favor of simplistic research models.

Today, HCI exists within and bridges among a large number of existing disciplines, including anthropology, cognitive science, computer science, educational technology/instructional systems, graphic design, human factors, library and information systems, management, psychology, and sociology. It also encompasses several new and emerging disciplines/professions, such as computer-supported cooperative work, informatics, interaction design, geospatial information systems, multi-modal systems/interfaces, ubiquitous computing, usability engineering, and virtual environments.

The scope of HCI has expanded dramatically over the past three decades. At its inception, HCI elaborated upon empirical studies of professional programming skills by applying more sophisticated cognitive theories. It extended attention to non-professional computing skill domains, such as text editing; examined early stages of skills acquisition, as well as asymptotic skills; and developed a more direct linkage between empirical studies and theories and the design and development of new technologies and applications.

The research community was tiny at the start, a few dozen people worldwide. But during the first half of the 1980s it grew rapidly. Although it is sometimes said that the personal computer (PC) revolution caused HCI, the vision of HCI was already established and many of the pioneering projects were well under way when the PC revolution helped to catapult HCI to prominence in the computer industry and in computer science and other disciplines bearing on the computer industry.

Indeed, HCI has been so successful and has grown so prodigiously that it could soon disappear as such. Until the mid-1990s, the intellectual center of gravity for HCI was clearly the ACM's Special Interest Group on Computer-Human Interaction (SIGCHI). Since then, there have been so many concurrent developments in so many diverse communities that it is increasingly difficult to point to HCI as such. Although some might fret about these developments and others might rejoice, they are clearly markers of the impact and importance of the intellectual and technical issues at the heart of HCI.

TENSIONS ABOUT MULTIDISCIPLINARY SCIENCE

I believe that a balanced tension of concern with innovative science and innovative technology has persisted through the years to keep the HCI field intellectually exciting and impactful. The scope and variety of this work is by now staggering. Two handbooks of HCI have been published in the past ten years, each with more than sixty chapters (Helander et al., 1997; Jacko and Sears, 2002). A few years ago, I collected fifteen diverse examples of research programs in HCI science and theory in an edited book, but there could easily have been two or three such volumes (Carroll, 2003).

This exciting admixture of innovative technology development and innovative science is itself inherently problematic. Science and technology development have different values, different methods, and incommensurable results. There are many traditional pitfalls and routes to failure.

In HCI this tension is surely exacerbated by the fact that most of the science in HCI has been social and behavioral, whereas the technology is in computing, communications, and media.

We should acknowledge the obvious stereotypes as they pertain to HCI: Technologists sometimes *do* have a tendency to be blinded by the mere fact that they had an exciting idea and got something to work. Their visions of how people might make use of a new technology or of how the technology might affect people can be stunningly naive. On the other hand, social and behavioral scientists often are delighted to have found any stable result. The work may be based on parlor-game research paradigms unrepresentative of anything people actually do, or superficial surveys and demographies elaborately confirming common sense. The result may be a meager statistical indication with dubious practical significance. Social and behavioral scientists often cultivate purple prose to make any result seem like a fundamental revelation about human nature, and yet at the same time many also manage to avoid drawing any implication specific or concrete enough to really help technology developers.

How should we think about this tension? What should we do about it? Early on in the development of the HCI field, there was a substantial amount of deliberate strategizing about this. The original vision of HCI articulated this tension and committed to harnessing and cultivating it as a defining characteristic. For example, in the early years of the flagship ACM CHI Conferences, the relative participation from cognitive science and computer science constituencies was an annual conference management topic. From a contemporary perspective, this balancing seems to leave out many important constituencies, such as media and sociology, but at the time this was radical and visionary, and it entailed a bit of explicit tuning.

I have come to see the tension between the science and the technology development work bearing on HCI as a permanent feature, and actually a desirable state of affairs. Resolving this tension would necessarily entail fundamental revisions in one or the other, and it is not clear that anyone has an idea of how to make that work out (but vide supra). Conversely, the success of HCI over the past thirty years suggests that this tension, if it can be harnessed as a resource, can be stimulating and productive.

ALLEN NEWELL AND "HARD SCIENCE"

Allen Newell was one of the most prominent early leaders in human-computer interaction. In 1975, with Herbert Simon, he had won ACM's Turing Award, the most prestigious award in computing, for fundamental contributions to programming languages, artificial intelligence, and human cognition. In the mid-1970s, he had initiated a project with (then graduate students) Stuart Card and Thomas Moran that resulted in the first major theoretical characterization of HCI, the GOMS model (for *g*oals, *o*perators, *m*ethods, and *s*election rules; Card, Moran, and Newell, 1983). Indeed, the Card, Moran, and Newell book explicitly, and quite presciently, described the consensus vision of the field sketched above.

In April of 1985, Newell delivered the opening plenary address at the CHI conference. His topic was the question of whether and how psychology could play a significant role in HCI. This topic was at once ambitious, controversial, and divisive. It was ambitious because psychology itself is a broad and fragmented science, thus describing its possible roles in a complex multidisciplinary area such as HCI is not a small undertaking. It was controversial because Newell described a paradigm for HCI that purported to reconcile the tension between HCI technology development and the social and behavioral science of HCI, essentially by better conforming the latter to the former. It was divisive because it aggravated that tension through a rather aggressive rhetoric of raising the question of *whether* psychology could contribute to HCI, or whether it literally would be "driven out" of HCI.

In the talk, and in the subsequent paper co-authored with Stuart Card (Newell and Card, 1985), Newell adopted a metaphorical Gresham's Law: hard science drives out soft science. He stated his concern that psychology, while crucial to a successful HCI, could still be driven out by harder HCI sciences, specifically by computer science. Obviously, everything about this argument hinges on the definition of science. Initially, he vaguely characterized hard science as "quantitative or otherwise technical" (Newell and Card, 1985, p. 211). From this he derived three key desiderata for a science of HCI: task analysis, calculation, and approximation. Campbell and I attacked this conceptual foundation as shallow, arguing that this notion of "hard" excluded much of the essential scientific base of HCI—including most of computer science.

Newell's talk and the subsequent paper had a great impact on me. I felt at the time—and still do—that Newell was a great leader in HCI with respect to his relentless focus on science and theory. But I did not like this talk for many reasons. First and foremost, in my opinion, Newell's metaphor panders to and exploits irrational and pathetic fears that have chronically plagued the social and behavioral sciences. To that extent, I feel that couching the issue the way he did was a disservice, since it trades on fears about professional inadequacy, engages emotional discourses, and distracts attention from substantive discussion about what sort of research programs lead to scientific progress.

Newell's hard science slogan actually raises two different, though related, fears: One is the fear that soft science is just poor science, and that it deserves to be driven out of HCI (and everywhere else), the second is that soft science is not consistent with, or useful to hard science, and that it will be ignored and ineffective in a hard science–dominated HCI.

With respect to the first fear, it is no secret that social and behavioral scientists are sometimes embarrassed by the messiness and ambiguity in their own research materials. Ceteris paribus, all scientists would prefer to carry out investigations with the simplicity and elegance of the Michelson-Morley experiment, and be able to report fundamental properties of nature with precision and accuracy. However, the philosophy of science has progressed much since the heydays of positivism a century ago. Then, hysterical concerns about the proper form for scientific inquiry led to behaviorism, which stymied progress for fifty years. Possibly because of this legacy, many social and behavioral scientists are well aware that one methodological paradigm does not fit all scientific inquiry, and indeed that quantification and abstraction can sometimes destroy the object of study.

In some ways the second fear is worse than the first, which can be argued against historically and intellectually. The second fear evoked by Newell's hard science slogan is a warning to social and behavioral scientists that if they want to participate effectively in HCI, to have impact on human-oriented computer technology, then they must speak the hard science language of the technologists. And this warning, even though it is wrapped in constructive suggestions about how to move the science forward, is coming from an ACM Turing Award winner and professor of computer science at Carnegie-Mellon University—one of the top universities for computer science. In other words, the warning that hard science technologists might disregard and denigrate soft science contributions is coming from a source who has impeccable credentials with respect to those hard science computer technologies.

SOFTENING UP HARD SCIENCE

Newell's CHI 85 talk was written up as an article in the journal *Human-Computer Interaction* with his former student Stuart Card. In 1986, Robert Campbell and I replied to that article, and Newell and Card responded to our reply. Campbell and I had agreed in advance not to respond further, but the debate did not quite end there. Newell's last book, his 1990 *Unified Theories of*

Cognition, included some discussion of theory in HCI. I was invited to participate in a multiple-review discussion of the book in *Behavioral and Brain Sciences* in 1992, and Newell briefly replied to my review comments. Allen Newell died on July 19, 1992.

In this debate, there would appear to be two key questions. The first concerns whether there is or was a problem in HCI with respect to the utilization or inclusion of psychology (and, by extension, the "even softer" sciences that joined in the interdisciplinary HCI project since 1985, anthropology and sociology in particular). The second question is whether what Newell called "hardening of the science" is desirable, feasible, or effective as a solution path.

With respect to the first question, Newell made three arguments (Newell and Card, 1985, pp. 212–214; Newell and Card, 1986, pp. 255–257). First, he argued that hard science can already be seen to drive out soft science, as engineering drives out human factors, and as operations research (in the sense of linear programming, queuing theory, etc.) drives out studies of values and culture in management. Second, he argued that hard science ignores, bypasses, and diverts attention from soft science, as programming language research ignores the psychology of programming and as artificial intelligence ignores the nature of human intelligence. Finally, he argued that the apparent utilization of soft science is often nothing more than common sense, as in the case of usability guidelines.

To the contrary, and even though things could of course be better yet, engineering did not drive out human factors, nor did operations research drive out management studies. The psychology of programming remains strong; in 2004 Alan Kay received the ACM Turing Award for Smalltalk, a programming language and environment with an explicit, articulate, and consummately "soft" psychological rationale. Indeed, the soft areas whose epitaphs Newell wrote twenty years ago are stronger and more vital in HCI today than they were then, and to a considerable extent, they are more qualitative (softer, in Newell's sense). In fact, to a stunning extent, the most active areas of theory development in HCI today are broad, conceptually rich, and quite soft: activity theory, critical theory, distributed cognition, ethnomethodology, phenomenology.

In their response to Campbell and me, Newell and Card (1986) entirely abandoned their aggressive rhetoric of "hard science" and of psychology being "driven out." They argued instead for "technical theories" in HCI, defining these as formal, manipulation-oriented, idealization-based, and cumulative. And more had changed than merely rhetoric. Newell and Card (1986) explicitly state that formal theories need *not* be quantitative, and that manipulation-oriented theories should support *reasoning* as well as calculation. Their new notion of idealization-based theories broadens their limited concept of approximation in Newell and Card (1985) with a richer and more standard concept. Indeed, only their notion of cumulation, which they see as a fairly mechanical summation and abstraction across local theories, seems problematically limited and naive.

My revisionist view, as I look back at this discussion, is that Newell was always primarily interested in the *second* question. He wanted to help define a particular approach to technical theory in HCI that could better integrate computer science and cognitive science in a computational framework. I think he became intrigued by the Gresham's Law metaphor, and in effect got carried away with his own rhetoric. In my 1992 review of *Unified Theories of Cognition*, I trumpeted the same themes Campbell and I had raised six years before. But I think Newell had had enough, he merely said my review extended him little intellectual generosity. I'm sorry now that it wound up that way.

NEW DIRECTIONS IN THEORY AND SCIENCE

In my view, the most important consequence of Newell's talk and the subsequent papers was the consequent heightening of interest in HCI science and theory. Through the 1980s, many new scientific ideas entered the HCI mainstream. Newell's vision provided a touchstone that helped to evoke and sharpen many alternate proposals.

One source of new scientific ideas was differentiation within the original cognitive psychology community of HCI. For example, during the early 1980s, a great deal of work had been done on the learning and comprehension problems of novice users. This was the decade of the PC, and it seemed that the whole world was struggling with DOS and its application software. These informal and qualitative studies were beyond the realm of routine cognitive skill, beyond the realm of GOMS as a technical theory, but also beyond the extension of GOMS envisioned in Newell's talk. However, learning and problem solving are definitely within the scope of cognitive science, raising issues such as abductive reasoning, learning by exploration, external representations, and the development of analogies and mental models. Moreover, these were the user issues that were driving the industry. Newell's vision marginalized this work, but that directly helped to energize and orient the articulation of alternative cognitive psychology and cognitive science paradigms in HCI (see, for example, the collection of papers in Carroll, 1991).

Another source of new scientific ideas was the growing multidisciplinary constituency of cognitive science itself. Social psychologists, anthropologists, sociologists, and philosophers participated in establishing cognitive science in the late 1970s. During the 1980s there were significant reciprocal interactions between cognitive science and HCI. Some of these were paradigmatically soft in Newell's sense. For example, Suchman's (1987) study of photocopier use described a variety of usability problems with advanced photocopier user interfaces. She considered the interaction between the person and the machine as a sort of conversation that frequently fails because the participants do not understand one another. She used this study to develop an important critique of planning as it had been viewed in cognitive psychology and artificial intelligence. This was a paradigm case of cognitive science, and in particular of HCI as cognitive science. Suchman brought field study concepts, techniques, and sensibilities from anthropology, ethnomethodology, and sociology. She applied them to a real problematic situation of human-computer interaction, and her results provided very specific guidance for both developing better user interfaces for photocopiers and better theories of planning.

A third source of new scientific ideas was the increasing internationalization of HCI in the United States. This was facilitated by several IFIP conferences held in Europe, and by initiatives within major computer companies. An example was Bodker's (1991) application of activity theory to HCI. Activity theory was originally developed in what is now Russia; its applications to work and information technology were pioneered in Scandinavia. It integrates the analysis of individual behavior and experience with interpersonal cooperation (including division of labor) and culture (including tools and socially developed practices). Its foundation is Marxism, not cognitive architecture. It addresses the achievement of particular goals in the context of broader motivations, human development, and social systems. Activity theory and cognitive science are not incompatible, but they embrace different underlying values and they prioritize conceptual and methodological issues differently. For example, in activity theory, understanding mental representations per se is a secondary issue.

A fourth source of new scientific ideas was technology. The personal computer, and its word processing and spreadsheet software, were instrumental in the original emergence of HCI. In the latter 1980s and throughout the 1990s, software and systems to support computer-supported cooperative work (CSCW), sometimes called groupware, became increasingly important. Networked computing became more differentiated and sophisticated. In the early 1990s the World Wide Web became available, and within a few years became a universal infrastructure for networked personal computing. Technological support for graphics and visualization, including virtual environments and augmented reality, and for audio and video became far more advanced and accessible. Handheld computers and cellular telephones allowed the use of computing to become increasingly mobile and ubiquitous in everyday life. These technology developments increased the salience of scientific issues in interpersonal communication, coordination, and collaboration, in browsing, search, and information integration, and in many facets of visual perception.

A fifth source of new scientific ideas is design. HCI is about the design of interactions and the hardware, software, and information systems that support interactions. As Newell put it in his CHI 85 talk, "design is where the action is." Design is where the action is, at least in part, because applying science proactively to guide design work is an unsolved problem, in HCI and elsewhere. Bringing scientific concepts, methods, and techniques into design practices was always a defining commitment of HCI. However, Newell's hard science program seriously underestimated the complexity of design.

Ironically, in calling attention to design, Newell helped to propel the field past his own program. During the 1990s, the original focus on applying HCI science to design was radically augmented by attempts to extract or construct technical and practical knowledge *from* design work. Design rationale became a complement to technical science. More recently, designers themselves have become a significant professional constituency in HCI, not only as practitioners, but also as researchers. Now, design case studies are a significant type of codified HCI knowledge, as evidenced by new ACM conferences such as Designing Interactive Systems (DIS).

All of these developments contributed to a scientific foundation far more rich, far more diverse than the starting points of the early 1980s. From the mid-1990s, the scientific foundation of HCI encompassed nearly all of social, cognitive, and behavioral science. Students and scientists from many disciplines bought their research interests and expertise to HCI. The tremendous range of empirical methods and scientific concepts in routine use in HCI has been a source of strength as the field grew to address new problems and issues encompassing new technologies and new applications. Newell should be credited as helping to launch this endeavor.

THE ESSENTIAL TENSION

From the vantage point of twenty years on, I still find this debate interesting and useful. Campbell and I took the Gresham's Law analogy more seriously than Newell might have originally intended. Gresham's Law says that "bad" (overvalued) money drives "good" (undervalued) money out of circulation. The appropriate response to Gresham's Law is not to reconcile ourselves to a world in which money is overvalued, rather it is to correct distortions in value. On Newell's analogy, the remedy for the risk that hard science might drive out soft science in HCI (and elsewhere) is also to correct distortions in valuation.

Through the miracle of hindsight, we know now Newell's concern that psychology might be "driven out" of HCI was needless. The scientific base of HCI is actually far more eclectic and far softer, in Newell's sense, than it was in 1985. His proposals for technical theories, a.k.a. hard science, in HCI did not lead to an expansion and generalization of the GOMS research program. Cognitive modeling is no longer the touchstone paradigm for HCI. It is a niche paradigm, seen as relevant to the design and evaluation of highly routine human-computer interactions. But the issues that Newell raised and the discussion that he initiated nurtured a sustained and diverse focus on science and theory in HCI. Through the past two decades this made HCI an intellectual beacon to its near-neighbor disciplines human factors, information systems, and software engineering.

Since this is a personal reflection, I will add that I learned much in the course of working out these arguments. It gave me a far more strategic view of HCI research. I also personally enjoyed the fact that although this was a sharp debate in many respects, it was constructive and professional among the combatants. In 1987, a year after this exchange was published, Newell wrote a letter to my managers at the IBM Watson Research Center. I never saw the letter, and have heard only a few brief references to its content, but immediately thereafter I enjoyed several years of uninterrupted research support from IBM for a project in user interface theory and design. It was a tremendous boost to my career and to those of several of my co-workers.

This brings me back to the inevitability and inherent good of interdisciplinary tension. I believe that to a considerable extent the debate about hard versus soft science is a debate about our confidence in our discipline and in our own research programs. One of the saddest experiences this debate has caused for me is witnessing unconfident social and behavioral colleagues wilt in the face of the term "soft science." But perhaps one must confront this discomfort, and work through it, in order to be able to contribute fully to the HCI project. We might ironically credit Newell's metaphor with providing the raw material for therapy and personal development in our field.

In his later work, Thomas Kuhn (1979) elaborated his well-known concepts of scientific revolution and paradigm. He acknowledged that tumultuous periods of revolution sometimes persist, and that scientists "like artists [...] must occasionally be able to live in a world out of joint." He called this the essential tension: If periods of crisis go on long enough, scientific communities may pursue what Kuhn calls extraordinary science, in which assumptions are questioned, conventions are abandoned, and innovative practices become routine.

I have come to believe that the tension between relatively discursive, qualitative, and conceptual social-behavioral science and relatively formal, quantitative, and device-oriented computer science is inherent and abiding in HCI. It should be regarded as a resource to the field and not (only) as a source of interdisciplinary conflict. I see this as a primary cause for the vitality and productivity of HCI as an interdisciplinary endeavor. Further and finally, I think people are attracted to HCI in part because it is exciting to live in a world out of joint, and to participate in an extraordinary science.

ACKNOWLEDGMENTS

I am grateful to Jonathan Grudin, Bonnie John, Irene Petrick, Steve Sawyer, and Alistair Sutcliffe for comments and discussion during the preparation of this paper.

REFERENCES

Bødker, S. *Through the Interface: A Human Activity Approach to User Interface Design*. Hillsdale, NJ: Erlbaum, 1991.

Card, S.K.; Moran, T.P.; and Newell, A. *The Psychology of Human-Computer Interaction*. Hillsdale, NJ: Erlbaum, 1983.

Carroll, J.M. (ed.). *Designing Interaction: Psychology at the Human-Computer Interface*. New York: Cambridge University Press, 1991.

Carroll, J.M. The path is well-worn and the trenches are deep: review commentary on Allen Newell's *Unified Theories of Cognition*. *Behavioral and Brain Sciences*, 15 (1992), 441.

Carroll, J.M. (ed.). *HCI Models, Theories, and Frameworks: Toward a Multidisciplinary Science*. San Francisco: Morgan-Kaufmann, 2003.

Carroll, J.M., and Campbell, R.L. Softening up hard science: reply to Newell and Card. *Human-Computer Interaction*, 2 (1986), 227–249.

Helander, M.; Landauer, T.K.; and Prabhu, P.V. (eds.). *Handbook of Human-Computer Interaction*, 2nd ed. Amsterdam: North Holland, 1997.

Jacko, J., and Sears, A. (eds.). *The Human-Computer Interaction Handbook: Fundamentals, Evolving Technologies and Emerging Applications*. Mahwah, NJ: Lawrence Erlbaum Associates, 2002.

Kuhn, T.S. *The Essential Tension: Selected Studies in Scientific Tradition and Change.* Chicago: University of Chicago Press, 1979.

Newell, A. *Unified Theories of Cognition.* Cambridge, MA: Harvard University Press, 1990.

Newell, A., and Card, S. The prospects for psychological science in human-computer interaction. *Human-Computer Interaction,* 1 (1985), 209–242.

Newell, A., and Card, S. Straightening out softening up: response to Carroll and Campbell. *Human-Computer Interaction,* 2 (1986), 251–267.

Newell, Allen, and reviewers. Precis of *Unified Theories of Cognition. Behavioral and Brain Sciences,* 15 (1992), 425–492.

Rosson, M.B., and Carroll, J.M. *Usability Engineering: Scenario-Based Development of Human-Computer Interaction.* San Francisco: Morgan-Kaufmann, 2002.

Suchman, L.A. *Plans and Situated Actions: The Problem of Human-Machine Communication.* New York: Cambridge University Press, 1987.

EDITORS AND CONTRIBUTORS

Ritu Agarwal, PhD, is professor and Dean's Chair of information systems at the Robert H. Smith School of Business, University of Maryland, College Park. She is also the director of the Center for Health Information and Decision Systems. Dr. Agarwal has published more than seventy papers on information technology management topics in journals such as *Information Systems Research*, *MIS Quarterly*, *Management Science*, *Communications of the ACM*, and *Journal of Management Information Systems*, and has made presentations at a variety of national and international conferences. Her current research is focused on how organizations derive value from information technology through adoption, diffusion, and creative use; IT in the health-care sector; and the design and structuring of IT activities. Professor Agarwal is currently serving as a senior editor for *Information Systems Research* and an associate editor for *Management Science*.

Corey M. Angst is a PhD candidate in the Decision and Information Technologies Department at the Robert H. Smith School of Business, University of Maryland. His interests are in the transformational effect of IT in the health-care industry and technology usage in the health-care sector. Prior to pursuing this degree, Angst worked for ten years as a mechanical engineer in both technical and marketing roles, most recently with the DuPont Company. Angst has presented papers at several academic conferences and has several papers under review within the IS and medical informatics fields. He has a BS in mechanical engineering and an MBA from the University of Delaware.

Izak Benbasat, Fellow of the Royal Society of Canada, is Canada Research Chair in information technology management at the Sauder School of Business, the University of British Columbia, Canada. He was CANFOR professor of management information systems from 1991 to 2000. He served as associate dean of faculty development from 1996 to 1999, and associate dean of research from 2001 to 2002. Professor Benbasat received his BA in business administration from Robert College, Istanbul, and his master's and PhD in management information systems from the University of Minnesota. He is a past editor-in-chief of *Information Systems Research*, and currently a senior editor of the *Journal of the Association for Information Systems*. His current research interests include the investigation of human-computer interaction for electronic commerce; he is particularly interested in designing interfaces for product understanding, recommendation agents, and collaborative shopping.

Robert P. Bostrom is the L. Edmund Rast professor of business at the University of Georgia. He teaches in management information systems (MIS) and management areas. He is also president of Bostrom & Associates, a training and consulting company focusing on facilitation and the effective integration of people and technology. Bob holds a BA in chemistry and an MBA from Michigan State University, an MS in computer science from SUNY at Albany, and a PhD in MIS from the University of Minnesota. Besides numerous publications in leading academic and practitioner journals, he has extensive consulting and training experience in the areas of MIS management, MIS design, organizational development, facilitation, leadership, and digital collaboration.

His current research interests are focused on high-performing individuals, facilitation, leadership, digital collaboration, technology-supported learning, and effective design of organizations via integrating human and technological dimensions.

Glenn J. Browne is an associate professor and the James C. Wetherbe professor of information technology at the Rawls College of Business Administration at Texas Tech University. He received his PhD from the Carlson School of Management at the University of Minnesota. His research focuses on cognitive and behavioral issues in information requirements determination, systems development, e-business, and managerial decision making. His articles have appeared in *Management Science, Organizational Behavior and Human Decision Processes*, the *Journal of Management Information Systems, MIS Quarterly, IEEE Software*, and other journals.

John M. Carroll is the Edward Frymoyer Chair professor of information sciences and technology at the Pennsylvania State University. His research interests include methods and theory in human-computer interaction, particularly as applied to networking tools for collaborative learning and problem solving. He has written or edited fourteen books, including *Making Use* (MIT Press, 2000), *HCI in the New Millennium* (Addison-Wesley, 2001), *Usability Engineering* (Morgan-Kaufmann, 2002, with M.B. Rosson) and *HCI Models, Theories, and Frameworks* (Morgan-Kaufmann, 2003). He serves on nine editorial boards for journals, handbooks, and series; he is a member of the U.S. National Research Council's Committee on Human Factors and editor-in-chief of the *ACM Transactions on Computer-Human Interactions.* He received the Rigo Career Achievement Award from ACM, the Silver Core Award from IFIP, the Goldsmith Award from IEEE, and was elected to the CHI Academy. He is a fellow of the ACM, HFES, and IEEE. In 2003 he received the CHI Lifetime Achievement Award from ACM.

Boreum Choi is a researcher at the Human-Computer Interaction Laboratory, Yonsei University, Korea. She has been involved in the mobile Internet user survey, the Mbiz survey in Korea, and the WMIS project worldwide. She is interested in cultural aspects of mobile Internet usage and interaction design. Her papers have appeared in *International Journal of Human-Computer Interaction, International Journal of Mobile Communications*, and other related journals and conferences. Her current project is a cross-cultural study of localization strategies to export mobile Internet services.

Alan R. Dennis is professor of information systems and holds the John T. Chambers chair of Internet systems in the Kelley School of Business at Indiana University. His research focuses on the use of computer technologies to support teams, on knowledge management, and on the use of the Internet to improve education. He received a bachelor's degree in computer science from Acadia University in Nova Scotia in 1982, an MBA from Queen's University in Ontario in 1984, and a PhD in management information systems from the University of Arizona in Tucson in 1991. He is the author of more than a hundred research papers, as well as four books—two on data communications and networking, and two on systems analysis and design. He is the publisher of *MIS Quarterly Executive* and serves on the editorial boards of *Journal of Management Information Systems, Journal of the Association for Information Systems, Journal of Computer-Mediated Communication*, and *International Journal of e-Collaboration*.

Jerry Fjermestad is an associate professor in the School of Management, New Jersey Institute of Technology. He has published in *JMIS, DSS, Group Decision and Negotiation, International Journal of Electronic Commerce* and several other journals and conferences. His current research is on customer relationship management, virtual teams, and outsourcing.

Dennis Galletta is an AIS fellow and professor of business administration at the Katz Graduate School of Business, University of Pittsburgh. He obtained his doctorate from the University of Minnesota. His research involves human factors, electronic commerce, and user training, especially with a focus on user attitudes, behavior, and performance. His articles have appeared in journals such as *Management Science, Information Systems Research, Journal of Management Information Systems, Journal of AIS, Decision Sciences, Communications of the ACM, Data Base, Information & Management,* and *Accounting, Management, and Information Technologies.* He serves or has served on several editorial boards, including those of *Information Systems Research, MIS Quarterly, Data Base, Information Systems and eBusiness Management,* and *Cycle Time Research.* He embarked in fall 1999 on an around-the-world trip with Semester at Sea, teaching IS courses aboard ship. While on land, over the years he served as the AIS VP of Member Services, ICIS Treasurer, AIS Council Member, general chair of the first AMCIS Conference, and, most recently, co–program chair of AMCIS 2003. He was co–program chair for ICIS 2005 and is editor-in-chief of *AISWorld.*

Monica J. Garfield is an assistant professor in computer information systems at Bentley College. Her research focuses on the use of IT to enhance creativity, the impact of technology on group interactions and knowledge creation. She also works in the area of telemedicine with regards to socio-technical issues that impact the implementation of telemedicine networks. She holds an AB from Vassar College, an MBA and MS from Boston University, and a PhD in MIS from the University of Georgia. Her work has appeared in such journals as *Information System Research, Journal of Management Information Systems, MIS Quarterly,* and *Communications of the ACM.* She is also the editor of the AISWorld Net's Data Base Course Web site.

Raymond M. Henry is an assistant professor in the department of management at Clemson University. He earned his PhD in information systems from the University of Pittsburgh. His current research focuses on IT governance, systems development, project management, and the use and development of information sources. His work has appeared or is forthcoming in research outlets including *Information Systems Research, Journal of the AIS,* and *Communications of the ACM,* as well as many national and international conferences.

Starr Roxanne Hiltz is distinguished professor, department of information systems, College of Computing Sciences, New Jersey Institute of Technology. She conducts research on applications and social impacts of computer technology, publishing widely in journals including *JMIS, MISQ, Communications of the ACM,* and *Management Science.* Her research interests currently include group support systems (particularly, support for virtual teams), asynchronous learning networks, and pervasive computing.

Se-Joon Hong is an associate professor of management information systems in the Business School of Korea University. He obtained his PhD in information systems from the Graduate School of Industrial Administration (GSIA) at Carnegie Mellon University. His current research interests are ubiquitous computing, IT adoption and diffusion, and human factors in information systems. His work has been published or is forthcoming in *Information Systems Research, International Journal of Human Computer Studies, Communications of the ACM, Decision Support Systems,* the DATA BASE for Advances in Information Systems, Electronic Markets, and others.

Geoffrey S. Hubona is an associate professor in the department of computer information systems at Georgia State University and a visiting associate professor in the department of information systems at Virginia Commonwealth University. He holds a BA in psychology from the University of Virginia, an MBA from George Mason University, and an MA in economics and a PhD in MIS from the University of South Florida. He previously held faculty positions at Virginia Commonwealth University and at the University of Maryland, Baltimore County. His research focuses on human-computer interaction as it applies to 3-D visualization and Internet usability, direct brain-computer interfaces, and the user acceptance of information technologies. His research has been published (or accepted for publication) in *ACM Transactions on Computer-Human Interaction*, *IEEE Transactions on Systems, Man, and Cybernetics*, *Part A: Systems and Humans*, *The DATA BASE for Advances in Information Systems*, *International Journal of Human-Computer Studies*, *International Journal of Technology and Human Interaction*, and *Journal of Information Technology Management*.

Jinwoo Kim is professor of HCI in the School of Business at Yonsei University, Korea. He also directs the Human Computer Interaction Lab at Yonsei University. His research interests include three types of issues (navigation structures for interactive systems, the cross-cultural value of IT and its impact on usability, and evaluation metrics and framework for digital contents) in three different domains (traditional e-Business systems, mobile Internet, and digital TV). He has published several papers in *Information Systems Research*, *Decision Support Systems*, *International Journal of Human Computer Studies*, *International Journal of Human Computer Interaction*, *ACM Transaction on Human Computer Interaction*, *Communications of ACM*, and other journals; he has also presented his research at related conferences.

Inseong Lee is a researcher at the Human-Computer Interaction Laboratory, Yonsei University, Korea. He has been involved in the mobile Internet user survey, the Mbiz survey in Korea, and the WMIS project worldwide. His current project is a cross-cultural study on localization strategies to export mobile Internet service. His papers have appeared in *International Journal of Human-Computer Interaction*, *International Journal of Mobile Communications*, *Journal of Electronic Commerce Research*, and other related journals and conferences. His interests are in the areas of cultural and usability factors that have substantial effects on mobile Internet usage behaviors.

Scott McCoy is assistant professor of MIS in the Mason School of Business at the College of William and Mary. He earned his PhD in information systems from the University of Pittsburgh with a major in MIS and a minor in telecommunications. His research interests include HCI, cross-cultural issues in IS, IT in developing countries, and telecommunications policy. He teaches HCI, telecommunications, and e-commerce.

Bjørn Erik Munkvold is professor of information systems in the department of information systems, Agder University College, Norway. He was previously a systems consultant and researcher in a number of industries, including banking, pulp and paper, and telecommunications. His main research interests are organizational implementation of information technology, computer supported co-operative work, and information systems research methodology. He has published articles in journals such as *European Journal of Information Systems*, *Communications of the AIS*, *Database for Advances in Information Systems*, and *Journal of Organizational Computing and Electronic Commerce*. He has authored a recent book entitled *Implementing Collaboration Technologies in Industry: Case Examples and Lessons Learned*. Professor Munkvold currently serves on the editorial boards of *Information & Management* and *International Journal of E-Collaboration*, and is co-editor of *Scandinavian Journal of Information Systems*.

Kazuaki Naruse is the chief specialist of smart card marketing for Toshiba Corporation. Since joining Toshiba, he has developed numerous systems such as smart card, security, and financial applications. From 1998 to 2003, he was the research director of the electronic commerce promotion council of Japan (ECOM). He directed the Mobile EC working group. Since 2003, he has acted as the chairperson of worldwide mobile Internet survey (WMIS), organizing international research projects. He completed his master's degrees in applied physics at Waseda University in 1979 and electronic engineering at Yale University in 1986. He is currently in the doctoral course on informatics at the Graduate University for Advanced Studies.

Rosalie J. Ocker is a Visiting Scholar in the College of Information and Technology at Pennsylvania State University. She received her PhD from Rutgers University in computer and information science in 1995. Her research interests include computer-mediated communication, group creativity and innovation, and customer relationship management (CRM). She is the principal investigator for a multi-year research grant sponsored by SAP America, Inc. on customer relationship management (CRM) readiness. She has published her research in journals such as the *Journal of Management Information Systems* and *Group Decision and Negotiation*, and in various conference proceedings including those of the Hawaii International Conference on Systems Science and the American Conference on Information Systems and Decision Sciences.

Lorne Olfman is dean of the School of Information Systems and Technology and Fletcher Jones chair in technology management at Claremont Graduate University. Lorne came to Claremont in 1987 after graduating with a PhD in business (management information systems) from Indiana University. He also holds a bachelor's degree in computing science, a master's degree in economics (both from the University of Calgary), and an MBA from Indiana. His extensive work experience includes computer programming, economic analysis of government airport policy, and computer model development of financial plans for a telecommunications company. His research interests involve how software can be learned and used in organizations, the impact of computer-based systems on knowledge management, and the design and adoption of systems used for collaboration and learning. He has published articles on these topics in journals including *MIS Quarterly*, *Journal of Management Information Systems*, and *Information Systems Journal*. He has always taken an interest in using technology to support teaching and has been using the Internet to facilitate classes for more than a decade. A key component of his teaching is his involvement with doctoral students. He has supervised thirty-nine students to completion. He is an active member of the information science community. He regularly reviews papers for journals and conferences, and was in consecutive years the program chair and general chair of the Association for Computing Machinery's Conference on Computer Personnel Research. He also coordinated mini-tracks of the Hawaii International Conference on System Sciences for ten years.

Gary M. Olson is the Paul M. Fitts professor of human-computer interaction and associate dean for research in the School of Information, University of Michigan, where he is also professor of psychology. He received his BA (1967) in psychology from the University of Minnesota, and his PhD (1970) in psychology from Stanford University. After serving in the Navy, he moved to the University of Michigan's psychology department in 1975. In 1996, he also became a charter faculty member of the new School of Information. For the past fifteen years, he has conducted research in the areas of human-computer interaction (HCI) and computer-supported cooperative work (CSCW). His current focus is on how to support small groups of distributed people working on difficult intellectual tasks. This research has involved both field and lab studies. He has published more than a hundred articles and papers, and has edited three books. He is a member of the CHI Academy, and in 2006 received, with his wife, Judith S. Olson, the CHI Lifetime Achievement Award.

Judith S. Olson is the Richard W. Pew professor of human-computer interaction at the University of Michigan. She is a professor in the School of Information, the Business School, and the psychology department. She got her PhD in psychology at the University of Michigan, and then held a postdoctoral fellowship at Stanford University before returning to Michigan as a faculty member. Except for three years at Bell Labs and a year at Rank Xerox Cambridge, UK, she has been at Michigan her entire professorial life. Her research focuses on the technology and social practices necessary for successful distance work, encompassing both laboratory and field study methods. She has served on a number of editorial boards and panels for both the National Research Council and the National Science Foundation. She was one of the first seven inductees into the CHI Academy, and in 2006 received, with her husband, Gary M. Olson, the CHI Lifetime Achievement Award.

Peter Polak is an assistant professor of computer information systems in the School of Business Administration at the University of Miami. He earned his PhD in information systems from the University of Pittsburgh with a major in MIS and a minor in telecommunications. His research interests are in the areas of human-computer interaction, Internet technologies, electronic commerce, electronic auctions, and telecommunications.

Adriane B. Randolph is a doctoral candidate in the department of computer information systems at Georgia State University. She is a National Science Foundation graduate research fellowship award recipient, KPMG doctoral scholar, and Southern Regional Education Board doctoral scholar. In addition, she is a member of the Association for Computing Machinery and the Association for Information Systems. Her research interests focus on human-computer interaction, assistive technology, and user-centered design. In particular, she is working with brain-computer interfaces in the Georgia State University BrainLab. Prior to returning to academia, she was a consultant with Accenture, one of the world's leading IT and management consulting firms. She holds a BS from the University of Virginia in systems engineering.

Mary Beth Rosson is professor of information sciences and technology at Pennsylvania State University. Her research interests include scenario-based design and evaluation, the use of network technology to support collaboration, especially in learning contexts, and the psychological issues associated with use of high-level programming languages and tools. She is co-author of *Usability Engineering: Scenario-Based Development of Human-Computer Interaction* (Morgan Kaufmann, 2002), author of *Instructor's Guide to Object-Oriented Analysis and Design with Application* (Benjamin Cummings, 1994), as well as numerous articles, book papers, and tutorials. Dr. Rosson is active in both ACM SIGCHI and ACM SIGPLAN, serving in numerous technical program as well as conference organization roles for the CHI and OOPSLA annual conferences.

Radhika Santhanam is a Gatton endowed professor in the School of Management, College of Business, at the University of Kentucky. Using a variety of research methods, Dr. Santhanam has investigated issues relating to the effective use of resources invested in technology. From a micro-perspective, her research in the area of human-computer interaction has investigated methods by which training and better system design can improve users' understanding and utilization of information systems. From a macro perspective, her research has proposed methods by which organizations can select and track investments in information systems in order to make effective use of organizational resources. She has published her research in several journals and currently serves on the editorial boards of *MIS Quarterly* and *Decision Support Systems*.

Sharath Sasidharan is completing his PhD in information systems at the Gatton College of Business and Economics at the University of Kentucky. He holds a BTech in electrical and electronics engineering from the University of Kerala in India and an MBA from the University of Glasgow in the United Kingdom. His major research interests include issues related to human-computer interaction, organizational acceptance of technology, ERP systems, e-learning, online training, and information systems accessibility for the disabled.

Maung K. Sein is professor of information systems at Agder University College, Norway. A PhD graduate of Indiana University, his current research interests are information and communications technology in national development, IT in the public sector, and, e-government. He has conducted research in end-user training, human-computer interaction, conceptual database design, systems development methods, data warehousing, computer personnel, and IS management. He has published widely in such prestigious journals as *Information Systems Research, MIS Quarterly (MISQ), Communications of the ACM, The Information Society*, and *Human-Computer Interaction*. He has conducted workshops and seminars on different aspects of research methods at several universities in the United States, Norway, Finland, and Tanzania. He has served or is serving on the editorial boards of *MISQ, MISQ Executive, Communications of the Association of Information Systems*, and *E-Service Journal*. He has also chaired and served on program committees of several international conferences.

Conrad Shayo is a professor of information science at California State University, San Bernardino. Over the last twenty-three years he has worked in various capacities as a university professor, consultant, and manager. He holds a PhD and a master's in information science from Claremont Graduate University. He also holds an MBA in management science from the University of Nairobi, Kenya, and a bachelor of commerce in finance from the University of Dar-Es-Salaam, Tanzania. His research interests are in the areas of IT assimilation, performance measurement, distributed learning, end-user computing, organizational memory, instructional design, organizational learning assessment, reusable learning objects, IT strategy, and "virtual societies." Dr. Shayo has published these and other topics in various books and journals. Currently, he is involved in developing reusable learning objects and Web-based learning-game simulations. He is also a co-editor (with Dr. Magid Igbaria) of the book *Strategies for Managing IS/IT Personnel*.

Detmar W. Straub is the J. Mack Robinson distinguished professor of information systems at Georgia State University. He has conducted research in the areas of e-commerce, computer security, technological innovation, and international IT studies. He holds a DBA in MIS from the University of Indiana and a PhD in English from Penn State University. He has published over 110 papers in journals such as *Management Science, Information Systems Research, Journal of Management Information Systems, MIS Quarterly, Organization Science, Communications of the ACM, Journal of Global Management, Information & Management, Communications of the AIS, Academy of Management Executive, Sloan Management Review*, and *Journal of Global Information Management*.

Kar Yan Tam received his PhD in management information systems from Purdue University. He is a professor of MIS at Hong Kong University of Science and Technology. He has also held a research scientist position at EDS, where he worked in the area of software engineering method-ologies and tools. His research interests include information technology applications and elec-tronic commerce. He has published extensively on these topics in major information systems and management science journals and is currently on the editorial board of more than six journals.

Heikki Topi is an associate professor of computer information systems at Bentley College. His cur-rent research focuses on human factors and usability issues in data management, systems analysis and design and Web search, management and commercial utilization of advanced telecommunications technologies with a special emphasis on wireless applications, and the effects of time availability on human-computer interaction. His research has been published in a number of information systems and information science journals, and he is the co-editor of *Auerbach's IS Management Handbook*.

Duane Truex III, an associate professor in the GSU CIS department, researches the social impacts of information systems and emergent ISD. He is an associate editor for the *Information Systems Journal*, has co-edited special issues of *The DATA BASE for Advances in Information Systems* and is on the on the editorial board of the *Scandinavian Journal of Information Systems*, the *Journal of Communication, Information Technology & Work*, and the *Online Journal of International Case Analysis*. His work has been published in sixty refereed and scholarly jour-nals, IFIP transactions, edited books, conference proceedings, and professional reports. An active member of the IFIP WG 8.2, he was the co-program chair of the 2004 Manchester UK conference on IS research methods.

Murray Turoff is distinguished professor of information systems at the New Jersey Institute of Technology. For more than three decades Dr. Turoff has been active in research and development associated with the use of computers to aid and facilitate human communications. Credited as "the father of computer conferencing," he designed the first computer conferencing system while working in the Office of Emergency Preparedness in the executive offices of the president of the United States in the late 1960s. Currently he is interested in large-scale "social decision support systems," which incorporate Delphi type methods into a dynamic real-time communication process for large numbers of users. He is also currently working on the design of Emergency Preparedness Management Information Systems.

Joseph S. Valacich is the Marian E. Smith Presidential Endowed Chair and the George and Carolyn Hubman Distinguished Professor in MIS at Washington State University. He was previ-ously an associate professor with tenure (early) at Indiana University, Bloomington, and was named the Sanjay Subhedar Faculty Fellow. He has conducted numerous corporate training and executive development programs for organizations, including: AT&T, Boeing, Dow Chemical, EDS, Exxon, FedEx, General Motors, Microsoft, and Xerox. He previously served on the edito-rial board of *MIS Quarterly* (two terms) and is currently serving on the boards at *Information Systems Research, Decision Science*, and *Small Group Research*. He was the general conference co-chair for the 2003 International Conference on Information Systems (ICIS) in Seattle and was the vice-chair of ICIS 1999 in Charlotte. His primary research interests include technology-mediated collaboration, mobile and emerging technologies, e-business, human-computer interaction, and distance education. He has published more than fifty refereed articles in journals such as *MIS Quarterly, Information Systems Research, Journal of Management Information Systems, Management Science, Journal of the AIS, Academy of Management Journal, Decision Science, Organizational Behavior and Human Decision Processes,* and *Journal of Applied Psychology.*

Jijie Wang is a PhD student in the department of computer information systems at Georgia State University. She holds a BBA in accounting from Peking University, and a MS in CIS from Georgia State University. Her research interests include software project management, software engineering, computer-mediated community, and open source software development.

Ping Zhang is associate professor at the School of Information Studies, Syracuse University. She earned her PhD in information systems from the University of Texas at Austin. Her research appears or will appear in journals such as *Behaviour & Information Technology (BIT)*, *Communications of ACM*, *Communications of AIS (CAIS)*, *Computers in Human Behavior*, *Decision Support Systems*, *International Journal of Human-Computer Studies (IJHCS)*, *International Journal of Electronic Commerce*, *Journal of American Society for Information Science and Technology*, and the *Journal of AIS (JAIS)*. With Dov Te'eni and Jane Carey, she co-wrote an HCI textbook for non-computer science students, *HCI: Developing Effective Organizational Information Systems* (John Wiley and Sons, 2007). Dr. Zhang has received several Best Paper awards at IS conferences, an excellence in teaching award from the University of Texas at Austin, and an outstanding service award from AIS SIGHCI. She is associate editor for *IJHCS* and *CAIS*, and a guest co-editor for *JMIS, JAIS, IJHCS, IJHCI,* and *BIT*. She is a co-founder and the first chair (2001–2004) of the AIS SIGHCI.

Ilze Zigurs is a professor and the Mutual of Omaha distinguished chair of information science and technology in the College of Information Science and Technology at the University of Nebraska at Omaha. Her research examines design and implementation of groupware for making teams more effective. She has published in such journals as *MIS Quarterly*, *Journal of Management Information Systems*, *Journal of Organizational Computing and Electronic Commerce*, and *Group Decision and Negotiation*. She is co-editor with Laku Chidambaram of a book entitled *Our Virtual World*, which examines both positive and negative impacts of the Internet on individuals, organizations, and society. Professor Zigurs serves as editor in chief of *e-Service Journal*, and was formerly a senior editor for the *MIS Quarterly* and department editor for the *IEEE Transactions on Engineering Management*.

SERIES EDITOR

Vladimir Zwass is the Distinguished Professor of Computer Science and Management Information Systems at Fairleigh Dickinson University. He holds a PhD in Computer Science from Columbia University. Professor Zwass is the Founding Editor-in-Chief of the *Journal of Management Information Systems*, one of the three top-ranked journals in the field of Information Systems; the journal has celebrated twenty years in publication. He is also the Founding Editor-in-Chief of the *International Journal of Electronic Commerce*, ranked as the top journal in its field. Dr. Zwass is the author of six books and several book chapters, including entries in the *Encyclopaedia Britannica*, as well as of a number of papers in various journals and conference proceedings. He has received several grants, consulted for a number of major corporations, and is a frequent speaker to national and international audiences. He is a former member of the Professional Staff of the International Atomic Energy Agency in Vienna, Austria.

INDEX

T - #0276 - 101024 - C0 - 246/174/26 [28] - CB - 9780765614872 - Gloss Lamination